AJ handbook of building enclosure

CI/SfB(9-)

Editors, authors and consultants

The authors of each section will be credited at the start of that part of the handbook in which their material appears. The following four consultants have been retained to advise on certain aspects of the building fabric's design on which they have expert knowledge. In addition, the editor wishes to thank Michael Rostron and Jan Sliwa for their help and advice.

Elder   Hodgkinson   Pugh   O'Brien

The editor of this handbook is A. J. ELDER RIBA, *architect in private practice, in collaboration with the Architects' Journal Technical Section and various authors. He has also been responsible for part of the work as author of sections 3, 7 and 9.*
ALLAN HODGKINSON, *structural engineer in private practice, consultant on structural considerations*
BRIAN PUGH, *qs in private practice and visiting lecturer in building economics at London University's School of Environmental Studies, consultant on cost considerations*
TURLOGH O'BRIEN, *materials specialist with Ove Arup & Partners and visiting lecturer at London University's School of Environmental Studies, consultant on use and performance of materials*

AJ Handbook of
Building Enclosure

CONSULTANT EDITOR
A. J. Elder RIBA

The Architectural Press, London

Editor's preface

The handbook system

In recent years it has been the practice of the Architectural Press to republish in book form certain Handbooks and other technical material which it is felt members of the building team will want to consult regularly and which for this reason they would want to have in a form more permanent than bound-up issues of the *Architects' Journal*. Publications which have been produced in this way include the AJ *Handbook of Urban Landscape*, the AJ *Metric Handbook*, the AJ *Handbook of Fixings and Fastenings*, and the AJ *Legal Handbook*.

People who have bought this book and who are not AJ readers will want some introduction to the method in which information is presented. It should be explained that when a handbook is published in the AJ the material does not appear continuously nor in batches of equal size. The information is however carefully structured into coherent units. These consist of three types of presentation: Technical Studies, Information Sheets and Design Guides (see Presentation of Information below).

At the beginning of every major section a chart is given, showing its relationship to material on previous pages and to that which is still to come, so that readers can keep track of the way the content is organised.

This book

The material comprising this book is a revised and updated version of the Handbook of Building Enclosure which was published in the AJ from mid-1971. It was designed to be used as a comprehensive guide to the enclosure problems of any project.

The text was not originally published in its correct sequence although filing under the CI/SfB system was suggested. However, a reassembly of the subject matter into a textually more coherent form has been one of the editors' aims in producing a book version. In addition the following steps have been taken:

1 Each section has been returned to its original author for checking and correction.
2 A considerable amount of feed-back in the form of letters and reference material received from many sources has been incorporated either by the original author or the editors.
3 New information received since the original publication dates has been incorporated and other information updated.
4 Additional information designed to clarify possible obscurities has been added by the editors.

Readers may notice one major omission from this list, namely the question of costs. This is deliberate, especially in view of the very rapid cost escalation which has recently occurred and which is still producing unpleasant surprises. To bring the costs up to date was, after due consideration, considered pointless. It poses the immediate question 'what

ISBN 0 85139 275 X
First published in book form 1974
© *Architectural Press* 1974
Printed in Great Britain
by Diemer & Reynolds Ltd, Bedford

date?'—presumably the date on which the particular author does the work; then whilst the book is being edited, assembled, printed etc. these new costs are already passing out of date again. It was therefore thought better to leave the rates as they were originally published and simply state that they should be treated as approximately correct (there is no such thing as absolute accuracy in pricing) at about the turn of the year 1971/2. Any qs should be able to produce a factor by which the rates should be multiplied to bring them up to the desired period. Even in their unmodified form they remain useful as a means of comparing relative costs of various systems. It is of course quite possible that some materials have become more costly at a faster rate than others: indeed some may not have increased at all due to improved manufacturing techniques offsetting normal cost increases: in general however the relativity or ratios of one cost to another tend to remain unchanged to any significant degree.

Another important change which has been continuing since the AJ series was first published is metrication. This is now virtually complete and in general all quantities are now given in metric terms. There may be a few imperial survivors and also a few metric quantities which by their clumsiness still display the fact that their origins lie in the Imperial past. There are also a few examples where both figures are given: these are simply perpetuated from the original series as being still, possibly, of some slight use.

Amendment to Building Regulations

The technical information given in this handbook is based on the Building Regulations 1972. After the main body of the book had gone to press, these Regulations were amended by the Building (First Amendment) Regulations 1973, coming into operation on 31.8.73. These amendments have *not* been incorporated in the Handbook, and readers are advised to consult The Guide to the Building Regulations 1972, 2nd Edition (1973) by A. J. Elder (Architectural Press) for up to date information on all matters affected by the Building Regulations.

As a general guide, the 1973 amendments deal principally with:

a an extension of the range of building types in respect of which local authorities acting under delegated powers may in certain circumstances dispense with or relax the provisions relating to structural fire precautions in buildings (regulation 7);
b the substitution of a revised Part E (Structural fire precautions). Some of the previous remain; but elsewhere there have been drafting changes and various substantive changes. The main substantive changes include 1. provisions permitting the use in certain circumstances of electro-mechanical or electro-magnetic devices susceptible to smoke to hold fire-resisting doors open, and 2. amendments to the provisions relating to the penetration of structure by pipes imposing more onerous requirements on pipes made of non-combustible materials which would soften or fracture at a temperature of 800°C and less stringent requirements on pipes of certain combustible materials in particular those made of unplasticised polyvinyl chloride (regulation 16 and Schedule 1);
c the introduction for the first time of regulations (Part EE) relating to means of escape in case of fire from certain flats, maisonettes, offices and shops in new buildings (regulation 17 and Schedule 2);

d the introduction of provisions requiring the erection of barriers around floors and roofs of buildings used as vehicle parks (regulation 18);

e amendments permitting certain domestic oil-burning appliances to be exempted from some of the provisions for the prevention of fire which have applied hitherto (regulation 25); and

f an amendment restricting the types of gas appliance which may be installed in a bathroom for heating water for a bath (regulation 26 and 27).

Also, references to various technical publications which are incorporated with the Building Regulations 1972 have been brought up to date as at 30th September 1972.

Scope

The title of the handbook published may mislead some readers into thinking that the handbook deals only with the building's external shell. In fact it covers *all* space-enclosing elements of the building fabric, both external and internal: floors, walls, roofs and ceilings. Whenever possible, these are dealt with as *whole elements* (eg 'external wall' would include secondary elements such as doors and windows, and finishes) to encourage designers to think of these elements in terms of their overall performance.

Arrangement

It will be seen from the diagram below that this handbook deals with its subject in three broad parts. The first part deals with building enclosure *generally;* it gives an overall view of the functions of the building's physical fabric, and gives specific guidance on two constraints which apply to the design of the physical construction as a whole: cost and dimensional considerations.

After this general introduction the handbook divides its subject into two broad element-groups: *external envelope* and *internal space division.* The former covers all those elements separating the internal volume from the external environment: lowest floor, external walls and roof. The latter covers those elements subdividing the building's

internal volume: suspended floors and ceilings, and internal partitions. Each of these two parts of the handbook is introduced by a general technical study examining the functions of that particular element group, the problems involved and trends in solving the problems; this general technical study is followed by specific studies and information sheets on the elements involved.

By approaching the problem in this way, starting at the most general level and proceeding gradually to more detailed aspects, it is hoped to overcome the inconsistency and inadequacy, characteristic of much present-day design.

Presentation of information

Information is presented in three kinds of format.

Technical studies are intended to give background understanding and to summarise general principles. They also include information that is too general for direct application. Information sheets are intended to give specific data that can be applied directly to design.

Design guides are intended to remind designers of the proper sequence in which decisions required in the design process should be taken. They also contain concise advice and references to detailed information required at each stage. The general pattern of use, then, is first to read the relevant technical studies to understand the design aims, the problems involved and the range of available solutions. The design guides and information sheets are then used as design aids; the former to ensure that decisions are taken in the right sequence and that nothing is left out; the latter as sources of data and design information.

Sequence of decisions

Design guides are based on the following broad sequence of decision-making. This reflects the underlying approach of the handbook as a whole, which is that design should start with the users' needs, and proceed from general decisions on the building's performance as a whole to increasingly detailed decisions on elements and components.

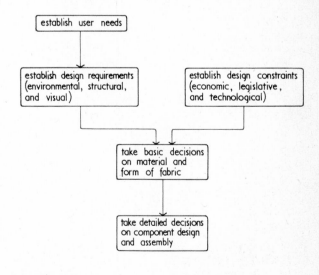

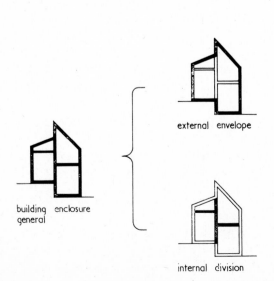

external envelope

building enclosure general

internal division

Sources

A source of information, regarded as a necessary reference, will be listed in the bibliography at the end of the technical study or information sheet; sources mentioned in the text, but not regarded as being necessary references, will be described either in the text or in a footnote; they will not be repeated in the list of references at the end.

Contents

References and keywords

The handbook is divided into three parts:
Building enclosure: general
External envelope
Internal envelope

Keywords are used for identifying and numbering technical studies, information sheets and design guides; thus: technical study ENCLOSURE 1: information sheet EXTERNAL ENVE-LOPE 2; information sheet PARTITIONS 2; and design guide INTERNAL DIVISION.

Section 1 **Building Enclosure: General**

Section 1 Building enclosure: General

Relationship to rest of handbook

The table and diagram on this page show the contents of the handbook as a whole, with the present section highlighted.

Scope

This initial section of the AJ Handbook of Building Enclosure provides an introduction to the design of the building's fabric, at the most general level. It does not deal with the design of any particular part of the building shell: rather, it is intended to give an indication of the basic functions the building fabric is intended to perform, and of the factors which must be taken into account in designing it.

The first technical study in this section looks at one important, and much neglected function—that of environmental control—and shows how the development of modern transparent, lightweight building enclosures has given rise to problems of environmental control. The next study outlines the fundamental design approach that will underlie the rest of the handbook. Then follow two information sheets giving data on two constraints which apply to the design of the building shell *as a whole*, rather than to particular elements: dimensional coordination, and cost planning.

On the basis of this general introduction, section 2 and subsequent sections then go on to deal with the building in greater detail as the diagram below shows.

References and keywords

The keyword by which this section is identified is ENCLOSURE. For a further explanation see page 6.

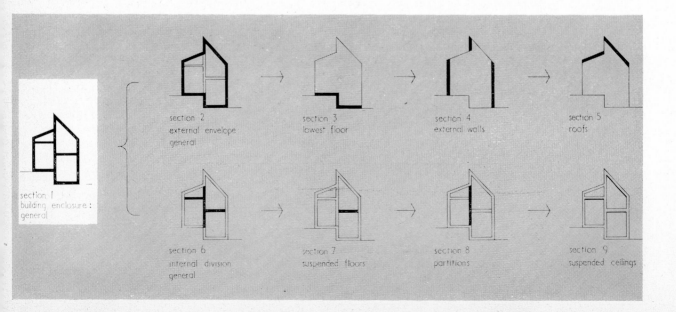

section 1
building enclosure: general

section 2
external envelope
general

section 3
lowest floor

section 4
external walls

section 5
roofs

section 6
internal division
general

section 7
suspended floors

section 8
partitions

section 9
suspended ceilings

Technical study
Enclosure 1

Functions of building enclosure

The purpose of this initial technical study is to set the scene for the more detailed sections which will follow, by sketching in broad outline the purpose of building enclosure; by drawing attention to the environmental problem which has arisen in connection with buildings in recent decades; and by indicating an approach which will, in the view of the editors, help designers to avoid some of the present problems and improve the performance of buildings. Many of the aspects touched upon in this general study will be examined in greater depth in subsequent sections of the handbook

1 Introduction

1.01 Subject of handbook

The subject of this handbook is the design of building fabric, and detailed information will be given, in its various sections, on materials, components and products, and on the design, assembly and finishing of these commodities to form a completed building shell and its internal sub-division.

1.02 Poor building performance

It is important for the designer, before getting involved in the minutiae of building construction, to form an understanding of the fabric's functions as a whole: the present paradoxical situation of poor building performance in an age of unprecedented technological expertise can be traced partly to the general lack of an overall, explicit design philosophy or system to govern, and give coherence to, the multitude of detailed decisions which shape the evolving building design.

Such a situation could not exist in design fields where the price of failure is disaster. If a supersonic aircraft, for instance, were to be designed without the discipline of an overall set of controlling functional requirements against which detailed decisions could be tested constantly, the resulting catastrophe would be spectacular. In the case of buildings, the consequences of haphazard decision-taking are less newsworthy: the building merely causes misery to its inhabitants by leaking, overheating, admitting noise, or by streaming with condensation. These inconveniences are more easily ignored than air disasters so architects tend to muddle on in their bad old ways, paying scant regard to the complaints of buildings' users. And the problems mentioned above are with us constantly.

1.03 Need for coherent approach

There are signs that users' and clients' dissatisfaction with the poor performance of many modern buildings will become gradually too vocal to be ignored. In the past, architects have been liable to litigation usually only if a building suffered some specific failure or breakdown in fabric or services, or caused physical injury to a user. However, in a recent American case an architect was taken to court for designing a school which severely overheated

in summer—ie for failure of *overall* environmental performance—and the client was awarded substantial damages.

As this trend grows (and it is certain to following the recent revision of CP3 chapter 11*, and the present climate of increasing consumer militancy), architects will have to overhaul their present haphazard procedures, think in a more disciplined way about the functions of the building fabric and the services it incorporates, and ensure that every decision taken—both by themselves and by the growing body of consultants, specialist manufacturers and subcontractors whom they direct—is compatible with the desired (and explicitly formulated) end result.

2 Functions of building

2.01 Need for environmental control

Why does man build? Most of the reason can be summed up in the phrase 'environmental control'. People need shelter from wind, dust, and the various forms of precipitation; they require certain conditions of temperature, humidity and air movement if they are to be physically comfortable; they require security and, at certain times, privacy (which may be visual or aural, or both); they like views of the world outside; they dislike excessive noise; they desire certain conditions of light and dark at particular times; they require appropriate physical surfaces for their activities and the arrangement of their possessions; and they need cooking, drinking, sanitary and storage facilities.

The main purpose of building has always been to provide an environment that will minister to these needs. It is our success in controlling or modifying the natural environment that has enabled mankind to progress gradually from an existence of bare survival to one of ease and comfort.

2.02 Two methods of control

In his efforts to achieve environmental control, man has always had at his disposal two kinds of resources he could manipulate to modify those aspects of the natural environment which did not suit him: physical barriers and energy[1].

---

* This code lays down, for the first time, standards of thermal insulation in relation to control of internal environment

2.03 Physical barriers

The simplest form of barrier between man and climate is clothing **1,2**. The cloth is a membrane which modifies the relatively hostile external climate to produce a more acceptable 'microclimate' inside, giving the wearer protection against wind, sun, rain, snow or dirt, and providing him with more comfortable temperatures as well as privacy. On this simple level a tent can be seen as an extended form of 'clothing', providing the same kind of climate modification and privacy as clothes by acting as a membrane between man and climate **3**. The principal function of clothing is to entrap a layer (or several layers) of air around man's pitifully unprotected body, which then provides good thermal insulation in the same way as cavity walls and double glazing. This works equally well both ways ie whether it is excessive cold or heat which calls for modification.

In the case of other forms of physical shelter such as caves, or houses **4 to 5**, it is still possible to see them as climate-modifying enclosures analogous to tents or clothes, but the analogy cannot be taken too far because the addition of significant *mass* to the substance of the enclosure gives it special properties not possessed by thin fabric membranes. In addition to becoming relatively immovable, the enclosure also begins to acquire the highly important thermal characteristic of heat storage capacity.

In any but the most temperate climates, the latter property plays a vital role in providing comfortable living conditions. In hot weather the massive structure of a dwelling will absorb solar heat during the day, thereby keeping the inside relatively cool; it then radiates the stored heat into the interior at night (if the night is warm, the unwelcome effect of this thermal radiation can be counteracted by providing adequate through-ventilation). On the other hand, in cold weather the structure will slow down the rate of heat loss from sources of warmth inside the building to the outside, thus helping to keep the interior warm. Heavy structure acts, in fact, as a sort of thermal flywheel. Clothes, tents, and massive enclosures are all examples of the use of physical barriers to help provide the kind of environment man needs or desires.

2.04 Energy

However, physical barriers cannot provide light (although they can control it), and while they can conserve heat, they cannot generate it. For these purposes, man has exploited the second of the two kinds of resources available to him—energy. The earliest method of using energy to temper the natural environment was the camp fire which produced both heat and light (and, to a limited extent, security). It has been succeeded by the growing use of increasingly sophisticated methods of exploiting combustion and, more recently, other forms of energy; and today the average citizen in an industrialised society disposes of several kilowatts of environmental energy in his home.

2.05 Human needs

The history of the built environment, then, is the history of man's manipulation of two resources, physical enclosure and power, to produce an environment suitable for his cultural and psychophysical needs*.

* The term psychophysics refers to the relationship between physical stimuli and sensory events, eg the relationship between physical conditions of air temperature, radiative temperature, humidity and air movement, and the subjective sensation of thermal comfort

1

2

3

4a

4b

6

5

Simplest form of barrier between man and climate is
clothing. Phillipino farmer's palm leaf cone-hat and cape **2**
give shelter from rain and sun; Persian muleteer's black felt
garment **1** protects from snow and wind. Functional analogy
between clothing and simple forms of building enclosure is
clearly demonstrated by these examples. **2** has similar
function to leaf-covered hut, but on different scale; **1** is
climate-modification membrane similar in some ways to
3 Tibetan nomad tents, also made of black felt.
Massive forms of enclosure, such as caves **4** or thick-walled
dwellings **5**, have characteristic of heat storage capacity in
addition to thermal insulation qualities. This enables them to
absorb heat during day and radiate it into dwelling at night.
On the other hand thatched roofs **6** give excellent thermal
insulation, but low heat storage capacity; heat transmission is
therefore reduced, but not distributed over a period of time
as with **4, 5**

7a

7b

3

9

10

*Thermal advantages of massive, small-apertured construction
which characterised European architecture for centuries both
in cold climates (**7** shows 15th century, **8** 19th century
examples) and warm **9**, are sacrificed by modern light-clad,
large-windowed buildings **10***
*Vernacular building often exploits limited technological
resources to produce highly effective environmental
performance, eg thatched roof of Samoan chief's house **11**
protects from heat of sun, but as climate is mild air is
allowed to circulate freely through dwelling. At night, or when
weather is bad, roller blinds can be let down. In arctic
conditions of northern Canada, trail igloo **12,** built from
readily available material in 45 min, offers minimum
access to wind, maximum internal volume for minimum
surface area and provides surprisingly warm interior*

11

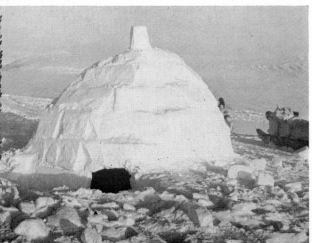

12

Just what these needs are constitutes one of the most
complex problems facing designers and environmental
planners; and their present level of competence in respond-
ing to these needs leaves much to be desired.

3 The environmental problem

3.01 Environmental performance of buildings

The important point is that most of the failings of modern
buildings mentioned in 1.02 are failings of *environmental
performance*. Public dissatisfaction is not merely with the
apparently exorbitant cost of building construction and
maintenance; it is a growing complaint that too many new
buildings provide a disappointing environment both for
those who live or work inside them, and for those who use
the streets and urban spaces formed by them.

To understand how this environmental problem has arisen,
it is necessary to trace briefly certain trends which have
appeared in building within the past two centuries, and
especially since the last war. It is in this recent history of
new aesthetic ideals, new building types, and rapidly
changing building technology that the major causes of our
problems can be found; and we will not be able to put
matters right until we understand where we went wrong.

3.02 Traditional building

Massive enclosure

European buildings of the kind dignified by the description
'architecture' (mainly churches and dwellings for the
well-to-do; the poor survived as best they could in hovels,
shacks and huts for the most part) have tended for several
millennia to consist of massive forms of enclosure. The
reasons for this preference were mainly structural and
technological (thick walls were better able to resist the load
and thrust of the heavy pitched roofs required to give
protection against snow), perhaps cultural, and possibly
environmental (the high heat storage capacity and good
thermal insulation value of thick walls were valuable
commodities both in the cold winters of northern Europe
and the hot summers of southern Europe).

Judged by the available technological resources of their
time, these buildings functioned well environmentally.
Those in cold climates had large, massive fireplaces which
stored heat during the day and radiated warmth into the
dwelling at night after the fire had died; and the thick outer
walls helped conserve this warmth **7, 8**. Those in hot climates
were shaded from the sun and were provided with good
through-ventilation; and the massive construction helped
to moderate temperatures inside **9**. Also both types benefited
from the good acoustic insulation and security associated
with the thick-walled, small-apertured structure.

Vernacular tradition

The reasons for their environmental success can be traced
not only to the kind of construction used but to another
factor which applies to pre-industrial vernacular building
generally. This is that in such societies there are relatively
few building types changing relatively slowly, and they are
erected by craftsmen with a deep understanding, born of
familiarity, of the kind of building desired, the materials
available in the locality, the techniques of using them, and
the local climatic characteristics. In such a situation of
familiar, well understood and gradually evolving building
'models', the fabric of the building tends to be well adapted
to its functions and to climatic conditions, and a generally

accepted vocabulary of materials usage comes into being, enabling ordinary builders to avoid problems of bad weathering and visual deterioration **13**.

3.03 The industrial revolution

The 18th century saw the beginnings of a radical disturbance of traditional society, and the effects of this revolution on the built environment were as far reaching, and as mixed, as those on the social order. In many respects the consequences of the industrial revolution have proved, ultimately, to be almost miraculously beneficial. Whereas life for most people in pre-industrial societies was short, physically miserable and intellectually limiting, we take for granted in contemporary Europe standards of comfort, well-being and freedom which are very unusual by historical standards.

Loss of coherence

However, we have suffered too. In the architectural context, proliferation of new building types and new inadequately understood materials and methods, building ever faster to keep up with population and economic growth, substitution of formal controls (eg codes, regulations and zoning rules) for the previous informal controls which expressed a consensus of opinion on the way buildings ought to be built, and satisfying the modern craving for novelty and change, have all combined to disorder the previous underlying unity of purpose, and competence of execution, in creating a built environment.

3.04 New building forms

One of the main contributory factors to the present environmental problem mentioned in 3.01 is the radical change which the new technologies of the industrial revolution brought about in building structure. It has been shown how European architecture had traditionally been structurally reliant on massive walls which yielded great incidental benefits in terms of thermal and, to some extent, aural comfort. The development of cast-iron and steel framed building structures in the 19th century, followed by reinforced concrete framed structures in the 20th, put an end to this situation. European architecture found itself liberated from the loadbearing wall, and new buildings with thin-framed façades and large windows began to appear in the second half of the 19th century **14**.

Abolition of solid wall

Soon the theorists of a new architecture began to explore—in drawing board projects and a few real buildings—the possibilities of this liberation and to exploit the potential of the skeleton structure. Two powerful ideas emerged from these explorations: the glass sheathed, almost totally transparent building in which the solid wall was not merely abolished but ostentatiously *shown* to have been abolished (for instance, the Bauhaus **15**), and the tall tower block in which advantage was taken of the steel or concrete frame to provide city dwellers with the fresh air and the wide views which seemed so infinitely desirable in the dark, satanic cities of that time. In many cases (for instance, the prophetic sketches produced by Mies Van der Rohe around 1920) both ideas are combined, and we see the tall, sheer glass-skinned tower block which has since become almost an archetype of modern urban architecture **16**, **17**.

Problems of environmental control

The aesthetic and social motivations which produced this dream-image of tall, airy towers set in park-like surroundings, were admirable; but the attempts to

realise this vision in post-war architecture have caused immense problems in environmental control.

If unprotected from the sun, glassy, large-windowed buildings suffer from enormous solar heat gain in summer, leading to high internal temperatures. If the building has a lightweight structure (as tends to be the case with industrialised building), the low thermal capacity of the building aggravates the problem, and large, rapid temperature fluctuations can occur inside the building with little delay between a temperature change outside the building and a corresponding change inside. This is a striking contrast to the situation in traditional, relatively massive enclosures where the building tends to 'iron out' and delay temperature changes, so that the heat of the day is not radiated into the building until night-time when it is less of a nuisance or even a benefit. These new buildings produce great cooling and ventilation problems. In buildings near roads or in urban areas opening the windows for ventilation may let in so much noise and dirt that the inmates prefer to stifle. In high rise buildings opening the windows may create intolerable wind and draught problems.

In winter such buildings will suffer from a converse problem due to the high rate of heat loss.

Enclosure versus energy

Once mistakes of this kind have been made in the design of the building's fabric, and it fails to act effectively as the climate-modifying membrane described in 2.03, the architect has no recourse but to call in the services specialist. Unnecessarily elaborate, expensive and frequently inadequate air-conditioning and heating systems, which are difficult to operate and maintain, are commonly provided today to make up for deficiencies in thermal control which could quite cheaply and effectively have been dealt with by the building's fabric. It is in this context that the changing relationship between our reliance on properly designed enclosure and our reliance on energy, as methods of environmental control, must be seen.

In the past we relied largely on a sensibly designed building fabric to provide us with comfort and amenity, augmented by fire providing light and additional warmth. It is inevitable that we should now be moving towards an increased use of energy for these purposes, as our needs become more complex, our standards rise, and our expertise in handling energy grows. In such conditions it may be cheaper to use energy than physical structure for many purposes of environmental control and manipulation.

Unnecessary complication

But these considerations do not justify the present situation in which the fabric of the building is often designed with flagrant disregard for the needs of the users, necessitating the addition of expensive services (vulnerable to mechanical breakdown and operational difficulties) to make the building comfortable. In addition these energy supplies are costly in use and the recent brouhaha over a possible world energy shortage suggests the need for a reversion to fabric control with correspondingly reduced energy consumption.

3.05 Influence of post-war technology

It has been shown how the transformation in building *form*, in the past century or so, has given rise to problems of environmental control because new forms were adopted without adequate understanding of what the consequences would be. Since the war these problems have been aggravated by the rapid adoption of new *materials* and *assembly techniques*, again without adequate understanding of the likely consequences.

13a

13b

13c

13 *Finnish log boathouse* **a**; *Iraqi reed guesthouse*
b; *Czechoslovakian wood-shingled belfry* **c**; *Greek and
Italian tiled domes* **d**, **e**; *and Iranian mud-brick mosque*
f *demonstrate appropriateness and beauty of form sometimes
achieved by anonymous pre-industrial builders*

13d

13e

13f

Lightweight construction

For example, the on-site assembly of large prefabricated
building components favours the adoption of lightweight
construction. The problems of thermal control which have
resulted from this trend have already been mentioned
in 3.04.

The lesson is not that industrialised building or lightweight
construction are necessarily bad. Provided the consequences
of decisions are carefully thought about, there need be no
problem. A proper mix of light and heavy components,
considered use of sunbreakers and heat-absorbent glazing,
proper insulation of the external skin of the building, an
effective ventilation system that will not conflict with the
need to exclude outside noise, and a lighting, heating and,
perhaps, air-conditioning system designed as a whole
concept with no internal conflicts and inconsistencies, will
produce a building which can maintain comfortable internal
conditions at low cost. The criticism is of the tendency
shown in post-war building of hastily, even enthusiastically,
adopted new techniques and materials without sufficient
understanding of their limitations and consequences.

Condensation

The same lesson can be drawn from the prevalent problem
of interstitial condensation—the kind that occurs *inside* the
material of building elements rather than on the surface.
This troublesome effect is a result not only of the materials
used in a wall or roof but also of the sequence in which they
occur. Wall panels or roofs consisting of thermal insulation
near the inside face and an impermeable outside face
virtually invite interstitial condensation; and new types of
walls and flat roofs have given rise to endless problems
because they are used with insufficient understanding of
their thermal and vapour resisting characteristics.

Visual deterioration

Finally, there are the effects of misunderstood or inadequately controlled technology on the visual quality of
our environment. These have probably done more to
alienate the general public from modern architecture than
even the psychophysical failings of new buildings.

The observer does not require an architectural training to
perceive the giantism of scale, monotony of form, and
crudity of detail which characterise much of our recently
built environment **18** and which can be traced partly to
architects' willingness to have the form of building components dictated by manufacturing and production considerations, and to have the form of the buildings themselves
dictated by site assembly considerations, such as easy crane
runs. All too often buildings, which were aesthetically
mediocre even when new, are further marred by progressive
streaking, staining and discoloration due to faulty detailing
of unfamiliar materials **19**.

3.06 Causes of dissatisfaction

Admittedly this catalogue of failures presents a one-sided
picture: there is no doubt that people today enjoy housing
and working conditions which are superior, from a psycho-
physical point of view, to those available to the mass of
society in the past (whether they are aesthetically superior
is, however, another matter). What is wrong is that performance falls so far short of the standards we have come to
expect in this age of technological wizardry. An attempt will
be made in the various sections of this handbook to indicate
a coherent approach to the design of the building fabric,
which will, it is hoped, eliminate some of the mistakes
described in earlier paragraphs.

14

*Skeleton-framed construction of 19th century ended need for
loadbearing walls and revolutionised building form* **14.**
*Exciting aesthetic possibilities of lightness and transparency
were exploited further in real buildings such as Bauhaus* **15,**
and projects such as Mies's glass tower, 1920-21 **16.** *Latter
created archetype now being realised throughout world* **17.**
*But new construction technologies tend, if allowed to get out
of control, to produce crude, monotonous building form* **18**

15

16

17

18

4 A coherent approach

4.01 Human needs

There can be only one starting point for any examination of building design—the user. A rational approach must begin with an examination of human needs; these were summarised in 2.01.

4.02 Environmental performance standards

Many of these needs will not necessarily be quantifiable (for example, privacy requirements, outlook, appearance and character of environment); but there are several kinds of psychophysical need which can, in principle, be translated into quantified environmental standards. For instance, appropriate physical conditions for thermal, aural and visual comfort could in many cases be specified ('visual' is used here in a restricted sense, and refers only to lighting. On this basis, a specification can be developed for the environmental performance required of the building fabric—for example, thermal insulation value and capacity of the external envelope (either whole-wall elements, including wall, windows and finishes, or whole-roof elements, including roof, rooflights and roof finishes); or the acoustic attenuation of internal partitions (including openings, and taking account of joints between components). The ultimate standards to be realised are those which will provide reasonable comfort for humans (or animals or suitable storage for goods) appropriately active for that particular part of the building. This will involve not only resistance standards for elements of buildings but a proper balance between these and the corrective effect of energy installations. The storage capacity of the element will also be important.

Overall design discipline

Once environmental performance standards of this kind have been laid down as comprehensively as possible, together with other quantifiable requirements and constraints such as structural and fire safety, cost and durability, the design team will have a precise brief against which the evolving design of the building fabric can be constantly evaluated, to ensure that the completed building will create the environment the users really require.

No longer ought the walls, for instance, be designed by one group of men guided by their own technical preoccupations and nothing more detailed than a U-value as an environmental performance standard; and the windows by another group of designers with very different technical preoccupations and an equally vague environmental brief. Instead an external wall ought to be seen as a membrane between outside and inside, which is required to modify the external macroclimate (including noise, heat, wind and so on) to produce a *defined range of conditions* inside; and every component in the wall (including the joints connecting different components) will be designed to play its part in performing the required function. Only in this way will conflicts and inconsistencies be avoided in the design of the building fabric, and the services engineer be relieved of the burden of having to design machinery to cancel out the mistakes made by the architect.

Inadequate data

It is not suggested that all the desired psychophysical qualities of the internal environment can be fully specified in this precise, detailed way at present. Probably it will never be wholly possible, and we will always be dependent on the skills of environmental designers who have acquired, through training and experience, an intuitive appreciation of environmental parameters (lighting, heating, noise and so on) which cannot be fully quantified.

The present lack of adequate data for this purpose is not only due to an insufficiency of research effort; even more distressing is the ease with which this type of research has tended to be divorced from the reality of building, thus leading to unreliable results. Experimental 'subjects' can be tested in a 'respectable' scientific manner in a laboratory by workers who do not have any experience of building design; consequently the results often do not reflect reality. A typical outcome of standards developed in this way is a single figure (eg temperature) when in reality a range of values would be satisfactory for users and would be inescapable in a real building. The inevitable result is either that pointless expense is incurred in trying to achieve an unrealistic objective, or that designers abandon any attempt to achieve the objective.

There are signs that the situation is improving: BRS is developing standards and methods, particularly in the thermal field, that promise a real advance on the existing situation. Also current architectural education is producing a new generation of architects who will be able to play a more effective role in the development of standards than has been possible in the past.

This handbook

For the present, this handbook must restrict itself to indicating the desired approach and encouraging designers to think of the building fabric in the right way. An attempt will be made to provide this encouragement and to provide, where possible, useful data.

5 Reference

1 BANHAM, R. The architecture of the well-tempered environment. London, paper 1973, Architectural Press [(E6)] £2·25

19 *Faulty detailing, based on inadequate understanding of materials, tends to cause further visual deterioration of buildings aesthetically mediocre even when new*

Technical study
Enclosure 2

An approach to design

This technical study analyses the design problems involved in producing a solution for the building's fabric, and indicates the general approach that will be adopted in this handbook

1 Design process

1.01 Requirements and constraints

An examination of the design process will show that two kinds of information are incorporated in the evolving building design, which have to be reconciled with each other. They are clients' and users' *requirements*, ie what they want or need, and the *constraints* acting upon the solution, ie factors which control or tend to prevent the fulfilment of these requirements.

1.02 Building form

These moulding influences will control the design of the building from the very earliest stages, when the basic arrangement of volumes and spaces is being planned, leading to the determination of the building's general *form*. This earliest stage of design is outside the scope of the present handbook so the designer is referred to the AJ series on Building types[1] and Building spaces (internal)[2] for relevant guidance.

1.03 Building fabric and services

Once the general form of the building has been determined, the next step is to design the building's *fabric* and the incorporated environmental[3] and utility[4] services*. It is at this stage that the present handbook becomes relevant and will begin to be used in detail; and here the same pattern of *requirements* and *constraints* will be apparent.

2 Design requirements

2.01 Environmental requirements

It has already been stated in technical study ENCLOSURE 1

that design requirements must be derived from an analysis of the building's users and their needs. The purpose of the building and the activities to be carried out in each of the spaces within it must be analysed; these will influence not only the psycho-physical conditions to be provided, but also such aspects of environment as floor-to-ceiling heights, window heights, worktop heights, partition spacings, service provision, resilience and nature of floor and wall surfaces and so on, all of which will affect the building fabric. The *users* must be defined in terms of numbers, age, sex, and any other special characteristics that might influence their use of the building, eg physical disability, kind of clothing worn, or even status and personality. The nature of the users' occupancy—permanent or temporary, continuous or intermittent, active or sedentary the intervals and periods involved—must be established.

Once this information has been collected, user needs can be determined. They are those mentioned in 2.01 of technical study ENCLOSURE 1: shelter from wind and dust, rain and snow; visual and aural privacy and, to be balanced against this, the need for view and communication; security from intruders and fire; appropriate conditions of light (and dark); thermal comfort; fresh air; circulation, including access and egress; suitable surfaces for activities and arrangement of possessions, tools, and so on. The *environmental functions* of the building's fabric can now be established.

2.02 Structural requirements

A second set of design criteria can be derived, partly from user needs, and partly from storage, plant and equipment requirements. These are the *structural functions*, the need of the building to make provision for certain loadings, both static and dynamic.

Design of the building structure generally is covered by the AJ Handbook of Building structure[5], and will not be dealt with here in depth. However, it is essential to consider structural functions when designing the building's fabric (consulting the Handbook of Building structure when necessary), and the interaction between structure and enclosure where appropriate. This handbook also gives

---

* This separation of the design process into clear-cut sequential stages is theoretical; in practice the designer must to some extent consider building form, fabric and services simultaneously. But it is more convenient to deal with them in separate handbooks

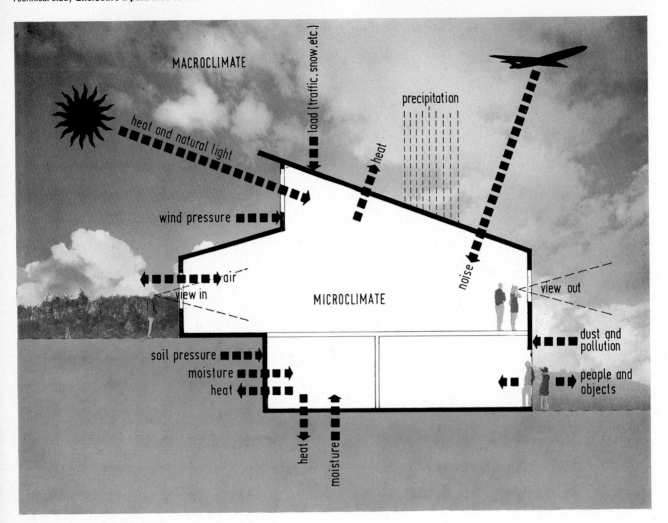

1 *External envelope of building acts as selective filter separating internal volume from external environment, exercises environmental control by modifying various aspects of macroclimate to produce more acceptable microclimate. Also serves structural functions (resisting various loads) and controls access and egress*

guidance in those instances where the elements of enclosure serve a structural purpose too, eg loadbearing walls which enclose space and carry the building elements above.

2.03 Aesthetic requirements

There is also appearance to consider: the *aesthetic function*. After excessive preoccupation with appearance at the cost of environmental performance, during the Modern Movement's earlier years, we may now be entering an era of total preoccupation with environmental performance at the expense of appearance. In fact, both aspects are of vital importance and to ignore or devalue either leads to unwelcome consequences. In this handbook consideration of aesthetic theory is largely left out, not because it is thought unimportant, but because there is not enough space to deal with this complex and controversial subject. The only aspect of the visual function that will be covered is weathering and prevention of visual deterioration generally.

3 Design constraints

3.01 Cost

The cost target will be a major constraint controlling fulfilment of the design requirements. Capital, running

and maintenance costs, must be borne in mind: unfortunately, taxation considerations favour low capital and high maintenance costs, whereas it might be more rational in a perfect world to reverse the relationship. For general guidance on cost considerations in the design of building enclosure elements, see information sheet ENCLOSURE 2.

3.02 Dimensional basis

Another important constraint is the limitation on dimensions to be used in setting out the building vertically and horizontally and in sizing components. The aim of the official dimensional co-ordination programme, now well under way, is to evolve a range of related dimensions for the sizing of building components and assemblies, and for the buildings themselves, so that components such as bricks, tiles, windows, doors, wall panels and partitions may be bought from any manufacturer and fitted together on site without cutting or 'stretching' and with a minimum of site labour. Guidance on controlling lines and dimensions etc is given in information sheet ENCLOSURE 1.

3.03 Statutory regulations

These cover health and safety. If relevant, guidance will be given in each section of this handbook. In general, however,

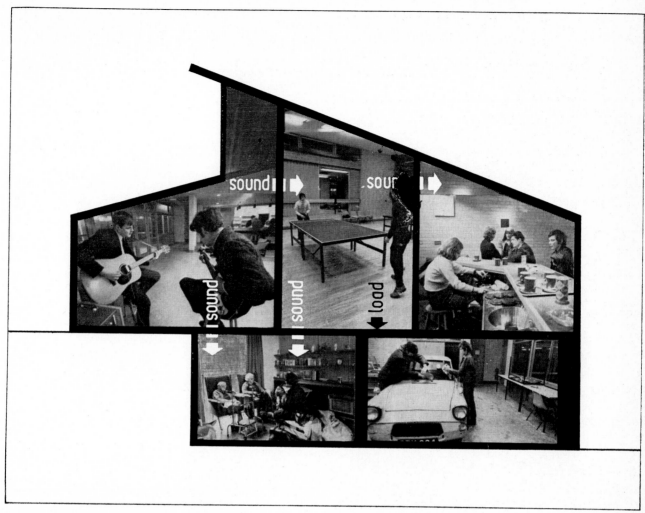

2 *Internal subdividing elements control sound transmission between internal spaces, provide privacy and control internal circulation. Also serve structural and fire control functions*

legislation on structural safety is dealt with in the AJ Handbook of Building structure[5], and legislation on health in the AJ Handbooks of Building environment [3] and Building services[4]. Also the Guide to the Building Regulations 1972[6].

3.04 Design life and adaptability

The client's projected life for the building will influence choice of materials and finishes; and the degree of adaptability, eg of internal partitioning, will affect structure, enclosing elements, and services, and the way they are related to each other. So the client's real intentions and requirements must be established. But it would be wrong to tailor the building too rigidly to the projected lifetime: 'temporary' buildings tend to linger on for decades so they must remain safe and pleasant for as long as they are in use; conversely, 'permanent' buildings often need to be adapted or demolished much sooner than expected. More will be said on this aspect in later sections of the handbook; probably the most useful advice that can be given in this general introduction is to stress the necessity of avoiding solutions tailored too tightly to any set of assumptions. Designing for complete adaptability, using sophisticated demountable elements, could be extremely expensive and may turn out later to have been unnecessary; and designing a 'tight-fit' solution, using a non-adaptable fabric, may be equally foolhardy. A reasonable compromise must be aimed for.

3.05 Manufacturing and erection considerations

The speed and ease of erection and assembly will obviously exercise a degree of control on the enclosure's design. Dimensional and weight limitations imposed on components by handling difficulties and the effect of crane swings and crane runs on layout must be considered.

It must not be forgotten however that consideration of such matters involves consultation with the contractor at the design stage, a process only possible with special contractual procedures such as fee contracts.

At the same time the designer should heed the warning given in 3.05 of technical study ENCLOSURE 1. Ultimately the design of components, and their assembly to form the completed environmental shell, should be determined by the needs of the people who have to use the building and look at it, not by the needs of batch-production jigs, assembly lines, or of site cranes.

4 Arrangement of Handbook

4.01 Two major groups of elements

Most buildings can be seen in terms of two major groups of elements: those forming the external envelope **1** of the building (which act as a 'filter' between external environment and internal space); and those which subdivide the internal volume of the building **2**. The functions, particularly environmental ones, of these two groups of elements are so distinct from each other that this handbook treats them separately.

Therefore, the handbook is divided into three broad sections, as shown in **3**. After the initial *general* section (including the present technical study), which provides an introduction to the handbook and is quite brief, the subject is dealt with in terms of *external envelope* (comprising basement/lowest floor, external walls and roofs) and *internal subdivision* (comprising suspended floors, internal partitions and suspended ceilings).

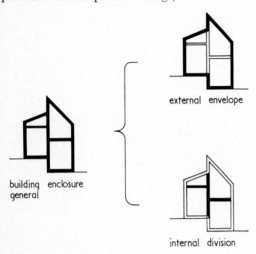

external envelope

building enclosure
general

internal division

3 *Handbook of Building enclosure deals with space-enclosing elements in three broad groups: general, ie all aspects relevant to fabric as a whole; external envelope; and internal division*

5 References

1 AJ *guides to building types:*
Garages 25.3.64 to 15.4.64; educational buildings 2.12.64 to 23.12.64; housing 26.5.65 to 23.6.65; office buildings 2.5.73 to late 1973, to be republished as a book; shops 2.2.66 to 16.3.66; factories 6.4.66 to 15.6.66; car-parking buildings 22.6.66 to 6.7.66; industrial storage 12.9.73 onwards; health and welfare buildings 16.11.66 to 25.1.67; theatres 1.2.67 to 8.2.67 and 17.5.67; cinemas 1.3.67 to 22.3.67; pubs 29.3.67; sports halls 5.4.67 to 10.5.67; swimming baths 14.6.67 to 26.7.67; churches 9.8.67 to 18.10.67, subsequently republished as a book; laboratories 1.11.67 to 27.12.67; college and university buildings 10.1.68; libraries 21.2.68 to 28.2.68 see 8 below; hostels 10.4.68 to 1.5.68; animal housing 29.5.68 to 12.6.68; hotels 17 and 24.6.70, subsequently republished as a book

2 AJ *guides to building spaces (internal):*
Cooking spaces 17.4.63 to 12.6.63; sanitary spaces 26.6.63 to 17.7.63; laundry spaces 14.8.63 to 4.9.63; storage spaces 11.9.63 to 16.10.63; garage spaces 6.11.63 and 20.11.63; eating and drinking spaces 22.4.64 to 10.6.64; general practice surgeries 17.8.66 to 21.9.66; dental surgeries 28.9.66; and spaces for the old and disabled 19.10.66 to 2.11.66

3 AJ Handbook of Building environment [(E6)]: (AJ 2.10.68 to 13.8.69)

4 AJ Handbook of Building services and circulation [(5–)]: (AJ 1.10.69 to 5.8.70 and 16.9.70)

5 AJ Handbook of Building structure [(2–)]: (AJ 8.3.72 to 5 September 1973: to appear in book form Spring 1974.

6 ELDER, A. J. The guide to the Building Regulations 1972, London, 2nd edition, 1973. Architectural Press.

7 PITT, P. H. and DUFTON, J. The guide to the London Building (Constructional) Bylaws 1972. London, 1973. Architectural Press

8 THOMPSON, GODFREY. Planning and design of library buildings, London, 1973. Architectural Press

9 HAM, RODERICK. Theatre planning. London, 1972. Architectural Press

10 LAWSON, FRED R. Restaurant planning and design. London 1973. Architectural Press.

11 LAWSON, FRED R. Principles of catering design. London 1973. Architectural Press.

Information sheet
Enclosure 1

Dimensional considerations

At the earliest design stages the architect should establish a dimensional framework for the building fabric as a whole (including external envelope and internal subdivision) to ensure that dimensionally co-ordinated components and assemblies can be incorporated without trouble. This information sheet, based on the relevant BS documents and including information supplied by JAN SLIWA, *summarises the dimensional considerations which must be taken into account; it represents the first category of design constraints (see technical study* ENCLOSURE 2)

1 Need for dimensional discipline

1.01 Traditional building

With traditional building techniques, the space-enclosing elements of the building were usually manufactured and assembled on site. This gave the designer great freedom in selecting dimensions and sizes for the building; eg structure and walls were made in situ either of formless materials such as concrete, or of small, cheap components such as bricks; both can be assembled on site to virtually any specified dimensions without much trouble. Also secondary elements, such as doors or windows, tended to be made to specified sizes on site by craftsmen on a one-off basis.

In addition to the dimensional freedom they allowed the designer, traditional building techniques did not place much emphasis on accuracy, because there was always a following trade to make good the deficiencies of the previous one. If the structural frame was inaccurate, the bricklayers constructing the infilling panels could easily pull in, or stretch out, the brick courses to suit and cut bricks where necessary. Irregularities in the brickwork could, in turn, be made good by the plasterer, and inaccuracies in the plastered surface could be disguised by scribing the timber trim to the plaster face. Also, with one-off fabrication, components could be made to the actual sizes of openings as measured on site, so that small departures from the figured opening sizes shown on the drawings were of little importance.

1.02 Component building

However, with component building, the manufacturing and assembly processes are separated; the former being transferred from the rough and ready conditions prevailing on building sites to the controlled environment of the factory where labour can be employed more efficiently and higher manufacturing standards attained.

The use of large, prefinished components affects building design in two ways. First, the problem of accuracy becomes extremely important: this is true regardless of whether the building method employed is industrialised or semi-traditional. If the component turns out to be oversized in relation to the opening left for it, it cannot be cut to size as bricks can be. On the other hand if it is undersized, problems of jointing will arise. And if the builder attempts to overcome these problems by setting up the component first and 'building round' it, instead of inserting it in a preformed opening, numerous problems arise: not only is early incorporation of prefinished components in the building carcass undesirable because of the likelihood of subsequent damage to them, but a rigid and possibly uneconomic operational sequence might be imposed on the building programme, and failure of the component to arrive at the right moment may delay everything else.

So the use of prefabricated components demands close attention to the question of accuracy and tolerances, hitherto lacking in the building industry. Not only that; if the full benefits are to be derived from off-site prefabrication of components, long production runs are desirable so that expensive plant can be exploited to the full with a minimum of resetting of jigs, moulds and assembly lines. Inevitably this imposes the need for a certain degree of standardisation and 'variety reduction' in component manufacture. Automated manufacturing plant under computer control may reduce this need for standardisation in future, but that is of little comfort to present-day designers.

1.03 Dimensional discipline

These two factors—the need for agreed and rigorous standards of accuracy, and for agreed ranges of component sizes to allow reasonable production runs—confront the building industry with a major challenge; and the official dimensional co-ordination programme, which is currently under way, provides a basis on which the challenge can be met.

2 Dimensional co-ordination

2.01 General principles

Purpose

The programme, which started in 1966 with the publication of BS 4011, was intended to achieve co-ordination of the dimensions of *building spaces*, and the sizes of the *components* incorporated in the buildings. The idea is that if the dimensions of the building are related to the dimensions of available components (with proper allowance for joints and tolerances), the designer will be able to set out the positions of walls, floors, partitions and so on in such a way that when he later comes to select and specify the components of which they are composed all will fit together harmoniously without any need for costly specials, cutting to fit, or packing-out, even though the components may come from different manufacturers.

Sequence of decisions

First the designer determines, from user and other requirements, the minimum sizes of the spaces within the building, eg floor-to-ceiling heights; sill, window head and door head heights; service spaces within ceilings; column spacings; wall spacings; door and window widths, and so on. He can then select, from the horizontal and vertical *controlling dimensions* **1** given in 2.02, the officially recommended dimensions best suited to his purpose. The three-dimensional framework thus created will accept standardised components and assemblies. It can be filled in a variety of ways, so the second step is to select appropriate *basic sizes* **2, 3** for the components which are to be used (see 2.03). Finally, the joints between components must be considered, not only to establish the method of jointing, but also to allow decisions to be taken on questions of tolerances and accuracy, so that the *working sizes* of components (as distinct from the basic sizes, which are nominal and take no account of joint dimensions, tolerances etc) can be established. This is the most problematical of the three broad decision-groups listed here, because of the lack of helpful official guidance; and the problems involved are discussed in 2.04.

2.02 Controlling dimensions

Definitions

Controlling dimensions are the dimensions between key reference planes **1**. *Vertical* controlling dimensions are recommended for floor-to-roof and floor-to-floor heights, floor-to-ceiling heights, heights of floor zones and roof zones, heights of door and window heads and sills, and changes in level. *Horizontal* controlling dimensions are recommended for spacings between loadbearing walls, or structural columns, and they may be measured either between axes or between the boundaries of zones, as shown in **5**. The key reference planes are represented by *controlling lines*. Zones contain the structure of the floor, roof, wall or column, and may also contain finishes, services, and (where appropriate) allowances for camber and deflection. However building components, or their finishes, may be placed outside the zone boundaries provided the use of co-ordinated components is not inhibited as a result.

Application

Tables I to VIII give ranges of recommended dimensions for the spaces within various building types; adherence to these recommendations is essential if the designer is to ensure that dimensionally co-ordinated components can be used for the construction of the building fabric. It will be seen from the tables that some of the dimensions, eg floor-to-floor height for local authority housing, are mandatory (see table V, which shows controlling dimensions for housing).

2.03 Component dimensions

Basic principles

Once the basic dimensions of the spaces within the building have been selected in accordance with tables I to VIII, the

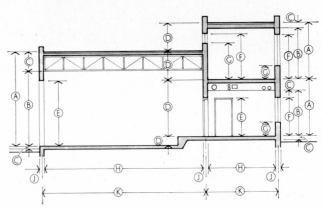

1 *First step in designing dimensionally coordinated building is to select from tables I to VIII appropriate controlling dimensions A floor-to-floor and floor-to-roof heights; B floor-to-ceiling heights; C heights of zones for floors and roofs; D changes of level; E doorset head heights; F window head heights; G window sill heights; H horizontal spacings between zones, and J widths of zones; or alternatively K axial spacings (not necessarily in this order)*

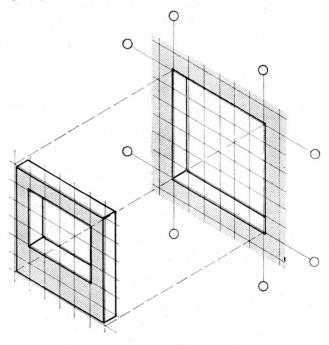

2 *Second step is to establish, within chosen controlling dimensions, a three-dimensional framework of basic sizes for components*

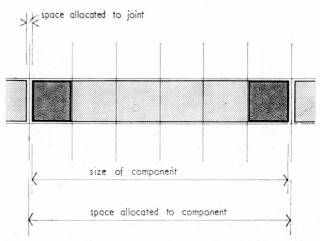

3 *Third step is to decide on accuracy, tolerances and joint widths, and establish working sizes of components*

next step is to design or select the components which will be assembled within these basic spaces to form the building enclosure.

Preferred sizes

The basic sizes must be decided in accordance with the hierarchy of preferred units laid down in BS 4011[1]: first preference is 300 mm and second preference is 100 mm. For dimensions below 300 mm (but not above—see **4**) there is a third preference of 50 mm, and a fourth of 25 mm. The reasoning behind these preferred sizes is that their general adoption will help the manufacturing and assembly industries achieve greater efficiency and greater economy by reducing the variety of component sizes.

The above are basic sizes, not working sizes; consequently they make no allowance for joints or tolerances. The latter are of vital importance in component building, because of the impossibility of cutting to fit on site, and are dealt with below.

2.04 Joints and tolerances

Basic principles

The modular grid established by the controlling lines, and by the basic sizes within the controlling lines, delineates the spaces *into* which the components have to fit **2**, **3**; the component must always be undersized in relation to the space grid. However, the amount by which the component needs to be undersized is one of the most difficult problems facing the designer today, because of the dearth of reliable information. Two main factors are involved: the amount of space required for the joint to perform its linkage function effectively; and the amount of space required to make allowance for inaccuracies, thermal, drying or other movement.

Joints

The purpose of the joint is to link adjoining components in such a way that the assembly as a whole will satisfactorily perform its functions of environmental control (eg sound and heat insulation, or moisture exclusion), structural stability and safety, and good appearance. With traditional building techniques this presents little problem: the wet-laid mortar joint can be adjusted, within wide limits, to whatever thickness is required to fill the space between the two components; once it has dried and cured, it has physical properties similar to the brick or concrete units linked by the joint, so that the assembly functions effectively as a single unit.

With component building and dry jointing techniques, the problem becomes much more complex. The joint may consist of a mastic filler, a gasket, or a third member, or any combination of these.

Therefore, joint and component are dissimilar physically in contrast to the traditional situation described above; ensuring that the joint will perform satisfactorily in every

way becomes a tricky, technological problem. Also, the design of the joint should not impose an unacceptable left-to-right, or right-to-left, operational sequence on component assembly; this might interfere with the contractor's programme and lead to difficulties with the installation of the last component or corner components. Finally, the width of joint is usually not as freely adjustable, without impairment of its functional performance, as a traditional mortar joint. So deciding on width of joint between prefabricated components is a problem requiring careful study; it is not enough to apply rules of thumb and manufacturers' advice; the performance of the assembled building fabric as a whole must be considered, involving problems of accuracies and tolerances which will control it.

Tolerances

The tolerance should allow for three kinds of inaccuracies: those of manufacture, setting-out on the building site, and faulty positioning of the component in relation to the setting-out lines. The tolerance should also make allowance for movement in the structure and component, due for example to loads, or thermal expansion and contraction.

Unfortunately the official documents purporting to give guidance on these matters (notably PD 6440[4] and 6445[6]) are inadequate[12]. The former, in particular, starts at the wrong end of the problem. Instead of examining the degree of accuracy *desirable* for the most critical parts of the building enclosure to function properly, and then deriving a hierarchy of fits and accuracies for the rest of the building fabric and specifying how these accuracies are to be achieved (both in the factory and on site), it starts by accepting the crude degree of accuracy characteristic of present-day in situ construction, and transfers this to component technology. Moreover, it is left to the individual designer to specify his own accuracies and tolerances, which leaves the field wide open for confusion and disagreement when components from various sources are combined in one building.

Until more useful advice and guidance from official bodies such as BSI becomes available, designers will have to assess as best they can the *manufacturing tolerance* (obtained from the makers of the component) and the *position tolerance* (obtained from an understanding of site assembly procedures), taking care not to accept unduly gross standards of inaccuracy. In particular, the fairly primitive standards of accuracy which have hitherto characterised the setting-out and assembly of the building on site are not good enough for component building, and we are likely in future to see the architect specifying not only the dimensions of the building, but also the means of setting out and the instrumentation to be used to ensure that critical datum lines and positions of components are accurate.

Working size

Once a minimum gap required for jointing technique has (*continued on p272*)

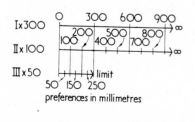

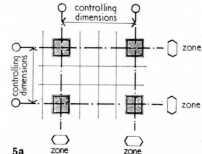

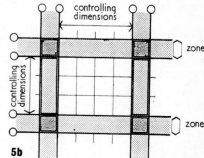

4 *First, second and third preferred dimensions for spaces and components, in mm; fourth preference (not shown) is 25 mm*

5 *Horizontal controlling dimensions quoted in tables* I *to* VIII

Table I *Controlling dimensions for offices*

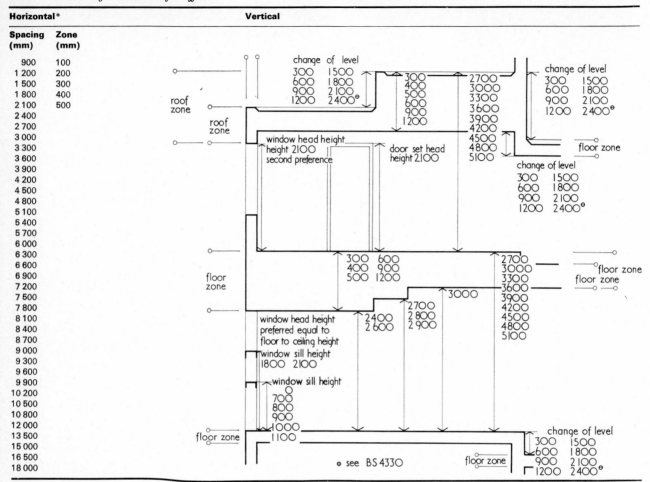

Horizontal*		Vertical
Spacing (mm)	**Zone (mm)**	
900	100	
1 200	200	
1 500	300	
1 800	400	
2 100	500	
2 400		
2 700		
3 000		
3 300		
3 600		
3 900		
4 200		
4 500		
4 800		
5 100		
5 400		
5 700		
6 000		
6 300		
6 600		
6 900		
7 200		
7 500		
7 800		
8 100		
8 400		
8 700		
9 000		
9 300		
9 600		
9 900		
10 200		
10 500		
10 800		
12 000		
13 500		
15 000		
16 500		
18 000		

*Dimensions to be read in conjunction with **5**; spacings are between centre lines, or zone boundaries, depending on method of setting-out adopted

Table II *Controlling dimensions for shops*

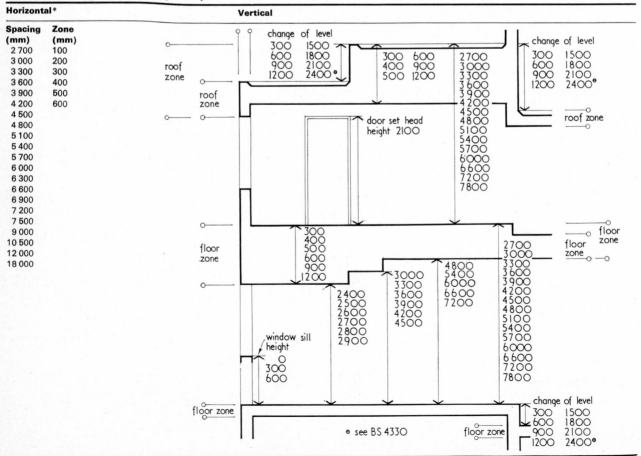

Horizontal*		Vertical
Spacing (mm)	**Zone (mm)**	
2 700	100	
3 000	200	
3 300	300	
3 600	400	
3 900	500	
4 200	600	
4 500		
4 800		
5 100		
5 400		
5 700		
6 000		
6 300		
6 600		
6 900		
7 200		
7 500		
9 000		
10 500		
12 000		
18 000		

*Dimensions to be read in conjunction with **5**; spacings are between centre lines ,or zone boundaries, depending on method of setting-out adopted

Table III *Controlling dimensions for educational buildings*

Horizontal*		Vertical
Spacing (mm)	**Zone (mm)**	
1 800	100	
2 400	150 (see BS 4330)	
2 700	200	
3 000	250 (see BS 4330)	
3 600	300	
4 200	600	
4 500		
4 800		
5 400		
6 000		
6 300		
6 600		
7 200		
8 100		
8 400		
9 000		
9 600		
9 900		
10 800		
11 700		
12 000		
12 600		
14 400		
16 200		
18 000		

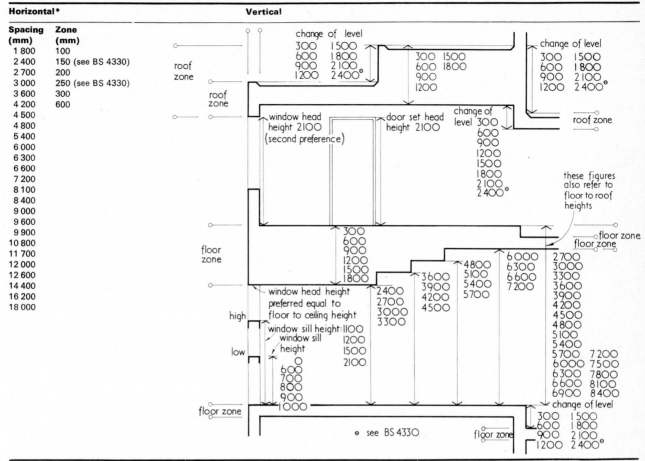

*Dimensions to be read in conjunction with 5; spacings are between centre lines, or zone boundaries, depending on method of setting-out adopted

Table IV *Controlling dimensions for hospitals*

Horizontal*		Vertical
Spacing (mm)	**Zone (mm)**	
2 700	100	
3 000	200	
4 200	300	
4 500		
5 400		
5 700		
6 000		
6 300		
8 700		
9 000		
9 300		
9 600		
11 700		
12 000		
12 300		
12 600		
12 900		
13 200		
17 400		
18 600		
19 800		

Dimensions to be read in conjunction with 5; spacings are between zone boundaries

Table v *Controlling dimensions for housing*

Horizontal*		Vertical
Spacing (mm)	**Zone (mm)**	
800	100	
900	200	
1 200	300	
1 500	400	
1 800		
2 100		
2 400		
2 700		
3 000		
3 300		
3 600		
3 900		
4 200		
4 500		
4 800		
5 100		
5 400		
5 700		
6 000		
6 300		
6 600		
6 900		
7 200		
7 500		
7 800		
8 100		
8 400		
8 700		
9 000		
9 300		
9 600		
9 900		
10 200		
10 500		
10 800		
11 100		

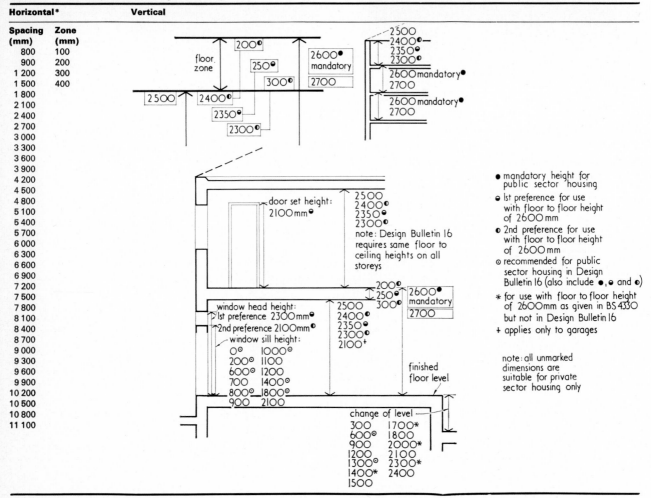

● mandatory height for public sector housing

◒ 1st preference for use with floor to floor height of 2600 mm

◓ 2nd preference for use with floor to floor height of 2600 mm

⊙ recommended for public sector housing in Design Bulletin 16 (also include ●, ◒ and ◓)

* for use with floor to floor height of 2600mm as given in BS 4330 but not in Design Bulletin 16

+ applies only to garages

note: all unmarked dimensions are suitable for private sector housing only

*Spacings are between boundaries of zones for loadbearing walls and columns **5**; axial spacing is not recommended for public sector housing. Dimensions greater than 7200 mm apply to pitched roof construction

Table vi *Controlling dimensions for farm buildings*

Horizontal†		Vertical
Span (mm)	**Bay spacing (mm)**	
First preference: 3 000	3 000	
3 000	4 800	
4 800	6 000	
5 400		
6 000		
6 600		
7 200		
7 800		
9 000		
10 800		
13 200		
14 400		
18 000		
20 400		
Second preference:		
2 400		
3 600		
4 500		
15 600		
Third preference:		
2 700		
3 300		
3 900		
4 200		
6 300		
8 400		
9 600		
10 200		
11 400		
12 000		
16 800		
19 200		
19 800		
21 600		

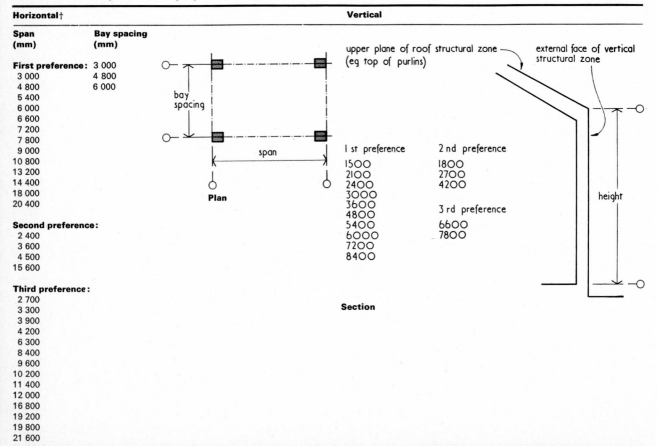

1 st preference	2 nd preference
1500	1800
2100	2700
2400	4200
3000	
3600	3 rd preference
4800	6600
5400	7800
6000	
7200	
8400	

*Information from the Agricultural Land Service, Wolverhampton (see *Agriculture*, December 1970 to January 1971)
†Span dimensions to outer faces of structural zones; length or bay spacing dimensions to centre lines of structural zones

Table VII *Controlling dimensions for hotels*

Horizontal*		Vertical
Spacing (mm)	**Zone (mm)**	
1 800	100	
2 100	200	
2 400	300	
2 700	400	
3 000	500	
3 300	600	
3 600		
3 900		
4 200		
4 500		
4 800		
5 100		
5 400		
5 700		
6 000		
6 300		
6 600		
6 900		
7 200		
7 500		
9 000		
10 500		
12 000		

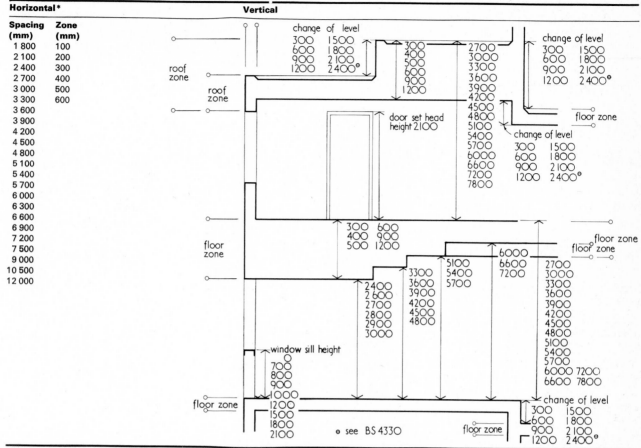

*Dimensions to be read in conjunction with **5**; spacings are between centre lines, or zone boundaries, depending on method of setting-out adopted

Table VIII *Controlling dimensions for industrial buildings*

Horizontal*		Vertical
Spacing (mm)	**Zone (mm)**	
3 000	100	
4 500	200	
6 000	300	
7 500	400	
9 000	500	
10 500	600	
12 000		
13 500		
15 000		
16 500		
18 000		

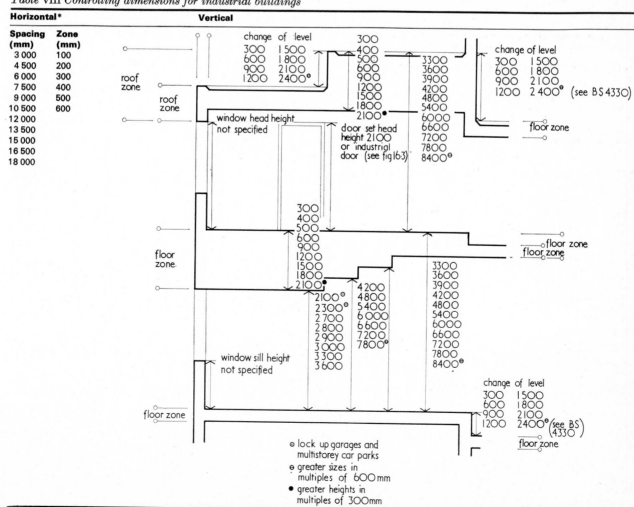

*Dimensions to be read in conjunction with **5**; spacings are between centre lines, or zone boundaries, depending on method of setting-out adopted

been established (as explained in 'Joints' above) plus an allowance to take into account site inaccuracies in positioning the component and an allowance to take into account manufacturing inaccuracies (as explained above), it is possible to specify the *working size* of the component by using the methods set out in BS 3626:1963. The working size will be specified in terms of a maximum and a minimum size; eg a component of basic size 900 mm, and a working size of 890 mm ± 5 mm, would be permitted to be of any size between 885 mm and 895 mm, so the joint width would range between 10 mm and 30 mm as tolerance extends both sides of grid line.

The above brief notes are intended only to summarise the principles involved in component and joint design. More detailed guidance will be given in later sections of the handbook.

3 Checklist

3.01 Functional spaces

Establish, from user and other requirements, desired values for the following critical dimensions:
- Floor-to-ceiling heights
- Heights of zones for floors and roofs
- Floor-to-floor and floor-to-roof heights
- Junction of higher and lower buildings in relation to roof zone
- Changes in level
- Window sill heights
- Window head heights
- Door set head heights
- Wall and column spacings.

3.02 Controlling dimensions

Select, from the officially recommended ranges of dimensions given in tables I to VIII, the most suitable co-ordinated equivalents for the values established in 3.01.

3.03 Basic sizes of components

- Consider effect of functional requirements, eg environmental and structural performance, on basic sizes
- Consider effect of manufacturing, transport and assembly factors on basic sizes
- Consider effect of cost factors on basic sizes
- Consider appearance
- Decide basic sizes of components and assemblies in accordance with preferred dimensions quoted in 2.03.

3.04 Accuracies, tolerances and joints

- Consider minimum and maximum joint widths for satisfactory environmental, structural and visual performance of joints
- Consider manufacturing inaccuracies
- Consider site setting-out and assembly inaccuracies
- Consider relative movement in structure and components
- Establish hierarchy of fits and tolerances for structure and fabric of building as a whole (see 2.04).

3.05 Working sizes of components

- On basis of 3.04, establish manufacturing sizes and tolerances for all components and assemblies.

4 References

BRITISH STANDARDS INSTITUTION
1 BS 4011:1966 Basic sizes for building components and assemblies [(F4)]
2 BS 4330:1968 Recommendations for the co-ordination of dimensions in building: controlling dimensions [(F4j)] *metric units*
3 PD 6432 Recommendations for the co-ordination of dimensions in building: arrangement of building components and assemblies within functional groups, part 1:1969 Functional groups 1, 2, 3 and 4 [(F4)]
4 PD 6440 Draft for development: accuracy in building, part 1:1969 imperial units; part 2:1969 metric units [(F6)] *£1·80 each*
5 PD 6444 Recommendations for the co-ordination of dimensions in building: basic spaces for structure, external envelope, and internal subdivision, part 1:1969 functional groups 1, 2 and 3 [(F4j)] *£2*
6 PD 6445 Recommendations for the co-ordination of dimensions in building: tolerances and joints, the derivation of building component manufacturing sizes from co-ordinating sizes [(F4j)] *metric units*

MINISTRY OF PUBLIC BUILDING AND WORKS
7 DC 4 Recommended vertical dimensions for educational, health, housing, office and single-storey general purpose industrial buildings. 1967, HMSO [(F4j)]
8 DC 5 Recommended horizontal dimensions for educational, health, housing, office and single-storey general purpose industrial buildings. 1967, HMSO [(F4j)]
9 DC 6 Guidance on the application of recommended vertical and horizontal dimensions for educational, health, housing, office and single-storey general purpose industrial buildings. 1967, HMSO [(F4j)]
10 DC 7 Recommended intermediate vertical controlling dimensions for educational, health, housing and office buildings, and guidance on their application. 1967, HMSO [(F4j)]

11 MINISTRY OF HOUSING AND LOCAL GOVERNMENT Circular 31/67 Vertical dimensional standards in housing. 1967, HMSO [(81 (F4j)]
12 SLIWA, J. Accuracy, tolerances, joints: confused advice from BSI. *Architects' Journal*, 4 March 1970, p553 [(F6)]

Information sheet
Enclosure 2

Cost considerations

Dimensional considerations and costs are the most important of the constraints on design listed in technical study ENCLOSURE 2. *The first of these has been covered in information sheet* ENCLOSURE 1; *in this information sheet* BRIAN PUGH *deals with the second. The aim here is restricted to outlining the effect of design decisions on costs. More directly applicable cost information on specific element-groups will be given in later sections of the handbook*

1 Introduction

1.01 Available methods

There is a great deal of computer-aided research now in progress, which aims to assess and compare building costs at early design stage: eg West Sussex employ a system which covers design and building process from inception to feedback of information from completed building. A more general application of this system may well represent the future pattern of design and construction processes. If these systems result in relating pricing more closely to actual operations, in reducing uncertainties and enabling risks to be more easily identified and shared between client and contractor, then estimating, cost planning and cost control can become much more accurate and effective. For the moment, however, most architects must design without very sophisticated aids, must assess the cost implications of their decisions with the data available and have their designs priced on the basis of the documentation and tendering methods still in general use. Therefore this sheet is based on prevailing design and building situations, and it aims to provide a guide to the factors influencing the cost of design decisions in general and of building enclosure in particular. It attempts to identify the elemental costs which may be less variable than others and the influence these might have on design approach. Finally, it emphasises the care required in applying historical pricing data to design proposals.

2 Cost and price

2.01 Terminology

In this information sheet, the term *price* will be used to denote the prices contained in competitive or negotiated tenders or estimates obtained from contractors, subcontractors and suppliers. The term *cost analysis* will be used, although it would be more correct to describe these published analyses as price analyses, particularly as they are usually based on tenders and not on final accounts. The term *cost* will generally be used to denote a contractor's or subcontractor's book costs plus overheads. Cost will also be used in a more abstract sense when considering examples of size and shape, and for this purpose it is assumed that differences between one shape and another would be reflected perfectly in the costs and not be subject to the varying conditions of actual building operations.

2.02 Tendering procedures

The limitations of contractors' pricing under present methods of tendering should be appreciated. Average rates are used widely with little detailed consideration of design factors which could have drastic effects on labour constants and constructional methods. Determination of construction methods, plant selection, resource allocation and outline programmes is often a rough and ready process based on assessments of bulk quantities.

The difference in price between projects which have been deliberately designed for economy of construction and those which are difficult to construct, is inadequately reflected in tenders, particularly when competition is keen.

Average pricing and crude planning also obscure the real effect of post-contract variations, and if architects and qss sometimes show an unwarranted reluctance to leave the relative safety of subclause 11(4) of the 'RIBA' contract for the insecurities of 11(6)[2], they are not helped by contractors' inability to isolate the costs of particular operations.

The alternative methods of obtaining tenders with varying degrees of competition and estimation, can be studied in *Tendering procedures and contractual arrangements*[1]. Unorthodox tendering methods do not always result in a higher price to the client. In many cases where continuity of work and guaranteed programmes are available, and where the client's requirements are very specialised, a semi-competitive or controlled cost plus method can produce a cheaper price to the client in the end. But at present, competitive tenders with traditional documents will still produce a lower initial price for the majority of projects (even if the final cost is somewhat greater).

2.03 Improved methods

Tendering documents with an operational format may become more acceptable in the future and many new procedures are already in use, but in the meantime the following factors would help to improve traditional tendering methods:

1 Consultants should be more aware of operational implications of designs and decisions, and these should be made clearer to contractors in drawings and tender documents.

2 Wherever possible, subcontractors should be selected earlier and identified in the tendering documents.

3 Clients and consultants should appreciate that although contractors may be well equipped to solve site problems, they should not be expected to be clairvoyants as well and to cover any unreasonable risks in their prices.

Table I *Effect of plan size and proportions on cost of enclosing wall element*

	Shape A	B	C	D	E
Perimeter (m)	12	24	40	80	100
Area (m²) of enclosing walls (£8 per m²)	36	72	120	240	300
Floor area (m²)	9	36	100	400	400
Wall/floor ratio	4·0	2·0	1·2	0·6	0·75
Cost (£) of enclosing wall element per m² of floor area	32·00	16·00	9·60	4·80	6·00

Table II *Effect of plan shape on cost (£) of substructure and primary elements (all shapes are the same area ie 400 m²)*

	Shape F	G	H	J
Floor slab (£4 per m²)	1600	1600	1600	1600
Perimeter foundation (£9 per m)	900	720	1080	1170
External wall (£8 per m²)	2400	1920	2880	3120
Flat roof (£8 per m²)	3200	3200	3200	3200
Roof edge (£3 per m)	300	240	360	390
Internal foundation* (£7 per m)	—	140	—	—
Internal wall (£5 per m²)	—	300	—	—
Total cost	8400	8120	9120	9480
Cost per m² of floor area	21·00	20·30	22·80	23·70

*An internal foundation is assumed to run across the width of shape **G**

Table III *Actual savings achieved by reducing length of* **F** *to 30 m*

	Cost £
Floor slab 100 m² at £4	400
Perimeter foundation 20 m at £9	180
External wall 60 m² at £8	480
Roof 100 m² at £8	800
Roof edge 20 m at £3	60
Total	**1920**

Note: this is less than ¼ of the floor area (ie £2100)

Table IV *Additional cost of small bay added to* **F**

	Cost £
Floor slab 25 m² at £4	100
Perimeter foundation 10 m at £9	90
External wall 30 m² at £8	240
Roof 25 m² at £8	200
Roof edge 10 m at £3	30
Total	**660**

Note: this exceeds the *pro-rata* increase based on floor area (ie £525)

3 Design factors

3.01 Size and shape

Certain basic principles apply to the cost effects of size and shape. There has been much emphasis in cost planning on the significance of perimeter/area ratios and wall/floor ratios. The implications of these are shown in the following illustrated examples:

Example 1

Taking simple building shapes and considering only the cost of a typical enclosing wall, say 3 m high (assumed for this purpose to be identical in all cases), the measurements, ratios and costs obtained are shown in table I. This example (ignoring all other design implications) illustrates one cost aspect of size and the difference between square and rectangular shapes. For any given area the shortest enclosing perimeter is produced by a circle. Although in the past this has been discounted as an economic proposition, with the development of new techniques, eg inflatables, it should not be overlooked.

Example 2

Table II illustrates the effect on cost for single-storey 3 m high enclosures with different shapes but all of the same area. To make the example more realistic other elements have been introduced, and in one case an internal loadbearing wall is indicated to maintain the theoretical maximum roof span. As before, other design implications have been ignored. Although no account has been taken of the possible savings in **H** and **J** due to shorter roof spans, the example indicates a likely difference between **G** and **J** of £3·40 per m² of floor area which might represent more than the cost per square metre of floor coverings in a building.

Example 3

There are many dangers in the use of total costs per square metre of buildings, when increases and reductions in floor area are being considered. The percentages of total costs in buildings which are affected by changes in area are considered in a later section, but an example of the caution needed can be demonstrated by showing the effect of changes in **F** in table II. **F** costs £21/m² for the elements included. Assume that to keep within a cost limit, the total of £8400 has to be reduced by at least £2100. It is tempting to say that this represents 100 m² and that the saving can be achieved by reducing the length of the building by 10 m. Of course the actual saving would be less, as shown in table III.

Example 4

Similar caution is needed when considering the addition of protrusions, bays, link corridors and other small or narrow spaces, as these invariably cost much more per square metre of floor area than might be expected. Assume that a small room or bay is to be added to **F**. The bay is 25 m² which at £21/m² would cost £525, but the cost is likely to be much more, as shown in table IV. The roof cost might be less because of the shorter span, but even so, the cost per square metre of such a bay is still likely to be higher than that of the main building.

Example 5

If the effects of size and shape in relation to cross-section and number of storeys are considered, it is obvious that the total design situation becomes much more complex, but certain basic implications should be appreciated. Assuming that a total inflexible floor area could be contained either in a single storey or in several storeys, the diagrams in table I will show different basic effects.

Given a square shape, **D** would represent a single-storey building of 400 m²: **C** would represent one floor of a four-storey building with the same total floor area of 400 m². So the area of enclosing wall of **D** is 240 m² and for each storey of **C** it is 120 m², which multiplied by four gives a total area of enclosing wall for **C** of 480 m². In short, the wall/floor ratio has doubled by accommodating the same total area in four storeys instead of a single storey. From single-storey to two-storey and single- to three-storey, increases in wall/floor ratio are 41 and 73 per cent respectively. But as each storey is added the increase becomes less and less until at 10 storeys it is about 5 per cent only per storey added. This is all fairly obvious and is unaffected by size, as can be seen by applying this process to **A** and **B** in the same example. It is also unaffected by shape, if the relative proportions of length and breadth are maintained and no set-backs or projections are incorporated.

If the proportions become more uneven as the storeys are increased, then the increase in wall/floor ratio is much greater. Conversely, if the proportions are made more even, then the increase is less marked and sometimes the wall/floor ratio can be reduced, but to achieve this at the lower range of heights, a drastic change of shape is needed. In traditional hostels and similar kinds of buildings, where the width tends to remain constant, an increase in the number of storeys with the total floor area maintained naturally results in the proportions becoming more even, but the additional vertical circulation can cause a reduction in functional areas.

In these examples the enclosing walls have been emphasised but the relative costs of other elements, particularly the roof, are affected considerably by the number of storeys, especially at the lower range of heights.

Example 6

If **C** and **D** (of table I) are again taken as models, it is obvious that the area of roof to cover **D** in single storey is four times that required to cover **C** in four storeys, although the total floor area is the same in both cases. The cost of the floor element is also a major factor in considering differences between numbers of storeys, because in most cases a suspended floor is more expensive than a ground floor slab. To illustrate some of these effects, the relative costs of enclosing walls, roof and floors might be as shown below. In table V, **C** and **D** are taken as models with an assumed storey-height of 3 m. Obviously floor and roof spans could be different in the two models, and changes in the frame or loadbearing walls would be significant in a more detailed study. These costs show that although the wall/floor ratio of **C** is double that of **D** and the floors cost more, these effects are balanced by the difference in roof costs. If the external wall is assumed to be glass curtain walling (which might cost £30/m² of surface instead of the £8 used in the example), **C** would be over £5000 more expensive than **D** and the wall/floor ratio would be particularly significant.

Table V Relative costs of four- and one-storey solutions

	C (4 storeys)		D (1 storey)	
	Total cost £	Cost (£) per m² of total floor area	Total cost £	Cost (£) per m² of total floor area
Ground floor slab (£4/m²)	400	1	1600	4
Suspended floor slab (£6/m²)	1800	4·5	—	—
External wall (£8/m²)	3840	9·6	1920	4·8
Roof (£8/m²)	800	2	3200	8
Roof edge (£3 per m)	120	0·3	240	0·6
	6960	17·4	6960	17·4

Table vi *Relative costs of one- and two-storey solutions (all shapes same floor area—400 m²)*

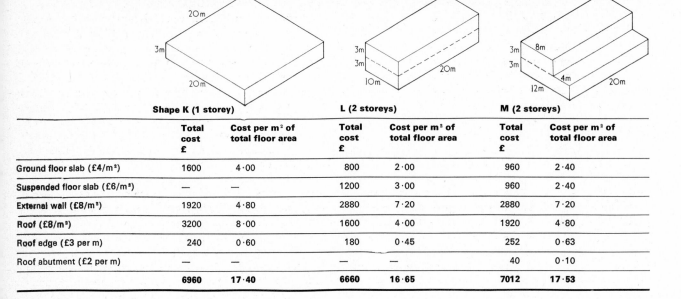

	Shape K (1 storey)		L (2 storeys)		M (2 storeys)	
	Total cost £	Cost per m² of total floor area	Total cost £	Cost per m² of total floor area	Total cost £	Cost per m² of total floor area
Ground floor slab (£4/m²)	1600	4·00	800	2·00	960	2·40
Suspended floor slab (£6/m²)	—	—	1200	3·00	960	2·40
External wall (£8/m²)	1920	4·80	2880	7·20	2880	7·20
Roof (£8/m²)	3200	8·00	1600	4·00	1920	4·80
Roof edge (£3 per m)	240	0·60	180	0·45	252	0·63
Roof abutment (£2 per m)	—	—	—	—	40	0·10
	6960	17·40	6660	16·65	7012	17·53

Example 7

The occasions when total floor area is fixed and number of storeys is flexible are infrequent because of site and planning constraints. In the cheap or medium cost-range of buildings a square shape is not easy to achieve in more than a single storey because of ventilation and lighting problems. The solution often considered involves a different area at each level and this creates set-backs and overhangs. Taking **K** as a basic model of a single-storey building, two variants of a two-storey solution with the same total floor area are shown in table vi.

A major factor in solutions similar to **M** (apart from stairs), is the extra cost of a beam to support the front wall of the upper storey, if the internal supports cannot be adjusted suitably. So the cost of roof abutment (skirting, cavity gutters, etc) might seem less important, but when set-backs, balconies, means of escape and similar external areas are created, the costs of the abutments as well as the edges can become particularly significant, especially in housing designs.

Comparison of external wall costs in table vi shows that the change from single-storey to two-storey produces an increase of over 41 per cent (see example 5), due to the departure from the square shape of **K**. The saving in roof cost in **L** outweighs the increase in external wall and floor costs, but this does not apply to **M** where the set-back occurs.

If model **M** were stood on its head (producing an overhang) and only the same simple costs were applied, the total cost would be £7072. This would not take account of the considerable extra cost of the projecting floor slab, insulation to the exposed soffit, cold-bridging safeguards and other design problems caused by overhangs.

Example 8

A particularly important factor in housing design is the cost of an end wall in a terraced or linear situation. If **O**, **P** and **Q** in **1** are each considered to represent terraces of either two-storey houses or four-storey maisonettes all of constant width and depth, the structural cost of each dwelling includes, in addition to the front and rear walls and one party wall, a share of the extra cost of facing one end wall and a whole faced wall at the other end. The front-to-back depth of the dwellings affects the cost of

this situation, but an average extra cost over two storeys for facing one end wall and a whole faced wall at the other end could be approximately £400. Therefore the share per dwelling in **Q**, whether a two-storey house or maisonette, is £50. In **P** it is £100 per dwelling, and in **O** £200 per dwelling. If **N** represents a two-storey detached house, the enclosing walls can cost £350 (£400 less £50) more per dwelling than for a two-storey terrace house in **Q**. This example takes account only of walls, but obviously strip foundations, roof edges and other details are affected in the same way and, depending on the number of storeys, tend to further increase the cost of dwellings in short terraces or blocks.

In housing design the fact that external walls are usually more expensive than internal walls is significant when considering the relationship of frontage to depth and the effect of staggered terraces.

In blocks of heights affected by recent structural regulations*, the measures which have had to be adopted to strengthen cross walls have upset some of these established notions of cost, and in cases where dwelling blocks have fairly complex sections, a frame might provide the cheaper structural solution. But party walls still have to be of a certain thickness to comply with other regulations, and the opportunity to combine this requirement with loadbearing capacity must still remain an attractive economic proposition.

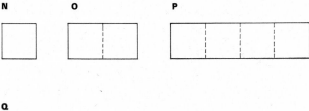

1 *Cost effect of terrace lengths*

*Regulations D19, D20 and D21 of the Building Regulations 1972 concern all building over five storeys in height (for this purpose the number includes the ground storey, but not basements) and are additional to the controls exercised by the rest of Part D (Structural Stability)

Example 9
No account has been taken of windows in all the models presented because of the many factors influencing window sizes, making it difficult to incorporate realistic window situations into the limited number of examples. Windows are an expensive element. Even a standard opening window of wood or metal with normal glazing can cost between two to three times more per unit area occupied than the average external-faced brick wall, when the formation and trimming of the opening are taken into account.

This factor is very important when changes in wall/floor ratio are being considered. When shapes of designs are changed from deep or square to narrow or rectangular (or in housing design from narrow front to wide front), it is often assumed that, in theory, the proportion of window to solid wall can be reduced. This reduction is often achieved when the window concept is that of punched openings. But when the concept is that of continuous horizontal strip windows or of a large element of window wall, then the proportion of window to solid tends to remain very similar whatever the shape of the design. The ratio of total window area to total perimeter area is an important cost factor, a point illustrated in 6.03.

Summary
The model situations presented in this section are extremely simple compared with the complexities faced in actual design, but the tendencies described are real enough and their significance should be recognised and used early in the design process.

3.02 Specification and standards

Standards
The price or cost of an element is particularly affected by the standard of performance required. Where materials or in-situ elements are described in catalogues, or can be inspected, or are the subject of Agrément certificates, BS specifications or consortia quotations, value for money or fitness of purpose can be judged with some confidence. Made-up components or in situ operations cannot be so easily pre-judged in this way, and difficulties may arise from problems of fitting components together.

Finishes
In attempting to achieve the desired standards of appearance of components or elements, the full cost implications must always be recognised. For example difficulties in achieving appearance or finish often arise with in-situ concrete. The difference in cost between an off-the-shutter 'fair face' finish and a board-marked, or ultra-smooth, or special colour or textured finish can be considerable.

It is rarely possible to achieve particular standards on the cheap and it is unreasonable to expect a contractor to maintain uniformity of colour and texture in exposed concrete or brick joints without using special cements, aggregates or sand, or special shuttering or pointing as a separate operation.

Tolerances
Incompatibility of tolerances is another source of considerable extra cost. Normal tolerances may be specified for brickwork or in-situ concrete, but it is then often assumed that standard components or made-up components with apparent repetition of similar sizes, such as windows or door frames, can be fitted perfectly into openings without use of cover fillets and fillers, and without having to spend more on site labour, in making adjustments, scribing or general

bodging, often costing more than the component itself.

Drilling of holes in components for screw or bolt fixings can usually be done more cheaply in the shop than on the site, but hopes that shop-drillings of, say, windows, sills, frames and other similar components will line up either with each other or with holes in steel frames or pockets and fixing blocks in site concrete have often been too optimistic with disastrous effects on costs.

Sheet materials, which have to fit into openings or frames, can sometimes be cut or formed to slightly different sizes to suit differences in tolerance without too much extra cost, but this is not always the case: eg for armour-plate glass there is sometimes a fixed charge of about £6 for each different-sized pane (however minute the difference), and it can be appreciated what the cost implications would be if every pane had to fit exactly into frames or openings which are apparently of the same size but are in fact subject to normal permitted tolerances.

The effect of waste is not always properly taken into account. In the case of board or sheet materials, where the fitted sizes are obviously very different from standard sizes supplied, the waste factor is usually apparent. Sometimes fitted sizes are calculated very carefully in an attempt to avoid any waste at all, but it is often forgotten that saw cuts, inevitable breakages, rough edges on brittle materials can make a nonsense of this intention where the fitted sizes are critical.

Standardisation
In the past the difference between the price of a standard component and a purpose-made one has often not reflected the true difference in manufacturing costs. Specials were often supplied at relatively low cost as a good-will service to designers, or formed such a large proportion of the output that the true difference between standard and special was not apparent.

In more recent times, changes of attitude by manufacturers and the development of consortia, bulk-purchasing arrangements and guaranteed programmes have produced a big price difference between standards and specials. Of course, the price of specials depends entirely on the methods of manufacture and quantities involved. The cost of special moulds, dies, machine tools and cutters spread over a large quantity can sometimes be almost insignificant, but where small quantities are involved the fixed costs can be prohibitive: eg with certain methods of producing bricks, the mould cost might be about £10 and the difference between spreading this cost over a few dozen bricks, as compared with hundreds or thousands, can be appreciated.

Future developments may make it possible to produce any run of specials at no more cost than standards; but this is not likely to be achieved soon.

4 Operational factors

4.01 Introduction

Many disputes can be avoided if thought is given to the effect of particular design details or decisions on actual site operations. The following examples illustrate the effect of design decisions on construction methods, use of plant, productivity, insurances and so on.

4.02 Examples

Basements
The design of basement walls and the method of waterproofing can drastically affect the contractor's approach to

construction. Propped cantilever design of basement walls or externally applied membranes may prohibit the strutting of earth retainers off the basement walls and may virtually demand sheet piling or large excavation with sloping sides.

Formwork

The number of times that formwork can be used is an important factor in pricing concrete. Use can be restricted by designs which require continuous propping through all floors of a building. Where special forms are required, eg fibreglass or plastic for waffle slabs, they must be re-used as much as possible. The designer should consider ways of maintaining adequate propping of ribs, which still permit removal of forms in a shorter time. Another design feature which has caused problems is the incorporation of alternate timber and concrete floors in dwelling blocks, where propping off the timber is not permitted, thus adding considerably to the cost of formwork (but probably not to the extent of making all concrete floors cheaper).

Use of plant and manpower

The effect of design decisions on the use of plant is not always appreciated. Certain specifications which appear to be economic, result in costly restrictions on site. An example is the use of polythene dampproof membranes under ground floor slabs without designing in proper protection. The contractor may find that his work over the area of the slab is so restricted by the need to avoid damaging the membrane, that it would pay him to adopt a more costly membrane or provide an extra blinding or bed at his own expense.

Craneage and scaffolding are frequently affected more than is foreseen. A design for cladding which can be erected from the inside may well be thought to obviate the need for outside scaffolding, but this design needs the most careful scrutiny to ensure that there is not some minor feature of fine finish, flashing or jointing which cannot possibly be executed from inside.

The use of precast concrete components is closely linked to craneage. Precast concrete may well be chosen for speed of construction or a certain standard of surface finish. But it is essential to ensure that the weights of the components permit the use of an economic crane which can reach the necessary positions at permitted boom or jib ranges.

Restricted sites sometimes prohibit the use of cranes of a size or type which design demands. Conditions on site may prohibit the use of heavy lorries and equipment and this should also be considered at design stage.

Productivity

This may be adversely affected by apparently economic design decisions. In an attempt to reduce prices, different strength concretes are often specified for members which are close together; or different mortar strengths or different blocks or bricks are incorporated into a single length of wall. The effect of changing from one material to another in a single operation can be far greater in cost than apparent savings in the different materials.

Cast-in services

The casting of services into concrete is sometimes an attractive proposition and while it can be economic, the effect on pouring operations and the need to provide location or fixing blocks should not be overlooked in the cost appraisal.

Protection

This is often overlooked and can add considerably to cost. Concrete cast very close to faced brickwork, particularly in internal situations, may involve irremediable damage to finished surfaces. The contractor should be warned so that the appropriate precautions are taken and priced.

Hidden costs

An example of inconsistencies in specification will show how hidden costs are not always appreciated. A specification may demand that a building is properly glazed before certain finishes or fittings commence, but if the glass specified is particularly costly, eg sealed double units, the contractor may find it impossible to insure against breakages, and the cost of replacements could well be ruinous.

Summary

These and many similar examples show that design decisions affect site operations as well as specification and quantities, and that adequate forethought can forestall a large number of post-contract problems.

The whole of the foregoing highlights the need for architects to either (a) be trained in site operational systems and costs or (b) to consult the builder at design stage, making necessary a special form of contract permitting early appointment or (c) have the services of a specialist site-cost consultant. This last alternative suggests the development of a totally new kind of animal with a new role to play in the construction team.

5 Cost in use

5.01 Implications for public sector

Capital or initial costs are often given greater emphasis than running costs or costs in use. This is because of limitations imposed on capital expenditure by the nature of the cost limits which apply in the public sector. These limits are related to annual or essentially short term budgeting dictated by the uncertainties of the national economy, and the likelihood of changes in political opinions and policies. Although public cost limits generally permit the design of basic structures to last the 60 years of the public loan repayment period, repayments of capital and interest, maintenance and other running costs are usually financed out of annual revenue. Replacements of major building elements, when they occur, are financed out of revenue, reserve funds, or are the subject of special loans.

The effect of these arrangements is generally to preclude consideration of spending in excess of cost limits now, in order to save expenditure in the long term. The only specific exception to this is district or central boiler chamber heating schemes for housing, where proof of economies in the long term enables extra capital expenditure to be approved. There has been more flexibility in some sectors recently which permits greater freedom of action at regional or local level, but policies relating to costs in use seem unlikely to change at present.

5.02 Implications for private sector

In the private sector similar attitudes often prevail and although these may stem from the same basic economic situation, they can be more easily explained in commercial terms. When interest rates are high, and the future can be heavily discounted due to continuing inflation, extra spending now (to save expenditure later) is discouraged. This tendency can be greatly influenced or modified by grants and tax allowances, effect or inflation and scarcity value of particular types of property.

5.03 Cost-in-use calculations

Where these comparisons can be made, they are usually calculated by simple accounting techniques. That is, the capital expenditure is amortised over the expected life of the component or building and the annual repayments of capital and interest so calculated are compared with the anticipated differences in annual running and maintenance costs. In the private sector the calculations are usually more complicated and involve consideration of taxes, grants, allowances, depreciation and the return on investments.

More sophisticated discounting techniques are not widely used, except at research level for appraisals of new building concepts and in consideration of the cost benefits of expenditure on motorways, airports, new towns etc. Discounting and the use of discounted cash flow techniques is increasing in the commercial sector but is not widely applied at present. Discounting techniques[3] can make significant differences to calculations of cost in use. Such techniques are highly sophisticated and beyond the realms of the architect's training. Possible future results are also at the mercy of unknown factors such as a change of government or at least government policy. Clearly if cost figures are to be examined in this kind of detail, close consultation with the client's accountants would be essential.

Design considerations

When costs in use are compared with the capital costs of design options the following factors should be considered:
1 Repayment and interest on loans for the investment and accumulation of funds for future expenditure
2 Rates, taxes, allowances and subsidies affecting return on investment
3 Annual periodic maintenance costs, eg painting, washing down, overhauls and inspection, gardening, minor repairs
4 Replacement costs, eg floor coverings, roofing, lighting bulbs and tubes, mechanical plant, major repairs
5 Cleaning costs, eg daily cleaning, periodic window cleaning
6 Fuel and power costs, eg fuel and power for heating, cooling, ventilation, lighting, lifts and other equipment
7 Staffing costs, eg boiler room staff, lift attendants, caretaking, security staff (including overheads on labour)
8 Insurances for fire, damage, theft, personal injury
9 Functional costs, eg flexibility, effects on production, staff comfort and turnover, prestige.

As regards initial capital cost, interest rates and repayment periods are of vital concern. Interest rates are now high and tend to restrict capital expenditure, but the effect is modified if the repayment period is very long because annual costs are less although total expenditure is greater in the end. Short term loans increase the annual outgoings and this is important when rehabilitation of property is being considered as against rebuilding, where repayment periods are often very different.

Heating and air conditioning systems should always be evaluated in terms of cost in use, type of fuel being an important factor. Calculations for those studies are influenced by shape and size of buildings, choice of enclosure materials, window areas and type of glazing, all of which affect heat losses or gains. Mechanical ventilation and artificial lighting costs must also be considered in relation to shape, layout, and ability to provide natural ventilation or light at perimeter or roof level.

The capital costs of internal finishes, claddings and roof coverings should be compared more often with costs in use arising from cleaning, maintenance and durability. The capital and running costs of fire and security precautions can be compared with the variations in premiums for insurance which changes in proposals will produce.

Some cost factors involved in flexibility, particularly where they relate to partitioning of spaces, can be easily assessed; but when the factors include the effects of future major alterations, discounting techniques are best employed to make appropriate decisions.

6 Elemental costs

6.01 Variable and 'fixed' costs

Patterns can be found in the relative cost of elements in various building types, particularly in percentage of total cost devoted to services. But the value of these comparisons is limited by differences in cost limits, standards, methods of construction, heights and shapes of different buildings of the same type. Individual published cost analyses show relative values of elements and these provide a reasonable basis for a cost feasibility model or an initial cost plan. It is often very difficult to isolate the true cost of a frame. This requires careful appreciation of the relationship between the frame elements and foundations, building enclosure, internal floors and space divisions. Certain elemental costs, eg floor and ceiling finishes, can be related directly to the total floor area of the building. Others, eg partitions, doors, fittings, sanitary installations and even service installations, may be consistent in buildings of similar function, variations in cost per square metre of total floor area being more obviously due to differing standards rather than to building shape.

If a proportion of the cost limit or target can be allocated to cover standards of internal finish, fittings and service installation, then the main design effort can be concentrated on testing the feasibility of achieving various forms of enclosure and structure within the balance of the cost limit. In the public sector, minimum areas and standards are often predetermined by regulations. In the private sector (depending upon the quality of the brief) similar decisions related to functional requirements can also be made at an early stage.

Many internal elemental costs can be set quite firmly. Others can be set with upper and lower limits of feasible and acceptable costs, to provide flexibility in balancing the cost limit. Some designers prefer to develop their schemes as an integrated whole and the establishment of internal elemental costs at a very early stage might encourage too ready an acceptance of traditional layouts, and perpetuate stereotyped solutions of functional requirements. Where the clients' brief, cost limits and design time permit, there can be advantages in keeping all elemental costs flexible for as long as possible. However it is usually necessary to concentrate the design effort on matters of the greatest uncertainty as early as possible.

Public sector housing, where cost limits are rigorous and space requirements mandatory, can provide a good example of the advantage of establishing certain 'fixes' within cost limits at an early stage.

Example 1

Given a brief for three-person two-bedroom flats, the effect of containing these under different site density conditions can be considered. Assuming a high density of 510 persons per hectare in an urban situation in south-east England with an average of three persons per dwelling, the current metric yardstick would give a cost target for the superstructure (without adding any part of the 10 per cent tolerance) of approximately £3800 per dwelling.

The minimum net area of each three person flat, including

storage, would be 60 m². (There are mandatory standards for fittings and equipment and it is assumed that whole dwelling heating is to be provided.)

The cost per dwelling (excluding balconies, stairs and public areas) of internal elements of the desired standard can be established before the building form is considered at all. Typical costs for these elements are shown in **2a**. Suggested total of soil, waste and service costs, are also shown, but it is assumed that the extra cost of services, associated with high density dwelling blocks, is contained within the balance of the cost limit indicated.

The balance of the cost target (£2340 or approximately 62 per cent) is available for this extra service cost, and for the building enclosure and structure, plant rooms, balconies, stairs, lifts and all public areas in the superstructure. Under present conditions the difficulties of designing within the yardstick are only too apparent but there has been scope within highest density cost limits, to consider a wide variety of forms and arrangements ranging from individual tower blocks to complex medium rise deck schemes.

Now consider the cost target calculated for a lower density site in the same region, with the same type of flat and the same average number of persons per dwelling. For a density of 240 persons per hectare, the metric yardstick gives a cost target for the superstructure (again without adding any part of the 10 per cent tolerance) of £2868 average per dwelling.

Assuming that the standards of the internal elements are to be maintained, it will be seen from **2b** that the balance of the cost limit is now only £1408 or approximately 49 per cent. In this situation it should not be difficult for the designer to appreciate very quickly that even if he cuts the internal standards to an irreducible minimum, a great deal of design effort and consultant time would be wasted in pursuing ambitious concepts which are obviously incapable of achievement within the balance of cost available.

'Fixed' costs are not entirely independent of the final form of the building and the structural materials, but experience will enable weightings or provisional forecasts to be applied.

6.02 Element relationships

A proportion of partitions in large dwellings and other building types are often formed by loadbearing walls; wall finishings are affected by shape, structural materials and proportions of window and external door openings; floor and ceiling finishes are affected by the type of structural floors and roofs and the provision of service spaces. In complex dwelling blocks the distribution costs of all services are considerably affected by plan and section form. The capacity of heating and ventilating plant and outlets, and levels of artificial lighting are affected by form, structural materials and proportions of window opening. In the case of housing, each dwelling is self-contained and 'fixed costs' can be assessed for each different type and size. Other types of building often include many different kinds of functional space. These spaces should be treated separately so far as 'fixed costs' are concerned, particularly when the standard of finish, fitting out and servicing and the quantities of partitions and doors and heights of spaces are likely to vary. This is usually the approach in hospital or university cost planning and is equally useful for other types of building. In the early design stages, client's brief or designer's intentions may change. If this 'departmental' approach can be applied, it enables adjustments to cost models to be made at the correct cost level for different parts of the building without having to adjust the averages of elemental costs for the building as a whole.

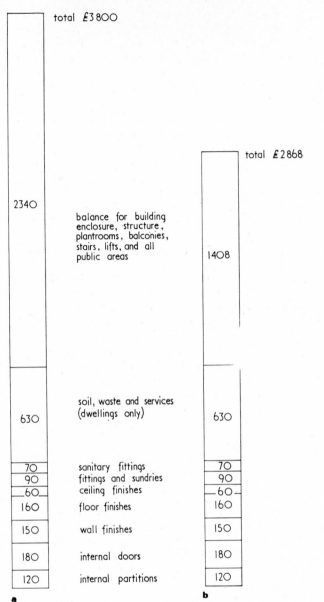

2 *Fixed and variable costs in similar dwellings at different densities;* **a** *at 510 people per hectare,* **b** *at 240 people per hectare*

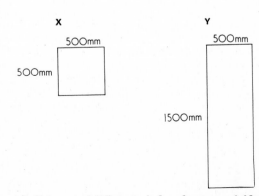

3 *Comparison of all-in cost of different window shapes; see 6.03*

An appreciation of relative costs of different spaces in buildings is essential either when discussing all-in floor area rates at feasibility stage, constructing early cost models, or assessing the effect of changes in spaces without detailed cost plan adjustments. The effect of adding or subtracting small areas on a limited range of elements, were shown in para 3.01. There, cost differences were relatively minor and nothing like the dramatic variations which are sometimes apparent when all elements and differences of function are taken into account. The following examples illustrate the careful appreciation that is needed.

Assume that the addition or omission of area is being considered to the bedroom of a dwelling or to a school classroom, after a provisional cost model or cost plan has been evolved. The all-in average cost of the gross area of flat dwellings or secondary school (including normal foundations but excluding external works) might be of the order of £54 and £68/m² respectively. Providing that changes in area do not involve addition of some structural irregularity, the cost per square metre of bedroom or classroom area to be adjusted, might only be worth 50 per cent of the gross cost rate, ie about £27 and £34/m² respectively. The reason for this is that many of the elemental costs that contribute to the total cost per square metre are unaffected by the change, eg the cost of sanitary fittings, kitchen fittings, many services, lifts and in the case of the school, other highly serviced and fitted areas, eg laboratories, domestic science areas and changing rooms. Basic mechanical plant costs are also unlikely to be affected by minor changes in area.

A similar effect would be apparent if, say, extensions or reductions to the length of a conventional office block for letting were being considered. In this case the differences between the cost per square metre of the area affected and the overall cost per square metre would be accounted for by the fact that the costs of lifts, vertical circulation, wcs, entrances and basic plant costs may remain unchanged.

6.03 Use of cost analysis data

In the use of published cost analyses it is essential to interpret reasons for differences in elemental costs. It should be possible to identify 'fixed' costs (see 6.01) and see how far they are related to the quality of the building and to what extent they were affected by structural or enclosure elements. Much time can be saved at very early design stages, when cost appraisals are being compared, perhaps unfavourably, with the all-in rates per square metre of updated published analyses of similar buildings, if it is appreciated that the client's brief requires a higher standard than that of the building in the analysis.

It is also essential to appreciate the broad effects of size, shape and height when considering the enclosure elements.

Example 1

When comparing the cost of proposed elevational treatments with those in a published analysis, the wall/floor ratio must also be compared. A published analysis may be within the same total cost per square metre as the proposed elevation, but the actual costs will be quite different if the analysis shows a wall/floor area ratio of 0·80 and the proposed elevation shows a ratio of 0·40. This sort of difference is not unusual in similar types of building: eg when an 'open' office and an orthodox office are being compared, if the 'open' office tends to be square and the orthodox office rectangular. In this case, the difference in the cost of the elevation for the open office (particularly if the window area to wall area ratio is reduced), can offset the extra cost of engineering services which are usually necessary.

Example 2

The roof element in a single-storey building may easily account for 10 per cent of the total cost per square metre whereas the same type of roof in a 10-storey building may obviously only account for about one per cent and this can vitally affect design decisions.

All-in component costs

When considering the standard that can be afforded for a particular element, great care should be taken to appreciate the effect of perimeter to area ratio on the all-in element unit rate. That is, the costs per square metre of the surface or area of component or materials which appear in cost analyses and price books.

The following examples will illustrate the differences that shape and size can make.

3 shows two different sized windows **X** and **Y**, both of which are assumed to be galvanised steel fixed lights with similar treatment to brick openings at head, sill or jambs, and similar weights of sheet glass. The all-in costs including the window, glass, painting and formation of the opening are approximately £30/m² for **X** and £17/m² for **Y**, of the area occupied. An extreme example has been given and obviously if **Y** were horizontal instead of vertical, the head and sill costs would be much greater. Also, although the cost per square metre of large windows is generally less than that of small, the increase in glass weight required for a very large pane may make the larger window more costly per square metre of all-in cost.

Perimeter costs are also extremely important. The all-in cost of an asphalt roof covering say 30 m × 10 m, including water check and edge trim costs, might be about £3·30/m², whereas a small roof or a balcony 3 m × 2 m with an upstand skirting all round of the same specification is likely to be about £6/m².

7 References

1 MCCANLIS, E. W. Tendering procedures and contractual arrangements. London, 1967, RICS [(A4t)]

2 AJ Legal Handbook. London, 1973, Architectural Press. [(Ajk)]

3 STONE, P. A. Building design evaluation: costs-in-use. London, 1967, Spon Ltd [(Y4)]

4 NISBET, J. Cost planning and cost control (AJ 3, 10 and 24.11.65)

Section 2
External envelope:
General

Section 2 External envelope: General

Building enclosure		Reference keywords
Section 1	**Building enclosure: General**	ENCLOSURE
Section 2	**External envelope: General**	EXTERNAL ENVELOPE
Section 3	**External envelope: Lowest floor and basement**	LOWEST FLOOR
Section 4	**External envelope: External walls**	EXTERNAL WALLS
Section 5	**External envelope: Roofs**	ROOFS
Section 6	**Internal division: General**	INTERNAL DIVISION
Section 7	**Internal division: Suspended floors**	SUSPENDED FLOORS
Section 8	**Internal division: Partitions and walls**	PARTITIONS
Section 9	**Internal division: Ceilings**	CEILINGS
	Design guide Appendix A: Legislation Appendix B: Specialist advice	DESIGN GUIDE
Appendix 1	**Summary of references**	ENCLOSURE: REFERENCES
Appendix 2	**Index**	ENCLOSURE: INDEX

Relationship to rest of handbook

The above table shows the contents of the handbook as a whole, with the present section highlighted.

Scope

Section 1 of the AJ Handbook of Building enclosure provided, at the most general level, an introduction to the design of the building's fabric. It did not deal in detail with any specific element or assembly of elements, but was intended to give an understanding of the functions of the *total enclosure*, and to provide data on two design constraints applying to the enclosure as a whole—dimensional considerations and cost considerations.

Section 2 is also general in scope, but less so than section 1. It provides an introduction to the first of the two major groups of elements that constitute the building enclosure—the *external envelope*. It will be followed by a series of specific sections giving design guidance on each of the element-groups included in the external envelope. The relationship between the various sections will be apparent from the diagram at the foot of the page.

Section 2 is relatively brief and consists of a single technical study and one information sheet. The technical study is intended to develop in greater detail the analysis of the functions of building enclosure given in technical study ENCLOSURE 1; and to isolate the ones pertaining specifically to the external envelope (those pertaining to the internal subdividing elements will be examined similarly in section 6). It is hoped that this study will give architects an understanding of the overall set of purposes they are trying to achieve when taking detailed design decisions on the elements described in sections 3 to 5.

The technical study is followed by an information sheet (External Envelope 1) providing usable data on the thermal and acoustic performance of a selected range of roof and wall constructions. This is included in Section 2 because its data concerns the environment performance of the external envelope as a whole. It is hoped that it provides practical design data not easily available elsewhere.

References and keywords

The keyword by which this section is identified is EXTERNAL ENVELOPE; those for the other sections are shown in the table. See the notes at the beginning of this handbook p6 for an explanation of how keywords are used to identify the sections of this handbook.

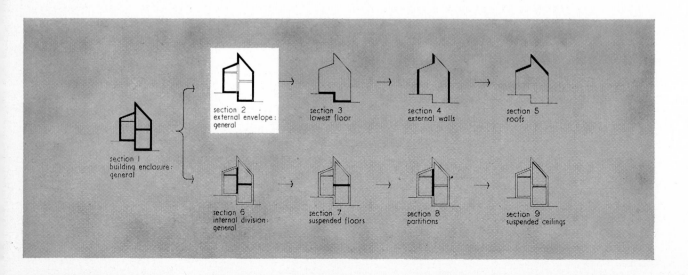

Technical study
External envelope 1

Functions of the external envelope

This technical study is intended to provide an introduction to the design of lowest floor/basement, external walls, and roofs, by describing in broad outline the functions of the building's enclosing skin. It draws attention to four basic functions: environmental control, security, structural support and visual performance. The first of these is analysed in some detail because of the inadequate attention frequently given to this important aspect of building design.
Sections 1 to 5 are by MARITZ VANDENBERG; *section 6 by* SUSAN DAWSON

1 Introduction

1.01 Scope of technical study

It has been explained that this handbook as a whole is divided into three basic parts: first, a section dealing with the functions and design of the building fabric as a whole; then a group of sections dealing with those elements forming the external skin of the building; finally a group of sections dealing with those elements subdividing the internal space of the building.

The present technical study is an introduction to the *second* of these basic parts, giving the designer an overall view, on a general level, of the considerations involved in designing the external skin of the building: lowest floor, including basement; external walls, including windows and doors, claddings and finishes; and roofs, including rooflights and roof finishes. The study will be followed by detailed sections on each of the groups of elements mentioned above.

This approach is in line with the underlying strategy of the handbook, which is that the detailed problems cannot be understood or solved without an understanding of the whole. A useful start cannot be made on window, wall or cladding design until the functions of the wall-element as a whole have been analysed and understood; and before that can be done, there must be understanding of the general functions of the complete 'breathing skin' which envelopes the building, of which the wall forms part. What, then, are the essential functions of this external envelope?

2 Human needs

2.01 Logical starting point

Building design begins and ends with human needs, unless the building concerned is intended to house non-human activities, such as industrial or agricultural processes, or to perform a storage function. Every design decision should be subservient to this controlling purpose. So the starting point of building design should be a rigorous analysis of user requirements; and the aim throughout the process of design and construction should be to ensure that the completed building will perform in the desired way, and play its part in creating the desired conditions for those inside it and those using the external spaces influenced by it.

2.02 Contribution of external envelope

It is useful to analyse the functioning of the building as a totality in terms of six major element-groups: structure, external envelope, internal subdivision, services, fittings and furnishings, and external works. In some ways each of these represents a distinct design problem, but all interact with each other and contribute to the overall performance experienced by the users. Therefore it is not possible to design any of them in isolation; the architect must constantly bear in mind that the particular part of the building he happens to be dealing with must play its part in ensuring that overall performance is in accordance with the desired standards.

In this total picture the external envelope's major function is *environmental*, ie to intervene between the external environment and the internal volume of the building, and to modify the former to produce as nearly as possible the internal conditions the building's users require. It has other purposes as well; eg it may have a *structural* function, that of holding up the building above it; and it certainly has a *visual* function in its appearance to passers-by, and its contribution towards the creation of a pleasant land or townscape is a major function of the building exterior. Architects are usually aware of the structural and aesthetic functions of the building envelope. The former are dealt with in great detail by many building construction manuals, and the latter receive lavish attention in glossy books and periodicals.

However, the environmental function has only recently begun to receive its due share of attention; and many architects, while being well equipped to handle building designs of traditional types, which have developed gradually and represent basic 'models' well suited to climatic conditions and users' needs, are less effective in dealing with environmental design when faced with new and comparatively unfamiliar building types, and new building techniques and materials. In these circumstances, traditional solutions and knowledge derived from previous experience become less relevant, and a new approach is needed, based upon a theoretical understanding of fundamental principles, and an ability to apply them to design.

Increasingly, architects will require an understanding of the complex interactions which occur between external climate, the internal climate, and the building envelope separating the two. For this reason, the latter subject will be examined in some detail in the following paragraphs.

3 Climate-modification function

3.01 Local climate and endoclimate

It has been stated above that the external skin of the building intervenes between external environment and internal volume; in general in this handbook the former will be referred to as the *local climate*, and the latter as the internal or *endoclimate*. The *local climate* is a given situation —certain prevailing conditions of radiative and air temperature, precipitation and humidity, air movement, light, noise, dust and pollution, aspect and prospect—none of which is likely to be exactly in accord with the needs and desires of the people for whom the building is being designed for other than very limited periods of time, if that. So the desired *endoclimate*, which the building is intended to create, is an ideal situation. The conditions described above must be modified to bring them within a range of values that will be satisfactory to users, and the users should be given the means to modify still further one or more of these conditions, when they wish, to suit their changing needs or simply their moods, inclinations and preferences.

Taking the physical conditions necessary to produce thermal comfort as an example of the kind of control required, the most recent research indicates that office workers, wearing their ordinary day clothes, will be comfortable if indoor globe temperature keeps within a 4°C band centred on the monthly mean: if short-term variations, such as hourly or daily fluctuations, move outside this band, a significant proportion of people will begin to complain of discomfort. Therefore the building must be designed to keep short term fluctuations within this range for, say, 95 per cent of the time, regardless of temperature variations occurring outside; and this requires much closer attention to the thermal performance of walls, windows and roofs, to control of solar heat gain, to usable ventilation, and to heating and cooling installations, than has been usual hitherto. Also, the same temperatures do not suit all the people all the time, valid though they may be as averages; so those inside the building should be able to adjust the prevailing internal temperature within certain limits to suit their personal needs.

The above example relates to thermal comfort; similar examples could be adduced for acoustic and visual comfort, or for ventilation needs. In each case designers should equip themselves with a much clearer understanding than they had in the past of the psycho-physical needs of building users, and of the kind of modifications of local climate necessary if the endoclimate is to be acceptable.

3.02 'Breathing skin'

This kind of environmental control is brought about mainly by two of the functional groups of building elements listed in 2.02: the external envelope and the environmental services. The former is the first line of defence, modifying

climatic conditions by means of its physical properties, eg thermal insulation and inertia, vapour permeability, degree of air-tightness, and sound insulation. When this modification is not enough to produce the required internal conditions, further modification must be effected by lighting, heating, ventilating and cooling services, ie by the use of *energy* as opposed to *physical structure* (see also 2.02 technical study ENCLOSURE 1).

Both these methods play their part, but it is important to understand that dependence on the physical enclosure is cheaper, more reliable, and often more effective than the application of energy; where the 'skin' of the building has been badly designed, and fails to play its part in reducing the undesirable characteristics of the local climate, the services are sometimes incapable of putting matters right. Even if they are capable of doing so, they are likely to be expensive and subject to maintenance and operational difficulties. Therefore it is essential that the first line of defence (physical enclosure) be exploited to the maximum, leaving the second line of defence (environmental services) to cope with as small a challenge as possible; this is the way to produce an effective, economical and trouble-free building.

Barrier and filter

In analysing the climate-modifying functions of this 'breathing skin' which encloses the building, it is apparent that it acts in two ways: certain physical variables are excluded altogether (as far as this is possible); others are admitted, but selectively. So in some respects the building's skin acts as a *barrier*, in some respects as a *filter*.

Those aspects of the external environment to be excluded altogether, as far as this is possible, are water and the various forms of pollution. On the other hand, light, heat, sound and air are dealt with selectively, being allowed to penetrate the external envelope wholly, partly, or not at all, in accordance with the needs and desires of the users. Each of these entities is dealt with individually in the following paragraphs.

3.03 Water

Water in its free liquid form must be excluded from the interior altogether by the building's external envelope. On the other hand, water vapour is always present in both local climate and endoclimate, as well as within the fabric of the envelope, and here the function of the envelope will be one of control rather than that of total exclusion. Basically there are three methods of keeping the building's interior dry **2**.

Permeable barriers

The first is to employ a *permeable barrier* thick enough to allow the water that has penetrated the outer face to evaporate in dry periods before it has reached the inner face in appreciable quantities. This was a traditional solution **1** for walls; but while it may be satisfactory for countries with comparatively dry climates, it performs poorly in the long, damp British winter. Moreover, the thickness necessary for such a barrier to be effective is far in excess of what is required structurally. So the solid permeable wall has been superseded by other methods of construction.

Air gaps

The second method is to employ a double skin separated by a *continuous air-gap* (cavity) to break the capillary paths along which water may travel from the outside to the interior. This method is now used widely for external walls.

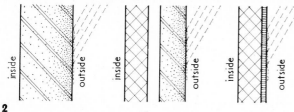

1 Traditional method of water exclusion is permeable wall, relying on thickness for effectiveness; this is now superseded by cavity construction and forms of cladding incorporating impervious barriers **3**
2 Three methods of water exclusion: permeable wall; cavity wall; impervious barrier. Dotted shading indicates water penetration

Provided careful attention is given to avoiding bridges, eg badly detailed lintels, or lumps of mortar adhering to wall ties, which may carry water across the cavity, double-skin walls exclude unwanted moisture effectively and economically.

A cavity or air-gap will not provide effective control of vapour diffusion, however, unless it is ventilated. It is partly for this reason that suspended ground floors (relying on the cavity between ground and floor structure to prevent entry of moisture) have become less popular. To prevent water vapour from the ground diffusing through the floor into the building's interior, the cavity has to be well ventilated, which results in high heat losses. Consequently this form of floor construction has been superseded by the use of impervious barriers in many cases (there are also other contributory factors).

Impervious barriers

The third method of control—the *impervious barrier*—is becoming increasingly common **3**; it can be very effective, provided proper consideration is given to certain problems which have led to many cases of building failure over the past few years.

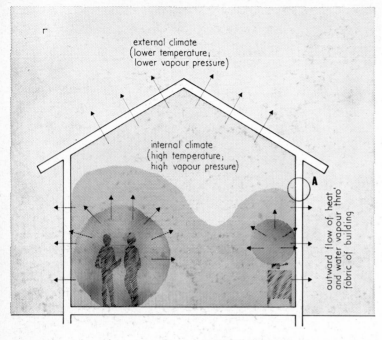

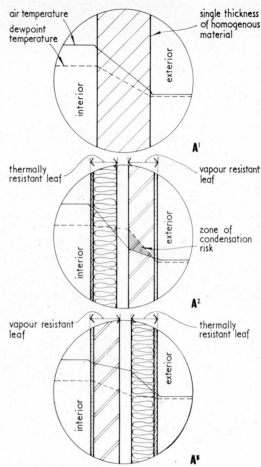

4 *Shows outward flow of heat and moisture through envelope of building, and effect of different sequences of materials on condensation risk. Placing vapour-resistant barrier on outside, and thermal insulation near inside face, invites interstitial condensation*

Cracking and jointing problems

The first problem is that of cracking. Many commonly used impervious materials may crack if subjected to thermal and other movement. If this happens, water shed by adjacent surfaces penetrates the crack, soaks into the underlying fabric and is prevented from drying out again by the impermeable skin: the results can be imagined. This problem can occur with external walls, but is particularly troublesome with flat roof finishes such as asphalt. Joints in impermeable materials also tend to be troublesome, for much the same reasons as those described above, unless carefully designed and constructed.

Condensation problems

The second problem is one that arises if the barrier, in addition to being impervious, is also to a high degree resistant to the passage of water vapour. The principles which underlie interstitial condensation (the formation of condensation within the fabric of the building envelope) are too complex to be described fully here. They may be summed up by the following broad generalisation: condensation risk will be negligible if structural temperature is high and vapour pressure* is low; if, on the other hand, structural temperature is low and vapour pressure high, there will be a severe condensation risk.

In winter (which is when condensation tends to be a problem) both air temperature and vapour pressure are higher inside the building than outside—the former because of the presence of heating installations and other heat-producing bodies inside the building enclosure, the latter because transpiration, cooking and washing add a certain

*'Vapour pressure' is one way of expressing the moisture content of air: the higher the vapour pressure, the higher the moisture content

amount of moisture to that already present in the air which has been drawn into the building from the outside. Therefore it is helpful to visualise the internal volume of the building in winter as a reservoir of heat and water vapour, both of which are constantly trying to diffuse outward through the external envelope to the colder, drier air outside **4**. Both temperature and vapour pressure must drop within the thickness of the envelope from the values prevailing inside the building to those prevailing outside **4A¹**. The crucial question is which of the two variables is reduced first, and this depends on the sequence of materials constituting the envelope.

For example, if the envelope is a composite construction, the inner skin being vapour-resistant **4A³** but allowing the passage of heat, and the outer skin being an effective thermal insulator, it is obvious that the fabric of the envelope will be relatively warm and dry, because the heat from the building's interior is allowed to penetrate the thickness of the fabric and is held there by the outer insulant, while vapour is excluded from it by the internal vapour barrier. In this case risk of condensation will probably be low. On the other hand, if the impermeable barrier is on the *outside* and the thermal insulant on the *inside* **4A²**, the situation will be reversed: vapour will be allowed to diffuse into the fabric of the envelope, but heat will be kept out, creating the very combination of conditions (high vapour pressure and low temperature) which invite interstitial condensation.

Unfortunately, designers with insufficient understanding of the principles underlying condensation tend to employ just this latter sequence of materials. After all, the outside face of the wall or roof is the logical position for the impermeable barrier from the weather-exclusion point of view. This

5

5, 6 *Examples of vernacular roof forms, corrugated palm leaves and clay tiles, consisting of overlapping units of locally available material. In principle this remains an effective roofing technique; modern pitched roofs of overlapping units are probably more trouble-free than flat roofs*

6

explains many of the recent failures of new kinds of composite wall-panel, and flat roofs, incorporating impermeable barriers as the chosen method of water-exclusion. It also demonstrates the need for caution when employing this method.

In floors, however, impermeable barriers are effective against rising damp, and they may be used without any of the reservations which have been expressed above. The reason for this is that floors do not lose heat in the same way as walls and roofs because the ground beneath the floor acts to some extent as a heat accumulator; so in this case the impervious barrier is the indicated method of water-exclusion.

Roofs, walls and floors

Summing up the use of the three methods of water exclusion and vapour-diffusion control described in the above para-

graphs, the following are the typical applications in various parts of the external envelope:

Roofs, if flat, must be provided with an impervious covering. This can be some sort of mastic, impregnated felt, or metal sheet. In the case of mastic or impregnated felt, problems of cracking due to movement, and the risk of condensation due to presence of water vapour trapped beneath the impermeable membrane, must be considered. On the other hand, pitched roof coverings need not be completely impervious but can consist of overlapping units **5**, **6** of reasonably impervious materials, backed by a lining (sarking) to prevent entry of wind, wind-driven snow or rain.

Walls are best constructed on the cavity principle. Alternatively, or in addition to provision of an air-gap, an impermeable barrier may be used, but careful thought must then be given to jointing and to prevention of cracking; and if the barrier is vapour-resistant, condensation risk must be considered, and the precise sequence of materials becomes a critical factor. (See Information sheet which follows.)

Floors should incorporate an impervious barrier to exclude rising damp; so should basement walls. However, the latter can also exploit the air-gap principle with a wet outer skin and a dry inner skin separated by a drained cavity.

3.04 Dust and pollution

Atmospheric pollution (dust, grit, smoke, and harmful chemicals in the external air) is the second aspect of the external environment which should, if possible, be excluded from the interior of the building altogether. In fact this ideal is difficult to attain, because the need to exclude atmospheric pollution is liable to conflict with the need to admit air. Where the local site climate is relatively unpolluted, and the internal endoclimate would not be unduly affected by low concentrations of dust and so on, considerations of economy will probably prevail, and access of unfiltered air will be allowed. But in other cases it may be necessary to design the environmental envelope in such a way that it will allow air to pass through it, while barring airborne pollutants; this would involve the use of filters and forced ventilation. The decision must rest on an analysis of local site climate, the required endoclimate, considerations of economy and the interaction of hygiene with ventilation requirements.

3.05 Air

In the case of water and pollution, the function of the environmental envelope is essentially that of a barrier. But in the case of air the function is not one of exclusion, but one of controlled access to suit the needs and desires of the people inside the building.

Local climate
As before, the first step is to analyse the site climate—a task rendered difficult in this instance by the inadequacy of the available methods. Probably the most that can be done at present is to obtain data on typical wind velocities and prevailing wind directions from the nearest meteorological station, to try to gain an understanding of the effect of site topography on wind flow from local experience, and to consider the likely patterns of air flow over the surfaces of the proposed building form, by studying the typical examples given in Section 2 of the AJ Handbook of Building environment[3]. These investigations (preferably supported by wind-tunnel tests **7**) will enable the architect to gauge the likelihood of troublesome patterns of air turbulence in the spaces surrounding the building, and to consider the problem of ventilation of the building interior.

Endoclimate
The purposes of ventilation are to provide air for breathing, to dilute and remove from the interior smells such as cooking or body odours, to provide cooling in summer, to increase the low moisture content or in cases where there are an excess of moisture sources inside to remove moisture-laden air from the interior in winter. The arrangement of smoke-free exits in case of fire must be considered too.

Building envelope
The proper disposition and sizing of openings in the external envelope to allow for the required patterns of air infiltration

is at present more a matter of judgment based on experience, and of satisfying the Building Regulations, than of scientific calculation.

In general, natural ventilation is appropriate in the case of low buildings with relatively small rooms. For winter ventilation, openings should be at high level, whereas for summer ventilation and cooling they should be at low level to induce air movement at working height. Tall buildings cannot be ventilated satisfactorily by natural ventilation, owing to stack and wind effects, so mechanical services must be relied on rather than openable windows. The same applies to building interiors too heavily populated for natural ventilation (more than one person per $3 \cdot 5$ m^3, and any room occupied by more than 50 people), to interiors requiring special conditions, and, most important, to buildings where pollution of the external air, or external noise conditions, are such that the windows cannot be opened for ventilation without causing a nuisance to those inside. The latter is an important example of interaction between two quite different aspects of environmental control—in this case, noise or pollution control, and ventilation.

There are several possible answers in such cases. If the noise source is localised (as in the case of a motorway on one side of a block of flats), the building envelope on that side could be made relatively soundproof by reducing ventilation openings to a minimum **12**, and designing them carefully to attenuate the noise as much as possible. Alternatively, it might be necessary to forgo natural through-ventilation altogether and to rely on forced ventilation. But whatever the solution, the problem of conflict between air admission and noise exclusion must be given far more attention than it has received in the past; and this will have a major influence on the form of the external envelope.

3.06 Light

Local climate
First, the available light should be studied: this will be influenced by orientation, slope of site, obstacles such as trees or other buildings, and local seasonal variations in sunlight.

Endoclimate
Then an analysis must be made of lighting requirements inside the building; both official recommendations (such as BS CP 3 Chapter 1; or the IES *Code*) and special users' requirements will be relevant. Detailed lighting calculations are covered by the AJ Handbook of Building environment[3], and will not be dealt with in the present handbook. It is appropriate here to draw attention only to those basic decisions that will have an effect on the design of the building enclosure.

Natural versus artificial lighting
Once users' needs have been established, the first main decision, is the relative contributions to be made by natural and artificial lighting. Natural lighting has some desirable features: it is liked by building users, it often gives better three-dimensional modelling of objects than artificial lighting and its colour-rendering is the norm to which we are accustomed.

But natural lighting does have disadvantages which must be taken into account. It is variable, it penetrates the building to a limited depth only, and there are important interactions between natural light and other aspects of environmental control, which may cause problems; eg the

use of large windows for improved light may result in excessive solar heat gain in summer and excessive heat loss in winter. Or there may be a conflict between the size, shape and position of windows required for adequate lighting, and those giving the most satisfactory views or elevational appearance. On the basis of considerations such as these, a decision must be made on which of the following permutations of natural/artificial lighting is to be adopted:
● Total reliance on artificial lighting (ie a wholly window-less interior);
● Artificial lighting as main source of illumination, with small windows to improve three-dimensional modelling qualities of light, and also to give views of outside (windows may be 20 to 25 per cent of façade area);
● Natural lighting as one source of illumination, permanently supplemented by artificial lighting (PSALI) where rooms are too deep to be lit adequately by the windows (maximum room depth usually about 10 m);
● Natural lighting as main source of daytime illumination (maximum room depth usually about 6 m).

Openings in envelope
It is on the basis of these decisions balanced against other factors, such as appearance, ventilation, noise control, thermal control and so on, that the sizes and dispositions of openings in the external envelope can be determined. The following points should be kept in mind.
Tall windows admit light further into a room than wide ones, but at the cost of greater glare; the latter can be counter-acted by means of a horizontal baffle extending outwards from the top of the window.
Windows in one wall of room only may give excessive contrasts; if possible, windows should also be included in an adjacent wall, or (less desirably) in the opposite wall. A wall composed totally of reduced-transmission glazing, or clear glazing plus shades or blinds, gives better visual comfort than a large window surrounded by a wall, because it avoids the harsh contrast between window and adjacent wall panels. If small windows are used to provide vision of the outside rather than light, vertical slit windows are preferable to long horizontal ones.

3.07 Heat

Local climate
The two most important thermal components of the site

7 *Wind-tunnel tests are valuable method of investigating wind-flow patterns created by building envelope*

climate are the *air temperature* and *radiant conditions*. In the case of air temperature, winter and summer design temperatures must be established. In the case of radiation intensities, the major determining factor will be latitude; but cloud cover, atmospheric pollution, and the presence of vegetation and other buildings will modify the intensity by providing shading. Two other aspects of site local climate, which influence thermal conditions, are *air movement* and *relative humidity*. Information on all these variables is given in the AJ Handbook of Building environment[3].

Endoclimate
The usual aim, in specifying the desired endoclimate, is to provide conditions compatible with human thermal comfort. In some instances, eg laboratories, factories, and agricultural buildings, the overriding purpose will be to provide conditions suitable for research or manufacturing processes, storage and so on; but these special cases need not be discussed in detail here.
Human thermal comfort is a complex phenomenon. The body produces heat which must be dissipated in such a way that body temperature remains at its correct level. This requires not merely that the correct *amount* of heat be lost, but also that the correct *balance* be maintained between the three forms of heat loss that occur: radiation, convection and evaporation. Heat loss by radiation depends on the temperatures of the physical surfaces surrounding the body; heat loss by convection depends on air temperature and rate of air movement; heat loss by evaporation depends on air temperature, relative humidity and air movement. The contribution of each of these forms of heat loss is not fixed; if one is unsatisfactory this may, within certain limits, be compensated for by the others. If, for instance, mean radiant temperature is rather lower than the desired value, a modification of air temperature can restore conditions of thermal comfort, but only within certain limits.
It must be understood that there is no magic value, or range of values, that will satisfy everyone all the time. Age, sex, and the sort of conditions users are accustomed to, as well as the activities to be carried out, clothing worn, and the time of year (see 3.01) will have an influence on the particular physical conditions deemed by users to be comfortable. So the most that can be realistically hoped for

is to provide conditions that will satisfy a stated majority of users, and to provide a degree of control that will enable users to adjust conditions to suit their individual inclinations, within certain limits. More detailed data will be found in section 4 of the AJ Handbook of Building environment[3].

The first step must be to specify the users of the proposed environment in terms of age, sex, and any other characteristics that may be relevant; to specify the activities that will take place, eg heavy manual, light manual or sedentary activities, and the kind of clothing likely to be worn; and to decide what kind of environment is to be provided—stimulating or relaxing, minimal comfort or luxurious, and so on. On the basis of these factors, a range of values can be decided for air temperature, radiant conditions, air movement and relative humidity. These are dealt with more fully in the relevant sections of the AJ Handbook of Building environment [(E6): AJ 18 and 25.12.68 to 8.1.69], and summarised in section 7 of that handbook (AJ 6.8.69).

Building enclosure

The environmental control services of the building will be relied on considerably to make the desired modifications in local climate. If internal air temperature is to be maintained at a comfortable level, for instance, the provision of additional heat will almost certainly be required in winter, and artificial cooling may be required in summer; and if the humidity of the external air is too high for comfort, there is no way of reducing the water content except by means of mechanical plant. But building form and fabric can make a substantial contribution towards creating the desired conditions, if properly designed, and the following notes summarise what the architect should have in mind when designing the external envelope.

Air temperature can be moderated considerably by building enclosure—in winter by reducing heat loss from the interior, and in summer by excluding solar heat. Both of these moderating properties depend on the thermal transmittance characteristics of the enclosing elements, ie transmission of heat from one side to the other by convection, conduction and radiation; and heat build-up in summer depends, in addition, on solar heat gain, ie the unaltered passage of solar radiation into the building interior where it warms the internal surfaces. Standards of thermal insulation have been rising in recent years, partly because of the accompanying saving in fuel costs, partly because of the increased availability of effective thermal insulants and partly because of people's increased expectations of comfort.

In general a high degree of insulation is desirable for external walls and roofs, but the amount of money spent on insulation should not be allowed to get out of proportion. As a guide, the amount worth spending *increases* with the temperature difference required between interior and exterior, with the costs of space heating and with duration of heating season. It *decreases* with amount of incidental internal heat gain from sources such as industrial processes, high lighting levels and large numbers of occupants, because the generation of 'free' heat inside the building obviously lessens the importance of heat loss through the fabric. Average transmission values for various constructions are given in section 27 of the Metric Handbook; and data will also be given later in this handbook.

However, thermal performance of the building fabric is not merely a problem of the *rate* of heat transfer from one side of the enclosing element to the other when a steady condition has been reached; an additional factor of great importance is the *rapidity* with which changes on one side are passed on to the other. A building enclosure of low thermal capacity, ie of lightweight construction, will allow external temperature changes to be reflected internally with almost no time lag. This will necessitate a cooling or heating installation which can respond rapidly to changing conditions, and with sufficient capacity to bring about an effective change in the short time available. On the other hand, building enclosure of high thermal capacity, ie of relatively massive construction, will tend to delay temperature changes in the endoclimate and spread them out over some time, thereby reducing the capacity and rapidity of response required of the thermal installation. It is important to understand that thermal insulation does not give thermal capacity—in fact, as good insulation is usually associated with low density materials and high thermal capacity is associated with high density materials, the two properties tend almost to be mutually exclusive. Packing additional lightweight insulation into an aluminium curtain wall will reduce rate of heat transmission, but will not significantly increase thermal capacity.

Unfortunately there is no simple method of quantifying the thermal capacity of a building, and judgment must be the basis of dividing enclosures into broad categories of short, medium and long thermal response. The use-pattern of the building will be one of the factors deciding whether the response of fabric ought to be short, medium or long. A fairly large heat-storage capacity is desirable for continuously occupied buildings for reasons of thermal comfort and economy of servicing. For intermittently occupied buildings, which need to be heated quickly, low capacity is preferable. For continuously occupied buildings like housing a high thermal capacity is desirable especially in climates with warm days and cold nights. The building stores the solar heat during the day without transmitting it to the interior. At night this stored heat is given off, either helping the heating system or making its use unnecessary, **8, 9, 10, 11.**

A third factor (after thermal insulation and thermal capacity) to be considered, when thinking about internal temperatures, is solar heat gain. Many modern buildings are over-glazed, sometimes for aesthetic reasons, sometimes because of desired day-lighting levels. In addition to the very high thermal transmission coefficient of glass, causing high rates of winter heat loss and summer heat gain, there is the problem of solar heat input which can greatly aggravate cooling problems, if insufficient attention has been given to orientation, external shading devices and so on. Finally, it should be remembered that most heat losses from buildings can be attributed to ventilation and escape of warm air at door and window edges.

To sum up what has been said above, thermal transmission, thermal capacity, solar heat gain and rate of air infiltration are the four characteristics of the external envelope, which will influence internal air temperature, so they ought to be taken into account when investigating the effect of building enclosure on internal climate.

Internal surface temperatures are the second of the parameters of the physical environment, which will influence thermal comfort. Ideally, the average temperature of internal building surfaces should be equal to, or preferably higher than, air temperature. In practice this is difficult to achieve and the aim should be to approximate as closely as practicable to the ideal by providing well insulated walls, and by avoiding, if possible, large cold surfaces, such as unprotected windows, which would cause radiant heat loss from the human body towards the cold surfaces.

Air movement is the third parameter, and all that needs to

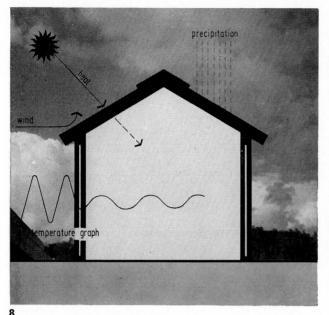

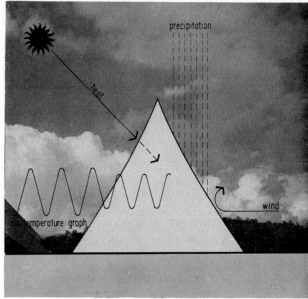

8

8, 9 *Show effect of different types of enclosure on internal temperature fluctuations.*
10, 11 *Show probable temperature variation in small-apertured, long-response enclosure, compared with that*

9

in highly-glazed, short-response building. Latter would make it almost impossible to keep temperatures within vomfort zone, even with expensive plant.

be said here is that rate of movement should be variable rather than uniform. It should be about 0·10 m per s in winter, and more rapid in summer (see 3.05).

Relative humidity is the fourth of the physical determinants of thermal comfort, and should normally be kept between 30 and 65 per cent. The main implication for the design of the external envelope is that a sufficient rate of air escape should be ensured in winter to prevent excessive build-up of moisture in the microclimate. Provision of permanent strip ventilators to the tops of windows (300 mm² per 100 m³ of room space) would be a partial safeguard.

Interaction
The above notes provide a summary of the ways in which proper design of the building's external envelope can ensure that excessive demand is not made on the environmental control installation in providing conditions of thermal comfort inside the building. It will be seen that the most

important considerations are avoiding excessive areas of glazing, careful attention to orientation and solar shading of windows, adequate thermal insulation to prevent excessive heat loss, provision of adequate mean radiant temperature and provision of appropriate thermal capacity.
Thought must also be given to the interaction between thermal and other aspects of environmental control. Natural lighting, external views and solar heat gain; exclusion of outside noise and admission of air for cooling; provision of insulation and avoidance of condensation are all interrelated problems and must be considered together.

3.08 Noise

Local climate
The main sources of external noise are railways, traffic and aircraft. An analysis of local site climate will indicate the degree of noise nuisance to be expected from these and other sources.

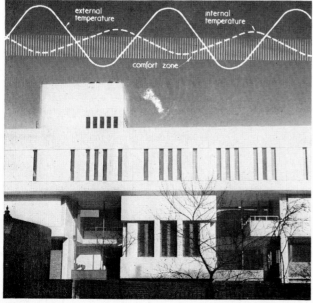

10

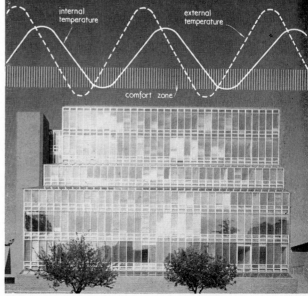

11

Endoclimate

In most buildings, maximum permissible background noise level will be determined by speech interference considerations. In specialised buildings, such as auditoria, more stringent requirements will apply. Recommended standards are given in section 5 of the AJ Handbook of Building environment (technical study SOUND 2, AJ 22.1.69; and information sheet SOUND 3, AJ 5.2.69).

Building envelope

Buildings of traditional construction are likely to give adequate noise attenuation in most cases, as long as the windows are closed. The real problem in these instances is not so much that of finding forms of construction that can reduce external noise levels to desirable internal levels, but rather that of reconciling the conflicting needs of noise reduction and ventilation, ie finding means of admitting air through the external envelope while excluding sound. In some cases specially designed baffled windows may be required; in others it may be necessary to design one or more of the building elevations without ventilation openings, and to rely on mechanical services for ventilation, as described in 3.05; or with small openings only **12**.

When dry construction such as system building is used, problems may arise even when windows are closed, or in the absence of openable windows, because air paths through the envelope are provided by dry joints. With these buildings all joints between elements must be sealed with mastic or air-tight gaskets, if significant noise reduction is required. Careful design and site supervision will be necessary.

If conditions are severe enough, not only will the use of openable windows be ruled out, but fixed windows too may require special consideration. Sealing is a first step and

double glazing would improve sound reduction even more. In the latter case, spacing between panes should be at least 150 mm and preferably 200 mm; and an absorbent lining in the cavity would improve its performance. However, prevention of condensation in the cavity is a problem with double glazing.

3.09 Interaction

The above paragraphs give an indication of the ways in which the building's external envelope provides a comfortable internal endoclimate by filtering, and in some cases by barring access to a wide range of environmental factors such as water, dust, air, light, heat and sound.

Attention has been drawn in several instances to the importance of *not* isolating one particular aspect of design. Unfortunately fragmentation of approach is a common characteristic of 20th century technology: a complex problem is divided into separate strands and each is tackled individually, probably by different specialists or specialist teams. On one level, this approach has led to spectacularly successful results. Thus, modern structures, modern lighting equipment, modern heating and cooling equipment, modern vapour-resistant barriers, modern thermal insulants and modern glazing each attain standards of performance that are practically miraculous by historical standards. But the overall performance of all these marvels, when assembled to form a single building, sometimes leads to aesthetic or environmental results which would have shamed our ancestors. The problem is lack of overall control and integration; the subsystems dominate the total system, are sometimes inconsistent with each other and occasionally even counteract one another.

12 *Where noise source is highly directional, as with motorway, orientating building so that it faces away from source, and careful design of openings in walls, can mitigate nuisance*

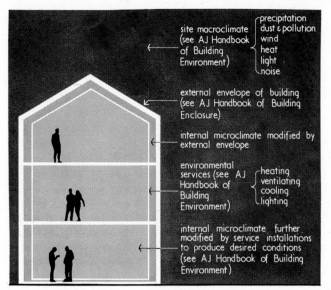

site macroclimate (see AJ Handbook of Building Environment) — precipitation, dust & pollution, wind, heat, light, noise

external envelope of building (see AJ Handbook of Building Enclosure)

internal microclimate modified by external envelope

environmental services (see AJ Handbook of Building Environment) — heating, ventilating, cooling, lighting

internal microclimate further modified by service installations to produce desired conditions (see AJ Handbook of Building Environment)

13 *Building enclosure is first line of defense in modifying external climate; environmental services second line of defense. Both must be designed to work together to produce required conditions*

The answer, to sum up all that this study has said so far, must be to analyse as carefully as possible the local site climate, to specify in writing as accurately as possible the desired endoclimate and to bear in mind that building *fabric* and building *services* must work together to produce the necessary modification of the external environment **13**. Particular care must be taken to ensure that the fabric functions as effectively as possible, leaving to the mechanical and electrical services only those functions (mainly lighting, to some extent heating and possibly ventilation and cooling) that the physical enclosure cannot cope with. Services are expensive to install and run, liable to operational, maintenance and control problems, and building users may be subjected to highly unpleasant conditions in the event of breakdown or power failure, if undue reliance has been placed on environmental services.

4 Security function

4.01 Access and egress

In addition to allowing controlled passage for air and radiation, as described in 3.05 to 3.08, the external envelope of the building must do the same for physical objects—people and goods. Unlike environmental control, this aspect of building function is well understood by most architects, and no more need be said about the general functions of doors, hatches and shutters in this technical study. Detailed information on design will be given in the relevant information sheets later in the handbook.

4.02 Security

There is one frequently neglected or inadequately understood specialised aspect of access and egress, ie security of the occupants of the building against attack and security of objects within the building against theft, which deserves some attention here. This kind of security (and shelter) were probably the main motives that prompted early man to start erecting buildings; and while we no longer require protection against predatory beasts or hostile tribes, there

is no doubt that fear of burglary or nocturnal attack is present in the minds of many householders—huge sums of money are lost every year through theft. So effective control of unauthorised access is a major function of the external envelope.

Attention has already been drawn to the two complementary methods of environmental control—by physical structure (the fabric of the building) and by energy (the building services)—and it has been stated that the best design strategy is to plan the fabric of the building to achieve as much of the required effect as possible. This general principle applies with equal force to the specific problem of making the building secure.

Intrusion can be detected and controlled by organisational methods (patrols, night-watchmen, control of entrances and so on) or by electrical and electronic services of varying degrees of sophistication. But if the physical envelope of the building has been badly planned, leaving weak points vulnerable to attack and hidden from view, these methods will be expensive and possibly inadequate. Therefore the following general design strategy should be adhered to in designing the external envelope of the building; more detailed advice will be found in section 13 of the AJ Handbook of Building services and circulation[3].

First, the primary enclosing elements should have a structural strength appropriate to the degree of security required. For instance, lightweight industrialised wall construction can in some cases be dismantled easily, so it would present a security problem if used in a building containing objects of great value. Similarly, a flat roof of timber boarding covered by bituminous felt offers little resistance to a determined intruder, and would be unsuitable for many building types and occupancies.

Second, particular attention should be given to the secondary elements in the roof and walls (windows, doors, rooflights) as these are the usual points of entry. In fact it is almost impossible to make them burglar-proof; the best that can be hoped for is to make them secure enough to discourage the casual burglar, and to rely on additional organisational and electronic methods for protection where this is deemed justified.

Third, and perhaps most important, every attempt must be made to ensure that the most vulnerable points, if these cannot be eliminated, must be in clear sight of the public or under permanent supervision. Given privacy and time, a determined intruder can probably penetrate any but the most sophisticated security barrier, but without these aids he is handicapped: eg exit doors can be fitted with sturdy locks and bolts on the inside, except for the last door by which the occupant leaves, which can be locked from the outside only. Therefore this is a vulnerable point and should be located in a well supervised area, preferably in public view. There are a few special building types (eg banks) where security is of overriding importance and specialists must be used to provide high strength, highly sophisticated forms of enclosure.

5 Structural function

5.01 Introduction

So far two sets of functions of the external envelope have been examined: environmental control, and control of access to and egress from the interior of the building. There is a third deserving mention—the structural function. The structural function is the ability of the envelope to resist loads of which there are two kinds.

Dead loads comprise the weight of the building fabric which is supported by the envelope. In the case of a loadbearing wall, for instance, the dead load will be the weight of the wall itself above the part under consideration, and that proportion of the weight of other floors, roofs and so on which are supported by it. In non-loadbearing construction, dead loads are carried by structural members provided specifically for that purpose, and the vertical space-enclosing element is not subjected to any dead load.

Dynamic loads include traffic on roofs, wind loads acting against walls or roofs and any other loads due to movement of people or objects, or to natural forces, eg snow loads and earth tremors. All elements of building enclosure are subject to dynamic loads of one kind or another, which should be considered at design stage.

In general, structural functions are dealt with in the AJ Handbook of Building structure*, and will not be considered in detail in the present handbook.

6 Visual function

6.01 Failure in appearance

The external skin of a building is bound to change in appearance, depending on the nature of the materials used and the conditions of exposure. Such changes should be anticipated, otherwise they may cut across the designers' original concept of the building's appearance.

Materials change in different ways, according to their nature and surface characteristics. Porous materials—the traditional external skin of brick or stone—change mainly by accumulating dirt and organic growths on their surface. Impervious materials—metals and plastics—may react to exposure by internal chemical change. Thin films or coatings, on the other hand, may fail and reveal a contrasting surface beneath. Designers should be aware of the weathering implications of these different types of material.

The responsibility for change of appearance of metals and plastics lies rather with the manufacturer than with the architect (who is nevertheless still responsible for selecting materials suitable for the conditions anticipated, lifespan and so on) whereas the main area of architectural responsibility for changes in appearance lies in correct detailing of porous materials, and general design control.

Acceptable change might be defined thus: a building when new produces patterns of light and shade (according to the position of the illuminant), reflection and texture. Weathering which emphasises this pattern is acceptable but a change which is contrary to the original intention is not.

6.02 Control of change in appearance

There are many ways in which designers can control weathering effects on materials to avoid unacceptable disfigurements. Causes of change—dirt and organic growths—cannot be eliminated, but their distribution on a building face can be predicted and controlled reasonably well. The methods of control are constant, but their application will vary according to the particular location, material or detail. Weathering effects can be *camouflaged* by colour or broken up by texture. They can be *controlled* by modelling the building shape or treating the surface finish to provide a deliberate preferential path down which water will run. Third, the element causing streaking, ie water flow, can be *eliminated* by detailing for adequate drainage from the face.

* The first part of an AJ series on building structures was published on 8.3.72 and continued through to late 1973. It will be reissued in book form in 1974 as AJ *Handbook of building structure*.

13 *Bold, deliberate modelling on the facade of the Mathematics Building, Liverpool University, has been emphasised by the 'shadow' effect of dirt and wind*

Camouflage

Some materials already possess built-in methods of control by virtue of their inherent texture, colour and or properties of water absorption. Smooth stones, such as granite and some marbles, are virtually impervious and so resist weathering in the same way as impervious materials. Dark coloured materials, eg Staffs blue bricks or creosoted timber, possess properties of camouflage. Dirt accumulation will not be apparent as the dirt colour is similar to that of the material. Brickwork is unique in possessing properties of colouring which vary slightly from brick to brick and provide camouflage for differences in dirt accumulation that might be noticed on a panel of uniform colour.

Light but textured materials, eg rough stone and concrete with exposed aggregate, resist streaking by breaking up the flow of water down the face. In general, the stronger the texture, the greater the resistance to streaking. Very large texture becomes pattern or modelling. Dirt accumulates in the sheltered areas of the modelled surface, but is eroded by wind from the exposed areas. In **13**, sheltered undersides of the tetrahedrons are dirty and exposed faces are clean.

Staining from dirt is more apparent on materials of light colouring and smooth yet porous finish, eg concrete and Portland stone. Concrete can be darkened, modelled or textured to camouflage the surface. Also careful design and detail of the façade will prevent some uneven dispositions of water and dirt.

Control

Uneven distribution of dirt by wind and rain occurs at changes of exposure, plane and material. Changes of plane at the tops and sides of tall buildings cause alterations in wind speed, resulting in the upper parts being washed. On exposed sites and on façades facing the prevailing wind, the wind speed is sufficient to wash the whole face, but on protected sites, away from the prevailing wind, differential washing will be apparent **15**. This washing is most noticeable on tall buildings faced with light-coloured materials such as concrete. The surface finish of concrete can be treated by exposing the aggregate, bush hammering or by configured

14

14 *Horizontal pc concrete balconies, repeated on each floor of these flats at Roehampton, have undergone a change in appearance which must be very different from the designer's original intention*

15 *Large scale shadow effects at Roehampton. The exposed side of the building (right) has been completely washed, whereas the sheltered side (left) is much darker, with staining at the upper face where wind force is greatest*

15

formwork. The larger the aggregate, the more effective it will be in breaking up the flow of water and deposit of dirt. But it will not disguise bad detailing, and large areas of strongly textured concrete may affect building scale.

Detailing

Wind and rain combined cause large scale disfiguration and affect the appearance of the whole building, while rain alone changes the appearance of small scale details. Rain causes run-down lines where the vertical flow of water is interrupted by a change in plane due to horizontal elements, or where the flow of water is increased by change of material, particularly impervious materials.

Horizontal elements include parapets, eaves and string courses, balconies and, in particular, the external expression of rc floors and frames. Such elements, repeated on each floor of tall buildings, will suffer from differential wind exposure, as described previously **14**. Only camouflage by darkening the element will prevent staining.

On lower buildings, streaking within the horizontal element must be prevented. The path of water and dirt can be controlled by providing vertical channels for drainage; an example of this is the use of vertical ribbing on concrete eaves and string courses. Alternatively, the vertical path could be disguised or broken up by the use of texture. Protection by overhangs of horizontal elements is not effective as the material is protected from washing and will darken; it would be wiser to use dark-coloured concrete in the first place. A smooth, totally washed finish might be achieved by splaying the element outwards for maximum exposure to washing. Staining can also be prevented by eliminating the flow of water down the face.

Paradoxically the uneven staining resulting from classical detailing with large cornices and other features in a traditional material like Portland stone can be a positive asset in some circumstances. Typical of this effect are St Paul's and Wren's City churches, which before cleaning exhibited the dramatic contrast between soot-blackened areas where protected by overhangs and the pure white of the stone where it was unprotected and washed by rain. The black areas below overhangs gave the effect of deep shadow only seen in climates where bright sunshine is the norm as contrasted with London's generally neutral light. This was probably unintentional on Wren's part, as he could hardly have foreseen the concentrated air pollution which eventually produced these effects. It would be nice, to think that the old boy foresaw and designed for such conditions. Here is a case where enthusiastic preservationists have succeeded in getting facades cleaned and restored with consequent loss of powerful and beautiful contrasts which were produced by properly controlled weathering.

Rain contacting a porous façade runs down and is gradually absorbed into the surface. On an impervious material, such as glass, rain is not absorbed but flows down rapidly until it reaches a horizontal surface or an absorbant material which will show strong run down lines. Adequate sill details throw water away from the face immediately below the window, but this may streak the face farther down. The flow of water can be eliminated from the outside face by using internal drainage channels below windows. The problem could also be solved by using impervious surfaces where water and dirt flow concentrates. Windows positioned vertically in line with an impervious material, such as paint or vitreous enamel between (forming 'slots' in otherwise uninterrupted brickwork), conform to this idea **16**. Such vertical features tend to be favoured in present design and, although they may have come about for other reasons than control of weathering effects, they do in fact represent one logical way of achieving such control.

16 *Vertical arrangement of porous and impervious elements —in this case brick and glass—is one method of preventing staining*

7 References

General
1 BUILDING RESEARCH STATION Principles of modern building: volume 1. 1964, HMSO [(9–) (E1)] *£1*
2 BUILDING RESEARCH STATION Principles of modern building: volume 2. 1961, HMSO [(9–) (E1)] *87½p*

Environmental control
3 AJ Handbook of Building environment (AJ 2.10.68 to 13.8.69) [(E6)]
4 BURBERRY, P. Environment and services. London, 1970, Batsford [(E6)] *£2·50, paperback £1·60*

Weathering
5 WHITE, R. B. The changing appearance of buildings. 1967, HMSO [(9–) (S)] *£1·05*

Information sheet
External envelope I

Environmental performance data

Technical study EXTERNAL ENVELOPE 1 *emphasised the importance of the climatic control function of the building's external envelope, and pointed to the neglect frequently suffered by this aspect of building design.*
The present information sheet is an attempt to help remedy this situation, by providing architects with simple methods for establishing at an early design stage the likely performance of the building in three major respects: condensation risk, heat loss and noise insulation. A summary of the steps to be followed, in each case, is given in the checklist at the end of the information sheet; and worked examples are provided of all the procedures described. The methods were developed at the Functional Design Laboratory, Department of Architecture, Bristol University, by RICHARD LINNELL *in collaboration with* BRIAN DAY *and* PETER BURBERRY

1 Scope

This information sheet is intended to aid architects with decision-taking at a formative stage of design, by providing information on the likely environmental performance of alternative building forms, or fabric types.

The following aspects of environmental performance are covered:
● Condensation risk (see 2)
● Heat loss (see 3)
● Acoustic performance (see 4).

The information relates to the performance of the building's *external envelope* only; ie external walls, including windows and doors, and roofs.

Similar data for the internal subdividing elements will be published in section 6 of the Handbook.

2 Condensation risk

Figures **1** and **2** indicate graphically the condensation risk associated with various wall and roof constructions. The condensation zone is that part of the wall or roof in which the structural temperature (continuous line) falls below the dew-point temperature (broken line). Readers wishing to know more about the underlying principles of condensation, and methods for determining condensation risk in particular forms of wall or roof construction not shown here, are advised to consult a series of three articles published in the AJ in 1971[9], or, if a briefer reference is required, BRS Digest 110[3].

In **1** and **2** the computations have been based on the recommendations of CP 111 Chapter 2[6], so the following conditions have been assumed:
● Normal exposure
● Normal domestic occupancy

● External air temperature 0°C (-6°C for roofs)
● External relative humidity 100 per cent (saturated)
● Internal air temperature 20°C
● Internal relative humidity 48 per cent (ie a moisture vapour excess of 0·0034 kg/kg over saturated outdoor air at 0°C).

In addition, it has been assumed that foil-backed plasterboard is fixed so that the foil backing forms an unbroken vapour barrier; and all vapour barriers shown in the structure are fixed so as to be continuous and unbroken; although not all 100 per cent proof against vapour, they are effective in reducing the vapour pressure.

3 Heat loss

3.01 Heat loss computation

If the U-value of each element of a building's construction is known (comprehensive tables will be found in, for instance, the AJ Metric Handbook), the rate of heat loss for the building as a whole can be established by room-by-room analysis, multiplying in each case the area of each particular type of construction by its U-value, and by the temperature difference between the air in the room and the air on the other side of the construction. Individual results for each type of construction are summed to give total heat losses for rooms, and these can then be used to select appropriate room-heating appliances. In the same way, the total heat loss for *all* rooms can be calculated, and used to select an appropriate central heating plant.

However, the present handbook deals only with the building fabric and not with services installations; so readers requiring guidance on the latter problem should consult the AJ Handbook of Building environment section 4 THERMAL PROPERTIES (AJ 18.12.68 to 8.1.69) and section 8 HEATING SERVICES (AJ 2.4.69 to 28.5.69).

1 *Condensation risk associated with various forms of wall construction, calculated on the basis of* CP 3, *chapter* II.

Shaded area indicates zone of condensation risk, where structural temperature (solid line) falls below dew-point temperature (broken line)

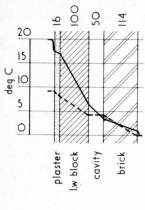

No special problems

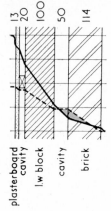

No special problems

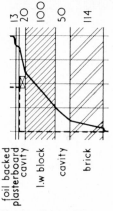

No special problems

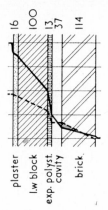

No special problems

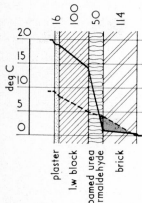

Possible problems

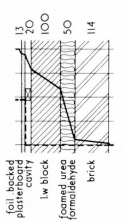

Possible problems

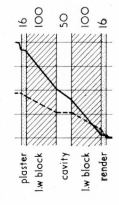

No special problems

No special problems

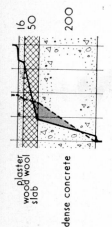

Serious problems

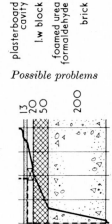

No special problems

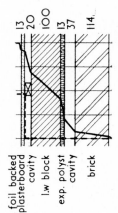

No special problems

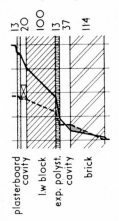

No special problems

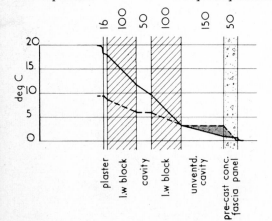

No special problems
(drain outer cavity)

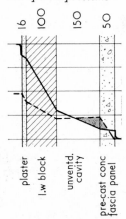

No special problems
(drain cavity)

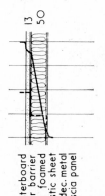

*Problem; condensation
may saturate insulation*

1 *Condensation risk associated with various forms of wall construction (continued)*

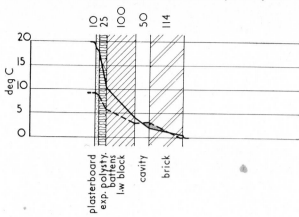

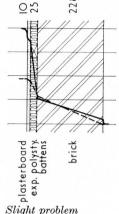

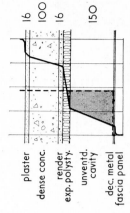

No special problems

Slight problem

*No risk if cavity drained;
otherwise serious problem*

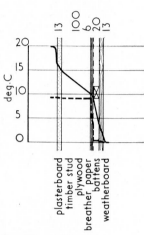

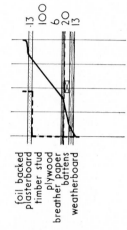

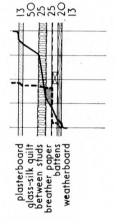

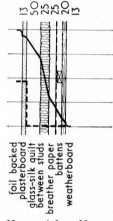

Possible problems

No special problems

Severe problems

No special problems

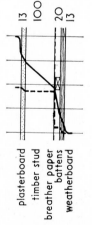

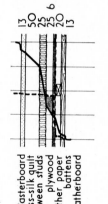

Possible problems

No special problems

Severe problems

No special problems

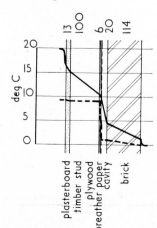

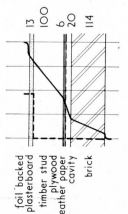

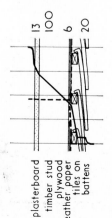

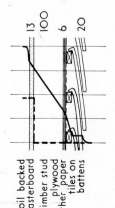

No special problems

No special problems

Slight risk

No special problems

2 *Condensation risk associated with various forms of roof construction, calculated on the basis of* CP 3, *chapter* II. *Shaded area indicates zone of condensation risk, where structural temperature (continuous line) falls below* dew-point temperature (broken line). First two examples are pitched roofs, remainder are flat*

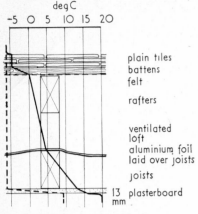

deg C
-5 0 5 10 15 20

plain tiles
battens
felt

rafters

ventilated
loft
aluminium foil
laid over joists

joists

13 plasterboard
mm

No condensation. No special problem. If pitch is less than 20°, vapour barrier should be included immediately above plasterboard

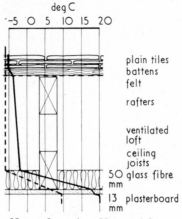

deg C
-5 0 5 10 15 20

plain tiles
battens
felt

rafters

ventilated
loft
ceiling
joists
50 glass fibre
mm

13 plasterboard
mm

No condensation. No special problem. If pitch is less than 20°, vapour barrier should be included between plasterboard and insulation

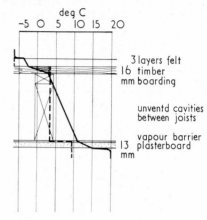

deg C
-5 0 5 10 15 20

3 layers felt
16 timber
mm boarding

unventd cavities
between joists

vapour barrier
13 plasterboard
mm

Considerable risk of condensation damage to timber boarding and joists if cavity is unventilated

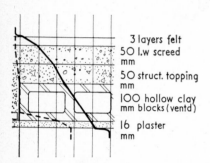

3 layers felt
50 l.w screed
mm
50 struct. topping
mm
100 hollow clay
mm blocks (ventd)

16 plaster
mm

No condensation. No special problem. Cavity in hollow blocks must be ventilated

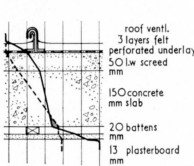

roof ventl.
3 layers felt
perforated underlay
50 l.w screed
mm

150 concrete
mm slab

20 battens
mm
13 plasterboard
mm

Slight condensation risk in very severe conditions. Should not cause trouble

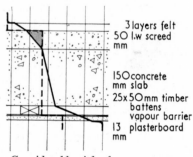

3 layers felt
50 l.w screed
mm

150 concrete
mm slab
25 x 50 mm timber
battens
vapour barrier
13 plasterboard
mm

Considerable risk of condensation occurrence

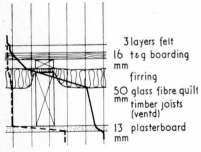

3 layers felt
16 t&g boarding
mm
firring
50 glass fibre quilt
mm timber joists
(ventd)
13 plasterboard
mm

No condensation. No special problem. Cavity must be ventilated

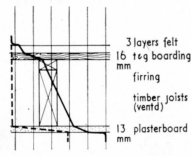

3 layers felt
16 t&g boarding
mm
firring

timber joists
(ventd)

13 plasterboard
mm

No condensation. No special problem. Cavity must be ventilated

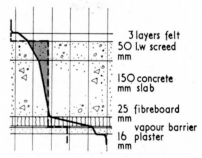

3 layers felt
50 l.w screed
mm

150 concrete
mm slab

25 fibreboard
mm
vapour barrier
16 plaster
mm

Considerable risk of condensation occurrence in slab and screed

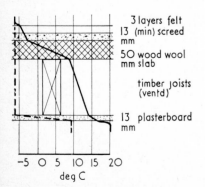

3 layers felt
13 (min) screed
mm
50 wood wool
mm slab

timber joists
(ventd)

13 plasterboard
mm

-5 0 5 10 15 20
deg C

No condensation. No special problem. Cavity must be ventilated

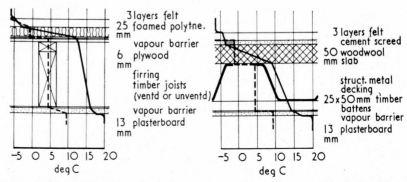

3 layers felt
25 foamed polytne.
mm
vapour barrier
6 plywood
mm
firring
timber joists
(ventd or unventd)
vapour barrier
13 plasterboard
mm

-5 0 5 10 15 20
deg C

No trouble if insulation is properly protected by vapour barrier

3 layers felt
cement screed
50 woodwool
mm slab

struct. metal
decking
25 x 50 mm timber
battens
vapour barrier
13 plasterboard
mm

-5 0 5 10 15 20
deg C

Slight risk of condensation damage

* *Vapour barriers are not always 100 per cent proof, particularly polythene sheet, though this may be waterproof. Aluminium foil (properly jointed) is virtually 100 per cent proof, hence diagram 1 shows the dewpoint up to the barrier as the same as the outside air. The barriers shown in diagram 2 are not meant to be foil but polythene or other partially effective material permitting some passage of vapour.*

But it must be emphasised that these two aspects of building design, fabric and services, are closely interlinked, and that it will be expensive—perhaps impossible—to provide a comfortable thermal environment by means of sophisticated services, if mistakes have been made in designing the building fabric. So it is important that the thermal performance of proposed building enclosures be checked at an early design stage, unless the building is of traditional construction with relatively massive walls of low u-value, and with a low ratio of glazing to solid wall.

3.02 Simplified methods

Because heat-loss calculations (see AJ information sheet HEATING SERVICES 13, 28.5.69) are time-consuming, they often go by default as architects have not got the time or patience to carry them out. Therefore a series of charts and tables are provided on the following pages, enabling architects to short-circuit the usual onerous computation procedures, and determine quickly and easily the likely effect of any design decision on heating costs, at an early design stage. Account is taken of a wide range of variables, and the architect can see at a glance the effect of choosing alternative values for any particular variable.

The tables give approximate heat losses based on a number of fundamental building characteristics (area, shape, window/wall ratio, approximate u-value), and may be used at a very early design stage, prior to drawing.

Once a number of alternative possibilities have been explored in this way, and a suitable concept has been chosen, the basic design can be developed in detail by using the charts.

3.03 Use of tables I to IV

Maximum rate of heat loss

As a basis for estimating size of heating installation required, tables I and II provide a quick method of comparing the *maximum rate of heat loss* from detached and terrace dwellings of various shapes, sizes and insulation values. Tables III and IV give additional values which allow the computation to be extended to end-dwellings in a terrace, and to staggered terraces. The figures assume the following conditions:
● Normal exposure
● External temperature 0°C; internal air temperature 20°C
● Ventilation rate two air-changes an hour
● u-value of single-glazing 5·60 W/m² deg C; double-glazing (6 mm cavity assumed) 3·00 W/m² deg C
● 'Low insulation' refers to the following u-values: walls and roofs 1·50 W/m² deg C; floors 0·86 W/m² deg C
● 'High insulation' refers to the following u-values: walls and roofs 0·50 W/m² deg C; floors 0·86 W/m² deg C
● In table III and IV, end walls and staggered walls are assumed to be unglazed.
● Perimeter ratio (table I) = $\dfrac{\text{Perimeter of building}}{4 \times \sqrt{\text{plan area}}}$
● Plan ratio (table II) = ratio of depth of dwelling to length of exposed facade
● Percentage glazing in table I is percentage of *total* wall area occupied by windows or glazed doors; but in table II it refers to percentage of *opposite exposed facade walls* occupied by windows or glazed doors.
If values other than those given in the tables are needed, they may be found by interpolation. If an average temperature other than 20° is required, then the maximum rate of heat loss should be divided by 20 and the result multiplied by the new temperature difference.
Take, for example, a house which has all the characteristics of that in the worked example given at the end of table IV,

except that an external temperature of −5°C would be more appropriate than 0°C. Temperature difference is therefore 25° rather than 20°; which means that the problem is worked through exactly as in the worked example, and the end result 14·11 kW is divided by 20 and multiplied by 25. The answer is therefore 17·64 kW·

Seasonal heat loss

If it is desired to establish *seasonal heat loss* (as a basis for estimating likely fuel costs), it will be necessary to feed the maximum rate of heat loss, found from the tables, into chart E. The seasonal heat loss concept takes account of both heat losses and heat gains (from sunshine, occupants and so on) throughout the heating season, and allows an estimate to be made of heat requirements for the whole of the heating season. A worked example is given with chart E.

3.04 Use of charts A to E

Dwellings

As a subsequent step to using the above tables, a rather wider range of variables and values can be investigated with some accuracy by making use of this series of charts.
Chart A and B
Charts A and B refer to dwellings (detached in the case of A; terraced in the case of B) and assume the following conditions:
● Normal exposure
● External air temperature 0°C; internal air temperature 20°C
● u-value of single-glazing 5·60 W/m² deg C; double-glazing (6 mm cavity assumed) 3·00 W/m² deg C
● Percentage glazing is the percentage of the *total* wall area occupied by window or glazed door
● In chart B, a ventilation rate of two air-changes an hour is assumed and percentage glazing is the percentage of opposite exposed *facade* walls of terraced dwellings, and does not include for glazing in the end walls of the terrace. Worked examples are given on each of the charts.
Chart D
The factors found by using the previous two charts must be multiplied by the total dwelling area to find the *maximum rate of heat loss*. Chart D provides a simple method of doing this, and its use is illustrated by the worked example printed on the same page.
Chart E
Finally, if it is desired to establish from the maximum rate of heat loss what the *seasonal heat loss* would be, this can be done using chart E. Again, the method is explained by means of a worked example. The value found will be approximate only, and does not include for heat gains from occupants and their activities. For normal occupancies, approximately 3·8 × 10⁹ Joules should be subtracted from the seasonal heat loss, for each person occupying the dwelling.
On the basis of the above calculations, it will now be possible to estimate both boiler sizes, and fuel costs.

Larger buildings

So far the charts have dealt with dwellings only: for larger buildings, maximum rate of heat loss may be calculated by using chart C. Maximum building dimensions accommodated by this chart are from plan area 900 m² and height 48 m, to 2500 m² and 15 m. Assumed conditions are as for charts A and B, and the chart is used in the same way, except that it is not necessary to carry out the multiplication exercise (rate of heat loss × area), using chart D, at the end; in this case, the multiplication is incorporated within the chart.

Table I *Detached dwelling approximate maximum rate of heat loss in kilowatts*
This table can be used at earliest design stage, to assess effect of alternative building forms, degrees of insulation and window : wall ratios, on building's heat loss characteristics*. Once basic decisions have been taken, chart A *can be used for more detailed investigations.* SG *denotes single glazing;* DG *denotes double glazing*

perimeter ratio 1·O   perimeter ratio 1·O7   perimeter ratio 1·16   perimeter ratio 1·35   perimeter ratio 1·5O

Area of dwelling (m²)	Per cent glazing	Insulation — perimeter 1·0				perimeter 1·07				perimeter 1·16				perimeter 1·35				perimeter 1·50			
		Low SG	Low DG	High SG	High DG	Low SG	Low DG	High SG	High DG	Low SG	Low DG	High SG	High DG	Low SG	Low DG	High SG	High DG	Low SG	Low DG	High SG	High DG
Single floor																					
30	20	4·75	4·23	3·34	2·82	4·91	4·35	3·45	2·89	5·13	4·52	3·59	2·98	5·57	4·86	3·88	3·17	5·92	5·13	4·11	3·33
	40	5·58	4·53	4·37	3·33	5·80	4·68	4·55	3·43	6·08	4·87	4·78	3·57	6·69	5·27	5·27	3·86	7·16	5·59	5·65	4·08
	60	6·40	4·83	5·40	3·83	6·68	5·00	5·65	3·97	7·04	5·22	5·98	4·15	7·80	5·68	6·66	4·53	8·40	6·04	7·20	4·84
	80	7·23	5·13	6·43	4·33	7·57	5·33	6·75	4·51	8·00	5·57	7·17	4·74	8·92	6·09	8·05	5·22	9·64	6·50	8·74	5·60
Single floor																					
45	20	6·48	5·84	4·60	3·96	6·69	6·00	4·73	4·04	6·94	6·20	4·90	4·15	7·49	6·62	5·25	4·39	7·92	6·95	5·53	4·57
	40	7·50	6·21	5·86	4·57	7·77	6·39	6·08	4·70	8·12	6·63	6·36	4·87	8·85	7·12	6·95	5·22	9·43	7·51	7·42	5·50
	60	8·51	6·58	7·11	5·19	8·85	6·79	7·42	5·36	9·29	7·06	7·82	5·58	10·22	7·62	8·65	6·05	10·95	8·06	9·31	6·42
	80	9·52	6·95	8·37	5·81	9·93	7·19	8·77	6·02	10·46	7·49	9·28	6·30	11·59	8·12	10·35	6·89	12·47	8·62	11·20	7·35
Single floor																					
60	20	8·13	7·39	5·79	5·05	8·36	7·57	5·95	5·15	8·66	7·80	6·14	5·28	9·29	8·29	6·55	5·55	9·79	8·68	6·88	5·76
	40	9·30	7·82	7·25	5·76	9·62	8·03	7·50	5·91	10·02	8·30	7·83	6·11	10·87	8·87	8·51	6·51	11·54	9·32	9·06	6·83
	60	10·47	8·25	8·70	6·48	10·87	8·49	9·06	6·68	11·37	8·80	9·51	6·93	12·45	9·45	10·48	7·48	13·29	9·96	11·24	7·90
	80	11·64	8·68	10·16	7·19	12·12	8·95	10·61	7·44	12·73	9·29	11·20	7·76	14·02	10·02	12·44	8·44	15·05	10·60	13·42	8·97
Two floors																					
60	20	8·09	7·04	5·87	4·83	8·41	7·29	6·09	4·97	8·84	7·62	6·36	5·15	9·72	8·31	6·95	5·53	10·43	8·85	7·41	5·83
	40	9·74	7·64	7·93	5·83	10·18	7·94	8·29	6·05	10·75	8·32	8·75	6·32	11·96	9·13	9·72	6·89	12·90	9·76	10·49	7·35
	60	11·39	8·25	9·99	6·85	11·95	8·59	10·49	7·12	12·67	9·02	11·13	7·49	14·19	9·94	12·50	8·25	15·38	10·67	13·57	8·86
	80	13·05	8·85	12·04	7·85	13·72	9·23	12·69	8·20	14·59	9·72	13·52	8·66	16·42	10·76	15·27	9·61	17·86	11·57	16·66	10·37
Single floor																					
75	20	9·73	8·90	6·96	6·13	9·99	9·10	7·13	6·24	10·32	9·36	7·34	6·38	11·02	9·91	7·80	6·68	11·58	10·34	8·17	6·92
	40	11·04	9·38	8·58	6·92	11·39	9·61	8·86	7·09	11·84	9·92	9·23	7·31	12·79	10·55	10·00	7·76	13·54	11·05	10·60	8·12
	60	12·34	9·86	10·21	7·72	12·79	10·13	10·60	7·94	13·35	10·47	11·11	8·23	14·55	11·20	12·19	8·84	15·50	11·77	13·04	9·31
	80	13·65	10·34	11·83	8·52	14·18	10·64	12·34	8·80	14·87	11·02	13·00	9·15	16·32	11·84	14·39	9·91	17·46	12·49	15·48	10·51
Two floors																					
75	20	9·49	8·32	6·94	5·77	9·86	8·60	7·18	5·92	10·33	8·97	7·49	6·13	11·32	9·74	8·14	6·56	12·11	10·35	8·65	6·89
	40	11·34	9·00	9·24	6·89	11·84	9·33	9·64	7·13	12·47	9·75	10·15	7·43	13·82	10·65	11·24	8·08	14·88	11·36	12·10	8·58
	60	13·19	9·67	11·54	8·02	13·81	10·05	12·10	8·34	14·62	10·54	12·82	8·75	16·31	11·57	14·34	9·60	17·65	12·38	15·55	10·27
	80	15·04	10·35	13·83	9·15	15·79	10·77	14·56	9·54	16·76	11·32	15·49	10·05	18·81	12·48	17·45	11·12	20·42	13·39	19·00	11·96
Single floor																					
90	20	11·29	10·38	8·09	7·19	11·57	10·60	8·28	7·31	11·94	10·88	8·52	7·46	12·71	11·48	9·02	7·80	13·31	11·95	9·42	8·06
	40	12·72	10·91	9·87	8·06	13·10	11·16	10·18	8·24	13·60	11·49	10·58	8·48	14·64	12·19	11·43	8·97	15·46	12·74	12·09	9·37
	60	14·15	11·43	11·65	8·93	14·64	11·72	12·09	9·18	15·26	12·10	12·65	9·49	16·57	12·90	13·83	10·15	17·61	13·52	14·76	10·68
	80	15·58	11·95	13·43	9·80	16·17	12·28	13·99	10·11	16·92	12·71	14·71	10·50	18·50	13·60	16·23	11·33	19·76	14·31	17·43	11·99
Two floors																					
90	20	10·84	9·56	7·97	6·68	11·24	9·87	8·23	6·86	11·76	10·27	8·57	7·08	12·85	11·11	9·28	7·55	13·71	11·78	9·84	7·92
	40	12·87	10·30	10·49	7·92	13·41	10·66	10·93	8·18	14·11	11·13	11·49	8·51	15·58	12·11	12·68	9·21	16·74	12·89	13·62	9·77
	60	14·89	11·04	13·00	9·15	15·58	11·46	13·62	9·50	16·46	11·99	14·41	9·94	18·31	13·11	16·08	10·88	19·78	14·00	17·40	11·62
	80	16·92	11·78	15·52	10·39	17·74	12·25	16·31	10·82	18·80	12·85	17·33	11·37	21·05	14·11	19·48	12·55	22·82	15·11	21·18	13·47
Three floors																					
90	20	11·42	9·85	8·40	6·83	11·91	10·23	8·73	7·04	12·54	10·72	9·14	7·32	13·88	11·75	10·01	7·89	14·93	12·57	10·70	8·34
	40	13·90	10·76	11·49	8·34	14·57	11·20	12·03	8·66	15·42	11·77	12·72	9·07	17·22	12·98	14·18	9·93	18·65	13·93	15·33	10·61
	60	16·38	11·66	14·57	9·85	17·22	12·17	15·32	10·28	18·30	12·83	16·29	10·82	20·57	14·20	18·34	11·97	22·37	15·29	19·95	12·88
	80	18·86	12·57	17·66	11·37	19·87	13·14	18·62	11·90	21·17	13·88	19·87	12·58	23·92	15·43	22·50	14·01	26·09	16·65	24·58	15·15
Single floor																					
105	20	12·82	11·84	9·21	8·23	13·12	12·08	9·41	8·36	13·52	12·38	9·67	8·53	14·34	13·02	10·21	8·89	15·00	13·53	10·64	9·17
	40	14·37	12·41	11·14	9·17	14·78	12·68	11·47	9·37	15·31	13·04	11·90	9·63	16·44	13·79	12·81	10·16	17·33	14·39	13·53	10·59
	60	15·91	12·97	13·06	10·12	16·44	13·29	13·53	10·38	17·11	13·70	14·13	10·72	18·53	14·56	15·41	11·44	19·65	15·23	16·41	12·00
	80	17·46	13·54	14·98	11·06	18·09	13·89	15·59	11·39	18·90	14·35	16·36	11·81	20·61	15·32	18·00	12·71	21·96	16·08	19·30	13·42
Two floors																					
105	20	12·15	10·77	8·97	7·58	12·59	11·10	9·25	7·77	13·14	11·54	9·62	8·01	14·32	12·45	10·39	8·52	15·25	13·17	11·00	8·92
	40	14·31	11·57	11·69	8·92	14·91	11·96	12·17	9·20	15·68	12·46	12·77	9·56	17·27	13·53	14·06	10·32	18·53	14·37	15·08	10·92
	60	16·53	12·37	14·41	10·25	17·27	12·82	15·08	10·62	18·22	13·39	15·93	11·10	20·22	14·61	17·73	12·12	21·81	15·57	19·16	12·92
	80	18·71	13·17	17·13	11·58	19·61	13·67	17·99	12·05	20·75	14·32	19·08	12·65	23·17	15·69	21·40	13·92	25·09	16·77	23·24	14·92
Three floors																					
105	20	12·72	11·02	9·41	7·71	13·25	11·43	9·75	7·94	13·93	11·96	10·20	8·23	15·37	13·08	11·14	8·85	16·51	13·96	11·89	9·34
	40	15·40	12·00	12·74	9·34	16·11	12·48	13·32	9·68	17·04	13·10	14·06	10·12	18·99	14·40	15·64	11·06	20·52	15·43	16·88	11·79
	60	18·07	12·98	16·07	10·97	18·98	13·53	16·88	11·43	20·14	14·23	17·93	12·02	22·60	15·72	20·14	13·26	24·54	16·90	21·88	14·24
	80	20·75	13·96	19·40	12·61	21·84	14·58	20·45	13·18	23·25	15·37	21·79	13·91	26·22	17·05	24·63	15·46	28·56	18·37	26·88	16·69

**Use of table is explained in 3.03, and worked example at end of table* IV

Table II *Centre terrace dwelling: approximate maximum rate of heat loss in kilowatts*
This table can be used at earliest design stage, to assess effect of alternative building forms, degrees of insulation and window: wall ratios, on building's heat loss characteristics*. Once basic decisions have been taken, chart B *can be used for more detailed investigations.* SG *denotes single glazing:* DG *denotes double glazing*

plan ratio 3:1   plan ratio 2:1   plan ratio 1·5:1   plan ratio 1:1   plan ratio 1:1·5

Left axis: Area of dwelling (m²) — Per cent glazing

Area / floors	%	3:1 Low SG	3:1 Low DG	3:1 High SG	3:1 High DG	2:1 Low SG	2:1 Low DG	2:1 High SG	2:1 High DG	1·5:1 Low SG	1·5:1 Low DG	1·5:1 High SG	1·5:1 High DG	1:1 Low SG	1:1 Low DG	1:1 High SG	1:1 High DG	1:1·5 Low SG	1:1·5 Low DG	1:1·5 High SG	1:1·5 High DG
Single floor 30	20	3·09	2·94	2·25	2·10	3·24	3·05	2·35	2·17	3·37	3·15	2·44	2·22	3·58	3·32	2·58	2·32	3·84	3·52	2·75	2·43
	40	3·33	3·02	2·55	2·25	3·53	3·16	2·71	2·35	3·70	3·28	2·86	2·43	3·99	3·47	3·09	2·57	4·35	3·71	3·38	2·74
	60	3·56	3·11	2·85	2·39	3·82	3·27	3·08	2·52	4·04	3·40	3·28	2·64	4·41	3·62	3·61	2·82	4·86	3·89	4·01	3·05
	80	3·80	3·20	3·14	2·54	4·12	3·37	3·44	2·70	4·38	3·52	3·70	2·84	4·82	3·77	4·12	3·07	5·36	4·08	4·64	3·36
Single floor 45	20	4·45	4·26	3·26	3·07	4·63	4·40	3·38	3·15	4·79	4·53	3·48	3·22	5·05	4·73	3·66	3·34	5·37	4·98	3·87	3·47
	40	4·74	4·37	3·62	3·25	4·99	4·53	3·83	3·57	5·20	4·68	4·00	3·47	5·56	4·91	4·29	3·64	6·00	5·21	4·64	3·85
	60	5·03	4·47	3·99	3·43	5·35	4·67	4·27	3·59	5·61	4·83	4·51	3·73	6·06	5·10	4·91	3·95	6·61	5·43	5·41	4·23
	80	5·32	4·58	4·35	3·61	5·70	4·80	4·72	3·81	6·03	4·98	5·03	4·00	6·57	5·28	5·54	4·26	7·23	5·66	6·18	4·61
Single floor 60	20	5·78	5·57	4·25	4·04	5·99	5·73	4·39	4·13	6·17	5·87	4·51	4·21	6·48	6·11	4·71	4·34	6·85	6·40	4·95	4·50
	40	6·12	5·69	4·67	4·24	6·41	5·88	4·90	4·38	6·65	6·05	5·10	4·50	7·06	6·32	5·43	4·69	7·57	6·66	5·84	4·93
	60	6·45	5·81	5·09	4·45	6·82	6·03	5·42	4·63	7·13	6·22	5·70	4·79	7·65	6·54	6·16	5·05	8·28	6·92	6·73	5·37
	80	6·79	5·94	5·51	4·65	7·23	6·19	5·93	4·88	7·61	6·40	6·29	5·08	8·23	6·75	6·89	5·41	9·00	7·18	7·62	5·81
Two floors 60	20	4·76	4·46	3·69	3·39	5·06	4·69	3·89	3·52	5·32	4·89	4·06	3·63	5·75	5·22	4·34	3·82	6·27	5·63	4·68	4·04
	40	5·24	4·63	4·29	3·68	5·65	4·91	4·62	3·88	5·99	5·14	4·90	4·04	6·57	5·53	5·37	4·32	7·28	6·00	5·94	4·66
	60	5·71	4·80	4·88	3·98	6·23	5·12	5·35	4·23	6·67	5·38	5·74	4·45	7·40	5·83	6·40	4·82	8·30	6·37	7·20	5·28
	80	6·19	4·98	5·47	4·26	6·81	5·33	6·07	4·59	7·34	5·63	6·58	4·87	8·22	6·13	7·42	5·33	7·31	6·74	8·46	5·89
Single floor 75	20	7·10	6·86	5·23	5·00	7·34	7·04	5·39	5·09	7·54	7·20	5·52	5·18	7·88	7·47	5·74	5·33	8·29	7·79	6·01	5·51
	40	7·48	6·99	5·70	5·22	7·80	7·21	5·97	5·38	8·07	7·40	6·18	5·51	8·53	7·70	6·55	5·73	9·09	8·08	7·01	5·99
	60	7·85	7·13	6·17	5·45	8·26	7·38	6·54	5·66	8·61	7·59	6·85	5·83	9·10	7·94	7·37	6·12	9·89	8·37	8·00	6·48
	80	8·23	7·27	6·64	5·68	8·72	7·55	7·11	5·92	9·14	7·79	7·51	6·16	9·84	8·18	8·18	6·52	10·70	8·67	9·00	6·97
Two floors 75	20	5·77	5·43	4·50	4·16	6·11	5·69	4·72	4·31	6·40	5·91	4·91	4·43	6·87	6·29	5·22	4·64	7·46	6·74	5·60	4·89
	40	6·30	5·63	5·16	4·49	6·76	5·93	5·53	4·71	7·15	6·19	5·85	4·89	7·80	6·63	6·37	5·20	8·59	7·16	7·02	5·58
	60	6·84	5·82	5·83	4·81	7·42	6·17	6·35	5·10	7·90	6·47	6·79	5·35	8·72	6·97	7·52	5·76	9·73	7·58	8·42	6·27
	80	7·37	6·02	6·50	5·14	8·07	6·41	7·16	5·50	8·66	6·74	7·72	5·81	9·65	7·30	8·67	6·32	10·86	7·99	9·83	6·96
Two floors 90	20	6·77	6·40	5·30	4·93	7·14	6·68	5·54	5·09	7·45	6·93	5·74	5·22	7·98	7·33	6·09	5·45	8·62	7·83	6·51	5·72
	40	7·35	6·61	6·02	5·28	7·85	6·95	6·43	5·52	8·28	7·23	6·77	5·72	8·99	7·71	7·35	6·06	9·86	8·29	8·05	6·48
	60	7·94	6·82	6·75	5·64	8·57	7·21	7·32	5·96	9·10	7·53	7·80	6·23	10·00	8·08	8·61	6·68	11·10	8·74	9·59	7·24
	80	8·52	7·04	7·48	5·99	9·28	7·47	8·21	6·39	9·93	7·83	8·83	6·73	11·01	8·45	9·87	7·30	12·34	9·19	11·14	8·00
Three floors 90	20	6·43	5·98	5·13	4·68	6·88	6·33	5·43	4·87	7·27	6·63	5·68	5·04	7·91	7·13	6·10	5·32	8·70	7·74	6·62	5·66
	40	7·15	6·24	6·02	5·11	7·76	6·65	6·52	5·41	8·28	6·99	6·94	5·66	9·15	7·58	7·64	6·07	10·22	8·29	8·51	6·58
	60	7·86	6·50	6·91	5·55	8·64	6·97	7·61	5·94	9·29	7·37	8·20	6·27	10·39	8·03	9·19	6·83	11·74	8·85	10·40	7·51
	80	8·58	6·76	7·80	5·99	9·51	7·29	8·70	6·48	10·30	7·74	9·46	6·89	11·63	8·49	10·73	7·58	13·25	9·40	12·28	8·43
Two floors 105	20	7·75	7·35	6·09	5·68	8·15	7·66	6·34	5·86	8·50	7·92	6·57	6·00	9·06	8·37	6·94	6·25	9·75	8·90	7·40	6·55
	40	8·38	7·58	6·87	6·07	8·93	7·94	7·31	6·33	9·38	8·25	7·68	6·55	10·15	8·77	8·30	6·91	11·09	9·39	9·06	7·36
	60	9·01	7·81	7·66	6·45	9·70	8·23	8·27	6·80	10·28	8·58	8·79	7·09	11·24	9·16	9·66	7·58	12·43	9·88	10·73	8·18
	80	9·64	8·04	8·44	6·84	10·47	8·51	9·23	7·27	11·17	8·90	9·90	7·64	12·34	9·56	110·2	8·25	13·77	10·37	12·39	8·99
Three floors 105	20	7·33	6·84	5·87	5·38	7·82	7·22	6·19	5·59	8·23	7·54	6·47	5·77	8·93	8·08	6·92	6·07	9·78	8·74	7·48	6·44
	40	8·10	7·12	6·83	5·85	8·76	7·56	7·37	6·17	9·33	7·94	7·83	6·44	10·27	8·57	8·59	6·88	11·42	9·34	9·52	7·44
	60	8·87	7·40	7·80	6·32	9·71	7·91	8·55	6·75	10·42	8·34	9·19	7·11	11·61	9·06	10·25	7·71	13·06	9·94	11·56	8·44
	80	9·64	7·68	8·76	6·80	10·66	8·26	9·73	7·33	11·51	8·74	10·55	7·77	12·94	9·55	11·92	8·52	14·70	10·54	13·60	9·44
Two floors 120	20	8·73	8·30	6·87	6·44	9·16	8·63	7·15	6·63	9·52	8·91	7·39	6·78	10·12	9·38	7·78	7·04	10·87	9·96	8·27	7·36
	40	9·40	8·55	7·71	6·85	9·98	8·93	8·18	7·13	10·47	9·26	8·57	7·36	11·29	9·81	9·24	7·76	12·30	10·48	10·05	8·24
	60	10·08	8·79	8·55	7·26	10·81	9·24	9·21	7·63	11·43	9·61	9·76	7·94	12·46	10·24	10·69	8·47	13·73	11·01	11·83	9·11
	80	10·75	9·04	9·39	7·67	11·63	9·54	10·23	8·14	12·38	9·96	10·95	8·53	13·63	10·67	12·15	9·18	15·16	11·53	13·61	9·98
Three floors 120	20	8·21	7·69	6·61	6·08	8·74	8·10	6·95	6·31	9·18	8·44	7·24	6·50	9·92	9·02	7·73	6·82	10·83	9·72	8·32	7·21
	40	9·04	7·99	7·63	6·59	9·75	8·47	8·21	6·92	10·35	8·87	8·69	7·21	11·35	9·54	9·51	7·69	12·59	10·36	10·50	8·28
	60	9·86	8·29	8·66	7·09	10·76	8·84	9·47	7·54	11·52	9·29	10·15	7·92	12·79	10·06	11·29	8·56	14·34	11·00	12·68	9·35
	80	10·69	8·59	9·69	7·59	11·77	9·21	10·73	8·16	12·69	9·72	11·60	8·64	14·22	10·59	13·07	9·44	16·09	11·65	14·86	10·42

**Use of table is explained in 3.03, and worked example at end of table* IV

Table III End of terrace: approximate maximum heat loss from solid end wall of terrace in kilowatts. To be used in conjunction with table II (add this value to centre-terrace dwelling heat loss, for maximum heat loss from end of terrace dwelling)

Plan ratio = ratio of depth of dwelling to length of exposed facade

plan ratio 3:1 plan ratio 2:1 plan ratio 1·5:1 plan ratio 1:1 plan ratio 1:1·5

Area of dwelling (m²)	Number of floors	Low wall insulation	High wall insulation	Low wall insulation	High wall insulation	Low wall insulation	High wall insulation	Low wall insulation	High wall insulation	Low wall insulation	High wall insulation
30	1	0·65	0·22	0·53	0·18	0·46	0·15	0·38	0·13	0·31	0·10
45	1	0·80	0·27	0·65	0·22	0·57	0·19	0·46	0·15	0·38	0·13
60	1	0·92	0·31	0·76	0·25	0·65	0·22	0·53	0·18	0·44	0·15
	2	1·31	0·44	1·07	0·36	0·93	0·31	0·76	0·25	0·62	0·21
75	1	1·04	0·35	0·85	0·28	0·73	0·24	0·60	0·20	0·49	0·16
	2	1·46	0·49	1·20	0·40	1·04	0·35	0·85	0·28	0·69	0·23
90	2	1·60	0·53	1·31	0·44	1·13	0·38	0·93	0·31	0·76	0·25
	3	1·96	0·65	1·60	0·53	1·39	0·46	1·13	0·38	0·93	0·31
105	2	1·73	0·58	1·41	0·47	1·22	0·41	1·00	0·33	0·82	0·27
	3	2·12	0·71	1·73	0·58	1·50	0·50	1·22	0·41	1·00	0·33
120	2	1·85	0·62	1·51	0·50	1·31	0·44	1·07	0·36	0·87	0·29
	3	2·27	0·76	1·85	0·62	1·60	0·53	1·31	0·44	1·07	0·36

Table IV Staggered terrace: approximate maximum heat loss from solid stagger walls between terrace dwellings in kilowatts. To be used in conjunction with table II (add this value to centre-terrace dwelling heat loss, or end of terrace heat loss, for total maximum heat loss)

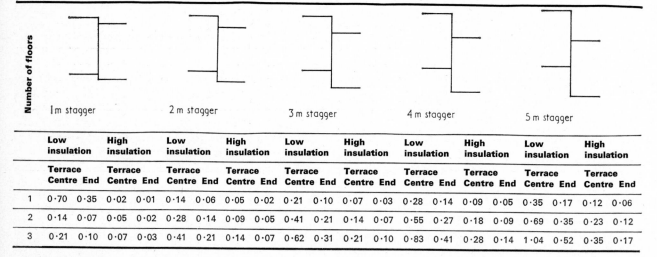

1m stagger 2m stagger 3m stagger 4m stagger 5m stagger

Number of floors	Low insulation Terrace Centre	End	High insulation Terrace Centre	End	Low insulation Terrace Centre	End	High insulation Terrace Centre	End	Low insulation Terrace Centre	End	High insulation Terrace Centre	End	Low insulation Terrace Centre	End	High insulation Terrace Centre	End	Low insulation Terrace Centre	End	High insulation Terrace Centre	End
1	0·70	0·35	0·02	0·01	0·14	0·06	0·05	0·02	0·21	0·10	0·07	0·03	0·28	0·14	0·09	0·05	0·35	0·17	0·12	0·06
2	0·14	0·07	0·05	0·02	0·28	0·14	0·09	0·05	0·41	0·21	0·14	0·07	0·55	0·27	0·18	0·09	0·69	0·35	0·23	0·12
3	0·21	0·10	0·07	0·03	0·41	0·21	0·14	0·07	0·62	0·31	0·21	0·10	0·83	0·41	0·28	0·14	1·04	0·52	0·35	0·17

Worked example

TABLE 1 Find approximate maximum rate of heat loss from detached dwelling of the following fundamental characteristics: total dwelling area is 90 m² and there are two floors (therefore plan area = 45 m²); perimeter ratio is 1·16; external walls are 40 per cent single-glazed, 60 per cent solid; u-values are 1·25 W/m² deg C for roof, and 1·20 W/m² deg C for solid portions of wall.

Step 1: Locate row in table representing dwelling area of 90 m², and 2 floors (it is the eighth row from the top); and select line representing 40 per cent glazing (it is the line marked 40).

Step 2: Windows are single-glazed and u-values 1·25 and 1·20 are (according to instructions in 3·03) regarded as *low insulation*. Select therefore, under the diagram *perimeter ratio* 1·16, the specific column headed *Low insulation* SG, and read off figure at intersection with row selected in step 1.

Maximum rate of heat loss is seen to be approximately 14·11 kW; this forms a basis for estimating capacity of heating plant required to maintain comfortable internal temperatures in the above dwelling when external temperatures are at their lowest. If heat loss is deemed acceptable, architect can proceed to detailed design with some confidence, using chart A to investigate the effect of more detailed decisions on fabric design. But if rate of heat loss found above is deemed to be unacceptably high, alternative plan sizes and shapes, u-values, and window: wall ratios should be tried out, until a satisfactory basic design has been achieved.

OTHER TABLES Table II, for centre-terrace dwellings, is used in exactly the same way as table I, except that *plan ratio* (see 3.03) is substituted for perimeter ratio. If an end-of-terrace dwelling is being investigated, use table II as above; then find rate of heat loss from solid end wall by using table III, and add the two figures together to find total heat loss. Table III does not cater for end-walls containing windows. If a staggered terrace is being investigated, again start by using table II, plus if necessary table III; and add on rate of heat loss from stagger walls, found from table IV.

Heat loss calculator chart A: detached dwellings

Once a fundamental design concept has been chosen on the basis of the approximate heat loss figures given in table I, a more detailed investigation can be made by using the charts below. They allow the effects of different permutations of building dimensions, U-values, ventilation rates, and window: wall ratios on the building's heat loss characteristics to be assessed.

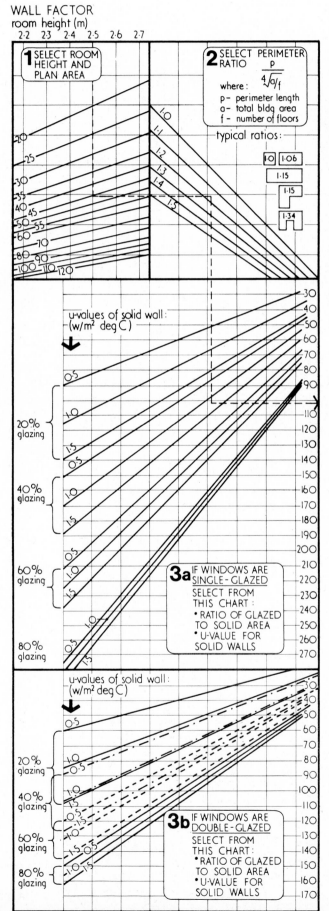

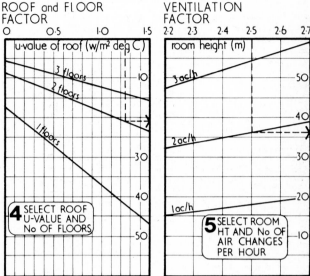

Worked example

Calculate heat loss from the following detached dwelling. Dwelling area is 90 m²; there are two floors; plan area is 45 m². The plan is L-shaped, and a comparison with the diagrams shown with step 2 above, indicates that perimeter ratio is 1·15. Ventilation rate is average (therefore taken at two air-changes per hour). External walls are 40 per cent single-glazed, 60 per cent solid; and U-values are 1·20 W/m² deg C for solid portions of walls; 1·25 for roof; and 0·86 for lowest floor. Room height is 2·5 m average.

● Make first start on *room height* scale on left of page; drop vertical line from 2·5 m to intersect 45 m² plan area line. From here draw a line at right angles to the first, to meet the 1·15 *perimeter ratio* line (interpolated between 1·1 and 1·2). Drop another vertical line from this point to meet the theoretical line representing 40 per cent single-glazing and a solid-wall U-value of 1·20 W/m² deg C (interpolated); and read off the *wall factor* on the vertical right-hand scale: 102

● Make second start on *roof U-value* scale; from 1·25 W/m² deg C drop a vertical line to intersect line representing two floors, and read off *roof and floor factor* on right-hand vertical scale: 21

● Make third start on *room height* scale on right of page; from 2·5 m room height, drop vertical line to intersect 2 ac/h line, and read off ventilation factor on right-hand vertical scale: 36

● Now add up the wall factor, roof and floor factor, and ventilation factor, found in the above three operations (102 + 21 + 36 = 159); and multiply the answer by the total dwelling area 90 m² (159 × 90). The multiplication can easily be carried out by using chart D, and it is seen that *maximum rate of heat loss* is 14·5 kW. This figure will assist in sizing of heating plant for the dwelling. If it is desired also to make an estimation of fuel cost, *seasonal heat loss* can be found by using chart E (see worked example included with E).

Heat loss calculator chart B: terraced dwellings

Once a fundamental design concept has been chosen on the basis of the approximate heat loss figures given in tables II to IV, a more detailed investigation can be made by using the charts below. They allow the effects of different permutations of building dimensions, u-values and window: wall ratios, on the building's heat loss characteristics to be assessed.

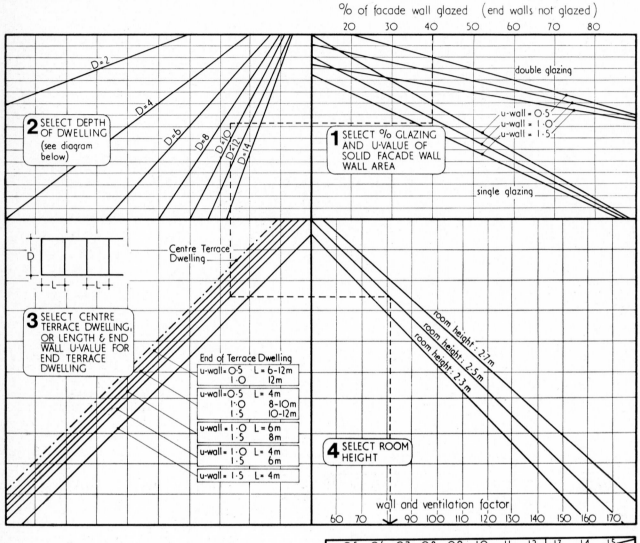

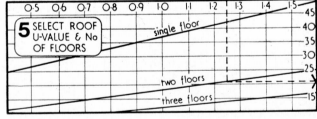

Worked example

Calculate heat loss from the following end-of-terrace dwelling. Dwelling area is 90 m²; there are two floors; plan area is 45 m². Façade length is 5 m, and depth of dwelling 9 m. Ventilation rate is average, and therefore taken at 2 ac/h. External walls are 40 per cent single-glazed, and 60 per cent solid (this applies to opposite exposed façade walls only, and assumes end wall to be without apertures; see para 3.04). u-values are 1·20 W/m² deg C for solid portions of all external walls; 1·25 for roof; and 0·86 for lowest floor. Room heights average 2·5 m.

● Make first start on *percentage of facade wall glazed* scale, and follow line through successive steps as shown above, ending by reading off the *wall and ventilation factor*: 82

● Make second start on *roof u-value* scale, follow line through number of floors, and read off *roof and floor factor*:

21

● As with chart A, add up the factors found in the above two operations (82 + 21 = 103); and multiply the answer by the total dwelling area 90 m² (103 × 90). The multiplication can easily be carried out by using chart D, and it is seen that *maximum rate of heat loss is 9·3 kW*. This figure will assist in sizing of heating plant for the dwelling. If it is desired also to make an estimation of fuel cost, *seasonal heat loss* can be found by using chart E (see worked example included with E).

Heat loss calculator chart C: office buildings, schools and flats

It is possible to evaluate the effects of alternative building dimensions, U-values, and window: wall ratios on building's heat loss characteristics, by using the charts below. In this case, unlike calculators A and B, no table of approximate values has been provided for preliminary assessments.

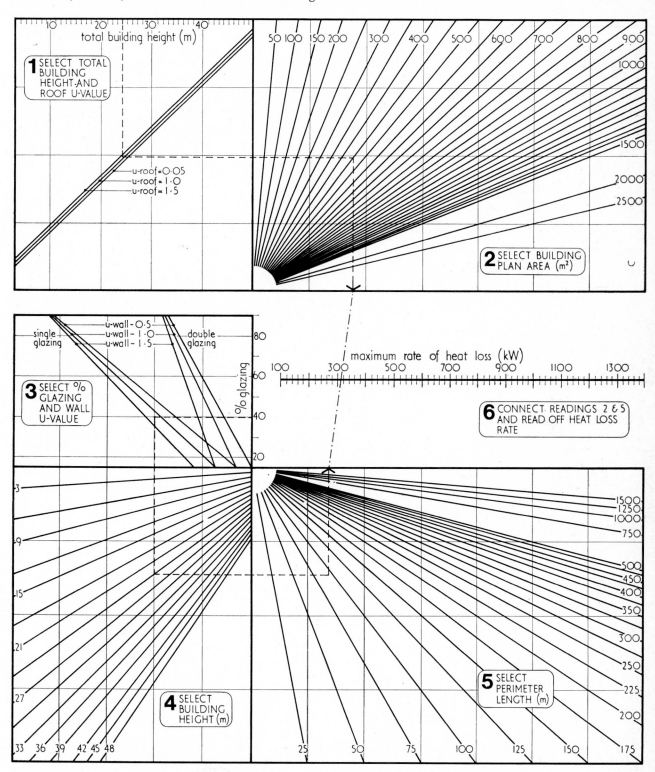

Worked example

Calculate heat loss for the following building. Plan dimensions are 15 m × 30 m (a rectangle); therefore plan area is 450 m². Building height is 24 m. External walls are 40 per cent single-glazed, 60 per cent solid; and U-values are 1·20 W/m² deg C for solid portions of walls; 1·25 for roof; and 0·86 for lowest floor.

Make first start on *total building height* scale, and follow

through to end of step 2. Make second start on *percentage glazing* scale, and follow through to end of step 5. Then connect values found at end of steps 2 and 5; point at which this line intersects central scale gives maximum rate of heat loss = 310 kW. Note that it is not necessary with this chart to multiply chart result by building area, as with charts A and B.

Chart D: multiplier to be used in conjunction with charts A and B

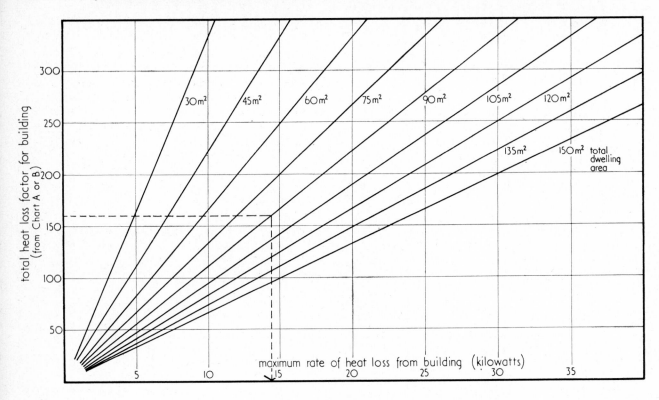

Chart E: maximum rate of heat loss converted to seasonal heat loss

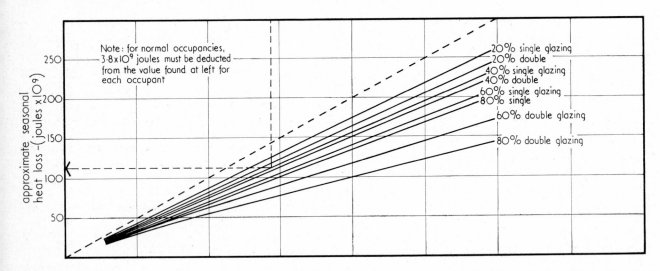

Worked examples

CHART D This chart is simply an aid for carrying out the multiplication required at the end of charts A and B; see the worked examples included with these charts. The value found at the end of A or B is fed in on the left-hand vertical scale, and carried through horizontally to intersect the appropriate *total dwelling area* line. From this point, a vertical is dropped to the bottom scale, and *maximum rate of heat loss* is read off. For example, the value found at the end of chart A was 159; if followed through on chart D, it is seen that maximum rate of heat loss is 14·5 kW. This figure will assist in the estimation of size of heating plant required for the dwelling.

CHART E This enables the maximum hourly rate of heat loss, given by the previous chart, to be converted to total heat loss for the whole of the annual heating season; this *seasonal heat loss* figure allows cost of fuel to be estimated. Method

of use is to drop a vertical line from *maximum rate of heat loss* scale (14·5 kW, if we follow through the worked example started on chart A, and carried through to D above) to intersect the relevant *percentage glazing* line. Approximate seasonal heat loss can then be read off on left-hand vertical scale. This must be corrected to allow for heat gains from the occupants and their activities, by subtracting (for normal occupancies) $3·8 \times 10^9$ per occupant. If the present dwelling has 4 occupants, seasonal heat loss is therefore approximately $[113 — (4 \times 3·8)] = 97·8$ Joules $\times 10^9$.

Table v Range of external noise levels at locations in which traffic noise predominates

Group	Location	Noise climate dBA* Day 10 per cent	Day 90 per cent	Night 10 per cent	Night 90 per cent
A	Arterial roads with many heavy vehicles and buses (kerbside)	80	68	70	50
B	Major roads with heavy traffic and buses Side roads within 15 to 20 m of major or arterial roads	75	63	61	49
C	Main residential roads Side roads within 15 to 20 m of heavy traffic routes Courtyards of blocks of flats, screened from view of heavy traffic routes	70	60	55	44
D	Residential roads with local traffic only	65	56	53	45
E	Minor roads Gardens of houses with traffic routes more than 100 m distant	60	51	49	43
F	Gardens and courtyards in residential areas well away from traffic routes	55	50	46	41
G	Places of few local noises and only very distant traffic noise	50	47	43	40

*10 per cent column gives noise levels exceeded for 10 per cent of time; 90 per cent gives levels exceeded for 90 per cent of time. Former should be used for design purposes

Table vi Range of external noise levels at locations in which aircraft noise predominates

Location	Approximate noise level
Within 1·5 km of take-off path, 0 to 5 km from beginning of runway	100–130 PNdB*
Within 1·5 km of take-off path, 5 to 15 km from beginning of runway	90–110 PNdB
Below large jet in 'stack' at 1550 m ht	80–90 PNdB
Within 1·5 km of landing path, 0 to 5 km from touch-down point	90–115 PNdB
Within 1·5 km of landing path, 5 to 15 km from touch-down point	85–100 PNdB
Within 1·5 km of landing path, 15 to 30 km from touch-down point	80–90 PNdB
Between 1·5 and 3·0 km from landing path, 0 to 30 km from touch-down point	75–87 PNdB
Within 1 km of ground maintenance running and warming up	75–100 PNdB

*This figure represents peak noise level

Table vii Range of external noise levels at locations in which railway noise predominates (London area)

Location	Noise climate dBA* 10 per cent	90 per cent
Track side	91	67
Within 8 m of track	91	70
9 to 18 m from track (full view)	85	70
9 to 18 m from track (screened)	82	76
18 to 45 m from track	79	67
45 m+ from track	79	63

*See footnote to table V

4 Acoustic performance

4.01 Introduction

It is not easy to predict the noise climate of an environment, nor the subjective assessment by users of that noise climate. And the methods of calculating and presenting the effect of even a simple sound source on an environment are so complex that, as in the case of heat loss calculations, architects frequently prefer to rely on unaided judgment rather than attempt the necessary arithmetic.

In the pages that follow, an attempt has been made to present methods which will allow architects to make a quick assessment at an early design stage of the order of sound insulation required for a building in a particular noise environment.

Average values are used to describe both sound environment and sound reduction. This will give useful and satisfactory results in most cases, but where noise sources have predominant frequency characteristics (ie emit sound mainly over a limited frequency range†), or where the sound reduction at certain frequencies is well below the average value over the 100 to 3250 Hz range, the method may not be satisfactory. For such cases the effect of any insulation should be checked at all frequencies.

The terms dBA and PNdB used in the following calculations refer to scales for measuring complex sounds, which are weighted towards certain frequencies and correlate fairly well with subjective assessments of loudness. Further explanation of the basic principles of sound is given in the AJ Handbook of Building environment section 5 SOUND (22.1.69 to 12.2.70); but the present information sheet is self-contained and can be used without reference to other sources of information.

Computation method

The charts and tables follow the logical sequence of operations to be carried out in determining the required insulation value of a room's external envelope against the external noise climate, and consist of three groups:

● Calculation of likely *external* noise climate

● Establishment of what would be an acceptable or desirable *internal* noise climate

● Determining whether the proposed external envelope construction has the required insulation value to bring about the required modification of external noise levels.

If the external envelope does not have the necessary insulation value, its construction must be modified until the required performance is achieved. The charts and tables provide a quick and easy method of carrying out the necessary checks as part of the design process.

4.02 External noise climate

Tables v to vii and graphs **3** to **6** give basic information on various external noise sources, and the effects of distance, barriers and other noise sources on the likely external noise climate. They are intended to be used in the following way:

● For locations where *traffic noise* is the predominating source of nuisance, table v gives average dBA values to describe the noise climate. Because the noise source is continuous in nature, it is described in terms of the 10 and 90 per cent levels (the former level being exceeded for 10 per cent of the time, and the latter being exceeded 90 per cent of the time). The 10 per cent figure should be taken to

†An example of such a noise source is a band saw; whereas traffic noise is an example of noise which is spread over a fairly wide range of frequencies, and to which 'average' values may be applied with some confidence.

represent the external noise climate for the purposes of design, when the provision of suitable indoor conditions is the objective.

No allowance need be made for distance from noise source; this factor has been taken into account in the table.

Where more information is available on vehicle density and speed, the graphs in **3** and **4** may be used instead of the more generalised data given in table v. The 10 per cent noise level kerb-side from **3** should be corrected for distance by consulting **4**, and the shielding effect of acoustic barriers may be taken into account by using **5** and **6**

● For locations where *aircraft noise* is the dominant source of nuisance, table vi gives peak noise levels. These are more appropriate for intermittent noise sources, building up to very high peak levels, than the 10/90 per cent description used in the previous instance

● For locations in which *railway noise* predominates, table vii may be used. As with road traffic, noise levels are given in terms of 10 and 90 per cent dBA levels; and the former should be used when designing for the attainment of suitable indoor conditions.

To find the average noise level of the external noise climate, *all* the major noise source components must be considered and added together. Sound levels cannot be added up in a simple arithmetic way, but must be added using **7**; the method is explained in the caption.

4.03 Indoor noise climate

Having established the likely external noise climate, the next step is to decide on the desired indoor climate.

Table viii gives some recommended internal 10 per cent noise levels, ie levels that should *not* be exceeded for 90 per cent of the time. These values may not provide satisfactory conditions for everyone, and other values may be substituted if this seems called for by the particular design situation.

4.04 Design of external envelope

Having established both the existing *external* noise climate (4.02), and the desired *internal* noise climate (4.03), the architect can now proceed with designing an external envelope which will give satisfactory acoustic insulation. In some cases the designer will wish to start by first determining the average insulation value required of the envelope, and then choosing proposed forms of construction using this value as a guide; in other cases he will already have chosen proposed forms of roof, wall, door and window construction by the time the present information sheet is used, and will wish to check whether his design is acoustically satisfactory.

In the first instance, nomogram **8** provides a quick method for determining average insulation values required in particular situations.

Once, however, a proposed form of construction has been decided upon, whether on the basis of **8** or on other grounds, an acoustic check can be carried out as follows, to ensure that the required insulation value is achieved.

All sound transmission paths should be considered, as indicated in **9**; and the external envelope's performance analysed in the following two steps:

● First, each of the planes exposed to the external noise climate, and enclosing the internal space, should be taken in turn, and the average insulation value of each determined. Where the plane consists of a single uniform construction (eg a solid wall without apertures), there is no problem, and the value may be taken direct from tables ix to xii. But where the plane consists of two or more different materials, or different forms of construction (eg a

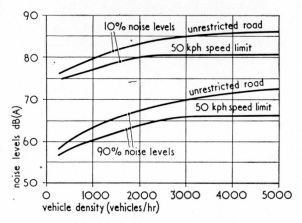

3 *If sufficient information is available on vehicle density and speed, above graph may be used to establish traffic noise level, in preference to table v. 10 per cent level should be used, and kerb-side noise level read off on left-hand vertical scale; this value must be corrected for distance using* **4**

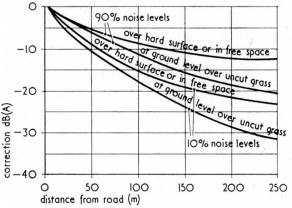

4 *Reduction in sound level with distance from sound source, to be used in conjunction with* **3**. *For example, if a dwelling is situated 100 m from a road carrying 2000 vehicles an hour (speed limit 50 km/h), what will be the traffic noise level at the dwelling? From* **3**, *it is seen that 10 per cent kerb-side level is 80 dBA; from* **4**, *that corrected value is 80 − 15 = 65 dBA (intervening area is hard-surfaced)*

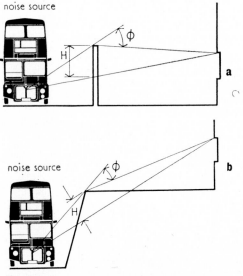

5a, b *Effective geometry of two types of acoustic barrier; for calculation of noise shielding effect, see* **6**

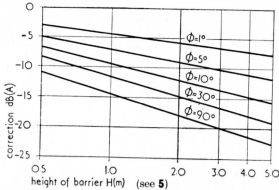

6 *Shielding effect of barriers shown in* **5***; correction shown on left-hand vertical scale must be applied to noise source intensity. For example, arterial road kerb-side sound level is seen, from table* v*, to be 80 dBA (value exceeded for 10 per cent of the time during the day); if a barrier as shown in* **5b** *intervenes between noise source and dwelling, with h = 2 m, and* φ = 7°*, corrected noise level at dwelling will be (80 − 10) = 70 dBA*

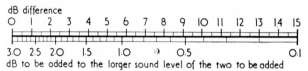

7 *Scale for adding dB. To add two sound levels, find difference between them and locate difference on upper scale. Increment that must be added to larger of the two levels may then be read off lower scale opposite. For example, to add 40 dB and 45 dB: difference between values is 5 dB; find 5 dB on upper scale, and read off on lower scale value* 1·3 *dB. Combined value of 40 dB and 45 dB is therefore* 45 + 1·3 = 46·3 *dB*

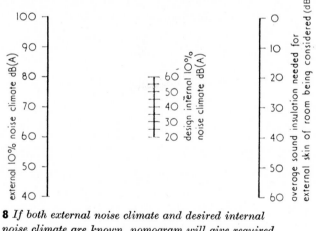

8 *If both external noise climate and desired internal noise climate are known, nomogram will give required insulation value. To use nomogram, lay straight-edge across diagram, connecting relevant values on left-hand and centre scales; required value can then be read off on right-hand scale*

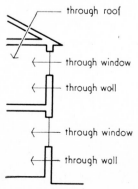

9 *When computing noise insulation value of building envelope, all transmission paths must be considered*

Table VIII *Recommended internal 10 per cent noise levels for dwellings**

Situation	Day	Night
Country areas	40 dBA	30 dBA
Suburban areas	45 dBA	35 dBA
Busy urban areas	50 dBA	35 dBA

*Noise level exceeded for only 10 per cent of time

Table IX *Typical insulation values for external walls*

Description	Approx sound insulation†
114 mm brick outer skin, 50 mm cavity, 100 mm l/w concrete block inner skin, plastered internally	50–53 dB
228 mm brick, rendered externally, plastered internally	50 dB
100 mm l/w concrete block outer and inner skins, rendered externally, plastered internally	50 dB
200 mm dense concrete, thermal insulation and plaster on inner face	50–53 dB
150 mm dense concrete, thermal insulation and plaster on inner face	49 dB
Timber-frame construction, 114 mm brick face	45–49 dB
Timber-frame construction, weatherboard, hung tiles or other lightweight cladding	34–37 dB
Timber-frame construction, lightweight cladding, absorbent quilt between studs	39–42 dB
Timber-frame construction, lightweight cladding, absorbent quilt between studs, resilient mountings to internal plaster	44–47 dB

Table X *Typical insulation values for windows*

Description	Approx sound insulation†
Wide open window	5–10 dB
Slightly open window	10–15 dB
Closed window, (capable of being opened)	15–20 dB
Sealed single-glazed window, 10 kg/m² (32 oz) Staggered opening double-glazed window	20–25 dB
Sealed single-glazed window, 6·3 mm plate Well fitting double-glazed window, 10 kg/m²	25–30 dB
Sealed single-glazed window, 9·5 mm plate	30 dB
Well fitting double-glazed window, 6·3 mm plate	30–35 dB
Sealed double-glazed window, 10 kg/m² Sealed single-glazed window, 25 mm plate	35–40 dB
Sealed double-glazed window, 6·3 mm plate Sealed double-glazed window, 10 kg/m² one leaf, 6·3 mm plate the other	40–45 dB
Sealed double-glazed window with leaves out of parallel. 9·5 mm plate one leaf, 12·6 mm the other	45–50 dB

Table XI *Typical insulation values for external doors*

Description	Approx sound insulation†
44 mm hollow core door, with normal gaps 44 mm glazed door, with normal gaps	15–18 dB
44 mm hollow core door, sealed edges	25–28 dB
57 mm solid core door, with normal gaps	20–25 dB
57 mm solid core door, sealed edges	30–35 dB
Double doors separated by an entrance lobby with absorbent surfaces. External door: 44 mm glazed door, unsealed. Internal door: 57 mm solid core door, sealed edges	45–50 dB

†Average value over 100 to 3250 Hz frequency range

wall containing a window), the *average* insulation value of the various materials must be found. This can be done using **10**, following the instructions given in the caption.

● Then, once an average insulation value has been established for each of the enclosing plane-elements, each such surface must be considered as a separate noise source (as, for example, in **9**). The indoor noise climate immediately inside each of these surfaces must be established, by subtracting the noise reduction, due to the skin, from the external noise level; and all the individual noise levels calculated in this way must then be added up logarithmically, using **7**.

Readers who find this explanation difficult to follow in the abstract should study the worked example given below.

4.05 Worked example

It is desired to determine whether the sound insulation of a first floor bedroom in an urban two-storey dwelling will be adequate. The following is the step by step procedure:

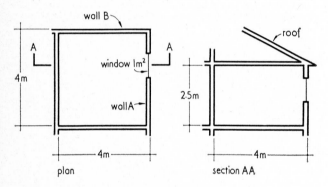

plan   section AA

1 Establish external noise climate
There is a heavily used arterial road next to the dwelling; from table v (group A), the external noise climate at night is therefore determined as 70 dBA.

2 Decide desired indoor noise climate
From table VIII, a level of 35 dBA is recommended for this environment at night.

3 Determine average insulation values of proposed envelope
Wall construction is 114 mm brick outer skin, 50 mm cavity, and 100 mm lightweight block with inner skin plastered internally. From table IX, approximate sound insulation over 100 to 3250 Hz frequency range is 50 to 53 dB. The lower figure will be assumed, to be on the safe side = 50 dB. The window is a single-glazed sealed window, of 9·5 mm plate glass. From table x, approximate sound insulation over 100 to 3250 Hz frequency range = 30 dB.
The roof is pitched tiled, with lath and plaster ceiling on timber joists; and mineral wool pugging (15 kg/m²) between joists. From table XII, approximate sound insulation over 100 to 3250 Hz frequency range = 38 dB.

4 Determine internal noise climates due to each plane exposed to external noise environment
● WALL A: Ratio of window area to wall area = 1 : 9
Difference in insulation values (50−30) = 20 dB
Reduction in the higher insulation value due to the window (from **10**) = 10 dB
Average insulation therefore 50−10 = 40 dB
Indoor noise level due to wall A (70−40) = 30 dB.
● WALL B: Indoor noise level due to wall B (70−50) = 20 dB.
● ROOF: Indoor noise level due to roof (70−38) = 32 dB.

Table XII *Typical insulation values for roofs*

Description	Approx sound insulation*
Pitched tiled roof, lath and plaster ceiling on timber joists	35 dB
Pitched tiled roof, lath and plaster ceiling on timber joists. Mineral wool pugging (15 kg/m²) between the joists	38 dB
Pitched tiled roof, lath and plaster ceiling on timber joists. Sand pugging (85 kg/m²) between the joists	45 dB
Flat concrete roof. 100 mm reinforced concrete slab with 50 mm l/w screed	45 dB
Flat hollow clay tile roof. 100 mm slab with 50 mm l/w screed	49 dB
Flat timber joist roof. T & G boarding roof deck, lath and plaster ceiling	34–39 dB
Flat timber joist roof, T & G boarding roof deck, lath and plaster ceiling on resilient suspension mountings	43–48 dB
Flat timber joist roof, T & G boarding roof deck, lath and plaster ceiling, mineral wool pugging (15 kg/m²) between joists	37–42 dB
Flat timber joist roof, T & G boarding roof deck, lath and plaster ceiling, sand pugging (85 kg/m²) between joists	44–49 dB

*Average values over 100 to 3250 Hz frequency range

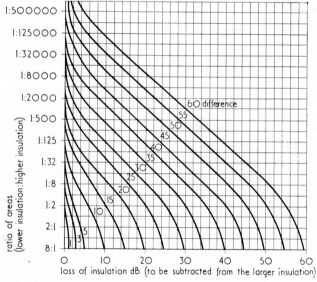

10 *Chart for estimating average sound reduction index of wall if latter consists of areas with different sound reduction indices (eg a wall containing a window). First, find difference between noise insulation values of two wall areas, from tables IX to XI. Second, find point of intersection between curve representing this difference, and horizontal line representing ratio of their areas. Third, read off amount to be subtracted from larger index value on bottom axis; this gives average sound reduction index for complete wall. For example, wall of total area 10 m² consists of 8 m² cavity wall (sound insulation 50 dB, from table IX) with 2 m² window, taken to be wide open for purposes of calculation (sound insulation 5 to 10 dB, from table x; say 5 dB). Ratio of lower insulation area (window) to higher insulation area (wall) is therefore 1 : 4; and difference in insulation values is 50 dB − 5 dB = 45 dB. Reading down vertically from point of intersection between 45 dB curve, and 1 : 4 horizontal line, loss of insulation dB is found to be 38 dB. Subtract this from larger value. and average sound reduction index for complete wall is 50 dB − 38 dB = 12 dB*

5 Add up individual noise levels logarithmically, using 7, to give actual internal noise level

The figures to be added are 30 dB + 20 dB + 32 dB. The difference between 30 and 20 is 10; find 10 on the upper scale of **7**, which gives a reading of 0·4 on the lower scale. If this is added to 30, the sum of 30 dB + 20 dB is found to be 30·4 dB. To this must be added 32 dB; and the same procedure as above is repeated. The difference between 30·4 and 32 is 1·6; find 1·6 on the upper scale of **7**, which gives a reading of 2·3 on the lower scale. If this is added to 32, the internal noise level is found to be 34·3 dB. This is slightly lower than the desired level of 35 dB, and the insulation value of the structure is therefore adequate to maintain the average indoor background noise level below the recommended level.

It must again be emphasized that the above are *average* noise levels over the whole range of frequencies from 100 to 3250 Hz, and that these may not give satisfactory results in cases, for example, where the external noise source emits sound mainly over a limited frequency range (see 4.02), in which case the insulation values of the structure should be checked at *all* frequencies. The method is however satisfactory for traffic noise.

5 Checklist

5.01 Condensation risk within fabric

● Check whether steady-state conditions assumed in 2 may be considered to apply to building under consideration

● If they do, compare proposed external wall and roof constructions with those illustrated in **1** and **2**, to ensure that no condensation risk exists

● If however the above conditions do *not* apply, or proposed construction is *not* among those illustrated, carry out arithmetic or geometric check[9].

5.02 Heat loss from dwellings

● For quick check of maximum rate of heat loss from detached or centre-terrace dwellings, consult tables I and II

● For quick check of maximum rate of heat loss from end-of-terrace dwellings, or staggered terraced dwellings, consult, in addition, tables III and IV

● If more detailed investigation of effects is desired, use charts A (detached dwellings) or B (terraced dwellings); and chart D

● If it is desired to deduce, from maximum rates of heat loss found above, the approximate *seasonal heat loss*, use chart E.

5.03 Heat loss from larger buildings

● To find maximum rate of heat loss, use chart C.

5.04 Insulation against noise

● Calculate likely external noise climate. For *road traffic noise*, use either table V, or **3** to **6**; for *aircraft noise*, use table VI; for *railway noise* use table VII

● Decide on acceptable internal noise climate, using table VIII

● Check whether proposed external skin of building will give sufficient insulation to produce required internal conditions. Method is explained in 4, 5

● If required performance is not met, modify design of external skin.

6 References

1 BRITISH STANDARDS INSTITUTION BS CP 3; Chapter II: 1970. Thermal insulation in relation to the control of environment [(J2)]

BUILDING RESEARCH STATION
2 Digest 108 Standardised U-values. 1969, HMSO [(J2)]
3 Digest 110 Condensation. 1969, HMSO [(I6)]

4 INSTITUTION OF HEATING AND VENTILATING ENGINEERS Guide. London, 1970, The Institution [(J)]
5 DIAMANT, R. M. E. Thermal and acoustic insulation of buildings. London, 1965, Iliffe [(J) (M)]
6 BRITISH STANDARDS INSTITUTION BS CP 3; Chapter III: 1960. Sound insulation and noise reduction [(M)]
7 NATIONAL PHYSICAL LABORATORY Noise. Final report of Wilson Committee. 1963, HMSO [(M5)]
8 DAY, B. F., FORD, R. D., and LORD, P. Building acoustics. London, 1969, Elsevier [(M)]
9 BURBERRY, P., DAY, B. F., and LOUDON, A. G., Condensation in buildings. *Architects' Journal*, 1971, May 19, p1149-1159; May 26, p1201-1208; June 2, p1265-1269. [(I6)]

Section 3
External envelope: Lowest floor and basement

Section 3 External envelope: Lowest floor and basement

Building enclosure		Reference keywords
Section 1	**Building enclosure: General**	ENCLOSURE
Section 2	**External envelope: General**	EXTERNAL ENVELOPE
Section 3	**External envelope: Lowest floor and basement**	LOWEST FLOOR
Section 4	**External envelope: External walls**	EXTERNAL WALLS
Section 5	**External envelope: Roofs**	ROOFS
Section 6	**Internal division: General**	INTERNAL DIVISION
Section 7	**Internal division: Suspended floors**	SUSPENDED FLOORS
Section 8	**Internal division: Partitions and walls**	PARTITIONS
Section 9	**Internal division: Ceilings**	CEILINGS
	Design guide Appendix A: Legislation Appendix B: Specialist advice	DESIGN GUIDE
Appendix 1	**Summary of references**	ENCLOSURE: REFERENCES
Appendix 2	**Index**	ENCLOSURE: INDEX

Relationship to rest of handbook

The table and diagram show the contents of the handbook as a whole, with the present section highlighted.

This section should be used in conjunction with section 2 EXTERNAL ENVELOPE: GENERAL, which analyses the functions of the whole external skin of the building, and there-fore provides a background against which the functions of the lowest floor can be better understood.

Scope

This is the first of the sections of the handbook giving detailed design and construction guidance on one specific element-group: in this case, the lowest floor and all other parts of the external envelope situated below ground level. Problems of structural strength, which will be particularly important if a basement is included, or if the lowest floor is suspended above ground level, are not given detailed consideration in this handbook; these come within the ambit of the AJ Handbook of Building structure.

References and keywords

The keyword by which this section is identified is LOWEST FLOOR; those for other sections are shown in the table. See the notes at the beginning of this handbook (p6) for an explanation of how keywords are used to identify sections in this handbook.

Author

A. J. Elder is a partner in Elder, Lester & Partners of Yarm, Yorkshire. In 1966-67 he was president of the Northern Architectural Association. He has acted as an AJ consultant and is author of the Guide to the Building Regulations 1972.

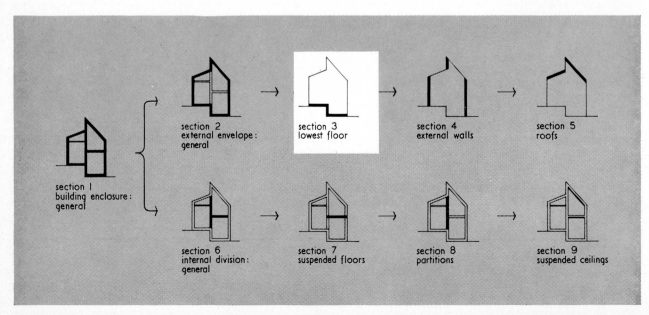

section 1 building enclosure: general

section 2 external envelope: general

section 3 lowest floor

section 4 external walls

section 5 roofs

section 6 internal division: general

section 7 suspended floors

section 8 partitions

section 9 suspended ceilings

Technical study
Lowest floor 1

Functions of the lowest floor

In this technical study A. J. ELDER *examines the functions of the lowest floor, and the factors which will determine its position, form and finish. This study is concerned only with general principles; more detailed practical guidance on the various floor types will be found in the subsequent information sheets*

1 Position of lowest floor

The purpose of this technical study is to examine the functions of the building's lowest floor, and to describe the factors determining the form and position of the floor relative to the ground. The main problem at planning stage is to decide the level of the lowest floor in relation to ground level. At one extreme the solution may be a basement; at the other, the floor may be suspended above ground. Between these two situations lies a whole range of intermediate positions **1**, the most common one being that in which the floor rests directly on the ground at a level requiring the minimum of excavation or fill.

1.01 Floor at ground level

This type of ground floor involves the fewest constructional problems so it is usually the cheapest solution and the best one to adopt unless there are good reasons against it.

Historical background
This has been the most common position for the lowest floor of the building historically, except in areas where climatic factors, such as extremes of heat or cold, or flooding have led to raised or dropped floors being used **2** to **6**. Early buildings probably had floors of beaten earth, which were acceptable because the shelter provided by the building above kept them dry. Animal skins would have provided some insulation and damp prevention and, in a sense, were the predecessors of carpets.

As man's technological skills grew, the use of stone and ceramics gradually developed; floors became yet another place for the artist craftsman to display his skill and command over a wide range of materials, such as natural marbles and manufactured ceramics in tile or mosaic form. The principal characteristic of this art form, distinguishing it from other adornment of buildings, was its lack of modelling as it had to be flat to serve its function, and the artist's skill had to be exercised to make the most of this medium.

In the UK, due perhaps to our scarcity of natural marbles, the stone-slab or clay-tile floor was almost universal until comparatively modern times. In much English cottage architecture the ground floor consisted of burnt clay tiles, frequently laid in a chequer-board pattern of black and red and usually laid direct on sand on the ground.

The main characteristic of all such floors through the ages has been that none of them made any attempt to control the passage of moisture from the ground below through the floor into the building—perhaps not an important consideration in some climates where early development took place, but one essential to comfort in the UK. The idea of making a solid floor waterproof to allow for a wide range of finishes, or of leaving a space below the floor to enable ordinary joist and board construction to be used, is comparatively recent. The use of timber was confined mainly to upper floors. However, wood blocks bedded in pitch on lime concrete were often used from the 18th century onwards.

1.02 Floor below ground level

Recessing the building into the ground creates so many structural and operational difficulties and problems of water exclusion, that basements should be avoided except where the special circumstances described in 1.04 warrant the trouble.

Historical background
One reason for dropping floor level below ground in pre-industrial vernacular building, is the thermal control this gives in conditions of extreme heat or cold. For instance, Matmata dwellings of the Sahara are built below ground and the heat capacity and insulation provided by the enclosing layers of earth provide internal conditions cooler than anything that could be achieved by building on the surface. At the other climatic extreme, the igloo is also partly sunk below ground **3**, the main living area being approached via a semi-sunken tunnel.

In both desert and arctic conditions the problem of damp is of relatively minor importance; but in European building, water exclusion is one of the major problems associated with floors below ground level. Basements have been used in European architecture in the past, eg the medieval church crypt, but until recent times no attempt has been made to form the basement as a waterproof tank. Instead reliance was placed on building in suitable ground with a low water-table, and often the basement was sunk only partly into the ground beneath a raised ground storey.

With development of the Renaissance's urban terraces, the practice of placing the lowest floor roughly half a storey

1 *First problem at planning stage is to decide position of lowest floor relative to ground*

below ground level **4** became virtually universal, but even then tanking was not used, the problem of ground water being dealt with by providing an 'area' outside the building which could be drained. This was also convenient for the provision of a service access to the lower floor, and the necessary excavation automatically provided a suitable level for foundations.

In very cold countries a basement was frequently considered useful as a location for the central heating plant, especially when natural circulation of hot water was the normal system. Such basements were not habitable rooms and a small amount of seepage could be tolerated, provided this could be drained away.

1.03 Raised floor

Raising the building above the ground so that the lowest floor becomes a suspended floor (but distinguished from the internal suspended floors by the fact that it intervenes between internal and external climate) is a characteristic technique of modern architecture. The current popularity of buildings on stilts can be traced partly to aesthetic fashion and partly to the fact that the additional cost involved is a much smaller fraction of the total for modern skeleton-framed high rise buildings than for traditional low rise: also the space formed beneath the building can often be used for vehicle circulation and parking. Nevertheless, even today, raising the building in this way is expensive: a suspended floor of this kind can cost three times as much as a floor at ground level.

Historical background

There are examples **2**, **6** of primitive or vernacular buildings on stilts, eg the Seminole houses of Florida. In some cases floors were raised for protection against floods, insects or rats, and sometimes the motivation was environmental—to avoid rising damp, or to provide better air circulation through the building. But in other cases it must be admitted that vernacular builders were prompted probably by the same motives of social prestige and aesthetic appeal as those which seduce trendy modern architects!

1.04 Choice of position

The above are the three basic positions in which the lowest floor of the building may be situated. What are the factors determining which position is chosen? Planning and circulation considerations and site conditions will exercise most influence. People enter a building more conveniently at ground floor level, so those internal zones of the building, eg reception areas, public restaurants and shops, that the public want to reach easily will tend to be located at or near ground level.

This basic consideration, balanced against factors such as ground slope, road and pedestrian walkway levels, legal restrictions on total building height, and ratio between required floor area and available site area, will establish whether or not there is a need for recessing the building into the ground, or raising it above ground level.

The major constraint upon choice of position will usually be cost. In the centre of large cities, basements may be carried several storeys into the ground and still be practical financially because of the extremely high land values that might be several times the unit cost floor area of the building; and modern systems of ventilation and lighting can overcome problems that existed previously, making available below-ground accommodation for carparking, storage and service installations.

Nevertheless, basements and raised floors are expensive and should be avoided unless there are good reasons for having them. In the case of basements, there are considerable structural and operational difficulties in working below ground in a typical central area where the building occupies the whole site and is flanked by existing party walls of the adjacent buildings. Specialist techniques and careful management are required. In addition, waterproofing remains an expensive problem, and one liable to be a source of future trouble. In the case of raised floors, such a floor can cost three times as much as a conventional floor bed, and there may be problems of thermal insulation and condensation which do not apply to solid floors.

The relative importance of the additional costs involved in dealing with these problems depends on the total number of floors in the building. For instance, in a single-storey factory or warehouse, in which the cost of the floor element is a large part of the building enclosure's total cost, any additional expenditure on the floor would cause a comparatively large increase in overall cost. In a high rise block, where the cost of one particular floor is a small part of the total cost, an expensive lowest floor would be less important **7**.

2 Functions of lowest floor

Having decided the basic position of the lowest floor relative to ground level, the architect can proceed to more detailed design problems, such as construction, finish and exact floor level. Consideration of these questions must start with an analysis of the functions of the floor.

Basically there are three functions to be considered: structural support, environmental control and appearance. The last of these is outside the scope of the present handbook and general comment on the first two functions (particularly on environmental control) will be found in technical study EXTERNAL ENVELOPE 1, in addition to the notes following below.

2.01 Support

The main function of any floor is to provide a level surface capable of supporting people, furniture, equipment, and possibly wheeled traffic or internal partitions. These functions will influence both the construction and the finish of the floor chosen.

Floor *construction* will be influenced strongly by the imposed loads which the floor will have to support, and by site conditions (see information sheets LOWEST FLOOR 2 and 3). On the other hand, floor finishes usually contribute little or nothing to the floor's structural strength. However, they do contribute to the support function by protecting the structural floor from wear and corrosion, and by providing a comfortable and safe surface for the users. See information sheet ENCLOSURE 2.

2.02 Environmental control

Water exclusion

Water in its free liquid form must be excluded from the interior of the building, and the passage of water vapour through the envelope must be controlled. There are two methods of ensuring that ground floors and basements fulfil these functions: an air-gap (cavity) **8**, or an impervious barrier (damp-proof membrane) **9**.

The principle of the *air-gap* has been exploited in traditional construction by the suspended timber ground floor. The air space below the floor is a highly effective barrier to rising

2

*Traditional position for lowest floor is at ground level. But sunken floors **3** (igloo) or raised buildings **5** (Indian tree dwelling), **6** (farm outhouse in Essex) and storage buildings in **2** (Kenya village) have sometimes been used to give protection against climate, insects or rodents.*

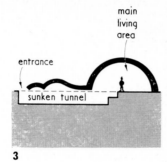

3

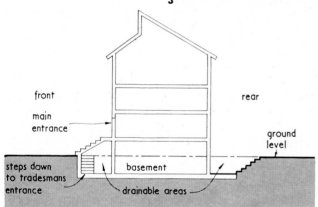

4

5

6

damp. Nevertheless, this form of floor construction is becoming less common. Not only is it comparatively expensive, but there is a danger of dry rot unless the under-floor space is well ventilated, and provision for the latter causes unacceptable rates of heat loss through the floor.

A more recent exploitation of the cavity principle is the use of cavity-retaining walls and stooled floor tiles in basements forming a continuous drained gap to intercept the passage of ground water into the building. However, normally a membrane would be required in the wall and floor construction, in addition to the cavity. The *impervious barrier* principle is usually applied to basement construction in the form of asphalt tanking, and to solid ground floors in the form of an asphalt or pitch continuous damp-proof membrane (see information sheets LOWEST FLOOR 1 and 2).

Heat

BS CP3 Code of Functional Requirements, chapter VIII, *Heating and thermal insulation*, recommends a U-value of 1·14 W/m² deg C for the floors of dwellings. In the case of concrete floors laid directly on the ground, this value will be usually obtained automatically, owing to the low rate of heat loss to the ground. But special precautions may be required around the perimeter of the building, especially where wall construction is thin, or if the foundation projects beyond the perimeter of the enclosing walls. Underfloor heating, too, may make additional precautions essential.

In the case of suspended floors, with a ventilated air space below, heat loss will be much higher than with solid floors; so checks must be carried out on U-values of proposed constructions and additional insulation may be required (see information sheet LOWEST FLOOR 3).

Sound

Sound transmission through the lowest floor will be a problem only where buildings are raised above noisy areas such as railways, roads, parking or industrial areas. If the suspended floor is a concrete slab, as it probably will be, it should perform satisfactorily — most of the noise will enter the building via windows and light claddings, rather than through the floor.

Vibration insulation, such as resilient mounting, may be required where the lowest floor rests on the ground, and there is a source of vibration, eg a railway or mechanical plant, in contact with the ground.

Acoustic absorption characteristics of the floor finish will have an important influence on internal room acoustics, and will require careful consideration.

3 Floor and construction

3.01 Choice between continuously supported or suspended floor

Floors at or near ground level can either be continuously supported by the ground itself, or by fill (in which case they are usually referred to as 'solid floors'); or they can be supported from the foundation system (in which case they are usually referred to as 'suspended floors'). The former are dealt with in information sheet LOWEST FLOOR 2, the latter in information sheet LOWEST FLOOR 3. The considerations which govern choice between the two types are:

● Desired floor level in relation to site levels
● Bearing capacity of ground
● Floor loading required
● Nature of foundations
● Availability and cost of suitable fill

Floor level in relation to site levels

The need for a floor level some distance above the site level can arise due to sloping ground, loading bay requirements, or flood water levels **11** to **13**. In such cases, the cost of the large amount of fill required must be balanced against the cost of a suspended floor. Normally, with only a nominal depth of hardcore fill, a continuously supported floor is cheaper than a suspended one (assuming there are no special

7 *Importance of lowest floor cost varies with building form; effect on total building cost would be substantial in* **a**, *but negligible in* **b**

7a   7b

problems of loading, soil subsidence and so on); but if depth of fill exceeds 600 or 700 mm, the suspended floor will tend to become cheaper. Detailed cost checks will be required.

Bearing capacity of ground

On normal soil, the need for a suspended floor purely on grounds of soil-bearing capacity will seldom occur. Only in the case of certain warehouses (for example, those in which voidless goods, such as paper, might be stored in stacks of considerable height) will unit loads on the floor approach the limits imposed by soil bearing capacity.

On the other hand, buildings of this type are frequently placed on sites where several feet of fill overlie the original ground. The fill may be mostly refuse and the original ground itself may consist of poor bearing material such as silt. It is quite common for industrial estates to be located on this type of ground which has in the past been unusable. In such cases, the problems posed by the foundations of the building will almost certainly involve the use of piles and, if anything other than a lightly loaded floor is needed, it will almost certainly have to be a suspended floor spanning between pile beams. Even so, there is a saving to be made over the normal suspended floor in the cost of shuttering or formwork, as the ground will usually be good enough at least to support the self-weight of the floor slab during construction.

Some cases will inevitably be marginal and the final choice may have to be left to the client, after having informed him of all known circumstances. For instance, it might be possible for the client body to accept a degree of settlement rather than face the additional cost of a fully suspended floor, which may be of considerable significance in the cost plan of a single-storey building.

Superimposed loadings on floors

These are laid down in the Building Regulations.

Nature of foundations

The type of foundations used will influence the decision on floor type. There are three principle conditions to be considered:

In the case of *normal loadbearing foundations*, the ground will usually be adequate to support the ground floor which will, therefore, be of normal solid construction and have no connection with the structure of the building above. In such cases a separating joint should always be made between the edge of the floor and the main walls or structure.

If *piled foundations* are used, the ground may still be good enough to support the ground floor, depending on loadings and so on, in which case the above notes will apply, although care will be needed in relating the ground floor construction to pile connecting beams which are usually considerably higher than normal foundations. But on the other hand, where piles are being used the ground may not be adequate to support the ground floor construction, in which case it will have to be treated as a suspended floor. In the case of *concrete raft foundations*, at or near ground level, the raft itself will usually form the ground floor, requiring the addition only of suitable screeds and finishes to provide a satisfactory floor surface. Screed must be deep enough to take services.

Availability and cost of fill

Availability and price vary considerably from region to region. It is difficult to generalise, but as already mentioned, if depth of fill exceeds 600 to 700 mm, the continuously supported floor may no longer be the cheaper option.

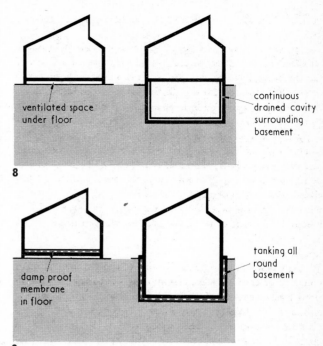

8

9

8, 9 *Two methods of waterproofing: air-gap and impervious barrier*

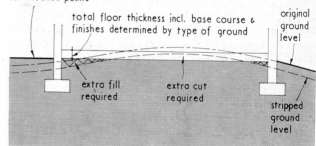

10 *Method of fixing ground floor level*

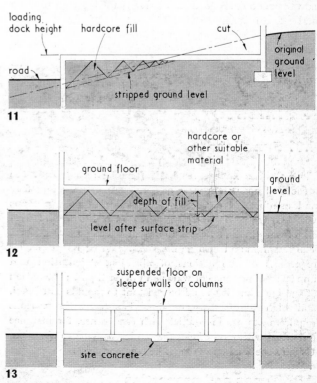

11

12

13

11, 12 and **13** *Raised ground floors on sloping site* **11,** *and on level site. In most cases* **12** *will be cheaper than* **13,** *except if depth of fill exceeds about 600 to 700 mm*

3.02 Effect of finish on floor construction

The proposed floor surface finish has a considerable effect on the form of construction adopted for the lowest floor. If the finish is to be laid integral with the floor slab, or while the concrete is green, risk of 'lifting' is reduced, but difficulties are created for the builder as the floor finish is usually complete quite early in the contract and runs a correspondingly high risk of damage. Granolithic or terrazzo finishes can also be laid at a late stage in the job, but success in achieving a properly bonded, crack-free floor is then dependent on taking appropriate precautions to ensure the cleanliness of the original slab, and working in accordance with procedures laid down in Codes of Practice and the recommendations of the Cement and Concrete Association. There have been frequent failures with this type of floor finish.

Where the finish is to consist of one of the various forms of concrete or ceramic tiles, the approach is to try to achieve proper adhesion of the tile-bedding material to the concrete subfloor by taking appropriate precautions as regards cleanliness and key. The alternative is to introduce a spreading membrane, usually building paper, at slab-surface level and introduce separating strips of Ebonite or similar material which extend from the top surface of the tile down to the membrane, dividing the area of tile and bed into completely separate sections small enough to ensure that no curling occurs as a result of drying shrinkage.

This type of floor finish has much to recommend it where there is risk of settlement in the floor slab. The effect in this case would certainly be much less than in an in situ type of floor finish, such as granolithic and terrazzo.

If the desired floor finish is to be one of the thin, flexible types, such as linoleum or pvc, requiring a smooth flat surface, a damp-proof membrane and screed are essential and care must be exercised in following the proper Code of Practice for screeds, otherwise the same sort of difficulties can arise as those which can occur with granolithic finishes. The subject is treated in more detail in information sheet LOWEST FLOOR 2. A good alternative to the use of membrane and screed in such cases is a 19 mm layer of mastic asphalt which serves as both waterproof membrane and screed as it provides an excellent smooth surface for the laying of thin flooring materials. It also eliminates any possible difficulties with shrinkage or curling of screeds.

4 Finishes

4.01 Functions

Floor finishes have three basic functions: to protect the structural floor from wear or corrosion; to provide safety and comfortable conditions for pedestrian (and perhaps wheeled) traffic, ie warmth, quietness, resilience and freedom from slipperiness; and to provide an attractive surface. The finish should also be *durable*, retaining its properties regardless of the actions of abrasion, indentation and impact; the presence of water and other liquids; the action of sunlight; and it should be resistant to moulds and fungi, and high temperature or fire. Sometimes the various requirements are in conflict with each other, for instance quietness with ease of cleaning and resistance to abrasion. Usually the final choice must be a compromise.

4.02 Types and properties

The following are the main types:
1 Hard jointless, eg granolithic and terrazzo
2 Hard tile and slab, eg concrete, terrazzo and ceramic
3 Resilient jointless, eg patent resins
4 Resilient sheet and tile, eg line, rubber and pvc
5 Wood, eg block and strip
6 Carpet.

These types and their properties are dealt with in more detail in section 7 of the handbook, SUSPENDED FLOORS.

5 Checklist

5.01 Position of lowest floor

Establish from planning requirements, site topography and soil conditions, whether lowest floor is to be:
● At ground level
● Below ground level, ie basement
● Above ground level

5.02 Functions of lowest floor

Establish, from site conditions and user requirements, the required:
● Support functions (loadbearing capacity and surface characteristics)
● Environmental control functions (water exclusion, thermal performance and acoustic performance)
● Appearance

5.03 Floor level

● Decide exact floor level in relation to ground

5.04 Floor construction and finish

Decide from site conditions, structural requirements and cost considerations:
● Whether solid or suspended floor
● Floor construction
● Floor finish

6 References

1
b BUILDING RESEARCH STATION Principles of modern 2uilding: volume 1. 1964, HMSO [(9–) (E1)]
b BUILDING RESEARCH STATION Principles of modern uilding: volume 2. 1961, HMSO [(9–) (E1)]

Information sheet
Lowest floor 1

Basements

This information sheet gives guidance on basement design, and on the alternative systems of waterproofing available. It does not attempt to cover comprehensively the multitude of waterproofing details arising from various constructional situations. For these, reference should be made to the publications listed at the end

1 Introduction

1.01 Definitions

The Building Regulations 1965, with amendments, lay down precise rules regarding ground storeys and basements. Generally (that is to say when considering all parts of the Regulations except part E) a ground storey is one in which the floor is at or about, but not below, ground level. A basement storey is then defined as the storey below the ground storey **1,** but where there is no ground storey a basement storey can still exist if the building is only a single floor and the floor level is below the ground level **2a.** On sloping sites it is possible to have a basement storey which is, in fact, entirely above ground level, if the storey above it is at or near ground level on the higher part of the site **2b.** The recent Sixth Amendment introduced a new definition of ground and basement storeys, which is applicable only to part E (Structural Fire Precautions). In this case a ground storey is one in which the floor level is nowhere more than $1 \cdot 2$ m below the adjacent ground level, and a basement storey is any storey below this **3.**

1.02 Need for basements

The factors which will decide whether or not a basement is required, have been described briefly in 1.04 of technical study LOWEST FLOOR 1. The conclusion was that basements cause so many problems of excavation, construction and waterproofing, all of which are reflected in the building's cost, that they are best avoided unless their use can be justified by good reasons.

2 Functions of basement enclosing elements

2.01 Structural functions

Basement walls have to be designed to resist both *vertical* dead and imposed loads from the building above; and *horizontal* imposed loads due to earth and, in some cases, water pressure. Basement floors may also have to resist upward water pressure from below. The following brief notes explain the basic principles; as with all structural matters, more detailed information will be found in the AJ Handbook of building structure (to be published in 1974).

Earth pressure
Basement walls have to be designed to hold back earth pressure. The typical retaining wall **4** is a cantilever resisting earth pressure by converting this into pressure on the ground below the base. However, such a condition is rarely encountered in basements where the walls are usually

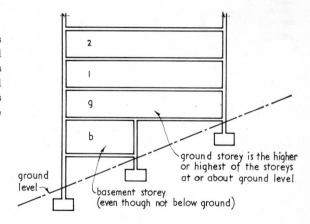

1 *Interpretation of 'single-storey'*

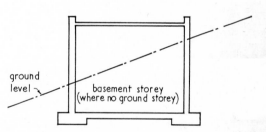

2a *Building with no ground storey*

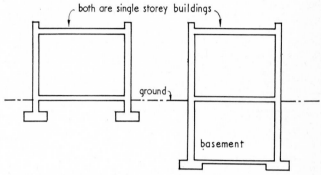

2b *Definition of storeys on sloping site*

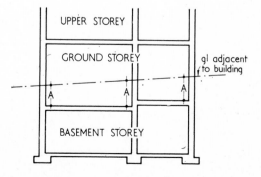

3 *Definition of basement in part* E *of Building Regulations: A not to exceed $1 \cdot 2$ m at any point*

stiffened by a number of other structural members, and stability is improved by the supporting members and structure of the building above **5a, b**.

Water pressure

A much larger force exerted on the structure is likely to be the static head of water depending on the height of the water table above basement floor level **6**. In the circumstances shown the force acting against the wall equals $\dfrac{X^2 \times 1000 \text{ kg}}{2}$ per metre run. This force can be considered as acting from a point $\frac{1}{3}X$ above basement floor level. The upward force created by water pressure on the underside of the floor helps offset the load exerted on the ground by the building and during construction precautions may have to be taken against the possibility of the whole basement floating upwards in high water table conditions.

Therefore, it is important to establish the maximum height of the water table. In gravels and sandy soils this is not difficult and the height is usually reasonably constant. In clay soils the only safe assumption is that the water may rise almost to ground level. The movement of water in fissured clays is extremely erratic so it is possible to excavate for a basement and encounter no ground water at all, only to find after construction of the basement that the water table is well up near the surface of the ground. The probable reason for this is that in excavating for the construction the fissures which permit water movement are sealed off and what virtually amounts to a waterproof clay 'tank' is formed. Subsequently when the structure is complete, and the space around is back-filled with suitable hard material, the clay 'tank' will hold rainwater which might rise to less than a metre below the outside ground level **7**. Although the actual extent of this rainwater may be only a metre or less outside the basement, it will still exert the same static head pressure as an unlimited stretch of water.

Another possible reason could be that the new construction has been built in the path of underground moving water, thereby creating a dam effect. If the back-fill is porous and a suitable outlet is available, it may be possible to drain away this water, or at least reduce the level. Alternatively, a sump, kept clear by an automatic pump, may be formed outside the basement to receive the water drained from the outside of the walls.

2.02 Water exclusion

Problems of water exclusion can be seen in terms of two basic situations. Where it can be assumed without doubt that the water table will never rise above the floor level of the basement, so the wall will never be under water pressure, the problem will be the relatively simple one of preventing water entry by capillary action. However, this is a risky assumption, and an expensive failure could result if it turned out to be wrong. The recommendation of cp 102[10], clause 301, that it should always be assumed that there will be positive water pressure at some stage, is sensible.

Therefore the second situation will be the one assumed to exist, ie that the basement wall is under water pressure, so that the water is forced through the construction. cp 102, clause 303, recommends that a positive water head of not less than a third of the total basement depth be assumed for normal single-storey basements. However, site investigations should be carried out whenever there are indications that special problems may exist, eg in clay soils.

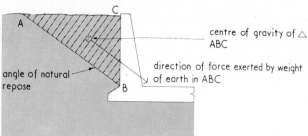

4 *Retaining walls act as cantilevers, resisting earth pressure by converting it into pressure on ground below base*

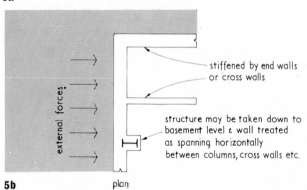

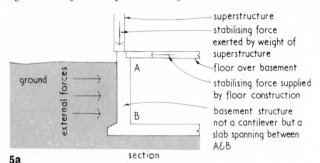

5 *However, basement walls usually act as slabs spanning between other structural members, rather than as cantilevers*

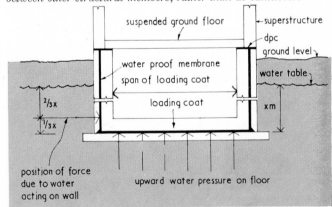

6 *Water pressure may be exerted on basement structure both horizontally, and vertically upward.*

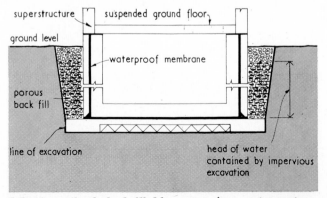

7 *In clay soils, the back-filled basement pit can act as water tank, in which head of water may build up after completion*

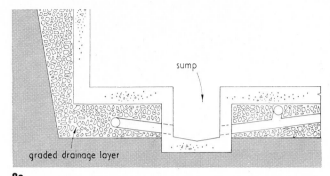

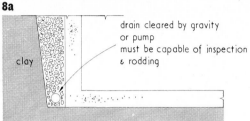

8a

8b

8 *Subsurface drainage is wise precaution where water table is likely to rise above top of wall footings*

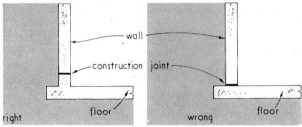

9 *Upstand detail recommended for joint between wall and floor of waterproof concrete construction*

2.03 Chemical resistance

Soil and ground water samples should be tested in accordance with CP 2001[12] for aggressive chemicals such as sulphates (originating most commonly in clay soils) and acidic waters (found in peat soils). If such chemicals are present, an impervious membrane or special cement in the structural concrete, may be required.

2.04 Thermal insulation

This is not usually a problem. Walls and floors below ground do not lose heat in the same way as those exposed to the air, as the ground acts to some extent as a heat accumulator; so heat loss is of minor importance.

3 Waterpoofing systems

3.01 Selection

A range of waterproofing systems are described below. The method chosen will depend largely on three factors.

Basement use

If the basement is to be used for *human occupation*, or for the accommodation of sensitive equipment or for certain kinds of storage, construction will need to be not only waterproof but vapour-proof. Effective and uniformly distributed ventilation may reduce the need for this, but is not always easy to achieve. Vapour-proof construction is best achieved by a combination of 3.03 and 3.04 plus a vapour barrier, or by 3.05. If the basement is to be used for *services accommodation* only, or for non-critical storage, or

for car-parking, vapour-proof construction is not required, and method 3.03 will probably be the most suitable.

Cost

The most important cost differences between alternative options usually arise not so much from the waterproofing itself, as from operational aspects such as excavation (either a splay-sided crater requiring backfill; or a straight-sided excavation requiring temporary supports or sheet piling), propping and sheet piling.

Operational conditions

The constraints of site conditions may rule out the use of certain methods.

3.02 Site precautions

One or both of the following precautions may be useful adjuncts to the methods described subsequently (especially 3.03), if there is a head of water, or the possibility of one.

Reduction of surface water entering into adjacent ground
Where possible the ground should slope away from the building for a distance of about 3 m to divert the surface run-off and to prevent water from standing near or against the walls. Surfaces near walls should preferably be paved. On sloping sites it is usually desirable to construct a cut-off land drain on the high side to lead water around the building to a lower level. Rainwater from the roof of the building and from impervious external wall surfaces, if any, or paved areas, should generally be collected in a separate drain and diverted away from the building and should not be allowed to enter the ground near the walls.

Subsurface drainage around basement walls and under floor
Water may be prevented from remaining in contact with basement walls or floors for long periods by installing a system of drainage round the wall footings or beneath the floor or both together **8a, b.** Provision of drains around the perimeter of the basement is recommended for any site where the ground water table is likely to rise above the top of the footings. These drains should be placed beside the wall footing and should be graded to an open outlet or storm water sewer or to a sump within the building and pumps provided. Drains should be porous or laid with open joints, and should be covered by a graded filter starting with coarse stone around the pipe and changing gradually to material a little coarser than the surrounding soil. Detailed design for a graded filter is discussed in clause 1.84 of Civil Engineering Code of Practice 2, *Earth retaining structures.*

3.03 Integral waterproofing

Engineers are fond of saying that good concrete is waterproof and needs no additives. However, there are a number of proprietary materials which can be used to assist in producing waterproof concrete. They usually work on the principle of making the concrete more workable with low water/cement ratios, thus enabling high-density and low-permeability concrete to be placed without the risk of creating voids. Placing must be done with the aid of a poker-type vibrator.

When this system is used great care is needed in forming the construction joint between floor and wall. This is usually a weak spot, and it is better to form an upstand (sometimes called a kicker) of 150 mm or so, cast integrally with the floor **9.** The risk of leakage at this point can be lessened by using a patent water bar of heavy rubber or, more usually today, of plastic, placed in construction joint **10a, b**. Even then, great care in the mixing and placing of the concrete is absolutely essential. The water bar itself must be either prefabricated to the shape of the basement plan or cut and welded on site, and here again care is needed to ensure water-tightness at welds or other joints.

Positions of construction joints should be shown on structural drawings, with maximum area of wall or slab between joints 50 m², and maximum length of pour between joints 10 m. Minimum thickness 230 mm for wall 3 m high; 300 mm for wall 5 m high.

3.04 Drained cavity

This method requires considerable space, and requires regular pumping; but if these disadvantages are acceptable, it is recommended as the most successful water-exclusion method currently available. If vapour-proof construction is required, the most effective combination is a waterproof concrete wall (see 3.03), a drained cavity and an inner leaf with vapour barrier.

Any leakage through the first line of defence would be intercepted by the second line of defence—the air-gap **11**. Moreover, this method has an advantage in that the outer leaf can be inspected for leakage before the inner leaf is built and necessary remedial action carried out; and that fixings can be made to walls without risk of puncturing or weakening the waterproofing system.

3.05 External membrane

The advantage of the external membrane is that it is both waterproof and vapour-proof. The disadvantages are that external membranes are difficult to execute, and extremely difficult to repair if failure occurs. There are two methods of application:

The first **12** is external application. It has the distinct disadvantage that the floor membrane must be laid first, followed by the loading coat and wall construction before the vertical membrane can be placed, necessitating a construction joint which can be a weak point in the system. It also necessitates excavating to provide enough working room outside the basement. The membrane must never be left unprotected against damage from the back-fill. The second method **13** is preferable: the whole membrane can be placed in one operation and built up at the angle between the vertical and horizontal for extra security; and it is protected against damage by the brickwork skin.

For the membrane itself, asphalt is used almost universally (to BS 1097: 1966[6] and BS 1418: 1966[7]) usually in three layers of 10 mm each, building up to about 30 mm total thickness. It is a reliable material in suitable conditions, but has, unfortunately, little flexibility at normal temperatures encountered below ground, and is easily cracked by quite small building movements. This is the principal disadvantage of the membrane system because if a crack does occur, the ground water may move a considerable distance from the crack behind the inner retaining wall or floor structure before showing itself at a weak point in the latter. This makes tracing the leak a difficult and costly business.

There have been a few attempts in the past to overcome this problem by substituting a more flexible material based on heavy bituminous felt and bitumen. Usually the work was carried out by specialist firms and long term guarantees of watertightness were given. This proved hazardous as, apart

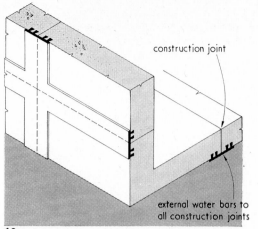

10a

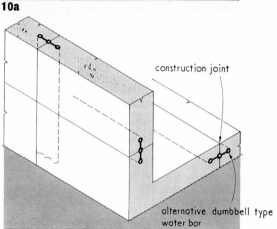

10b

10 *Two types of water bar*

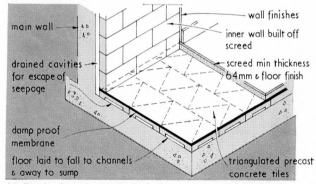

11 *Drained cavity method of waterproofing is highly effective; main disadvantage is need for regular pumping of sump (not shown)*

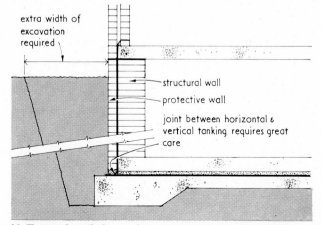

12 *External asphalt membrane, externally applied. Joint between floor and well membranes, which must be applied in successive stages, can be weak point. For this and other details, Mastic Asphalt Advisory Council publications and CP 102 recommendations must be followed*

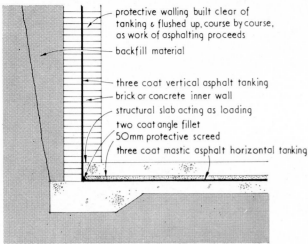

13 *External asphalt membrane, internally applied. Internal wall must be able to resist water pressure; gap between membrane and internal wall must be grouted solid to prevent membrane being pushed off outer wall*

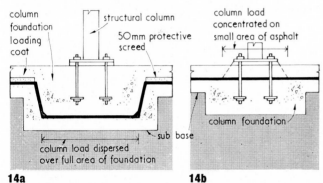

14a **14b**

14a *Load is dispersed over larger area of membrane than in* **14b,** *and membrane is not pierced by holding-down bolts*

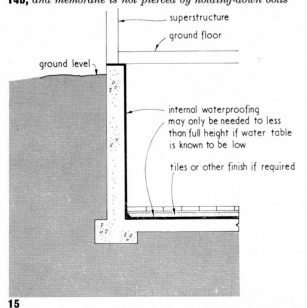

15

wall thickness

16

15 *Nowadays internal rendering is recommended for remedial work only, and is a specialist skill*
16 *Preferably services should not penetrate basement walls. If they do, flanged sleeve is essential*

from settlement, there was always the risk of mechanical damage by workmen other than those of the specialist, and the guarantee system had a short life only, proving too expensive for the firms concerned.

Bitumen emulsions and solutions are sometimes used, but fail to bridge joints or cracks in the concrete, and the same applies to coal-tar epoxy coatings, although the latter are tougher. They are best used on waterproof concrete. A new type of membrane based on a bitumen/polythene laminate appears to be quite successful, but is easily punctured by back-fill or by the bricklayer's trowel.

In future the best line of approach to the membrane system may well be based on heavy pvc sheeting with sealed joints. This is tough and the risk of mechanical damage is probably smaller than with bitumen-based materials, but the chance of the membrane being pierced, for instance by the end of a reinforcing rod, still exists and great care in use would always have to be exercised.

For detailing **14** and specification of external membranes, CP 102: 1963[10] is an essential reference.

3.06 Internal membrane

Superficially, this seems to be the least logical system of all as it involves applying a waterproof membrane to the inside of the basement where the pressure of ground water from the outside will tend to force it off. It has been used widely as a means of waterproofing in the past, but nowadays it is regarded mainly as a remedial treatment (see CP 102 chapter 8).

There are a number of proprietary systems based on cement/sand mixes with additives, which can be applied even to damp surfaces and remain firmly adhered and dry out rapidly. A normal thickness is about 20 to 25 mm on walls, usually applied in two coats; and a little more on floors to allow for wear or mechanical damage, although when complete any wearing surface, such as tiles, can be placed on top of the waterproofing layer. The work is best carried out by specialists, but materials are available for use by normal plastering contractors to whom some supervision or advice is usually offered by the manufacturer of the additive. Application by a specialist firm is clearly preferable and such firms are usually prepared to give an unqualified guarantee of water-tightness, provided their recommendations are accepted by the architect.

A normal application of this system is shown in **15** but if the water table is known to be a reasonable distance below ground level, it may not be necessary to carry the waterproofing to the full height. The system has many advantages: for those applications where the need is only to prevent entry of water by capillary action, and where no water pressure exists (but see 2.02); and where failure would not be disastrous. It may be a little costlier than integral waterproofing, but it is certainly cheaper than an asphalt membrane. Furthermore, if a leak occurs it is immediately detectable and easily cured. Finally it provides quite a good finish, normally acceptable for the usual basement usages.

3.07 Penetrations

Usually it is better to avoid penetrating the basement structure with pipes or cables by bringing the mains into the building at some other point, where no basement exists, and feeding down into the basement as necessary. If it is essential for services to penetrate basement walls, the usual technique is to introduce a sleeve with a flange welded on the outside to act as a water bar **16**. The position of the

(in figure 2 labels)
protective walling built clear of tanking & flushed up, course by course, as work of asphalting proceeds
backfill material
three coat vertical asphalt tanking
brick or concrete inner wall
structural slab acting as loading
two coat angle fillet
50mm protective screed
three coat mastic asphalt horizontal tanking

(figure 14 labels)
column foundation loading coat
structural column
50mm protective screed
column load concentrated on small area of asphalt
column foundation
sub base
column load dispersed over full area of foundation

(figure 15 labels)
superstructure
ground floor
ground level
internal waterproofing may only be needed to less than full height if water table is known to be low
tiles or other finish if required

flange will vary according to the system of waterproofing being used, and with internal waterproofing may not be necessary at all. With integral waterproofing the flange will usually be in the centre. With a membrane, the flange may be sandwiched between two of the three coats of asphalt, or sealed against the outside of the membrane with bitumen or a suitable sealing mastic. It is then necessary to caulk between the pipe or cable and the inside of the sleeve.

4 Checklist

4.01 Functional requirements

Consider the following functional requirements of the basement walls and floor:
● Structural requirements (dead and imposed loads)
● Water exclusion requirements (waterproofing only; or water- and vapour-proofing)
● Heat insulation

4.02 Site conditions

Investigate the following conditions:
● Soil type, movement and so on
● Water table and underground water paths
● Presence of harmful chemicals

4.03 Basement construction

Consider construction of:
● Floor
● Walls

4.04 Waterproofing systems

Decide on basis of proposed use of basement, costs and site conditions, which of following systems to use:
● Integral waterproofing
● Drained cavity
● External membrane
● Internal membrane
Decide whether site drainage is required.

4.05 Detailing

Decide details of:
● Construction
● Waterproofing
● Penetration of waterproofing system

5 References

1 Building Regulations 1972. 1972, HMSO [(A3j[

2 Building Standards (Scotland) Regulations. 1963, HMSO [(A3j)]

3 London Building Acts 1930-39 London Building (Constructional) Bylaws 1972, 1973, GLC [(Ajn)]

4 BUILDING RESEARCH STATION digest 90 Concrete in sulphate-bearing clays and ground water. 1968, HMSO [Yq (S)]

BRITISH STANDARDS INSTITUTION
5 BS 743:1966 Materials for damp-proof courses [(9–) Yy (I2)]

6 BS 1097:1966 Mastic asphalt for tanking and damp-proof courses (limestone aggregate) [Ps4 (I2)]

7 BS 1418:1966 Mastic asphalt for tanking and damp-proof courses (natural rock asphalt aggregate) [Ps4 (I2)]

8 BS 3235:1964 Test methods for bitumen [Ys1 (Aq)]

9 BS CP 101:1963 Foundations and substructures for non-industrial buildings of not more than four storeys [(1–)]

10 BS CP 102:1963 Protection of buildings against water from the ground [(I2)]

11 BS CP 303:1952 Surface water and subsoil drainage [(52·5)]

12 BS CP 2001:1957 Site investigations [(11) (A3s)]

MASTIC ASPHALT ADVISORY COUNCIL
13 Model specification for mastic asphalt in building. 1965, the council [Ys4]

14 Application of mastic asphalt: tanking, roofing, flooring paving. 1966, the council [Ys4]

Information sheet
Lowest floor 2

Section 3 **Lowest floor and basement**

Solid floors

The factors which will determine whether the lowest floor is to be suspended, or laid directly on the ground, have been set out in technical study LOWEST FLOOR 1. If the choice is a fully-supported concrete slab, this information sheet should be used. The succeeding sheet gives information on suspended floors

1 Introduction

1.01 Scope

This information sheet deals only with floors that are continuously supported either by the ground itself, or by fill material **1**. Floors which are structurally supported from the foundation system (ie suspended) are dealt with in information sheet LOWEST FLOOR 3, even when they are at ground level and have no open space below them.

1.02 Choice between solid and suspended floor

The considerations which will determine whether a floor at ground level is to be continuously supported or suspended are the following:
- Floor level in relation to site levels
- Bearing capacity of ground
- Floor loading required
- Nature of foundations
- Availability and cost of suitable fill

They have been examined in 3.02 of technical study LOWEST FLOOR 1, and the discussion will not be repeated here. It is assumed that a choice has been made, and that the need at this stage is for practical design data on the chosen floor type.

2 Functions of floor

The functions of lowest floors generally have already been analysed in technical study LOWEST FLOOR 1. The following notes apply specifically to continuously-supported floors at ground level.

2.01 Support

The concrete bed's function is to transmit to the ground the loads imposed on it. In practice most superimposed loads are applied locally, ie as point loads, and the concrete bed, by spreading the load, ensures that the ground's bearing capacity is not exceeded. The latter is established by site investigation; loads are specified in the Building Regulations[1].

2.02 Exclusion of water

Historically it has not been customary to provide damp-proof courses to floors where the finishes would not be affected by damp, eg granolithic, ceramic tile, terrazzo, but now the Building Regulations 1965 (clause c3) make this obligatory, excluding excepted buildings. 'Excepted buildings' are those used wholly for accommodating goods

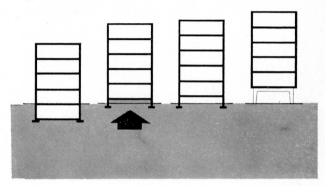

1 *Arrow indicates floor-types dealt with in this information sheet*

or machinery, where the occupants are engaged in supervision or maintenance; or buildings where compliance would not increase protection of the occupants' health, eg factory buildings where the essential processes involve wet floors, so that prevention of rising damp would make no difference. Consequently, except for the examples listed above, a continuous damp-proof membrane is a necessary part of any floor in contact with the ground and is no longer a matter of choice.

2.03 Chemical resistance

Clause c3 of the Building Regulations lays down that the hardcore used must not contain soluble sulphates or other matter that might cause damage to the floor. However, site tests may show aggressive chemicals to be present in the soil below the hardcore, eg sulphates in clay soils or acidic water in peat soils, in which case an impervious membrane or special cement in the concrete may be required.

2.04 Heat insulation

Normally no special precautions are required as the ordinary domestic type solid floor has a U-value of about $1 \cdot 13$ W/m² degC and the natural tendency of heat to rise, coupled with the fact that below-ground temperatures tend to stay constant at about 13°C, mean that losses through the ground floor represent a minor proportion only of the total heat loss. Thus special insulation measures are not economically justifiable. The exception to this is when electric floor-warming is used and measures must be taken to prevent loss of heat to the ground or to the exterior. Even then the only serious loss occurs around the perimeter owing to conduction through the floor to the external walls and thence to the atmosphere. In such cases it is usual to insulate with some suitable rigid material, such as 25 mm polystyrene or polyurethane, for a distance of a metre or so in from the perimeter and also between the edge of the slab and the wall, in which position the insulation also acts as an expansion joint **2**.

3 Floor construction

3.01 Base course and fill

Functions

Where continuously-supported floors are used, it is usual to strip the surface soil at least a nominal 150 mm to remove organic growth, and then to lay a *base course* of hardcore, or some other suitable material (see table 1), intended to perform the following functions:
- Build up levels as required
- Spread point loads over a greater area
- Restrict or reduce capillary movement of water from the ground upwards
- Provide insulation
- Supply a suitable dry surface for the placing of concrete

Now that the Building Regulations require a continuous damp-proof membrane for most solid floors, the third of the above points is much reduced in importance. Given good ground and dry weather, there seems no reason why the site concrete should not be placed directly on the ground and the hardcore omitted.

Additional material over and above the base course thickness (which could be anything from 0 to 250 mm) may be required to make up levels because of site conditions and topography. Such material is usually known as *fill* and may differ slightly from the base material, as it has somewhat different functions:
- To be inert
- To be capable of full compaction
- To be as cheap as possible

Lateral interlocking strength is not important here as it is in the base course.

Types

Table 1 shows the various types of material available, and indicates their suitability for use as a base course or general fill material. Costs, depending on location, vary so much that no useful indication of comparative costs can be given.

Requirements

The basic requirements for both base course and fill materials are that they should be chemically and physically

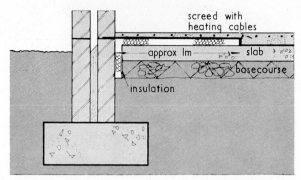

2 *Edge insulation of electrically heated floor. Perimeter insulation may also be used in unheated floor if floor slab extends beyond outer wall, or if latter is of thin lightweight construction, causing excessive heat loss by conduction to outside atmosphere*

stable (whether wet or dry), should be incombustible, free from organic material and excessive dust and (subject to the provisions above) free from sulphate and other constituents that could have a deleterious effect on concrete. The material should be cube-shaped and able to pass a 125 mm diameter ring; it should be so graded that it can be consolidated into a compact but free-draining fill.

Laying

The fill should be compacted thoroughly, in layers not exceeding 150 mm in consolidated thickness, by means of a smooth-wheeled roller weighing not less than 5 tonnes, or a vibrating roller providing the equivalent compacting capacity, or by means of power rammers where the roller cannot obtain access. The top of the final layer of fill should be blinded with finer material to the same specification, and rolled to a firm and even surface true to form. It may be necessary to blind with sand or other suitable material to achieve a surface smooth enough to avoid the risk of penetrating polythene sheet laid to receive the concrete slab. A special case of fill is necessary in mining areas where a sand bed is sometimes placed under a reinforced concrete ground slab to allow the ground to move laterally under the slab without tearing it apart.

Precautions against chemical attack

Some materials, especially clinker and pulverised fuel ash (pfa) may contain soluble sulphates that can attack concrete. Materials containing less than 0·2 per cent sulphate (as SO_3) can be used without special precautions. If a greater percentage exists, or if the fill is not tested, the underside of the concrete slab should be protected by a sheet of 1000 gauge polythene; or sulphate-resisting cement may be used.

Table 1 Types of fill material

Material	Description	Suitable for base course	Suitable for fill	Notes
Hardcore	Broken brick and other non-organic building waste	Yes	Yes	
Slag	By-product of steel industry	Yes	Yes	May contain soluble sulphates
Shale	Naturally-occurring soft slaty material or mining waste. Should be well burnt; otherwise may not be inert		Yes	
Pfa	Pulverised fuel ash; by-product of large boiler installations		Yes	May contain soluble sulphates
Dolomite	Soft, broken limestone, generally 75 mm down to dust		Yes	
Hoggin	Natural mixture of gravel and sand; must be free-draining with just enough clay to bind the fill	Yes	Yes	May contain soluble sulphates
Clinker	Furnace waste, similar to slag; must be well burnt		Yes	
Stone	Broken stone or quarry waste of any type containing hard sharp material	Yes	Yes	

Table II *Guide to base course and slab thicknesses*

Design conditions	Soil type	Domestic and small buildings				Industrial buildings		
		Suggested foundation type	Base course thickness mm	Slab thickness (unreinforced) mm	Slab thickness (reinforced) mm	Suggested foundation type	Base course thickness mm	Slab thickness (reinforced) mm
Slab on existing natural ground	Stable (well-graded sand or gravel)	Strip footing	0 to 100	100	100	Pad footings (columns) Strip footings (walls)	0 to 100	150
	Normal (poorly-graded sand average clays)	Strip footing	0 to 100	120	100	Pad footings (columns) Strip footings (walls)	150	150
Slab on cut or excavated ground	Unstable (organic soil, soft clays, peat)	Raft or short bored piles	100 to 150	Unsuitable	120*	Piles	150 to 230	180*
Slab on fill or made-up ground	Compacted sand and gravel	Strip footing, raft or piles, depending on quality and depth of fill	Not required	Unsuitable	120*	Strip footing, pad footing or piles, depending on quality and depth of fill	Not required	150*
	Compacted average soils		0 to 100	Unsuitable	150*		150	180*
Slab with soft underlying strata		Raft or short bored piles	100 to 150	Unsuitable	120*	Piles	150 to 230	200*
Mining subsidence area	Unstable until subsidence completed	Raft	150 to 200 (coarse sand)	Unsuitable	150*	Special design to suit movement	150 to 200 (coarse sand)	200*
Water table within two-thirds of a metre	Stable	Strip footing	150	120	100	Pad footings (columns) Strip footings (walls)	150	150
	Normal	Strip footing	150	150	120	Pad footings (columns) Strip footings (walls)	150	150
	Unstable	Raft or short bored piles	150	150	120*	Piles	230	200*

*It may be necessary to suspend the slab, in which case the base course thickness may be reduced to provide only a good surface on which to form the concrete slab, or a blinding concrete may be used

3.02 Concrete slab

Functions
The slab has two main functions:
● To transmit the superimposed loads to the supporting ground, spreading point loads to ensure that the bearing capacity of the ground is not exceeded
● To receive a floor finish appropriate to users' needs.

Design
Thickness and reinforcement are decided by an analysis of existing soil condition, fill material and type of loading. In the case of domestic and small buildings, this will be based on experience, but in industrial work with heavy local loading, a design basis may be employed similar to that in rigid road-paving construction. Table II is a guide to typical situations.

The concrete quality may be 1:3:6 in the case of domestic works on stable ground, but will generally be a 1:2:4 nominal mix by volume with not less than 282 kg of cement per m^3 of finished concrete with a cube strength not less than $21 \cdot 0$ N/mm² at 28 days. If the concrete surface is to be the finished surface in industrial applications, then there should be not less than 309 kg of cement per m^3 of finished concrete with a cube strength not less than $28 \cdot 0$ N/mm² at 28 days; and to minimise dusting limestone should not be permitted as an aggregate.

Reinforcement, if specified, usually has a square mesh, but an oblong mesh may be used for special design purposes. The reinforcement serves the following purposes:

● To prevent cracking and limit the size of cracks
● To prevent lipping at construction joints or cracks
● To act as normal structural reinforcement to spread local loads

Mesh is usually supplied in sheets $4 \cdot 8$ m $\times$ $2 \cdot 4$ m or in rolls $2 \cdot 4$ m wide and 48 m long. BS references A98, A142, A193, A252 and A393 cover a range of square meshes (about 203 mm square) from weight $1 \cdot 54$ to $6 \cdot 16$ kg/m². A good, general purpose mesh placed in the top of the slab to control cracking is A142 at $2 \cdot 22$ kg/m² but this can be calculated on BS CP 114 shrinkage basis of steel area being not less than $0 \cdot 12$ per cent of the cross-sectional area of the concrete slab in each direction. A concrete cover of 37 mm minimum must be provided where the concrete is in contact with the ground, and cannot be less at the top of the slab without risk of the mesh appearing on the surface during placing of the concrete.

If the reinforcement is in the centre, it should be equally effective in resisting bending (concave) or hogging (convex) moments, both of which are likely to occur with uneven settlement or deflection under local loadings **5**. In practice the concrete would crack severely before the reinforcement became effective, therefore where there is doubt as to the likely amount of settlement it is best to reinforce both top and bottom.

Bay sizes and joints
In domestic work the areas involved are usually determined

by room sizes, so it is not necessary to define limits of concrete slabs.

Industrial work may be of such magnitude as to be comparable with road and airfield construction, so the specification will be directed to the type of plant to be employed and the type of joints. At one end of the scale, a machine may lay a bay width of 5 to 7 m in a length of 40 to 80 m, in which case intermediate contraction joints would be essential. At the other end of the scale, hand placing with poker or beam vibrators might be as little as 3 to 5 m bay width and be cast in alternate bay construction with construction joints between adjacent bays. Bays should be broken down by contraction, expansion or construction joints to a 1½:1 side ratio maximum.

Expansion joints with a 19 mm filler material should be provided at the junction of walls, columns and machine bases, but are unlikely to be required in the body of the floor except in very large industrial works.

Construction joints are provided at the sides of the bays by the containing screed and at the end of the length of placing, if this is not an expansion joint.

Contraction joints **7** in continuous placed slabs must be provided at regular intervals to control the shrinkage cracking of the slabs. The joint spacing may vary from 5 to 10 m depending on bay width and placing length.

In industrial work transfer of load across the joint is important. In the contraction joint this is achieved by the interlocking of the aggregate across the small width crack which forms, but in the case of the expansion joint it must be achieved by transfer steel dowels, and in the case of the construction joint by steel dowels **8** or, if the slab is deep enough (175 mm minimum), by a keyed joint in the edge face of the slab.

Junctions with external walls

There are two points the designer should bear in mind.

First, the joint is in some ways similar to joints between adjacent slabs, being a point at which expansion or contraction can be absorbed; allowance should be made for this. Second, it is a point at which differential settlement may occur, especially in the case of a ground-supported slab adjacent to a pile-supported wall **6**. This must be allowed for by ensuring that the slab is in no way adhering to the wall, otherwise bending stresses will be set up and the slab could crack.

There is a third point to be considered—that of continuity between the damp-proof membrane in the floor and the dpc in the wall—but that is dealt with in 3.03. When raft construction is used, a different situation exists; **11** shows a suitable arrangement with the damp-proof membrane positioned below the slab.

Junctions with internal walls

There are two basic alternative relationships. First, where the wall penetrates the floor **12**, which usually occurs with normal spread footings on poor ground, or where the wall is heavily loaded and possibly pile-supported.

Second, where walls are not heavily loaded and the ground is reasonable, a thickening of the slab may suffice **13** or, in preference to this, the slab may be maintained at the same thickness and merely provided with additional reinforcement at the bottom to spread the load.

3.03 Water-exclusion systems

As stated in 2.02, floors resting on the ground are now required by the Building Regulations to incorporate an effective damp-proof barrier. It should be noted that water-proof barriers are not necessarily vapour-proof. For

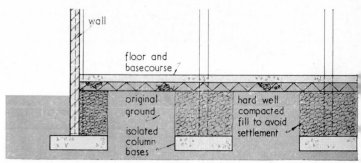

3 *If heavy loads necessitate large footings, careful back-filling is required to avoid settlement of slab above footings*

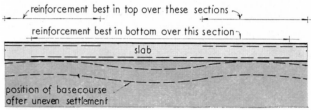

4 *Reinforcement positioning if likely pattern of settlement is known*

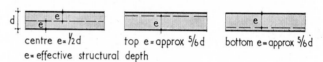

centre e = ½d   top e = approx ⁵⁄₆d   bottom e = approx ⁵⁄₆d
e = effective structural depth

5 *Effective structural depths of reinforcement in various positions; minimum concrete cover of 37 mm is required in all cases. Centre reinforcement will counteract both convex and concave bending, but effective depth is much reduced*

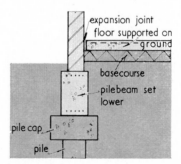

6 *Expansion joint between wall and floor makes allowance for differential movement*

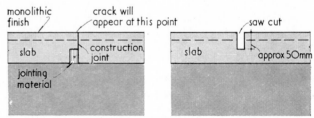

7 *Two methods of forming joint in slab*

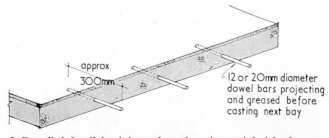

8 *Dowelled detail for joints where there is special risk of differential settlement of adjacent slabs*

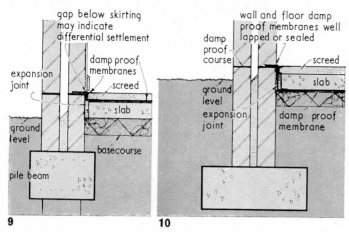

9, 10 *Continuity between membrane in floor, and dpc in wall, is essential*

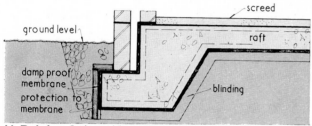

11 *Raft foundation with membrane below slab. Protection of membrane by blinding is essential*

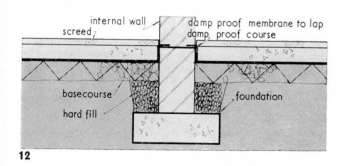

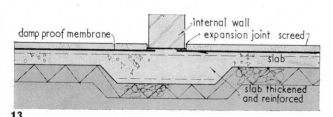

12, 13 *Two alternative relationships between internal wall and floor: either slab is interrupted* **12**, *or continuous* **13**. *Thickening of slab in* **13** *is traditional detail of dubious value; constant thickness may be preferable*

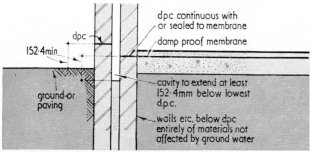

14 *Building regulation requirements*

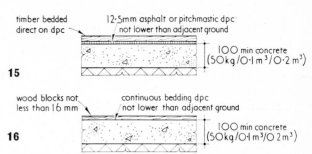

15, 16 *Damp-proofing incorporated in floor finish*

instance, the lighter weights of polythene sheeting come in the former category, but not in the latter: nothing less than 500 gauge is acceptable, and preferably 1000 gauge polythene should be used where it is to be the only protection against vapour penetration. Ordinary light-gauge pvc sheeting is quite satisfactory if it is used exclusively as a separating membrane between base course and slab, to prevent loss of fines when the concrete is being placed, and if no vapour-proofing function is intended.

Membranes are of two types, preformed sheeting, and in-situ coatings. *Sheet membranes* can include bituminous felt, heavy reinforced building paper and polythene. They may be placed either below or above the concrete slab; if placed below, care must be taken to ensure that there are no sharp projections in the base course; the latter may be blinded with sand or lean mix concrete to avoid this. Also care must be taken to avoid damage by reinforcement.

Membranes placed below the slab have two advantages. First, they serve the dual purpose of vapour-proof membrane and separating layer (to avoid leakage into the base course); and second, they keep the slab dry, in which condition it is a better insulator, especially if a lightweight aggregate is used. The slab can then be used as the storage medium for off-peak electric floor heating.

From the foregoing, it may be seen that membranes below slab have considerable advantages, but the above-slab type are more usual, probably because of the difficulty in ensuring that no damage occurs to the membrane placed below the slab. Regardless of whether the membrane is above or below the slab, it must be married to the dpc in the wall by lapping or sealing together. This will be made easier if materials of a similar nature are specified for both. *In-situ coatings* are usually either hot-poured bitumen, required by the Building Regulations to be at least $3 \cdot 2$ mm thick, or cold-applied bitumen/rubber solutions applied in not fewer than three coats by brush or spray. In situ membranes are usually placed above the slab, because the blinded base course is not a good enough surface to receive them. They then require a loading screed which, because it is completely de-bonded, must be at least 50 mm thick. When wood blocks are used as a finish, the pitch or bitumen in which they are bedded is considered acceptable under the Building Regulations as a damp-proof membrane, provided that the mastic is not less than $12 \cdot 5$ mm thick **15**, and that it is not situated below the adjacent ground. Alternatively, if the mastic is less than $12 \cdot 5$ mm, eg with wood blocks dipped in hot bitumen or pitch and then laid direct on the screeded slab, the wood must be at least 16 mm thick **16**.

3.04 Screeds and finishes

The functions of floor finishes and the categories of types available are listed in 4.01 of technical study LOWEST FLOOR 1, and need not be repeated here. Nor is it proposed to duplicate the comprehensive information on specific finishes, laying techniques and so on, which will be given in section 7 of this handbook—SUSPENDED FLOORS starting on page 275.

The intention in the following notes is to cover only those few situations specific to floor slabs in contact with the ground. There are two factors which differentiate treatment of solid ground floors from suspended floors:
● The solid floor may consist of an unreinforced, or lightly reinforced, concrete slab supported on fill; this can cause cracking, caused by movement, which will not occur with reinforced concrete suspended floors
● There will be moisture present below the ground floor slab, but not under a suspended floor.
The detailing of finishes and screeds applied to solid ground floors will have to take these problems into account.

Control of cracking
Screeds may be formed in three ways:
● So as to be monolithic with the floor slab (either an applied finish, laid while the concrete is green, or a self-finish formed on the surface of the slab)
● Bonded to, but not monolithic with the slab
● Separated from the slab by a membrane (probably, but not necessarily, serving as a vapour barrier)
Whichever system is used, appropriate joint details will have to be provided in the floor finish, in positions that coincide with the expansion, construction and contraction joints formed in the concrete slab below. As already explained in 3.02 *Bay sizes and joints*, this will apply mainly to industrial buildings, rather than to domestic work. In the case of reinforced concrete, slabs will be cast in much larger bays and instead of joints in screed and slab coinciding, as described above, it will be necessary to provide intermediate joints in the screed only where monolithic floors or underfloor heating are used.

Control of moisture
This has already been dealt with in 3.03. As stated under *in-situ coatings*, the damp-proofing may in certain circumstances be incorporated in the floor finish rather than in the slab; **15** and **16** indicate alternative methods which are deemed to satisfy c3 of the Building Regulations. The latter should be consulted if it is proposed to use these details.

4 Checklist

4.01 Functional requirements

Consider the functional requirements of the floor:
● Structural (imposed loads)
● Users' requirements (levels, finishes)
● Water exclusion
● Thermal insulation
● Incorporation of services, machine mountings, ducts

4.02 Site conditions

Investigate:
● Soil type and condition (see table II, first and second columns)
● Presence of harmful chemicals
● Levels

4.03 Base course and fill

Determine:
● Depth of topsoil to be removed
● Thickness and material of base course, if any
● Thickness and material of fill, if any

4.04 Floor slab

Decide:
● Thickness, concrete mix, and reinforcement, if any
● Bay sizes, expansion, contraction and construction joints
● Relationship with walls

4.05 Waterproofing systems

● Decide damp-proofing material, and position within floor

4.06 Thermal insulation

● If required, decide material, position, thickness, waterproofing

4.07 Floor finish

Decide floor screed type, and finish, bearing in mind:
● Users' requirements
● Overall thickness required for incorporation of services
● Effect of thermal insulation and damp-proofing
● Effect of drying shrinkage
● Effect of chosen finish on floor construction and contractor's programme

6 References

1 Building Regulations 1965, including all amendments up to sixth amendment. 1970, HMSO [(A3j)]
2 Building Standards (Scotland) Regulations 1963. 1963, HMSO [(A3j)]

GREATER LONDON COUNCIL
3 London Building Acts 1930-39 Constructional by-laws, amended to December 1970. 1970, The Council [(Ajn)]
4 Development and Materials Bulletin 10/2 Damp-proofing solid floors. 1967, The Council [(13) (12)]

BUILDING RESEARCH STATION
5 Digest 9 (first series) Building on made-up ground. 1949, HMSO [(11)]
6 Digests 63 and 64 Soil and foundations: parts 1 and 2. 1965, HMSO [(16) (L4)]
7 Digest 67 Soil and foundations: part 3. 1966, HMSO [(16) (L4)]
8 Digest 54 Damp-proofed solid floors. 1968, HMSO [(13) (12)]
9 Digest 90 Concrete in sulphate-bearing clays and ground water. 1968, HMSO [Yq (S)]

BRITISH STANDARDS INSTITUTION
10 BS CP 101: 1963 Foundations and substructures for non-industrial buildings of not more than four storeys [(1-)]
11 BS CP 102: 1963 Protection of buildings against water from the ground [(12)]

12 SHACKLOCK, B. W. The design of concrete ground floor slabs. London, 1968, Cement and Concrete Association [(13) Yq]

Information sheet
Lowest floor 3

Suspended floors

This information sheet covers those cases in which the lowest floor of the building is suspended, ie spans between supporting structures, instead of resting on the ground. It divides such floors into three basic categories: timber floors at approximately ground level, concrete floors at approximately ground level and elevated concrete floors

1 Introduction

1.01 Scope

This information sheet deals with all floors that span between supporting structures, and that form the lowest floor of the building, intervening between the external environment and the internal volume of the building **2**. Floors of this kind can be either at or near ground level, in which case they perform functions similar to those of solid ground floors, or they can be elevated well above ground level to create an open or partially open usable space below the building **1**.

In the former case, the suspended floor and the solid floor are alternative ways of achieving the same object, and the factors determining which of the two floor types is chosen are the following:
- Floor level in relation to site levels
- Bearing capacity of ground
- Floor loading required
- Nature of foundations
- Availability and cost of suitable fill

These have been examined fully in 3.02 of technical study LOWEST FLOOR 1, and the discussion will not be repeated here. It is assumed that the choice has been made, and that the need at this stage is for practical design data on the

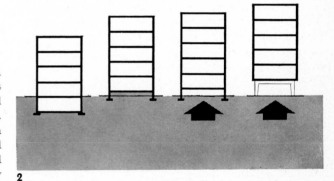

2

1 *Arrows indicate floor types dealt with in this information sheet. Floors laid directly on the ground (or on fill) are covered in the previous information sheet*
2 *Lowest floor may be suspended above ground level, leaving open usable space below*

chosen floor type. This design guidance is given in para **2** to **4** below.

On the other hand, if the floor is elevated well above ground level, it must necessarily be a suspended structure, and there is no need for the above kind of choice; design data for floors of this kind are given in para 5.

2 Floors at ground level: functions

2.01 Support

The floor must provide a level surface capable of supporting people, furniture, equipment, perhaps wheeled traffic and possibly partitions. The superimposed loadings to be provided for are laid down in schedule 5 of part D2 of the Building Regulations.

2.02 Exclusion of water

The space below the suspended floor, and the use of dpcs in sleeper walls, will prevent the entry of water in its free liquid form by interrupting the paths along which water could travel to the interior of the building. But if the entry of water *vapour* is to be controlled effectively, the underfloor cavity must be well ventilated too (see also technical study LOWEST FLOOR 1, 2.02) in the case of timber floors. On the other hand, if a concrete slab is used, underfloor ventilation will not be required and is best omitted, in view of the high rate of heat loss associated with it.

2.03 Thermal insulation

In the case of a suspended concrete slab with an unventilated underfloor space, heat loss is unlikely to be a problem, and usually there will be no need for special measures to be taken. But the ventilated underfloor space required for suspended timber floors (not only to prevent diffusion of water vapour from the ground into the building, but also to avoid fungus growth) creates problems of heat loss, and this is one reason for the currently reduced popularity of this form of construction. See 3.03.

3 Timber suspended floors at ground level

3.01 Construction

Between the first and second World Wars the ground floor of the average small domestic house was usually suspended, and consisted of tongued and grooved softwood boarding on joists and sleeper walls **3a**. Site concrete was usually down at foundation level and the finished floor level at least 300 mm above ground. This left a generous gap below the ground floor joists, which often proved useful to electricians or central heating engineers carrying out later improvements. The honeycomb sleeper walls would probably be about eight courses high and capped by a 4½in × 3in wall plate. Joists would be no less than 4in × 2in whatever the span. Timber was seldom treated (except perhaps to char the ends of joists built into walls) and the 4½in × 3in wall plate was built into the external walls just like a course of bricks at ground, upper floor and roof levels. This now seems a dubious practice, since abandoned, but most likely for reasons of cost rather than because of the risk of fungal attack. Usually great care was taken to provide adequate ventilation, but the quality of site concrete was not always good enough to prevent some form of organic growth starting. Dpcs were usually of hot pitch, slate or lead. The second World War brought about a change in the value and availability of materials. Timber floors were replaced largely by concrete slab construction, finished with materials

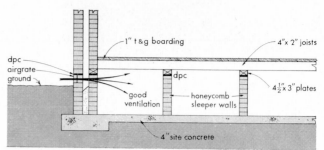

3a *Traditional pre-war suspended timber floor*

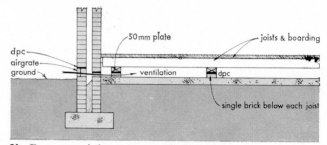

3b *Post-war minimum cost equivalent of 3a*

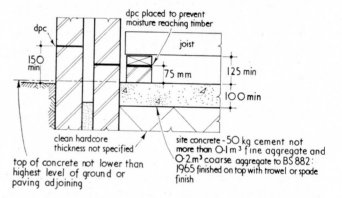

4 *Requirements of 1972 Building Regulations for suspended timber floors are satisfied by this construction*

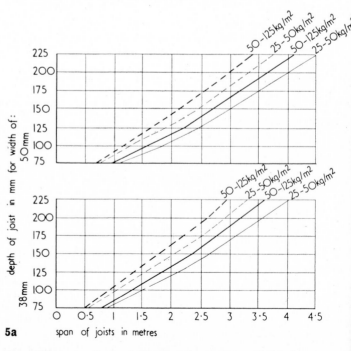

5a

5a *and* **5b** *(opposite page) Graphs for superimposed floor load of 1·44 kN/m² and dead loads of 25 to 50 kg/m² and 50 to 125 kg/m², giving alternative joist sizes, spans and spacings. Solid lines indicate 400 mm joist spacings; broken lines indicate 600 mm spacings. Values for other dead loads or joist spacings can be found by interpolation*

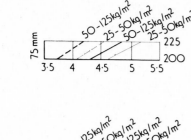

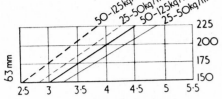

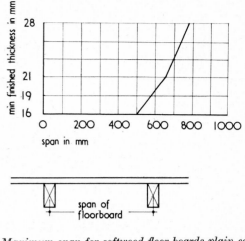

5b

6 *Maximum span for softwood floor boards plain edged or tongued and grooved according to finished thickness.*
NOTE *Boards are to comply with* BS 1297:1970.

such as thermoplastic tiles which quickly became available in a variety of colours. A virtue was made of necessity and advantages were found in such floors, mainly because they were vermin- and rot-proof and had improved thermal resistance and draught excluding properties. However, they were hard and cold to the touch and, although they were suitable for rugs, they provided no means of fixing for the traditional English fitted carpet or carpet square and surround. Their lack of 'nailability' was a considerable defect.

Today timber floors are again used to a limited degree **3b**. They can seldom be justified on grounds of cost, except perhaps for domestic buildings on sloping sites; but they are popular with many people because of their slight flexibility underfoot, and their convenience for the fixing of coverings. Suspended timber floors satisfy the requirements of the Building Regulations (clause C4) if constructed as shown in **4**. Alternative joist sizes, spans and spacings for houses occupied by a single family and having not more than three storeys as defined in Clause D2 (3) and set out in Schedule 6 of the 1972 Building Regulations. These graphs allow the available alternative possibilities that will satisfy the Building Regulations for this class of building to be assessed rapidly. Table I gives metric softwood sizes from which selection should be made.

Floor boards are required by the Building Regulations to comply with BS 1297:1970, and should be tongued and grooved timber **7**. For spans see **6**.

3.02 Prevention of beetle or fungal attack

It is essential that the ground below the floor is sealed properly by a concrete slab of 100 mm minimum thickness **4** (or by other effective means) and that the space between is well ventilated. Treatment of the timber against beetle or fungal attack is also advisable. There are available on the market many proprietary preparations for this purpose, some of which involve treatment in kilns under pressure so that the timber has to be treated before delivery to site. Some preparations can be applied on site, but even when the material is kiln-treated, site treatment is still required if the timber has to be cut to length leaving exposed ends. There is also a number of firms which specialise in treating timber which has been attacked. On request these firms will make a technical inspection of the damaged timber work and recommend treatment to be carried out by their own specialist operators. Guarantees against a recurrence of beetle or fungal attack are given provided that all the work recommended is actually carried out.

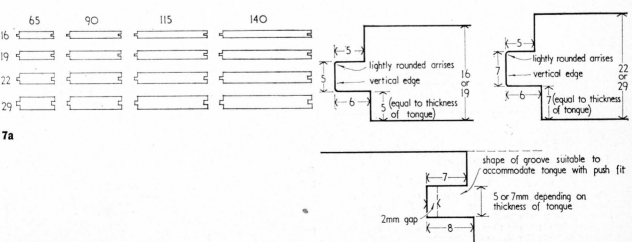

7a

7a, b *Floor board sizes and profiles*

7b

3.03 Insulation

Insulating boards, quilt or reflective foil should be used to improve the U-value of the floor to the required degree. The value should be no higher than $1 \cdot 42$ W/m² deg C (Reg. F6), and a value lower than this is preferable. Table II gives typical values.

3.04 Screeds and finishes

The floor boarding is normally the floor finish, and screeds on timber bases are seldom required. If they are, the timber base should be protected by bitumen felt or building paper. Galvanised chicken netting or light expanded mesh should be fixed to the base at about 200 mm centres.

4 Concrete suspended floors at ground level

4.01 Construction

The floor construction may take several forms:
On a *level site* with a raised ground floor, the choice may depend on the type of foundation being used. In good ground, strip footings and sleeper walls may be chosen as the most economical system **8**. In poor ground the choice may lie between a raft and piles. If a raft is used sleeper walls would again provide a suitable support system for the floor **9**. The use of piles leaves open the alternative of forming a pile beam grid at ground level and again using sleeper walls **10**, or allowing the piles to project from the ground and constructing a beam and slab structure at actual floor level **11**. This system involves providing form-work for the top section of the piles and would be considered a rather unusual structural system.
On *sloping sites* a need may arise for a stepped type of

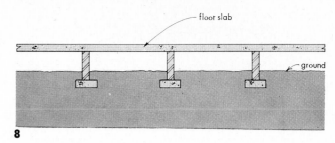

8

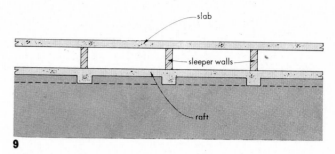

9

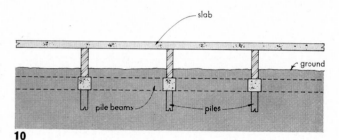

10

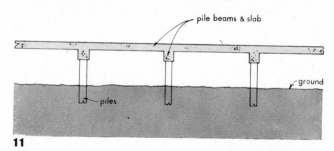

11

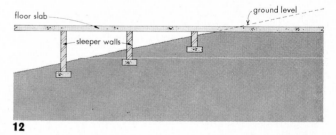

12

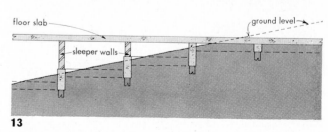

13

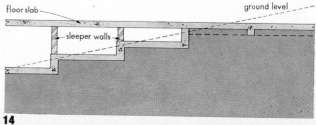

14

Table I Metric softwood sizes in mm

38 × 75	44 × 75	50 × 75	63 × 150
38 × 100	44 × 100	50 × 100	63 × 175
38 × 150	44 × 150	50 × 125	63 × 200
38 × 175	44 × 175	50 × 150	63 × 225
38 × 200	44 × 200	50 × 175	
38 × 225	44 × 225	50 × 200	75 × 200
		50 × 300	75 × 300

Table II U-values of various floor constructions

Floor	W/m² deg C
1 Concrete on ground or hardcore fill	1·13
1 plus grano, terrazzo or tile finish	1·13
1 plus wood block finish	0·85
2 Timber boards on joists, space ventilated one side	1·70
2 plus parquet, lino or rubber cover	1·42
3 Timber boards on joists, space ventilated on more sides	2·27
3 plus parquet, lino or rubber cover	1·98
3 plus 25 mm fibreboard under boarding	1·08
3 plus 25 mm corkboard under boarding	0·95
3 plus 25 mm corkboard under joists or forming cavity	0·79
3 plus 50 mm strawboard forming cavity (between joists)	0·85
3 plus double sided aluminium foil draped over joists	1·42

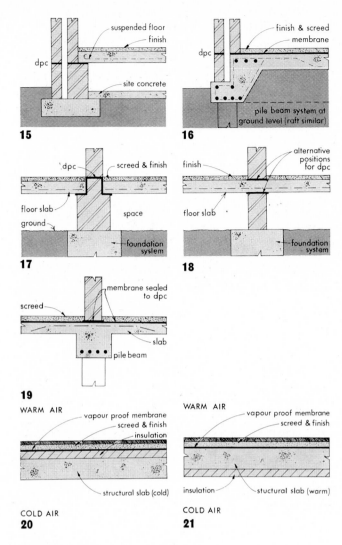

15

16

17

18

19

20

21

8 *Sleeper walls on strip footings*
9 *Sleeper walls on raft foundation*
10 *Sleeper walls on piled foundation*
11 *Pile beam and slab on projecting piles—the latter is an unlikely solution*
12 *Foundation system on sloping site with good ground. If ground is not of satisfactory quality, piles* **13** *or raft foundations* **14** *are alternative solutions*
15 *Footings (or pile beams) below a raised floor*
16 *foundation system at ground floor level*
17 *to* **19** *Alternative relationships between floor slab and internal walls;* **17** *slab interrupted by walls;* **18** *continuous slab;* **19** *pile beam system*
20, 21 *Insulation above structure* **20**, *and below* **21**

construction at site level, and similar alternative systems to those described in the last paragraph will be available for consideration depending on the quality of the ground and the proposed loading **12 to 14**.

4.02 Relationship to external walls

Again this is dependent, to a large extent, on the type of foundation which is in turn dictated by ground conditions and topography. The situation differs from the ground-supported slab in that the wall and floor are both supported from one and the same foundation system, and hence no question of differential settlement arises. Furthermore, if the floor is suspended above a space (as in **15**) and not merely laid using the ground as formwork **16**, there will be no need of a damp-proof membrane, and the lapping or sealing of this to the wall dpc does not arise.

4.03 Relationship to internal walls

These may either penetrate the slab or be built off it. Where a sleeper wall system is used, the internal walls will normally serve to subdivide the suspended floor system **17**. However, this may create difficulties with the coursing of brickwork or blockwork. If the foundation is a pile beam system at ground level, then the relationship is as at **19**.

4.04 Waterproofing

If the floor is not in contact with the ground, no damp-proof membrane will be required; but if it is, the Building Regulations' provisions described in 2.02 of information sheet LOWEST FLOOR 2 will apply.

4.05 Resistance to chemical attack

If the floor is in direct contact with the ground, it must be ensured that the ground does not contain water-soluble sulphates (a danger with clay soils in particular) or other harmful chemicals. If these are present, an isolating membrane or the use of special cement may be necessary.

4.06 Thermal insulation

As table II shows, the required value of $1 \cdot 13$ W/m^2 deg C is usually arrived at without any need for special measures to be taken.

4.07 Screeds and finishes

These will be dealt with in section 7 SUSPENDED FLOORS (see AJ 21.7.71 p60 at the beginning of this handbook), and the information will not be duplicated here.
The one point of difference which may arise between floor finishes on suspended floors subdividing the building internally and a suspended floor forming part of the external envelope is that created when the latter is in contact with the ground. There is then a problem of damp-proofing that would not exist with internal floors, and this may affect the floor screed or finish. The notes in 3.04 of information sheet LOWEST FLOOR 2 will then apply (see 'control of moisture' and **15** and **16** in that sheet).

5 Elevated lowest floors

5.01 Definition

What is meant by elevated lowest floors is shown in **1**.

5.02 Characteristics

In such cases the lowest floor of the building has most of the characteristics of a suspended ground floor, so many of the design considerations already dealt with will apply; particularly those relating to screeds, finishes and relationships with the external walls.

5.03 Exclusion of water

Obviously at external walls care must be taken to avoid water or vapour penetrating the floor via the supporting structure at first floor level. In such cases a detail very similar to a pile-supported structure will be needed, but with the ground floor column supports replacing the piles **20**. Protection against penetration from below is scarcely necessary as even heavy rain is seldom driven upwards. However, there will be a need for a vapour-proof membrane mainly to guard against interstitial condensation. Such a membrane, if constructed to lap or seal to the dpc, will also ensure against penetration through the concrete structure from the ring beam or structural system around the perimeter.

5.04 Thermal insulation

The principal additional protection required by such floors is heat insulation, without which the floor temperature of the lowest floor in the building might be uncomfortably low compared with the upper floors through which heat loss normally does not occur. Complaints of cold feet have been frequent from the occupants of first floor flats where the buildings have an open ground floor. The insulation can be positioned either above or below the structural floor and its position in relation to the vapour-proof membrane is important if damage from interstitial condensation is to be avoided.

When insulation is used it normally provides the greater part of the total thermal resistance of the floor. Thus the temperature change across the thickness of the insulation forms the largest part of the total temperature difference between the inside and the outside of the structure. Consequently, if the insulation is placed below the floor, the actual structural floor slab itself will maintain a temperature fairly close to that of the interior. If the insulation is placed above the structural floor, the slab itself will tend to approximate to the external temperature and as a result be a good deal colder. The job of the vapour-proof membrane is to prevent the warm air with its greater moisture content passing through the insulation, which is normally porous, and touching the cold face of the structural slab where condensation might take place. Thus if the insulation is positioned above the floor, it is best placed below a vapour barrier that will prevent the moisture-laden internal air passing through to reach the cold concrete upper surface **20**. If the insulation is positioned below the structural floor, the floor itself should remain reasonably warm and interstitial condensation is unlikely to occur at all. However, it could occur under extreme conditions, depending on temperature, relative humidities and efficiency of insulation. Thus a vapour barrier is best positioned above the slab **21**.

If the insulation above the floor is of the board type, eg polystyrene or polyurethane, no particular problems should be encountered with the screed. However, if the insulation is a glass fibre or mineral wool quilt, the screed should be at least 64 mm thick and incorporate a light reinforcement such as galvanised chicken wire.

6 Checklist

6.01 Functional requirements

Consider the functional requirements of the floor:
- Users' requirements (level, finish, and so on)
- Structural (imposed loads)
- Exclusion of water
- Thermal insulation
- Incorporation of services, machine mountings, ducts and access openings

6.02 Suspended timber floors at ground level

Decide:
- Level of floor in relation to ground
- Floor construction, insulation, finish

6.03 Suspended concrete floors at ground level

Decide:
- Level of floor in relation to ground
- Method of support
- Whether waterproofing, insulation, or precautions against chemical attack are required
- Screeds and finishes

6.04 Suspended concrete floors raised above ground

Decide:
- Level
- Construction
- Thermal insulation methods

7 References

1 Building Regulations 1972. 1972, HMSO [(A3j)]
see also:
ELDER, A. J. Guide to the Building Regulations 1972. London, 1972, Architectural Press £2·25 (A3j) (F7)
2 GREATER LONDON COUNCIL London Building Acts 1930-39
PITT, R. H. and DUFTON, J. The Guide to the London Building (Constructional) Bylaws 1972 and the London Building Acts. London, 1973, Architectural Press £2·75.
3 Building Standards (Scotland) Regulations 1963. 1963, HMSO [(A3j)]
4 BUILDING RESEARCH STATION Digest 18 The design of timber floors to prevent decay. 1970, HMSO [(23) Hi (S4)]

BRITISH STANDARDS INSTITUTION
5 BS 1282:1959 Classification of wood preservatives and their methods of application [Yu3]
6 BS CP 98:1964 Preservative treatment for constructional timber [Yu3]
7 BS CP 101:1963 Foundations and substructures for non-industrial buildings of not more than four storeys [(1–)]

Section 4
External envelope:
External walls

Section 4 External envelope: External walls

Relationship to rest of handbook

The table and diagram show the contents of the handbook as a whole, with the present section highlighted. Section 2 provided a general introduction to the more specific sections following, so it is recommended that the present section be used in conjunction with section 2.

Scope

This section, like the preceding one, gives guidance on detailed design and construction for one specific element-group. In this case, the subject is the group of elements which forms the vertical enclosing skin of the building above ground: external walls; windows, doors and other secondary elements contained within the walls; and the finishes to all of these.

Problems of structural strength, which are especially important when the external walls have a loadbearing function, are not given detailed consideration in this handbook; they are covered in the AJ Handbook of Building structure.

References and keywords

The keyword by which this section is identified is EXTERNAL WALLS: use of keywords is explained on p6.

Authors

The coordinating author of this section is DAVID KIRBY DiPArch, ARIBA of Thorne Barton & Kirby, assisted by Philip Lancashire MA, ARIBA, Paul Martin and Howard Nash BA, BArch.

Lancashire   *Martin*   *Nash*

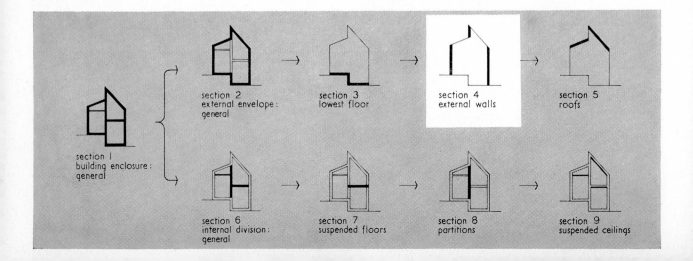

section 1
building enclosure:
general

section 2
external envelope:
general

section 3
lowest floor

section 4
external walls

section 5
roofs

section 6
internal division:
general

section 7
suspended floors

section 8
partitions

section 9
suspended ceilings

Technical study
External walls 1

Trends in wall design

This technical study introduces section 4 by drawing attention to the enormous increase in complexity of the task facing the modern architect, in comparison with the form-givers of previous ages. Partly this is a reflection simply of the increased complexity of society, but it is due also to the recent substitution of rapid change for slow evolution in the creation of building form. This places an unprecedented burden on the designer, for he must solve instantly, on a basis of theoretical understanding, the kinds of problems previous generations solved gradually on a basis of cumulative practical experience. The study is by
MARITZ VANDENBERG

1 The importance of walls

To most people walls are buildings. Walls define outside and inside space. They keep the outside out; and if they do not always keep the inside in, at least they are somewhere between. They also contribute more than any other element to the image and appearance of the building. And they create, to the observer at ground level, streetscape and townscape.

Public opinion, as reflected in newspapers and magazines, (and comments overheard) does not much like modern walls and wallscapes but hankers nostalgically after the walls of the past. Comparisons are not always fair, because there is a tendency to compare the best of the past with the worst of the present **1a** and **b**; nevertheless it must be admitted that the public has cause for complaint. These days we seldom achieve the richness and variety combined with the human scale and overall harmony shown, for example, in **2**. What we achieve instead is visible on the right of the photograph.

2 Design trends

2.01 Traditional design

Why is it that expensively-trained professionals, with the accumulated knowledge of past ages at their fingertips, find it so difficult to achieve the results that were within the reach of unsophisticated traditional builders?

Perhaps the major reason lies in the fact that the traditional builder operated within a very limited area of choice—most of his design problems had been solved by his predecessors

to the satisfaction of the community, and his own task was therefore relatively simple.

In primitive societies, for example, there is very little specialisation either in building type or in technical knowledge. The average member of such a society is perfectly capable of building his own house, and he works within a received tradition of building form and strict constraints of available materials and construction techniques which leave him with very few design decisions. The building he erects represents a model which has developed gradually over generations, being adjusted constantly until it satisfies most of the cultural and psycho-physical requirements and technological constraints of a fairly static society. In such circumstances the builder need not be an original thinker to produce a good building: most of the problems have been solved for him, and he erects a standardised model which has stood the test of time and which the community knows it likes.

In more advanced societies, in which a greater degree of differentiation and specialisation has developed, there may be a larger number of building types, buildings will be erected by tradesmen rather than the owner himself, and there will be greater variability in building technique. In such societies the builder has a rather larger degree of freedom to take design decisions and therefore has more problems to solve; but even though some of the specifics of design are variable, there is still a broad consensus of opinion (shared by owner, builder and society at large) on the basic building model which reflects a common heritage and hierarchy of values.

2.02 Modern design

Today the above constraints have largely disintegrated.

Social and technical specialisation has generated a vast and growing range of building types: increasingly often the problem of building form must be solved anew in any particular instance. Also, technological progress has greatly widened the designer's area of choice. Instead of being restricted to one way of building walls, perfected by succeeding generations, he can choose between a score of methods, many of them of recent origin and imperfectly understood.

Finally, the shared value system of traditional society, reflected in a commonly-held image of what walls ought to look like, has decayed. Instead, we place a premium on originality and novelty; there is a craving for the new which has undermined the evolutionary basis of building.

The architect today therefore is faced with a vastly more complex challenge than any of his predecessors. He has available to him an almost infinite array of possible design options; and instead of being able to rely on precedent he is thrown back on his own judgment and theoretical understanding of fundamental principles to guide him to the right decision.

Unfortunately, the transition from designing by instinct to designing by method is proving very difficult, and changes in the external wall over the past few decades clearly demonstrates the unfortunate consequences of this failure to come to terms with a new situation.

2.03 The dominance of fashion

What we have seen is an ever-quickening cycle of fashions, each adopted hastily without proper understanding of its likely performance, and dropped equally hastily for some new fashion before the lessons of the previous one have been incorporated in an evolutionary design tradition.

First came the curtain-wall phase, when post-war technology responded to architects' demands for lightness and transparency by producing the off-the-peg sheath wall, usually highly glazed. It seemed to some that here was a new vernacular material, appropriate to the twentieth century— a sophisticated form of cladding, all sleek metal, glass and synthetic rubber gaskets, which could be mass-produced to exacting standards and used by the modern architect as naturally as builders of previous generations used stone, brick or timber.

This trend got a powerful boost from buildings such as Lever House and the Seagram building, which were undeniably handsome. Thus a fashionable image was created, and curtain-walled buildings sprang up all over the world **3**.

But two things were wrong: this new form of cladding was being applied largely as fashion, with little thought given to performance and behaviour; and whereas the handsome façades of Lever House and the Seagram building had been carefully custom-designed, most of the off-the-peg copies were nondescript and aesthetically mediocre. Not only were the users landed with buildings that became overheated in summer and lost too much heat in winter, whose internal temperatures fluctuated too rapidly for the overworked heating and cooling installations to keep up; but the buildings in many instances looked gimcrack and attracted public dislike.

Then, in the '60s, a reaction set in—architects began to develop an increased liking for sculptured concrete. At first the tendency was to combine concrete, with strongly profiled surfaces or forms, with the large areas of glazing inherited from the curtain-wall aesthetic; but later the solid components tended to dominate, and a vogue developed for chunky-looking buildings exploiting the sculptural possibilities of concrete.

1a

1a, b Comparisons between old and new may seem unfair, but to the public they are undoubtedly justified
2 King Street, Bristol. The richness and variety of external facades, built over several centuries, have a human scale
3 Sophisticated curtain wall, all lightness and transparency, needs careful detailing to succeed aesthetically

1b

2

3

From the standpoint of environmental performance, these buildings **4** are certainly preferable to the thin-walled, unprotected glass boxes which now, mercifully, are no longer accepted as uncritically as in the past. But one suspects that the main stimulus for change did not derive from a desire to improve building performance but rather from the swing of the fashion pendulum.

Already there are signs of a coming vogue for moulded reinforced plastic wall panels **5** that will combine the sculptural advantages of concrete with lightness and ease of handling—and that will also sacrifice the thermal advantages of concrete to produce a new generation of quick-response buildings in which it is difficult and expensive to maintain thermal comfort (unless used with heavy lining).

Also, if it does come about that concrete claddings are superseded by plastics, it will mean that concrete, which has tended to weather very badly in the past because it was badly detailed, is going out of fashion just at the time when we may be seeing the beginnings of a vocabulary of concrete detailing which would weather gracefully.

2.04 Consequences of change

And so we have an architecture in which rapid fluctuations of style have replaced gradual evolution; in which there is a premium (in terms of professional and social prestige) on the exploitation of novel forms and materials. Probably such an approach is inherent in a society addicted to change and to technological challenge. But if it is to work, designers will have to adapt to a demanding new world of performance standards, design methodology and technological expertise, while never forgetting that the ultimate object of building technology is to create a pleasing and comfortable environment.

5

4 *Sophisticated use of concrete cladding which, by its weight and thickness, also provides good environmental control*
5 *This office, converted by Michael Lyall & Partners, looks as though it is built of concrete, but in fact it is clad with glass fibre panels*

4

Technical study
External walls 2

Section 4 **External walls**

Design data

The first step in designing the external wall must be the collection of all relevant data to formulate the criteria against which the evolving design can be tested constantly. This technical study outlines the three categories to be assembled: data from client and building users; data from site and locality; data on the economic, technological and legal constraints. The study is by MARITZ VANDENBERG

1 User requirements

1.01 Building type and purpose

The starting point of the design problem is usually the building type and purpose. The activities, processes, and storage functions to be accommodated within various building types, and their design implications, have been analysed in some detail in two series of AJ guides[1, 2]; these should be consulted.

1.02 Occupancy and occupants' requirements

First, the occupants of the building must be defined. This information will include *numbers* of occupants, and *type* of occupant (age, sex, status, and any other special characteristics which might influence the use of the building, eg physical disability, personality type, kind of clothing worn).
Second, the nature of their occupancy must be established. This information will include *duration* (permanent or temporary; continuous or intermittent; by night or by day; length of period, etc) and *nature* of occupancy (occupants' activities).
Occupants have requirements of various kinds that will influence the design of the external walls—space needs, environmental needs, security needs. This checklist gives categories of requirements on which information must be gathered, and references to AJ Handbooks in which guidance will be found.
● Space[1, 2] (eg room dimensions, window sill and head heights, window and door sizes)
● Security[3]
● Psychophysical[4] (thermal and aural comfort; ventilation needs; lighting needs)
● Privacy (both visual and aural)
● Views of outside desired
The designer should check that any preferences the client may have do not conflict with functional and economic requirements considered in subsequent paragraphs.

2 Data from site and locality

2.01 Site data

AJ guide to site investigation[12] contains a systematic procedure for identifying and recording all data necessary for designing a building for the site. Data on soil, site history and adjacent property may be relevant to wall design.

2.02 Climate

Data must be gathered on the conditions of radiative and air temperature, precipitation and humidity, air movement, light, noise, dust and pollution, and exposure to sunlight which prevail on the chosen site. Guidance on the kind of information to be gathered is given in the AJ Handbook of Building environment[4].

2.03 Availability of resources

Local building methods and materials, availability of skilled and unskilled labour, presence of specialist sub-contractors (eg precast concrete, roofing), availability and capacity of public utility services during construction, must all be assessed. Advice can be obtained usually from local architects.

3 Design constraints

Constraints are factors which control, or tend to prevent the fulfilment of design requirements, ie what the client and user need or desire. For example, the client may want a large window in a particular external wall, and find that the size of the window is limited by fire-safety legislation; or he may want curtain walling plus sun shades, and find that the cost allocation for external walls does not allow this. In each case the controlling factor acts as a constraint upon the preferred solution.

3.01 Cost allocation

The aim of cost planning is to break down the total cost estimate for the building into smaller parts **1** (based on knowledge of previously constructed projects) in order to ensure a well-balanced distribution of available finance. A further advantage in allocating a certain percentage of the total finance to each part of the building is that particular design decisions can be tested constantly against allocated target figures.
The principles of cost planning have been covered in detail in a previous AJ series[5]. Nevertheless, because of the extreme importance of this particular constraint, this information is augmented by technical studies and information sheets in appropriate sections of this handbook.
Thus information sheet ENCLOSURE 2 (Section 1), outlined the effect of design decisions on costs.
More specifically, technical study EXTERNAL WALLS 3 deals with costs in relation to external walls.

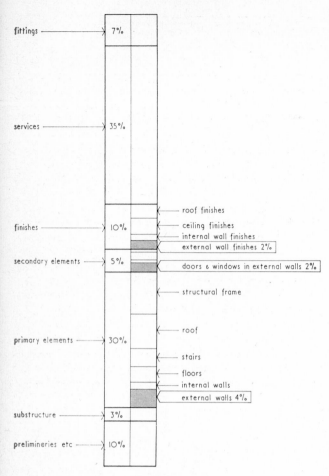

1 *Once total available finance for building as a whole is known, an analysis of similar buildings, previously constructed, will allow target costs to be established for external wall elements. Cost limits so established will be an important constraining influence on design options available to the architect*

3.02 Dimensional basis

If prefabricated components are to be incorporated in the proposed building, then it must be ensured that the dimensions of the building fabric are compatible with the preferred dimensions and controlling dimensions laid down in the official documents of the dimensional co-ordination programme. This will impose a severe constraint upon the dimensions selected for the spaces within the building, and upon the sizes of the components used.

The principles underlying the need for a dimensional discipline when designing the building fabric have been examined in information sheet ENCLOSURE 1 (Section 1) which also gave full details of the recommended ranges of controlling dimensions. This sheet should therefore be consulted. All that is required in the present information sheet is to provide some additional notes on problems likely to arise specifically in the design of the external envelope. Dimensional problems are particularly likely to arise with the detailing of corners, junctions, and abutments with other buildings, especially when a re-entrant is involved. There are two possible sources of difficulty.

The first is likely to occur when external claddings are placed *outside* the line of columns. Additional corner units may be required for salient corners, and re-entrant corners cause even more difficulty. In addition to special filler pieces to form the angle it will be necessary to use reduced-width cladding panels on one or both sides of the junction.

It is clear, then, that many problems of standardisation, interchangeability and jointing could be avoided by placing external claddings *within* the zone of columns **2**. Such a decision cannot be made simply on the basis of the factors described above, of course—the appearance, structural stability, and environmental performance of the assembly as a whole must be the deciding factors. But the dimensional considerations described here will be an important constraint upon the final decision.

Even if the components are located within the perimeter column zone, however, there is a second possible source of trouble because of the need to provide the external envelope with water-shedding projections such as profiled drips, mouldings and overlaps. These projections may transgress the boundary of the perimeter zone, again leading to problems particularly at re-entrant corners.

The important point in all these examples is what the effect will be on the possible degree of component standardisation. The larger the number of 'specials' required, the more expensive the components will be, and the greater will be the problems of sorting, matching and coding to ensure the right component is in the right place at the right time. It is therefore well worth devoting very careful attention, at the earliest design stages of the external wall, to the points outlined above, in order to achieve the maximum applicability of dimensional standardisation.

3.03 Statutory regulations

Structural regulations

These are dealt with in the AJ *Handbook of Building structure*[13].

Fire resistance regulations

The Building Regulations 1972

If the shape and size of the building and its position relative to the site boundary have been determined, minimum fire resistance of solid parts of the walls and maximum amount of 'unprotected area' are laid down in part E of the Regulations, which deals with fire resistance, combustibility and surface spread of flame. The governing factors are:

● Distance of external wall from relevant boundary

● Size and distribution of 'unprotected areas' (ie openings and areas of wall which have less than the required fire resistance or are faced with combustible material more than 1·0 mm thick)

● Purpose group of building

● Size of building or compartment

● Height of relevant part of wall

Detailed guidance on the effect of these provisions on external wall design is given in the *Guide to the Building Regulations* 1972[6].

London Building Acts 1930–39[8]

See part VI and part XI for requirements.

London Building (Constructional) By-laws 1972[9]

Guidance on the various statutory requirements for escape from buildings is given in a code of practice, *Means of escape in case of fire* (Document 3868) published by the Greater London Council.

Building Standards (Scotland) Regulations 1970[10]

The requirements for fire resistance, surface spread of flame and combustibility are set out in part IV. They are based on similar criteria to those of the *Building Regulations* 1972, although they differ in some details. Means of escape are set out in part E.

Other aspects

The Building Regulations 1972[7]
Light and air Part κ governs size of windows in habitable rooms in dwelling houses in relation to a 'zone of open space' outside the window which must be open to the sky. Note that any portion of the window within 1·22 m of the floor is discounted from the calculation.

Section κ4 deals with ventilation of rooms in dwelling houses. In general, if the window is used for ventilation, the ventilation area must not be less than one-twentieth of the floor area and the top of the opening not less than 1·75 m above the floor. External doors can be used for ventilation if they contain separate opening portions.

Thermal insulation External walls of dwellings shall, with the exception of any opening, have a thermal transmittance of not less than 1·70 W/m² deg C.

Moisture External walls shall resist the passage of moisture (section c8).

Railings on balconies, platforms, and so on shall not be less than 1·0 m high (section н6).

Materials Section в3 lists materials which are unsuitable without exception and those which are suitable only in certain circumstances.

London Building Acts 1930–39[8]
See clauses 6.01 to 6.09 for requirements for non-load-bearing enclosures.

London Building (Constructional) By-laws 1952[9]
Lighting and ventilation Clause 11.03 of the 1952 by-laws is still in force and stipulates requirements for lighting and ventilating rooms used for habitation or offices. In general, the superficial area of windows shall not be less than one-tenth of the floor area. In addition, either an area of window not less than one-twentieth of the floor area shall be openable or alternative means of ventilation shall be provided.

LCC By-laws for good rule and government
Access for maintenance The regulations set out in Document 4193 include a stipulation that no person may 'stand or kneel on the sill of any window for the purpose of cleaning or painting such window or for any purpose whatever, such sill being more than 1·829 m in height from the level of the ground immediately below it, without support sufficient to prevent such person from falling'.

The Building Standards (Scotland) Regulations 1970[10]
Light Part ʟ governs size of windows in dwelling houses and flats by means of a required daylight factor on the working plane, height of the window head above the floor, and floor area of the room.

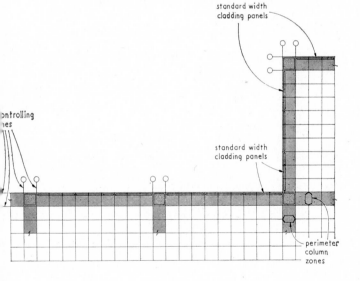

standard width cladding panels

standard width cladding panels

ontrolling
es

perimeter column zones

2 *Example of dimensional constraints on external wall design. These dimensional considerations allow maximum standardisation*

3 *Fire resistance Regulations exercise an important constraint on possible external wall configurations available to designers. Diagram indicates general effect of part E7 of Building Regulations 1965. For more detailed indication of provisions laid down, see The Guide to the Building Regulations 1972 (Arch. Press)*

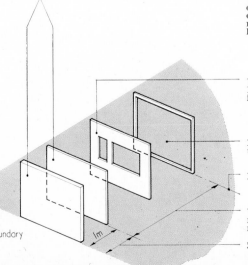

Wall must be free of openings or unprotected areas (with certain specific exceptions), must have the specified fire resistance from both inside and outside, external cladding must be non-combustible, construction must be entirely of non-combustible material (with certain specified exceptions relating to internal linings).

Wall may have openings and 'unprotected areas' as laid down in Schedule 9 of Building Regulations Part E7, need be fire resistant from inside only: if building is over 15 m high further requirements are laid down.

No controls, walls may consist entirely of opening or unprotected area, and there are no combustibility regulations.

Beyond this line no control is exercised.

Within this zone, controls on size of unprotected openings are progressively relaxed. Depth of zone will depend on wall height, size of building or compartment and building purpose group.

Zone of maximum control.

site boundary

1m

Air Part κ requires a ventilation area of not less than one-twentieth of the floor area in windows used for ventilating dwelling houses and flats. In some cases a permanent ventilator is required in addition.

Thermal insulation The thermal transmittance of solid external walls of residential buildings shall be not less than 1·70 W/m² deg C. If the walls contain glazed openings, the average thermal transmittance shall be not less than 2·38 W/m² deg C (j4).

Moisture External walls shall resist the passage of moisture (part G).

Access Part E stipulates requirements for access to windows and buildings for fire fighting and escape. This section requires windows above the ground floor of houses to be designed to be cleaned from inside unless they are accessible from a balcony or flat roof.

Exits Clause E7 governs width of exits and exit doors.

The Construction (Lifting Operations) Regulations 1961 and *The Construction (Working Places) Regulations* 1966
These Regulations (applicable to the UK) govern access to the wall by means of ladders, scaffolding, scaffolds or cradles suspended on cables and all lifting machines restrained by a guide or guides, provided that these are used for 'building operations'. They would consequently control the use of such equipment for any cleaning or maintenance work carried out by building operatives as part of a building contract but would not apply to routine window cleaning.

3.04 Design life and adaptability

The design life of a building can rarely be predicted with any degree of accuracy. Factors which cannot be foreseen at design stage, and which are beyond the architect's control, may prolong the useful life of a building far beyond its expected life ('temporary' prefabs lingering on decade after decade are a familiar part of the scene), or a structurally sound building may be torn down as a result of changes in land values, ownership, or technology.

If external walls are loadbearing brick, concrete or some similar material, the walls themselves will be extremely durable, and the main problem to be considered will be durability of a satisfactory appearance. Inadequate attention to detailing, or the use of materials which require frequent cleaning, could lead to very high maintenance costs, particularly in polluted areas.

Light claddings pose a different problem. They are often made of comparatively new materials, the durability and weathering qualities of which have not been tested over long periods of time. Also, with light claddings the structure and the external wall element are separate entities, and could have quite different life cycles—the claddings could theoretically be renewed, or replaced in response to changing needs, several times during the life of the structure.

Rather than try to decide on any limitations to the life of the cladding elements, a more realistic approach would therefore be first, to aim for flexibility in cladding, so that it can be adapted, renewed or replaced in response to future changes in circumstances; and second, to aim for minimal maintenance. At present, taxation considerations encourage low capital costs and relatively high maintenance costs, because the latter are an allowable charge against profits for taxation, whereas the former usually are not. This leads to enormous waste of money. It is shown in chapter 18 of

Light cladding of buildings[11] (an essential reference for all aspects of external wall design) that additional capital expenditure of £18 000 would be justifiable if maintenance costs could be reduced by £1000 a year. See also technical study 3. The method of capital financing may also affect the designed life. Loans for local authority housing have a 60-year repayment period which would therefore be the minimum designed life.

4 Checklist

4.01 Data from client/users

● Building type and purpose
● Building occupancy (numbers and types of occupants; duration and nature of occupancy)
● Occupants' requirements (space, security, psycho-physical, privacy, views)
● Cleaning and maintenance policy
● Clients' and users' preferences

4.02 Data from site and locality

● Site data (soil, site history, adjacent buildings)
● Site climate (heat, noise, light, air movement, precipitation, dust and pollution)
● Availability of resources

4.03 Economic, legal and technological constraints

● Cost allocation
● Dimensional basis
● Statutory regulations
● Insurance regulations
● Design life and adaptability
● Manufacturing, transportation and site assembly

5 References

1 AJ guides to Building types (see complete list at end of technical study ENCLOSURE 2, AJ 4.8.71)
2 AJ guides to Building spaces: internal (see complete list at end of technical study ENCLOSURE 2, AJ 4.8.71)
3 AJ Handbook of Building services and circulation, section 13 (AJ 17.6.70 to 5.8.70) [(5–)]
4 AJ Handbook of Building environment [(E6)]: (AJ 2.10.68 to 13.8.69)
5 Cost planning and cost control (AJ 3, 10 and 24.11.65) [sfB (1961) Ba7: CI/sfB (A14) (A3)]
6 ELDER, A. J. AJ Guide to the Building Regulations 1972. London, 1971, Architectural Press [(A3j) (F7)]
7 Building Regulations 1972, HMSO [(A3j)]
8 GREATER LONDON COUNCIL London Building Acts 1930–39 Constructional By-laws, amended to December 1970. London, 1970, The Council [(Ajn)]
9 LONDON COUNTY COUNCIL Document 3836 Code of Practice: means of escape in case of fire. London, 1954, The Council [(Ajn)]
10 Building Standards (Scotland) Regulations. 1970, HMSO [(A3j)]
11 ROSTRON, R. M. Light cladding of buildings. London, 1964, Architectural Press [(21)]
12 AJ Handbook of Building structure [(2–)] (AJ 8.3.72 to 5.9.73); to appear in book form in 1974.

Technical study
External walls 3

Wall costs

Technical study EXTERNAL WALLS 2 *outlined a range of constraints which influence external wall design. One of these—costs—could not be covered adequately in a few paragraphs, so more attention is given to it in this technical study by* DAVID KIRBY

1 Introduction

There is a wide variety in the cost of external walling as a proportion of building costs. In recent cost analyses the percentage has varied from about 6 per cent to 22 per cent. The range for housing is up to 27 per cent. The proportion clearly varies with the amounts spent on services, on other elements and on the ratio of wall area to building volume. Three examples from recent reports are considered.

1 *Hearts of Oak House, Euston Road*

2 Walls forming a high percentage of cost

Hearts of Oak House, Euston Road, London NW1

Comment

Double-glazed units, 3560 m², were used in the stainless steel curtain walling, a ratio of 1:3·4 of glazed area to total floor area. The architects, Kaye, Firmin & Partners, comment that the use of floor to ceiling glazing prevented the loss of 29·73 m² of floor area per floor, representing the loss of £400 000 of capital value to the building. Therefore the expensive specification (Glavertel 'Stopray') sealed double-glazing units with a thin deposit of gold powder on the inside face of the outer leaf is fully justified, and the support system of stainless steel clad curtain walling is consistent with a washable, low maintenance elevation. Ratio of total external wall area to floor area is 1:1·7. The low figure for partitions must mean that subdivision was left to tenant.

Summary of elemental costs

	Cost per m² £	Per cent of total
Preliminaries	13·78	8·43
Work below lowest floor finish	11·95	7·25
Structural elements		
Frame and upper floors	35·74	21·80
Roof and roof coverings	1·94	1·19
External walls (including windows and doors)	35·31	21·53
External brick walling	0·43	0·27
Internal doors	2·91	1·79
Partitions	0·75	0·46
Total of structural elements	**77·08**	**47·84**
Finishes and fittings		
Wall finishes	6·24	3·78
Floor finishes	3·23	1·96
Ceiling finishes	4·32	2·75
Decorations	0·32	0·22
Total of finishes and fittings	**14·11**	**8·71**
Services		
Sanitary appliances	0·43	0·24
Gas and cold water services	3·34	2·07
Heating and ventilation services	23·90	14·58
Electrical services	5·81	3·54
Special services	6·46	3·89
Drainage	0·65	0·41
Fixed equipment	2·80	1·70
Builder's work	3·44	2·12
Total of services	**46·82**	**28·57**
Total	**163·93**	**100·00**

3 Walls forming typical percentage of costs

Children's home, St Stephen's Road, London W5

Comment

Wall area costs are in three parts:
- 75 m² of cavity walling at £5·38 m²
- 176 m² softwood studding with glazed asbestos panels on plywood on polythene vapour barrier externally and 12 mm plasterboard, polythene vapour barrier and glass fibre insulation internally at £6·89/m²
- Single-glazed windows in galvanised metal frames in softwood subframes: 116 m² at £15·5/m².

The total external wall area of approximately 367 m² is a ratio of 1:1·3 of the total floor area. The walls provide an efficient envelope—also the structure—for a comparatively modest proportion of the building costs. Architects were Yorke Rosenberg Mardall.

- It should be noted that in the previous example (2) the windows and external doors are not separated and must be therefore included in the overall figure for exterior walls. Thus the true comparison is between 35·31 and a total of 9·26 for this building and 5·60 in the next building (4), still however a very significant difference. Note also the very high figure of 23·90 for H and V services in example (2) probably resulting from the choice of fixed glazing.

Summary of elemental costs

	Cost per m² £	Per cent of total
Preliminaries and insurances	4·23	6·33
Contingencies	1·70	2·55
Work below lowest floor finish	5·72	8·56
Structural elements		
Upper floors	5·88	8·79
Roof	4·36	6·52
Rooflights	0·82	1·26
Staircases	0·76	1·14
External walls	4·91	7·34
Windows	3·80	5·69
External doors	0·55	0·32
Partitions	2·24	3·35
Internal doors	1·49	2·38
Ironmongery	0·63	0·94
Total of structural elements	**25·54**	**38·23**
Finishes and fittings		
Wall finishes	2·13	3·19
Floor finishes	3·54	5·30
Ceiling finishes	0·95	1·43
Decoration	1·56	2·33
Fittings	4·36	6·53
Total of finishes and fittings	**12·54**	**18·78**
Services		
Sanitary appliances	1·39	2·08
Waste, soil and overflow pipes	2·29	3·42
Hot and cold water services	2·20	3·29
Heating services	5·14	7·69
Ventilation services	0·59	0·89
Gas services	0·25	0·37
Electrical services	3·95	5·91
Special services	0·15	0·22
Drainage	1·14	1·71
Total of services	**17·09**	**25·58**
Total	**66·82**	**100·00**

2 *Children's home, Ealing*

4 Walls forming low percentage of cost

Academic buildings, University of Surrey, Guildford

Comment

In this building by Building Design Partnership, the very low percentage of wall costs is due to the solid walling being confined to the lowest level. It consists of 1486 m² of cavity brickwork at £4·84/m². Remaining wall areas consist of mill finish aluminium horizontal glazing fixed between concrete panel edge beam units (not included). Single glazing and infill panels are included in the price at £22·33/m² with a total area of 2007 m².

The total of wall and window area is 3484 m² and compared with total floor area of 10 130 m² the ratio is 1:2·9. The building study in AJ 24.3.71 made the following comment on cost: 'The traditional elements of external walls have a ratio to windows of 1:1½. Together these two elements have a misleading perimeter to floor ratio as low as 0·3:1; but both these ratios exclude the perimeter detailing within the UBS cost, eg 5ft 6in high edge beams to upper floors.'

Services absorbed 39 per cent of the building costs, and with the large internal volumes and high demand for technical services it is doubtful whether a higher standard of wall specification would have resulted in economy in service provision. Although the average cost of external wall and window materials is higher than in the Hearts of Oak House, the lower wall/floor ratio produces a much lower percentage of the total cost for these elements, even after allowing for the fact that the children's home is a more highly serviced and expensive building.

Summary of elemental costs

	Cost per m² £	Per cent of total
Preliminaries and insurances	8·03	8·51
Contingencies	2·78	2·94
Work below lowest floor finish	8·97	9·50
Structural elements		
Frame, upper floors and roof construction	17·76	18·81
Roof coverings	1·93	2·04
Rooflights	0·02	0·02
Staircases	0·72	0·76
External walls	0·67	0·71
Windows	4·62	4·89
External doors	0·31	0·33
Partitions	3·68	3·90
Internal doors	0·63	0·67
Ironmongery	0·31	0·33
Total of structural elements	**30·66**	**32·46**
Finishes and fittings		
Wall finishes	0·07	0·07
Floor finishes	2·56	2·71
Ceiling finishes	4·13	4·37
Decoration	0·67	0·71
Fittings	0·09	0·10
Total of finishes and fittings	**7·50**	**7·96**
Services		
Sanitary appliances	0·40	0·42
Waste, soil and overflow pipes	1·53	1·62
Cold water services	1·44	1·52
Hot water	1·53	1·62
Heating services	4·62	4·89
Ventilation services	7·40	7·83
Gas services	0·76	0·80
Electrical services	11·48	12·15
Special services	6·68	7·07
Drainage	0·67	0·71
Total of services	**36·51**	**38·63**
Total	**94·45**	**100·00**

3 Academic buildings, University of Surrey, Guildford

5 Detailed assessment

The analyses of area and cost ratios and of previous building studies are an essential part of refining the choice of wall systems, but the final design process must depend on costing the preferred system in detail. This is done usually in association with a qs, but the following tables and illustrations will serve as a guide to relative costs at the design stage*.

* The figures quoted are derived mainly from Spon's *Architects' and builders' price book* 1971 or from AJ Costs and prices. They do not include preliminaries. Actual figures are used in preference to ratios or bar charts which can be derived only from past figures, and are therefore likely to go out-of-date as soon as actual figures

Table I *Framing*

	Cost £/m²
Timber framing 125 mm × 50 mm studs at 600 mm centres with 125 mm × 50 mm head and plate (check for diagonal bracing, plywood sheathing and fire stopping and adjust cost figure accordingly)	1·10

Table III *Claddings*

	Cost £/m²
Layer of double-sided building paper	0·20
Machine-made tiles on battens	2·90
25 mm tongued and grooved softwood boarding on battens	3·00
Add for knot, stop and prime, one undercoat and gloss paint	0·57
Cement- and sand-faced rendering	1·30
Glass mosaic *from*	7·85
Glazed ceramic mosaic *from*	9·10
Precast concrete facing slabs *from*	9·10
Faience stone, slate and marble slabs *from*	15·75

Table IV *Curtain walling and panels*

	Cost £/m²
Galvanised steel standard grid curtain walling	20·80
Anodised aluminium standard grid curtain walling	23·80
5 mm rough cast glass glazed into curtain walling	3·40
6 mm float glass glazed into curtain walling *from*	5·52
'Insulight' double-glazing units in panels *from*	11·43
Patent glazing with 6 mm Georgian-wired cast glass in aluminium bars	6·14

The depth of 479 mm seems excessive for a panel but **4** shows the reason: the use of heavy profiling for visual effect.

Table II *Masonry*

Specification	Inner leaf	Cavity	Outer leaf	Cost £/m²
'Standard' specification adequate structural performance for domestic work: better than minimum insulation	4in (100 mm) lightweight concrete block, in 1:1:6 mortar	50 mm width galvanised wire butterfly ties at 900 mm × 450 mm centres	4½in (112 mm) common brick at £10 per 1000 in 1:1:6 mortar	4·65
Considerably improved structural properties	4½in (112 mm) common brick	50 mm width galvanised wire butterfly ties at 900 mm × 450 mm centres	4½in (112 mm) common brick at £10 per 1000 in 1:1:6 mortar	5·15
Insulation improvements down to U-value 0·68 W/m deg C sufficient to justify economic check on heating system installation as well as running costs	Line inner leaf glass fibre in battens *or* polystyrene *or* polyurethane board	*or* fill cavity with urea-formaldehyde foam	As required	add up to 0·90 subject to specialist quotation
Improved appearance and weathering			Extra for fairface and pointing to standard specification	0·36
			As standard specification, but facings at £20 per 1000	5·70
			As standard specification, but facings at £50 per 1000	7·70
Fairfaced blockwork external walling or base for further cladding	4in (100 mm) lightweight concrete block in 1:1:6 mortar	50 mm cavity	4in (100 mm) lightweight concrete block in 1:1:6 mortar	4·54
Base for further cladding	Solid walling: 6in (152 mm) lightweight concrete blockwork		As required	2·79

4 *Row of cladding panels at Heathrow airport (architects: Pascall & Watson)*

Special facilities buildings, Debden, Essex (AJ 30.6.71) Scott, Brownrigg & Turner

Walls: 9in (228 mm) inner leaf fletton bricks: 76 mm cavity filled urea-formaldehyde foam; 4½in (114 mm) brick facings: 710 m² at £8·40/m².
N.B. Clearly a very high insulation (thermal) value was required.

Windows: rigid pvc extruded profiles with double-glazed units on inside and outside faces: 19·5 m² at £26·91/m².

Doors: 2⅛in (54 mm) teak in teak frames: 6·4 mm Georgian-wired glazed panels; draught excluders and thresholds; glazed doors £20·67/m²; solid doors £24 m².

5

Maternity unit, Royal Infirmary, Stirling (AJ 4.11.70) Keppie, Henderson & Partners

Windows: proprietary red pine timber frame, finished with decorative preservative; top-hung aluminium sashes (some double-glazed).

Walls: proprietary precast concrete cladding panel, integral polystyrene insulation, exposed white calcine flint aggregate finish externally, interior smooth finish for decoration, complete with synthetic rubber baffle, open drain joints: 663 m² at £15·88/m².
10½in cavity walling with 4in insulating block, 2in cavity, 4½in facing brick and concrete sills: £7·23/m².
Note much higher cost of modern factory made cladding (more than double).

6

Food Research Institute, Norwich (AJ 11.2.70) Feilden & Mawson

Cladding: 76 mm precast concrete exposed aggregate panels: £13·46/m².
Note—another example of higher costs of factory made units. Must be justified on other grounds.

Windows: prefabricated window and infill panels as shown: £19·73 m².

Walls: 11in (279 mm) cavity brickwork, in situ rc edge beams: £5·20/m².

7

Old people's housing, Glamorgan (AJ 26.5.71) Gammon, Williams & Partners

Windows: purpose-made treated softwood windows: £6·59/m².
External sill: brick on edge course, internally softwood window boards.
(Economy of cheap materials demonstrated).

Walls: 11in (280 mm) cavity loadbearing brickwork, common brick inner leaf, calcium silicate outer leaf: £5·79/m².
330 mm edge beams at floor levels, proprietary steel lintels, in situ rc lintels 4lb (1·8 kg) lead flashings with soldered corner pieces.
(Economy of traditional systems again demonstrated—use of other techniques must be justified on grounds other than cost.

Glazed screen: 175 mm × 75 mm softwood mullions at 860 mm centres; 125 mm × 75 mm hardwood sill, 125 mm × 75 mm softwood head and transoms: all timber treated; glazed louvre openings.

Infill panels: 12·7 mm asbestos, 25 mm polystyrene, plywood internal facing: £7·39/m².

8

Technical study
External Walls 4

Section 4 **External walls**

Design decisions

Technical study EXTERNAL WALLS 2 *covered the first stage in the design process—collection of the basic data; and technical study* EXTERNAL WALLS 3 *gave information on the comparative costs of alternative wall types. The present study suggests a possible sequence for taking design decisions on the nature of the wall; it should be used in conjunction particularly with technical study* EXTERNAL ENVELOPE 1 *in which the functions and performance requirements of the building's external skin were analysed in considerable detail. The final design stage, that of developing the detailed construction of the chosen wall type, will be covered by the various information sheets which follow this series of technical studies. The study is by* MARITZ VENDENBERG

1 Scope

This technical study covers the design stage at which the external wall's performance requirements are translated into a chosen wall type. The study is divided into three parts corresponding to the three design steps involved:
● Establishing performance requirements (para 2)
● Taking basic decisions on wall design (para 3)
● Taking more detailed decisions on wall design (para 4). The final design stage, the construction design of the wall assembly, will be covered by the relevant information sheet for the chosen wall type, rather than by this technical study which deals with general principles of building performance and not with the specifics of building construction.

2 Performance requirements

Using the information gathered, as described in technical study EXTERNAL WALLS 2, the following requirements of the proposed building can be established: environmental, security, structural and aesthetic. The purpose of design for each group of building elements (in this case, the external wall) will be to satisfy these requirements as much as possible within the constraints imposed by economics, available technology, legal requirements and so on.

2.01 Environmental requirements

Appropriate physical conditions must be defined for the following aspects of environment: (endoclimate)
● Thermal comfort, ie air temperature, radiant conditions
● Air, ie amount, purity rate of air movement and relative humidity
● Lighting (should be adequate for proposed uses and pleasant in quality: both natural and artificial)
● Privacy (both visual and aural)
● Prospect, ie occupants' desire for general or specific views of the outside.
Where appropriate, suitable standards can be established by applying the guiding principles set out in the AJ Handbook of Building environment and the guidance on user

requirements in para 1.02 of technical study EXTERNAL WALLS 2. To assist designers, table I summarises as concisely as possible generally applicable standards of natural lighting, sunlight penetration, air supply and noise conditions. These figures do not constitute a full specification for any of the aspects of psycho-physical comfort listed above, but by establishing minimum values for some of the most important variables involved, they will be of some help to designers, provided their limitations are understood.

2.02 Security requirements

The building must give the occupants security against unauthorised entry (see 4.02 in technical study EXTERNAL ENVELOPE 1) or other forms of attack (eg vehicle driving errors).

2.03 Structural requirements

Walls' structural functions will not receive detailed consideration in this section as they are covered fully in the AJ Handbook of Building structure. It is necessary only to remind designers that the major structural function of *loadbearing walls* is to support the weight of the structure above (a vertical deadload that can be established with considerable accuracy) as well as wind loads (in accordance with CP3 chap. v. part 2/1970) and loads due to occupants, furniture and so on (a vertical live load less easy to establish, and for which conventional figures are given in CP3 chap. v. part I/1967; whereas the major structural function of *non-loadbearing walls* is to resist horizontal wind loads only.

2.04 Aesthetic requirements

The visual satisfaction of those who will use the building and those who will see it from the outside as an element in the townscape should be respected. The problem of what constitutes 'good appearance' is thorny and controversial, and falls outside the scope of this handbook. But the problem of *retaining* the original appearance, or at least ensuring that it changes only in ways foreseen by the designer after the building is completed is an important aspect of building enclosure. Technical study EXTERNAL

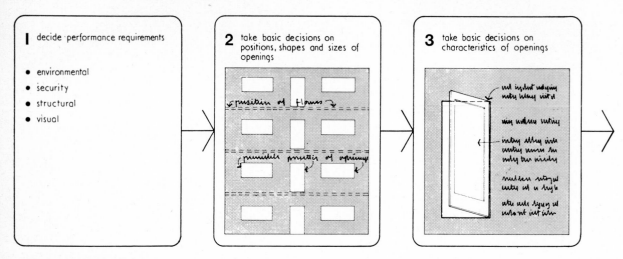

1 *Once the performance requirements for the external wall have been established (see para 2), the designer can follow the above sequence of decisions in designing the wall. Referring constantly to this diagram will help the reader keep track of the inevitable complexities of paras 3 and 4*

ENVELOPE 1 (6) outlined some of the principles of correct detailing for dealing with weathering.

3 Basic decisions

The major decisions to be taken at a relatively early stage of design, which will have not only a decisive influence on the building's appearance but will be likely to determine to a considerable degree its environmental performance, are the following:
● Sizes, shapes and positions of openings
● Treatment of openings, eg infill type, opening arrangements and protection from light, heat and water penetration
● Construction of solid portions of walls.
Each of these is dealt with in some detail below.

3.01 Openings: sizes, shapes and positions

Each internal space should be examined in terms of the following functional requirements; on this basis preliminary decisions can be made on the best position, size and shape for each opening in the building's external vertical skin.

Access and egress
In examining the need for access and egress by people, animals and goods through the external wall and deciding on suitable openings to serve these functions, the following points should be considered:
● Special needs, eg of disabled people and large objects
● Special functions, eg escape and access for cleaning
● Security requirements (these will influence both locations and sizes of openings)
● Legislation (Building regulations will impose limitations on openings in external wall, depending on proximity of wall to site boundary). Fire protection officers will often have requirements on egress.

Light and view
On the basis of factors such as those mentioned in 3.06 of technical study EXTERNAL ENVELOPE 1, a decision must be made on the proportion of natural/artificial lighting to be adopted. The greater the reliance on *natural lighting*, the more carefully window size, shape and position will need to be considered if the desired lighting conditions are to be

achieved, and the greater will be the problems of glare, heat gain and heat loss due to large areas of glazing. On the other hand, if major reliance is placed on *artificial lighting*, windows can be comparatively small and positioning will be less critical, thereby alleviating problems of environmental control although the problem of glare may be accentuated by the contrast between a small area of bright light and the surrounding comparative gloom. Occupants' desires for general views of the world outside and for vistas of specific objects are important factors in window design. The designer should study carefully the possibilities of conflict between view requirements and visual privacy requirements.

Sun
The psychological need for sunlight felt by many people is a factor quite distinct from natural lighting and should be considered separately (see table I). Prevention of overheating, particularly in interiors such as lecture rooms where occupants cannot change their positions, is vital.

Air
It must be decided how much reliance will be placed on natural ventilation, as opposed to air-conditioning or forced ventilation: 3.05 of technical study EXTERNAL ENVELOPE 1 indicates the main design factors to be taken into account.

Appearance
Obviously the wall's appearance influences sizes, proportions and dispositions of openings; but architects should ideally not allow considerations of appearance to outweigh other, equally important factors such as environmental performance and economy (although circumstances may change relativity, eg the wc window next to the prestige entrance).

3.02 Characteristics of openings

The preliminary layout of openings decided upon as a result of the above investigations must now be analysed more carefully to establish the functions of each opening, because some of the openings will have to perform multiple functions, eg light admission plus ventilation, or will have to perform selectively, eg admitting light but excluding heat, or allowing occupants to look out but preventing outsiders from seeing in. Also, the opening's functional performance must be reconciled with that required of the wall as a whole: for instance, if windows are very large, the whole wall-element may not reach the desired thermal resistance required for regulating internal temperatures.

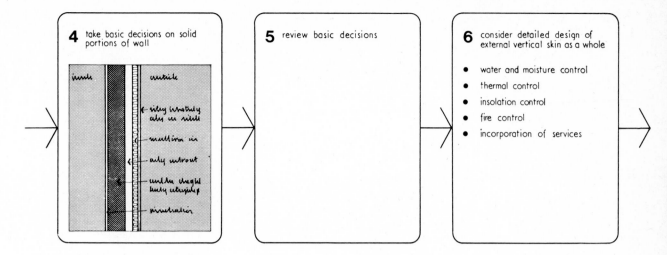

The following decisions have to be taken at this stage:
● Type of opening, eg fixed window or opening window, door or louvre
● Type of infill, eg transparent, translucent or opaque
● Additional features, eg protection devices against light or heat and special security devices.
The required analysis can be carried out under the following headings, using table II as a checklist.

Heat loss
Rates of heat loss through windows are high, and the benefits of low U-values for the solid parts of walls will be reduced by windows in the wall. Not only will this require increased performance from the heating installation, but it must be remembered that the radiation of body heat that occurs from the human occupant to the cold window surface has an adverse effect on thermal comfort. Heat loss through windows can be reduced by the following measures:
● Reduction in area of glass
● Use of multiple-glazing (double or triple) in preference to single-glazing
● Use of fixed windows in preference to opening lights
● Re-orientation of windows towards the south (but this may cause problems of heat *gain*, and may completely upset the major planning principles on which more important decisions have been taken); and reduction of exposure to wind
● Prevention of thermal by-pass through metal frames, and through solid sections of wall (stopped cavities) at the perimeter of openings ('cold bridges')
● Use of heavy curtains; but this will only assist at night as if drawn window is useless.

Heat gain
Whether this is a problem will depend on orientation of openings; shading by trees, other buildings, or projections from the building; and on the building's thermal capacity (lightweight enclosures will tend to overheat more easily than massive enclosures acting in the manner of an electrical condenser, or flywheel, absorbing energy when available (day) and discharging it later when colder (night)). Excessive heat gain can be reduced by the following measures:
● Reduction in area of glass
● Shading the windows by projections from the building, external blinds, louvres or shades
● Use of heat-absorbing glass
● Re-orientation of building
● Increased ventilation (natural or mechanical) and especially if introduced near windows

Sound transmission
Entry of noise into the building from outside is usually via windows (and especially open windows) rather than through walls or roof, particularly with traditional construction. Therefore, where an external noise source is present, it is more likely to be a nuisance if windows have to be opened for ventilation. Excessive noise entry can be reduced by the following measures:
● Re-orientation of window-wall away from noise source
● Use of fixed windows and mechanical ventilation
● Use of double-glazing preferably at least 150 to 200 mm apart
● Use of edge-sealing with opening windows.

Ventilation
Positions, sizes and method of operating vents must be decided, if natural ventilation is to be used.
Interior space should be protected from rain, snow and sleet; dust and pollution; and wind and air turbulance.
If sound transmission is of great importance mechanical ventilation in conjunction with non-opening fenestration may be the only acceptable solution.

Safety and access
Safety of occupants and window-cleaners must be considered. This will affect sizes, shapes and positions of the opening parts of windows, the method of opening and relationships of opening to fixed lights.

3.03 Solid parts of walls

Once tentative decisions have been made on the sizes, positions and arrangement of openings (3.01) and on the characteristics of each opening (3.02), only the solid parts of the vertical external skin are left to be decided. When this has been done, there will be a tentative design for the vertical external skin as a whole. Probably the major decision is whether the solid parts of the wall should be of 'heavy' or 'light' construction. Choice will be influenced by:
● Mass required for thermal capacity and sound reduction
● Degree of fire-resistance required
● Appearance required, eg solid or light looking appearance; modelling of wall surface
● Maintenance
● Structural, erection and assembly considerations.
● Availability of material (time)
Notes are given on each of these factors in the following paragraphs (for fire-resistance see 4.01).

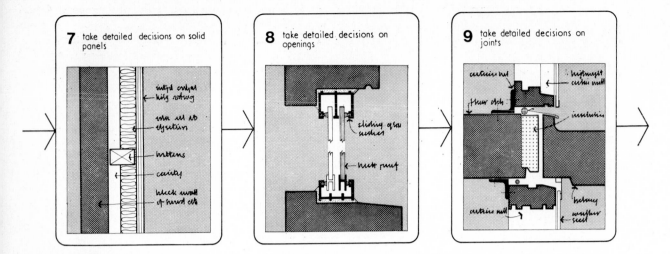

Thermal properties
Thermal capacity
It will be known at this stage whether the enclosure ought to be of high thermal capacity, ie 'slow-response'; low capacity, ie 'quick-response'; or an intermediate type (see table II and notes under 'Air temperature' in 3.07 of technical study EXTERNAL ENVELOPE 1). On the basis of this functional requirement for the wall element as a whole, and of the known ratio of window area to solid area in the proposed wall, the relative massiveness of the solid portions can be decided. The higher the required thermal capacity and the larger the proportion of window area, the greater the mass of the solid parts will need to be if the building is to perform satisfactorily. However it should be noted that the building's thermal capacity cannot be evaluated simply on an analysis of the wall elements; the relative massiveness of the building's entire physical fabric, including structure, floors and internal partitions, must be taken into account: all will contribute to the thermal capacity.

Thermal transmittance
On the basis of the now known ratio of window area to solid area, the mean U-value required for the wall as a whole can be reviewed and a suitable U-value for the solid portions established to give the necessary overall wall performance.

Acoustic properties
If a substantial degree of sound reduction is required between outside and inside, it is usually the windows, rather than the solid wall, that require the most careful consideration. For instance, if single-glazed opening windows have been specified, there is little point in spending time and money on reducing the noise transmission properties of the solid walling. But if enough attention has been given to arranging and detailing the openings, the presence of a noise source outside the building will influence the design of the solid parts of wall by favouring the use of relatively massive construction.

Appearance
This is an important factor, but the caution given in technical study EXTERNAL WALLS 1 should be heeded. If design decisions are dominated by superficial considerations of appearance unrelated to performance, the consequences are likely to be lamentable. Nevertheless it is in this field where the architect has training, experience, flair, feeling etc not acquired or often not understood by his associated designers and it is his job without allowing practical considerations to be forgotten to achieve good aesthetic results. Indeed it is still thought by some that the old theory of 'functionalism' (ie an effective design will look

well) still holds good.

Maintenance
Limits of annual expenditure on cleaning and maintaining wall surfaces will act as a constraint in selecting wall type. Maintenance includes renewal of finishes; cleaning; reglazing windows; and repairing and maintaining moving parts.

Structural, erection and assembly considerations
Structural function
At this stage the wall layout will be advanced sufficiently to show which parts of wall are available for structural functions. It may be necessary to modify the layout to suit the structural functions to be served; the effect of all such modifications on the non-structural functions of the wall should be checked (see 2.03).

Erection and assembly considerations
In many instances site conditions; local availability of labour, building materials and components, and special facilities; and contractors' resources will severely constrain choice of construction method, eg traditional/industrialised; heavy/light; small/large units; close tolerances/large tolerances; and so on.

3.04 Review of basic decisions

Preliminary decisions have now been taken on the following:
● Position, size and shape of each opening, and type of infilling
● General form and construction of solid portions of wall. The external vertical skin as a whole can now be reviewed and assessed, and final decisions taken on the relationship between the external wall and other building elements.

4 Detailed decisions

The performance of the wall and its parts ought now to be known, and the method of construction, cost, appearance and similar basic attributes will have been established in sufficient detail to enable architect and client to decide whether the wall type is basically satisfactory and acceptable. However, there are several other detailed decisions to be taken before the design of the whole wall assembly can be executed. The required analysis can usefully be carried out under the following headings:
● Whole wall element, ie vertical external skin as a whole, including solid panels, openings and joints
● Solid panels specifically
● Openings specifically

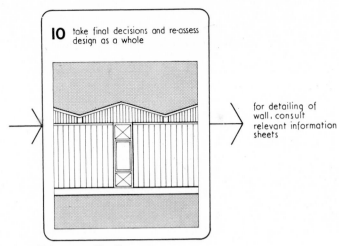

IO take final decisions and re-assess design as a whole

for detailing of wall, consult relevant information sheets

● Joints specifically
● Final decisions.

Each of these is examined separately in 4.01 to 4.05.

4.01 Wall as a whole

Water and moisture control

Rain exclusion

Of the three basic methods described in 3.03 of technical study EXTERNAL ENVELOPE 1, two will be suitable for modern conditions: a cavity wall or an impervious barrier. The former performs well and raises few problems of detailing; the latter may be subject to interstitial condensation, and usually requires a vapour barrier and a very high performance from joints.

Condensation

Risk of interstitial condensation is reduced by the following:
● Porous outer skin which allows water vapour to escape to outer air
● Ventilated and drained cavity
● Insulation incorporated near *outer* face of wall (not at inner face) so that heat from building interior is retained in wall and fabric remains warm
● Correctly-positioned vapour barrier. (See Information sheet External Envelope 1, section 2.)

Drainage

Thought must be given to passage and disposal of water collecting on or within wall as a result of rainfall or condensation. Collection of run-off can be made at base of wall, or at intermediate levels. Positions of downpipes, channels and gutters should be decided.

Thermal control

Methods should be chosen to achieve the degree of thermal insulation decided in 3.03 ('Thermal transmittance'). Available methods are:
● Rigid thermal insulating sheet or slab materials
● Low density insulating block wall materials
● Multi-leaf (cavity) construction
● Cavity with filling of insulating materials (use with great discretion—may create risk of water entry across cavity)
● Reflective surfaces. (Subject to loss of efficiency by becoming dirty).

Insolation control

If it has been decided under 3.02 ('Heat gain') to rely on sunshading devices to control insolation, more thought should now be given to their disposition, design and appearance.

Fire control

Fire-resistance and limitations on combustibility of solid parts of wall should be determined; these will depend on size of building or compartment; purpose group of building; height of wall and distance from site boundary; and numbers and sizes of openings in wall. The following factors require consideration (in relation to Regulations):
● Fire-resistance (from one or both sides; will depend on distance from site boundary, purpose group of building, and size of building or compartment)
● Combustibility and external surface spread of flame (will depend on height of relevant part of wall, distance from site boundary, and sizes and distribution of openings)
● Internal surface spread of flame (will depend on purpose group of building, size of room, and purpose of room, ie circulation or not)
● Fire stops (required in cavities, gaps in walls and junctions between compartments).

Incorporation of services

Distribution of services and their incorporation into the fabric of the building, making adequate allowance for access and future alterations (both of services and building fabric), requires careful consideration. Here the degree of flexibility required by the client/user must be carefully studied.

4.02 Solid panels

It will be known at this stage both what the basic *construction* of these is likely to be (heavy or light; large or small units, with or without secondary framing or backing; position of wall plane relative to structure; need for cavity, and general properties of materials to be used) and what the basic *sizes* of units are to be (sizes of units themselves and spacing of secondary framing). The detailed decisions that require to be finalised are the following.

Material/finish

Panels can either be *integral* (incorporating whole construction from external to internal surface), prefabricated away from final position or *assembled* in final position from separate components. Choice must be made of base materials; external and internal panel skins; insulating and other cores; secondary framing; and vapour barriers.

Considerations will include required mass; strength; thermal conductivity; combustibility and fire-resistance; dimensional stability; durability and weathering qualities; resistance to impact and other damage; appearance (texture and colour); available sizes; method of erection; availability of replacements; required profiles; and (a major constraint) cost. Similar consideration should be given to surface treatments, whether integral or applied, and it should be decided whether these should be incorporated during manufacture, eg exposed aggregate and vitreous enamelling; on site before assembly; or on site after assembly. Temporary protective finishes, eg paper or sprayed finish, should be considered.

Form

Shape and size must be checked against dimensional co-ordination requirements (information sheet ENCLOSURE 1) and manufacturing, transport and assembly considerations, in addition to the obvious requirements of performance and appearance. Tolerances must receive much closer attention than has been usual in the past (see above information sheet).

Thickness will be influenced particularly by strength requirements, eg handling and transport loads before erection, and wind and other imposed loads after erection; thermal conductivity requirements; mass requirements for thermal capacity and sound insulation; and by required profile at edges.

Edge profile will depend on jointing requirements; erection sequence and method, ie from inside or outside; method of support and attachment; junctions with adjacent components; and installation of last component.

Support and attachment

Panels can be self-supporting on main structure, eg brickwork; self-spanning and attached directly to main structural members such as beams, columns, cross walls; or supported on secondary framing members; or attached to a continuous backing. Attachment should be such that the panel is supported adequately and positioned accurately, that allowance is made for dimensional variations, and that thermal, moisture and structural movements are allowed for. Therefore anchorage devices should be adjustable in all directions, corrosion-resistant, strong enough for two-thirds of the fixings to be able to support the total load on the panel, secure and fire-resistant; and they should make allowance for movement.

Decisions to be taken are: type of anchorage, method of adjustment, material (unprotected steel or cast iron must be accessible for maintenance) and method of attachment to base material. For guidance on all these, see the AJ Handbook of Fixings and fastenings [Xt5] (AJ 24.3.71; 7 and 21.4.71).

4.03 Openings

It will be known at this stage what the size, shape and position of each opening is; the type, eg window, door or louvre; and the kind of infill required (transparent, opaque, fixed, opening and so on). The number and position of opening portions ought to be known as well as the necessary provisions for security, and protection requirements from light, heat and sound. The detailed decisions that require to be finalised are the following.

Method of opening

Opening leaf could be hinged, pivoted, sliding or removable. Its path of travel should be checked in relation to building structure and fittings, and to passing traffic.

Frame material and form

Wood sections give free choice of profile, and of ironmongery; low thermal transmission; low condensation risk; and ease of repair. On the other hand they are liable to decay and insect attack, and are subject to a high degree of moisture movement.

Metal sections are strong, dimensionally stable; complex sections are available and they may be very slender. On the other hand, they are liable to corrosion (less so if non-ferrous or properly protected) and have high thermal transmission rates.

Plastic sections have high resistance to corrosion, no moisture movement, low thermal transmission, low maintenance, and may have self-finish with integral colour. On the other hand choice of sections and fittings is limited but will no doubt increase as user demand increases. At the moment they are relatively expensive. Integral weather-stripping is a possibility.

Where frame profile is designed or selected by architect, attention should be given to strength, weather-resistance, weather-stripping, security, disposal of condensation run-off from glass and to fixing method of glass, eg from inside or outside. Jointing and gaskets should also be considered.

Infilling material and form

This will be governed by the function (or combination of functions) of the opening, which have been analysed in 3.02.

The infilling of an opening is a kind of filter, selectively admitting certain chosen aspects of the external environment, while excluding others. Thus a window might be required to admit light, but exclude heat; or allow the passage of air while excluding both light and heat; or allow the occupants of the building to view the world outside, while preventing passers-by from looking in: and similarly with doors. Therefore, types of infilling materials should be chosen for each opening, which will give the required performance within the available cost limit. For information on detailing, the relevant information sheet should be consulted.

Equipment

Method of operation must be decided for each opening (manual, by remote control or by mechanical control) and security and maintenance requirements taken into account. The following details can then be decided: suspension equipment (hinges, pulleys, pivots, counterbalances and tracks); security equipment (locks, latches, fasteners, levers, stays, sash stops, shutters, rails, bars and grilles); ventilation equipment (fixed and adjustable ventilators); miscellaneous equipment (curtain tracks, blinds, blind boxes and hooks for window cleaners).

4.04 Joints

The function of a joint is to connect adjacent components in such a way that the wall's overall performance is maintained. Therefore the joint must preserve, across the space between the adjoining components, the properties of the wall, such as thermal insulation, acoustic insulation, weather exclusion and structural strength, to a degree sufficient for the wall to function satisfactorily. In addition, the joint must allow for inaccuracies in the components or in the setting out and positioning of components; for some dimensional adjustment during erection; allow for easy maintenance of materials used in the joint, if this should be necessary; and allow in some instances for dismantling adjacent components for repair and replacement.

Joint size is likely to be a difficult decision in some instances because of the many factors to be taken into account (many of which are difficult to quantify at present owing to lack of information) while yet maintaining good appearance. See 2.04 of information sheet ENCLOSURE 1.

Joint shape may be pre-determined in some instances by the profile of a prefabricated component or product; where this is not so, shape of joint can be designed to take account of the following factors: magnitude and direction of anticipated movement in adjoining components; type of stress expected; need to protect seals; need to avoid thermal by-pass; assembly method of components (overlapping joint types may impose a left-to-right assembly sequence, or vice versa, or may create difficulties in placing the last component in position). Joint types are butt joint, lap joint (full lap or partial lap), mated joint (face-mated or edge-mated), or joints requiring a third member, eg cover strip or tongue.

Joint material will depend on stresses to which joint will be subjected (pressure, deformation, sunlight and corrosive substances); on performance requirements (water exclusion, thermal or acoustic insulation, ability to maintain properties under deformation and appearance) and on cost. For economical use of the more expensive sealing materials, it is acceptable to provide a filling of a cheaper sealant or gasket, and to point the exposed surface with a high-quality material.

Seals are of various kinds: non-curing soft seal (bituminous mastic, butyl mastic and polybutene mastic); curing soft

Table 1 Summary of environmental standards for various types of building enclosure

Use of enclosure	Daylight factor (per cent)	Sunlight penetration (hours)	Dry bulb air temperature (°C)	Ventilation rate (Changes/h)	Acceptable noise criteria (NC)
General spaces common to many building types					
Entrances	1	—	16	3	
Corridors	0·5	—	16	2	
Stairs and escalators	1	—	16	2	
Lifts and lift lobbies	1	—	16	2	
Lavatories	—	—	16 to 18	2	
Stores (General	—	—	10	½	
Cloakrooms	—	—	16	2	
Domestic spaces					
Living	1* (Over at least 8 m² and to at least half depth of room from main window)	1 Each day for at least 10 months. (Not including time when altitude of sun is less than 5°, or plan angle between plane of window and sun's rays is less than 22½°)	20 to 21	1½	35†
Bedrooms	0·5* (Over at least 6 m² and to at least half depth of room from main window)	As above	13 to 16	1	25†
Kitchens	2* (Over at least 5 m² or over 50 per cent of total floor area)	As above	16	Some mechanical extract for fumes is desirable (depends on circumstances)	
Educational spaces					
Class and lecture rooms	2	2 Morning sunshine desirable (see domestic for angular limits)	17	2	30
Assembly halls	2		14	1½	30‡
Art rooms	4§	North light	17	2	30
Laboratories	3§		17	2	30
Staff and common-rooms	1		17	2	—
Gymnasia	2		14	2	—
Dining-rooms	2		14	2	—
Other spaces					
Offices and banks	2 General 4 Machine rooms		20 19	2 2	30 to 35 private 40 to 45 general
Shops	—	—	19	2	40
Supermarkets	—	—	19	2 Mechanical ventilation may be needed	45
Restaurants	—	—	19	As above	35 to 45 ‡
Assembly and concert halls	1	—	19	Mechanical ventilation	20 to 25‡
Churches	1	—	16	1 to ½	25‡
Hospital wards	1	—	19	3	30
Factories	5 Top light may be essential to achieve this	Must sometimes be excluded	Work: 18 sedentary 16 light 13 heavy	Depends on process: extract may be needed	—
Large kitchens	2	—	—	Up to 20: mechanical extract normally needed	—

*Planning for daylight and sunlight gives a similar set of standards based on sky factor rather than daylight factor. Some architects may prefer sky factor as a standard as it is related to the design of the building, while daylight factor can be influenced by redecoration (see information sheet SUNLIGHT 2, AJ 23.10.68, AJ Handbook of Building environment [(E6)])

†For a standard of insulation appropriate to walls and floors between dwellings see chart 10 information sheet SOUND 3 (AJ 5.2.69) AJ Handbook of Building environment [(E6)]

‡In addition to noise levels special consideration of the form and finishes of the enclosure in relation to internal acoustics (see information sheet SOUND 5, AJ 12.2.69, AJ Handbook of Building environment [(E6)])

§Statutory minimum 2 per cent

Table II *Design checklist of wall properties to be considered*

Aspect	Relevant external conditions Guidance on specific values for actual sites is given in AJ Handbook of Building environment	Wall properties to be considered Wall performance should be such that desired internal conditions can be maintained in all likely external conditions. Guidance on detailed checks of factors likely to be important in AJ Handbook of Building environment	Relevant internal conditions Guidance on specific values for particular uses is given in table I, and in AJ Handbook of Building environment
Heat	**Air temperature** Design temperatures must be established for winter and summer **Radiation** from sun to building, and from building to clear night sky will depend mainly on latitude; and will be modified by cloud cover, air pollution, and shading by vegetation and other buildings **Wind** will affect external surface resistance and consequently thermal transmittance of wall **Rain and moisture** may affect transmittance	**Thermal transmittance** Building Regulations give minimum values for solid walls, but overall effect of solid and glazed areas should be taken into account. At this stage mean U-value for entire wall could be specified, to be reviewed when proportion of glazing to solid has been decided. Low U-values not only reduce heat losses, but also increase internal surface temperatures **Thermal capacity** Building of low thermal capacity will react quickly to warming or cooling effect of local climate or services installation; high thermal capacity will give slow reaction. High capacity indicated for continuously occupied and heated buildings, and where stable internal temperatures are desired. Low capacity indicated for intermittently occupied buildings, the fabric of which should be capable of quick warming-up. Latter effect may be obtained by low capacity lining to massive walls **Emissivity and absorptivity of external surfaces** will influence rate at which heat is absorbed from solar radiation during day, or lost by radiation to sky at night **Internal surface temperatures** Important determinant of thermal comfort (see 3.07 of technical study EXTERNAL ENVELOPE 1). Effect of cold window and other surfaces on thermal comfort demands attention **Proportion of glazing** affects overall transmittance and thermal capacity of wall, and governs admission of solar radiation which may create overheating problems. Orientation, external shading, and sun-control devices will affect performance as will internal finishes; eg carpets will warm up quickly, releasing heat into room, whereas solid hard floors may absorb substantial proportion of heat before releasing it into room	**Thermal comfort** depends on air temperature, mean radiant conditions, rate of air movement and relative humidity (see 3.07 of technical study EXTERNAL ENVELOPE 1) **Warm-up time** required: intermittent use demands rapid warm-up **Heating installations** Rate of heat output, nature of output and ease of control of probable installation must be taken into account when designing building fabric. Low output or slow-response systems cannot cope with temperature fluctuations of quick-response building; on the other hand large-output, quick-response systems are expensive and may not give thermal comfort because of nature of output eg warmed air systems may quickly give correct air temperature whilst leaving cold wall surfaces See also *Air* below: if overheating occurs, opening of windows is only recourse available to occupants of most buildings. So ventilation and thermal comfort must often be considered together. In turn this will necessitate consideration of *Noise* (see below); external noise sources may discourage opening of windows, leaving users in many cases with no means at all of counteracting overheating
Daylight, sunlight and prospect	**Latitude** (sun paths) **Topography and adjacent buildings**	**Windows** Orientation, shapes and sizes, and sun control devices, or special glazing, must be considered	**Daylight factor** required (see table I) **Sunlight** required admission or exclusion (see table I) **Glare** **Views** Occupants' desire to see outside
Air	**Wind** Prevailing *direction* and typical local *velocities* will be modified by presence of adjacent buildings and by site topography. Flow patterns can be investigated more effectively by wind-tunnel tests than by calculation **Pollution** Amount of dust, grit, smoke, or chemical pollutants in air, and positions of sources relative to building and wind direction	**Air infiltration** through window and door cracks, and through fabric of wall constitutes an important element in heat loss of most buildings **Window-opening areas and positions** Natural ventilation is effective only in low buildings with relatively small rooms. Also, problem of noise penetration will interact with that of ventilation in many instances **Ventilation openings other than windows,** eg flues and vents (see notes above) **Noise** Air turbulence set up by projections from building surface may generate noise, particularly in high buildings **Strength** Walls and claddings, and glazing to windows must be capable of withstanding likely wind velocities (see information sheet EXTERNAL WALLS 8)	**Rate of air change** Consider both hygiene and thermal requirements **Patterns of air movement** For summer ventilation and cooling, air movement should be induced at working height; for winter ventilation, openings at high level are preferable

Sound	**Noise sources**	**Transmission** In all cases transmission of total wall element (including openings), not merely solid part of wall, should be considered. Note that transmission may be from other spaces in building, as well as from outside	**Acceptable internal noise levels** Usually determined by speech-interference, but more stringent standards may apply, eg in auditoria (see table I)
	Topography and adjacent buildings Traffic—distance away		
			Acoustic performance of internal wall surfaces (to avoid echoes and reverberation and to give proper sound distribution in rooms such as class rooms and halls)
		Absorption of internal surfaces will affect acoustic properties of rooms; effect may be critical in specialised spaces such as classrooms, auditoria and general purpose halls which may be used for meetings	**Internal noise sources** which may give rise to airborne or structural transmission to other spaces in building
		Windows (opening) There is a close interaction, particularly in summer, between conditions of thermal comfort, ventilation and noise exclusion (see relevant paragraphs above). If windows are required to be opened for ventilation or cooling, noise transmission calculations for wall should be based on open-window situation	
Moisture	**Precipitation** (rainfall, index of driving rain and snow)	**Water exclusion** By permeable barrier, cavity, or impervious barrier (see 3.03 of technical study EXTERNAL ENVELOPE 1). Attention must be given to joints, hazard of water or snow retention (particularly where subsequent freezing can occur), and pattern staining due to surface modelling etc	**Vapour input** by building occupants and processes such as washing. Rate of moisture dissipation from building interior is governed by rate of air change; if latter is inadequate in winter, condensation risk will result
	Vapour in air (see also *Heat* above)	**Water run-off** Special provisions may be required, particularly in high buildings with impervious claddings (4·05)	**Relative humidity** should be maintained between 30 and 65 per cent for human comfort (some medical experts prefer 70 RH)
		Condensation resistance Structural temperatures within (or on) the wall fabric should always be kept above dewpoint temperature. It is important to position thermally-resistant components of composite walls near outside face, and vapour-resistant components near inside face (see 3.03 of technical study EXTERNAL ENVELOPE 1), and to carry out geometric or arithmetic checks (see 'Condensation in buildings' AJ 19.5.71, 26.5.71 and 2.6.71) to ascertain condensation risk. If there is unavoidable risk of condensation, suitable materials must be chosen to minimise nuisance and avoid deterioration of building fabric. Often it will be impossible to avoid condensation on window surfaces (even when double-glazed) and provision must be made to cope with water run-off from glass	
Fire	**Proximity** of site boundary, other buildings and special fire risks, eg car-parking* and flammable materials storage	**Flame spread,** particularly on internal surfaces **Combustibility**	**Fire risk** **Means of escape**
	Access for fire brigade	**Fire-resistance**	**Automatic sprinkler system**
Durability and dirt	**Pollution sources,** eg chimneys, traffic, industrial areas, salt spray from sea (in favourable topography may be carried well inland)	**Materials and finishes** Should be appropriate to site conditions, eg risk of vandalism	**Internal dirt sources,** particularly traffic past wall surfaces
		Constructional details should be designed to avoid build-up of corrosive or dirt deposits, and to allow easy cleaning of wall surfaces and windows	
		Window-cleaning Built-in equipment may be required	
Infestation		**Surfaces** should be smooth, impervious and easy to clean, and free from cracks which could harbour infestation	Special risks will be associated with certain building types or uses, and special requirements will apply to, eg hospitals, food stores
		Wall construction and materials Internal voids, eg services ducts, are particularly troublesome source of nuisance	
Security	**Ease of unobserved access**	**Wall construction** should be of physical strength appropriate to degree of risk, and adequate to resist accidental damage and deliberate attempts at vandalism or entry	**Nature of contents**
	Character of neighbourhood		**Degree of supervision**
			Burglar alarms
		Openings Doors and windows should be placed so as to minimise risk of entry, and equipped with locking devices adequate to degree of security required (see 4.02 of technical study EXTERNAL ENVELOPE 1)	

* Parked cars actually constitute a low fire load in comparison with say a whisky warehouse but good ventilation is important

seals (polysulphide rubber, curing butyl rubber, acrylic and polyurethane); and compression seals (butyl rubber, neoprene, hypalon, pvc, silicone rubber, metal strip pile or plush tape). *Gaskets* can be filler strip (inlock gasket); hollow tubes; applied beads, or enclosures; and method of forming corners must be decided, eg by site fusion (pvc only), shop welding, preformed angles, adhesive, or by rounded corners.

4.05 Final decisions

Detailed design decisions have now been taken on the design first of the whole wall element (4.01); followed by the solid panels incorporated in the wall (4.02); the openings (4.03); and the joints (4.04). It is now possible to undertake a final review of the design as a whole, before going on to the detailing of the wall assembly in accordance with the data given in the relevant information sheets. This review can be carried out under three headings: drainage, cleaning and maintenance, and assessment.

Drainage
The drainage system of the total wall assembly should be completed, and final decisions taken on sizes, positions and materials of channels, gutters and downpipes; outlet connections to surface water drainage system; and flashings and protective coverings. Rainwater disposal, condensation and cavity drainage should be considered. It should be remembered when calculating rainwater flow quantities that a tall building in conditions of driving rain will receive far more water on the wall facing the wind than on the roof—thus the correct position for collecting gutters may be at first floor level rather than roof eaves level (or both).

Cleaning and maintenance
Most of the decisions taken during the detailed design of the wall will have been influenced by client's maintenance policy. Materials will have been chosen with this consideration in mind, and some access to wall surfaces may have been provided (by projecting floors, or from opening windows).
Final decisions must now be taken on method of cleaning surfaces, and method of access. Methods of access should be provided both for cleaning and for occasional repair, and it should not be assumed that these methods will necessarily be the same. The following matters require consideration: supports for ladders (both at foot and at top); supports for cradles (roof runways, projecting supports, and whether supports are to be permanent or temporary); guides for cradle (vertical tracks and ropes); accommodation for equipment when not in use; water supply for washing (ideally by hose from bayonet fitted cocks on wall surface).

Assessment
A final check should now be carried out for satisfaction of performance requirements, compliance with legal provisions and for design faults. The following is a checklist of important points:
● Statutory requirements (fire, light, ventilation, thermal transmittance, escape and access for maintenance)
● Environmental requirements (amount and quality of daylight, heat gain and loss, sound reduction, ventilation and views of outside, balanced against need for privacy)
● Security requirements (with particular attention to location and burglar-proofing of windows/doors/louvres)
● Structural requirements (loadings)
● Aesthetic requirements (appearance when new, and avoidance of unacceptable changes in appearance due to

staining, chemical changes or physical damage)
● Travel of opening windows and doors
● Incorporation of services
● Trade sequence
● Cost
At this stage the basic design of the building's external vertical skin will be complete, and the detailing of the chosen wall assembly can begin, using the appropriate information sheet(s) as a guide to construction.

5 Checklist

5.01 Decide performance requirements

● Environmental requirements (see 2.01, and 3 in technical study EXTERNAL ENVELOPE 1)
● Security requirements (see 4.02 in technical study EXTERNAL ENVELOPE 1)
● Structural requirements (see 2.03)
● Aesthetic requirements (see 2.04).

5.02 Take basic decisions

● Sizes, shapes and positions of openings in walls (see 3.01)
● Characteristic of openings (see 3.02)
● Characteristics of solid portions of wall (see 3.03).

5.03 Review basic decisions

5.04 Take detailed decisions

● Detailed decisions on vertical external skin as a whole (see 4.01)
● Detailed design of solid panels (see 4.02)
● Detailed design of openings (see 4.03)
● Joints (see 4.04).

5.05 Take final decisions

● Drainage of wall (see 4.05)
● Cleaning and maintenance of wall (see 4.05).

5.06 Assessment

● Review and re-assess design as a whole before proceeding to detailing.

6 References

1 ROSTRON, R. M. Light cladding of buildings. London, 1964, Architectural Press [(21)]
2 AJ Handbook of Building environment [(E6)]: (AJ 2.10.68 to 13.8.69)
3 AJ Handbook of Building structure [(2–)] (AJ 8.3.72 to September 1973 to be published as a book in 1974).
4 ELDER, A. J. Guide to the Building Regulations 1972. London, 2nd edition, 1973, Architectural Press [(A3j)]
5 Cost planning and cost control (AJ 3, 10 and 24.11.65) [(A4)]

Information sheet
External walls 1

Masonry

This information sheet is concerned with the use of masonry in external walls. Masonry may be defined as a wall construction in which bricks or blocks are bonded together with mortar. Bricks may be of clay, sandlime, flintlime or concrete. Blocks may be of clay, aerated (gas) concrete, lightweight aggregate concrete, dense aggregate concrete, natural stone or cast stone*. The study is by HOWARD NASH

1 Types of external wall

1.01 Single leaf and solid walls

Masonry walls built before about 1930 are usually solid. These walls rely on a process of absorption and subsequent re-evaporation of rainwater close to the outer face (see 3.03 of technical study EXTERNAL ENVELOPE 1). Successful exclusion of damp depends on the absorptive capacity of the wall and its degree of exposure. External render effectively increases resistance to rain penetration, particularly the flow of water into cracks at perpends. Rendered walls of single-leaf concrete blockwork can be designed to exclude water and achieve required standards of insulation **1**. It is important to remember however that rendering which prevents water getting into masonry also prevents it drying out. Rendering is also notorious for cracking and even hair cracks will allow some water through. This then disperses into the masonry and since it cannot dry outwards, its only route is inwards. Unfortunate owners who have tried rendering (especially the cement/sand variety) as a cure for dampness inside have often finished up in a worse state than before. Other solid and single-leaf walls will however generally be confined either to low-grade buildings where

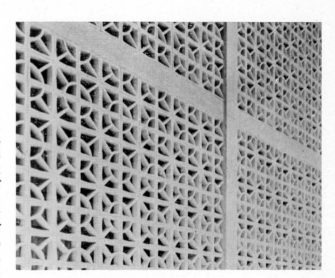

2 *Hollow blocks in screen wall*

periodic dampness is not critical or to screen walls of pierced or horizontally hollow blocks in areas where free ventilation is required, eg covered car-parking areas **2**.

The v-brick developed by BRS is designed to allow a cavity wall to be constructed as a single leaf and is an exception to the general rule **3**.

1.02 Cavity walls

The cavity wall is designed so that rainwater may penetrate to the inner face of the outer leaf. It therefore depends for its effectiveness upon methods of detailing and standards of workmanship that prevent water crossing the cavity and allow for discharge at the bottom.

The wide variety of performance standards that can be achieved by combining various materials for inner and outer leaves accounts for the continued use of cavity walling as infill to framed buildings in addition to use in simple and complex loadbearing masonry structure.

Design strength of a cavity wall of 112·5 mm brick leaves is less than that of a solid 225 mm wall by about 10 per cent at the lower end of the slenderness ratio scale and about 33 per cent less at the higher end, but depends in some degree on the compressive strength of the wall ties.

1.03 Composite walls

Masonry may be used as a backing to an external skin or may itself be used as an external skin. BS CP 111: 1964[1] draws a distinction between *faced walls* in which facing and backing are so bonded as to result in a common action under load, and *veneered walls* in which there is no common action. An example of faced walls is the traditional masonry

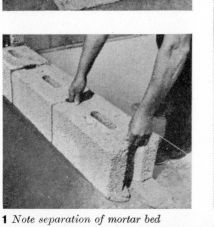

1 *Note separation of mortar bed*

* Concrete blocks will be discussed more fully in **information sheet** EXTERNAL
WALLS 2

3 BRS V-*brick*

technique of bonding ashlar facing work to brick or rubble backing **4** to form a solid wall. Typical veneered walls are illustrated in **5**, **6**. Rigid bonding of facing and backing where the materials tend to have different movement characteristics, eg brick and concrete, should generally be avoided. Cavity construction using wire ties will allow a certain amount of differential movement and is preferable.

1.04 Clad masonry walls

Single-leaf and solid masonry walls may be used as a backing to a cladding system. The brick or block leaf may support the cladding, eg tile hanging, weatherboarding, or may be added to improve thermal or fire performance of the cladding system, eg back-up walls to curtain walling, **7**, **8**.

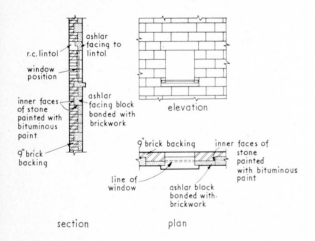

4 *Traditional facing technique*

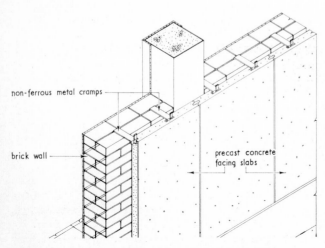

5 *Traditional method of attaching natural stone slabs to brickwork, equally applicable to concrete facing slabs*

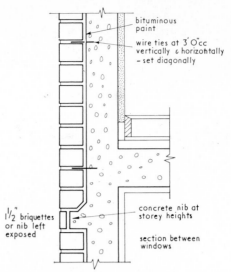

6 *Brick veneer*

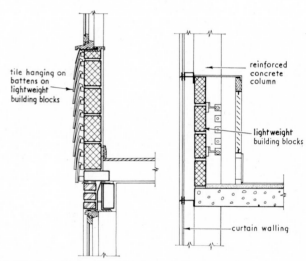

7 *Tile hanging on block back-up wall*
8 *Curtain walling on block back-up wall*

2 Bricks, blocks and mortars

2.01 Bricks and blocks

BS 3921[2] defines a brick as a walling unit not exceeding 337·5 mm long × 225 mm wide × 112·5 mm high. A block is a walling unit larger than a brick whose height does not exceed its length or six times its thickness. BS 3921 classifies bricks according to quantity, variety and type (table I). Concrete blocks are classified by BS 2028, 1364[3] according to form and type. Classification of type is now based on density and is irrespective of materials or methods of manufacture (table II).

A simplified guide to bricks is given in table III, while **9** is a guide to the textures of facing bricks. Table IV is a guide to concrete and cast stone blocks. More detailed information on concrete blocks is given in the AJ special issue on concrete blockwork[4].

2.02 Mortars

Mortar should combine good working properties with early development of strength. Mature strength should be no

Table I *Classification of bricks*

Variety Common; facing; engineering

Quality Internal; ordinary; special (low content of soluble salts)

Types
Solid Small perforations less than 25 per cent volume. Frogs less than 20 per cent volume

Perforated Small perforations greater than 25 per cent volume. Obtainable for both vertical and horizontal use

Hollow Holes through brick greater than 25 per cent volume. Obtainable for both vertical and horizontal use

Cavity Closed-end cavities less than 50 per cent volume

Table II *Classification of concrete blocks*

Types
A Greater than 1500 kg/m³ general use in building including below ground level dpc

B General use in building including below dpc in internal walls and inner leaves of cavity walls

C Primarily for internal non-loadbearing walls

Forms
Solid Cavities less than 25 per cent volume

Hollow Holes through block less than 50 per cent volume

Cellular Closed-end cavities less than 50 per cent volume

Special faces Profiled face or Special face on backing

Table III *Simplified guide to clay, silicate and concrete bricks*

Material	BS no	Manufacture	Varieties	Usual surface texture	Origin	Examples	Notes
Clay	BS 3921: Part 1: 1967 Part 2: 1970	1 Soft mud process (hand-made or machine-made)	Mainly facings	Sand-creased (hand-made or machine-made)	Mainly South-east England	Most multi-coloured stocks. London stocks	About 40 per cent of clay bricks are produced by semi-dry pressing. Most of these are made from Oxford clay. They owe their price competitiveness to the presence of natural fuel within the clay. Stiff plastic pressed and extruded wirecut bricks account for about 25 per cent of output
		2 Extruded wirecuts (subsequent pressing possible)	Commons Facings Engineering	Smooth Sandfaced Combed Dragged/rippled	General	Most Russets and Rustics	
		3 Semi-dry pressed	Commons Facings	Smooth Sandfaced Stippled	Mainly Cambridgeshire, Bedfordshire, Peterborough	Flettons	Apart from reversible movement, clay bricks are subject to permanent expansion. This expansion is largely taken up within a few days of firing but continues at a reduced rate over several years
		4 Stiff-plastic pressed	Commons Facings Engineering	Smooth Sandfaced Stippled	Scotland North-east England West Riding Lancashire Staffordshire South Wales	Staffordshire blues	
Calcium silicate (sandlime and flintlime)	BS 187: Part 1: 1967 Part 2: 1970	Pressed and autoclaved	Commons Facings Engineering	Generally uniform and fine but can be rough textured	North and central Scotland, North-east, north-west, south-east, south-west England, Midlands	—	Subject to fairly high reversible movement but largely unaffected by efflorescence, sulphates and frost
Concrete	BS 1180: 1944	Pressed and cured	Facings Commons	Rough texture can be produced by splitting	General	—	Subject to small irreversible shrinkage. Can be manufactured to close tolerances

Table IV *Concrete and cast stone blocks*

Material	BS no	Name	Aggregate	Curing	Notes
Concrete	BS 2028, 1364: 1968	Aerated (gas) autoclaved concrete blocks	Sand (Durox, Siporex) Pfa (Celcon, Thermalite)	Autoclaved only	All concrete blocks are subject to permanent drying shrinking. Aerated blocks are solid only
		Lightweight aggregate concrete blocks	Clinker Foamed slag Sintered pfa (Lytag) Expanded clay (Leca Aglite) Expanded shale and slate (Solite) Wood sawdust (Lignacite)	Air or steam cured Autoclaved CO₂ cured	Pfa stands for Pulverised fuel ash (a by-product generally from electricity generation)
		Dense aggregate concrete blocks	Natural gravels ⎱ to Granite ⎰ BS Limestone ⎱ 882: Local stones ⎰ 1965 Dense slag to BS 1047: 1952	Air or steam cured Autoclaved CO₂ cured	
Cast stone	BS 1217: 1947	Reconstructed stone	Aggregate is crushed stone of the type to be simulated		Although intended primarily as substitute for natural stone, reconstructed stone will generally behave as concrete, being subject to drying shrinkage. Texture is smooth and fine but blocks can be split to provide rough textured face

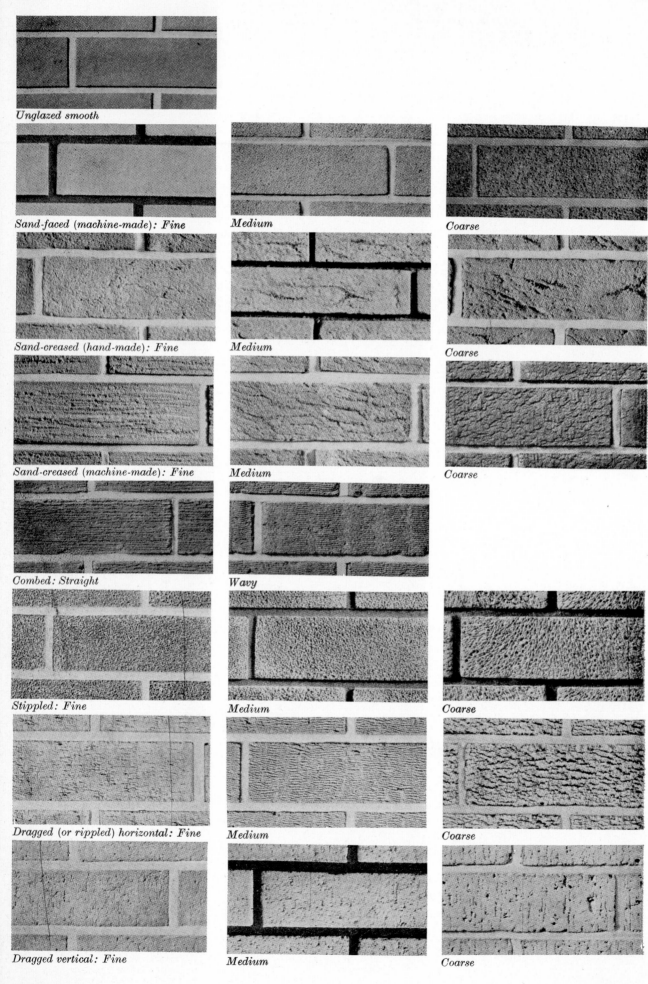

Unglazed smooth

Sand-faced (machine-made): *Fine*   *Medium*   *Coarse*

Sand-creased (hand-made): *Fine*   *Medium*   *Coarse*

Sand-creased (machine-made): *Fine*   *Medium*   *Coarse*

Combed: *Straight*   *Wavy*

Stippled: *Fine*   *Medium*   *Coarse*

Dragged (or rippled) horizontal: *Fine*   *Medium*   *Coarse*

Dragged vertical: *Fine*   *Medium*   *Coarse*

9 *Brick textures*

greater than is needed for structural design (see tables I and II, BRS Digest 58[22]) Loading tests on walls and piers have shown that strength of mortar has less influence on strength of brickwork than is generally supposed **10**. Since a weaker mortar more readily accommodates differential movement and distributes cracking as hair cracks at joints, the weakest suitable mix should always be chosen. Strong joints may cause cracking of blocks and bricks and spalling of the face. Mortar is, in effect, a multi-part adhesive, each part being chosen for different functions:

Sand is the basic filler and provides the body necessary to take up tolerances in size of bricks and blocks, inequalities in shape and adjustment between the module of the block and the size of the finished wall. It is also the principal colouring medium.

Cement is now the standard 'adhesive' element. High cement content gives high strength but provides rigid joints with associated problems. High cement content also gives a 'fat' mix which is easy to lay.

Lime is an alternative binder, not greatly used on its own because of slow setting times, cost and low strength. It must however be used when matching old work. It forms an excellent plasticiser which provides an easy 'fat' mortar with good early binding properties and a joint of good porosity and adequate strength.

Plasticisers are used to make mortar easy to lay. Careless or dishonest bricklayers may use excessive plasticiser to reduce cement content. (Although one of the objects of using such admixtures is to reduce the cement content and hence the risk of cracking).

2.03 Wall ties

BRS Digest 61[5] states: 'Wall ties are intended to share lateral forces and deflects between the two leaves. The butterfly type metal wall tie is the weakest in this respect and its use should generally be confined to two-storey work. (A solid galvanised twisted tie should otherwise be used.) Metal ties should conform to BS 1243[6].

2.04 Damp-proof courses

Dpcs should conform to BS 743[7] *Materials for damp-proof courses*. Reference may also be made to BS CP 102[8] (see table I, BRS Digest 77[9]).

3 Construction notes

3.01 Non-loadbearing infill panels

The structural properties of masonry are only partly determined by the separate properties of the bricks or blocks and the mortar. The units are strong in compression while the mortar is usually weaker and has greater elasticity. While both mortar and units themselves have considerable tensile strength, the interface of block and mortar in a completed wall has very little strength in tension. This is critical in non-loadbearing infill panels where resistance to lateral load from wind pressure or suction is not assisted by precompression from loads on the wall (the revision to BS CP 3 chapter 7[10] resulting in higher local design loads necessitated by wind has aggravated this problem yet further). Also the tops of such panels cannot generally be built up rigidly to the frame owing to the risks of:

● deflection in the frame
● shrinkage in the case of a reinforced concrete frame
● movement in the brickwork/blockwork **11**.

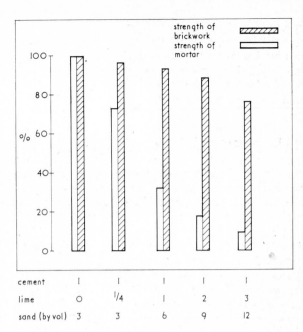

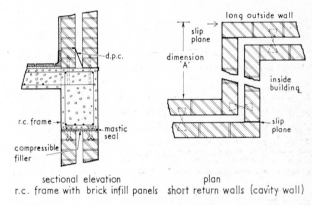

10 *Effects of mortar mix proportions on crushing strengths of mortar and brickwork built with medium-strength bricks. Strengths are shown relative to strength of 1:3 cement-sand mortar and brickwork with it*

11 *Brick infill panels*   **12** *Cavity wall returns*

However, it is sometimes assumed that this is exactly what is done.

Experiments are under way to help to find solutions to this ever-present difficulty. District surveyors in London have accepted the use of small vertical cantilever concrete members the combined thickness of the inner skin and the cavity, placed at about 6ft centres (1830 mm) or of a sill beam in reinforced concrete designed to span horizontally between the adjacent structural members of the frame. The brick wall is then allowed to span the short distance between floor and sill beam. Where large windows are supported on the sill of a small cavity wall, the sill itself, in either timber or metal, can be used as a beam spanning between the main structural members or between the special cantilever beams mentioned above. Alternatively, the panel can rest on the frame, have a soft mortar fill at its head as the frame connection, and steel ties into the structural frame from its sides with a soft pack at its joint with the structural frame.

3.02 Loadbearing cavity walls

BS CP 111[1] recommends that the outer leaf of loadbearing cavity walls should be supported at intervals of every third storey or every 9 m (30ft) so that differential movement does not loosen the ties. (Buildings of 12 m (40ft) or four storeys, whichever is less, are exempted from the recommendation.) These walls frequently occur at the gable end of loadbearing cross-wall buildings and the requirement for support can be met by projecting the floor slab through both leaves. When brick slips are used to conceal the slab it should be noted that the bearing area of the outer leaf is reduced **6**. See Product selection for architects: Clay bricks and blocks 2. Specification in practice[11] for discussion of problems associated with use of brick slips.

3.03 Movement joints

Vertical movements in walls are generally reversible, but horizontal movements may be reversible only if the wall does not crack as a result of the expansion or contraction. Movement may occur as a result of variations in temperature (reversible), variations in moisture content (reversible), permanent creep or shrinkage, movement in adjacent materials, deflections and settlement.

As a rough guide, long unrestrained walls of clay brickwork should generally be provided with 10 mm movement joints at about 13 m intervals. More frequent intervals of 6 to 8 mm will generally be necessary for calcium silicate bricks, lightweight concrete blocks and cavity walls of differing leaves.

At offsets and junctions in long walls movement can cause concentrations of stress to build up. Short returns of 675 mm or less are particularly subject to cracking **12**.

3.04 Formation of openings

The working load to be carried by a lintel over a small simple opening may generally be taken to include:
● the load of masonry contained within a 60° triangle with base equal to the effective span
● floor loads (if applicable), generally taken as a uniformly distributed load (depending on height above lintel).

Lintels are traditionally reinforced concrete, precast on site. Manufactured lintels are available in galvanised mild steel (Dorman Long) and prestressed concrete (Spanlite). The latter are one brick course deep and act with the masonry over to form a composite wall beam. BS 1239[14] covers manufactured cast concrete lintels. Simple rectangular lintels in reinforced concrete designed to a range of safe distributed loads can be found in technical tables[14]. More complex situations should be referred to a structural engineer.

4 Metrication and dimensional co-ordination

The BS metric brick format is 225 mm × 112·5 mm × 75 mm, being a metric rationalisation of the previous standard imperial brick. There are inevitable difficulties in using such bricks within a metric dimensional framework based on vertical and horizontal controlling dimensions that are multiples of 100 mm.

In public authority housing work, the mandatory floor-to-floor height of 2600 mm does not coincide with brick coursing at four courses to 300 mm, while the alternative of 34 courses to 2600 produces irregular dimensions at all intermediate levels (see AJ 8.9.71 building study p517-530). Various devices have been suggested to overcome problems in two-storey work **13**, but no solution is possible in blocks of flats and maisonettes unless the floor is expressed as a string course.

Because of these difficulties some manufacturers are producing metric modular bricks with a format of 300 mm × 100 mm × 100 mm and 200 mm × 100 mm × 100 mm.

14 *Third bond brickwork used in metric housing scheme*

Using 300 mm bricks laid in third bond, horizontal increments of 100 mm are possible, although a 200 mm brick must be used to complete at corners and around openings if cutting is to be avoided **14**. Alternatively 200 mm bricks only may be laid in half-bond. It should be noted that leaf thickness is only 90 mm with consequent effects upon slenderness ratios, thermal insulation and mass.

Semi-modular brick formats of limited availability are:
● 300 mm × 100 mm × 75 mm and 200 mm × 100 mm × 75 mm
● imported bricks based on three courses to 200 mm.

Calcium silicate bricks cannot be produced to a format of 300 mm × 100 mm × 100 mm but other modular sizes are available.

5 Frost attack, sulphate attack, efflorescence[29]

These are perennial problems with masonry construction, particularly where walls are exposed to continual wetting.

5.01 Frost attack

When water in masonry freezes, frost attack can have the following effects: surface crumbling of soft mortar; surface powdering of soft bricks; flaking or disruption of bricks or blocks with low frost resistance.

Materials to be used in exposed conditions, eg parapets, or work from ground to dpc, should be carefully specified. Raked joints should be avoided for masonry units with low frost resistance (eg fletton bricks).

5.02 Sulphate attack

Sulphate attack depends on the chemical action of soluble sulphates, which are present in varying quantities in most bricks, and tricalcium aluminate, a constituent of ordinary Portland cement. Continual wetting and drying of brickwork will cause the diffusion of salts in bricks into the mortar causing its expansion and ultimate disintegration. Precautions include:
● design to avoid the likelihood of repeated saturation of

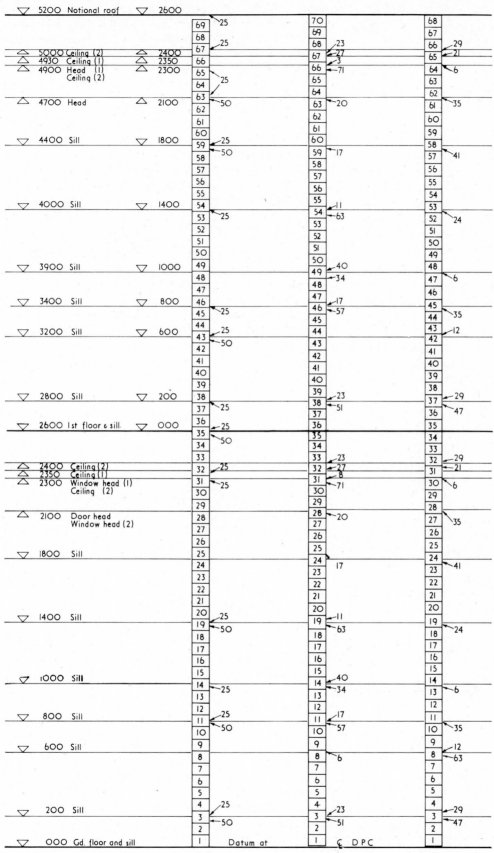

MOH & LG PREFERRED LEVELS   4 COURSES = 300 MM   35 COURSES = 2600 MM   34 COURSES = 2600 MM
(see also BS.4330: 1968)

BRICKWORK COURSING HEIGHTS

13 *Brickwork courses relative to preferred local authority floor levels show discrepancies which can occur in typical two-storey housing. Each number in vertical columns represents a 75 mm course. Bed joint is typically 10 mm thick (eg first column, course 3, occurs 50 mm below and 25 mm above 200 mm sill level)*

the body of the brickwork
● specification of sulphate-resisting cements or selection of bricks with low sulphate content where high degrees of exposure are inevitable **15**.

5.03 Efflorescence

Efflorescence is the most common defect. It is caused by crystallisation of salts derived generally from the mortar and/or brick, and is usually harmless though unsightly. Persistent efflorescence is an indication that water is able to percolate through the body of the brickwork, as commonly occurs in parapets of faulty design. Mortars which are denser and more impermeable than the brick cause water absorption and evaporation to take place predominantly through the brick, with the risk that any efflorescence will be concentrated where it is most unsightly **16**.

15 *Oversailing caused by moisture activity at dpc*

16 *Efflorescence*

6 References

BRITISH STANDARDS INSTITUTION
1 BS CP 111 Part 1: 1964 Imperial units; Part 2: 1970 Metric units. Structural loadbearing walls [(21·1) (K)]
2 BS 3921 Part 1: 1965 Imperial units; Part 2: 1969 Metric units. Standard special bricks [(Fg)]
3 BS 2028 and 1364: 1968. Precast concrete blocks [(Ff)]

4 GAGE, M. Concrete blockwork. *Architects' Journal*, 1970, April 8, p845–906 [(Ff)] *Special issue*
5 BUILDING RESEARCH STATION Digest 61 Strength of brickwork, blockwork and concrete walls. 1965, HMSO [(21·1) (K)]

BRITISH STANDARDS INSTITUTION
6 BS 1243. Metal ties for cavity wall construction [(21·1) t6]
7 BS 743: 1964. Metric units. Materials for damp-proof courses [(9) Yy (12)]
8 BS 102: 1963. Protection of buildings against water from the ground [(12)]

9 BUILDING RESEARCH STATION Digest 77 Damp-proof courses. 1966, HMSO [(9) Yy (12)]
10 BRITISH STANDARDS INSTITUTION BS CP 3: Chapter 7: 1970. Engineering and utility services [(5–)]
11 FOSTER, D. Clay bricks and blocks: specification in practice. RIBA *Journal*, 1970, April, p171–176 [Fg (A3u)]
12 BRITISH STANDARDS INSTITUTION BS 1239: 1956. Sills and lintels: cast concrete lintels [(31)Gy]
13 ASSOCIATION OF BUILDING TECHNICIANS Building technicians' diary. London, 1969, the Association [(Abd)] *p51*

BRITISH STANDARDS INSTITUTION
14 BS 1236 to 1240: 1956. Sills and lintels [(31) Gy]
15 BS 1217: 1945. Cast stone [Yf3]
16 BS 187: 1967. Calcium silicate (sandlime and flintlime), bricks [Ff1]
17 BS 1180: 1944. Concrete bricks and fixing bricks [Ff2]

18 HEAF, E. Building structure: masonry. *Architects' Journal*, 1967, May 3, p1081–1091 [(2–) Ge (A3)] *Design guide*
19 CLAY PRODUCTS TECHNICAL BUREAU Technical notes, vol 1, no 10 Movement joints in brickwork. London, 1966, the Bureau [(9–) Fy (S6)]
20 NATIONAL FEDERATION OF CLAY INDUSTRIES Efflorescence and staining of brickwork. Reprinted from *Brick Bulletin*, vol 3, no 5. London, 1920 [Fy (16)]

BUILDING RESEARCH STATION
(Following all published by HMSO)
21 Digests 16 and 17: Parts 1 and 2 Aerated concrete. 1961 [Yq6 (E1)]
22 Digest 58 Mortars for jointing. 1965 [Yq4]
23 Digest 89 Sulphate attack on brickwork. 1968 [Fg2 (S2)]
24 Digest 111 Lightweight aggregate concretes. 1969 [Yq 7 (K)]
25 Digest 123 Lightweight aggregate concretes. 1970 [Yq7]

26 WEST, H. W. H. Clay bricks and blocks: selection criteria. RIBA *Journal*, 1970, April, p169–171 [Fg (A3u)]
27 KIRKBRIDE, T. W. Loadbearing concrete blockwork for housing. RIBA *Journal*, 1968, November, p516–519 [814 (21·1) Ff]
28 BRICK DEVELOPMENT ASSOCIATION Loadbearing brickwork: design for the fifth amendment, 1970, London, the Association [(21·1) Ff (A3)]
29 FOSTER, D. Failures in brickwork. *Architects' Journal*, 1971, October 6, p767-776 [(21) Fg2 (5)]

Information sheet
External walls 2

Concrete

This information sheet is concerned with the uses of concrete in external walls. It includes descriptions of the types of concrete available, site and factory production methods and suggestions for use. The author is HOWARD NASH

1 Types of concrete

1.01 Conventional

Conventional dense concrete is suitable for most applications. Design limitations and steel cover are documented in the Building Regulations. The nature of the concrete will change with the proportions of the mix. Its colour and texture can be varied by the choice of aggregate and cement.

1.02 Lightweight

Lightweight concrete is made by omitting as much sand, gravel or crushed rock as possible and compensating by various manufacturing processes that result in several types described below. Advantages:
● Low thermal conductivity, so it has better heat insulation than conventional type
● Easily cut and nailed
● Good base for fixings
● Can be, perhaps, better left fairface for decoration.

Elimination of plastering
There is evidence that plaster does not always adhere to lightweight concrete owing to the difference in thermal expansion combined with moisture content, possibly because of particular site conditions. This would make it advisable to design to a fairface finish and eliminate the cost of plastering, not to mention another wet trade in the construction sequence. In this instance care must be taken with running of services as there will be no plaster to cover chases or discrepancies. Also door details may become more economic: sub-frames would be superfluous and frames would decrease in width.

1.03 Aerated concrete

Bubbles of air or gas are formed in a plastic mortar. After the material has set, this porous structure remains[1]. Major uses[2]:
● Concrete blocks
● Reinforced precast slabs for structural walls, floors and roofs
● Non-loadbearing precast slabs as infill to framed buildings. Generally requires protection from the weather by rendering or other surface treatment.

1.04 Lightweight aggregate concrete

Concrete in which aggregates such as clinker, foamed slag, expanded clays and shales and pumice are used.

Major uses:
● Concrete blocks
● Partially compacted for in situ wall construction (non-structural)
● Fully compacted and of strength suitable for reinforced construction, both in situ and precast. (Full compaction is necessary to give satisfactory bond and cover to reinforcement. Greater cover than for dense aggregate concrete is also necessary[3].)

1.05 No-fines concrete

Made either with a lightweight aggregate or a heavy aggregate such as gravel—by omitting the fine aggregate. In addition to the advantages of lightweight concrete generally, this has light shuttering, low drying shrinkage and resistance to water penetration by capillary action. Characterised by low tensile and shear strengths, light reinforcement is necessary over openings[4]. External rendering is essential to control penetration, plus detailing which ensures that such water as penetrates the render is discharged effectively at lintels and at the base of the wall.

2 Production methods

2.01 Site methods

Although conventional concrete is one of the most dense and seemingly impermeable materials in common use, rain exclusion is difficult to overcome. This is due to the high water run-off from the wall which may find its way to the interior through any local crack or defect. So control of shrinkage cracking by suitable reinforcement is essential (even if it is not required for structural purposes) or use of no-fines should be considered instead (see 1.05). Uniformity is a constant problem; it can only be achieved by careful supervision or accepted to be impossible; each pour is then distinctly separated. Sufficient gripping surface for each lift must be given. It is extremely difficult to achieve a perfect finish on both sides of the concrete.
Finishes to in situ concrete are covered comprehensively in an AJ special issue (14.2.68[5]). Small items such as lintels and sills may be precast on site.

2.02 Precast panels

Types used as facings **1**:
● Undersill cladding panels **2**
● Storey-height non-structural cladding panels **3**
● Structural cladding panels **4**

● Permanent shuttering **5**.

Types used as cladding:

● Those which are in effect the outer leaf of a cavity wall and are normally 50 to 100 mm thick, stiffened by projecting sills

● Those which are in the form of a 150 to 200 mm sandwich, incorporating an insulant, and to which no back-up walling is necessary.

Both cladding types may incorporate windows and other openings.

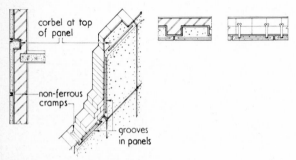

1 *Traditional masonry facing techniques not now in general use, but still suitable for small units, particularly those in difficult fixing locations*

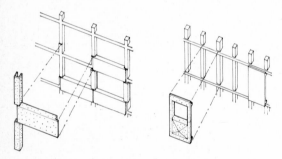

2 *Second fixed cladding: whole bay undersill panels with or without separate column-cladding units (left)*
3 *Second fixed cladding: storey-height wall panels with or without integral window openings (right)*

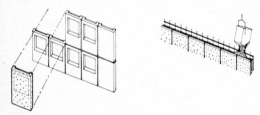

4 *Structural cladding units (left) here shown as storey-height but they may be greater. Alternative structural cladding system consists of separate column and beam units where beam also functions as undersill-cladding panel*
5 *Permanent shuttering to in situ concrete walling (right)*

2.03 Precast factory methods

Conventional methods of precasting wall units usually rely on horizontal casting **6**. Normally a 24-hour cycle is adopted, producing five castings from a mould in one week. According to the relative economics of the job, these are then lifted horizontally, after adequate curing, or, after minimum curing, the mould is rotated to allow the member to be lifted vertically. Development of industrialised building systems has resulted in further techniques.

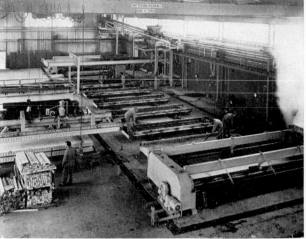

6 *Floor panel production shop*

7 *'Chevron' battery casting*

2.04 Battery casting

Panels are cast vertically between two finished faces of a 'battery' of moulds* large enough to allow a production rate compatible with the planned rate of erection. Further development by BRS has led to a technique of precasting by 'Chevron' battery casting units **7** that are L-shaped on plan.

2.05 Pressing

The pressing method of precasting panels depends on the pouring of a very wet mix concrete into an adjustable mould capable of achieving various sizes and edge profiles. Top and bottom mould faces are perforated and lined with filter materials so that when pressure is applied excess water in the mix is squeezed out, leaving a well-consolidated and cohesive panel. Immediately afterwards the panel can be lifted out of the mould by a vacuum pad **8** to **11**.

2.06 Spraying method

This method, also developed by BRS, is considered suitable for manufacturing small numbers of units, complex shapes

*Original continental system employed thin steel moulds. Later BRS developed similar battery system using concrete moulds cast vertically from two master moulds cast horizontally in conventional manner

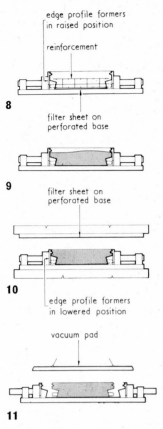

8 *Mould before concrete is poured in* (NB *edge profile-formers are raised). Lower filter paper and reinforcement have just been placed in position*

9 *Concrete has now been poured in and mould is ready to move into press*

10 *Immediately after pressing: concrete is now consolidated. Edge profile-formers are now in lower position, flush with top surface of concrete*

11 *Ready for lifting away. Mould backs have been retracted, taking profile-formers with them*

or cladding. Units are built up by spraying a series of layers of fine concrete. Insulants can be introduced during spraying and a good internal surface finish can be obtained by the use of a single coat of gypsum.

Table 1 Typical effect of mould utilisation on unit cost of production (storey-height panels)

No of castings	Mould material	No of moulds	Unit cost £
1	Timber	1	400
5	Timber	1	150
30 (average)	Timber	1	100
300	Timber	10	100
300	Steel	1	87

3 Economics of precast wall panels

Use of precast concrete wall panels requires careful evaluation of the relationship between costs of production, transport and erection. Unit size is determined by frequency of typical panels and crane capacity. The main factor determining production cost is the number of castings that can be produced from one mould (table 1). With the Jespersen system, Diamant[6] points out that while 10 types were found necessary with a unit weight of 450 kg, only eight were needed if 2270 kg units were used.

BRS have noted that with large panel construction (in housing) up to 70 per cent of the crane cycle is 'holding time'*.

The inherently stable L-shaped panel developed by BRS reduced the holding time substantially. A maximum of about 100 kg should be allowed for manual handling, after which mechanical handling is necessary. The position of the crane on site should be determined carefully to minimise the number of working positions and eliminate the need for scaffolding.

*Quote taken from BRS Open Day leaflet 23, 1971

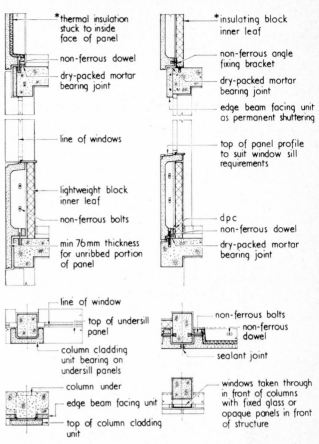

12 *Undersill panel and column-cladding details (*alternative insulating methods)*

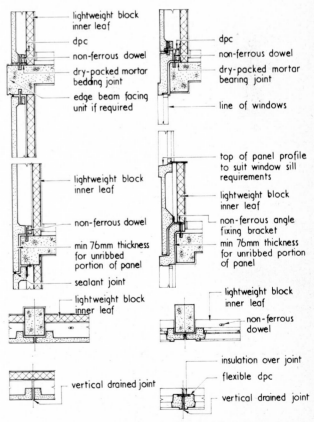

13 *Storey-height panels with and without window openings*

In **12** *and* **13** *the scale is too small to show all details but there should always be a dpc between the outer panel and back-up wall and drip holes at the base of the hollow space between outer panel and back-up wall to allow any penetrating moisture to escape* OUTWARDS

If the same finish is wanted on every surface, the particular process must be examined to discover if it is possible. If not, selected surfaces should be chosen. Choice of aggregates is important. If a special type is crucial, sufficient quantity for the entire job must be stock piled at the start and the probable extra cost taken into account at the budget stage. Where differing materials abut, their separate expansion and weathering characteristics must be studied and governed[7].

4 Walls incorporating non-structural concrete cladding panels

4.01 Under-sill panels

Typical general details for the use of under-sill panels are shown in **12**. The basic fixing method is by a loadbearing joint, continuous along the length of the panel, on the structural edge beam and with restraint fixings into the structural column through nibs at the ends of panels.

4.02 Storey-height cladding panels

Loadbearing fixings for storey-height panels may be by:
● Hanging from the top nib of panel
● Bearing on bottom nib of panel **13**.
Whichever fixing method is adopted, it is essential that the movement of the panel or of the supporting structure relative to the panel is able to be accepted by the members and their fixings without setting up adverse stresses.

5 Checklist

5.01 In situ concrete

1 Check effect of rain run-off and discoloration at changes of plane and surface—parapets, windows and junctions
2 Check information sheets on concrete finishes in AJ 14.2.68 to 26.3.69
3 Select materials, texture and pattern to meet design choice and production factors
4 Define tolerances at junctions with other production techniques. In situ concrete can vary in location, angle and surface and is difficult and expensive to adjust. And check possibility of using other components as permanent shuttering.

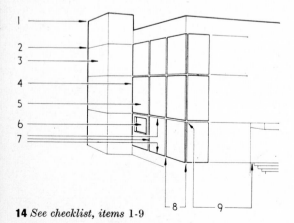

14 *See checklist, items 1-9*

5.02 Precast concrete

5 Design component size with comprehensive data on assembly techniques, cranage in factory and on site,

performance requirements and joint and tolerance specification
6 Design for selection of sub-assemblies to cost/performance requirements. Observe previous notes on water run-off, staining and streaking. Define responsibility for matching and fitting components
7 Define and specify tolerances in height, width, level, plane and to all surfaces. Establish that tolerances are realistic within desired cost limits and adequate for loading movement
8 Having defined tolerances, design joints—refer to AJ 15.11.67 p1231 and to BRS digests 36[9] *Jointing*, 37[9] *Mastics and gaskets* and 85[11] *Joints between precast concrete panels*
9 Design joints and sub-panels at angles and intersections.

6 References

BUILDING RESEARCH STATION
1 Digest 16 Aerated concrete, part 1: Manufacture and properties. 1969, HMSO, latest edition [Yq6 (E1)]
2 Digest 17 Aerated concrete, part 2: Uses. 1969, HMSO, latest edition [Yq6 (E1)]
3 Digest 111 Lightweight aggregate concretes, part 3: Structural application. 1969, HMSO [Yq7 (K)]

4 CEMENT AND CONCRETE ASSOCIATION Concrete practice in building construction. London, 1960, The Association [Yq]
5 GAGE, M. Guide to exposed concrete finishes. London, 1970, Architectural Press, paper £3·25 [(41) Yq]
6 DIAMANT, R. E. M. Industrialised building: Fifty International methods. Vol 1 1964, vol 2 1965, Iliffe Books (for *Architect and Building News*) [Elb] *vol 1 £3.15, vol 2 £3.50*
7 MURPHY, W. E. Jointing between precast concrete façade panels: Tolerances achieved in vertical joints. *Architects' Journal*, 1967, November 15, p1231–1234 [(21)]
8 WILSON, J. G. Bb15: Concrete facing slabs. London, 1959, Cement and Concrete Association [(41) Rf] *O/p*

BUILDING RESEARCH STATION
9 Digests 36 and 37 Jointing with mastics and gaskets: parts 1 and 2. 1963, HMSO [Yt4]
10 Digest 61 Strength of brickwork, blockwork and concrete walls. 1965, HMSO [(21·1) (K)]
11 Digest 85 Joints between concrete wall panels: Open drained joints. 1967, HMSO [(21) Gf2]
12 Digest 123 Lightweight aggregate concretes. 1970, HMSO [Yq7]
13 Digest 126 Changes in appearance of concrete on exposure. 1971, HMSO [Yq (S)]
14 Current paper 36/68 Battery case cladding panels. 1968, HMSO [(41) Rf (B2d)]
15 Current paper 73/68 Lightweight aggregates: Their properties and use in concrete in the UK. 1968, HMSO [Yp]
16 Current paper 30/69 Large panel structures. Notes on draft addendum 1 to CP 116 (1965). 1969, HMSO [(2–) Gf (K)]
17 Current paper 25/70 The use of cranes on low rise high density industrialised housing. 1970, HMSO [81 (E1e) (B3p)]

18 GAGE, M. Guide to exposed concrete finishes. London, 1970, Architectural Press, paper, £3·25 [(41) Yq]
19 Go-Con battery casting of concrete panels. *Architects' Journal*, 1971, May 5, p998–1002 and 1971, June 16, p1341 [Gf (B2d)]
20 BRITISH STANDARDS INSTITUTION BS CP 116: Part 1: 1965; Part 2: 1969. The structural use of precast concrete [(2–) Gf (K)]

Information sheet
External walls 3

Facings and renderings

This information sheet deals with finishes that embody cement, sand or lime coatings, used either as finishes in their own right, or as preparations for a range of facing materials that includes ceramic tiles and mosaics. The author is PHILIP LANCASHIRE

1 External renderings

1.01 Introduction

External rendering is the name given to two or more coats of cement/sand, or cement/lime/sand, applied to a building's external surfaces. External stucco finishes became popular with the development of 'Roman cements' in the 18th century, and were used widely in the Regency period. Later in the 19th century Roman cements were replaced gradually by Portland cement. Initially the extra strength and inflexibility of this material led to many failures, and the importance of maintaining some porosity in renderings is now recognised.

1.02 Functions

The functions of external rendering are:
● To achieve a particular aesthetic effect
● To cover an unsightly structure
● To increase the durability and reduce maintenance of a structure
● To assist in protecting the structure against rain penetration and other weather conditions.

1.03 Choice

The architect should specify materials, number of coats and manner of application, type of finishing treatment and colour. Choice of these will be governed by the following:
● Appearance
● Conditions of exposure
● Type of background to receive render.

Appearance required

A life of 60 to 100 years is possible for rendered finishes, but light-coloured or white finishes may require painting periodically, and cement paints must be repainted at intervals of three to 10 years. Oil-bound paints require renewal at intervals of four to five years; they are more expensive but more durable in town atmospheres than cement paints. Emulsion paints are not only cheaper but permit the sub-surface to 'breathe'. For external work acrylic emulsions are best as they have a degree of water resistance in themselves. Pebble-dash and roughcast are the least liable to change in appearance over long periods. Scraped finishes and some textured finishes in ordinary grey cement also change little in appearance. Types of finish are shown in table I.

Conditions of exposure

Table I (right-hand column) shows the suitability of various external renderings for various environments.

Type of background

Choice of external rendering is limited by properties of background, especially those of strength, porosity, resistance to water penetration and protection. Table II lists the properties of backgrounds, and suggests which types of rendering are suitable for them.

Methods of application

An external rendered treatment should not be less than two coats, each allowed to dry out and take up its initial shrinkage before applying the next.
● A spatter-dash coat, before the undercoats, may provide a good bond or reduce suction of the background
● Undercoats help to straighten or level an uneven surface, seal wall surface, prevent rain penetration, provide a surface of even suction and good adhesion for the finishing coats, and prevent 'grinning' of joints. An undercoat should not exceed 16 mm or be less than 10 mm in thickness in any part; if greater thickness is required to build up an even surface, additional undercoats should be used as necessary. Two undercoats will be required where the finishing coat does not provide a continuous solid layer, as in some machine-applied finishes and also on metal lathing
● Final coat thickness will be governed by texture required, but will normally be 6 to 9 mm thick. Finer-textured machine-applied finishes may be as thin as 3 mm.
The preparation and undercoat requirements for renderings are described in detail in 'External rendered finishes for walls'.[5] (BRS Digest 131.)

1.04 Detailing

As a guiding principle it should be assumed that a rendering will absorb a certain amount of moisture. So suitably-designed damp-proof courses and flashings should be provided to conduct moisture to the outside as rapidly as possible. Parapets should have copings, and continuous damp-proof courses should extend across all walls below the coping. At ground level the rendering should not bridge the dpc otherwise a capillary path may be formed for rising damp. This would cause sulphates in the soil to attack the rendering and the rising damp would be accompanied by staining. Movement control joints framed in walling or in joints between walling and framing members should be carried through the rendered surface.

Table I *Types of finishing treatment for renderings*

Appearance		Method of application	Characteristics	Suitability for various environments
Smooth (floated finish)		Surface is smoothed with a steel float	Likely to develop defects, including crazing, cracking and patchiness of appearance	All areas
Roughcast, wet-dash, spatter-dash or harling finish		A wet plastic mix is thrown on to wall with trowel or handscoop. Care should be taken to obtain wide but even spread. A range of coloured cements is available	Has no common defects and does not require maintenance (except possibly painting in polluted areas)	All areas, particularly rural or coastal
Pebble-dash or dry-dash finish		While material is still soft, a selected aggregate (eg calcined flint, spar or pea shingle) should be dashed on surface	Less susceptible to defects and deterioration than other types	All areas, particularly rural or coastal
Machine-applied finishes		Applied by hand-operated machines, cement guns and sprays (eg 'Tyrolean' or spattered finish). Machines are normally used with mixtures specially prepared by manufacturers	Does not craze but can become patchy or streaky. Small or hair cracks may appear but tend to be camouflaged by rough texture	Less suitable for urban conditions, as they show dirt
Scraped finishes		Obtained by scraping surface of rendering some hours after application to expose aggregate	Greater freedom from crazing and patchiness of appearance than smooth finishes	All areas, but coarser finishes less suitable in dirty urban atmospheres
Textured and ornamental finishes		Various ornamental patterns can be produced by treating freshly-applied final coat (eg ribbed, torn or stippled stucco, fan texture, English cottage texture)	Similar to scraped finishes	All areas; in dirty urban atmospheres tend to accumulate dirt, but are not so prone to streakiness as smoother finishes

Table II *Properties of background materials and their effect on choice of rendering*

Type of background	Properties	Notes
Dense, strong materials, eg high-density clay bricks, blocks, dense concrete (precast or in situ)	Low porosity, little suction and smooth surfaces that afford no mechanical key Usually weather-resistant in themselves Efflorescence of soluble salts is less likely than with more porous materials	Artificial bond, metal lathing or wire netting may be needed to provide good key. Use spatter-dash, hacking or bush hammering to prepare background. Rake mortar joints in brickwork
Moderately strong and porous materials, eg bricks and blocks other than dense types, lightweight products, medium density concretes	Relatively high suction, good mechanical key and good adhesion for renderings Usually weather-resistant in themselves Some backgrounds have high soluble salt content which may effloresce, thus causing damage to rendering	If suction is high or irregular, use spatter-dash first. Alternatively there are proprietary admixtures to assist key
Moderately weak and porous materials, eg lightweight concretes, aerated concretes and some bricks	Relatively low strength so more care needed in selection of rendering treatment than above types Possible risk of soluble salts with bricks	Rendering *must* be weaker than background or shrinkage will lead to shearing of surface of background If background very weak, pebble-dash, dry-dash, roughcast and hacking not advisable
No fines concrete	Many large voids but few small pores, give good mechanical key for rendering Should have sufficient strength to resist shrinkage stresses No capillarity, therefore no problems of excessive suction, and less risk of capillary transmission of water through wall	Provide weep-holes through rendering at suitable points immediately above horizontal damp-proof courses, to drain away moisture that may enter wall
Metal lathing of expanded metal; used as background in framed construction	No resistance to rain penetration so lathing must be protected	Three-coat work is essential, with dense and impervious mix for first coat to achieve resistance to rain penetration but avoid excessively strong mixes which will result in excessive drying shrinkage. The addition of reinforcement (eg hair or glass fibre) may assist

2 Facings: tiles and mosaics

2.01 Introduction

Historically, there has always been a division between walls that are 'fairfaced', ie assembled from materials attractive and durable enough to be left exposed to view and to the weather, and those built with less care and precision from materials that need to be covered by an outer facing (chosen for its better wearing qualities and preferred appearance). Tiles and mosaics are understandably popular as their hard impervious surfaces are both maintenance-free and vandal-resistant. A cautionary note must, however, be sounded. The original homes of mosaic facings were countries with low rainfall and no frost. Mosaics themselves will easily withstand these natural hazards but the method of fixing is all important. In particular insitu applications are for experienced expert fixers only. The country is littered with jobs where some or all of the original mosaic has come off. The intial considerations in making a choice of finish and fixing are:

- Appearance
- Cost
- Dimensional co-ordination
- Movement joints
- Type and preparation of background.

Appearance

Tiling and mosaics are available in a vast range of colour, texture and size.

Specification[13] part 2, p366–369 gives a comprehensive list of manufacturers of marbles, mosaics, floor and wall tiles, and catalogues showing colours and textures that can be obtained from them. Choice of size may depend on whether the whole building is to be covered with the material **1**, or whether it is to be used in panels only **2**.

Dimensional co-ordination

The type of tile or mosaic to be used should be decided early in the design stage to co-ordinate tile dimensions with door and window openings. Joints of 2 mm absolute minimum must be left between the tiles to receive the jointing material. Wider joints may be necessary where the tiles have to conform to a building module. In many ways a wider joint is preferable to a narrow one which may not allow jointing material to penetrate the full depth of the tiling.

Movement joints

Compressive stresses are set up in tiling and mosaic systems as a result of movement due to variations in strength of the materials and drying of backgrounds. They can also be caused by vertical settlement of the finish of a building.

Movement joints should be used at storey-height intervals horizontally, and approximately 3 m apart vertically. They should extend to the full depth of the tile and bed and should be a minimum of 6 mm wide. Non-rigid materials are available for movement joints, either in the form of a compound applied by a trowel or caulking gun, or as a prefabricated strip.

2.02 Application

Type of background

Some facings can be fixed direct to the background if it is very smooth, eg when tiles or mosaic are applied to sheets, boards, glazed bricks or tiles. If the background is unsuitable for direct fixing, then a floated coat is applied. Before receiving the floated coat, the background must be cleaned and prepared to receive the coat, and all initial drying shrinkage must have taken place. Summary of background properties in relation to floated coats and methods of fixing can be found in BS CP 212 Part 2[10] page 26-29.

Floated coat

Metal lathing fixed across the junction of different materials will minimise the risk of cracking caused by differential

1 *Rectangular white tiles cover all exterior faces of Newcastle Airport (Yorke Rosenberg Mardall, architects)*

2 *Natural stone mosaic infill panels under windows*

movement. It is however, always better to assume movement will occur and instead of trying to stop it to leave a suitable joint filled with a non-hardening elastic sealant. The risks of sulphate attack may be minimised by using a cement resistant to sulphate action, ie sulphate-resisting Portland cement, or high alumina cement in very severe conditions. If the thickness required is greater than 13 mm, it should be built up in two or more layers no greater than 10 mm thick. Two coats are also necessary, where thin bed fixing materials are used, to provide a firm and level surface.

Fixing materials

Sand/cement mortar

Sand and cement mortar is suitable for bedding vitrified tiles, earthenware tiles (exterior type) and mosaics generally. Tiles should be buttered evenly and tapped back firmly into position to ensure that the bed is solid over the whole of the back of the tile. Bed thickness of 7 mm is average and should not exceed 13 mm.

Often mosaics are assembled in the form of sheets, the tessarae being glued either face side down to paper, or bedding side down to nylon adhesive strips or net. Before bedded the fixing side of the mosaic sheet should be grouted with a cement slurry. After the sheets have been firmly beaten in and final straightening has been completed, a grout should be rubbed over the surface to fill voids in the joints.

Great care should be taken in the selection of additives such as plasticisers, waterproofers, fungicides and so on to ensure that they do not influence the adhesion or movement of the mortar adversely. The advice of the expert fixer is essential on this question.

Cement-based adhesives

These are good alternatives to sand and cement mortar bedding provided tiles are not keyed deeply or frogged. Greater speed at fixing can be obtained with both screeding and buttering methods. There are several proprietary adhesives available and specifiers should consult the manufacturers and the fixers for information on their use and suitability.

Other adhesives (thin bed)

Another increasingly popular system is to use a non-cementicious mastic type fixative. There are a number on the market with similar properties. It is essential that the background be smooth and accurate as there is no room for adjustment in the bed. This is probably only 2 or 3 mm thick and will always move in response to the background, avoiding breaking bond.

Grouting or pointing

To ensure lasting results, it is essential that particular attention be given to grouting and pointing. The general properties required are low shrinkage, low compressive strength, good adhesion and impermeability.

3 References

1 GRAY, W. S. and H. L. CHILDE. Concrete surface finishes. London, 1943, Concrete Publications (now Cement and Concrete Association), second edition [(41) Pq]
2 External rendering. London, 1970, Cement and Concrete Association, fifth edition [(41) Pq]
3 KEPPICH, A. Rendering. Cheddar, 1948, Callow & Keppich [Py]

2a

2b

2a *Welded wire fabric with cement rendering on top provides backing for tiles, while* **b** *shows method of laying facing tiles*

4 BRITISH STANDARDS INSTITUTION BS CP 221: 1960. External rendered finishes [(41) Py]
5 BUILDING RESEARCH STATION Digest 131 (first series) External rendered finishes. 1960, HMSO [(41) Pq4]
6 BESSEY, G. E. External rendered finishes for walls: National Building Studies bulletin 10. 1951, HMSO [(41) Py]
7 COWPER, A. D. Sands for plasters, mortars and external renderings: National Building Studies bulletin 7. 1950, HMSO [(41) Pp1]

8 BUILDING RESEARCH STATION Digest 58 Mortars for jointing. 1965, HMSO [Yq4]
BRITISH STANDARDS INSTITUTION

9 BS CP 212: Part 1: 1963. Internal ceramic wall tiling in normal conditions [(42) Sg 3]
10 BS CP 212: Part 2: 1966. External ceramic wall tiling and mosaics [(41) Sg]
BRITISH CERAMIC TILE COUNCIL
11 Recommended methods of fixing frost-resistant ceramic wall tiles. Stoke-on-Trent, The Council [(41) Sg3 (J2)]

12 Technical specification for ceramic wall tiles. Stoke-on-Trent, The Council [(A—) Sg3]

13 Specification. London, 1973, Architectural Press [Yy (A3)]

Information sheet
External walls 4

Panels

The use of external cladding panels can be traced back by historians into a respectable antiquity. However, the use of large, self-supporting units, hung on to the structure, and sometimes forming part of the structure, is a recent development and probably forms the most significant architectural mainstream development in the past 20 years. The author is DAVID KIRBY

Plastic cladding panels

Concrete cladding panels

1 Introduction

The reasons for the development of external cladding panels may be listed:

● The need to manufacture a large part of the building away from the site to speed construction time

● The need to find alternative constructional techniques to replace traditional on-site materials and techniques which may be in short supply

● Social, technical and economic pressures towards higher buildings, making traditional walling techniques too bulky, too laborious or too difficult to maintain

● As a response to the development of prefabricated building elements for the whole construction of the building, associated with improved cranage and other handling techniques.

It will be apparent from the buildings around us that the mainspring of development has been aesthetic; large panels and infill panels involve building methods requiring judge-

ment of objective and subjective factors. Most of the possible solutions can be rationalised with equal validity, and the initial choice of panelled construction will probably stem from the architect's personal response to the problem before him. After the initial decision, few techniques are so unencumbered by craft technique or by published information, and a careful analysis must be made of the effects of using panel form construction on the whole building.

For instance, there is the case of a panel design for a complex building in which the architects had used no modular grid and had employed several material techniques associated with changes of shape in the building, thus breaking any possible structural grid. Most panel construction techniques involve mould or jig processes where the increase in number of panel varieties can have a marked effect on panel cost. The design decisions which had been made and maintained were in conflict with the decision to use panels, thus resulting in a heavy increase in cost and design complexity.

2 Dimensions and tolerances[1]

Objects of using dimensional grid system:
● to reduce the number of component variations to a practical minimum; critically important when large panels are employed **1**: selection of dimensional grid systems is discussed in several publications and in Modular Society literature
● to provide an underlying dimensional system to which components can be related.
The accuracy of any manufactured component will vary in several ways **2**

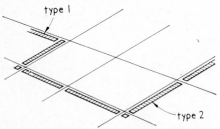

type 1

type 2

1 *Different panel types are required to deal with direction changes: number of varieties increases if panels of varying thickness are used*

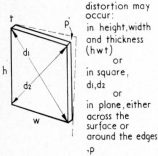

distortion may occur:
in height, width and thickness (h w t)
or
in square, d1, d2
or
in plane, either across the surface or around the edges ,p

2 *Probable manufacturing variations in accuracy*

In addition, when placed in position, a component will vary from its 'correct' location by being out of place, level and plumb. The components already in place for receiving a component and those placed afterwards will vary in similar ways. The accumulation of such errors will normally follow statistical principles, but without control their build up can be catastrophic. Accuracy is impossible—an exact 10 mm rod will not fit an exact 10 mm hole—and high accuracy becomes very expensive. In fact the more precise engineering becomes, the more tolerances and fits are defined to measurable limits, and the less likely one is to find the individual scraping and cutting in the manner that typifies high quality fitting work in the building industry. This subject is fully discussed in Jan Sliwa's articles (AJ 19.3.69, 23.4.70 and 16.9.70). Any manufacturer who claims to produce panels exactly to size is stretching his credibility gap too far.
The design of joints, discussed later, must account for panel tolerances, but the dimensional grid will affect (and be affected by) every design requirement of the building. Accommodating tolerances at joints is more difficult with larger panels as the number of joints is fewer.

3 Panels

3.01 Fire-resistance[2]

The former compulsory 'back-up' wall is no longer essential. The fire-resistance of the panel, measured from the inside in relation to glazing area and distance from the boundary, must be established as must surface spread of flame condi-

tions, both externally and internally. In buildings over 15 m high, check requirements for non-combustible panels[3].

3.02 Size

Take account of proposed material size limitations, requirements of height and width for frame, and thickness for frame fixing.

3.03 Insulation and insolation

High standards of insulation in thicknesses up to 24 mm can be achieved by using expanded plastics materials; any of the modern insulating materials will produce U-values of less than $1 \cdot 70$ W/m² deg C in thicknesses of less than $4 \cdot 8$ mm. Detail problems of condensation, cold-bridging and vapour pressure are more likely to cause trouble than heat loss itself. AJ 19.3.71, 26.5.71 and 2.6.71 should be consulted for detail design but the basic factors are shown in **3**.

3 *Condensate or moisture trapped in fabrication can produce vapour pressures capable of breaking down glue lines or breaking through surface films*

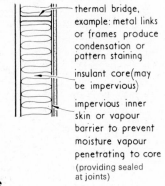

thermal bridge, example: metal links or frames produce condensation or pattern staining

insulant core (may be impervious)

impervious inner skin or vapour barrier to prevent moisture vapour penetrating to core (providing sealed at joints)

4 Panel types

4.01 Infill panels

Infill panels are supported fully by surrounding frames. Their use in framed cladding and curtain walling is well established and many types are available. The following factors should be taken into account in selecting and designing infill panels:
● well-insulated panels, exposed to strong sunlight can result in the build-up of very high (up to 130°C) surface temperatures. Such temperatures can cause high movement stresses in surface materials and glue lines
● glue lines between panels and insulants should be able to shear, otherwise strain build-up may result in buckling or blistering of surface material. This can be avoided by modelling surface materials to provide adequate rigidity while leaving the surface free to flex under thermal stress. Light-coloured surfaces will reflect sunlight and limit the problem.

4.02 Acoustic insulation

This should be consistent with the wall panel as a whole. A wall with acoustic insulant windows installed above 12mm of plastics foam and sheet steel would be a technical and economic nonsense.

4.03 Movement

Panels are subject to movement from wind, vibration and thermal change, of which the latter is the most significant: the range is shown in table I. In addition joints are affected by the frequency and rate of movement and may be subject to sudden, tearing stresses as a result of friction restraining the panel until the forces are large enough to push through and release the built-up stresses. Pumping movements

Table I Estimated temperatures on buildings in England

Construction	Temperature			
	Maximum		Minimum	
	°C	°F	°C	°F
Black glass Ceramic tiles Metal (insulated behind)	80	180	−25	−15
White glass Ceramic tiles Metal (insulated behind)	60	140	−25	−15
Black metal tray exposed behind clear glass and insulated behind	130	260	−10	15
Clear glass in front of dark insulated background such as tray above	80	180	−25	−15

Table II Materials

Outer face	Core	Inner face
Asbestos cement textured, enamelled, colour-coated	**Glass fibre** in various forms including patent laminate materials with bonded glass filaments (rigid or blanket)	**Plasterboard**
Steel enamelled, colour-coated, pressed to form shallow dish forms		**Plywood**
		Chipboard
	Paper resin honeycomb cores, straw, wood shaving and other waste products in resinous or cementitious bindings	**Asbestos-based boards**
Stainless steel		**Block and brickwork**
Aluminium anodised, colour-coated, pressed		**Vinyl sheeting**
	Chipboard plywood, blockboard	**Melamine/phenolic laminates**
Other metals copper, lead supported on back-up board panels	**Expanded plastics** irrethanes, polystyrene, phenolic foams, pvc (see BRS digest 93), mineral wool (rigid or blanket)	**Leather**
		Simulated leathers
Brickwork		**Timber and timber veneers**
Stone Ceramics, slate, marble	**Masonry** Brickwork, conc-blockwork (heavy or lightweight)	Any from first column
Plastics pvc, polypropylene		
Acrylics vacuum-formed, press-formed, extruded		
Glass-reinforced polyester (grp)		
Epoxy and polyester resins with decorative aggregates		
Melamine phenolic laminates (external grades only)		
Timber		
Concrete		

4 *Large concrete cladding panels at St Katharine Dock House. For detail see* **9** *which shows the drained joint used*

under wind forces are also possible, and can cause difficulties with some mastic jointing materials[4].

Where panels are secured in rebates with beads, fixing and sealing is a matter for detail discussion with the frame manufacturer and sealant supplier; for instance, fixing and sealing may be into rebates, using extruded neoprene sealing gaskets[5]. Most neoprene gasketing systems are designed to seal out water in driving rains of 160 km/h (100 mph) or more. They retain this ability for years because neoprene weathers well and resists permanent deformation. Its lasting resilience allows the gasket to absorb normal building movements without affecting its sealing function[6]. Panels may also require edge-to-edge jointing without intermediate frames. This can be difficult with thin panels, if edge clipping is visually unacceptable. Tongue and groove and overlap joints provide the necessary movement and dimensional tolerance.

5 Materials

Almost any combination of materials can be made into a panel, provided adequate attention is given to adhesives and vapour barriers: Table II.

5.01 Concrete

Concrete is probably the most common large cladding panel material and has been illustrated in Working Detail 164 (AJ 2.6.65)[7] showing panels at St Katharine Dock House. These are excellent examples of their type **4**.
Owing to their properties, concrete panels are sometimes made loadbearing, rather than used merely as a 'clip-on-wall'. Also they can be in the form of a sandwich section, usually with rigid fibrous insulation between two panels of concrete.

5.02 Other materials

In particular various forms of timber and sheet steel can be made up into large panels. These do not present abnormal problems and can be dealt with under the principles outlined in this and other information sheets **5** (see information sheets 6 and 7). In addition, thin sheet metal with massive use of plastics foam to form stressed skin laminates has been

5

6a

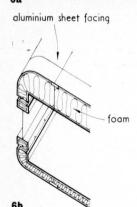

aluminium sheet facing

foam

6b

*5 Timber infill panels
designed to be demountable:
they butt flush against posts
and lintels, joint closed with
rubber gasket, and panels
bolted to posts
6a Elevation; 6b detail of thin
sheet metal used with plastics
foam to form stressed skin
7 Plastic panels used at
school in Daventry are
3·4 m high × 3 m wide.
Joints are over/underlap in
the horizontal*

the subject of intensive development by a few architects,
especially by Richard Rogers and Su Rogers **6a** and **b**.

5.03 Plastics

Since the construction of the GLC Paddington flats and the
development of their steel frame (SFI) system, plastics as
materials for large cladding panels have attracted the
attention of both architects and manufacturers. In theory,
plastics offer the advantages of light weight, precision
manufacture and choice of colour, in addition to the other
advantages offered by any panel-cladding system. In
practice, site crane use must be worked out fully and all
tolerances brought to the same standard before the advantage can be realised, and authorities' inevitable slow acceptance of new materials can be allowed to develop. However,
plastics offer a development potential which is not yet fully
realised and are worth serious consideration for any external
wall system **7**.

7

Manufacture

A number of manufacturers offer to make composite panels,
including facings, insulation, internal linings, windows and
fixing devices. This is probably the easiest way of obtaining
panels provided that a nominated supplier can be accepted
and that the experienced knowledge of a manufacturer can
be relied upon.

Several plastics manufacturers exist, most of whom would
be willing to undertake the panel fabrication. The majority
will be conscientious and well-intentioned and probably
excited by their own skill with new and exciting materials.
When considering such firms a check list might be drawn up:
● Is the factory large enough to fabricate, cure and store
components?
● Is it clean, dry, well ventilated and heated (dirt, wet and
cold can affect resin systems adversely)?
● Are general working conditions good?
● Are there enough experienced staff, including someone
with sufficient chemical training, to be able to measure
accurately, mix thoroughly and maintain quality standards?
● Who will make the moulds? The accuracy and finish of
the moulds will be better than the accuracy and finish of the
component. Mould-making requires accurate machinery and
experienced men, and can only be left to the plastics
manufacturer if he has these resources
● Have they previous experience of similar work? This
should entail manufacturing to specified tolerances, handling
large components and dealing as nominated suppliers to
general contractors under RIBA contract terms.
Consider the rigidity of the panel (during transport installation and in position). If a flat panel is desired, it may need
ribs or a slight camber. If shaped, often its form will make it
rigid enough.
● Make sure it is possible to remove the panel from its

mould, especially where inside corners are involved (a panel is *three*-dimensional)

● Decide which surfaces are to be mould surfaces and make certain these can be achieved.

Having selected and checked a number of manufacturers, a specification suitable for individual manufacturers must be arrived at. In the absence of standard specifications as guide lines, each problem must be considered carefully. Generally speaking, manufacturers of materials (resin and glass) will be anxious to protect their materials and will provide guidance.

Ask the manufacturer to provide full material specification —reinforcement, resin, any additive systems and details of manufacturing method stressing any important details which can affect quality of finished component. (A good idea is to arrange for the manufacturer's agent to call and inspect any vital stages in production—they are usually willing to provide this service free. Ask material manufacturers to check suitability of the system for the proposed application. Note that boats are not buildings! Although exposed to the elements they are often carefully washed and protected, repair is expected and willingly undertaken, and laminate breakdown may be attributed to an accidental blow or other local damage. There is an extensive literature on grp specification; the British Plastics Federation, 47-48 Piccadilly, London w1, has a building group that will give advice.

Fabrication and inspection should also be specified. Critical dimensions should be checked for accuracy and a minute examination of external surfaces undertaken. Pitting, the presence of exposed fibres, discoloration, small cracks and an uneven surface all indicate possible areas of weakness and potential danger. If in doubt, chemical tests of the curing of the resin system can be undertaken by independent research laboratories.

Having obtained a grp shell, the problem is to complete the work up to a finished building component. Ideally this should be by the same manufacturer: hence the desirability of going to specialist firms. Alternatively, an experienced joinery or metal-working firm should be responsible for the whole work, buying in the grp shell from the manufacturer. A number of artists and at least one specialist consultant firm exist to develop complete cladding systems.

This section has so far concentrated on large-scale panels of grp manufacture. Vacuum-formed thermoplastics, particularly acrylics and pvc, can also be used, but size has been restricted to available sheet and vacuum-forming machine sizes. The processes are particularly suited to producing a large number of similar components, assembled into framing **8**.

Jointing

The precision of plastics and the availability of mechanical fixings should make a wide variety of joints feasible. The present tendency is to regard the drained joint as ideal and, although this presents edge-moulding problems, its use is to be preferred (also see **7**).

It is important to avoid local concentrations of stress. These can arise from too few mechanical fixings, inadequate tolerances so that stress is thrown on to one or two points, overtightening of fixings and inadequate allowance for movement. Large washers, spreading bars, so that panels are clamped rather than pinched together, and loose fixings should be used. Extra reinforcement should also be provided.

8 *Clip-in clear acrylic panels enclosed the vast recreational interior of the Douglas Summerland solarium*

6 Wall panels

The idea of curtain walling composed of a series of frames and panels assembled on site is tending towards whole wall panels in which all walling elements, including doors and windows, are combined in a prefabricated element, fastened to the structure or adjoining components. However, there are many examples of plain wall panels, and ones which cover walls only partially, eg spandrel panels not set in frames. The use of such panels has made the questions of dimensional control and tolerance, outlined in previous paragraphs, particularly vital as there is no opportunity for introducing progressive tolerances which curtain walling assembly allows. Site installation must go direct from the general crude tolerances of structure (as much as ± 24 mm). to the requirements of factory-assembled components.

Problems of fire-resistance, size specification, thermal insulation, insolation, movement and acoustic insulation are broadly similar to those discussed under infill panels. Materials, fixing and jointing require particular attention.

7 Fixing and jointing

Except for those which are concrete system built, the manufacture of large panels is by no means as organised as the manufacture of curtain walling. Obviously this means that assembly procedures must be considered at the design stage to avoid the almost comic occurrence of four large panels all having to be 'sprung' into place, with several overlapping pieces of plastic film and a quantity of mastic. Even at only two storeys up on an exposed site on a windy day, confidence in the all-seeing wisdom of the architect can be reduced.

The preferred system of jointing for large panels is accepted by most to be the BRS drained joint. An example of this is shown in **9** (St Katharine Dock). This jointing system has been proved only for straight vertical joints, although examples are appearing, in which attempts to use it on the slope have been made. The introduction and general acceptance of this joint dates from the issue of the BRS digest 85 in August 1967. The rapidity with which the system has been accepted is an interesting commentary on those who criticise the building industry. Nevertheless, it is to be hoped that BRS will soon publish performance data on its success in performance, particularly as to the appearance of pattern staining behind the joint, the steps necessary to disguise movement internally and the success of gaskets

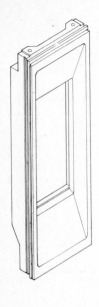

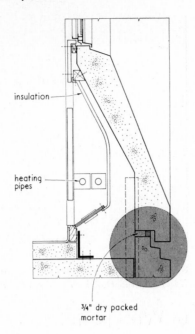

insulation

heating pipes

¾" dry packed mortar

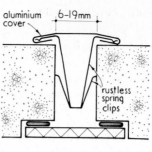

aluminium cover · 6-19mm

rustless spring clips

11 *Spring-retained cover strip in conjunction with drained joint: although shown here as external joint, principle of hidden fix cover strip is well established and used extensively, especially in light industry*

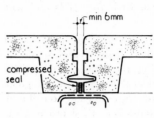

min 6mm

compressed seal

12 *Drained joint with flexible baffle and compressed seal: precision casting and location requirements appear to be even higher as compressed volume must be held to 25 per cent of its original. Assembly details to draw up one panel to next require considerable attention. Materials: baffle (as before); seal (bitumenised foam urethane strip)*

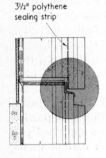

3½" polythene sealing strip

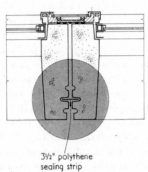

3½" polythene sealing strip

9 *Example of* BRS *drained joint: development of including services in wall zone which may free floor areas or make complex servicing independent of structural area*

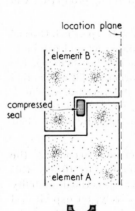

location plane

element B

compressed seal

element A

alternative seal

13 *Overlap joint with seal. Joint of this type allows ample tolerance at overlap which can be sized to manufacturing abilities. Overlap also acts as compressive jaw if one is used for location, in which case, element* A *being in place, element* B *is drawn back to it. This type of seal would work in principle internally and externally. Additional detailing would be required for weather sealing*

being located and retained under normal site tolerance conditions.

Problems of joints and jointing are common to all forms of external walling, but have become critical in cladding panels. Joint types have been the subject of extensive writing, and following is a brief summary of the types of solution available.

7.01 Dry Joints

Examples of dry joints are shown in **10** to **14**.

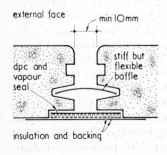

external face

min 10mm

dpc and vapour seal

stiff but flexible baffle

insulation and backing

10 *Drained joint with flexible baffle: edge detail requires precise casting; limited radius of baffle requires precise location.* BRS *suggests joint will vary even when finest casting techniques are used. Materials: baffle (suitable grades of extruded rubbers, eg neoprene or pvc); dpc and vapour; seal (same or polythene dpc material)*

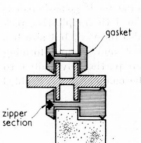

gasket

zipper section

14 *Gasket joint: this example—Saarinen's Technical Centre for General Motors at Detroit—shows extreme case of compression obtained in seals by zipper technique. General practice in this country has been to use smaller sections and employ metal sections for compression*

References for dry joints

1 POLE, C. T. Coverstrips for joints. *Architectural and Building News*, 1965, September 15, p517-518 [Yt4]
2 A selection of gasket manufacturers. *Specification* 1967. London, Architectural Press [Yt4] *p2/428*
3 BUILDING RESEARCH STATION Digests 36 and 37 Jointing with mastics and gaskets. 1963, HMSO [Yt4] *Essential references covering most aspects of subject*
4 DUPONT (UK) LTD Specification and guidance on 'neoprene' and 'hypalon' rubbers. 8 Breams Buildings, Fetter Lane, London EC4 [Yt4]

7.02 Sealed joints

It is recommended that sealed joints should be designed to avoid placing direct compression and tension on the seal. The aim should be to create sheer stresses, although compression and tension cannot be avoided entirely **15, 16a, b, c**. In most circumstances involving rigid elements, positive fixing and standard stressing, planar movement will exceed normal movement, and joint design should begin with this consideration.

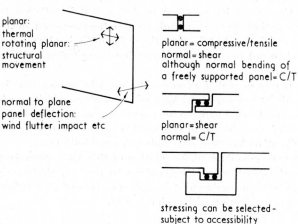

planar:
thermal
rotating planar:
structural
movement

normal to plane
panel deflection:
wind flutter impact etc

planar = compressive/tensile
normal = shear
although normal bending of
a freely supported panel = C/T

planar = shear
normal = C/T

stressing can be selected—
subject to accessibility

15 *Movement takes place in panel in these planes (left)*
16 *Different stresses are produced in joints of different types (right):* **a** *(top)*

butt joint—perhaps because it is worst case, most manufacturers emphasise it: **b** *(middle) lap joint;* **c** *(bottom) mated joint*

7.03 Lap and mated joints

These use similar principles but accessibility presents fresh design problems. Strip sealants and gun-applied strips prior to assembly can be used **17**.

● Preparation of joint surfaces may be difficult, or virtually impossible, after erection of the components
● Application of primer, if required, may be difficult
● It is difficult to control pressure build-up of the mastic in the cavity
● Owing to component and erection tolerances there will always be a danger that the mastic application will be too thin for effective performance
● It is impossible to inspect the sealant and very difficult to carry out remedial work.

Having indicated some of the practical difficulties associated with using mastics in lap joints, it should be noted that if by good design these can be overcome, then the long term performance of the sealing compound will be enhanced.

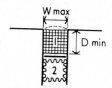

W max

D min

2

17 *Minimum butt joint in practice:* 1 *Sealant with preferred profile shown dotted; wherever possible joint would be better sheltered from erosion and sunlight.* 2 *Back-up material permits optimum proportions of* D *&* W. *Some manufacturers prefer this to be unbonded to* 1, *leaving* 1 *free to operate. Materials include polyethylene foam, urethane foam and traditional packings*

Where smooth metal or other non-porous surfaces subject to close tolerances are involved, the mastic seal can be used effectively as a bedding medium. This type of application is used mainly in curtain wall construction.

Lap joints are usually best dealt with by adopting a pre-formed gasket, eg of neoprene or other polymers, solid or foamed in a variety of sections. Allied in conception to gaskets are the pre-formed mastic strips which are flexible sealing compounds in strip form. They are a convenient and effective means of sealing lap joints in many components, and can be expected to give long trouble-free performance within the limits of their movement capability and resistance to aging. Mastic strips flow under pressure and are thus able to accommodate irregularities on the surface and the compressive force used in erection induces adhesion.

The essential pre-requisites for success with such sealing strips are smooth surfaces free from voids or protuberances, surfaces free from dust and moisture before application and strip mastic under continuous compression. Simple lap joints between components are shown in **18**; **x** illustrates the joint sealed with a mastic which looks good on a drawing but, for the reasons discussed, is almost impossible to achieve in practice; **a** and **b** show a possible satisfactory solution using a strip mastic. Sealant types are shown in Table III.

7.04 Frame and stop joints

The many complex forms of frame and stop joints, developed for curtain walling, panelling and windows, have developed correspondingly sophisticated assembly procedures using differing grades of sealant. Specialist guidance is necessary in this field and is usually supplied by sealant manufacturers, who provide a wide range of materials, with a high degree of objectivity.

Glazing joint detail

Many buildings are clad in relatively light non-loadbearing panels. Physical composition varies enormously from fully-compressed asbestos cement and vitreous enamel to glass and plastics. Often the panels are of sandwich construction incorporating insulating materials; many panels use glass backed by insulation and a metal tray. Panels of this type are particularly susceptible to large temperature variations[4]. Whether or not glass is employed in the construction of the panel, the method of fixing is usually that of a rebate in the frame and an external or internal bead. This type of joint is essentially a glazing joint detail: **19** shows typical details in **a** metal and **b** timber. The techniques used for sealing are the same as those used for beaded glazing, and the general principles given in BS CP 152: 1966 'Glazing and

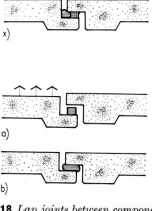

x)

a)

b)

18 *Lap joints between components*

Table III *Sealant Types*

	Form	Width (mm)	Depth (mm)	Butt joint movement tolerance %	Experience (years)	Life expectancy (years)	Adhesion
Oleo-resinous	Strip	50 (m)	6	2	50	5 to 10	Fair
	Knife	25	10	5 to 15			
	Gun	13†	13	15			
Butyl	Strip	50	6	2 to 10	20	10 to 15	Fair/good
	Knife	25	6	2 to 15			
	Gun	13†	6	5 to 15			
Acrylic	Gun	13	6	15	10	25†	Excellent
Polysulphide (one part)	Gun	13	6	15	5	20†	Good: excellent with primers
Polysulphide (two part)	Gun	51	6	15 to 33	25	25†	
	Pourable	51	6	15 to 33			
Silicone	Gun	13	6	50*	15	20†	

†Special grades
*Claim by manufacturers not made in references used for remainder of table

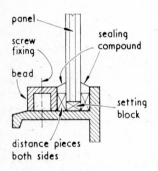

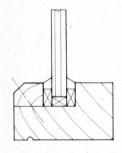

19a *Metal glazing joint detail*

19b *Timber glazing joint detail*

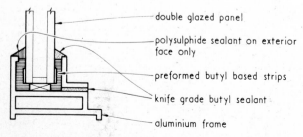

20 *Example of several types and applications of mastics used in one section*

fixing of glass for building' should be followed. Particular attention should be given to the following factors to ensure satisfactory performance:
● Adequate edge clearance to permit thermal movement of panel (consult manufacturer)
● Adequate support to base of panel, ie setting blocks
● Unless loadbearing mastic strips are employed in the joint design, an adequate number of distance pieces must be used to prevent movement of panel due to wind load vibration, or weight (bottom edge only)
● Care must be exercised in design and installation to ensure that the head is firmly fixed to the frame and, in the case of timber, to take steps (ie sealing of timber by primers and so on) to prevent warping due to excessive moisture movement
● Choice of sealing compound(s) must be appropriate for conditions of exposure; type of materials of which panels are constructed and the life expectancy of compound used must be considered in conjunction with the relative difficulty of replacement or maintenance and initial cost.
The compounds used for jointing of this type range from hand-applied, non-setting putties to mastics, elastomeric sealing compounds and strip-sealing compounds, used alone or in combination with each other **20**.

8 References

1 ROYAL INSTITUTE OF BRITISH ARCHITECTS The co-ordination of dimensions for building. London, 1965, The Institute [(F4j)]
2 FIRE PROTECTION ASSOCIATION Fire protection design guide: a handbook for architects. London, 1969, The Association [(R1)]
3 SCOTTISH DEVELOPMENT DEPARTMENT Building Standards (Scotland) Regulations 1963 Explanatory memorandum part 4: structural fire precautions. 1964, HMSO [(A3j)] (in Scotland)
4 MEIKLE, T. A. V. A guide to the use of sealants, part 1: Flexible joints. *Architect and Building News*, 1970, October, p55 [(Yt4)]
5 GROEGER, R. G. A guide to the use of sealants and mastics. *Architects' Journal*, 1968, June 5, Information sheet 1603/Dt4 [sfB 1961: (St4) CI/sfB (Yt4)]
6 DUPONT Building with elastomers. Switzerland [(Yt4)] p1
7 Working detail 164. *Architects' Journal*, 1965, June 2, p1321-1322 [sfB 1961: (21) Gf2 CI/sfB (21)]
8 Working detail 373. *Architects' Journal*, 1971, February 17, p371-372 [(41) Ri]
9 ALAN SILCOCK Protecting buildings against fire: background to costs. *Architects' Journal*, 1967, December 13 p1515-1519 [(R1) (Y2)]
10 Guide to the Building Regulations 1972, 2nd edition, 1973. (Architectural Press £2·25 covers England and Wales excluding GLC area)

Information sheet
External walls 5

Curtain walling

The success of curtain wall design depends largely on what information the architect gives to the manufacturer, and what checks are carried out on the manufacturer's detailed design in the workshop and on site. The author is PHILIP LANCASHIRE

1 Introduction

Curtain walls are non-loadbearing external walls with the following characteristics: they are often suspended in front of the structural frame, and their own deadweight and wind loads are transferred to the structural frame through point anchorages. Most curtain walls consist of a rectangular grid of vertical and horizontal members framing openings filled with inserts of glass and panels of other materials. The grid is expressed in elevation and gives the curtain wall façade its characteristic appearance.

Proprietary systems available are usually produced by metal window manufacturers. In exceptional circumstances, eg for very large buildings, special sections may be developed, but the architect must still rely on the manufacturer for technical guidance. Architects who consider using curtain walls must be able to evaluate available products and select the most suitable.

2 Information required by manufacturer

2.01 The following basic information is required by the manufacturer:

● Height and width of façade and total area. (Manufacturers are prepared to develop new extrusions and patterns for large buildings. As a rough guide, this service is available for orders over about 3500 m², or where curtain wall, fixing and glazing, is valued at around £100 000.)
● Interval between vertical members
● Floor to floor height
● Whether there will be a back-up wall

(The last three points help manufacturers to determine required strength and size of mullions. Back-up walls can often provide an additional point of support for mullions at all levels, thus reducing mullion size. Usually closer mullion spacing means a cheaper wall, the greatest economies—some manufacturers claim—being offered by

1a

1b

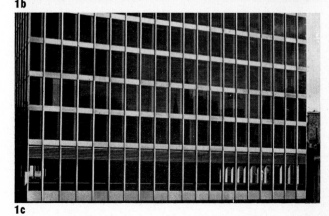

1c

1a, b, c *Shows three different types of curtain wall*

a module size of between 760 mm and 1200 mm. The popular module of 1200 m falls within this range, and is used widely because its multiple, 2400 mm, forms a useful minimum size unit when subdividing internal spaces. Where mullion spacings are over 1200 mm, glass costs and mullion sizes increase considerably. The following details must also be considered at an early stage.

- Insulation value
- Height of any false ceiling
- Location of mechanical heating and ventilating system
- Type of natural ventilation
- Type of infill panels
- Special requirements, eg incorporation of window-cleaning track into mullions.

Although the architect relies on the manufacturer's expertise, he must check that all criteria for a successful curtain wall have been observed at the design stage. An analysis of the problems in greater detail can be found in *Light cladding of buildings*[1].

3 Examine manufacturer's product

The following check list and subsequent information form a basis on which to examine the manufacturer's product or proposal:

- Visual suitability
- Loading
- Construction and assembly
- Joints and connections
- Insulation and moisture control
- Solar control
- Acoustic control.
- Modular sizes available.

3.01 Visual suitability

Grid proportions and the design of grid members may reflect structural reality; ie when principal grid members dominate, and secondary members are not emphasised. Hence many curtain walls have vertical emphasis **1a**, compared to horizontal **1b**. A grid in which mullions and transomes are of the same thickness implies either that the secondary members are over-dimensioned, or that the principal members are inconspicuously reinforced. This is often done by attaching mullions to the back-up wall, thus reducing their span and cross-section.

3.02 Loading

Although curtain walls have been defined as 'non-loadbearing external walls', they are loaded horizontally by wind force and vertically by their own dead weight. Wind loading is defined in BS CP3 chapter 5[2] (see also data on wind loading in *Guide to the Building Regs* 1972 pp24-33.

Design for wind loading depends on:

- Location of building
- Degree of exposure
- Height above ground.

Winds produce suction as well as pressure and these negative forces are important in detailing anchors, fixings and glazing beads.

Wind loading, particularly the severe loads experienced on high and exposed buildings, can cause considerable deflection in curtain walling members. Deflection may be both 'in' and 'out', alternating at high frequency. Com-

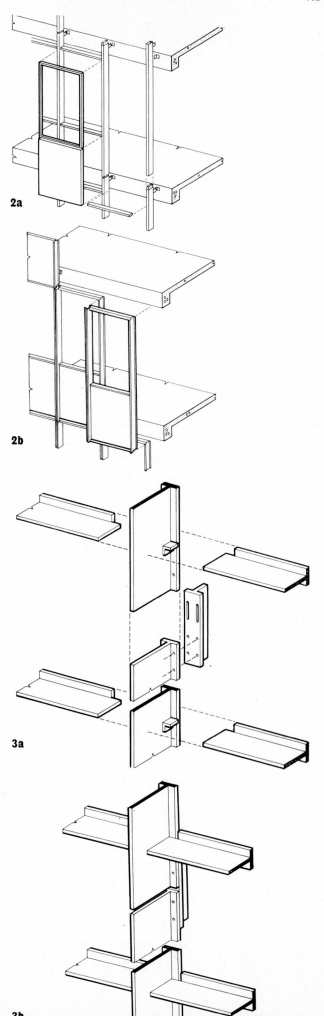

2a

2b

3a

3b

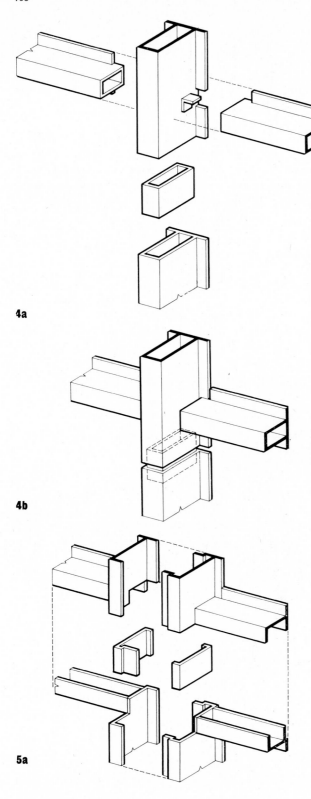

plex junction details are used to allow movement between sections, but it is important to check that panel, frame and other element details have been designed to work together. Many cases of leaking curtain walls are due to differential movement of this type. Complete theoretical analysis by calculation is very difficult and should be supplemented by static and dynamic load tests to reveal how the system will behave in practice.

3.03 Construction and assembly

Two basic forms of construction are illustrated in **2**; in **a** the system is assembled on site and offered to the frame; in **b** the windows themselves become the frame.

In both systems mullions are usually the principal members of the grid. Curtain walls are rarely supported by horizontal members because of design and structural disadvantages. Vertical members spanning from floor to floor must withstand axial stresses caused by self-weight, and bending caused by wind loads. Bending is in one direction only (compared with two, if principal members are horizontal), and it is in this direction that the mullion must have greatest stiffness and strength.

Order of assembly
Prefabricated components of grid systems—mullions, transoms and infill panels—are assembled in the following order:
● Mullions are mounted and aligned by connectors, adjustable in three directions and anchored to each floor
● Transomes are fixed in position between mullions
● Spandrel panels and windows are inserted, usually from outside.
Main advantage of this system is that components are easy to handle; disadvantages are time spent on site and need for scaffolding or special platforms to assemble the grid.

There are many different degrees of prefabrication in the construction of curtain wall frames, from the totally prefabricated (with spandrel panels and glazing already in place) to the empty frame, consisting only of framing members themselves into which spandrel panels and glazing are assembled on site. The more complete the prefabrication, the easier it is to carry out all site operations from inside the building, without scaffolding.

4a

4b

5a

2 *Site assembled system is offered up to frame* **a**; *or* **b** *system itself incorporates a frame*
3 *Diagram showing sleeve joint and tolerances:* **a** *before assembly;* **b** *after assembly*
4 *Diagram showing jointing between solid mullions and connections with transomes:* **a** *before assembly;* **b** *after assembly*
5 *Junction between four frames, illustrating principle of split mullion. Detail of type shown in* **2b**

5b

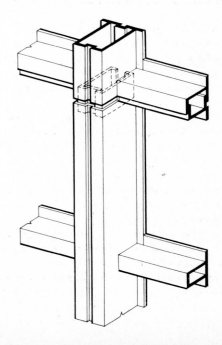

3.04 Joints and connections

Curtain walling consists of prefabricated elements finally jointed together on site. Joints at frequent intervals are necessary to enable components to be in sizes of manageable dimensions.

Frequent jointing will also reduce movement per joint, particularly thermal, in the system, and between the system and supporting system.

Joints between frame members

The metal components of every curtain wall must be allowed to expand and contract freely. Wood is an exception, as its low coefficient of thermal expansion reduces thermal stressing and members can be fixed together rigidly. Unless completely sealed however (by paint or other protective coating, maintained in good condition) wood is subject to considerable movement due to changes in moisture content. Differential changes due to patchy protection can produce twisting or warping, a most unpleasant state of affairs. In all other materials the problem of thermal expansion has a decisive influence on joint design.

Slip and spring connections are the two main types of jointing systems. These open and close in response to temperature changes. If temperatures fluctuate steadily, the components are in almost constant movement. Joints must also be weatherproof and permit safe and rapid construction. A slip connection is shown in **3a**.

Joints between frame and infill panels

Joints between frame and infill panels take the form of beads, gaskets and sealants. The following requirements must be met:
● Joints must be wind- and rain-proof (if inside of infill panel is sensitive to moisture, the edges should be protected)
● Self-weight of panels and wind loads must be transferred evenly to the frame
● Panels and framing members must be free to expand and contract independently (if subject to movement)
● Joints must tolerate structural movement
● Joints must allow for dimensional and alignment variations between shop and site.

3.05 Insulation and moisture control

Insulation problems

Cost of thermal insulation must be related to capital and running cost of heating and air-conditioning plant. The insulant must be positioned so that:
● Insulant is not saturated by condensation (see Information sheet External Envelope 1)
● Condensation is either prevented or occurs only where it can be collected and drained away. (For alternative methods of achieving this, see *Light cladding of buildings*[1].)
In the US condensation is often collected by a flashing and drained through open joints and weep holes **7**. Driving rain often forces its way upwards through weep holes (sometimes quite dramatically, as in the United Nations Secretariat building, New York, where a 75 mm head of water was once observed inside the wall). Alternatively the condensate can be drained with any other water that has forced itself past the joints into a gutter section discharging at low level via hollow mullions.

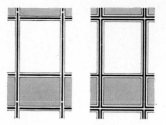

6a   **6b**

6 *Location of joints **a** in site-assembled system as shown in **2a**; and **b** in system incorporating frame as shown in **2D**. (In **b** joint is represented by white line between frames)*

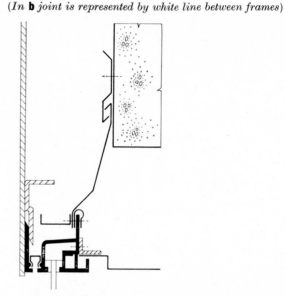

7a

7b

7 *Ceiling joint, Chase Manhattan Bank, New York: **a** as detail; **b** during erection*

8 *Aluminium fins projecting at right angles from glass face to shield the window from sun*

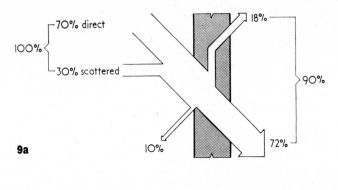

9a

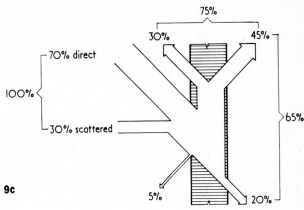

9c

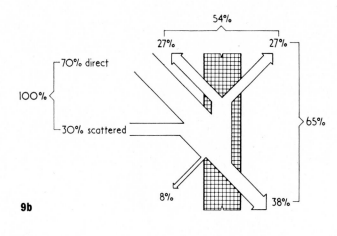

9b

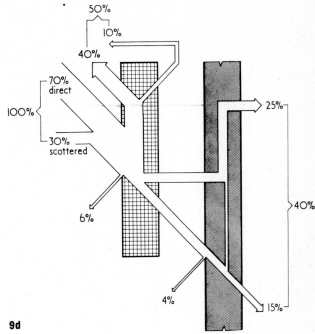

9d

3.06 Solar control

Solar control can be achieved by:

● External screens, louvres and other barriers which shade the curtain wall. (For detailed information on design, see AJ 2.1.63 Screens and louvres: General; and information sheet 1184 [sfʙ 1961 (35)] cɪ/sfʙ (22).) **8**

● Using the wall itself to screen the sun, eg sun-resisting glass.

● Internal screens, blinds and barriers; these are less effective than external barriers for although a blind may reflect radiant heat from the sun, it will itself become warm and reflect its own heat on to the occupants.

The efficiency of these methods is shown in **9a to e.** Not all methods are appropriate for tall buildings where high wind velocities and maintenance problems may restrict solar control devices to the plan of the glazing (producing the most characteristic of all curtain wall types, the unshaded building with heat-absorbing glass and full air-conditioning). Disadvantages of heat-absorbing glass are:

● Absorption of heat causes thermal stresses within the glass, requiring special glazing techniques

● Much of the energy absorbed by the glass passes into the building: it behaves like a panel radiator, unless it is ventilated, or used with double glazing.

A more recent technique is the development of glass that reflects, rather than absorbs, radiation by being coated with a thin transparent layer of evaporated metal.

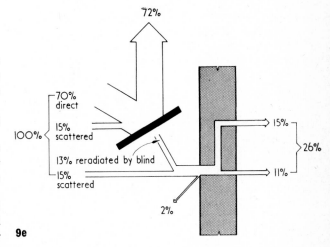

9e

9 *Efficiency of different means of controlling solar radiation*
a *Ordinary sheet glass*
b *Heat-absorbing glass*
c *Glare-reducing glass*
d *Panel of heat-absorbing glass freely suspended in front of glass*
e *Aluminium venetian blind freely suspended in front of sheet glass*

3.07 Acoustic control

Structure-borne sound

Noise can be transmitted from one level to another via vertical members of the façade. Common sources of this type of disturbance are:

● Window cleaners' cradle guided over mullions operating without rubber tyres

● Transmission of machinery noise from the building structure to the cladding via non-resilient mullion connectors.

Structure-borne sound can be prevented by isolating noisy machinery and joints between framing on resilient mountings, and insulating cleaning cradles on rubber tyres.

Air-borne sound

A light-weight cladding system offers no great mass to resist the penetration of sound. Weakest points in the system are:

● Transmission through the cladding from an external source

● Floor to floor transmission **10a**

● Room to room transmission **10b**.

Air-borne sound will penetrate the wall at its weakest point, namely the window. Reduce transmission either by reducing area of glazing, increasing glass thickness, and sealing the window, or by using double windows. Detailed calculations of the effect of these on decibel reduction can be found in *Light cladding of buildings*[1] (p141-144).

Airborne sound from internal sources can be considerably reduced by absorbents, especially at the weak points indicated in **10**.

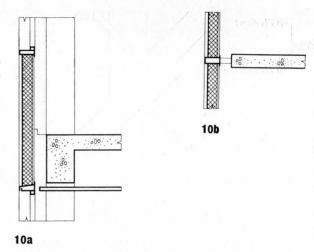

10a

10b

10a, b *In section* **a** *air-borne sound can travel between floors via space between slab and curtain wall. In plan* **b** *air-borne sound can travel between partitions, via space between column and curtain wall*

References

1 ROSTRON, M. Light cladding of buildings. London, 1964, Architectural Press [(21)]

2 BRITISH STANDARDS INSTITUTION BS CP 3: Part 2: Chapter V: 1970 Wind loads [(k4f)] £1

3 HUNT, W. D. The contemporary curtain wall. New York, 1958, Dodge Corporation [(21·4)]

4 Screens, louvres: General 3: Shading devices and masks; information sheet 1184. *Architects' Journal*, 1963, January 2 [sfB 1961: (35); CI/sfB (22)]

Information sheet External walls 6

Small unit claddings

This information sheet deals with claddings consisting of small elements fixed on to a structural support. Decorative claddings, eg sawn stone, precast slabs or sheet metal, cramped or slipped on to a backing wall, are also considered. Heavy stone and concrete claddings, and large sheet metal claddings have already been dealt with in previous information sheets. The author is DAVID KIRBY

1 Introduction

Traditionally claddings are used where the basic structure is unsuitable to resisting local environmental conditions. They are also used for visual reasons, to provide contrasts of material, colour and texture, or to express the difference between a visible structure and the infill area, eg in cross-wall construction **1**.

1.01 Function

Cladding should provide a near-impervious 'skin' to the structure, capable of resisting driven rain and wind forces from any direction. Traditional small unit claddings, such as slates or boards, perform this function and avoid condensation problems because of the ventilation provided by the many joints.

Rising standards of heating, insulation and construction require special attention to moisture vapour problems. Other types of small claddings, eg sawn stone fixed on to backing walls, have mainly decorative functions, and usually choice will depend on cost and the visual effect required by the architect or the local planning officer.

2 Structural support

Small unit claddings may be fixed either to a framed support, or to a block or brick support. Design of this system of support is shown diagrammatically in **2**.

Data on U-values and condensation risk associated with particular forms of construction will be found in information sheet EXTERNAL ENVELOPE 1; if the proposed form of construction is not included in the range of examples shown, U-value and condensation risk should be calculated (see 'Condensation in buildings', AJ 19.5.71, 26.5.71 and 2.6.71).

3 Types of cladding

Cladding should be selected in terms of:
● Appearance
● Cost
● Durability.

Table I lists types of cladding and gives data on appearance, fixing, cost and so on and refers to sources of additional information.

1 *Weatherboard cladding at Corby, used to provide strong contrast of colour and pattern (Corby Development Corporation architects)*

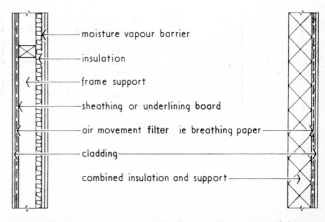

— moisture vapour barrier
— insulation
— frame support
— sheathing or underlining board
— air movement filter ie breathing paper
— cladding
— combined insulation and support

2 *Framed support (left) and block or brick support (right)*

Table 1 Types of small unit claddings

	Appearance	Method of fixing	Approximate cost £/m² (source: SPON'S 1971)		Durability	Useful references
Tile hanging Clay tiles Concrete tiles		Centre nailed on battens (see AJ Handbook of Fixings and fastenings, information sheet NAILS 1—(AJ 24.3.71)	Concrete tiles Machine made tiles Handmade clay tiles	2·50 2·90 3·65	Tiling generally guaranteed for 30 years; battens must be rot-proofed	Tile manufacturers' catalogues provide sections and details
Slate hanging Natural slate Asbestos slate		Centre nailed on battens (see above)	Welsh slates about Westmorland slates about	3·85 11·00	Life generally considered indefinite, if battens and nails will endure (use non-ferrous nails)	
Timber shingles Western red cedar Sweet chestnut (rare) Oak (rare)		Copper nails, galvanised nails, or silicone bronze nails (see above)				*Canadian red cedar shingles* and hand-split *shakes* (pamphlet published by the Council of the Forest Industries of British Columbia, Templar House, 81-87 High Holborn, London WC1)
Timber weather-boarding Varnished Painted Water-repellent finish		Nailed to battens, traditional details (see above)	Tongued and grooved softwood vertical boarding fixed on battens 3·00 Do Western red cedar 3·10 Timber preservative 0·26 Knot, stop, prime, one undercoat, one gloss 0·75		Boarding finishes require regular maintenance: timber preservatives every two to five years, paint every three to five years. Western red cedar can be left and is admired by architects in this condition but not generally by laymen	
Pre-coated weatherboarding Pvf-, pvfa- or pvc-coated board Pre-coated aluminium		Must be fixed to manufacturer's details: often grooves in planks are slid along fixing cleats (see AJ Handbook of Fixings and fastenings, information sheet CLADDING FIXINGS 8— (AJ 21.4.71)				
Stone and artificial stone claddings Natural stone Artificial stone Light precast concrete with exposed aggregate		Secured to backing wall by non-rusting cramps (see AJ Handbook of Fixings and fastenings, information sheet MASONRY CRAMPS 9— (AJ 21.4.71)	Stone from Faience slabs from	18·75 15·75	While most of these materials have indefinite life in themselves, these claddings provide one of the largest sources of trouble, with slabs breaking away, cracking or spalling at corners	
Metal clad dings Lead Copper Zinc Stainless steel Aluminium		Thin metal sheets are clipped to backing walls: side and end joints are formed by seaming or rolling, or by soldering or welding. Sometimes nailing is used with head protected by lead dot (lead only)	Metal sheet claddings on vertical walls and deep fascias are comparatively recent feature of modern designs, costs might be for: Copper 15·00 Lead 16·00 Aluminium 8·00		Stainless steel, copper and lead have outstanding resistance to weathering. Super purity aluminium has excellent resistance except in heavily polluted industrial atmospheres and care should be taken to check its suitability	The metal manufacturers maintain development associations which should be contacted for further information

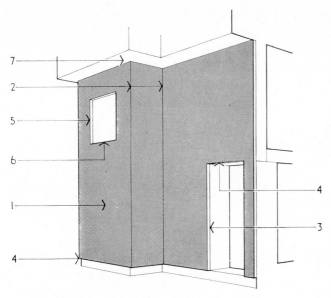

3 *Shaded area indicates cladding*

4 Design checklist

The location of points numbered in this checklist is shown in **3**.

1 Is preferred system resistant to local hazards, eg impact and abrasion resistance, particularly near ground level? Is cladding system suited to size of job and probable skill-level available?

2 Check angle details—traditional for traditional materials —but check that manufacturers of new materials supply necessary types of trim sections. Such sections may have to be ordered in advance with cladding and cannot be varied without causing some delay

3 Check junction details with other materials

4 Impervious claddings must allow for heavy run-off of rain. Sills, flashings, gutters, damp-proof courses and projecting lower courses must be detailed to cope with this run-off. Ground junction details require special attention. Few claddings can go down to ground level, so a plinth is required

5 Check opening details. Frame details must be located correctly in relation to cladding, if special trim is to be avoided

6 Check run-off below openings or at changes in detail. Heavy run-off may penetrate tile-type claddings or disfigure weatherboarding

7 Shading effects may lead to dust and dirt accumulation: the effect itself is unavoidable, but sudden changes of level and overhangs may cause undesirable patterning.

5 Building Regulations

Sections of the Building Regulations (England & Wales) 1965 which are relevant to cladding are (B3) 'Short-lived or unsuitable materials' and (E) structural Fire Precautions. Table II shows materials considered unsuitable for external use.

Section E7 of the Building Regulations refers to the position of external walls and its effect on claddings:

● Claddings on walls within 1·0 m of the boundary or exceeding 15·0 m in height must be entirely non-combustible with certain minor exceptions (see Reg. E7 and Schedule 9 of the Building Regulations 1972)

However, walls with combustible cladding are regarded as unprotected areas and limited accordingly. If the backing wall has the required fire resistance only 50 per cent of the area need be counted.

● On walls 1·0 m or more from a boundary and more than 15 m high, claddings up to 15 m high can be timber not less than 9 mm thick. Above 15 m all claddings must be Class 0 (surface spread of flame).

Table II *Short-lived cladding materials suitable for external walls*

Type of material	Suitability for external walls
Softwood boarding	Only that which is manufactured from: ● heartwood of timber (specified in table 1 to schedule 4) ● timber (specified in table 2 to schedule 4) subjected to preservative specified in table 3 to schedule 4 (with minimum thickness of 16 mm (except feather-edge boarding which should be 16 mm at thicker edge and 6 mm at thinner edge)
Plywood	Only external quality not less than 8 mm thick
Sheet steel	Only galvanised steel in accordance with Class 1A BS 2989 : 1967 or vitreous-enamelled, bitumen-coated or Type 200 BS 3088 : 1959
Asbestos cement sheeting	Only that conforming with BS 690 : 1963 or BS 4036 : 1966 or sheets which fail to comply with BS 690/1963 only because of their profile providing they comply with certain tests laid down in BS 690 as to extreme fibre stress. (See Building Regulations—Table to Regulation B3)

In Inner London, external cladding to a building is required to be 'of such materials, of such thickness and fixed and supported in such manner as the district surveyor may approve'. In many cases allowance must be made in the fixing of cladding for dimensional changes in the structural frame and thermal movement in the facing material. No statutory rules are laid down as there are many variables and each case requires individual consideration, but useful guidance may be obtained from the Concrete Society's data sheet, CSI 1 *The provision of compression joints in the cladding of a reinforced concrete building,* and the Brickwork Development Association's technical note vol 1, no 4, *Some observations on the design of brickwork cladding to multi-storey reinforced concrete framed structures.*

Information sheet
Extension walls 7

Sheet cladding

Large sheets of thin material, having rigidity provided by corrugation in various forms can be produced from a number of materials by economic continuous processes. The author is DAVID KIRBY

1 General

Sheet claddings have been associated mainly with industrial buildings where thin, lightweight basic weather protection is required. Light weight is important to enable cheap structures of maximum span to be provided: weather protection is basic (the object has usually been to keep rain off machines rather than to provide any sort of comfort conditions for men).

The advent of aluminium and various colour-coating processes and an increasing awareness of maintenance costs have led to a wider choice of finishes and some improvement in appearance. Rising heating costs and the need for increased environmental control during manufacturing processes have resulted in the basic sheeting being upgraded by the addition of insulation, lining and fire-resistant materials. In certain buildings it is also mandatory that the roof should comply with a statutory minimum standard laid down in 'The Industrial Buildings Roof Insulation Act'. This does not cover walls however, probably because they usually represent a comparatively 'small percentage of the total shell' area in the usual type of single storey factory or warehouse building.

With these improvements to the basic product, it is possible to achieve high standards of comfort within the building, and a certain crisp elegance of external detailing. However, few architects in this country have been able to break with the industrial image of sheet cladding and produce work up to continental standards, **5**.

2 Types of sheeting

Table 1 below lists the types of sheeting available with descriptions.

3 Design checklist

3.01 Weather resistance

All materials in Table 1 are resistant to normal weather conditions. Light claddings require particular attention where wind resistance and adequacy of fixings are concerned.

Large areas of impervious claddings produce heavy run-off from driven rain. Drainage at the wall base and drip protection at junctions and openings are necessary. Beads of moisture tend to hang at the ends of sheets and deposit dust and dirt. Joints should be masked where possible.

3.02 Thermal insulation and capacity

Large-span industrial and commercial structures have a high volume: surface ratio. The general preference of industrialists is for high-output warm-air unit heaters with a rapid response facility to heating change. Architects, probably poorly advised on the relative costs of insulation and heating should try, in a time of inflation and rising fuel costs, to persuade clients to allow them to improve insulation standards.

Check design for condensation and thermal bridge problems which may induce corrosion, particularly at frame rails and fixing points.

3.03 Occupancy and detail use of building

Sheet materials are subject to impact damage: asbestos cracks and breaks; metals dent or tear. Requirements of use factors should be checked; ie heights of vehicles, forklift trucks, handling equipment and storage heights. Pavement and ground level details should be considered carefully to keep hazards apart from buildings; brickwork is often used to resist base damage, while low and high level crash barriers cause less harm to errant vehicles.

3.04 Building details

Basic fixing details are described in manufacturers' information. Function and appearance problems arise at junctions, corners, angle-junctions with other materials and exposed structure.

Modular design of preferred sheeting is essential to accommodate sheet sizes and corrugated section intervals. Neat results are achieved by placing cladding between structure or panels of other materials, thus avoiding using manufacturers' cumbersome cover strips at corners.

3.05 References

References for design purposes, apart from manufacturers' catalogues, are rare. *The International Asbestos Cement Review* (published by Dr. H. Girsberger, Kirch Gasse 4c, Zurich, Switzerland) describes completed buildings, and the British Steel Corporation and the Zinc Development Association have published a handbook *Detailing coated-steel sheet: 1 Unframed non-loadbearing skins* (available from BSC Strip Mills Division, 151 Gower Street, London WC1).

4 Fixings

Sheet claddings are usually fixed to steel cladding rails which are secured in turn to the structural framework. Timber fixing rails may also be used.

With roof cladding in this country it is normal practice to bolt through the apex of corrugations (see AJ information sheet ROOFS 1 table I). With wall cladding it is preferable to fix in the valley, so that the fixing head can pull the sheeting back towards the rail of inner lining.

In addition to the bolts, the weight of sheeting is supported by hooks clipped over the rails **1**. Hookbolts are difficult to use and produce an untidy effect. A wide variety of hooks and self-tapping screws and bolts are available with plastic caps. These enable the sheets to be secured from one side only, but the sheet itself must be aligned carefully and clamped in place before the pilot holes are drilled **2a-d**. Plastic caps can be selected to match coloured sheets.

Metal sheeting is liable to flutter at the long edge of overlapping sheets. This can allow rain penetration and result in enlargement of fixing holes, eventually ripping the sheet from the framing. Seams must be screwed, bolted or riveted; self-tapping screws and pop- or sealed-rivets are typical types of fastening **3a-e**.

Various types of cladding with hidden fixings are offered by manufacturers. Two types are shown as illustrating two basic principles: **4, a** with one side of the sheeting secured into a tongue and groove type joint, suitably weathersealed, and **b** with a cover strip clipping over bolt heads, the cover strip being profiled to blend into the remainder of the sheet section.

5 Workmanship

Light claddings are particularly susceptible to poor workmanship. Site damage and careless handling; poor alignment and spacing of sheeting, overtightening or undertightening of fixings, omission of bolts and sealing sections can result in sheeting failure. Where fixings are prominent, good alignment is important. Cladding is usually fixed by specialist subcontractors; and there seems to be a shortage of good references on its design and specification, apart from manufacturers' catalogues.

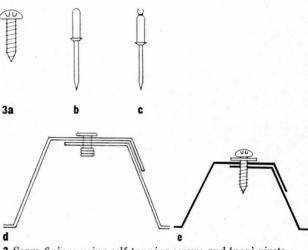

3a   **b**   **c**

d   **e**

3 *Seam fixings using self-tapping screws and 'pop' rivets*
a *Self-tapping screw for light gauge metal*
b *Sealed rivet, aluminium alloy*
c *Sealed rivet, monel metal*
d *Sealed rivet of types **b** and **c**, after fixing in sheeting*
e *Self-tapping screw in position*

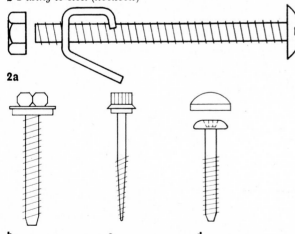

1a   **b**

1 *Basic fixing accessories for vertical sheeting*
a *Fixing on timber (screw)*
b *Fixing to steel (hookbolt)*

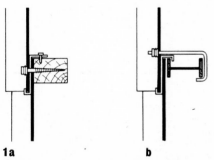

2a

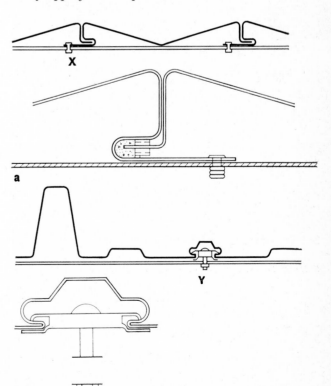

X

a

Y

b

4 *Secret fix details,* **a** *detail at* **X**; **b** *detail at* **Y**

b   **c**   **d**

2 *Clips and screws designed to produce a neat head on the external face of cladding*
a *Oakley clip for securing sheeting from the outside. A type of adjustable hookbolt; bent section hooks on to support while bolt secures sheeting (see **1b**)*
b *Self-tapping screw*
c *Self-tapping screw with integral plastic head, for steel*
d *Self-tapping screw with separate 'snap on' plastic cap*

5 *Water tower, Fulbourn Hospital, Cambridge*

Table I *Comparative information: sheet cladding types*

Material	Form	Durability and weathering	Upgrading
Aluminium	Corrugated profiles to BS 2855 Trough-section profiles to BS 3428 Other sections to individual manufacturers' standards. Sheet length up to 7·6 m	Durable, except in severely aggressive industrial atmospheres	Factory pre-painted finishes to BS 2660. Insulating and fire-resistant linings
Asbestos-cement	CP 143 Part 6: 1962 deals with corrugated a-c sheeting. Sections are to manufacturers' standards in sheets up to 1 m wide × 3 m long	Becomes ingrained with dirt and brittle with age; subject to impact damage: 40-year life if painted or otherwise protected	Linings to provide insulation and an improved internal appearance
Glass-reinforced polyester resin (grp) sheeting	Produced in standard sections to match other sheeting materials. Used mainly as translucent sheeting set in areas of other material owing to price. Materials amended to comply with 7th Amendment to Building Regulations†	When manufactured to BS 4154:1967, should be good for 15 to 25 years' life, but may yellow with age	Superior products can have surface layer of polyvinyl fluoride (pvf) to improve weathering. Double-skin linings can improve U-value to 3·06 W/m² deg C
Polyvinyl-chloride (pvc)	Pressed or extruded corrugated sheeting in standard sections to match other materials. Wire reinforcement added to produce sheeting with AA class 1 spread of flame rating	At least 15 years in limited range of natural, white and grey colours	Some manufacturers provide double-skin or patent interlocking systems
Galvanised corrugated steel	Corrugated sheeting to BS 3083. Mild steel is common material but iron sheet is available (see specification for gauge and span details)	Unless painted, life is limited to five to seven years. With maintenance, life may be 50 to 60 years. May also be coated with bitumen-asbestos mixture which gives long life span especially if used on galvanised profiles. Often considered adequate without galvanising	Insulant linings
Plastics-coated galvanised steel sheet	Variety of sections: sheet sizes up to 762 mm wide × 7620 mm long. Plastics may be film- or paste-coated	Good colour retention; low maintenance; colour ranges from BS 2660	Pvf film may be added to improve weathering. Manufacturers offer several comprehensive wall systems
Stainless-steel sheet*	Rolled or flat sheet sections—rare because of price	18.10.3 grade should always be specified in UK—life then indefinite	Linings as required

* See AJ special issue 22.4.70, p997
† Now incorporated into 1972 Regulations

Information sheet
External walls 8

External doors

This information sheet includes door types, modes of operation and materials. The author is HOWARD NASH

1 Function

An external door is a filter in the building envelope. Open, it should permit authorised passage. Closed, it may be expected to perform with the adjoining envelope as wall or window. Thus the door may affect the performance of the wall as a whole in respect of:

- Light
- Ventilation
- View
- Sound
- Security
- Privacy
- Heat loss and solar gain
- Exclusion of wind and rain
- Fire spread
- Air pressure (if inflatable structure).

2 Weather protection

The weather performance of external door openings is currently receiving considerable attention. The development of testing rigs for wind and rain penetration and the results of research into window performance, involving their use, is discussed in information sheet EXTERNAL WALLS 9.

Traditional good practice, illustrated diagrammatically in **1**, aims to *minimise* entry of wind and rain. With increased standards of comfort, *complete* sealing against entry of wind and rain is now required. Also door openings frequently have to be designed for severe exposure conditions and wind-eddying effects can occur around doors on to balconies, even on relatively low-rise buildings. This requirement represents a considerable design problem for the common domestic door, differing from that associated with windows in the following ways:

- Air-tight seals are more difficult to maintain on larger openings owing to the greater cumulative effect of any distortion
- Flush doors are particularly prone to distortion owing to the effect of temperature and humidity differentials across the door. Advanced designs incorporating insulation and vapour barriers are becoming available
- Simple compressive seals are more difficult to hold as openings become larger, and therefore have limited applica-

tion to doors. Check ability of closing device to restrain door in closed position, and of door to resist distortion

- Conventional ironmongery provides no restraint at top and bottom of door except by bolts which are cumbersome to use, and only operable from inside. Consider use of espagnolette-type lock or other suitable ironmongery to restrain door at head and sill, as well as centre
- Consider use of double doors to form air-lock.

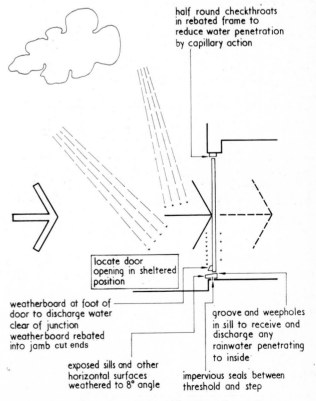

half round checkthroats in rebated frame to reduce water penetration by capillary action

locate door opening in sheltered position

weatherboard at foot of door to discharge water clear of junction weatherboard rebated into jamb cut ends

exposed sills and other horizontal surfaces weathered to 8° angle

groove and weepholes in sill to receive and discharge any rainwater penetrating to inside

impervious seals between threshold and step

1 *Schematic section showing traditional good practice. It is important, especially with inward-opening external doors, to ensure that the vertical frame rebates at each side finish forward of the threshold rebate or water bar*

3 Durability

3.01 Conditions of use

Consider effects of:
● Normal opening and closing
● Banging, kicking, slamming, bumping with carried articles, scratching by dogs, and so on.

3.02 Weathering

● Check suitability of hardwoods for exterior use. In particular consider tendency to warp especially where inside of door and outside are subjected to very different conditions, eg normal winter weather one side, heated atmosphere, say 20°C or more on other. In such cases sealer or finish to maintain even moisture content most important.
● Consider type of preservative treatment for all softwood (see BS 1282[1])
● Consider appropriate paint system for galvanised steel (see BRS digest 70[9])
● Select suitable anodized or post-applied finish for aluminium.

4 Access and egress

Consider type and volume of traffic and check:
● Minimum total opening width of all leaves in relation to peak flow (see AJ Handbook of Building services and circulation: Circulation 4[15]).
● Minimum clear opening width and height necessary (see **2**). These are defined by Building Regulations E10, E11, E12 for public buildings; and by specialised use, eg small wheelchairs require 2ft 8in minimum clear width (European standard 830 mm).

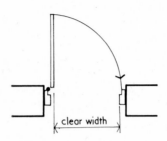

2 *Clear opening width not necessarily the stated width of door*

5 Type of door

Consider most appropriate type:

5.01 Pedestrian

● Side hung: inward opening, outward opening, or pivot (a)
● Straight sliding: manual or automatic operation (pressure switch, interrupted beam and so on) (b)
● Revolving (c)

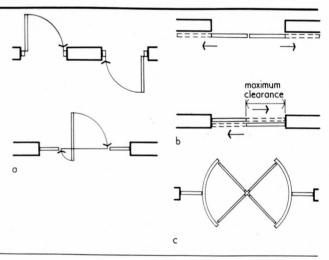

5.02 Industrial (horizontal)

Floor tracks may be subject to grit blockage, damage by traffic and icing up.

● Angle sliding (a)
● Folding: centre-folding or end-folding (b)
● Folding shutter (virtually unlimited size, generally cheapest type of industrial door for openings greater than 40ft (12 m), rapid opening but expensive to repair) (c)
● Flexible: rubber, pvc or neoprene (d)

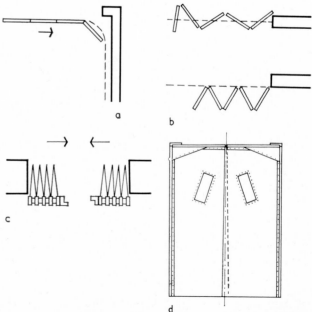

5.03 Industrial (vertical)

Absence of floor track an advantage with all vertical doors.

● Up-and-over (a)
● Centre-folding (b)

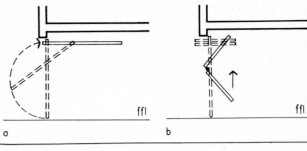

● Roller shutter (up to maximum 40ft wide × 30ft high (12 m × 9 m), most common industrial door, cheapest industrial door for middle range of sizes up to 35ft width (10·5 m) and relatively easy to repair) (c)
● Articulated panel or 'slideover' (relatively high first cost but good weatherseal possible) (d)
In both types slates may be wood or metal.

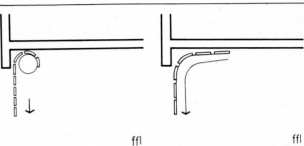

● Lifting panel (e)

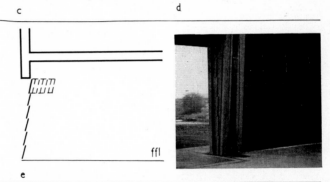

6 Materials

Consider most appropriate materials and methods of construction for door:

6.01 Timber

● Matchboarded doors (BS 459 Part 4: 1965[2]): Ledged, ledged and braced, framed, ledged and braced (a)
● Flush doors—exterior quality (BS 459 Part 2: 1962[2]) (b)
● Panelled and glazed wood doors (BS 459 Part 1: 1954[2]) (c)
● Louvred doors (d)

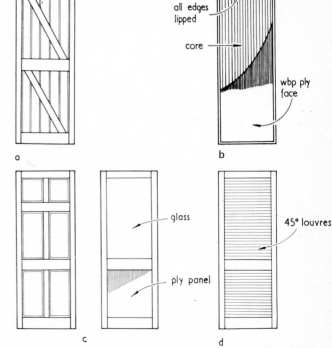

6.02 Galvanised steel

● Glazed steel casement doors compatible with galvanised steel windows to BS 990[4]. Available to standard size or formed from standard W20 universal sections (a)
● Horizontally-swaged galvanised steel panel doors for up-and-over operation (b)
● Steel-framed industrial doors with galvanised steel or aluminium alloy panels; also pressed metal fire doors, eg folding shutter doors see paragraph 5.02 (c)

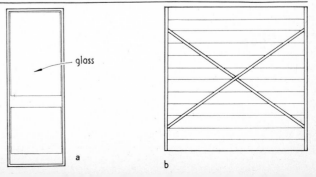

6.03 Aluminium

● Glazed entrance doors usually as part of shopfront system (a)
● Glazed domestic 'patio' doors, horizontal sliding (b)
● Cast aluminium doors to special design (c)

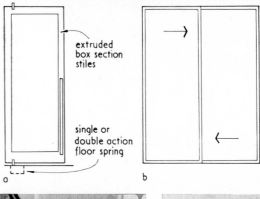

extruded box section stiles

single or double action floor spring

a   b

c

6.04 Stainless steel

● Glazed entrance doors usually as part of shopfront system. Stainless steel used in its own right or as cladding to mild steel, timber or aluminium, eg Midalinox stainless steel on aluminium extrusion (by Midlands Extrusions Ltd)

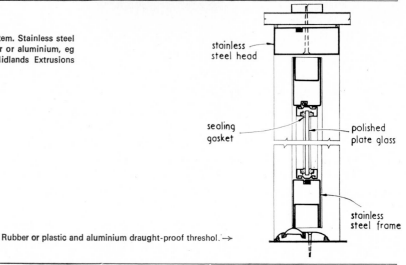

stainless steel head

sealing gasket

polished plate glass

stainless steel frame

Rubber or plastic and aluminium draught-proof threshol. →

6.05 Bronze

● Cast bronze doors to special design
● Glazed bronze doors fabricated from extruded sections

6.06 Glass

Toughened glass entrance doors
(Single or double, one- or two-way swing)

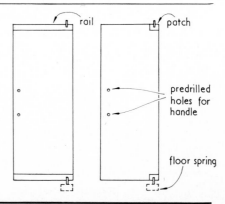

rail   patch

predrilled holes for handle

floor spring

7 Ironmongery

● Consider range of ironmongery necessary: hinges, latches, locks and bolts; letterplates, kicking plates, push plates and handles; door-closers and springs, bells, name and number signs
● Check ability of door to house all ironmongery securely without weakening door, eg flush bolts must be housed in doors not less than 45 mm thick
● Decide offset for handle unit (according to type)
● Ensure that closer can engage latch (if any) on self-closing fire doors.
● Ensure hollow core flush doors have solid packing where needed to receive furniture.

8 Security

● Check security requirements (see AJ Handbook of Building services and Circulation: Security 13[17])
● Check that strength of door and frame are comparable to standard of security provided by lock (and vice versa)
● Check that distance of lock from letterbox is minimum 400 mm to prevent illegal entry
● Where breakage of pane would give access to lock, consider use of toughened glass, wire-reinforced glass or high impact transparent plastic sheet (eg Perspex)

9 Safety

● Check perception of toughened glass doors by users; door must be easily recognisable
● Check that springs and closers do not make operation excessively difficult
● Consider safety and convenience of threshold/step detail for the elderly and disabled. Check access with prams. Consider use of detail illustrated, **3**.

10 Standard sizes

Sizes of standard doors and door sets have been issued by the British Woodwork Manufacturers' Association with the support of DOE. These are incorporated in a draft ISO standard, are widely used in Europe, and will almost certainly be used in the BS on doors due for publication very shortly. These proposals for external doors are to fill basic spaces 900, 1000, 1500 and 1800 mm long × 2100, 2400, 2700 and 3000 mm high.

11 References

BRITISH STANDARDS INSTITUTION
1 BS 1282: 1959 Wood preservatives and their methods of application [Yu3]
2 BS 459: Part 1: 1954 Panelled and glazed wood doors. Part 2: 1962 Flush doors. Part 4: 1965 Matchboarded doors [(32·2) Xi]
3 BS 2504: 1955 Wood doors and frames for milking parlours [(32) Xi]
4 BS 990: 1967 Steel windows [(31) Xh2]
5 BS 4471: 1969 Dimensions for softwood [Xi2]
6 BS 1186: Parts 1: 1952 and 2: 1955 Quality of timber and workmanship in joinery [Yi (A7)]
7 BS CP 151: Part 1 1957 Wooden doors [(32) Xi]
8 BS 3621: 1963 Thief-resistant locks for hinged doors [(32·2) Xt7]

9 BUILDING RESEARCH STATION Digest 70 Painting metals in buildings: 1 Iron and steel. 1966, HMSO [Vv]
10 The Building Regulations 1972 [(A3j)] especially E11 and E12.
11 Buildings Standards (Scotland) (Consolidation) Regulations 1970 [(A3j)] *also Explanatory memorandum 5 'Means of escape'*
12 London, Building Acts 1930-39: London Building (Constructional) Bylaws 1972: see also PITT, P. H. and DUFTON, J. The Guide to the London Building (Constructional) Bylaws 1972, London 1973, Architectural Press, GLC [(Ajn)] also GLC's booklet Means of escape, GLC publication 3863 (under revision; consult GLC); GLC CP Means of escape (multiple occupation); and *Explanatory memorandum 'Places of public entertainment'*
13 FARRANT, D. and HOWE, J. Product selection for architects: external doors. RIBA Journal, 1971, February, p73-78 [(31) Xy (A3u)]
14 Doors and windows. *Specification*, Vol 1, 1971, p316-325. Architectural Press [Yy (A3)]
15 Fire Regulations. Doors. *Architects' Journal*, 1970, March 18, p691-696 [(5–)]
16 Protection of openings. *Architects' Journal*, 1970, July 29, p271-276 [(5–)]
17 AJ Handbook of Building services. Security and fire. *Architects' Journal*, 1970, June 17 to August 5 [(5–)]

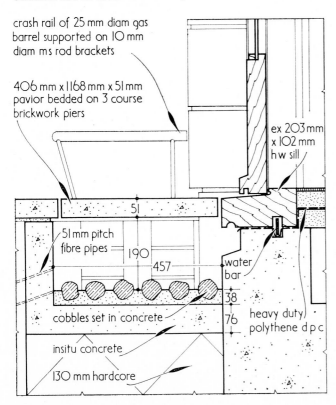

crash rail of 25 mm diam gas barrel supported on 10 mm diam ms rod brackets

406 mm x 1168 mm x 51 mm pavior bedded on 3 course brickwork piers

ex 203 mm x 102 mm hw sill

51

51 mm pitch fibre pipes

190

457

water bar

38

cobbles set in concrete

76

heavy duty polythene d p c

insitu concrete

130 mm hardcore

3 *Section through threshold detail for handicapped people.*
Scale 1 : 10 (Architect: Dennis Pugh Associates)

Information sheet
External walls 9

Windows

*This sheet gives information on window types and frame
sections as elements in the external building envelope.
It includes sections on glass and glazing, performance
requirements and references to ironmongery. The author is*
HOWARD NASH

1 Environmental functions of windows

1.01 Scope

The purpose of this information sheet is to examine the
functions of a window as an element in a building's external
fabric. It is not intended to be used for an examination of
the *environmental* functions of a window. This has been done
in the AJ Handbook of Building environment: appropriate
references are given in table x in the Appendix. Other AJ
material which will be found useful is listed in Appendix
table XI.

However, it may be useful to begin this sheet with a
summary of some of the more important environmental
factors to be considered, with an indication of the complex
interactions of various design decisions. The notes below
outline the key factors, and table I shows the interrelationships of window design decisions. This table is intended to
be used as a checklist rather than as a complete analysis of
each interrelationship. Dates of AJ references mentioned
below are given in the Appendix tables.

References to table I
1 Section 2 SUNLIGHT
2 Information sheet SUNLIGHT II
3 MARKUS, T. A. Significance of sunshine and view for office
workers. Paper in Proceedings of CIE conference 1965.
Rotterdam, 1967, Bouwcentrum International [(N7)]
4 STONE, P. A. Building economy. London, 1966, Pergamon
Press [(Y)]
5 OLGYAY, A., and OLGYAY, V. Design with climate. Princeton, USA, 1963, Princeton University Press [(E7)]
6 Information sheet THERMAL PROPERTIES 2 table I
7 BUILDING RESEARCH STATION Digest 68 Window design
and solar heat gain, 1971, HMSO [(31) (J2)]
8 Information sheet THERMAL PROPERTIES I part 3.
9 MINISTRY OF HOUSING AND LOCAL GOVERNMENT Homes
for today and tomorrow (Parker Morris report). 1961,
HMSO [81 (E2)]
10 BUTTON, D., and OWENS, P. Glass in façade design. Paper
at IHVE/BRS symposium *Thermal environment in modern
buildings* 29 February 1968 [(Ro)]

11 Information sheet THERMAL PROPERTIES 2
12 Section 5 SOUND
13 Section 2 SUNLIGHT
14 BRITISH STANDARDS INSTITUTION Code of Practice BS CP
3: Chapter I(B): 1945. Sunlight (houses, flats and schools
only) [(N7)]
15 SUNLIGHT and DAYLIGHT. Planning criteria and design
of buildings, HMSO [(N7)]

1.02 Environmental checklist

Lighting
Consider role of daylighting in the room lighting scheme.
Does the area and shape of glass proposed meet quantitative
standards (daylight factor) and qualitative standards
(glare, gloom)? Check AJ Handbook of Building environment information sheets SUNLIGHT 2, 6, 9, 11 and 12; and
Sunlight and daylight-planning criteria and design of buildings[1],
from which the following extract is taken.

'The normal multi-purpose vertical window, if it is to admit
daylight reasonably efficiently, needs to have a high window
head.
'This is particularly important if there is a high façade
opposite. A combination of a high opposing façade and a
low window head will tend to cut out light from the back
part of the room and make it impossible to see the sky
except from near the window; the deeper the room the
worse the effect will be. Increasing the width of the window
will not solve the problem.
'A *wide* window is however particularly useful in two
situations. First if the outside obstruction only extends
part way across the view, ie if there is light "round the side",
a window which extends laterally to allow this gap to be
seen will improve both the lighting and the view. Second,
if the room is wide and not deep, a wide window, though it
may not admit as much light as a high window, will distri-
bute it more effectively.
'In short, the optimum shape of the window is related to
the form of the obstruction outside and the shape of the
room. A high window is usually needed to give adequate
light and, particularly, to light a deep room where there is
a high continuous external obstruction. A wide window is

Table I *Interrelationships of window design decisions*

	Building shape[5]	Siting and orientation[5]	Window area[7,16]	External shading[2]	Internal shading[2]	Special glasses[4] (mainly affecting radiant energy)	Double glazing (affecting conductive energy)
Heat gain	Elongation of east-west axis increases solar gain less than elongation of north-south axis, or square plan form. Significance of cooling load due to heat gain through windows diminishes with increased building depth	Consider carefully incident radiation on facade orientations, as this has most significant effect on thermal balance[11]	Heat gain is proportional to glass area. Also consider interaction with noise[7]. In noisy surroundings windows tend to be kept closed, and heat loss due to ventilation is reduced. So heat gain may increase	Can be designed for total sun exclusion. Consider relative benefits of horizontal or vertical shading elements (depending on orientation)	Will obstruct direct radiation but unless highly reflective, will release absorbed heat rapidly to internal air	Wide range of special performance glasses diminish radiation by various degrees[2] (See table II)	Little effect unless special glass is incorporated as outer glazing, when comments are as for previous column
Heat loss	Significance of heating load due to heat loss through windows decreases with increasing building depth. Heat loss is proportional to surface area. Cube is efficient enclosure but not best shape for optimum heat balance	Topography of land can appreciably affect air flow and exposure. Exposure degree is related to orientation[8]. Stack effect in tall buildings increases window infiltration loss. Exposure increases with height	Heat loss is proportional to glass area. Only in Scotland is window area included in composite required wall U-value for statutory standards	No effect	Curtains and closed venetian blinds can marginally reduce U-value as well as radiant temperature	Little or no effect	Double glazing brings U-value to 2·8 W/m². Optimum separation is about 12 mm (½in). Little further benefit obtained from greater separation. Reduced heat loss probably not significant in cost terms (see below) but important for comfort
Visual daylight[1]	Daylit building is usually thermally capricious. Daylight for task illumination will determine narrow shape, but daylight for amenity will allow deep plan shape	Little effect except for presence of urban obstructions	Reduction of glass area usually means loss of task lighting; but natural amenity lighting is still possible	Fixed external shading diminishes daylighting, the degree depending on design	Good control—convenient if flexible natural lighting levels can be achieved during maximum radiation	Light transmission is related to total heat transmission[10]. Problems of colour rendering	No effect
Visual glare[2]	Shape has no effect on sky glare, but can cut out glare from low-angle sun	No effect on sky glare. Low-angle sun may penetrate from east to west (am) and opposite (pm)	Sky glare is little or not at all affected by glass area in walls	Can reduce sky and sun glare. Consider relative benefits of horizontal or vertical shading	Good control	Little effect on sun glare but they can contribute to control of sky glare	No effect
View out[3]	In high building view out from top floors may require different treatment of window shape than lower floors	This can be significant consideration in building conception	View out does not require large glass areas although it may be restricted	Does limit view out depending on design	Requires correct choice of shading type	View out is significant only if light transmission is below 20 per cent. Problems of colour rendering	No effect
Visual sunlight[1]	Little effect	Sun penetration should be carefully considered[13,14]	Sunlight effect is possible through small glass areas	Shading to exclude heat gain may exclude sun	Blinds and louvres can preserve 'effect' of sunlight	Benefit of sunlight is preserved	No effect
Noise	Incident sound energy on facade can be significantly masked by building obstructions	Incident sound energy can be significantly diminished by siting and orientation[12]	Effect of transmitted external noise is not directly proportional to window area but there is a relationship	Little or no effect	Little or no effect	No effect	Insulation increases with glass mass and spacing width. 100 to 200 mm width spacing is 5–10dB improvement on single glazed
Flexibility and control	Simple wide open spaces are easily adapted	No effect	Absence of continuous fenestration may limit flexibility	Can be made adjustable but such types are usually costly to install and maintain	Very good	No effect	No effect
Cost (capital and running)[4]	Difficult to estimate, but cost is related to thermal loading in relation to optimum building shape[4]	Good siting and orientation lead to significant reduction of services required and also some reduction of running costs	Glass and window frames are usually considerably dearer than the equivalent area of solid cladding. Running cost is high in terms of maintenance and thermal loss	Could significantly reduce services required in hot climates, hence running costs, but initial cost is high, particularly for movable shading. Maintenance of shading is expensive unless structural	Marginal reduction of services and running cost. Comparatively low initial cost, giving good visual benefit. Maintenance costs significant	Reduction of services depending on thermal properties of glass used. Initial costs generally proportionally to performance. Very low maintenance cost	Reduction of heating services and running costs. Consideration should include non-quantifiable benefits obtained from reduction of condensation downdraughts and cold radiation[9]

needed to light a wide room and to take advantage of a gap at the side of an external obstruction.

'As regards view: a high window head is usually necessary to include sky and cloudscape within it. Again a wide window may be needed where it can bring into the view gaps in the opposing buildings, but not where, for instance, it exposes a blank wall usually in shadow.'

Sunlight

Consider effect of sunlight on interior finishes and furnishings.

Solar heat gain

Consider how solar heat gain and time of day at which it occurs affects room temperature. Note increased 'greenhouse' effect (trapping of infra-red radiation) with double-glazing. Check AJ Handbook of Building environment information sheet THERMAL PROPERTIES 2.

Thermal insulation

Consider how glazed area affects U-value of *whole wall*. If contemplating double-glazing, consider what percentage of wall is glazed and whether equivalent reduction in heat loss could be effected more economically by other means. See technical study EXTERNAL ENVELOPE 1.

Example: heat loss through wall shown in **1a** could be reduced by approximately 26 per cent by any of the following measures:

● Use of double-glazed units with 15 mm air-space
● 25 per cent reduction in glass area **1b**
● Improvement of wall U-value from Building Regulations Standard $1 \cdot 70$ W/m²deg C to $1 \cdot 13$ W/m²deg C.

Check AJ Handbook of Building environment information sheet THERMAL PROPERTIES 1.

View

Consider occupants' requirements for view in relation to privacy: Where, for environmental reasons, glass area is reduced to 20 per cent or less of wall area, vertical vision strips may be preferable to horizontal windows as they present a cross-sectional slice of the view **2a** rather than a layer **2b.** Also vertical windows offer maximum change of view for a given change in the observer's position. However, vertical windows may also give less privacy (as in vertically-boarded fences). See also above, under 'Lighting'.

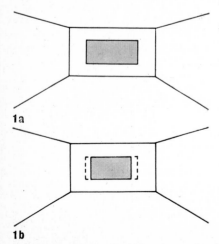

1a

1b

1 In **a**, *single glazed window is equal to 30 per cent of total area. Wall is insulated to Building Regulations Standard* $1 \cdot 70$ *W/m² deg C*
In **b**, *exactly the same reduction in heat loss of the total wall can be achieved, either by increasing the U value of the solid wall from* $1 \cdot 70$ *to* $1 \cdot 13$ *W/m² deg C, or by reducing the glazed area by 25 per cent, or by double-glazing*

Noise penetration

A relatively small glazed area has a radical effect on the sound reduction properties of a wall **3.** Check over-all sound insulation of whole wall using AJ information sheet EXTERNAL ENVELOPE 1. Sound insulation will be improved by:

● Heavier glass
● Double-glazing with 100 mm minimum air-space and sound-absorbent lining to reveals. To be effective all joints must be air-sealed. Different glass thicknesses for each leaf will avoid coincident natural frequencies. (NB preformed double-glazing units have little effect on sound insulation but those combining plate and sheet glass are better).

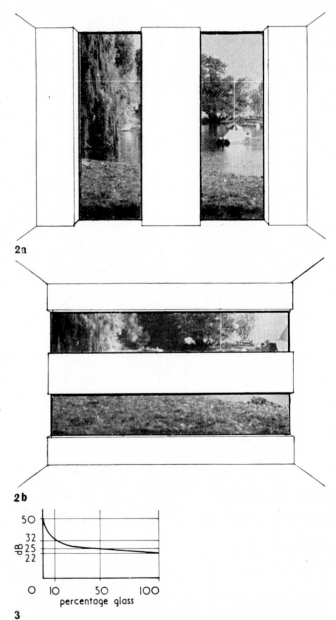

2a

2b

3

2a, b *The same view, seen through windows of different shape, may become quite different in appearance*
3 *Overall sound reduction of cavity wall (50 dB) with fixel single glazed area (22 dB) which varies in proportion to total area (AJ Handbook of Building environment information sheet SOUND 3)*

2 Types of windows

2.01 Opening type

Fixed windows

These are cheaper and simpler than opening windows, but they must always be cleaned from outside, unless there are opening lights adjacent.

Casements

Small top-hung casements **4a**, often placed above large fixed lights for by-law ventilation requirements, but built in permanent ventilators, are now available. Recently side-hung casements have tended to have increasingly large glazed areas and increasingly small sash sections **4b**. To prevent distortion, the glass should be thicker than normal, or even toughened. Large side-hung casements can be used as fire exit points **4b**.
One type of casement, **8** sometimes referred to as 'tilt and turn', opens in two different ways. Normally it provides ventilation as a bottom-hung casement with limited opening; but it can become an inward opening casement when the outside needs cleaning.

Pivots

Horizontal pivots are usually centre-hung **5a** so that the window can reverse for cleaning. Vertical pivots **5b** are usually off centre to prevent interference with curtains and blinds. All pivoted windows should have safety catches to prevent uncontrolled movement.

Louvres

Although in principle louvres **6** are a series of pivots, their characteristics are different. As much as 90 per cent of louvre area can be opened with little projection from the vertical plane. Louvres are ideal for kitchens and bathrooms where a stuffy atmosphere may have to be cleared quickly. Architects specifying louvred windows should always check with manufacturers that their windows have been properly tested and that the results justify their use in exposed situations.

Sliding windows

Sliding windows achieve 50 per cent opening of total window with no projection from the vertical plane. Vertical sliding windows **7a** (the double-hung sash) were developed in the 18th century and are still available—usually in aluminium. Horizontal sliding windows **7b** were developed more recently; though ones dating from the 18th century may still be found, usually where a high sill line was required. As the sliding parts are not exposed to the wind, sash sizes can be reduced or even omitted without using toughened glass. Water running down the face of horizontal sliding windows must be drained through channels. Sliding windows can be prevented from rattling, and air leakage reduced, by textile pile weatherstripping.

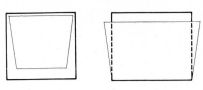

c *Top-hung casement,* **d** *bottom-hung casement*

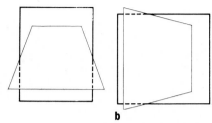

aa *Horizontal pivoted and* **b** *vertical pivot*

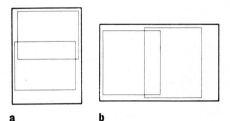

6 *Louvred window*

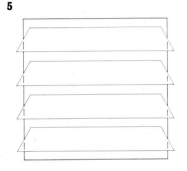

a   **b**
7a *Vertical and* **b** *horizontal sliding windows*

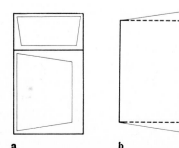

a   **b**
4ab *Side-hung casements*

8 *'Tilt and turn' casement window*

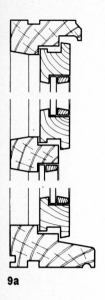
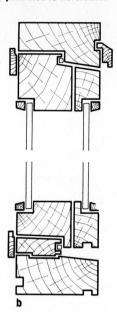
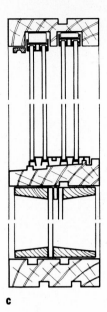
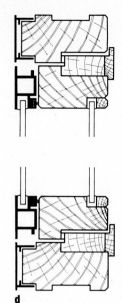
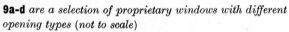

9a

b

c

d

9a-d *are a selection of proprietary windows with different opening types (not to scale)*
a *High performance metric joinery casement window, available with fixed or opening lower light, and adjustable ventilator in side hung sash*
b *Double glazed horizontal pivot-hung window, with sections based on Scandinavian practice. Venetian or pleated blinds can be incorporated between panels*
c *Double glazed sliding window with timber frame and extruded vinyl track. Drainage is through holes in vinyl*

cill track, and offset channels in timber. Above the vinyl head track is a foam cushion to prevent rattling. The fixed light below can be double- or single-glazed, as shown
d *Horizontal-pivot double-glazed coupled sash window, with stainless steel drawn on to extruded aluminium outer facings to frame. Outer sash is entirely extruded aluminium faced with stainless steel. Inner frame and sash is either softwood or hardwood. The coupled sashes rotate through 180° for cleaning. Venetian blinds may be incorporated in the cavity*

2.02 Timber frames

Softwoods used are mainly imported redwoods, while hardwoods suitable for external joinery include oak, iroko, gurjun, utile and teak. As sapwood can no longer be economically excluded from softwoods, preservative treatment is essential. This usually involves impregnation by water-borne or organic solvent type preservatives, either by pressure or double vacuum. A fairly clear line can still be drawn between inexpensive windows developed from the original EJMA ranges, and more sophisticated, mainly pivoted windows based on continental style ironmongery. Standard windows of the EJMA type are available in most opening arrangements and are based on the combination of a few sash sizes with various fixed lights. The chief feature of the more sophisticated timber windows is that they are available as large, undivided, glazed opening lights (up to 3·5 m² is common) incorporating, as standard, efficient weatherstripping and designed frequently as coupled sashes. Following the recent publication of BS DD4: 1971[3], the British Wood Manufacturers Association has announced the introduction by some of its members of 'high performance timber windows'.

Information on suitable timbers and properties is given in BS CP 153: Part 2[6], table II, and Forest Products Research Laboratory technical note 29.

Information on preservative treatments is described in Forest Products Research Laboratory technical note 4. Manufacturers prefer treatment by immersion, which can be done in the factory before assembly.

Finishes

● *Paint* is the traditional finish for wood, as it has good appearance and protection qualities. Advice on painting wood is given in BRS Digest 106. Factory finishes of polyurethane paint claim a useful life twice that of ordinary methods.

● *Clear varnishes* have improved recently, and a useful life of five to seven years is now possible.
● *Preservative stains* give a durable finish which cannot crack, also allowing timber to breathe. They can easily be renewed every three years.

References to timber windows

1 BUILDING RESEARCH STATION Digest 73. Prevention of decay in window joinery. 1966 HMSO [(31) Xi (S4)]
BRITISH STANDARDS INSTITUTION
2 BS 644 Part 1: 1951 Wood casement windows [(31·2) Xi]
3 BS 644 Part 2: 1958 Wood double-hung sash windows [(31·4) Xi]
4 BS 644 Part 3: 1951 Wood double-hung sash and case windows—Scottish type [(31) Xi]
5 BS 1186 Part 1: 1971 Quality of timber [Yi (A7)]
6 BS 1186 Part 2: 1971 Quality of workmanship [Yi (A7)]
7 BS 4471: 1969 Specifications for dimensions for softwood [Xi2 (A3)]
8 Production selection for architects: Timber windows. RIBA *Journal*, 1970, February [(31) Xh (A3y)]

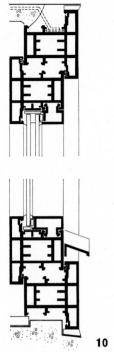

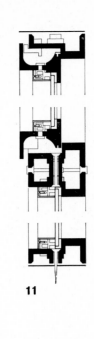

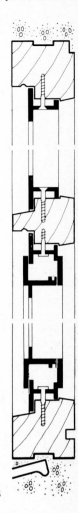

10 *Section of pvc casement window with masonry head and sill*
11 *Section of grp casement window with timber head and sill*
12 *Plastic window*
13 *Section through steel fixed light*

2.03 Plastics frames

Limited use is now being made of glass-reinforced polyester for complete frames, using tubular box-sections incorporating steel stiffening bars. Plastics are also used as cladding to timber and metal, providing a more durable finish than paint—at a price.

Plastic is also being used for complete frame sections in addition to its more proven use as cladding (see BRS Digest 70) and coating to timber and metal. Sections are often reinforced by steel stiffening bars. No painting is required but even the smallest metal fixing (ie screw) must be specified carefully as any rust or other weathering effect will be immediately obvious.

2.04 Bronze frames

Potentially, bronze is as versatile as aluminium, sections being produced by extrusion. The market is clearly limited to designs made to order by the material's expense.

Notes
● Extruded
● Purpose-made only; potentially as versatile as aluminium
● Flash-welded jointing
● Sand-blasted, fine-scratched, or lacquered finishes are possible.

2.05 Steel frames

Steel is not suited to the economic production of special sections, so the industry is oriented to the production of standard *windows* mainly for housing, industrial and agricultural buildings, and *universal sections* that can be used to make up most types of operable windows (except sliding). Rust-proofing is essential and will be achieved usually by hot-dip galvanising or zinc spraying. The latter has advantages, providing a good key for paint systems without the same need for etching as hot-dip galvanising. The main advantage of steel is its strength which enables large areas to be glazed with minimum obstruction **13**.

Notes
● Standards are covered in BS 990: Part 2: 1972 *Specification for steel windows generally for domestic and similar buildings:* Part 2 (metric units)[8]
● Recommendations for protective and decorative painting can be found in BRS Digest 70, second series, May 1966 and June 1966 [16,17]
● Re-rolling (hot rolling); forming (cold rolling also possible)
● Intricate and specials are difficult and costly to provide
● Cold-bridging is problem; condensation will cause deterioration of internal painted finish
● Adhesion of paint finish is a problem (degreasing and etch-priming recommended); high strength allows smaller frame member for large glazed areas
● Flash welding to galvanising for corner joints.

Finishes
Paint, pvc coating (factory-applied), flame-sprayed nylon, extruded pvc coating.

2.06 Stainless steel frames

Apart from being used as cladding to frames in timber or aluminium, stainless steel can be used as framing in its own right, sections being produced by brake-press folding or, roll-forming.
It is used more extensively in shop fronts **16** and prestige

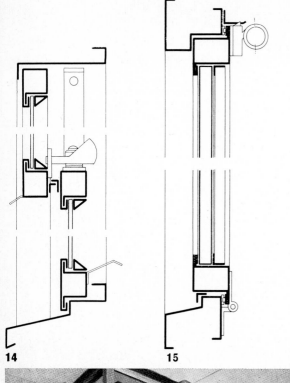

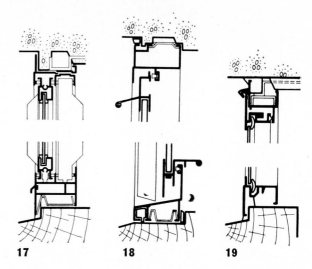

14 **15**

16

17 **18** **19**

14 *Section through stainless-steel double-lining sash window*
15 *Section through stainless-steel bottom-hung pivoted window*
16 *Stainless-steel shop front*
17 *Section through typical aluminium horizontal slider with masonry head and timber sill fixing*
18 *Section of typical aluminium frameless sash window with masonry head and timber sill fixing*
19 *Typical section of through head and sill of aluminium casement window, showing masonry head and timber sill fixings*

aluminium windows' success.

Most openable types can be produced in aluminium, although horizontal and vertical sliding sashes are the most well known. Assemblies of fixed and opening lights can be combined with timber frames. Aluminium has a high coefficient of expansion and high conductivity. More sophisticated designs incorporate thermal breaks. There is no BS for aluminium windows. Glazing can be a delicate operation so aluminium windows are normally factory-glazed with removable sashes.

Notes
- Extruded (allows intricate profiles)
- Mechanical and glued joints
- High strength: weight ratio
- High durability (washing only required)
- Normally pre-glazed in removable sashes.

Finishes
- *Mill:* the most economical, but must be detailed carefully to avoid staining.
- *Anodised:* three basic processes—conventional, Analok and Kalcolor/Alcanadox. Licences for these processes are issued to factories, ensuring quality control. Darker finishes can sometimes present problems if they appear in high wear areas where thicker film build-up on the surface renders it more vulnerable. Kalcolor/Alcanadox are self-colour processes resulting in a hard finish; colour consistency depends on metallurgy of section used. Analok is not as widely used; it is an added-colour (metal salts) process; colour consistency depends on metallic salt combination. There is always some difference in colour between sheet and extruded sections to the same specification.

Acrylic-coated: wash-down maintenance: can offer a durable finish, more economical than anodising.

Stainless-steel bonded: a thin skin of stainless over the aluminium gives the weathering performance of stainless steel, with some of the cost and flexibility advantages of aluminium.

office façades at ground floor level where it is important to achieve a high quality finish viewed at close range. It combines the strength of steel with a quality finish similar to aluminium (but better with polished finish) and its simple sections. Perhaps because it is used more extensively for economy reasons as a thin cladding on timber or extruded aluminium sections, more complicated sections are available in stainless steel (even from its roll forming process) than in ordinary steel.

Notes
- Cold rolling or brake-press formed (extrusion also possible)
- High durability even in marine industrial atmospheres
- Mechanical jointing etc

Finishes
Bright-polished, dull-polished, buffed, ground and bright annealed.

2.07 Aluminium frames

The great flexibility and precision of the extrusion process and the limitation of maintenance to regular washing only (except under certain climatic conditions) account for

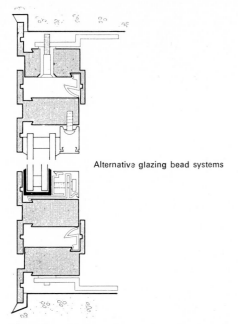
Alternative glazing bead systems

20 *Section through composite window showing masonry head and sill fixings*

2.08 Composite frames

It is logical to assume, while examining material performance, that ideally materials would differ in a single section in many cases: the most durable for the exterior and the most desirable for the interior. A section offering these conditions is available. The basic section **20** is formed from a steel-sheet shell with a modified rigid polyurethane core to combat internal condensation and add to the structural and insulative properties of the section. Materials and finishes offered as standard:
Interior: colourcoat pvc plastisol (white/black).
Exterior: colourcoat pvc plastisol (economy), colourcoat pvf2 white/bronze, type 316 stainless steel.

3 Window sizes

3.01 Steel windows

Basic spaces for steel windows
The Steel Window Association has defined the agreed Modular Basic Spaces for windows for:
● Housing (standard steel windows)
● Other building types (purpose-made steel windows)

The matrices
● Housing
The lengths of the basic spaces conform to BS 4011 first preference (300 mm), in increments of 300 mm. The heights of the basic spaces are derived from the preferred head and sill heights for public sector housing. Spaces larger than those in the basic matrix can be filled by combinations of the unit spaces **21**.

● Other building types
The lengths of the basic spaces conform to BS 4011 first preference in increments of 300 mm. The heights of the basic spaces are those indicated as first preference in the BSI matrices for basic spaces for health and office buildings, which can be filled by single units. Spaces larger than those in the basic matrix can be filled by combinations of the single units. Increased flexibility for modular spacings in increments of 100 mm is available by the use of fixed lights and box mullions.

Surrounds
Timber
● ex-75 mm × 75 mm timber adding 100 mm to the modular space.
● ex-50 mm × 75 mm timber adding 50 mm to the modular space.

Metal
Metal surrounds will also conform to preferred dimensions.

Lintels and sills
These may be contained:
● within the joint allowance between window and adjacent cladding unit
● within the basic space for the adjacent cladding unit. In this case they should penetrate the adjoining space in increments of 25 mm.

Windows and doors: domestic housing types
Outline spaces in **21** will be filled with single- or multi-pane standard window units. Details of types of casement and of work sizes are published by individual manufacturers. The Module 100 range is a development of the basic matrix and is available from the main steel window manufacturers **22**. Flexibility of the basic matrix is increased as follows:

Length
● By including one or more fixed light units 500 mm long in the composite window
● by including one or more pressed steel box mullions or partition covers in the assembly. Available in all matrix heights, these add 100 mm to length
● by applying a wood surround, adding 100 mm to length and height.

Height
● By combinations of basic units to fill the intermediate heights

eg $\frac{500}{500}:\frac{500}{700}:\frac{500}{900}:\frac{500}{1100}:\frac{500}{1300}:\frac{200}{1500}$

● by applying a wood surround, adding 100 mm to height. Thus all modular lengths and heights from 900 mm upwards can be achieved in increments of 100 mm.

Windows and doors: all other building types
Outline spaces in **23** are the preferred sizes to be filled with single-pane window units. Details of types of casement and of work sizes will be published by individual manufacturers. The metric w20 range is a development of the basic matrix and is available from main steel window manufacturers **24**. Flexibility to fill all modular spacings to BS 4011 second preference increments of 100 mm is provided as follows:

Length
● By using, either alone or in combination with the single-pane basic units, fixed lights available in increments of 100 mm
● by including one or more pressed steel box mullions or partition covers in the assembly. These are available with height increments of 100 mm and in widths which add 100, 200 or 300 mm to the length of assemblies.

Height
● By combinations of single-pane basic units

eg $\frac{300}{600}:\frac{300}{1100}:\frac{600}{11\,000}$

● by using 100 mm increment fixed lights either alone or in combination with the basic single-pane units.

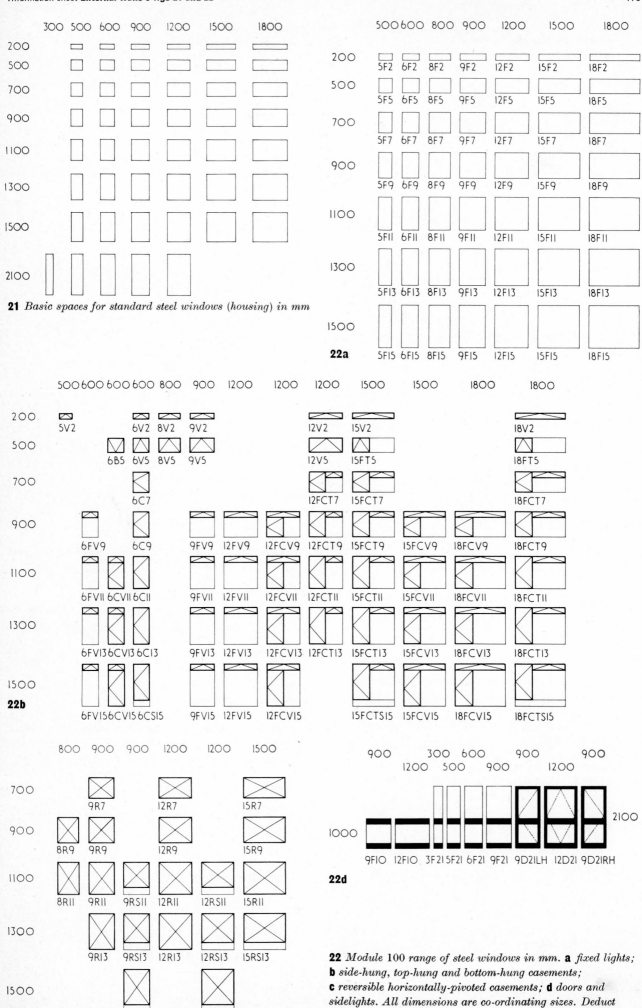

21 *Basic spaces for standard steel windows (housing) in mm*

22a

22b

22c

22d

22 *Module 100 range of steel windows in mm.* **a** *fixed lights;*
b *side-hung, top-hung and bottom-hung casements;*
c *reversible horizontally-pivoted casements;* **d** *doors and*
sidelights. All dimensions are co-ordinating sizes. Deduct
6 mm for work sizes

	600	600	600	600	900	900	900	1200	1200	1200	1500	1500	1800
300	6TH3				9TH3			12TH3			15TH3		
600	6TH6	6HP6			9TH6	9HP6		12TH6	12HP6		15TH6	15HP6	
900	6TH9	6SH9	6HP9		9TH9	9HP9		12TH9	12HP9		15TH9	15HP9	
1100	6TH11	6SH11	6HP11	6VP11	9TH11	9HP11	9VP11	12TH11	12HP11	12VP11	15TH11	15HP11	
1300		6SH13	6HP13	6VP13		9HP13	9VP13		12HP13	12VP13		15HP13	
1500		6SH15		6VP15		9VP15			12VP15				
2100					9SD21						15DD21		18DD21

24 *Metric W20 range in mm. Used mainly for heavy duty purposes*

	600	900	1200	1500	1800
300	□	□	□	□	
600	□	□	□	□	
900	□	□	□	□	
1100	□	□	□	□	
1300	□	□	□	□	
1500	□	□	□		
1800	□				
2100	□		□	□	

23 *Basic spaces for purpose made steel windows (other building types) in mm*

3.02 Aluminium windows

Basic spaces for aluminium windows

The Aluminium Window Association has issued sizes of basic spaces and ranges of aluminium windows, illustrated in **25a**. Details are available from individual manufacturers showing sections and work sizes.

Those spaces which include an additional ● are derived from the recommendations in MHLG design bulletin 16.

Window types and abbreviations (see 5)

1 Casement comprising a hinged or pivoted frame within its own outer frame **25b**
2 Slider comprising sliding panel(s) within own frame **25c**
3 Doors for occasional use comprising casement and sliders as in sections 1 and 2

D	DD	SD
single-leaf casement	double-leaf casement	single-, double- or triple-leaf slider

4 Fixed light F, a single frame prepared for glass or panel. ling. All windows shown in **25a** are available as fixed lights.
5 Spaces marked with the above abbreviations can be filled with the appropriate individual windows. All spaces can be filled with one-pane fixed lights or with combinations of individual casement and fixed light or individual slider and fixed light. Larger spaces can be filled by combinations of these units.
6 In addition to the sizes shown there is available a range of fixed lights with increments of 100 mm in both height and width together with vertical box mullions (open and closed), 100, 200 and 300 mm wide. These will provide a flexibility of 100 mm in both directions.

3.03 Wood windows

Basic spaces for wood windows

British Woodwork Manufacturers' Association proposals for basic spaces for standard wood windows are:
Widths: 600, 900, 1200, 1800, 2400 mm
Heights: 600, 900, 1050, 1200, 1500 mm

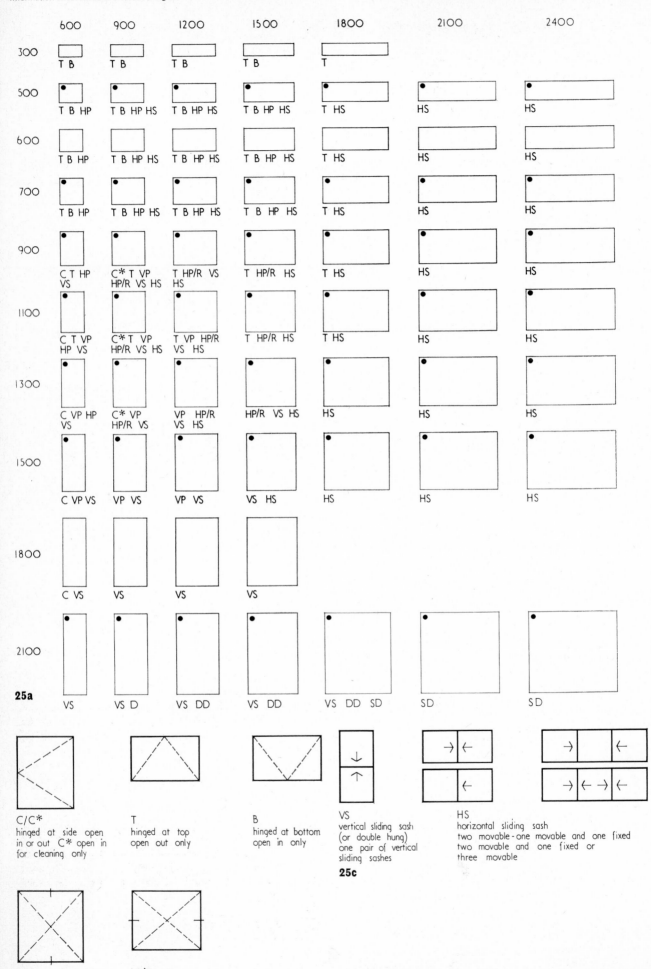

	600	900	1200	1500	1800	2100	2400
300	T B	T B	T B	T B	T		
500	T B HP	T B HP HS	T B HP HS	T B HP HS	T HS	HS	HS
600	T B HP	T B HP HS	T B HP HS	T B HP HS	T HS	HS	HS
700	T B HP	T B HP HS	T B HP HS	T B HP HS	T HS	HS	HS
900	C T HP VS	C* T VP HP/R VS HS	T HP/R VS HS	T HP/R HS	T HS	HS	HS
1100	C T VP HP VS	C* T VP HP/R VS HS	T VP HP/R VS HS	T HP/R HS	T HS	HS	HS
1300	C VP HP VS	C* VP HP/R VS	VP HP/R VS HS	HP/R VS HS	HS	HS	HS
1500	C VP VS	VP VS	VP VS	VS HS	HS	HS	HS
1800	C VS	VS	VS	VS			
2100	VS	VS D	VS DD	VS DD	VS DD SD	SD	SD

25a

C/C*
hinged at side open
in or out C* open in
for cleaning only

T
hinged at top
open out only

B
hinged at bottom
open in only

VS
vertical sliding sash
(or double hung)
one pair of vertical
sliding sashes

HS
horizontal sliding sash
two movable - one movable and one fixed
two movable and one fixed or
three movable

25c

VP
vertical pivot

HP/R
horizontal pivot
upper open in
lower open out
R is HP fully reversible

25b

25 *Aluminium windows:* **a** *basic spaces with notes on the types available, see notes on window types and abbreviations;* **b** *casements;* **c** *horizontal and vertical sliders*

4 Suspended glass assemblies

Toughened glass used without frames, mullions or transoms can form suspended assemblies to glaze large openings with no visual barriers. Non-ferrous metal patch fittings are used at the corner of each pane **26**, the whole then being hung from a continuous support at the top. Each pane supports the one below; failure of any two plates or members will not result in the collapse of the remainder. Glass fins are used to provide lateral support against wind load **27**. The head member from which the entire assembly is hung is firmly fixed to the building structure *which must be designed to take this extra load*.

Adjustable hangers are used to accommodate deflection of the head member, building tolerances and ease of installation. Thermal expansion (usually downward by nature of the assembly) must be allowed for by means of a channel detail at the sides and bottom. An extruded H-section in plastic or rubber installed during erection (or sealant gunned into the joint after erection) provides adequate weather-proofing **27**.

5 Glazing

5.01 Types of glazing

Types of flat glass are shown in table II. Plastics sheet materials scratch easily and have little fire resistance, high flame spread and high thermal expansion, so their use is currently confined to situations where special properties, eg impact resistance, are required. Where there are high labour costs and high vandalism rates, acrylics can be used economically for glazings, as resistance to breakage quickly pays for high installation costs.

Safety and security glazing

Laminated glass

Laminated glass consists of a layer of material, bonded under pressure between two sheets of glass. The laminate placed between gives the glass properties of protection from people or the elements, which it does not possess naturally.

● Polyvinyl butyral: this transparent laminate produces identical appearance to that of ordinary glass. Should be specified for areas needing protection such as glazing in high-rise buildings, doors and entrances, and in rooflights where falling pieces of glass may be dangerous.

Multi-pvb-laminated glass resists penetration from bullets. Suitable for screens in banking halls, prison windows and security vehicles. (Manufacturer: Thomas Bennett Ltd)

● Laminated glass with interlayer of plated steel wire. Used where security and vision are both essential, eg prisons, security vehicles (also for glazing on doors used as firestops).

Polycarbonate sheet

This material has been used widely in America and is claimed to have outstanding impact resistance—in fact it is guaranteed for three years against breakage by manufacturers. In appearance the material is similar to glass, and is fixed in the same manner.

Solar control glass

● Laminated glass with specially prepared polyvinyl butyral interlayer which reduces glare and solar heat gain. Available in limited range of colours.

● Laminated glass with interlayer which reduces ultra-

violet light.

● Glass which permits passage of most ultra-violet light for use in sun-rooms etc.

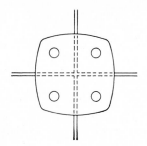

26

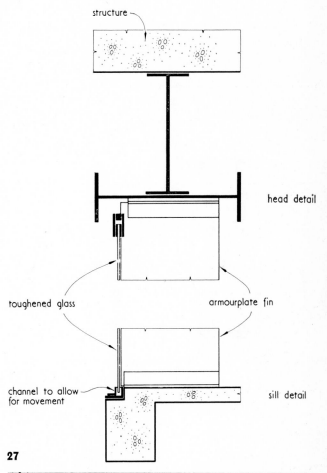

27

28

26 *Typical patch fitting to connect corners of four panes,*
27 *schematic head and sill detail of suspended glass construction,* **28** *use of suspended glass assembly at racetrack for mullion free view*

Table II *Types of glass*

Molten glass (the fusion of silica, soda and lime at 1490 to 1550°C) is formed by three processes:			
	Drawn Vertically-drawn surfaces are not always truly parallel	**Float** Truly flat glass with undistorted vision	**Rolled** (wired)	**Rolled** (textured)
Transparent	**Sheet glass** 85% light transmission **OQ** ordinary quality **SQ** selected quality **SSQ** silvering quality 2, 3, 4, 5, 5·5 mm thickness	**Clear float** 85% light transmission **GG** glazing glass **SG** selected glazing quality 3, 5, 6, 10, 12, 19, 22, 25 mm thickness	**Wired** 80% light transmission **Georgian-polished** square mesh **Diamond-polished** diamond mesh 6 mm thickness	**Patterned** special profiles for light refraction eg 'prismatic'
Translucent			**Wired** 75% light transmission **Georgian-wired cast** square mesh **Diamond-wired cast** diamond mesh 6 mm thickness	**Patterned** 70 to 85% light* transmission **Cathedral** specific texture 3, 5 mm thickness **Figured** pattern 3, 5 mm thickness **Reeded** parallel flutes† 3, 5 mm thickness **Rough cast** irregular texture one side only 5, 6, 10, 12 mm thickness
Solar control	**'Solarshield'** glass/pvb/glass laminated with bronze or gold metallic layer 6, 10 mm thickness (can also be made in float)	**Body-tinted** float glass green, grey or bronze **Spectrafloat** reflective metallic layer just below surface, bronze-coloured 6, 10, 12 mm thickness		**'Antisun'** rough cast or polished plate with blue green body tint 3, 5, 6 mm thickness **'Calorex'** blue-green tint 3, 5, 6 mm thickness
Toughened Resistance to impact and thermal shock 3 to 5 times greater than that of ordinary glass		**Armourplate** toughened float, including some solar control glasses		**Armourclad** (toughened cladding glass)—opaque **Armourcast** (toughened rough cast) **Armourglass** (toughened cathedral and figured)

* This section includes a very wide range of patterns usually applied one side only
† Reeded usually refers to **convex** profile, flutes to concave, both available in several widths

5.02 Methods of glazing

Direct glazing

While glass is used mainly in conjunction with a frame in timber or metal, direct glazing into concrete or masonry is possible **29**. Developments in frameless glazing include:
● Windows incorporating horizontal and vertical sashless sliders
● Direct use of toughened glass for hinged opening lights.
● 'Profilit'—a translucent sheet cladding capable of spanning vertically by using a U-shaped section giving increased resistance to wind loads. So glass walls of unlimited width can be constructed without mullions **30**.
● Hollow glass blocks with mortar jointing are available for the construction of infill panels. Panels up to 0·74 m² qualify for half-hour fire resistance. Adequate allowance for expansion at panel edges and top is essential.

Glazing materials

Two groups of glazing materials are distinguished in BS CP 152 1966[5]. Group 1 glazing materials are generally associated with traditional methods for glazing into timber and galvanised steel frames. Group 2 materials are generally associated with the more advanced techniques for fixing glass and other sheet materials into steel and aluminium frames, curtain walling systems and so on. With the exception of gasket glazing these techniques usually involve the use of glazing beads, which may be of the clip-on variety and which may apply mechanical compression to the joint. In all cases the use of setting blocks at the bottom of the pane and resilient location blocks around the sides and top is essential. These support the sheet so that it can be accurately set within the surround.

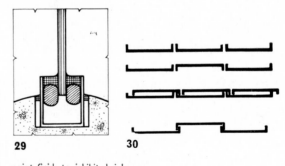

29 30

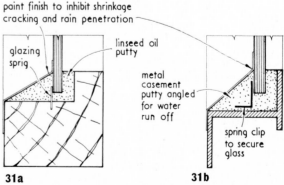

paint finish to inhibit shrinkage cracking and rain penetration

glazing sprig

linseed oil putty

metal casement putty angled for water run off

spring clip to secure glass

31a **31b**

29 *Glass set directly into concrete and cushioned by polythene foam strips.* **30** *'Profilit', fixed top and bottom into steel channels*
31 *Traditional method of glass,* **a** *in timber,* **b** *in metal*

Traditional methods

Traditional putty glazing is to timber or steel frames **31a,b**. The cheapest method has a life limited to 5-10 years and is not suitable where the pane has a perimeter greater than 4·8 m (3·6 m in exposed conditions). Beyond this size the use of glazing beads is necessary either internally or externally. This involves setting the glass in a suitable glazing compound prior to fixing the bead. As most non-setting compounds are non-loadbearing it is also necessary to provide distance pieces or spacers between the glass and the back of the rebate to prevent movement of the sheet and extrusion of the compound under wind load.

Modern bead-glazing techniques

More sophisticated glazing techniques have been developed to cope with one or more of the following problems:
● severe exposure to weather
● large undivided areas of glass
● installation from inside only (often required when security is important eg shop windows).
Generally these methods involve the use of a polysulphide or other elastomeric sealant. Such sealants have loadbearing characteristics that reduce distortion under wind loading. However they are expensive and while they can be used alone as in **25a**, a more economical alternative is to confine their use to that of a capping sealant **25b** to protect other glazing materials such as non-setting glazing compounds from damage.
Where it is necessary to glaze with no external access the technique illustrated in **25c** can be used. Here a pre-formed tape with integral distance pieces is used against the glazing stop. The elastomeric sealant is used with the head bead where it is protected against any loss of adhesion to the glass owing to exposure to sunlight. An extruded plastic slip acts as a distance piece and provides an easily cleaned internal finish.
More detailed information can be found in BS CP 152: 1966[5], publications of the Insulation Glazing Association and manufacturers[22]. See also AJ guide to use of sealants and mastics[24].

Gaskets

A limited use of gaskets for glazing is illustrated in **26** where the gasket replaces the capping sealant. This system is used mainly for factory glazing but may also be used for insular glazing. Gasket glazing relies on the fundamental property of rubber, ie it cannot be compressed, only displaced. The section design of the extension governs the direction and degree of displacement and must strike a balance between maximum sealing pressure with ease of installation. Gasket glazing is most familiar in car manufacture where H-section gaskets are used with a zipper strip to introduce the necessary compression **27a**. This type of gasket mounted on a flange has also been used in building. Alternatively Y-shaped sections may be used **b**. The latest development of CLASP Mark 5 takes advantage of the bulk of timber sections to generate a force couple capable of keeping glass in position without needing a zipper strip **c**.

5.03 Double Glazing

Heat loss

Heat losses through double glazing can be as low as half those through single glazing **2**. The air space between panes should be more than 15 mm, the cavity must be sealed or only sparsely ventilated and there must be no cold bridges in the form of uninterrupted metal framing from the inside to outside. The reduction in performance due to smaller cavities is shown in **28**.

Condensation

To prevent any obscuring of the glass, condensation within the cavity must be avoided. There are two ways of doing this:
● Seal the cavity thoroughly and ensure that the gas in it

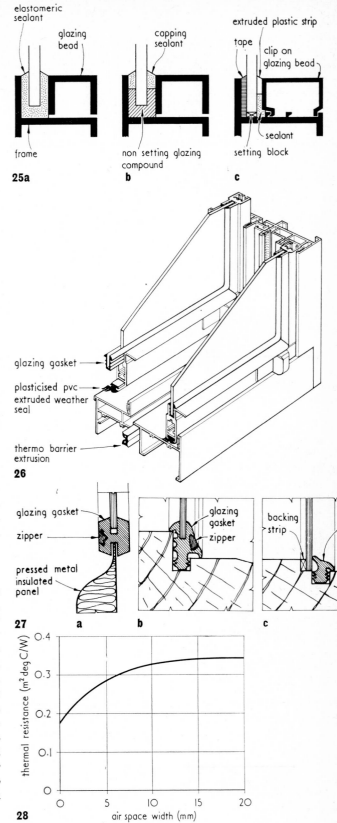

25a   **b**   **c**

elastomeric sealant *glazing bead* *capping sealant* *extruded plastic strip* *tape* *clip on glazing bead* *frame* *non setting glazing compound* *sealant* *setting block*

glazing gasket
plasticised pvc extruded weather seal
thermo barrier extrusion
26

glazing gasket *zipper* *pressed metal insulated panel* *glazing gasket* *zipper* *backing strip* *gla gas*
27   **a**   **b**   **c**

28   air space width (mm)   thermal resistance (m²degC/W)

25 *Elastomeric sealants can be used* **a** *alone, or* **b***, more economically, as a capping sealant, or as a head bead* **c** *where window is glazed from the inside*
26 *In this factory-made window, a glazing gasket replaces the capping sealant*
27 *Gaskets are most frequently seen in car manufacture* **a***, but have also been used in buildings* **b, c**
28 *Effect of air space width on thermal resistance of double-glazing under normal exposure conditions*

is dry at the time of sealing. This technique is limited to small cavities because (a) the unit needs to be mounted in a reasonable rebate in the frame and (b) changes in temperature cause changes of pressure or suction, which it does partially by bowing. The larger the cavity the more the glass bows, and this can damage the seal at the edges.

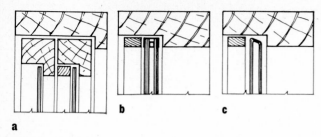

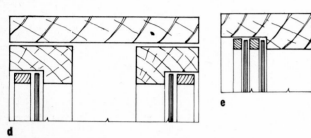

a

b

c

d

e

29a *Coupled window*
Factory-made double glazing units, **b** *bonded to metal*
spacers, **c** *all glass edges (glass to glass seal),* **d** *double window*
e *dual glazing*

● Ventilate the cavity to the outside. The air in the cavity takes up a temperature roughly midway between inside and outside air temperatures. Air entering the cavity from outside a building would normally be warmed and hence produce a drying régime in the cavity.

Fluctuating temperatures will cause air to be pumped in and out of the cavity, and unless the air passes through filters it will bring in dirt. Good proprietary filters will keep cleaning intervals to several years. Where windows have twin sashes the cavity can be opened for cleaning. This is the most appropriate solution for timber-frame windows where moisture migration into the cavity can be expected through frames. This, coupled with lower sealing standards to the cavity, requires more ventilation than is obtained by using filters. Ventilation of the cavity by edge cracks up to a millimetre will not produce a significant loss of thermal performance.

Sound insulation
Double glazing will improve sound insulation whatever the width of the cavity, but is much more effective with wide cavities of 100 mm or more (in effect two windows) especially if the reveal between is lined with sound absorbing material. The effect is also improved if different thicknesses or weights of glass are used for each pane, to prevent sympathetic vibration or resonance developing. This may also cut costs since the outer pane may need considerable

thickness to withstand wind loads whereas the inner pane being some distance away cannot assist structurally and hence can be of quite thin sheet glass. Cold bridges must be avoided also especially the risk of damp penetration into the back of the frame from the adjoining wall material.

6 Determination of glass thickness

On high-rise buildings or those in exposed areas, glass thickness must be calculated.
BS CP 152[5] 1966[5] contains a method for establishing the minimum glass thickness necessary to resist wind loads for vertical windows framed on all four edges. The method is applicable to:
● Single-glazed windows
● Coupled windows with air space up to 75 mm **29a**
● Factory-made double-glazed units with bonded metal-spacers on all glass edges **29b, c**.
Double windows **29d** and 'dual' glazing **e**, cannot be regarded as double-glazing for the purpose of computing glass size and must be determined as if the window were single-glazed.

Method of determining glass thickness
Determine maximum 3-second gust speed in m/s from Meteorological Office (MO3), London Road, Bracknell, Berkshire, or check by referring to the map in CP 3, chap V, Part 2, 1970 (wind loads) and make the appropriate adjustments for topography, location, etc.
● Adjust for local topography and heights as in table VI
● Translate gust speed to maximum probable wind loading from graph **30**
● Calculate glass factor to three decimal places
$$= \frac{\text{area of pane (m}^2)}{\text{perimeter of pane (m)}}$$
● Read off thickness from table appropriate to type of glass, table IV.

Example
Consider a clear plate glass window 1·80 m wide × 1·20 m high, 15 m above ground in a rectangular plan building
● The Met. Office has given a three-second wind speed of 40 m/s
● From table VI the correction factor corresponding to a height of 15 m for buildings with low obstructions is obtained. The three-second wind speed is: 40 × 0·93 = 37·2 m/s
● From graph **30** the probable maximum wind loading is then 128daN/sq m (ie 1280 N/m²)

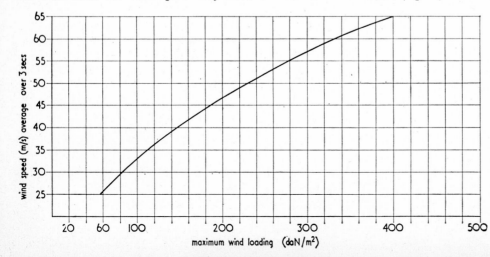

30 *Graph for determining maximum wind loadings to be expected at various wind speeds. The graph should be used only for buildings of rectangular plan and variations of this such as* L- *and* H-*shape. It is not applicable to curved buildings (1 deca newton = 10 N)*

Table III *Glass factors for coupled windows with a maximum air space of 75mm*

Glass factor for a wind loading (daN/sq m) of:												Min glass thickness mm
50	75	100	125	150	175	200	250	300	350	400	500	
Clear plate glass												
0·592	0·485	0·419	0·376	0·342	0·316	0·297	0·265	0·242	0·224	0·209	0·179	4·8
0·788	0·645	0·558	0·500	0·456	0·421	0·395	0·353	0·322	0·298	0·279	0·249	6
1·137	0·930	0·805	0·720	0·658	0·606	0·569	0·508	0·463	0·429	0·402	0·360	10
Sheet glass												
0·417	0·336	0·296	0·263	0·241	0·223	0·208	0·187	0·170	0·158	0·148	0·132	3
0·596	0·488	0·422	0·377	0·345	0·320	0·298	0·264	0·243	0·225	0·212	0·188	4
0·653	0·533	0·468	0·413	0·378	0·351	0·327	0·293	0·267	0·248	0·232	0·206	4·8
0·776	0·634	0·550	0·490	0·448	0·415	0·388	0·347	0·316	0·294	0·276	0·245	5·6
0·956	0·780	0·677	0·603	0·552	0·512	0·478	0·427	0·389	0·362	0·339	0·302	6

Table IV *Glass factors for single glazing*

Glass factor for a wind loading (daN/sq m) of:												Min glass thickness mm
50	75	100	125	150	175	200	250	300	350	400	500	
Clear plate glass												
0·520	0·426	0·368	0·330	0·301	0·278	0·261	0·233	0·213	0·197	0·184	0·157	4·8
0·692	0·567	0·490	0·439	0·401	0·370	0·347	0·310	0·283	0·262	0·245	0·219	6
0·996	0·816	0·706	0·632	0·578	0·533	0·500	0·446	0·407	0·377	0·353	0·316	10
1·300	1·066	0·920	0·824	0·753	0·694	0·651	0·581	0·531	0·491	0·460	0·411	12
Sheet glass												
0·366	0·295	0·260	0·231	0·212	0·196	0·183	0·164	0·149	0·139	0·130	0·116	3
0·524	0·428	0·371	0·331	0·303	0·281	0·262	0·234	0·213	0·198	0·186	0·165	4
0·574	0·468	0·407	0·363	0·332	0·308	0·287	0·257	0·234	0·218	0·204	0·181	4·8
0·682	0·556	0·483	0·431	0·394	0·365	0·341	0·305	0·278	0·258	0·242	0·215	5·6
0·840	0·685	0·595	0·530	0·485	0·450	0·420	0·375	0·342	0·318	0·298	0·265	6

Table V *Glass factors for factory-made double glazing units*

Glass factor for a wind loading (daN/sq m) of:												Max glass thickness mm
50	75	100	125	150	175	200	250	300	350	400	500	
Clear plate glass												
0·734	0·602	0·520	0·466	0·425	0·393	0·368	0·329	0·301	0·278	0·260	0·222	4·8
0·977	0·800	0·692	0·620	0·566	0·522	0·490	0·438	0·400	0·370	0·346	0·309	6
1·410	1·155	0·999	0·893	0·816	0·752	0·706	0·630	0·575	0·532	0·498	0·446	10
Sheet glass												
0·517	0·416	0·367	0·326	0·299	0·277	0·258	0·231	0·210	0·196	0·183	0·164	3
0·740	0·605	0·524	0·467	0·428	0·397	0·370	0·330	0·301	0·280	0·263	0·233	4
0·810	0·661	0·575	0·512	0·468	0·435	0·405	0·363	0·330	0·308	0·288	0·255	4·8
0·964	0·785	0·681	0·608	0·556	0·515	0·482	0·431	0·392	0·364	0·342	0·304	5·6
1·188	0·968	0·840	0·748	0·685	0·635	0·593	0·530	0·482	0·449	0·421	0·374	6

Table VI *Height correction factors*

Actual height above ground of window (m)	Correction factor: degree of obstruction		
	Nil*	Low†	Built-up areas‡
3 or less	0·85	0·83	0·80
5	0·91	0·85	0·80
10	1·00	0·90	0·80
15	1·04	0·93	0·84
20	1·06	0·97	0·88
30	1·09	1·00	0·91
40	1·14	1·03	0·96
60	1·18	1·10	1·02
80	1·21	1·14	1·06
100	1·23	1·16	1·09
150	1·28	1·22	1·15
200	1·31	1·25	1·19
250	1·34	1·29	1·22

(*continued from previous page*)

● The glass factor is:

$$\frac{\text{area of glass pane in sq m}}{\text{perimeter in linear m}} = \frac{1·80 \times 1·20}{2\,(1·80 + 1·20)} = 0·360$$

● From table IV, the first wind load above 128daN/m² is 150. Reading down this column the first factor above 0·360 is 0·401 and reading across to the right-hand column indicates that the minimum thickness is 6 mm.

*No material obstructions: large expanse of open grassland or water
†Relatively low obstructions, such as trees and two-storey buildings as in small towns
‡Built-up areas, with buildings generally more than two storeys high

7 Performance requirements

For any given conditions of exposure the following points should be considered in relation to weather performance:
● Air-tightness around opening lights
● Water-tightness around opening lights
● Deflection in frame from wind loads transmitted by the glass.

7.01 Weatherstripping

Fundamental to both improved air and water tightness is effective weatherstripping. To achieve higher performance, however, it is necessary to consider the joint between opening light and frame as a whole. Similar principles apply here as for other types of joint, and it is interesting to note that in the development of high performance timber windows, the 'drained joint' principle has been used. This type of joint was developed by BRS for concrete panels. The weatherstripping's role here is to provide an air-seal between the inside of the building and a 'cavity', sheltered by a check cover at the weatherface. The seal reduces air velocity in the cavity, thus allowing water to drain away, while the cavity protects the seal from the full impact of wind and rain. The weatherstripping, by improving air tightness, increases resistance to rain penetration.
Principal types of weatherstrips are:

Felt
Made from compressed wool and limited in use to channelled sections in which glass slides, or into which glass panels close. There are also limitations on lengths of material available (maximum shaped section 2 m). Felt weatherstrips also tend to be bulky.

Metal
Metals used for weatherstrips are usually stainless steel and phosphor bronze. The seal is made by the weatherstrip being held tightly against the moving part by its own spring action. Efficiency depends largely on straightness of the weatherstrip's sealing edge and evenness of opposing surface. The most suitable metal is stainless steel and, in general, metal weatherstrips are more useful on large sashes with heavy plate glass. Phosphor bronze should never be used with unprotected aluminium.

Wool or synthetic fibre-pile weatherstrip
This consists of a fibre-pile of wool or synthetic, mounted on a base. The air seal is made by the pile touching the opposing surface. The large number of individual fibres ensure a reasonably good seal and good sliding characteristics. Airtightness depends on pile height, width and density, but they also affect the force required to move the sash.
Fixing is usually achieved by sliding the weatherstrips into grooves in the sash or the frame. Alternatively the base of the weatherstrip can be bonded into position. This type of weatherstrip is possibly the most suitable for sliding sashes.

Plastics and synthetic rubbers
The most generally used are pvc and neoprene, preferably as buffer seals. Neoprene is preferable to pvc as it retains its characteristics over a long period: pvc tends to develop a transient set. There is no limitation on length and small extrusions can be made.
Natural rubber is unsuitable for this purpose.

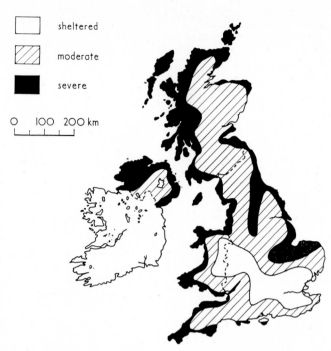

□ sheltered
▨ moderate
■ severe

0   100   200 km

31 *Map showing exposure zones. The* BSI *draft proposals (see p. 185) contain a much more detailed map (now in* CP 3, *chap.* V, *Part 2: 1970) which deals with wind speeds generally and is probably a better guide to local pressures than the system outlined on p. 182. Its use is now prescribed in the Building Regulations. A difficulty in use would be to convert the figures to the same basis as the factors given on p. 183 in tables* III *to* VI, *but this could be overcome by intelligent use of the system of design described in the* CP.

7.02 Methods of test and performance standards

Agrément Board scheme
The Agrément Board operates a scheme of window performance testing described in MOAT 1 *Windows* and Information sheet 1 *Windows*[2]. The scheme aims to define the suitability of a particular manufactured window type for use in various conditions by testing a sample window in a test rig. The rig simulates wind by air pressure, and rain by a defined pattern of water spray. In any such method of testing, two issues must be resolved:
1 Correlation between test conditions and conditions of exposure encountered in reality
2 Definition of standards of performance to be considered acceptable for a particular exposure category.
The board's scheme, which has been in operation since 1967, classifies three degrees of exposure—normal, moderately severe and severe, having 3-second gust wind speeds of 90, 100 and 115 mph respectively. These are related to geographical zones in accordance with climatological data current in 1967 **31**.
Standards of performance adopted are as follows:

Strength and stability
A window should not suffer permanent deformation or other damage when subjected to test pressures equivalent to the worst conditions of exposure (see table VII).

Air leakage
A window is acceptable if air leakage is below 60 m³/h/m² of openable light when subjected to test pressure of 10 mm water gauge.

Table VII *Strength and water resistance acceptance levels for windows in various exposure conditions*

Window height	Windows up to 10 m above ground level			Windows up to 30 m above ground level			Windows up to 60 m above ground level			
Degree of obstruction	Nil	Low	Built-up	Nil	Low	Built-up	Nil	Low	Built-up	
Zone A (sheltered)	150 4–16	150 4–16	150 4–16	200 16–30	150 4–16	150 4–16	200 16–30	200 16–30	150 16–30	Strength* Water resistance†
Zone B (moderate)	200 16–30	150 4–16	150 4–16	200 16–30	150 16–30	150 4–16	250 30–50	200 30–50	200 30–50	Strength* Water resistance†
Zone C (severe)	250 30–50	200 16–30	150 16–30	Special requirements may be necessary depending on local conditions						Strength* Water resistance†

*Pressure in mm water gauge at which no permanent deformation or damage may occur
†Pressure in mm water gauge. Lower value: must be water tight. Upper value: water penetration must not be excessive. Hatched areas: special requirements may be necessary depending on local conditions

Rain penetration

Tests for rain penetration are based on average wind speeds over 5 minutes. For each exposure condition, two pressure valves are given representing the:
1 pressure at which window must be watertight
2 pressure at which leakage should not be excessive.

The BSI draft proposals

Proposed draft performance standards for windows have been published recently by BSI[3]. Care must be taken to distinguish these proposals from the Agrément Board scheme, and the following differences should be noted:
● Methods of test are based on a rig constructed to BS 4315: Part 1: 1968[14], whereas the Agrément Board's test methods, although broadly similar, are in accordance with the European Union of Agrément
● Air leakage is measured in relation to length of opening joint rather than to area of opening light
● Rain penetration is assessed in relation to the pressure at which sustained leakage occurs, rather than to the dual standard adopted by Agrément
● Classification of exposure is as follows:
Sheltered—maximum 3-second gust velocity 40 m/s
Moderate—maximum 3-second gust velocity 45 m/s
Severe—maximum 3-second gust velocity 50 m/s
● Climatological data has been reviewed since 1967 and the degree of exposure is classified in accordance with BS CP 3: Part 2: Chapter v: 1970[4].
The BSI draft performance standards for air leakage and rain penetration are given in tables VIII and IX.
The Aluminium Window Association certifies horizontal and vertical sliding windows based on these standards, BSI acting as the testing agency.

Table VIII *Resistance to water penetration should not be less than the following values: window should be tested by method described in* BS 4315 *Part* 1

Exposure	Pressure differences up to which 'gross leakage' does not occur (mm wg)
Sheltered	5
Moderate	15
Severe	30

Table IX *Maximum air infiltration rate for three grades by method of exposure: window should be tested by method described in* BS 4315 *Part* 1

Exposure	Maximum air infiltration rate (m³/h/m length of opening joint)	Pressure difference (mm wg)
Sheltered	12	10
Moderate	12	15
Severe	12	20

8 Ironmongery

8.01 References

An AJ Ironmongery Handbook covering fittings and accessories for windows and doors is being prepared. In the meantime consult the previous element design guide: Accessories, ironmongery: General (AJ 14.2.62 p377-388) and associated information sheets 1068 to 1070. See also AJ Handbook of Building services and circulation, information sheet SECURITY 5 para 8 (AJ 29.7.70 p276). There is also an ironmongery section in *Specification* 1972 (Architectural Press). For the purposes of this information sheet, the following checklist may be useful.

8.02 Checklist

Determine:
● Insurance company's requirements
● Requirements of adjoining owners
● Fire requirements
● Insulation requirements (fastenings, gaskets)
● Window and frame and effect on ironmongery: method of opening; construction
● Cost limit for window fittings
● Type of fittings: suspension (hinges, pivots); security (bolts, fasteners); operative (handles, stays); draught-proofing (resilient, spring or cam action)
● Method of fixing
● Maintenance

9 Window checklist

Effect of external elements
● Wind loading (pressure and suction)
● Rain (associated with wind)
● Sunlight thermal insulation/glare
● Temperature change
● Atmospheric pollution
● Noise from without/within: traffic, aircraft, machinery.

Statutory requirements
● Daylighting Regulations
● Zones of open space
● Fire resistance
● Spread of flame
● Light for habitable rooms
● Air for ventilation
● Obstruction at ground level
● Any easements desired
● Means of escape.

User requirements
- Insurance: fire, theft, damage
- Security and safety requirements
- Maintenance: cleaning method, periodic refinishing, reglazing, repairs, lubrication of moving parts.

Design decisions (made prior to using this information sheet)
- Opening size: standard or special
- Sequence of erection (built in or fixed in).

Frame finish
- Durability for use, weather exposure
- Site applied (consider sequence)
- Factory applied (ensure protection)
- Ensure joint details maintain design standards of wall and window itself.

Specification
- Consider budget allowance
- Opening sizes and sections with respect to standard and specials
- Inclusion of: subframes, sills, blind boxes, condensation channels, weather bars, weepholes, lintels, mullions.
- Request sample for approval.

10 Cleaning and maintenance of windows and glazing

Design
The architect must make a decision about cleaning at design stage. He can:
- clean entirely from outside
- clean from inside
- clean partly from inside and partly from outside, gaining access to façade through individual windows.

Cleaning from outside
A variety of equipment is available for outside cleaning, ranging from a simple ladder (still recommended for small façades) to cradles and fully-automatic gondolas on high buildings. A travelling suspended cradle is the most suitable method of cleaning high buildings. It simplifies operations and ensures that the whole face of a building is accessible. Hand- and power-operated cradles of timber, steel, aluminium and glass-fibre reinforced-polyester plastics are available.

Gantry runways may be portable or permanent, but the latter is preferable. Vertical guide tracks should be fitted to mullions on the face of very tall buildings to stabilise the cradle, to prevent it swinging away from the building and to facilitate vertical movement. Provision should be made for storing the cradle, and it may be possible to run it directly into a storage bay through hatches in the face of the building. Rails for the cradle can project over the side of the building, or be mounted on the flat roof with a trolley and davits. Often a spray or sparge pipe can be fitted at the top of a tall building for automatic washing. On very large buildings window cleaning may be continuous.

Cleaning from inside
This involves care in designing and positioning openings **32**. Pivoted windows or side-hung windows on projecting or offset hinges may be used. Projecting hinges provide a gap between the casement and frame large enough to allow the outside surface of the glass to be cleaned. This gap should be not less than 100 mm. Pivoted windows should reverse a full 180° vertically or horizontally and should not foul blinds, curtains or interior fittings and furniture. The maximum pane width of fixed glazed areas horizontally

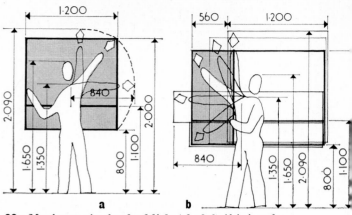

32a *Maximum size for fixed light (shaded) if it is to be cleaned from the inside (opening lights both sides),*
b *maximum interior reach*

adjacent to opening windows should not exceed 1200 mm (reached from both sides) or 600 mm (reached from one side). Permanent trickle or controlled ventilators in pivot windows obviate need for extra opening lights which are always a problem to clean.

Cleaning from inside may often inconvenience the occupants. Furniture has to be moved and work interrupted, and the cleaner may have to balance on sills or transoms, dangerous to both cleaner and window. Where internal access is not practical, permanent provision should be made for external cleaning. Cleaning and maintenance can often be carried out from projecting balconies, ledges or sills not less than 150 mm wide.

Permanent access to facade through windows
Balconies
Balconies must be designed to enable a ladder to stand at an angle of 1:4, allowing access to the bottom of it, and be as long as the glazing.

Masonry sills
A sill is a continuous ledge-like projection at the foot of a glass area, or at floor level. Normally the cleaner gains access through a window or door on each floor and is able to clean all the windows on that floor by moving along the sill. Sills should be a minimum of 630 mm wide. They are unsafe without permanent anchorage points for safety belts, so a continuous rail 900 mm above the sill, to which a safety belt can be attached, is essential. Also the runner must be positioned so that the cleaner can attach and detach himself when inside the building. Windows should not be higher than the reach of the cleaner. He may carry a short ladder, leather, scrim and bucket of water; therefore safety belt anchorage must be continuous so that he can slide the fastener along as he moves.

Travelling ladders
Ladders are usually made of metal, preferably aluminium, with fixtures top and bottom locating in a continuous rail or channel that allows them to slide along the façade. They are easy to detail unobtrusively and ladders can be demountable. They are very useful for long horizontal areas of glazing up to about 4·5 m high. The advantage over an ordinary ladder is that the cleaner is always a constant distance from the façade. There is no reason why this system should not be used on high-rise buildings, cleaning one floor at a time. Safety belts should always be worn, preferably fixed to a tensioned-wire lifeline fixed to the same rail or channel as the ladder, so that no disconnection is necessary when moving horizontally.

33 *Comparison of window types for internal cleaning access. Left-hand sketch shows good access, right-hand sketch shows difficult access. Lights being cleaned are shaded whether moveable or fixed*

Easy access   ### Difficult access

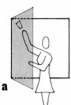

a   **b**

Side-hung casement **a**
opening in

b *opening out*

c   **d**   **e**

Bottom-hung casement **c, d**   **e** *opening out*
opening in

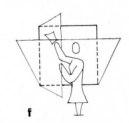

f

f *'Tilt and turn' casement*

g   **h**

g, h *Horizontal slide*

j   **k**

j, k *Horizontal pivot*   *Not fully reversible*
fully reversible

l   **m**

l, m *Vertical pivot*   *Not fully reversible*
fully reversible

CLEANING OPENING LIGHTS

Easy access   ### Difficult access

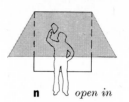

n   *open in*   **o**   *open out*

n, o *Top-hung casement*

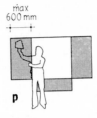
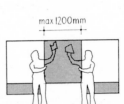
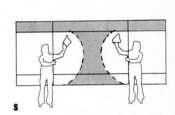

max 600 mm

p   **q**

max 1200mm

r   **s**

p, q, r, s *Fixed light adjacent*

CLEANING FIXED LIGHTS FROM INSIDE BY ACCESS THROUGH ADJACENT OPENINGS

11 Appendix

This appendix contains tables x and xi which list useful AJ material on window design.

Table x *References to information and guidance on window design contained in* AJ *Handbook of Building environment*

Title	Date and page nos	Applicability to window design
1 DAYLIGHT		
Design guide: Sunlight	16.10 68 (p887-898)	Design procedure for spacing and form of buildings, and design of rooflights and windows, to give adequate sunlight and daylight
Information sheet: Sunlight 1	23.10.68 (p951-954)	Definitions and units used in daylight calculations
Information sheet: Sunlight 2	23.10.68 (p955-957)	Recommended daylight factors
Information sheet: Sunlight 3	23.10.68 (p959-961)	Natural lighting survey techniques
Information sheet: Sunlight 4	23.10.68 (p963-968)	Natural lighting: use of models
Information sheet: Sunlight 5	30.10.68 (p1019-1036)	Sunlight: predicting sun's track. Gives method for determining sunlight through windows
Information sheet: Sunlight 6	13.11.68 (p1149-1152)	Daylight: Use of BRS daylight factor protractors
Information sheet: Sunlight 8	13.11.68 (p1157-1162)	Natural lighting: Use of perspectives. Explains principles of perspective used in Information sheets Sunlight 9 and 10
Information sheet: Sunlight 9	13.11.68 (p1163-1168)	Daylight and view: vertical perspectives for side windows. A method of measuring sky components

Information sheet: Sunlight 10 (revised)	6.8.69 (p327-332) *Supersedes sheet published 20.11.68 (p1217-1222)*	Sunlight: vertical perspectives. A method for showing position of sun in relation to view from a window
Information heet: Sunlight 11 (revised)	6.8.69 (p333-336) *Supersedes sheet published 20.11.68 (p1223-1226)*	Glare and solar protection (see also later references on screens and louvres)
Information sheet: Sunlight 12	20.11.68 (p1227-1234)	Window design and typical daylight distribution. Preliminary design sizing of windows

2 VENTILATION

Technical study: Air movement 2	27.11.68 (p1293-1298)	Wind flow over walls. Includes notes on windows and other openings
Design guide: Air movement	11.12.68 (p1413-1418)	Design procedure covering air movement for complete building, with sections on windows and enclosing envelope
Information sheet: Air movement 2	11.12.68 (p1421-1422)	Wind velocities
Information sheet: Air movement 3	11.12.68 (p1423-1426)	Typical wind patterns on building faces
Information sheet: Air movement 4	11.12.68 (p1427-1430)	Typical faults in designing and positioning buildings relative to wind conditions

3 THERMAL PROPERTIES

Technical study: Thermal properties 1	18 & 25.12.68 (p1485-1492)	Architect's role in design of thermal environment. Study of building fabric (including windows) in relation to building services and controls, and external climate
Design guide: Thermal properties	18 & 25.12.68 (p1493-1500)	Design procedure for deciding thermal environment including effect of windows
Information sheet: Thermal properties 2	8.1.69 (p117-123)	Prediction of solar heat gain through windows
Information sheet: Thermal properties 5	8.1.69 (p133-135)	Interrelationship of window design decisions
Information sheet: Heating services 11	21.5.69 (p1401-1414)	Thermal insulation and condensation

4 SOUND

Design guide: Sound	29.1.69 (p323-329)	Design procedure for noise control and room acoustics including effect of windows
Information sheets: Sound 2-5	29.1.69 (p335-344) 5.2.69 (p397-410) 12.2.69 (p457-470)	Standards, principles and practice of noise control, including effect of windows

5 ARTIFICIAL LIGHT

Design guide: Electric lighting	18.6.69 (p1665-1669)	This guide, with its associated technical studies and information sheets, is only marginally applicable to window design, but does deal with contribution made by daylight, and hence with window shape, size and position

Table XI *References to information and guidance on window design contained in other* AJ *articles (additional in table* X *)*

Title	Date and page nos	Applicability to window design
1 CONDENSATION		
Technical study: Condensation 1	19.5.71 (p1149-1159)	Control of condensation in buildings, which includes consideration of window design and ventilation
Information sheets:		
Condensation 1	26.5.71 (p1201-1208)	
Condensation 2	2.6.71 (p1265-1269)	
2 SCREENS and LOUVRES		
Element design guide: Screens and louvres	2.1.63 (p45-56)	This material is due for revision but in meantime is useful information and guidance on sun penetration and shading
Information sheets: 1182, 1183, 1184		

References

AGREMENT BOARD

1 Methods of assessment and testing 1 Windows. Hemel Hempstead, Herts, 1967, The Board [(31) (Aq)]

2 Information sheet 1 Windows. Hemel Hempstead, Herts, 1967, The Board [(31)]

BRITISH STANDARDS INSTITUTION

3 DD4 Draft for development Window performance. 1971 [(31)]

4 BS CP 3: Part 2: Chapter v: 1970 Wind loads [K4]

5 BS CP 152: 1966 Glazing and fixing of glass [Ro (D6)]

6 BS CP 153: Windows and rooflights. Part 1: 1969 Cleaning and safety. Part 2: 1970 Durability and maintenance [(3-)]

7 BS 952: 1964 Classification of glass for glazing and terminology for work on glass [Ro (Ah)]

8 BS 990: 1967 Steel windows generally for domestic and similar buildings [(31) Xh2] £1

9 BS 1236 to 1240: 1956 Sills and lintels [(31) Gy]

10 BS 1285: 1963 Wood surrounds for steel windows [(31) Xi]

11 BS 1422: 1956 Steel subframes, sills and windowboards for metal windows [(31) Xh2]

12 BS 1787: 1951 Steel windows for industrial buildings [27 (31) Xh]

13 BS 2503: 1954 Steel windows for agricultural use [26 (31) Xh2]

14 BS 4315: Part 1: 1968 Methods of test for resistance to air and water penetration: Windows and gasket glazing systems [(31) (I2)]

15 BS 4374: 1968 Sills of clayware, cast concrete, cast stone, slate and natural stone [(31) Gy]

BUILDING RESEARCH STATION

16 Digest 70 Painting metals in buildings; 1. 1966, HMSO [Vv]

17 Digest 71 Painting metals in buildings; 2. 1966, HMSO [Vv]

18 Digest 119 The assessment of wind loads; 1970, HMSO [(K4f)] (now superseded by CP 3 ch. v Part II: 1970 wind loads [K4])

OTHERS

19 Department of the Environment. Sunlight and daylight-planning criteria and design. 1972, HMSO [(N7)]

20 MARKUS, T. A. Function of windows: a reappraisal. *Building Science*, Vol 2, p97-121, 1967 [(31)]

21 Glass and glazing. *Specification* Vol 2, 1972. p429-460, Architectural Press [Yy (A3)]

22 INSULATING GLAZING ASSOCIATION Glazing requirements and procedures for double glazing units, 1. London, 1963, The Association [Ro5] *revised* 1968

23 LONGMORE, J. and ADDLESON, L. Product selection: float glass. RIBA *Journal*, 1970, September, p420-430 [Ro1]

24 GROEGER, R. G. A guide to the use of sealants and mastics. *Architects' Journal*, 1968, June 5 [Yt4] *information sheet* 1603

Section 5
External envelope: Roofs

Section 5 External envelope: Roofs

Relationship to rest of handbook

The table and diagram show the handbook's contents as a whole with the present section highlighted. Section 2 provided a general introduction to the more specific sections following, so it is recommended that the present section be used in conjunction with section 2.

Scope

This section of the handbook gives guidance on all aspects of roof design, and completes the group of sections dealing with the external envelope as a whole. The section starts by examining the brief and functional requirements for the roof, and goes on to consider structural form, decking, waterproofing and rooflights, and concludes with a cost guide.

Problems of structural strength are not given detailed consideration in this handbook; they are covered in the AJ Handbook of Building Structure.

References and keywords

The keyword by which this section is identified is ROOFS: use of keywords is explained on page 6.

Authors

The author of this section is HAROLD KING, RIBA, *an architect in private practice and lecturer in building technology at Newcastle University's School of Architecture. He has been assisted by* ERIC PARKES, BSC, CEng, *lecturer in civil engineering at Wolverhampton Polytechnic.*

King   *Parkes*

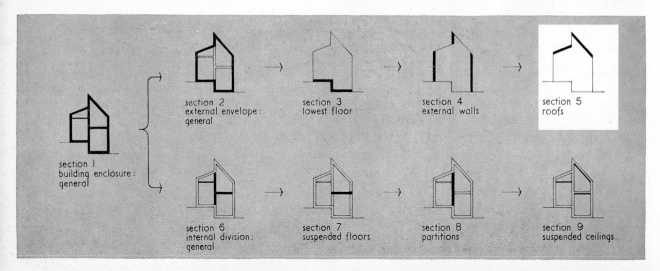

Technical study
Roofs 1

Section 5 : **Roofs**

A roof over one's head

In this short introductory technical study the editors draw attention to the paradox of technical limitations in the past having helped to produce exciting roof forms and roofscapes, whereas today technological expertise often helps to produce dull roof forms. Both aesthetically and functionally the roof has become a neglected element of the building; it deserves more attention in future

1 Roofs and roofscapes

1.01 Climatic problems

Whereas external walls are the building element most closely associated with the separation of spaces (inside from outside; public from private) and with the creation of streetscapes, the roof is the element most closely associated with the concept of shelter.

In common parlance 'not having a roof over one's head' is the equivalent of being homeless, at the mercy of the elements.

There is good reason for the close linguistic connection between roofs and shelter. In some climates, walls can practically be dispensed with as sheltering elements, or reduced to forms as elementary as screens and roll-up blinds **1**. Even in more rigorous climates they usually do not need to come up to the performance standards required of roofs.

On the other hand, roofs are an essential element of shelter (except in the most primitive communities, relying on windbreaks to protect them from the worst aspects of climate) and have to perform an impressive range of functions.

First, a roof must keep out water—perhaps continuous drizzle gradually soaking into the fabric; or violent downpours; and the rain might be accompanied by driving wind. Second, a roof has to give protection against the sun (not merely in the sense of screening solar radiation, but possibly also having to provide thermal insulation and thermal capacity); resist the destructive effects of radiation and alternate exposure to heat and cold; and moderate heat losses to acceptable limits.

1

1 *Walls can be dispensed with in mild climates, as in this Samoan chief's house, which relies on roller blinds to deal with bad weather; but the roof is an essential sheltering element*
2-5 *Various ways in which timber has been used for traditional roofing. Where rainfall is low, a flat roof can be supported on simple timber beams **2**. But in the northern European climate pitched roofs were essential;*

1.02 Structural problems

In addition to the function of exercising environmental control the roof is required to defy gravity by spanning across space. This may not be thought of as a major technological challenge in the present era of reinforced concrete and easily fabricated timber or metal trusses but for the primitive builder, relying on materials such as mud, stone, tree trunks and branches, leaves or grass the problem is daunting —particularly if the space to be spanned is large and substantial loads therefore are involved.

In areas where timber was freely available, the simplest traditional solution was the sturdy horizontal timber beam; this is both structurally effective (if the span is not excessive), and not dependent on advanced craft skills. It is a typical solution in many dry climates where flat roofs can be used **2**.

Prevalence of rain and the need to shed snow, however, necessitated a pitched roof and resulted in more sophisticated forms of construction. A typical example at the 'primitive' end of the range of forms is shown in **3**; **4** and **7**. **5** and **6** are examples in which a combination of factors (greater spans, availability of more advanced craft skills, and cultural forces) have produced more spectacular space-enclosing structural forms; one in brick, the other in stone. In areas where timber was scarce, or not used for building for other reasons, the problem was less easily solved. No other material available to pre-industrial builders has the tensile strength and other properties which allow it to be used in the straightforward ways shown in **1** and **2**; the problem had therefore to be solved by means of geometric form. Here lies a large part of the explanation of the traditional domed, arched and vaulted roof forms.

3 shows simple construction not requiring advanced craft skills;
4, 6 show application of more advanced craftsmanship in
Devonport dockyard building and virtuoso stonework
King's College Chapel, Cambridge. The latter is strictly
speaking a ceiling rather than a roof: it encloses space but
has no weather-excluding function
5 Clay bricks used in Iran, 7 flat stones in Italy; roofing
forms developed in areas where timber has traditionally been
scarce

4

3

5

6

7

8

9

8 *Golden Lane, London, an early post-war attempt to create a dramatic modern roof form for a tall building, has had few notable successors*

9 *In general, modern rooflines do not capture the interest and excitement of previous ones, evident in this view from Hyde Park towards Bowater House*

1.03 Roofscapes

The factors outlined above tended to produce rooflines that were full of interest: ordinary buildings in Britain and northern Europe normally had steeply pitched roofs, with a variety of textures created by small-unit claddings or thatch, enlivened by dormers and chimney stacks; and the skyline was punctuated by the dramatic spires and domes of more important buildings.

Today, roofing has become almost too easy, and the line of least resistance (for the designer) tends to lead to the ubiquitous featureless flat roof. Few are the buildings which have departed from the convention, and exhibit really exciting modern roof shapes. Golden Lane was a celebrated early example **8**, but it has not had many notable successors. All too often the contribution to the urban roofline made by the modern office block is in sad contrast to that of earlier buildings **9**. There are, however, logical reasons for this. The increase in height of buildings (even the typical earlier ten-storey London bylaw development) tended to make all roofs completely invisible from across the street. They can only make any visual impact when they can be seen from a distance **9**. Thus the often-used solution of strange shapes or cantilevers to house tanks, lift motors, washing lines or what you will. These could be seen from close to the building and given enough overhang. French renaissance builders met the same problem but with more moderate heights; their answer was the typical steeply sloping chateau roof with dormers, which as refined by Mansard was particularly popular in this country for many years. This roof helped in three ways: it increased the usable cubic content, added to the aesthetic effect of the roof as a feature, and let more light into the street (the bylaw aspect). Generally, steeply pitched roofs also give better weather protection.

1.04 A neglected element

We need to start paying more attention to roofs. Where the flat roof is the most appropriate solution, well and good; but it should not be taken for granted. And whatever the indicated solution, it requires more careful design than it usually gets. This applies aesthetically (think of the average flat roof seen from surrounding high building: the clutter of lift rooms and other services elements; the ponds of rainwater; the unpleasing surface appearance . . .) as well as functionally (leakage and condensation problems are all too frequent).

The roof is not a cheap element to be provided as best one can after most of the available finance and design skill have been lavished on the external façades; it is the most exposed, vulnerable and in some ways the most important weather-excluding element in the building. Again it must be remembered that in high-rise buildings the roof forms only a small part of the total enclosure; hence expensive materials may be used in insulation and weatherproofing with only a minor effect on overall cost. Furthermore in driving rain more water will fall directly onto the windward side of a high building than on the roof. This should be remembered, especially if a smooth non-absorbent facing material is being used.

Technical study
Roofs 2

The brief

The following is a concise statement by HAROLD KING *on the factors to be established at the brief stage plus any specific client requirements. Further stages of the contract will be discussed in the Design Guide*

1 Analysis of brief

1.01 Building type and purpose

Information regarding design parameters for roof elements, where building type and purpose are concerned, will be derived from the design brief. The range of structures to be considered will be determined by the spaces to be enclosed which will, in turn, indicate the appropriate construction. A roof is a primary element of enclosure: its form will have a dominant effect on the design as a whole. As the roof is the most exposed part of a building, the necessity of solving the associated aesthetic and technical problems is fundamental to a satisfactory total performance. The purpose group of the buildings classified in the table in Regulation E2 of the Building Regulations 1972 should be checked at an early stage to ascertain possible restrictions on the construction.

1.02 Required life and suitability for adaptation

The 'last a lifetime' philosophy is based on the present high cost of building set against the traditional fiscal policies o⁺ the nation. The concept of a limited life span for roo construction will be appropriate only so far as this concept applies to the whole building process. However, it would appear that the services, fittings, interior space dividers, and possibly external cladding units are more logical elements to consider with regard to short-term replacement, leaving the supporting structure and roof as the basic permanent elements. The possible exception to this is the planned replacement of the waterproofing layer after a given time span, set against an appraisal of its costs and maintenance over a given period.

Where adaptation is concerned, it is possible to construct the 'flat' roof so that it can become an intermediate floor when the building is extended vertically. In this case the waterproofing layer can be an expendable item set against a given time span, or alternatively the possibilities of a temporary roof should be considered. Requirements of

occupants on the top floor of a building must be checked, and any effect changes of use may have on rooflights or services should be ascertained.

In general terms, the more unusual or complex forms of roof call for special attention to detail where life expectancy is concerned. It is unwise to substitute cheaper roof coverings at cost plan stage without considering the effect this will have on the possible necessity of rethinking the structure and decking. Consistency of detail will not permit inferior parts, eg edge details or movement joints, to jeopardise a long-life design. As with other forms of construction, the causes of deterioration in roofing are due to the use of unsuitable materials and poor detailing, followed by inadequate supervision and inspection with perhaps, in some cases, too much faith being placed in specialised systems.

Bearing in mind that a roof is usually more vulnerable than other parts of the building to the effects of atmospheric pollution, solar radiation, heat loss to clear cold skies, and the action of rain, wind and snow, it is well to remember that the pitched roof form covered with traditional materials, such as slate or tiles, has proved itself over many years. The technical problems associated with the design of flat roof forms are still formidable and further research is necessary, particularly regarding the problems of water penetration, condensation, and moisture trapped during construction.

1.03 Security

Before issuing cover for building contents, insurance companies demand high standards of security, and the roof as a possible easy means of breaking and entering should not be overlooked. Rooflights that can be opened easily come to mind immediately, but also in roof-scaped buildings the possibility of illegal entry through escape and service doors should be avoided.

The Insurance Institute of London grades materials used in roof decking construction according to their ability to resist attack by intruders as follows:

Most likely: concrete, slates or tiles on close boarded timber; corrugated sheet iron fixed to steel trusses; and asbestos sheeting.

Least likely: slates or tiles on battens, unlined; with regard to rooflights, there may be a contradiction between the comparative straightforward detailing required for weather-proofing and the more complex details required for a high security risk.

1.04 Maintenance policy

Maintenance characteristics are a direct outcome of design decisions and these matters must be discussed with the client at the project's design stage. A specific maintenance policy should be predetermined, and the client should be advised where unwise economies would lead to unreasonably high maintenance costs. Large areas of glass require frequent attention and particular care must be exercised with regard to access for cleaning. Also there may be problems relating to privacy and/or security. Precautions should be taken against injury especially on sloping panes of glass.

Against this background the designer must solve the problems of maximum durability set against the restraints imposed. These restraints will be concerned with space utilisation suitability and appearance related to initial and maintenance costs over a predetermined period. However, the statistics of maintenance will vary according to the maintenance criteria adopted by the client relative to the building's age and the accounting conventions used. In general there is a lack of maintenance cost data available at present, but costs-in-use studies, sponsored by DOE, are being carried out to remedy this.

A Building Maintenance Cost Information Service is at present operated under the direction of Douglas Robertson, 47 Tothill Street, London sw1.

2 Checklist

2.01 Building type and purpose
● Check purpose group of building
● Analyse spaces to be enclosed

2.02 Required life, degree of adaptation, and maintenance
● Establish required life span of building as a whole and of roof in particular (if possible to forecast)
● Establish degree of adaptability required
● Check client's maintenance policy

2.03 Security
● Check insurance requirements

3 References

1 BRITISH STANDARDS INSTITUTION BS 3589: 1963, Glossary of general building terms [(9–) (Agh)]
2 MINISTRY OF PUBLIC BUILDING AND WORKS Report of a sub-committee of the Committee on Building Maintenance. The relationship between design and maintenance. London, 1970 Directorate of Research and Information [(W) (A3)]
3 The Building Regulations 1972 [(A3j)]
4 LEWORTHY, L. R. Security. *Specification* 1971: Vol 1, p1132–1141. London, 1971, Architectural Press [(4y) (A3)]
5 Handbook of Building services and circulation: Section 13: Security and fire. *Architects' Journal*, 1970, June 17 to August 5 [(5–)]

1 *Tange's suspended roof at one of his Olympic buildings, Tokyo*

Technical study
Roofs 3

Section 5: **Roofs**

Roof requirements

This technical study by HAROLD KING *draws attention to the basic principles associated with the functional requirements of roof assembly.*

1 Structural functions

1.01 Definitions

Technically a roof is either flat or pitched. In BS 3589: 1963 Glossary of general building terms, the roof is defined as 'flat' up to a pitch of 10 deg or less to the horizontal **1**. (NB 10° represents a slope of about 1 in 5·7)

1 *Up to* 10 *deg slope is defined as flat in* BS 3589

All roof elements must be designed so that there is adequate resistance of the whole or each part of the roof to failure by overstressing. It is also necessary to accommodate dimensional changes and to reduce movement within the roof construction to acceptable limits. Dimensional change may be due to changes in temperature or moisture content, or to chemical reaction between building materials in juxtaposition and in contact with moisture. Deflection must also be considered. A long span roof might deflect sufficiently to destroy the pattern of falls. Relevant Codes of Practice, British Standards[10-14] and advisory publications should be studied. A basic list will be found in the References (para 7.00).

Performance specification data should also be considered, reference being made to the master list of properties (CIB report 3, 1964) which provides a direct link between component design and material properties.

The AJ Handbook of Building structure deals with structural theories and problems associated with structure and to which further reference should be made for detailed information on these aspects of the roof elements.

The effect of wind pressure or suction on the roof form should be studied. Generally the local conditions at the edges or ridge of the roof will be critical for component parts of the roof, including fixings, and the total stability of the roof will take account of both overall and local pressures. To counteract suction on a low-pitched roof, particularly where lightweight materials are used for both covering and deck, special precautions should be taken to anchor the roof to the main structure (see BS CP 3 Part 2 Chapter V: 1970 *Wind loads*[13]).

Changes in design, use of new materials and new methods of construction may tend to move the roof system nearer to the critical point of failure and several insignificant defects can combine together to cause a major breakdown

of the roofing elements. This is particularly true of flat roof design. To avoid failure a careful choice of materials and components, and a competent specification of the method of construction must be made, followed by knowledgeable supervision and adequate inspection of the construction process.

2 Climate control

2.01 Weather exclusion

Roof construction must prevent entry of rain, snow and dust. Materials deemed unsuitable for the weather-resisting parts of a roof are listed in the table to B3 of the Building Regulations 1972[22].

Degree of rain penetration is related to amount of rain and associated wind speed. Maximum intensity of rainfall is a more important consideration than total quantity or duration. Maps showing an index of driving rain are included in BRS digest 23[5].

Sloping roof

On a roof slope, gravitational forces move water down the slope and tend to move moisture inward. As the slope decreases the resistance of gravity to the inward flow becomes less and therefore on roofs waterproofed by overlapping units laid dry, water penetration occurs when the slope or pitch in relation to the overlap of the units is insufficient.

Flat roof

On a flat or low-pitched roof, rain penetration can be prevented only by the use of a continuous watertight membrane. However, this is not always easy to achieve or maintain in practice. If a roof surface is designed to be level, ponding will inevitably occur as it is physically impossible to produce a flat surface over a large area and because most materials used for roof decking are flexible and will follow the shape of the material below.

This will lead to accelerated deterioration as shallow pools of water left behind cause local variations in temperature between the wet and dry areas of the roof, resulting in excessive differential thermal movement. This movement (plus accumulated acids left by evaporated rain) can cause breakdown of the roof surface, particularly in bituminous sheeting. The practical limits of screed thickness coupled with rational and economic gutter layout and reasonable downpipe positions usually impose some discipline on flat roof layout and maximum falls.

2.02 Thermal performance

The design of roofs in respect of thermal properties involves controlling heat loss and heat gain within the roof space and mitigating effects of extreme temperatures. Control is achieved by increasing the overall resistance to heat flow through the roof by using insulating materials between exterior and interior environments. Also, a light-coloured roof can be used to reflect solar radiation, thus controlling summer heat gain. The economic thickness of insulation necessary is determined by comparing two factors.
● The cost of the insulating materials plus installation
● The cost of installing and operating heating and/or cooling systems over a given period.
The service life of certain materials is dependent on the range of temperatures experienced. High temperatures increase the rate of deterioration of some materials by oxidative processes (soft bitumins and certain plastics.) High temperatures can also produce sufficient expansion of moisture-laden air between layers of the roof membrane to cause blisters and eventual break-up of the surface.
Daily and seasonal changes in air temperature, solar heating and cooling cause temperature variations sufficient to incur dimensional changes in roofing materials. As each part of the construction experiences a different temperature range and cycle, differential movements occur.

Position of insulation

Materials on the warm side of the insulation become warmer, and those on the cold side colder than they would otherwise be. Thus position of the insulation within the structure is important: with insulation on the inner side of the construction the roof deck and waterproofing layer suffer from a wide temperature variation, while the ceiling temperature remains relatively constant; with insulation on the outer side of the construction the temperature variation in all materials, except the outer membrane, is small. Very high surface temperatures can result from sun shining on externally-insulated roofs. Within this generalisation, the most economic method of construction is to place the insulation external to the supporting structure (immediately beneath the roof covering) for the following reasons:
● It insulates the structure and thus reduces stress due to temperature change
● It can be fully continuous and should eliminate cold spots in the construction
● It will help to control condensation by keeping all the construction, including its internal surface temperature, above the dew-point.
The theory may have to be modified in practice, and the most common alternative positions for insulation relating to roof elements are shown in **2**. Minimum standards of thermal insulation for roof elements are prescribed as follows:
● The Building Regulations 1972[22]: Ceilings and roof (together). u-value required = 1·42 W/m²deg C*
● Building Standards (Scotland)[23] Regulations 1970: Ceilings and roofs. u-value = 1·14 W/m²deg C (see also Scottish Development Department explanatory memorandum 9[25])*
● Thermal Insulation (Industrial Buildings) Act 1957[24]. The combined effects of glazed and solid parts of factory roofs are considered in Factory building study 11: *Thermal insulation of factory buildings*.
u-values of a selection of commonly used techniques for roof construction are given in table I and II (see also IHVE guide book A[3] 1970, and *Thermal insulation of buildings*).

*Note these standards which are mandatory apply only to dwellings.

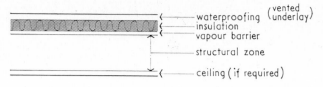

2a *Flat roofs: external (above deck) insulation. This minimises danger of thermal movement within structural zone and interstitial condensation. Structural zone protected against extremes of temperature; structure can act as heat store facility*

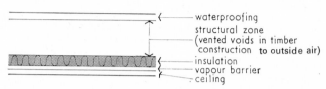

b *Flat roofs: internal (below deck) insulation. Room quickly responds to heat input (advantageous with intermittent occupancy)*

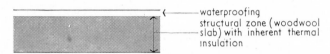

c *Flat roofs: structure has inherent thermal insulation properties. Exposed woodwool slab, ie with no ceiling or vapour barrier, should be used only where relative humidity is low (ie controlled mechanically). Alternatively a suitable vapour barrier is needed below*

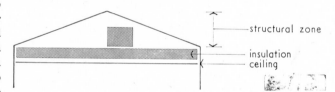

d *Pitched roof: with horizontal ceiling. Room quickly responds to heat input. Pipes or tanks in roof void require insulation. Roof void does not take heat from building*

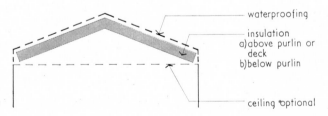

e *Pitched roof: with or without horizontal ceiling. Roof space is heat capacity factor of building*

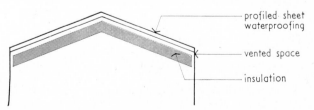

f *Pitched roof clad with lightweight profiled sheeting: where relative humidity within building is high (say more than 60 per cent), space between insulation and cladding must be vented*

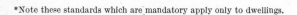

Table I *Selection of typical* U-*values for commonly used roofing techniques*

Pitched roofs	U-value (W/m³ degC)
Tiles on battens on sarking felt on rafters with 10 mm plaster board and skim ceiling	2·46
Tiles on battens on sarking felt on rafters with 25 mm glass wool, or mineral wool mat or quilt between ceiling joists	0·91
Tiles on battens on sarking felt with 25 mm expanded polystyrene fixed to underside rafters and eaves sealed; 10 mm plasterboard and skim ceiling	0·78
Corrugated asbestos cement sheeting on steel purlins unlined	7·90
Corrugated asbestos cement sheeting with lining of 12 mm fibreboard on light metal T-sections; over or below steel purlins	2·17
Corrugated asbestos cement sheeting; 25 mm expanded polystyrene over purlins	1·17
Corrugated asbestos cement sheeting; 25 mm expanded polystyrene under purlins with ventilated air space	1·00
BS type B corrugated asbestos cement sheeting sandwich construction with 25 mm glass fibre insulant	1·08
Do BS type C	1·19
Metal deck 12 mm fibreboard; three layers built-up felt system	2·17

Flat roofs	
Timber deck 25 mm thick on timber joists; three layers built-up felt system; 10 mm plasterboard and skim ceiling on underside of joists	1·82
Timber deck 25 mm thick on timber joists; three layers built-up felt roofing; 10 mm thick mineral wool quilt draped over joists	0·80
Timber deck 25 mm thick on timber joists; 50 mm expanded polystyrene; three layers built-up felt system; 10 mm plasterboard and skim ceiling on underside of joists	0·47
50 mm pre-screeded wood wool slabs on timber joists; 20 mm asphalt on sheathing felt; 30 mm mineral chippings	1·42
50 mm compressed straw slabs on timber joists; three layers built-up felt system	1·24
Metal deck; 50 mm expanded polystyrene; three layers built-up felt system	0·63
175 mm concrete slab plastered below 16 mm lightweight plaster screeded 50 mm (average) CHEECOLITE lightweight aerated concrete screed (480/560 kg/m³) above 60 mm cavity formed by clay blocks and 19 mm asphalt	0·17
100 mm in situ solid concrete roof; 38 mm sand/cement screed; 25 mm wood wool slabs; three layers built-up felt roofing	1·17
125 mm precast hollow concrete beams with 25 mm sand/cement screed; 25 mm fibre insulated board; three layers built-up felt roofing	1·19

Table II *Roofs (Recommended min* U *values for different internal temperatures)*

U-value (W/m² degC)	Internal temperature (°C)
1·7	20
1·9	17·5
2·4	15
2·8	12·5
3·4	10
4·4	7·5
6·2	5

2.03 Control of moisture movement and condensation

As with other parts of the building enclosure, the roof is vulnerable to the effects of moisture. Water from condensation and from water entering or trapped during construction will seriously affect the components of a roof system, leading to deterioration of materials with the possibility of subsequent breakdown and consequent inability to remain weathertight.

Surface condensation

The amount of water vapour contained in the atmosphere will vary according to the temperature and relative humidity of the air. The temperature at which saturation is reached is called the *dew-point* and warm air is able to contain more water vapour than cool air before it becomes saturated. This means that when air containing a given amount of water vapour is cooled by coming into contact with a cold surface, there will be a given temperature at which the water vapour will condense into water droplets on the surface. A high relative humidity (more than 80 per cent) will in fact cause mould growths on the surface of organic materials. In order to avoid surface condensation in the roof construction, insulation should be introduced so that the internal surface of the construction is at a temperature above the dew-point of the internal air. For more detail on risk of condensation see External Envelope 1 p60.

Interstitial condensation

In certain industrial processes and in buildings where there are numbers of people in a confined space, the internal climate will be warm and humid. In these circumstances the difference in vapour pressure of a cold external atmosphere and the warm damp internal conditions may be such that water vapour will move into and through the roof structure and condense within the structure as the temperature of the construction becomes less. This form of condensation is known as *interstitial condensation*. The resultant moisture will be a primary cause of deterioration. To prevent this a vapour barrier is necessary to control the vapour movement. The construction must be ventilated to the external air so that the moisture content of the air within the building or within the roof space is reduced, thus lowering its dew-point.

Positioning the vapour barrier

The most suitable practical position is to place the vapour barrier on the warmest side of the insulation where it will remain at a temperature above the dew-point of the air. The resistance to vapour flow required depends on the service conditions. There are a number of materials suitable for use as vapour barriers: asphalt-coated felts and papers; metal foils of copper or aluminium; polythene film; aluminium paint; asphalt coatings; some types of latex emulsion paints; exterior grade plywood; and cellular plastic insulation.

The tensile strength, pliability, tear resistance, ease of handling, and durability of the vapour barrier should be taken into account. The effectiveness of the barrier depends on it remaining unpierced and is thus determined by the design and care involved in its application and especially jointing. The barrier will be rendered ineffective by the presence of accidental openings. The methods used to counteract the effect of intentional openings are determined by the details of specific application.

Vapour barriers in ceilings and roofs

There is a great danger of openings being made in vapour barriers in roofs and ceilings where electrical fittings and services are installed. Openings also occur around service ductwork and chimneys. When the vapour barrier is pierced, the roof space must be ventilated. Special difficulties may be encountered in air-conditioning applications. A traditional sloping tiled roof is inherently able to control moisture as any accumulation of vapour caused by slight defects in the waterproofing can usually escape by diffusing through the roof. As the slope of the roof decreases, the rate of ventilation by natural convection also decreases, so in a flat roof system the effect of diffusion will be small and requires assistance from planned ventilation *to the open air* (not to the internal air).

Impervious outer coverings act as vapour barriers on the wrong, ie cold side, of the construction. In heated buildings of low inside humidity with impermeable exterior water-proofing, it is possible to control moisture vapour without using a vapour barrier provided that the material used for the roof deck is capable of holding moisture without dripping for reasonable periods until re-evaporation into the interior is possible. In these circumstances increase in heat loss due to the damp insulation should be recognised. (On the whole not to be recommended—better to protect insulation by vapour barrier.)

Moisture control

Control of moisture depends on an awareness of its source, and following control methods where appropriate:
● Materials protected during storage and application
● Construction moisture from wet finishing dispersed by ventilation before sealing by impervious finishes
● Roof surface to give adequate fall to allow quick drainage
● Moisture generated by occupancy to be isolated or dispersed by ventilation
● Critical interior surfaces kept warmer than dew-point temperature by sufficient insulation on the cold side, moist air to be prevented from reaching the cold surfaces by vapour barrier on the warm side.

Two vapour-resistant components together can constitute a vapour trap, as is the case with multi-layer built-up roofing, and in this instance water vapour within the construction must be able to escape to the cold side by means of air vapour paths and vents. This can be done either by the partial bonding of last layer of felt or by using a vented underlay, with outlets at edges or also at intervals throughout.

BRS Digest 51, *Developments in roofings*, discusses in detail the problems of water vapour in the roof deck, particularly in connection with lightweight screeds. This matter will be dealt with more fully in Information Sheet Roofs 1, Decking.

2.04 Natural light and ventilation

The method of providing natural lighting units for roofs can be selected from a wide range of components:
● Patent glazing (north light or continuous lower pitched)
● Lantern lights
● Dome lights
● Sky lights
Amount of light will be determined by the ratio of floor to glass area, having regard to the orientation. The distribution of light will be related to the arrangement and spacing of glazed surfaces.

To avoid glare, special glass may be used or the light screened from normal view within 40 to 45 deg to the horizontal.

2.05 Sound insulation

With regard to the roof element, the main noise source will be air-borne. Establish whether the requirement is to keep internal noise in, or external noise out and deal with directional effect by screening where possible. *See Principles of modern building*[1] vol II and BS CP 3 Chapter III: 1960 *Sound insulation and noise reduction*[11].

3 Drainage

Decide first whether the roof is to have concealed integral gutters or an exposed applied gutter system. The rate at which water will run off a roof is a fundamental question. Pitched roofing has a high rate of run-off and provided that

the detailing of overlap or jointing of the waterproofing element is satisfactory, the pitch is a significant contributory factor to roofing durability. The run-off from a flat roof is very slow and the consequent ponding will have a detrimental effect on durability.

Alternatively it is possible to design roofs to retain a considerable depth of water to protect and insulate the roof surface so that the construction has freedom from diurnal temperature change. The water must be deep enough to withstand evaporation and must not stagnate. This is difficult in practice; one problem is the weight of water on the roof. Even 300 mm of water will weigh 300 kg/m² or virtually equal to a floor loading rather than the usual roof loading.

BRS Digest 116 *Roof drainage* (first series)[8] and BRS Digest 34 *Design of gutters and rainwater pipes*[6] provide a basis for matching the flow load and capacity of gutters and outlets. After assessing the total flow load from the roof, the aim is to arrange for the pipes to discharge as near to full bore as possible: this allows outlet size to be reduced materially compared with traditional rule-of-thumb methods. The critical point in the design is the water's point of entry into the head of the pipe (ie the weir or point at which the flow changes from almost horizontal to vertical. The tapering conical outlets are meant to increase the lineal extent of the weir (perimeter) thus reducing the depth of water passing over and hence the risk of overflowing at this point. Proprietary outlets with wide-entry diameter tapering to the minimum size rwp produce the most efficient discharge system (see **3** for outlet to flat roof). Recommendations of BRS are: that the flow load from flat roofs and from roofs pitched up to 50 deg is calculated from the formula: flow

$$\text{load (litres/s)} = \frac{\textit{net area of roof (m}^2)}{50}$$

The flow capacity of gutters depends on cross-sectional area, frictional resistance and fall. Bends reduce the flow so that allowances of up to 25 per cent may have to be made. Flow capacities of a selected range of half-round gutters and associated recommended down pipe sizes are in table III.

Table III Flow capacities of level half round gutters with outlets at one end

Gutter size (mm)	True half-round gutters* flow (litres/s)	Nominal half-round gutters† flow (litres/s)
75	0·43	0·32
100	0·84	0·67
112	1·14	0·84
125	1·52	1·06
150	2·46	1·82

*Pressed steel to BS 1091 ; asbestos cement to BS 569
†Aluminium to BS 1430 ; cast iron to BS 1205

4 Fire resistance

4.01 Grading tests

Fire resistance of structural elements is measured by the length of time or notional period during which the element under test will resist a fire of prescribed severity without failure. In addition a roof must provide an adequate barrier to the spread of fire from neighbouring buildings (fire protection). The external fire exposure roof tests set out in BS 476: Part 3: 1958[10] classify the performance of the construction in relation to the ability to resist penetration of fire from an external source and the rate of spread of flame over the external roof surface.

A tested specification receives a designation consisting of two letters, eg AA CC AB. The first letter relates to penetra-

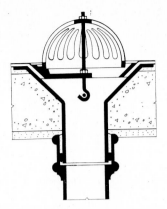

3 *Proprietary rainwater outlet for flat roofs*

tion and the second relates to spread of flame. Categories A to D in descending order of resistance are listed in each case. It follows that in theory there are 16 possible classifications, but about half only are practical possibilities. In general terms resistance to penetration has more significance than the rate of flame spread. Designations can be prefixed EXT F and EXT S. Plastics with low softening temperatures, such as pvc, will fall out of the test rig before they can be designated unless reinforced with wire mesh. This is taken into account in the Building Regulations 1972 E17 paragraphs (5) and (6)[22].

4.02 Mandatory requirements

Statutory controls are as follows:

For England and Wales: The Building Regulations 1972
Roof members are excluded from the category of elements of structure and thus are not required to have fire resistance. Roof decks must comply with the designations in BS 476: Part B[10] (see section E17 *Roofs*, and *Notional designations of roof constructions schedule* 10 in the Regulations for the type of construction permitted). In addition to the grading classifications other constraints apply, depending on the size of a building, its use, and the distance from the nearest boundary (see table IV for a selected list of permissible constructions). Provision is made for the acceptance of constructions not listed in the Regulations, provided there is evidence of a satisfactory test.

For Scotland: The Building Standards (Scotland) Regulations 1970
Roof members are excluded from fire-resistance require-

ments. Roof decks are required to resist external exposure to BS 476, or notional designations table 8 schedule 8, dependent on distance from nearest boundary.

For the area controlled by the GLC: The London Building (Constructional) By-Laws 1972
The slope of roofs is controlled and the materials to be used for finishes, gutters and roof glazing is specified.

Other Acts
The following acts, to which reference should be made where relevant, contain sections on fire protection: Thermal Insulation (Industrial Buildings) Act 1961[24]; Offices Shops and Railway Premises Act 1963[27]; and Factory Act 1961[16].

4.03 Compartmenting and fire venting

Fires may spread through roof and suspended ceiling spaces unless compartment walls are extended into the space and additional fire-stopping provided where necessary (see Building Regulations 1972, sections E1, 4, 8 and 14).
In single-storey factory buildings it may be difficult, because of user requirements, to compartment the working area. In these cases the rapid accumulation of smoke and heat at an early stage in the outbreak may be dissipated by the use of automatic ventilators that open on the outbreak of fire. The ventilators are used in conjunction with non-combustible screens within the roof space.

4.04 Fire fighting

For active defence against fire, consideration should be given to access by the fire brigade and to installation of automatic detector systems and sprinklers related to the roof elements. It should be remembered that the roof may form a means of escape in case of fire, so the district fire officer should be consulted at early design stage.

5 Access

Flat roofs to which access is provided for work other than maintenance must be protected with an adequate balustrade, parapet, or railing not less than 1·1 m high (see Building Regulations 1972 H6).
Roofs should be assessed for amount of traffic likely, and walkways should be provided in parapet gutters and for maintenance purposes over asbestos-sheeted and glazed roofs. Other roof forms may require special attention as some types of roof covering and insulation below can be easily damaged.

Table IV *Selection of permissible roof constructions (Building Regulations* 1972 E17)

| England and Wales | Minimum distance from boundary | | | |
	No limit	(6 m)	(12 m)	(22 m)
Exceeding (1500 m³)	AA AB AC	BA BB BC (AD)	AD	—
Factory or storage (in whole or part)	AA AB AC	BA BB BC (AD)	AD	—
Terrace housing	AA AB AC	BA BB BC (AD)	AD	—
Any other	AA AB AC	BA BB BC (AD BD CA CB CC CD) (Thatch), (wood-shingles), glass, self-extinguishing pvc** (undesignated)	AD BD CA CB CC CD Thatch, wood shingles, undesignated*	DA DB DC DD
Garage conservatory or outbuilding not exceed 40 m²	Glass, self-extinguishing pvc	—	—	—
Roof or canopy over balcony, verandah, open carport, covered way or detached swimming pool	Glass, self-extinguishing pvc**	—	—	—

*Distance from boundary must not be less than twice height of building
**Self-extinguishing when tested in accordance with method 508A of BS 2782: Part 5: 1965
Materials and designations in brackets are limited to areas not exceeding (3·0 m²) isolated from each other by areas of non-combustible material at least 1·5 m wide. Undesignated materials are those not designated in BS 476: 1958 because of low softening temperature, eg Univinyl

6 Checklist

6.01 Structural functions
● Definitions

6.02 Climatic control
● Weather exclusion
● Thermal performance
● Moisture movement and condensation control
● Natural light and ventilation
● Sound insulation
● Artificial light and ventilation

6.03 Drainage

6.04 Fire resistance
● Grading tests
● Mandatory requirements
● Compartmenting and fire venting
● Fire fighting

6.05 Access

7 References

1 DSIR Principles of modern building. volumes I and II. HMSO [(9–) (E1)]

2 NASH, C. D., COMRIE, J., BROUGHTON, H. F. The thermal insulation of buildings: Design data and how to use them. 1955, HMSO [(J2)]

3 INSTITUTION OF HEATING AND VENTILATING ENGINEERS IHVE guide book A 1970. London, 1970, Curwen Press [(1) (J)]

4 NASH, G. D. Factory building study 11 Thermal insulation of factories. 1962, HMSO [27 (J2)]

BUILDING RESEARCH STATION

5 Digest 127 An index of exposure to driving rain. 1971, HMSO [(I3)]

6 Digest 34 Design of gutter and rainwater pipes. 1963, HMSO [(52·5)]

7 Digest 108 Standardised U-values. 1969, HMSO [(J4)]

8 Digest 116 (first series) Roof drainage. 1958, HMSO [(52·5)]

9 Digest 119 The assessment of wind loads. 1970, HMSO [(K4f)[5]. Superseded by CP 3 Chapter V, Part 2, see below.

BRITISH STANDARDS INSTITUTION

10 BS 476 Part 3: 1958 External fire exposure roof tests [Yy (R4) (Aq)] *amended* 1959

11 CP 3 Chapter III: 1960 Sound insulation and noise reduction [(M)]

12 CP 3 Chapter I, Lighting. Part 1: 1964 Daylighting [(N)]

13 CP 3 Chapter V: Part 2 1970 Wind loads (K4)

14 CP 144 Roof coverings. Part 1: 1968 Built-up bitumen felt. Imperial units [(47) Ln2]. Part 2: 1966 Asphalt. Imperial units [(47) Ps4] *amended* 1967

15 BURBERRY, P. Environment and services: Mitchells building construction. London, 1970, Batsford [(E6)] £2·50

16 Factory Act 1968 [27 (Ajk)]

17 FIRE OFFICES COMMITTEE Rules for automatic sprinkler installation. 29th edition. London, 1968, Witherby [(68·5)]

18 MINISTRY OF TECHNOLOGY AND FIRE OFFICES' COMMITTEE Fire note 5 Fire venting of single-storey buildings. Post war building study 2 Fire grading of buildings. 1965, HMSO [(R)]

19 PWBS 30 Recommended minimum standards of day-lighting for offices. 1952, HMSO [32 (N7)]

20 CAPE UNIVERSAL BUILDING PRODUCTS LTD Technical manual 1970/71. England 1970-71, Page Bros [Yy (Abd)[3]

21 PRATT, A. W. Condensation in sheeted roofs. National Building Studies research paper 1958. 1960, HMSO [(27) (I6)]

22 The Building Regulations 1972 [(Ajk)]

23 Building Standards (Scotland) Regulations 1970 [(A3j)]

24 Thermal Insulation (Industrial Buildings) Act 1957 [27 (Ajk)]

25 SCOTTISH DEVELOPMENT DEPARTMENT Explanatory memoranda 4 to the Building Standards (Scotland) Regulations 1963, HMSO [(A3j)]

GREATER LONDON COUNCIL

26 London Building (Constructional) By-laws 1972. [(Ajn)]

27 Offices Shops and Railway Premises Act 1963 [(Ajk)]

28 SCOTTISH DEVELOPMENT DEPARTMENT Explanatory memorandum 9 Resistance to the transmission of heat. 1963, HMSO [(A3j)]

29 KING, H. and EVERETT, A. Components and finishes. London, 1970, Batsford [(9–) (E1)]

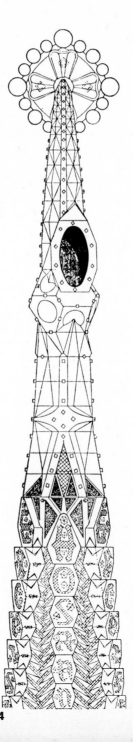

4 *Gaudi's Sagrada Familia: glazed tile and glass mosaics used in roof which becomes total building element*

Technical study
Roofs 4

Section 5 **Roofs**

Structural form

In this technical study by ERIC PARKES, *the large number of different roof forms available have been classified into natural groups (table I), and information presented as concisely as possible on each of these groups in turn (table II).*
It is possible to give guidance on the reasonable range of spans for some roof forms, eg timber joists, but others, for instance tension structures, lack built examples and therefore are dealt with by outlining the main features and indicating sizes of those already constructed or projected. Cross references to decking and waterproofing have been given in the classification index, so that the structure may be thought of, not in isolation, but as part of a complete roof assembly. More detailed information is given in AJ *Handbook of Building structure*[14]

1.01 Key to decking classification in table I

a Asbestos cement
Asbestos cement hollow decking profiles to BS 3717 (usually insulated).

b Compressed straw slabs
Compressed straw building slabs to BS 4046.

c Lightweight concrete panels
Lightweight reinforced concrete in thin precast panels.

d Profiled metal decking
Steel decking from steel sheet galvanised to BS 2989.
Aluminium decking from alloys to BS 1470.
Metal decking with pvc and other coatings.
(Decking is usually overlaid with insulation sheeting.)

e Timber
Softwood tongued and grooved boarding.
Plywood (see BS 3493).
Chipboard (see BS 2604 Part 2).
(Timber used in accordance with BS CP 112).

f Wood wool slabs
Unreinforced wood wool slabs to BS 1105 Type B.
Edge-reinforced wood wool slabs.
Pre-screeded (cement/sand slurry) wood wool slabs.
Pre-felted or waterproofed wood-wool slabs.
Edge-reinforced wood wool structural units (combined beam/slab).

1.02 Key to waterproofing classification in table I

g Asphalt
Mastic asphalt for roofing to BS 1162 or BS 988 (limestone aggregate).

h Built-up felt
Roofing felts to BS 747.
Proprietary bituminous sheet roofing systems.
Aluminium or copper faced bituminous felt.

j Liquid finishes
Brush- or spray-applied liquid and semi-liquid finishes.
Epoxy polyurethane resins.
Styrene.
Butadiene.

k Profiled metal, plastics or asbestos sheeting
Corrugated asbestos cement sheets to BS 690.
Profiled protected metal sheeting.
Composite profiled sheets; steel/plastic.
Steel-cored corrugated asbestos.
Galvanised corrugated steel sheet to BS 3083.
Corrugated aluminium sheet to BS 2855.
Troughed aluminium building sheet to BS 3428.
Profiled clear or translucent plastic sheeting.

l Sheet metal roofing
Aluminium sheet or strip to BS 1470.
Rolled copper sheet or strip to BS 2870.
Plain sheet zinc roofing to BS 849.
Lead sheet or strip to BS 1178.
Factory-bonded prefabricated panels faced with copper, aluminium, zinc or lead (combined deck and finish).

m Single-layer flexible sheet
Proprietory roofing systems using:
Asbestos bitumen
Glass fibre reinforced bitumen
Vinyl asbestos
Bitumen polymers
Neoprene
Pitch polymers
Composite sheets.

n Slates, tiles or similar
Roofing slates to BS 680.
Plain clay roofing tiles and fittings to BS 402 (including BS 550).
Concrete roofing tiles and fittings, and concrete single lap roofing tiles to BS 473.
Asbestos cement slates to BS 690.
Shingles.
Thatching.

Table i *Classification index*

Structural form Type	Profile	Timber	Steel	Concrete	Aluminium	Plastic	a Asbestos cement	b Compressed straw slabs	c Lightweight concrete panels	d Profiled metal decking	e Timber	f Wood wool slabs	g Asphalt	h Built-up felt	j Liquid finishes	k Profiled metal, plastics or asbestos sheeting	l Sheet metal roofing	m Single layer flexible sheet	n Slates, tiles or similar
							Decking (see para 1.01)						Waterproofing (see para 1.02)						
Beams and slabs		●	●	●			Slabs are integral structure and deck ●	●	●		●	●	●	●†	●		●†	●†	
Lattice and similar girders		●	●	●			●	*●	*●	*●		*●	●	●†	●	●	●†	●†	
Trusses		●	●				*●			*●	*●	*●	●	●	●	●	●	●	●
Portal frames		●	●	●	●		*●		*●	*●		*●	●	●	●	●	●	●	●
Space frames		●	●		●		●	●	●	●	●	●	●	●	●		●	●	
Shell roofs		●	●	●	●	●	Integral structure and deck or special deck units						●	●	●		●	●	
Folded plates		●	●	●	●		Integral structure and deck						●	●	●			●	●
Arches		●	●	●	●		*●	*●	*●	*●	*●		●	●	●	●	●	●	●
Tension (cable) structures			●				Special deck units						Special applications (must be flexible)						
Cable-stayed (suspended) roofs			●				Special deck units						Special applications (flexibility important)						
Inflated membrane structures			●			●	Integral construction Requires continuous pressurisation and air lock entry						Integral construction						

† On flat roofs these materials must be laid to falls
* With intermediate purlin support where required
N.B. The ommission of a marker (●) below any particular application does not necessarily mean that this material cannot be used, but simply implies that its use would not be normal or usual

Table II *Types of roof forms*

BEAMS AND SLABS

Type	Profile	Notes and application
Timber		
Sawn joist		Reasonable range of spans up to about 4 m
Laminated		Economic range starts somewhat below the maximum for sawn joists and up to about 15 m
Plywood web		Standard beams available up to 15 m (refer to manufacturers' tables)
Stressed skin panels		'Skin' attached, usually by gluing, to members forming box beam. Deck resists bending across main span with consequent reduction in timber sizes. Convenient to prefabricate using standard size plywood panels
Steel		
Angles		Angles and Z-sections are commonly used as purlins rather than beams, so are 'deck' members.
Z-sections		Sections are usually hot rolled in mill but all except I sections are also produced by cold rolling or pressing and are lighter.
Channels		Other steel sections shown are more commonly used as beams, although in particular circumstances they may be used as part of decking system. It is usual to calculate the load on the member and then refer to 'safe load tables' to ascertain size of member required. These tables are published by British Constructional Steelwork Association[16] and are available in metric form
I-section		
Open web beam		
Castellated beam		Proprietary sections available up to spans of about 30 m (refer to manufacturers' tables for loadbearing capacity). May be fabricated from angles, channels, tubular sections solid rods, etc, for any specific span
Concrete (reinforced)		
Solid flat slab		Reasonable range of spans up to about 8 m
Waffle slab		Reasonable range of spans above about 7 m span (2 way span)
Beam and slab		Suitable spacing of beams to give economical slab, which may span either one or both ways and assist beam strength by increasing compression area.
Precast slabs		See manufacturer's tables for standard panels or design for non-standard
Precast beams		Proprietary sections normally used. Maximum span varies from 5 to 20 m depending on make. 2 types shown—beam and infill and simple beam. Neither require propping.
Precast planks		Planks used as permanent shuttering which also contributes strength. In situ concrete topping provides remainder of strength required. Propping at mid span or more closely always needed until concrete develops strength.
Composite construction		Concrete slab connected to steel beams by shear pins welded to top flange. Both slab and beams act as monolithic section

LATTICE AND SIMILAR GIRDERS

Type	Profile	Notes and application
N or Pratt		*Steel:* wide range of spans may be used. Girder may be fabricated from various sections, though square and circular hollow sections are most frequently used now. Girder depth may be designed to coincide with floor to roof and ceiling heights
		Timber: available with non- laminated chords up to about 18 m span. Above 18 m span laminated timber chords are likely to be used. In US spans over 100 m have been built
Warren		*Concrete:* usually precast units post-tensioned
		All these types are convenient for taking roof slab on top and ceiling on bottom boom leaving space between (subject to layout of girder members) for services.
Howe		
Vierendeel		Vierendeel girder is available in steel and concrete only
		Normally used where rectangular spaces are needed for services (eg rectangular ventilation ducts) or other purposes.
Triangular lattice		Triangular lattice gives stability and rigidity in three dimensions; slopes used for glazing

TRUSSES

Couple		*Timber:* low pitch span up to about 4 m. Steep pitch span up to about 14 m. Using laminated timber sections (at close centres)
Close couple		*Timber:* sawn span up to 5 m; with hanger span up to 6 m (at close centres)
	Tie	
		Steel: with lattice rafters; hangers and tie bar, spans up to about 20 m
Trussed rafter		*Timber:* with or without central hanger; up to about 10 m span
Standard fink (or Belgian) truss		In timber or steel up to about 10 m maximum span (similar to TRADA domestic types) with purlins under rafters of truss—every fourth rafter trussed (usually by doubling with struts between)
Double fink truss		*Timber:* 5 to 14 m span (similar to TRADA industrial)
		Steel: 8 m to 15 m span

Type	Profile	Notes and application
Howe truss		*Steel and timber:* up to 10 m
Double Howe		*Steel and timber:* 8 to 15 m
Fan truss		*Steel:* up to 8 to 15 m
French truss		*Steel:* 12 to 20 m
French truss (variations for long spans)		These long span trusses have been largely superseded today by portals, lattice girder and similar large span systems
North light roof trusses		*Steel:* up to 5 m
		5 to 15 m
Saw tooth		*Steel:* generally about 5 m span between longitudinal lattice girders
Umbrella		*Steel:* up to about 13 m span between longitudinal lattices
Bow string		*Timber and steel:* 20 to 40 m normal, although much larger spans have been done in US using timber
Scissors (variations of)		*Timber and steel:* general range of spans about 6 to 13 m

PORTAL FRAMES

Type	Profile	Notes and application
Pitched fixed portal		All joints, including connection to foundation, are rigid and transmit bending moments as well as forces. This is economical in frame itself, but gives worst loading conditions to foundations. Site connections not always convenient to make, particularly in timber and precast concrete
Two-pin portal		Pinned or hinged joints at foundation level eases loading condition, ie no moments are transmitted to foundation. Some economy is sacrificed, however, in that maximum moment in frame is increased
Three-pin portal		Maximum bending moment in frame is increased further, but in timber and precast concrete it is relatively easy to shape section to give maximum material where it is required. With rolled steel sections this is not always economical to do. Three-pin frame is also better able to resist differential deflection of foundations
		Timber: Hollow boxed plywood or laminated frames; spans up to about 50 m
		Concrete: Precast (normally standard spans are used because expense of shuttering for specials). Standard spans up to about 20 m, specials up to about 40 m
		Steel: Up to about 80 m span, fabricated from solid web, castellated, lattice, and structural hollow sections
Mansard		*Timber:* Laminated—up to about 30 m span
		Steel: Large spans could be achieved but not usually required in this shape
North light (modified)		Standard precast frames available up to about 13 m span
		Steel: Up to about 13 m span
Monitor roofs		Used either as roof structure or as subframe on top of main structure
Cantilever frame		Normal portal but cantilevered over on one or both sides

SPACE FRAMES

Single-layer grid Singly curved		Curve forming cylindrically-shaped roof
Cross vault		Intersecting cylinders forming cross-vault
		Timber: Up to about 50 m maximum
		Concrete: Up to about 50 m maximum
		Steel: Large spans possible

Type	Profile	Notes and application
Doubly curved		Example shows six hyperbolic paraboloid surfaces forming roof on hexagonal plan. Wide variety of shapes and sizes is possible
Domes		*Timber:* 25 m diam domes have been constructed
		Metal: Steel and aluminium ribbed domes up to about 300 m
		Plastic: Sandwich construction 45 m
Double-layer grid		
Two-way		Roof structure consists of series of lattice girders spanning at 90 deg to each other
Three-way		Uniform stress distribution (compared with two-way grids) allows flexibility in design. (Example: roof at Bilancourt, Paris, about 50 m square)
Lattice units		Formed of prefabricated latticed units bolted or welded together
Rectangular prisms		30 m plus in steel and aluminium
Triangular prisms		30 m plus in steel and aluminium
		Commercially available double-layer space frame in tubular steel can span 152 m clear

SHELL ROOFS

Singly-curved shells

Type	Profile	Notes and application
Barrel vault (symmetrical)		Diaphragms commonly used to stiffen shell against deformation. Other methods of stiffening may be used, ie internal arch beam, external arch beam, tie bar, etc
		Timber: Plywood and laminated 10 m span
		Reinforced concrete: 40 m long × 14 m wide
North light barrel vault		North light form may be single-span, single-bay, multi-span, multi-bay, as with symmetrical barrel vault
		Reinforced concrete: 30 m × 10 m wide
		Prestressed concrete: 40 m × 12 m wide
Tilted cylinders		Similar spans to above
Intersecting cylindrical surfaces		Generatrix in one or more planes, variety of plan shapes possible
		Timber: Plywood up to 10 m span
		Reinforced concrete: Up to 20 m

Type	Profile	Notes and application
Rotational shells		
Dome	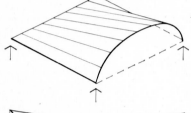	*Timber:* 25 m domes have been constructed with laminated ribs and two layers of tongued and grooved boarding *Concrete:* Ring beam at bottom may be prestressed *Metal:* Steel and aluminium ribbed domes up to 300 m designed (sphere may be cut to form straight line plans)
Other rotational forms		Intersecting rotational shells may be formed to various plan shapes
Translational shells	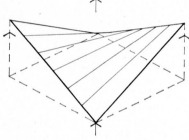	Suitable for in situ or precast concrete. For example 8 m square precast shell was used for supermarket building in US (crane-hoisted). Translational shell is a plane curve moving parallel to itself along another plane curve

Anticlastic shells (Saddles)

Conoid		Roof surface is formed by series of straight lines, which simplifies formwork for in situ concrete shells and enables timber to be used economically for timber shells. Convex curve in one direction forms arching action, concave curve in other direction acting as tension member. Systems of two or more 'hypar' surfaces, intersecting or conjoined, may be used to form one roof. About 30 m × 40 m reinforced concrete shell constructed in US. Timber shells somewhat smaller
Hyperbolic paraboloid		NB: some types of shell roofs have been built using plastic sandwich construction

FOLDED PLATE SYSTEMS

Prismatic folded	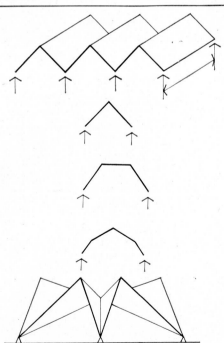	Suitable for prefabricated roof decks—wide variety of forms possible. Stressed skin plywood panel construction up to about 14 m span. Metal stressed skin units may also be used; reinforced concrete and plastic sandwich construction also possible in many shapes
		Intersecting plates to polygonal plan shown; many other forms may be used

Type	Profile	Notes and application
Pyramidal folded	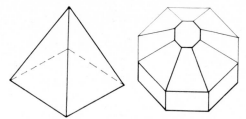	
Folded frame	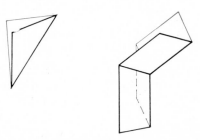	Suitable form for stressed skin plywood panels, concrete, plastic sandwich panel

ARCH STRUCTURES

Two-pin	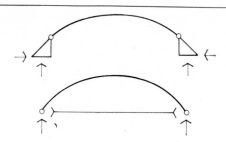	Horizontal thrust may be taken to foundation level by buttressing or relieved by use of tie bar. Laminated timber and steel boxed lattice construction up to about 90 m span
Three-pin		Similar in principle to 3 pin portal.
Cantilever	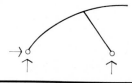	Cantilevered lengths have been constructed in laminated timber and prestressed concrete up to about 20 m, and using high tensile steel lattice truss up to about 50 m

TENSION (CABLE) STRUCTURES

Suspended cable		Suspended cable in tension is very economical but aerodynamically unstable with light deck. It may be stabilised by increasing dead weight or by pretensioned stabilisation cables
Pretensioned cables	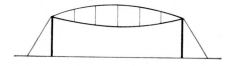	Stabilisation cable above or below suspension cable, parallel struts between
	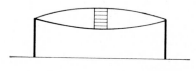	Cables on circular plan, tension drum in centre and compression ring on outside
	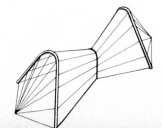	Transverse stabilisation cable stresses suspension cable and resists deflection

Type	Profile	Notes and application
	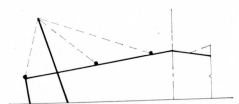	130 m diam suspended roof at Madison Square Gardens has two-storey building above cables

CABLE-STAYED (SUSPENDED) ROOFS

Cable-stayed cantilever		130 m span Tulsa Exposition Centre (100 m clear between supports) is of this type. Long spans and variety of forms possible

INFLATED MEMBRANE STRUCTURE

Inflated membrane structure

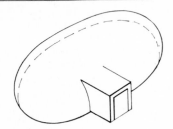

Thin sheet steel welded and inflated for aircraft factory about 400 m diam in US. Pvc-coated nylon membranes up to 100 m × 30 m

Requires continuous pressurisation and air lock at all entry points to maintain +Ve pressure inside.

Bibliography

General

BRITISH STANDARDS INSTITUTION

1 BS CP 3: Chapter V: Part 1: 1967 Dead and imposed loads [(K4)]

2 BS CP 3: Chapter V: Part 2: 1970 Wind loads [(K4f)]

3 BS CP 112: 1967 Structural use of timber [(2–) Yi (K)] £2

4 BS CP 114: Part 2: 1969 The structural use of reinforced concrete in building [(2–) Eq4 (K)] £1·50, *metric*

5 BS CP 115: Part 2: 1969 Structural use of prestressed concrete in building [(2–) Yq (K)] *metric*

6 BS CP 116: Part 2: 1969 Structural use of precast concrete /(2–) Gf (K)] £2, *metric*
A unified code replacing CPs 114, 115 and 116 has been recently published and should now be used.

7 BS CP 117: Part 1: 1965 Composite construction in structural steel and concrete: Simply-supported beams in building [(2–) Gy (K)]

8 BS CP 118: 1969 The structural use of aluminium [(2–) Yh4 (K)] £3

9 BS 449: Part 2: 1969 The use of structural steel in building [(2–) Gh2 (K)] £1·50, *metric*

10 BS 1161: 1951 Aluminium and aluminium alloy sections [Hh4]

11 Building Regulations 1972 HMSO [(A3j)]

12 ENGEL, H. Structure system. London, 1968, Iliffe [(9–) (E1)] *o/p*

13 FOSTER, J. Stroud Mitchell's advanced building construction: The structure. London, 1963, Batsford, 17th [(9–) (E1)] £1·50

14 AJ Handbook of Building structure. *Architects' Journal*, 1966, December 14 to 1967, June 28 [(2)Ba4] *to be revised and republished in* 1974 *in book form.*

Concrete

15 REYNOLDS, C. E. Reinforced concrete designer's handbook. London, 1971, Concrete Publications Ltd, 7th edition [(2–) Gf (K)]
Also publications by Concrete Society Ltd, 52 Grosvenor Gardens, London SW1, and individual manufacturers giving properties and safe load tables of precast concrete units

Steel

16 Steel designer's manual. London, 1966, Crosby Lockwood, 3rd edition [(2–) Yh2 (K)]
Various publications including safe load tables by British Constructional Steelwork Association Ltd, 87 Vincent Square, London SW1 (metric edition)

Timber

Several useful publications are available from:
Timber Research and Development Association, Hughenden Valley, High Wycombe, Bucks
Finnish Plywood Development Association, 56 Haymarket, London SW1
Council of the Forest Industries of British Columbia, 81 High Holborn, London WC1
Timber Trade Federation of the United Kingdom, 47 Whitcomb Street, London WC2
Publications are also available from individual manufacturers, eg Corrply beams design guide, by Rainham Timber Engineering Co Ltd

Aluminium

17 INSTITUTION OF STRUCTURAL ENGINEERS Report on the structural use of aluminium. London, 1962, The Institution [(2–) Gh4 (K)]

Information sheet
Roofs 1

Decking

This information sheet deals with prefabricated units for the sub-structure of a flat or sloping roof. Decking provides support for the waterproofing layer or units, and usually incorporates insulation. On this page are discussed various types of proprietary decking. Beginning overleaf is a table of comparative information for the various general categories

This is the first of six Information Sheets all by HAROLD KING. *No 7, on costs, is by* BRIAN PUGH.

1 Introduction

Technical data concerning span and thickness is given for roofs to which there is access only for maintenance purposes. The fire rating of the decking is usually classified according to the weathering finish applied. Surface spread of flame classification is given where this is relevant to the ceiling finish.

The following decking types are covered in table I:

- Asbestos cement
- Compressed straw slabs
- Lightweight concrete panels
- Profiled metal decking
- Timber
- Wood wool slabs.

2 Proprietary decking

There are several composite decking materials and proprietary decking systems available. The following are typical.

Concrete

Reinforced concrete hollow purlins spaced at, say, 1000 mm to support standard decking units: wood wool, asbestos, metal, compressed straw slab and similar (Concrete Ltd).

Lightweight autoclaved aerated concrete 550 kg/m³ reinforced (Siporex = Costain Concrete Ltd).

Precast, inverted reinforced concrete T-beams with hollow infill blocks grouted with in situ topping laid to falls (Qualcrete Ltd).

There are a tremendous variety of roof systems based on precast concrete (or light precast concrete) beams either placed together at spaced out with an infill of wood wool, light concrete or other suitable short span insulating materials, either standing independently or requiring the integral strength of a structural topping with the consequent need for propping at mid span or more frequent intervals during construction. The variety is virtually as wide as that in patent floor systems based on concrete, the main difference lying in the (normally) lighter loading but additional desirability of thermal insulation.

Metal

Special steel ribs to span up to 4·5 m in conjunction with infill of compressed straw slabs to provide clear soffit (Stramit Ltd).

Aluminum extrusion units with self-locking weather-tight seal, forming combined beam and roof cover for span up to 7 m: no sealants required (Spanfast—Weathertight Structures Ltd).

Timber

Timber lightweight beams for flat roofs spanning up to 15 m with precut tongued noggings to receive decking slab (Teeten—Newsum Timber Engineers Ltd).

Timber lightweight troughed decking units with plywood webs for flat roofs to span up to 13 m, usually with plywood decking (Trofdek—Newsum Timber Engineers Ltd).

Insulated composite roof deck of softwood and plywood boxed structure with glass fibre insulation and integral plywood ceiling; for spans up to 9 m (FPA Pichmastic Ltd, Northply roof deck—Northern Asphalt Division)

Composite decking slab: 6 mm exterior grade finish plywood deck bonded to 13 or 19 mm polyurethane foam insulation, with polythene-coated kraft liner board soffit as vapour barrier. In 2440 mm × 1220 mm sheets (Purldeck—ICI Ltd Agricultural Division).

Table I Comparative information on decking systems

Classification CI/SfB	Description	Standards	Physical data	(U-value) thermal transmittance	Fixing and jointing	Diagrams
Asbestos cement **(27·1) Nf6**	Interlocking asbestos cement box section, for flat roof construction, usually with insulation mat incorporated **1**. Sheets are manufactured from cement asbestos fibre and water using Hatschek process and moulded to shape. Two sections riveted together to form decking unit. Standard units and finishing units available; also special section for adjustment to 'out-of-square' roofs. Range of accessories include gutter sections, stop ends and fascia angles.	Manufactured from Portland cement to BS 12 : 1958 BS 3717 : 1964 *Asbestos cement decking* BS 1494:1951 *Fixing accessories for building purposes* BS CP 199 : 1968 *Roof deckings : Part 1 Asbestos cement.* **Fire rating** Will not support combustion.	Standard units : Lengths : 1829 to 3048 mm in 305 mm increments Width : 502 mm overall (406 mm net cover) Depth : 152 mm Thickness of asbestos sheet : 9·5 mm Weight : 51·2 kg/m² as laid for roofing (including insulation mat).	Decking units with glass fibre insulating mat or equivalent with three layers bituminous roofing. U = 0·95 W/m² deg C.	Fixed by PK self-tapping screws, woodscrews or decking clips with nuts, bolts and washers to steel, concrete or timber supports **2, 3**. Minimum bearing 50 mm. Ends of units butt joined over centres of supporting members.	insulation mat **1** locking nut **2** locking nut **3** 1 **Decking unit** 2 **Fixing to steel beam** 3 **Fixing to concrete purlin**
Compressed straw slabs **Rj3** **(27) Gh**	Slabs manufactured from selected straw by patented method of heat with pressure (trade name Stramit). Available in several grades : 50 mm thick—roofing grade with bitumen liner to both faces ; roofing grade slab with bitumen liner for decoration on underside ; roofing grade slab with bitumen liner one face and liner on underside to give class I spread of flame. 53 mm thick—each grade as above, but with first layer of felt (fibre based or glass fibre) factory-applied.	BS 4046 : 1966 *Compressed straw building slabs.* **Fire rating** Class I if required.	Standard width : 1200 mm (±3 mm) Standard lengths : 1800, 2400, 2700, 3000 and 3600 mm Standard thickness : 50 mm (+3 mm ; −1 mm) Special sizes cut if required Weight : 18·5 kg/m², 39·0 kg/m² with three layer felt and 9·5 mm chipping Safe span : supports at 600 mm centre Flat roof with three layer bituminous felt roof dressed with chippings.	Flat roof : three layer bituminous felt roof dressed with chippings 50 mm compressed straw slabs on timber joists, with 9·5 mm plasterboard with skim ceiling U = 1·02 W/m² deg C.	Each edge of slab must be fully supported and fixed in accordance with manufacturers' instructions. Strength of slab lies in 1200 mm width, so long edges of slab must run with lines of support, nogging tees supporting short sides **4**. Slabs nailed to timber by means of 100 mm galvanised nails at 300 mm centres. When supported on steel or precast concrete purlins, galvanised steel tees (gauge according to span) and special purlin clips are used. Joints are taped with 100 mm wide strips of bitumen scrim bonded to deck, before final waterproofing layers are applied. Where slabs are cut on site, edges must be sealed with special tape. Close co-ordination is required during fixing of	bitumen scrim over joints A noggin tee taper firring 100 mm galvanised nails at 300 mm crs **4** tapered firring air vent dpc **5** air vent soffit continuous ventilation of roof void by use of fillets on top of the joists dpc **6** 4 **Used as flat roof decking** 5 **Alternative verge details at A** 6 **Continuous ventilation to roof void by use of fillets on top of joists**

7 Typical section
8 Steel decking
9 Steel decking with soffit

	Description	Standards / references	Sizes and properties	Thermal properties	Notes
Lightweight concrete panels **Gf4** (Precast and/or prestressed rc beams and slabs or in situ rc slabs where slab structure and deck are integral are not included in this classification.)	Lightweight reinforced concrete in thin precast panels: usually autoclaved aerated concrete. Standard slabs supported on steel or concrete main beams, lattice girders, portal frames or space frames. Reinforcement is treated against corrosion with coating of bitumen, or cement/rubber/casein slurry.	BRS Digests 16 and 17 *Aerated concrete.* **Fire rating** Will not support combustion.	Standard sizes accepted by most manufacturers are as follows: Length: up to 6400 mm Width: 508 and 609 mm Thickness: increments of 25 mm Weight: 75 mm slabs 36 to 66 kg/m². Safe span: to design requirements.	Should be calculated from manufacturers data. Thermal conductivity (K) varies from 0·12 to 0·19 W/m deg C for densities 480 to 800 kg/m³.	Preferably laid to falls so as to avoid need for screeds. Bitumen emulsion primer should be applied to top surface of slabs as soon as possible after laying to prevent absorption of rainwater.
Profiled steel and aluminium sheet to form decking units with or without flat soffit **Steel and aluminium decking with pvc or other coatings** **(27)Gh**	Roll-formed sheeting in various gauges. Galvanised steel decking from hot-dipped, continuously galvanised steel sheet; gauges 1·20, 0·9 and 0·7 mm (18, 20 and 22 swg). Length as required. Aluminium decking from alluminium alloy grade NS 3 H; gauges 1·20 and 0·90 mm (18 and 20 swg) available in smooth or embossed finish. Coated deckings: laminated vinyl 0·30 mm thick on steel; pvc coating 0·20 mm thick on steel; colour coating 0·05 mm thick on steel or aluminium.	Steel decking from sheet steel galvanised to BS 2989: 1967 Aluminium decking alloys to BS 1470:1969 **Fire rating** Class 0	There is range of profiles available for various load/span relationships. Calculations are made in accordance with Metal Roof Deck Association code of design (to CP 3 Ch. V *Dead, imposed and wind loads*). Units are from 25 to 85 mm deep and will span up to 4000 mm **8, 9**. Weights: steel decking from 6·80 to 15·10 kg/m²; aluminium decking from 2·95 to 5·35 kg/m², excluding insulation and weather-proofing.	Metal decking does not provide sufficient thermal insulation, so non-structural insulation board should be introduced on top of decking. Where insulation is not vapour-proof, vapour barrier must be introduced below insulation **7**. Typical U-values (W/m² deg C) for selection of insulation materials on metal decking: 20 mm fibre board—1·45 25 mm fibre board—1·28 25 mm cork board—1·16 25 mm glass fibre—0·96 25 mm expanded polystyrene—0·96 35 mm expanded polystyrene—0·75	Sheets are fixed with minimum end lap and minimum bearing on supports of 50 mm. Side lap is secured at 460 mm centres. Aluminium decking must be isolated from supporting steel work by bitumen felt strips. Vapour barrier felt is laid by mopping flat upper part of deck with bitumen. Minimum lap on longitudinal joints is 50 mm with fully sealed end laps of 150 mm. Insulation layer is bedded in bitumen bonding with panel joints staggered. Insulation must be protected against rain. Metal decking, insulation, and waterproofing is best installed by specialist roofing subcontractors.

Continuation of notes for lightweight concrete panels:

deck and application of waterproofing, and it is good practice for both deck and waterproofing to be fixed by specialist roofing subcontractor. Where compressed straw slabs are used as decking in conjunction with separate ceiling, it is essential that roof void is vented adequately. This can be done for simple flat roof construction by introducing cross bearers and providing a 3 mm continuous space behind the fascia round roof's perimeter **5, 6**. Roof vents must be introduced where roof span exceeds 12 m, and care must be taken to ensure that no pockets of stagnant air remain in roof void. Where cavity brickwork is used, cavity must be closed at top by means of a dpc to prevent discharge of moist air into roof space. Manufacturers do not subscribe to practice of unventilated roof cavities coupled with vapour seals owing to initial difficulties of establishing complete seal during construction and subsequent problem of ensuring that seal is maintained after building is handed over.

Classification CI/SfB	Description	Standards	Physical data	(U-value) thermal transmittance	Fixing and jointing	Diagrams
Timber	Softwood boarding; plywood sheathing grade; and chipboard to BS 2604/1970	*Timber* sub-structure in accordance with BS CP 112 : 1967 *The structural use of timber* (£2)	*Timber*: plain edge boarding, minimum 25 mm nominal thickness. Tongued and grooved boarding minimum 19 mm nominal thickness, optimum width 100 mm.	Softwood boarding, chipboard and plywood decking does not normally provide sufficient insulation, so is usually used in conjunction with non-structural insulation sheet or quilt.	*Timber:* construction should be soundly braced to minimise effects of relative movement of timber. Ventilation should be provided in roof void and it is best to specify all structural timbers to be pressure-treated by preservative as protection against wood-boring insects and wood-rotting fungus. When plain edge boards are used, they should be nailed at each edge to prevent curling (see **10**). All nails must be punched below surface.	
Softwood boarding Hi Plywood Ri4 Chipboard Rj4		Plywood to BS 3493 : 1962 *Information about plywood* Chipboard to BS 2604 : Part 2 : 1970 *Resin-bonded wood chipboard*. Metric BS 1811 : Part 2 : 1969 *Methods of test for wood chipboards and other particle boards*. Metric. Includes test procedure for moisture content of particle boards (wood chipboard, flaxboard and hempboard).	As specified, boarding to span 450 mm between supports. *Plywood:* sheet sizes commonly stocked. *Birch* (Finland) : metric equivalents of imperial sizes	Boarding should be 16 mm minimum thickness and insulation can be placed just below it on joists or under joists as a ceiling. There are a wide variety of materials which will bring the U-value down to the regulation maximum of 1·42 W/m² °C, eg fibreglass or mineral wool quilt 19 mm thick, fibre, insulation board 19 mm, expanded polystyrene 12·5 mm, etc	*Plywood:* panels should be placed with face grain at right-angles to supports and laid with 2 mm open joint. Where fascia is used, this should be fixed first and plywood nailed over. Where felt roofing is to be laid, plywood must be first primed with bitumen. Prefabricated stiffened panels and stressed skin plywood panels **11, 12,** allow reduction in size of framing members. Stiffened panels are economical over 2·5 to 6 m spans and stressed skin over 3·5 to 7 m spans. Stressed skin panels will span up to 12 m.	**10** Nailing of plain edge timber decking **11** Stiffened plywood roof deck panel **12** Stressed skin roof deck panel **13** Chipboard laid along main supports **14** Chipboard laid across supports
			Length Width 1220 mm x 1220 mm 2240 mm x 1220 mm 1525 mm x 1525 mm 3050 mm x 1525 mm (maximum sheet length available 3660 mm) *Fir* (Canada) : standard sheet—metric equivalent of imperial size			
		Fire rating Fire rating is Class III but can usually be improved to Class I by use of special paints. Regulation E17 of Building Regulations 1972 Part III Schedule 10 designates as AA all roofs covered with aluminium copper, zinc lead, mastic asphalt or steel sheet laid on timber or steel joists and either t & g or plain edge boarding, chipboard of any thickness or 9·5 mm plywood	Metric Length Width 1200 mm x 1200 mm 2400 mm x 1200 mm 1500 mm x 1500 mm 1500 mm x 3000 mm (maximum sheet length available 3600 mm) Thicknesses (normally used for decking): 9, 12, 18 and 21 mm.			
			Length Width 2440 mm x 1220 mm (maximum size available 3048 mm x 1524 mm) Metric size (to order) Length Width 2400 mm x 1200 mm Thicknesses (normally used for decking): 8, 12·5, 16 and 19 mm. Sheets should be nailed at maximum 150 mm centres along main supports and at 300 mm centres along intermediate supports. (If main support centres exceed 900 mm, then nailing centres		*Chipboard:* sheets are normally laid along main supports with noggins under short sides **13**. Spanning properties of sheets are improved if they are laid across several supports **14**. Nailing is at 150 mm centres.	

overlap joint

plywood

glue line

10

plywood

softwood framing

interlock joint

11

nailing at 150 mm crs

main supports

nailing at 150 mm crs

noggins

main supports

12

15 Structural unit
16 Wood wool slab decking units for use with space frames
17 Typical fixing accessories:
a trimming units;
b drive screws and washers; c roof slab nails; d fixing clip by roofing contractor, bent on site; e fixing clip welded to steelwork before delivery, bent on site; f eaves brackets (to detail); g duct unit; h cartridge-assisted nails (shot fixing)

Classification CI/SfB	Description	Standards	Physical data	(U-value) thermal transmittance	Fixing and jointing
	Table II Minimum requirements for fir plywood sheathing for flat and sloping roofs **Thickness Spacing of supports**		should not exceed 150 mm throughout.) Where staples are used, these should be divergent type, narrow crown, 18 swg, galvanised or equal, spacing half that for nails. (Information from Plywood Manufacturers Association of British Columbia.) Tongued and grooved fir plywood also available. (see table II). *Chipboard* (imperial board sizes are supplied as standard, with imperial dimensions rounded up to nearest 5 mm). Length 2440 mm x width 1220 mm can be taken as standard. Medium density (550 to 650 kg/m³) standard chipboard is used for decking. Alternatively, (see next column)	Instead of wood high density flaxboard or hempboard can be used. Chipboard is susceptible to moisture movement and if moisture content is greater than 20 per cent, physical deterioration may occur and board will be liable to fungal attack. Sheet sizes in each case given as guide; manufacturers should be consulted for full information.	More rigid deck is possible using tongued and grooved flooring grade chipboard laid as **14**, when noggings can be omitted. Joints should be taped with bitumen scrim and deck temporarily protected from weather until final waterproofing is laid.

Thickness Spacing of supports

Thickness	Panel edges supported:		Panel edges unsupported
	by noggins between main supports	by H-clips, t & g plywood spline etc	
8 mm	600 mm	400 mm	300 mm
9 mm	800 mm	600 mm	400 mm
12 mm	1200 mm	800 mm	600 mm
16 mm	1370 mm	1200 mm	800 mm
19 mm	1500 mm	1370 mm	1200 mm

Thickness	Nail length	Staple length
8 mm	38 mm	22 mm
9 mm	38 mm	28 mm
12 mm	42 mm	38 mm
16 mm	50 mm	50 mm
19 mm	57 mm	—

Classification CI/SfB	Description	Standards	Physical data	(U-value) thermal transmittance	Fixing and jointing
Wood wool slabs **(27) Gj8**	Randomly distributed shredded wood fibres petrified by chemical impregnation, bound with cement and compressed into slabs. Various types of interlocking reinforced slabs are produced, which have longitudinal edges lipped with tongue and groove, galvanised steel channels to improve load/span performance. Channel reinforced structural units are also produced for long spans **15**. Alternative surface and soffit finishes are available (see **19**).	BS 1105:1963 *Unreinforced wood wool slabs up to 3in thick* (type B for roof decking) sets down minimum standards. **Fire rating** Class I	Imperial standard work sizes (approximate metric equivalent—mm):	Three layers built-up felt roofing on screed 50 mm slab flat roof decking laid on timber joists Plasterboard and skim ceiling 0·97 W/m² deg C	Slabs are fixed by means of roof slab nails, drive screws and washers, special clips, or cartridge-assisted nails, as applicable. Manufacturers' fixing instructions must be followed. Slabs are supported at edges or roundtrimmed openings by pressed steel T-, C- or H- sections. Eaves brackets are supplied to detail and there are special ducts or wiring or similar services. See **17** for typical fixing accessories. Structural supports must provide minimum bearing of 50 mm for ends of each slab. Factory-applied finishes eliminate need

Length	Width	Thickness
1829	610	38
		64
1829	610	51
2032		
2134		
2438		
1829	610	76
2032		
2134		
2438		
3048		
3429	610	102
3810		

Classification CI/SfB	Description	Standards	Physical data	(U-value) thermal transmittance	Fixing and jointing	Diagrams
			Metric modular work sizes proposed by Wood Wool Slab Manufacturers Association (mm): Length Width Thickness 1800 600 68 2400 51 (50) 2700 64 (65) 76 (75) 102 (100) 3000 102 Maximum spans for unreinforced slabs used as flat roof decking (mm): Thickness Span 38 450 51 600 76 900 102 1200 (imposed load 0·75 kN/m²) Channel reinforced slabs: Thickness Span 51 2100 76 3600 102 4000 Channel reinforced structural units: Example—unit 600 mm wide and 150 mm deep will span up to 6000 mm. Safe span limits are given as guide and manufacturers should be consulted. Slab types: unreinforced, edge-reinforced, edge-reinforced structural units (combined beam/slab), pretextured (cement sand slurry), prefelted, smooth soffit. Unreinforced square units are made for decking to space frames **16**		for site applied bases, but where plain surface slabs are used, deck must be prepared to receive waterproofing. Joints are filled with cement sand slurry and minimum thickness 1·4 mm cement sand screed applied. Screed mix should be as dry as possible and should be 'cut' into 3 m panels before setting to predetermine positions of shrinkage cracks. Screeds can be laid to falls from maximum thickness say, 57 mm. Slabs must be propped adequately to prevent excessive deflection due to unset screed. On slopes of more than 20 deg screed is omitted and cement/sand slurry used instead. Insulating strips can be used at joint to eliminate cold bridge with channel reinforced slabs. Manufacturers produce slabs which have 25 mm thickness of wood wool over channel (see **18**). Where pre-felted slabs are used, this should not form part of waterproofing system except by specific approval of roofing contractor. Wood wool slabs are commonly used as permanent shuttering to in situ concrete roof decks.	**18 Methods of overcoming 'cold bridge' to combat condensation in humid conditions** **19 Fixing detail to flat roof, parapet gutter** **20 Fixing detail to flat roof, eaves** 18 roof covering, 75mm woodwool slabs, I-beam unit, 50mm gutter sole, u beam — 19 aluminium trim, timber fillet, dpc, roof finish, screed to falls, woodwool slabs, dpc, open web metal joist — 20

Information sheet
Roofs 2

Section 5 : **Roofs**

Insulation

This information sheet, which should be read in conjunction with Information sheet ROOFS 1 *and* ROOFS 3, *summarises properties of insulants and indicates methods of fixing*

1 Non-structural insulation

When a decking unit does not in itself provide sufficient thermal insulation, a non-structural insulation material is introduced. The most commonly used materials are: wood or cane fibreboard; natural or regranulated cork sheet; mineral fibreboard; bonded sheet materials based on glass fibre; and expanded or extruded polystyrene in sheet or slab.

The board is usually placed on top of the decking immediately below the waterproofing. A vapour barrier (see AJ Technical study ROOFS 3, 2.03 should normally be included and placed immediately below the insulation.

Roof screeds

Water trapped in roof screeds is a potential source of danger because it causes:

● blistering and eventual breakdown of waterproofing due to vapour pressure

● reduction in the efficiency of thermal insulation

● staining and deterioration of internal surfaces.

Main sources of screed moisture are:

● condensation from within building

● rainwater during construction period

● mixing water.

See Technical study 'Flat roof failures' (AJ 30.6.71 p1489 and 7.7.71 p37).

To minimise these effects, one of the following techniques should be used, preferably the last:

● The base layer (in a multi-layer roofing system) of waterproofing should be isolated by using a vented underlay, and there should be escape ducts at eaves and abutments

● There should be partial or frame bonding of base layer

● Proprietary breather vents should be installed, used and spaced in accordance with the manufacturers' instructions. In addition the screed should be laid as dry as possible and be provided with temporary drainage holes at low points in the slab. Alternatively a dry, lightweight roof insulation screed could be used where conditions permit. There are limitations on the use of dry insulation screeds, and they should always be laid by specialist roofing contractors who should be consulted at design stage.

● The screed may be separated from the structural concrete by a cavity formed by a layer of clay blotter blocks normally $62 \cdot 5$ mm thick. This base receives an aerated lightweight concrete screed leaving a cavity, thus producing a composite element similar in character and performance to a normal cavity wall, but horizontal not vertical. The cavity is ventilated either at the perimeter only or by special mushroom-type vents in the general area. The system has enormous advantages over directly-applied screeds since:

1 The drying time required during construction is greatly reduced.

2 The cavity will continue to operate as vent and permanent guard against interstitial condensation.

3 The cavity adds notably to the total thermal resistance.

4 No vapour barrier is necessary since any vapour penetrating the structure is dispersed by the cavity ventilation.

5 To cut the construction drying time still further, heat drying (blowing air at 85 deg C through the cavity), is very effective in drying both screed and structural concrete, enabling waterproofing to be carried out much sooner. The whole process is a job for specialists, at time of going to press one firm (see Table I) who use aerated concrete as the insulating screed. It could obviously work just as well for other light weight mixes. Vermiculite is one possibility since its water retention is notorious, mitigating its many advantages.

Table I Properties of insulation materials and screeds

Description CI/SfB	Standards	Physical data	K value* (thermal conductivity) k = W/m°C	Fixings and jointing
Foamed glass (27) Ro9 (J2)				
Honeycomb structure of pure borosilicate glass, milled and foamed to 18 times its original volume. Manufactured in slab or board form in two grades : T2 for roofs with normal foot traffic ; S3 for roofs with heavy traffic such as car decks. For flat or low-pitched slopes (0%—15%, or 0°—8°). Foamed glass is totally impermeable, so no vapour barriers are required.	Agrément Board certificate 71/83/C **Fire rating** Incombustible	Standard units : *Slabs* 300 mm × 450 mm 600 mm × 450 mm (thickness from 40 to 130 mm) *Boards* 1200 mm × 60 mm (thickness 40 to 60 mm) Density : 128 to 143 kg/m³	T2 = 0·046 S3 = 0·049	Joints between slabs are made with hot bitumen

Table I (*continued*)

Description CI/SfB	Standards	Physical data	K value* (thermal conductivity) k=W/m°C	Fixings and jointing
Corkboard (47) Rj1				
Boards made by compressing and baking granules of cork, natural resin acting as binder	**Fire rating** Combustible	Standard sizes: 914 mm × 304 mm 914 mm × 608 mm (thickness 12·7 to 101 mm) Density: 96 to 288 kg/m³	0·04	Used as lining and fixed by adhesives, cement slurry or nails
Expanded polystyrene (27) Rn7				
Beads of polymerised styrene are combined with blowing agent and moulded under pressure, to form rigid lightweight material. Available in following grades: EHD for roofs subject to constant foot traffic and metal deck roofs HD for roofs not subjected to foot traffic SD for roof lining in industrial and farm buildings RD for ceiling and soffit insulation in protected situations ISD for impact sound insulation beneath floating and suspended floors.	BS 3837: 1965 *Expanded polystyrene board for thermal insulation purposes* EPPMA Code of Practice **Fire rating** SE type meets class 1 spread of flame	Standard board sizes: width 600 and 1200 mm; length 1200, 1800 and 2400 mm; thickness 13, 19, 25·4 and 51 mm Density: EHD = 32 kg/m³ HD = 24 kg/m³ SD = 16 kg/m³ RD = 16 kg/m³ ISD = 16 kg/m³	0·03	Lightweight sheet roofs: it may be fixed between sheeting and purlins, or beneath purlins **1a, b.** For spans up to 600 mm, minimum thickness of 12·7 mm recommended, although thicker boards can be used if required. Maximum span recommended is 914 mm, which requires 38·1 mm thick board

1a Over-purlin insulation   **1b** Under-purlin insulation

Description CI/SfB	Standards	Physical data	K value*	Fixings and jointing
Fibre insulating board (47) Rj1				
Rigid board made from wood or vegetable fibre pulp. Can be supplied laminated or bitumen bonded	BS 1142: 1961 *Fibre building boards* **Fire rating** Combustible: class IV surface spread of flame undecorated (can be raised to class 1 with certain decorative treatments)	Standard units: width 610, 915, 1220 mm; length 1220 to 3660 mm; thickness 12 to 25 mm Density: not over 400 kg/m³	0·05	Nailed or screwed to battens or joists, or in metal sections. Also as permanent shuttering to concrete or lining to solid backgrounds by dab fixings
Glass fibre insulation				
Flexible mat of bonded fibrous glass	**Fire rating** class 1	Standard sizes: Width: 1200 mm 6 m × 75 mm 8 m × 65 mm 10 m × 50 mm 15 m × 40 mm 20 m × 20 mm Density: 12 kg/m³	0·03	Used on underside of roof between joists, supported by ceiling board. Air space between insulation and roof deck should be freely ventilated at eaves
Rigid slab of bonded fibrous glass	**Fire rating** class 1	Standard units: width 600 mm; length: 600, 900, 1200 mm; thickness: 12·5, 19 mm; Density: at least 80 kg/m³	0·03	Used with screeded flat roofs Maximum compression under load of 3830 N/m² is 10%
Screeds (47) Pp3 (J2)				
Lightweight expanded clay aggregate screed	BS 3797: 1964 *Lightweight aggregate for concrete*	Available in two grades: *Coarse* Particle size: 20 to 10 mm Density: 320 to 385 *Medium* Particle size: 10 to 3 mm Density: 320 to 410	0·133	Dry loose screed requires topping of 1:4 cement/sand mix, 32 mm thick, to receive felt or asphalt. Dry screeds should always be ventilated to release possible moisture
Bitumen-bonded aggregate screed	-	Density: 481 kg/m³	0·144	Usually laid with waterproofing layer, as both are proprietary products. Bituminous felt vapour barrier should be laid underneath, and solar reflective treatment on top (trade name: BIT-AG)
Lightweight air entrained concrete on cavity formed by clay blocks and vented	Agrément Certificate 70/67	Available in 2 densities 480/560 Kg/m³ and 960/1040 Kg/m³ according to traffic intensity	0·09/0·12 and 0·23/0·30 (screed only)	Usual average: total thickness 140 mm including cavity. Great advantage in speed of drying out. Vapour barrier not necessary because of vented cavity. (Trade name Cheecolite)

* K-values are given for insulation materials, so that they can be included in U-value calculation of whole roof

Information sheet
Roofs 3

Waterproofing

This information sheet, by HAROLD KING *explains methods of handling the all-important problem of water penetration. Properties of suitable materials for waterproofing are isted in table* II *to* IV

1 Introduction

Roof shape and roof pitch determine range and type of waterproofing techniques which can be used.

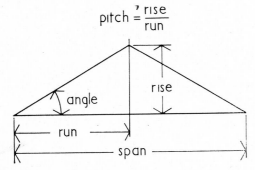

$$\text{pitch} = \frac{\text{rise}}{\text{run}}$$

1 *Roof pitch*

Roof pitch
This is the angle or slope to the horizontal which can be shown as $\frac{\text{rise}}{\text{run}}$. Run is normally half span in symmetrical roofs.
Pitch expressed as a fraction is useful for setting out as it indicates the relationship of rise to span, **1**.

Table I shows recommended roof pitch for some commonly used materials.

Roof fall
For flat roofs pitch is usually indicated by the fall to which

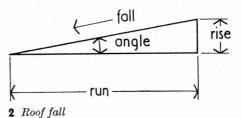

2 *Roof fall*

the material must be laid to shed water. The fall is expressed as the relationship between the rise and a given run of roof, usually 1000 or 3000 mm.

Table I *Recommended roof pitches for materials in common use*

Waterproofing	Pitch	Angle (deg)	Rise in 1000 mm run (mm)
Asphalt: lead and copper (with drips)	1/80	$\frac{3}{4}$	12
Built-up bitumen felt: zinc (with drips)	1/60	1	17
Corrugated asbestos cement sheeting (with sealed end laps)	1/5½	10	180
Copper and zinc (with welted end seams)	1/4	13¾	250
Interlocking concrete tiles	1/3	17½	333
Corrugated asbestos cement sheeting (with 150 mm end laps)	1/2½	22½	400
Slates: minimum 225 mm wide Single lap tiles	1/1½	33 35 }	660
Plain tiles (BS CP 142 allows 35 deg for concrete	5/6	40	830

Table II Properties of waterproofing materials

Description CI/SfB	Standards	Physical data	Notes on laying	Proprietary products
Asphalt	BS 1162: 1162, 1410, 1418: 1966 *Mastic asphalt for roofing (natural rock asphalt aggregate)*	Mastic asphalt consists of aggregate with bituminous binder. It is manufactured in blocks which are reheated on site before laying.	On all horizontal surfaces asphalt is laid on sheathing felt to BS 747: Part 2: 1970, type 4 A (i), bitumen based in 'wet' construction, pitch based on 'dry'.	
(47) Ys4	BS 988: 988, 1097, 1076, 1451: 1966 *Mastic asphalt for roofing (limestone aggregate)*		*Flat roofs:* two coats of equal thickness totalling 20 mm: fall 12 mm in 1000 mm.	
Asphaltic cement and aggregate. Composition of asphaltic cement is variable so specification should indicate requirements in accordance with tables set out in appropriate BS.	BS 1446: 1962 *Mastic asphalt for roads and footways (natural rock asphalt aggregate)* * BS 1447: 1962 *Mastic asphalt for roads and footways (limestone aggregate)* * **Necessary where roof takes vehicular traffic, eg car-parking* BS CP 144: 1966 *Roof coverings: Part 2 Mastic asphalt.*		*Sloping roofs:* various techniques according to deck construction and degree of slope. Slopes of more than 30 deg require three coats totalling 22 mm thickness. *Reservoir roofs:* three coats of equal thickness totalling 30 mm; with upstands to form tanking. Surface should be dressed with reflective chippings to control solar heat gain. Some specialist contractors offer 'brush on' two-coat solar-reflective treatment in small range of colours having high reflection coefficient (eg Briggs Amasco 'Reflexsol'). Where there is continuous foot traffic, asphalt is protected by concrete or asbestos tiles (300 mm × 300 mm × 25 mm) or* 25 mm protective screed usually incorporating bitumen joints in both directions. Breather vents are recommended to allow safe release of vapour pressure in deck when necessary. *Smaller for asbestos tiles.	
	External fire designation AA.			
Built-up felt roofing	BS 747: Part 2: 1970 *Specification for roofing felts:* class 1 fibre base; class 2 asbestos base; class 3 glass fibre base.	Bitumen felt supplied in rolls, designated by weight, and in following finishes to BS 747: Part 2: 1970.	For flat roofs three-layer specifications are recommended; for pitched roofs two-layer specification can be used. On roofs of 10° or less, *first layer* is laid starting at, and parallel with, lower edge of roof or eaves, and at right-angles to direction	Several proprietary systems of built-up roofing use thin metal foil bonded to cap layer as roof finish. These are not single-layer roofing materials, but are bonded to one or more underlays. Following finishes are produced: pure copper, high purity aluminium, stove-enamelled aluminium, and
(47) L	BS CP 144: Part 1: 1968 *Built-up bitumen felt* 11 m or 22 m in length.	Class: A, saturated; B, fine sand finish; C, self-finish; D, coarse sand surfaced; E, mineral surfaced; F, reinforced; G, venting base layer.	of fall. On roofs over 10° felt is laid up slope at right-angles to eaves. For all decks except timber, felt is secured to deck by hot bitumen compound using 'roll and pour' method. For timber decking first layer is secured by clout nails at 50 mm centres along laps, and by stagger nailing at 100 mm centres	textured (granule-faced) aluminium. Techniques used are similar to those for conventional built-up roofing. Several contractors also specialise in their own proprietary 'vented underlay' systems.
Bitumen felt roofing generally, including proprietary systems and aluminium- or copper-faced bitumen felt.	**External fire designation** *Flat roofs* Any bitumen felt roofing with following surface meets AA designation:	*Fibre-based felt* has great flexibility and is used for low cost specifications. *Asbestos-based felt* is relatively inert and provides improved fire resistance. *Glass fibre-based felt* has high dimensional stability, is proof against decay and is specified for high quality work.	over sheet. *Subsequent layers* are bonded by 'roll and pour' hot bitumen method. First layer felt may be fully or partially bonded (see **1**) according to deck construction. Minimum fall 17 mm in 1000 mm. On pitched roofs (10° or more) one single heavy layer with mineral finish is sometimes used. See notes on methods of controlling vapour pressure,	Problem of 'trade following trade' must be carefully considered where built-up felt roofing techniques are concerned, and wherever possible deck and waterproofing should be carried out as continuous operation by same specialist contractor, in accordance with established CPs. Where this is not possible, following should be pre-planned: 1 Work programmed so that substructure, including abutments, vertical surfaces and verge and eaves construction, plus projections through
	• bitumen-bedded stone chippings at least 12·5 mm deep • bitumen-bedded tiles of non-combustible material • sand-cement screed • macadam. *Pitched roofs* Fire designation depends on type of decking.	Numerous specification permutations are possible with three classes and seven surface finishes listed (see *Built-up felt roofing*—London, 1971, Felt Roofing Contractors Advisory Board).	Information sheet 1 para 4, and take appropriate action. Vented base layers are recommended for most decks (except timber boarding) in case moisture is trapped during construction. Top layer of felt should be dressed with about 10 mm of reflective chippings. To prevent chippings puncturing felt underfoot, raised duckboards should be provided for maintenance. Where foot traffic is expected, surface should be protected by using concrete or asbestos promenade tiles or screed with V joints bitumen filled. Normally main roof surface will have stone chipping finish, edges and upstands will be in mineral-surfaced felt and gutters in self-finished felt. Structural movement must be accommodated by movement joints in structure, detail being related to amount of movement expected.	decking is completed before roofing contractor begins work 2 Subject to drying out periods, substructure should be covered by roofing contractor as soon as possible to protect deck and building from weather 3 Roofing must be protected from damage by subsequent trades 4 Layer must follow layer as soon as possible otherwise delay may lead to suspect adhesion 5 Surface treatment should be applied as soon as possible

1 Patterns of partial bonding of first layer felt

perimeter ventilation

Liquid finishes

(47) Vr·4

Multi-coat specification of liquid or paste material to build up to specified thickness of waterproofing membrane. In building terms these materials are relatively new, having been developed over past 10 to 15 years, mainly in US. Architects are continually in search of all-weather, jointless, tough, lightweight, elastic, fully maintenance-free roof waterproofing which can be used on any type of deck to cover any shape of roof. To tempt specifier, various sprays or brush-applied polymeric materials are available.

See manufacturers' literature

These specialist materials are best applied by specialist manufacturers. Spray finish is usually more satisfactory than brush application.
The system illustrated below (Evode Ltd) is also used to repair all types of roof coverings. 2

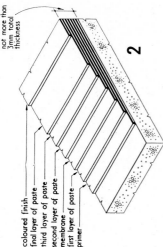

coloured finish
final layer of paste
third layer of paste
second layer of paste
membrane
first layer of paste
primer

not more than 3mm total thickness

2

Brush or spray applied waterproofings are based on following:

● Neoprene and Hypalon elastomers: Hypalon is trade name given by Du Pont Co (UK) Ltd to their coloured and ozone-resistant synthetic rubber which is available in liquid or sheet form. Neoprene is an elastomer that has been used in various forms (seals, adhesives, bearing pads and so on) for 40 years. They have been reported satisfactory in use (in US) on complex roof shapes over period of 10 years. Multi-layer specifications are usual (five to eight coats). Inflatable fabric structures have been waterproofed successfully with Neoprene and Hypalon synthetic rubbers.

● Plastisol pvcs: these are fluid dispersion of pvc with plasticisers. Loss of plasticiser has been reported from pvc compounds over several years in use, causing membrane to become brittle.

● Styrene-Butadient latex: more recently developed as brush/spray-applied finishes. These compounds are water based which makes them simple and safe to use. Apart from obvious risks of frost or heavy rain immediately after application, extended weathering tests have given satisfactory results.

● Epoxy polyurethane resins

● Asphaltic bituminous paste

Some proprietary systems

Adhesive Solutions Limited: multi-coat cold fluid applied coatings based on Neoprene and Hypalon. (Rufepake)

Evode Ltd: Multi-layer built-up asphaltic bituminous paste system, cold applied and incorporating reinforced fabric membrane.

Molecular Metals Group: liquid styrene-butadient, spray applied.

Plastics & Resins Ltd: semi-liquid-twin pack epoxy polyurethane resins brush applied (Polaroof).

Shell Composites Ltd: liquid bitumen glass fibre reinforced, spray applied, also used to repair old roofs (Flintcott Monoform).

Belzona Molecular Systems Laboratories: liquid molecular compound reinforced with flexible fibres, which cures in contact with carbon dioxide to form flexible and elastic polymeric film for repair of tile, slate, asphalt, bitumen or corrugated metal roofing.

Liquid Plastics Ltd: a fluid or soft paste water-based plastics copolymer (Decadex). May be used on virtually any sub-base, requires primer and two coats which may be applied on successive days. Sets at low temperatures; remains elastic and highly resistant to all dilute acids and alkalis. Range of colours available. Rated Class I and (s) AA (BS 476). A variant is Decadex Firecheck which may be used direct on combustible structure to improve the fire rating of the whole roof, making some structures acceptable under Building Regulations which would otherwise be rejected; also Palidux for use on surfaces permanently under water (eg reservoir type roofs).

Manufacturers should be consulted for information on physical properties, performance specification data.

Single layer flexible sheeting

(47) Tr·4

Proprietary systems fully supported on decking using synthetic materials in sheet form.

Manufacturers should be consulted for information on physical properties and performance specification data. Roof sheeting in this category is usually based on synthetic rubber with various methods of reinforcement or, alternatively, an asbestos bitumen thermoplastic membrane.

Agrément certificates where noted. Substructures must be constructed in accordance with good building practice, as laid down in BS CP 144: Part 1: 1968

External fire designation: Usually EXT. F.AA according to decking, but see manufacturers' literature.

These are specialist materials and must be laid by specialist contractors who have trained personnel in jointing and laying techniques. Preparation and construction of deck are important factors in performance; thin and flexible roof membrane requires very smooth deck surface. Method of application relates to adhesion and jointing. Systems having most easily managed sheet and simplest jointing techniques (which do not need to rely too heavily on site conditions at time of laying) will be most satisfactory. Key to success is skill and ease with which joint is made.

Some proprietary systems:

Evode Ltd: one-ply neoprene sheeting + liquid finish (Evoprene).

Hardman & Son & Co Ltd: rubber bituminised woven glass cloth, lapped joints sealed with primer (Pitchkote).

Hatcham Rubber Co Ltd: site-applied single-layer flexible rubber sheeting. or factory-applied laminated sheeting to prefabricated decking, site jointed by sealed overlap. Choice of polymers according to requirements of application from butyl, neoprene, hypalon, ethylene-propylene, nitrile/pvc (Princeway).

Marley Ltd: 1·02 mm thick vinyl sheet backed with asbestos paper. Butt jointed over gap filling adhesive sealed by special tape. Technique incorporates deck venting system for use on roof decks containing moisture (Marleydek—Agrément certificate 68/16).

Permanite Ltd: 1·5 m thick bitumen-polymer sheet for single-layer application to prefabricated decking units under factory-controlled conditions. lap jointed on site. (Or as top exposed layer on two- or three-layer built-up system.) (Permabit 60)—Agrément certificate 70/73.

Polysar International: polyisobutylene sheet and glass fibre reinforcement. Storey Bros: 0·76 mm thick prefabricated butylite membrane on base layer of 0·64 mm thick bituminised felt bonded to perimeter with special

Table II Properties of waterproofing materials

Description Cl/SfB	Standard	Physical data	Notes on laying	Proprietary products
Single layer flexible sheet contd.				adhesives and covered with 40 mm thick layer of 10 mm chippings (Uni-sheet roofing—NBA appraisal certificate for use on housing). The Nuralite Co: asbestos bitumen thermoplastic membrane, secured by special adhesive and joint sealing compound (Nuraphalte), and asbestos bitumen laminate sheets formed to shape by heating and joined by special compounds under heat and pressure. Flexible when warm; brittle when cold. Roll cap or twin-rib system of jointing also available bonded to chipboard or plywood decking (Nuralite—Agrément certificate 69/29). Jointing details similar to traditional lead sheet. The Ruberoid Co Ltd: Fibre-reinforced pitch polymer plastic: not used as exposed layer; must be surfaced with 12 mm stone chippings in situ or 305 mm square asbestos cement tiles. Can be used as underlayer to macadam for roof carparks (Hyload 75); and asbestos fibre impregnated with neoprene laminated to Tedlar white pvf film—as cap sheet to Ruberoid built-up systems (TNA 200). Uni-Tubes Ltd: asbestos backed 0·51 mm thick Hypalon sheets secured by neoprene latex adhesive, butt jointed and weatherproofed on site by heat-welded joint and sealing tape. Alternatively selvedge laminate available which forms 38 mm lapped joints heat welded on site (sealing tape not required): six colours (Uni-roof—Agrément certificate 68/19).
Profiled sheeting (47) Ny ● Corrugated asbestos cement sheeting. ● Steel-cored corrugated asbestos cement sheeting. ● Profiled and plastic coated steel sheet. ● Corrugated and troughed aluminium building sheet. ● Profiled clear or translucent plastic sheeting. These sheets are in form of single lap, single-layer corrugated coverings self-supporting over purlins. Sheets overlap to extent depending on roof pitch, sheet section and degree of exposure. Lower pitches can be used if lap is increased and/or sealed with mastic.	*Corrugated asbestos cement sheets to BS 690: 1963 Asbestos-cement slates, corrugated sheets and semi-compressed flat sheets: Galvanised corrugated steel sheet to BS 3083: 1959 Hot-dipped galvanised corrugated steel sheets for general purposes. Troughed aluminium building sheet to BS 3428: 1961 Troughed aluminium building sheet. Corrugated aluminium sheets for general purpose to BS 2855: 1957 Corrugated aluminium sheets for genera purposes. BS 4154: 1967 Corrugated plastic translucent sheets made from thermo-setting polyester resins (glass fibre reinforced). BS 4203: 1967 Extruded rigid pvc corrugated sheeting. CP 143 Sheet roof and wall coverings: Part 1: 1958 Aluminium, corrugated and troughed; Part 2: 1961 Galvanised corrugated sheet; Part 6: 1962 Corrugated asbestos-cement.* External fire designation *Asbestos sheeting: EXT S.AA** (BS 476 Part 3)	*Corrugated asbestos cement sheeting* The Asbestos Cement Manufacturers Association and BSI have agreed results of study of requirements of metric dimensioning and dimensional co-ordination. Profile dimensions will be expressed in rounded metric equivalents. Certain profiles have been redesigned and are marketed as 'metric modular' units. Standard metric lengths are as follows: 3050, 2900, 2750, 2600, 2450, 2425, 2275, 2125, 1975, 1825, 1675, 1525, 1375 and 1225 mm. Manufacturers should be consulted regarding range in which various profiles are produced. *Corrugated steel sheets* Available in wide range of profiles and with various protective coatings. Zinc coatings: electrolytically deposited zinc, provides base for plastic coatings; hot-dip galvanising as self-finish or as base for further coatings. Organic-coatings: colorcoat steel (British Steel Corporation, South Wales Group). Pvc plasticol—heat-cured pvc (vinyl) coating 0·2 to 0·4 mm thick. Wide colour range, embossed finish. Special range for agricultural applications. *Corrugated and troughed*	*Corrugated asbestos cement sheeting* Fixing by hook bolts, patent screw clips, pistol-fired studs, Oakley clips, or drive screws, according to material and shape of purlin. Fixing accessories should be in accordance with BS 1494: *Specification for fixing accessories for building purposes: Part 1 Fixings for sheet, roof and wall coverings.* Supporting structure must be of adequate design and conform to relevant BSs and CPs. Properly-constructed walkways should be provided to give access for maintenance. *Asbestos cement: fixed in accordance with BS CP 143: Sheet roof and wall coverings: Part 6 Corrugated asbestos cement.* All fixings should have 8 mm diam, have no hole nearer than 38 mm to any edge, and all holes pre-drilled to receive fixings. Type of mastic seal and method of laying should be specified by manufacturers: 4° pitch is recommended only for limited number of profiles; manufacturers should be consulted. *(see lap treatment table below)*	Colorsteel (British Steel Corporation Northern & Tubes Group): pvc-coated galvanised steel; textures surface; 15 colours. Galvaprime (British Steel Corporation Scottish & North-west Group): green/grey paint-on galvanising (mainly for agricultural application; low cost finish). Stelvetite (British Steel Corporation Scottish & North-west Group): pvc coating, on galvanising G or R range for external application. Cellactite (Cellactite Co Ltd): mild steel sheet coated with high temperature blended bitumen plus asbestos bitumen layer bonded under heat and pressure; 12 colours. Galbestos (H. H. Robertson (UK) Ltd): multi-layer construction; zinc-coated steel bonded with asbestos fibres; bitumenous layer; polyester facing; six colours. Sheets listed can be used for walling and roof cladding; usually supplied and fixed as proprietary system by specialist contractors. Sheeting requires insulation either over or under purlins, unless composite insulated cladding is used. Metal sections are available in lengths up to 12 m, which permit their use on moderate span low-pitch roofs without end laps. Non-proprietary systems should not be used except in conjunction with Strip Mills Division of British Steel Corporation, 151 Gower Street, London WC1. In addition to profiles illustrated, there are some proprietary roofing systems utilising galvanised or plastics-coated sheet and incorporating interlock jointing system.

Lap treatment table (from *Notes on laying*):

Roof pitch	Lap treatment
Normal and sheltered sites	
4°	Side and end laps sealed in accordance with manufacturer's instructions
10° to 15°	150 mm sealed end laps; and sealed side laps
15° to 22½°	150 mm sealed end laps (or 300 mm unsealed)
Over 22½°	150 mm unsealed end laps
Exposed sites	
10° to 15°	300 mm sealed end laps with extra fixings; and sealed side laps
15° to 17½°	150 mm sealed end laps and sealed side laps
17½° to 25°	150 mm sealed end laps

Profiled sheeting contd

according to surface application.

Polyester resin glass fibre (reinforced): EXT S.AA* or EXT S.AB according to manufacture. Also, F.R. grade which has self-extinguishing properties and does not support combustion.

Rigid pvc (upvc— 'unplasticised'): self-extinguishing when tested in accordance with method 508A of Part 5 BS 2782, and permitted to be used on roofs more than 6 m from any boundary (Building Regulations 1972 Reg E 17. Nearer to boundaries it can be used for roofs of garages, conservatories, open car ports, covered ways and swimming pools.

Rigid pvc reinforced with wire mesh: EXT S.AA* (BS 476 Part 3).

*Prefix S: for use on sloping roofs

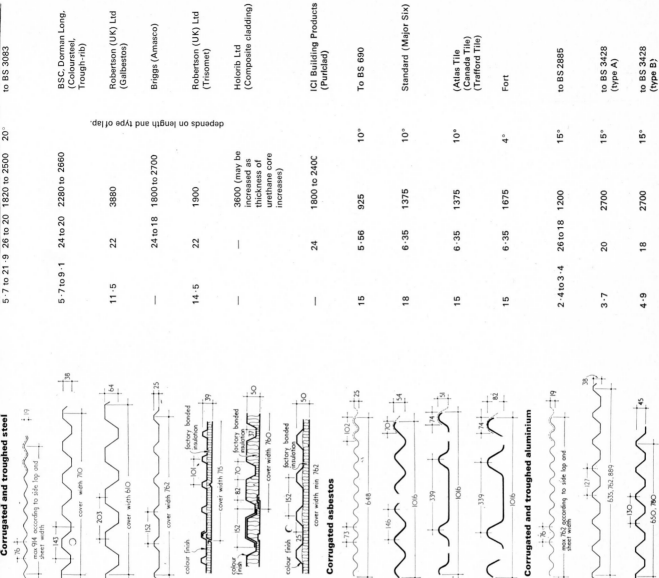

Corrugated and troughed steel

bS3, with plain, embossed or aked enamel colour finish. Full range of accessories is available, including corrugated sheeting with small slit louvres for permanent ventilation. Aluminium alloy fixings are preferable but galvanised fittings may be used in non-corrosive atmosphere. Copper base or brass fixings must not be used.

profiled clear or translucent plastics sheeting
Corrugated plastics roofing sheet is manufactured in profiles compatible with corrugated metal or asbestos roofing sheet. Manufacturers should be consulted regarding particular applications. Sheeting can be grouped as follows:
● Glass fibre-reinforced polyester resin sheets (GRP) (BS 4154) manufactured in various weights. Natural sheet is translucent but there are few tinted and semi-opaque colours. Trade names: Cascalite, Estalite, Filon, Stypolight, Unilux.
● ('Unplasticised') rigid pvc sheet (upvc) to BS 4203. In clear or opal corrugated or troughed in limited range of profiles. Clear sheets are available tinted. Trade names: Corolux, Corolite, Osmaglaze.
● Pvc sheet, wire-reinforced: clear pvc sheet reinforced with galvanised wire mesh. Trade names: Vistaglaze, Wirelon.
Corrugated steel cored asbestos sheet: as for asbestos roofing.

Corrugated asbestos

Corrugated and troughed metal and plastics sheeting: lightweight sheets require secure fastenings to resist wind suction.
BS CP 143 is relevant code for aluminium corrugated and troughed sheet, and galvanised corrugated steel 76 mm profile. For steel cladding sheets other than standard profile (to BS 3083), criteria set down in CP 143 should still be used for comparison with manufacturers' fixing data.

Corrugated and troughed aluminium

Weight	swg/gauge	Length (mm)	Min pitch	Reference / trade name
5·7 21·9	26 to 20	1820 to 2500	20°	to BS 3083
5·7 to 9·1	24 to 20	2280 to 2660	depends on length and type of lap.	BSC, Dorman Long. (Coloursteel, Trough-rib)
11·5	22	3880		Robertson (UK) Ltd (Galbestos)
—	24 to 18	1800 to 2700		Briggs (Amasco)
14·5	22	1900		Robertson (UK) Ltd (Trisomet)
—	—	3600 (may be increased as thickness of urethane core increases)		Holorib Ltd (Composite cladding)
—	24	1800 to 2400		ICI Building Products (Purlclad)
15	5·56	925	10°	To BS 690
18	6·35	1375	10°	Standard (Major Six)
15	6·35	1375	10°	(Atlas Tile) (Canada Tile) (Trafford Tile)
15	6·35	1675	4°	Fort
2·4 to 3·4	26 to 18	1200	15°	to BS 2885
3·7	20	2700	15°	to BS 3428 (type A)
4·9	18	2700	15°	to BS 3428 (type B)

Table II Properties of waterproofing materials cont.

1 Nut and Bolt Method
A hole is drilled through two or more overlapping sheets. The joint is secured by nut and bolt, and waterproofing is effected by fibre, bitumen or plastic washers.

2 Self-Tapping Screws
This method obviates the use of a securing nut on the underside. Screws are driven through the metal and thread themselves in the sheeting. Waterproofing by fibre, bitumen or plastic washers.
✳Quick and direct. Application from one side only. Can be obtained with coloured plastic heads.

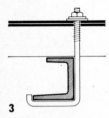

3 Hook Bolt
The most commonly used method. Waterproofing is effected by fibre, bitumen or plastic washers.

4 Oakley Clip
In effect, an adjustable hook bolt. The holes in the clip can either be threaded or not. If not, a securing nut is used. A great variety of clip shapes can be fashioned, so as to fit any purlin at any angle. Waterproofing by fibre, bitumen or plastic washers.

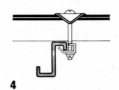

5 Drive Screws
Drive screws can be hammered into wood or metal purlins. They are made watertight with fibre or plastic washers.

6 Stud Welding
A recent method that eliminates bolts and drilling. Steel studs are welded upright to the purlins and the sheeting is impaled on the studs by means of a rubber hammer. A locking cap is then punched on to the projecting part of the stud. This secures the sheet and makes the hole watertight.

7 Pistol-fired Stud
Bullet-shaped stud is fired through the sheet and into the purlin. Waterproof.

Table III Properties of sheet metal roofing (fully supported)

	Aluminium			Copper					Lead			Zinc				
CI/SfB ▶◀	**(47) Mh 4**			**(47) Yh 5**					**(47) Mh 8**			**(47) Mh 7**				
Description	Sheet and strip from: SI (99·99% super-purity) flashings SIA (99·8% purity) and SIB (99·5% purity) special work SIC (99·0% purity) normally specified NS3 or NS4 (alloys) if more strength is required			Hot- or cold-rolled sheet or strip 'Dead soft' temper for traditional roofing ¼H for copper strip roofing					Milled sheet (cast sheet for repairs to old roofs)			Rolled zinc in sheet or strip from either commercial zinc or from alloy containing small amounts of copper and titanium Sheets are rolled to zinc gauge which rises in number with thickness				
Standards	BS 1470 : 1969 *Wrought aluminium and aluminium alloys: Plate, sheet and strip* BS CP 143 : Part 7 : 1965 *Sheet roof and wall coverings: Aluminium*			BS 2870 : *Rolled copper and copper alloys, sheet, strip and foil* BS CP 143 : Part 4 : 1960 *Sheet roof and wall coverings: Copper*					BS 1178 : 1969 *Milled lead sheet and strip for building purposes* BS CP 143 : Part 3 : 1960 *Sheet roof and wall coverings: Lead*			BS 849 : 1939 *Plain sheet zinc roofing* BS CP 143 : Part 5 : 1964 *Sheet roof and wall coverings: Zinc*				
External fire designation	AA			AA					AA BA (on plain edge board decking)			AA				
Physical data **Gauge (swg)**	22	20	18	30	26	24	23	22	**(Nearest equivalent swg)**			**(Nearest equivalent swg)**				
									14	12	11	23	22	21	20	9
Thickness (mm)	0·71	0·91	1·22	0·31	0·45	0·55	0·61	0·7	2·13	2·56	2·99	0·61	0·71	0·81	0·91	1·01
Approx weight **(kg/m²)**	1·92	2·47	3·39	2·82	4·08	5·00	5·45	6·35	24·4	29·3	34·2	4·32	5·04	5·76	6·48	7·20
									Code No			**ZG**				
									5	6	7	12	13	14	15	16
	Satisfactory	Normally specified	Heavy duty	Patterned and for long strip technique only	Economic: for long strip technique	Best quality work			General roofing work Light gauge for flashings, soakers. Heavy for gutter soles, etc.			General roofing work As for lead				

Table III Sheet metal roofing contd.

	Aluminium	Copper	Lead	Zinc
Sheet sizes (mm): **Length**	Max 3660	1220 1830 2440	4500 to 12 200	2450 or 2130
Width	Max 1220	610 910 1220	2100 to 2750	910
Coil strip	457 and 610 wide to max 11 m long	Cut to any width or length (usually 24 swg) to max coil weight approx 51 kg		
Weathering	Light grey in rural atmospheres; black in industrially-polluted atmospheres; avoid contact with copper or copper alloys	Over five to 20 years develops patina; bright green in rural atmospheres to black in polluted atmospheres; 'pre-patinated' sheets now available	Matt grey; light and dark shading according to exposure	To grey colour; resists corrosion in marine atmospheres, but unsuitable for use in very heavily polluted atmospheres
Laying and fixing	Sheet metals are laid in bays with long side of sheet parallel to fall of roof. Sheets are turned up against abutments and protected by cover flashings. Relative malleability determines form of joints which are made in direction of fall—longitudinal; and across fall—transverse. Method of jointing must make provision for thermal movement. Maximum size of fixed sheet limited by its rigidity, to avoid wind lift and drumming			
Underlay	BS 747 Type 4a ii on timber: 0·5 mm polythene sheet on concrete decking	BS 747 Type 4A ii or equal proprietary	BS 747 Type 4A ii or waterproof building paper class A to BS 1521	BS 747 Type 4A ii
Minimum fall	17 mm in 1 m	17 mm in 1 m	12 mm in 1 m	17 mm in 1 m
Joints: *(See p321 for diagrams)* *Pitched roofs* Longitudinal	Standing seam or wood roll	Standing seam or wood roll	Hollow roll for pitch greater than 15°	Standing seam or wood roll
Transverse	Double-lock welt or single-lock welt for pitch greater than 40°	Double-lock welt or single-lock welt for pitch greater than 45°	Single lap: 15° 584 mm 20° 457 mm 25° 355 mm 30° 304 mm	Single-lock welt: pitch greater than 15°
Flat roofs Longitudinal	Standing seam or wood roll, or extruded aluminium cover strip	Standing seam or wood roll	Wood roll	Standing seam or wood roll with standard machine-formed capping
Transverse	Double-lock welt: sealed where pitch is less than 20° Drips at max 3 m centres: where pitch is less than 5°	Drips at max 3 m centres: where pitch is less than 5°	Drips at max 2·75 m centres	Beaded or welted drips at max 2·25 m centres
Guide to bay sizes *Standing seam or wood roll techniques:* **Length (mm)**	3050 2440 ⎫ 20 swg	1830 ⎫ 24 swg for	3040 ⎫ on pitched	2300 or 1975 ⎫ on pitch
Width (mm)	457 610 ⎬ for pitched roofs	540 ⎬ pitched and flat roofs	675 ⎬ and flat roofs	835 ⎬ and flat roofs
Length (mm)	3660 2440 ⎫ 22 swg for flat			
Width (mm)	475 610 ⎬ roofs (unworked sheets)			
Further information from:	Aluminium Federation, Portland House, Stag Place, London SW1	Copper Development Association, 55 South Audley Street, London, W1Y 6BJ	Lead Development Association, 34 Berkeley Square, London, W1X 5DA	Zinc Development Association, 34 Berkeley Square, London, W1X 5DA

Table III Sheet metal roofing contd.

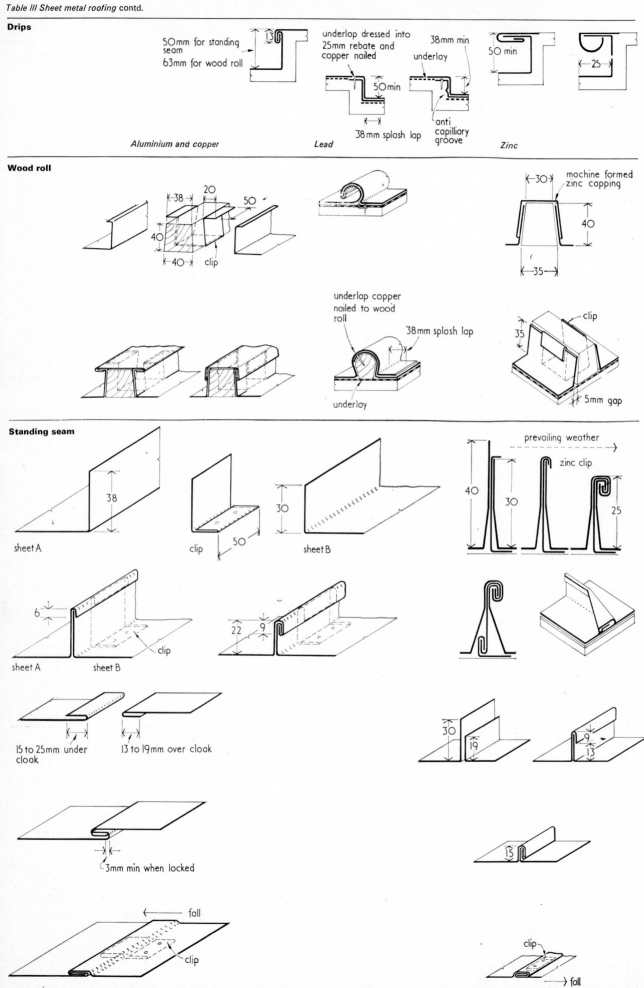

Drips

50mm for standing seam
63mm for wood roll

underlap dressed into 25mm rebate and copper nailed

38mm min
underlay

50 min

50 min

25

50 min

38mm splash lap

anti capilliary groove

Aluminium and copper   Lead   Zinc

Wood roll

38   20   50

40

40   clip

machine formed zinc capping

30

40

35

underlap copper nailed to wood roll

38mm splash lap

underlay

clip

35

5mm gap

Standing seam

38

sheet A

clip   50

30

sheet B

prevailing weather

zinc clip

40   30   25

6

sheet A   sheet B   clip

22   9

30
19

9
13

15 to 25mm under cloak   13 to 19mm over cloak

30

15

3mm min when locked

fall

clip

clip

fall

Flat troughed (47) Nf2 BS 473/550: 1967 **External fire designation AA*** cross section	Concrete	44	413 × 330, or 419 × 333, or 381 × 229	25 to 29	Variable: min 76	Min 30	22 if on (b) type supporting construction (last column)	As above	As above
Deep trough section (47) Nf2 BS 473/550: 1967 **External fire designation AA*** cross section	Concrete (acrylic finish available)	49	413 × 330	38	Variable: min 76	Min 30	Min 15 on (b) type supporting construction	Every tile nailed	As above
Slate tile (47) Nf2 BS 473/550: 1967 **External fire designation AA*** a. variation of a.	Concrete	51	413 × 330, 430 × 380	38	Variable: min 76	Min 30; max 45	Min 17½; max 45	Nibs hooked over battens: no nails, but lower ends clipped down at verges and eaves and all tiles clipped in exposed locations (see BS CP 3, Chap 5)	20 mm × 40 mm to 25 mm × 50 mm battens at 356 gauge maximum above felt draped over rafters
Wood shingles (47) Ni 2 Use restricted (see Building Regulations 1972, E17) roof section	Western red cedar (teak, oak, fir used infrequently in UK)	Very low	Varies 406 × 102 to 304 wide (tapered) in common use	Butt joints: min side lap	152 (double lap)	Min 30 (127 mm gauge, 406 mm shingles)	20 if 95 mm used	Centre nailed with 32 mm × 15 gauge copper nails, 13 mm to 25 mm from edges, two nails to each shingle	25 mm × 40 mm battens at 127 mm gauge: no felt; rafters at 600 to 750 mm centres
Thatch (47) Nj 3 As for wood shingles 	1 Norfolk reed 2 Combed wheat reed 3 Hand-threshed long wheat or rye straw	—	Not applicable	—	—	50 to 55	Reeds: min 45 Others: min 50	Bundles stitched to battens with tarred twine, or stapled down with hazel staples or iron hooks holding horizontal hazel rods or binders (see local usage)	20 mm × 50 mm battens forming 300 mm squares, or at 200 mm gauge over bitumen roofing felt (untearable)
Bitumen felt strips (47) Ps 5 **External fire designation BB or CC** according to specification 	Asbestos- or fibre-based bitumen felt (mineral surfaced)	—	Horizontal lapped strips Notched or profiled at lower edge to simulate slated roofing	According to type				Strips laid on close boarding and nailed with non-corroding nails to gauge recommended for roof pitch. Follow manufacturer's instructions	

* On timber rafters with or without underfelt on boarding, wood wool slabs, compressed straw slabs, wood chipboard or insulating fibreboard.

Information sheet
Roofs 4

Section 5 **Roofs**

Rooflights

This information sheet is concerned with the provision of natural lighting units as part of the roof structure. On this and the following page relevant standards and Regulations for rooflights are discussed. Table III starting on page 234 gives comparative information on the various types

1 General

These units are usually assembled using dry glazing techniques. For environmental considerations relevant to the provision of natural roof lighting see AJ Handbook of Building environment.

1.01 Sun control and light transmission

Tinted plastics and Calorex or other similar anti-sun glass are available; blinds and louvres can also be used. Manufacturers should be consulted for data. (A list of manufacturers, who currently produce rooflights to the proposed ranges of metric co-ordinated sizes, is given for guidance only in para 5.)

2 Standards

There are no British Standards for rooflights. The Glass Benders Association and the Patent Glazing Conference have submitted separate proposals set out in PD 6444 Part 1 *Basic spaces for structure: external envelope and internal sub-division.* These are shown in tables I and II.

Table I: Rooflight (one piece) co-ordinating spaces*

Width	450	600	750	900	1050	1200	1350	1500	1800	2100	2400
1800									◇		
1500							✱				
1350					◇						
1200						✱			◇		◇
1050					✱		◇				
900				✱	◇	□			□		
750			✱	◇	□						
600		✱	□								
450	□										
300	◇		◇								

Length

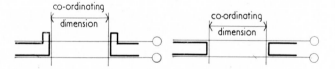

key
□ builder's kerb required for rooflight to this co-ordinating space.
◇ no builder's kerb required for rooflight to this co-ordinating space.
✱ = □ + ◇

Table II: Rooflight (single unit) co-ordinating spaces*

Width	600	900	1200	1800	2400	3000	3600
3600							▲✱
3000						△▲●✱	△▲●✱
2400					■△▲○●✱	■△▲○●✱	△▲●✱
1800			□■△○●	□■△▲○●✱	■△▲○●✱	■△▲○●✱	△▲●✱
1200	□■○	□■○	□■△▲○●✱	□■△▲○●✱	□△▲●✱	□△▲●✱	△▲●✱
900	□■○	□■○	□■○	■○	■○	■○	
600	□■○	□■○	□■○	■○	■○	■○	

Length

key
□ Flat or minimum pitch opening rooflight
■ Flat or minimum pitch fixed rooflight
△ Single pitch or back pitched lean to lantern light
▲ Multi-pitch lantern light (with vertical upstands) and multi-pitch skylight (without upstands)
○ Also in spans of 600, 900, 1200, 1800 and 2400 mm, in 600 mm length increments from 3000 mm upwards
● Also in spans of 1200, 1800, 2400, and 3000 mm, in 600 mm length increments from 3600 mm upwards
✱ Also in spans of 1200, 1800, 2400, 3000 and 3600 mm, in 600 mm length increments from 3600 mm upwards
* Gives manufacturers' proposed component ranges submitted to functional
group panels, adapted from PD 6444. December 1969 (metric units)

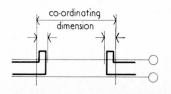

3 Codes of Practice

The following are relevant:
BS CP 145: *Glazing systems* (Part 1) *Patent glazing* (metric version expected in 1973).
BS CP 3: Chapter 1: *Lighting: Part 1 Daylighting: spacing, size and shape of rooflight* (metric version expected in mid 1972).

4 Regulations

4.01 England and Wales 1972

E17 permits parts of a roof designated AA, AB or AC to be placed any distance from the boundary of the roof. Check with Building Inspectorate for interpretation of part F in respect of the required thermal insulation of the rooflight kerb, to verify that standard kerbs are acceptable.
Roof materials of other designations may be used according to size, distance from boundary and each other. In addition glass and rigid pvc sheets may be used over small garages and car ports (not exceeding 40 m²) regardless of situation.

4.02 Building Standards (Scotland) Regulations 1970 and 1971

D18 specifies the requirements of roofs with regard to fire designation, relative to their distance from the boundary.

4.03 London Building (Constructional) Amended By-laws (no 2) 1964

Rooflights and glazing of translucent material classified not less than AD are permitted, provided that their area does not exceed 2·787 m² and that they are not less than 914 mm from the boundary of the roof.

4.04 Fire designation of materials

Glass fibre reinforced polyester resin and wired pvc
(fire rated AA, BS 476 part 3)
Their use is restricted under the Building Regulations 1972 and the Building Standards 1970 Scotland. Under the London Building (Constructional) Amending By-laws (no 2) 1964, covering the inner London boroughs (the former area of the LCC, excluding north Woolwich), they may be used when, in the district surveyor's opinion, the material is durable and suitable for the purpose.
Council consent is required where grp and wired pvc rooflights are to be used on a building to which section 20 or part V of the London Building Acts (Amendment) Act 1939 apply. The Building Regulations 1972 apply in the outer London boroughs of the GLC area.

Acrylic,
(fire rated DD, BS 476 part 3)
Clear or opal acrylic material has a burning rate the same as medium density timber and is acceptable if the following conditions are fulfilled:
Under the Building Regulations 1972 E17 (4) and the Building Standards 1970 Scotland, part IV 38 (2c), acrylic rooflights may be used 22 m and over from the site boundary, if the area of each skylight does not exceed 3 m² and the skylights are at least 1·5 m apart. Acrylic rooflights are not permitted in the inner London boroughs.

Pvc
(rated as extinguishing when tested in accordance with method 508A of BS 2782: 1970)
In the Building Regulations 1972 Regulation E17 permits the unrestricted use of pvc rooflights on the roof of a building, provided that the part of the roof where it is used is not less than 6 m from the site boundary. The boundary is accepted as being the centre line of any street, river or canal which abuts on to the site.
Pvc rooflights may be used at less than 6 m from the site boundary to form the roof of a garage, conservatory or outhouse with a floor area not greater than 40 m². It makes no difference whether the building is detached or not. They may also be used as the roof of a canopy over a balcony, veranda, open car-port, covered way or detached swimming pool without any restrictions.

4.05 Ventilation, insulation and condensation prevention

Manufacturers should be consulted for performance specification data. Condensation is usually controlled by means of trickle-ventilation gaps, channels or the use of an absorption seal. Condensation is less likely to occur when insulation is increased by double glazing.

5 Manufacturers

The following is a list of manufacturers currently producing rooflights in proposed range of metric co-ordinated sizes:
D. Anderson & Son Ltd, Cordar Division, Elders Walker & Co., William Cox Ltd, English Electric Co Ltd, Gardiner Aluminium Ltd, G. & B. Gardner & Newton Ltd, Greenwood Airvac Ventilation Ltd, Heywood Williams Ltd, E. D. Hinchliffe & Sons Ltd, A. G. Hudson (bent glass) Ltd, T. & W. Ide, Marley Ltd, New Guildford Decklights Ltd, Pillar Patent Glazing, Robin Architectural Products, R. Seddan & Sons Ltd and Vulcanite Ltd.

Table III *Comparative information*

Types and description		Materials or construction	Notes
Plastics		Glass fibre reinforced polyester resin (grp): translucent, clear, tinted or opaque	*Fixing:* by special security clamps or clips; bases purpose-made pigmented grp or metal; or builder's upstand kerbs
	1 Circular **2 Square**	Acrylic Pvc: clear, tinted, opaque or wire-reinforced (supplied single-skin, or double-skin for increased thermal insulation)	*Alternative bases* Fixed base Vent base: hit and miss or louvred (both pole or remote control)
	3 Rectangular **4 Hexagonal**		*Hinged opening:* automatic venting systems available linked with fire detector devices; continuous or connected base units available for large areas of roof-lighting
	5 North light **6 Barrel**		
Domelights in glass		6, 10 or 12 mm rough-cast or wired-cast glass	Fixed by security clamps in galvanised mild steel or aluminium liners, or to builders upstand kerbs in concrete or wood. Standard plan sizes: Spherical rough cast domes
	7 Spherical **8 Rectangular**		Diameter (mm) Thickness (mm) 450, 600, 750 6 900, 1050, 1200 10 1350, 1500, 1650, 1800 12
Dormer lights		Traditional timber-framed with timber or metal windows; single units or continuous	Requires careful integration of traditional trades, from carpenter, joiner, plumber, tiler, glazier
	9 Gabled **10 Flat-roofed**		
		Dormer in one piece. Glass fibre-reinforced plastics moulding	Not widely used
Glass/concrete		Translucent toughened-glass lenses, specialist design, required for rc framing units	Can be used on flat roofs or to form lantern lights or barrel lights
	11 Pedestrian loadbearing and non-loadbearing		
	12 Translucent toughened glass lenses; specialist design required for rc: framing units		
	13 Anti-condensation pedestrian loadbearing heat and sound insulation lenses		

Metal-framed

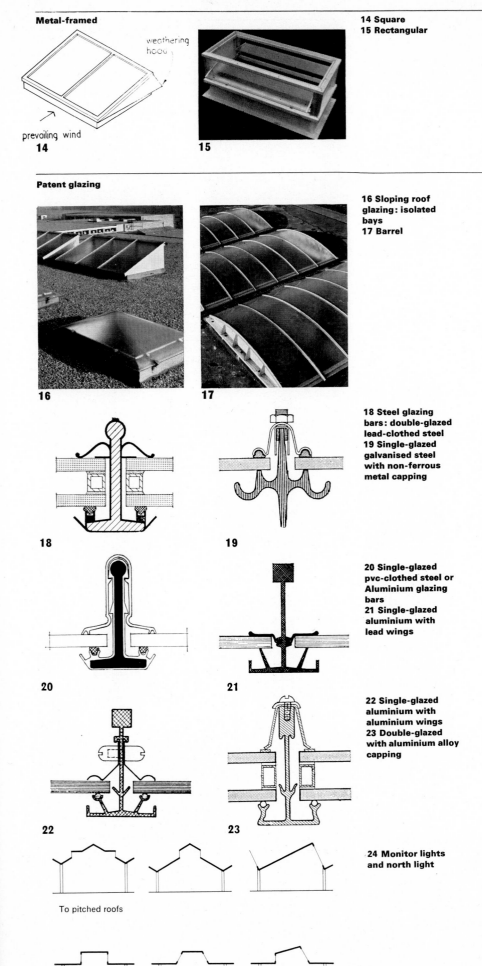

weathering hood

prevailing wind
14

15

14 Square
15 Rectangular

Decklights with glazing at low angle to load: factory-glazed and sealed. Fixed or opening: louvre or pivot vents or access hatch. Manufacturers of decking units, eg wood wool slab, asbestos-cement or profiled metal sheet, offer co-ordinated rooflight systems

Patent glazing

16

17

16 Sloping roof glazing: isolated bays
17 Barrel

18

19

18 Steel glazing bars: double-glazed lead-clothed steel
19 Single-glazed galvanised steel with non-ferrous metal capping

20

21

20 Single-glazed pvc-clothed steel or Aluminium glazing bars
21 Single-glazed aluminium with lead wings

22

23

22 Single-glazed aluminium with aluminium wings
23 Double-glazed with aluminium alloy capping

To pitched roofs

24 Monitor lights and north light

24 To flat roofs

May be glazed both sides as shown or one side only to give directional light

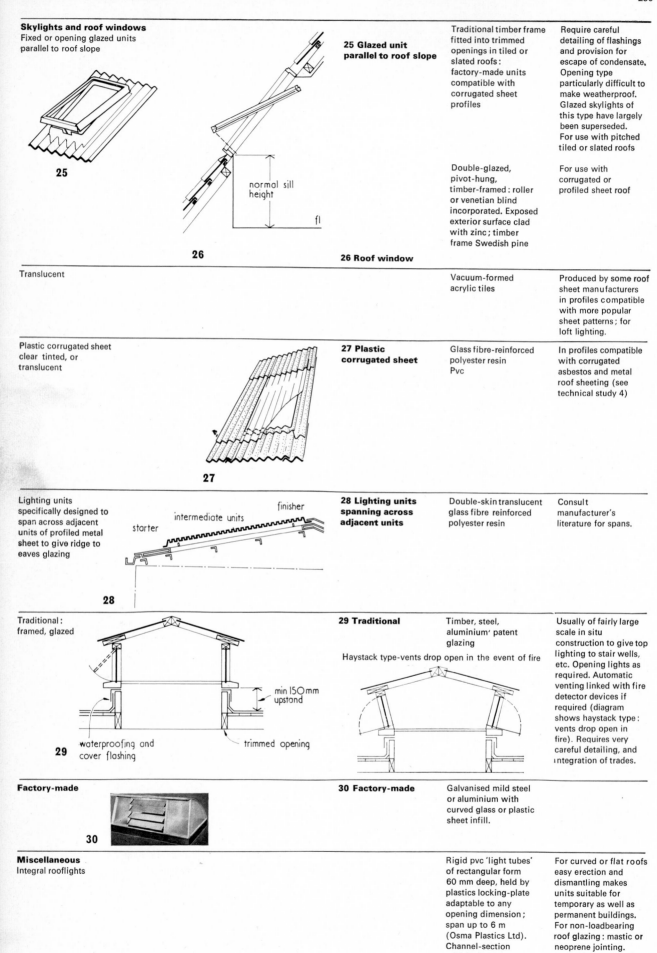

Skylights and roof windows Fixed or opening glazed units parallel to roof slope	**25 Glazed unit parallel to roof slope**	Traditional timber frame fitted into trimmed openings in tiled or slated roofs: factory-made units compatible with corrugated sheet profiles	Require careful detailing of flashings and provision for escape of condensate. Opening type particularly difficult to make weatherproof. Glazed skylights of this type have largely been superseded. For use with pitched tiled or slated roofs
	26 Roof window	Double-glazed, pivot-hung, timber-framed: roller or venetian blind incorporated. Exposed exterior surface clad with zinc; timber frame Swedish pine	For use with corrugated or profiled sheet roof
Translucent		Vacuum-formed acrylic tiles	Produced by some roof sheet manufacturers in profiles compatible with more popular sheet patterns; for loft lighting.
Plastic corrugated sheet clear tinted, or translucent	**27 Plastic corrugated sheet**	Glass fibre-reinforced polyester resin Pvc	In profiles compatible with corrugated asbestos and metal roof sheeting (see technical study 4)
Lighting units specifically designed to span across adjacent units of profiled metal sheet to give ridge to eaves glazing	**28 Lighting units spanning across adjacent units**	Double-skin translucent glass fibre reinforced polyester resin	Consult manufacturer's literature for spans.
Traditional: framed, glazed	**29 Traditional**	Timber, steel, aluminium' patent glazing Haystack type-vents drop open in the event of fire	Usually of fairly large scale in situ construction to give top lighting to stair wells, etc. Opening lights as required. Automatic venting linked with fire detector devices if required (diagram shows haystack type: vents drop open in fire). Requires very careful detailing, and integration of trades.
Factory-made	**30 Factory-made**	Galvanised mild steel or aluminium with curved glass or plastic sheet infill.	
Miscellaneous Integral rooflights		Rigid pvc 'light tubes' of rectangular form 60 mm deep, held by plastics locking-plate adaptable to any opening dimension; span up to 6 m (Osma Plastics Ltd). Channel-section wired-cast, or cast-glass units 262 mm × 41 mm (Profile Glass Ltd)	For curved or flat roofs easy erection and dismantling makes units suitable for temporary as well as permanent buildings. For non-loadbearing roof glazing: mastic or neoprene jointing.

Labels within diagrams:

25

normal sill height
fl
26

27

starter intermediate units finisher
28

min 150 mm upstand
waterproofing and cover flashing trimmed opening
29

30

Information sheet
Roofs 5

Rainwater goods: materials

This information sheet describes materials for gutters, for pitched roof drainage, downpipes and accessories, and lists relevant British Standards and Codes of Practice and additional sources of information

1 Asbestos-cement

This is still the cheapest material for rainwater goods even when the cost of initial painting is included, but the cost of maintenance of paintwork should also be taken into account. However, it is not essential to paint asbestos-cement and many architects like its natural colour when new. Unfortunately, its appearance deteriorates when exposed.

Its brittle nature makes it unsafe to stand on and liable to break if it receives a sharp knock or other sudden stress. Unfortunately this characteristic tends to increase with age and a member which might seem quite tough when fixed can become increasingly brittle over the years. Detailing by manufacturers in this country has never been of a high standard and the effect produced by asbestos-cement rainwater goods on houses is not as attractive as that of many of the other materials.

However, there is one new range which is unsocketed, relying on a wide, pressed-metal bolted bracket joint and jointing compound. This is neater than the clumsy socket joint. Valley and parapet gutters are available in asbestos-cement; warning notices should be provided to comply with the Factories Act in case they are used for access. It is a long-life material if protected from damage by people. A range of glazed colours applied in the factory is now available, at an extra cost of 60 per cent for downpipes and 90 per cent for gutters[1-3].

2 Rigid bitumen-bonded asbestos sheet

This material is suitable for supported box, valley and parapet gutters. It is easy to form to required shapes and join with a blow lamp, and has a long life. Its coefficient of expansion is $18 \cdot 8 \times 10^6$ per deg C ($2 \cdot 5$ mm per 3 m for 30 deg C temperature difference)[4, 5].

3 Concrete

Precast

Two or three concrete manufacturers produce precast concrete eaves gutter units of slightly varying sections. Usually the problem is to conceal the joints. Longer sections, if reinforced in situ, can serve as lintels over wide openings (a combined eaves gutter and lintel spanning from cross-wall to cross-wall in one length is available).

Gutters are made waterproof by lining them internally with bitumen felt with sealed lapped joints. There are no falls to outlets. Advantages claimed are the elimination of two courses of brickwork, savings in timber and site labour, elimination of separate lintels at eaves level. Outlets are supplied to suit any of the standard downpipes on the market in other materials[6].

4 Metal

Aluminium [7-9]

Cast aluminium rainwater goods, while of greater strength than sheet or strip gutters, use a different alloy that is liable to pit in marine or corrosive atmospheres. Painting is unnecessary except in these circumstances, but a whitish film will form over the aluminium in time which may not be visually acceptable. This material can be anodised to external quality standard, or even colour-anodised or Aluchromed (a proprietary protective finish giving a greenish appearance). This may have to match an aluminium roof finish and could present matching up problems.

Cast iron [10, 11]

Half-round and ogee-pattern gutters are standard, but box-section gutters and downpipes can also be obtained. Cast iron will corrode if not painted inside and out but has a long life, if well maintained, and is not subject to electrolytic action from roofs of metals such as copper. Inside, pipes with bituminous coating inside and out are used, and joints should be sealed. Heavy or medium grades to BS 416 are most suitable for this purpose. Bright permanent-glazed coloured rainwater goods can be obtained from Vitreflex Ltd, Dafen, Llanelly, South Wales, who produce a vitreous-enamelled cast iron and pressed steel range. Care is needed on site to ensure the sections are not chipped before fixing.

Copper [12, 13]

It is essential to use either copper or a non-metallic material for rainwater disposal from a copper-covered roof to avoid electrolytic action. Half-round, ogee or rectangular sections are standard and must be strengthened with copper $12 \cdot 7$ mm diameter tubes or rods of equivalent strength, soldered in place at a maximum spacing of 380 mm centres. Downpipes are usually solid drawn round, but can be made up to a required section by folding or bending and welding the joints. BS 1431 also covers round pipes of this kind of 2, $2\frac{1}{2}$, 3 and 4in (50, 64, 76 and 100 mm) internal diameter, and rectangular pipes $2\frac{1}{2}$in (64 mm) wide $\times$ 2in (50 mm) deep and $3\frac{1}{2}$in (89 mm) wide $\times$ 3in (76 mm) deep. Wrought sections are all specials; size is therefore to detail.

Galvanised pressed steel [14-18]

This material is short-lived unless well maintained by painting. It is particularly suitable for valley and parapet gutters for industrial type roofs. Light gauge gutters in 18 gauge ($1 \cdot 22$ mm swg) mild steel are available in half-round and ogee patterns as fascia gutters. Heavy gauge is available for box, valley and parapet sections.

Downpipes are standard at 20Bg (10 gauge), but a lighter range can be obtained in 24Bg (14 gauge) if required. All should be heavily galvanised at works (see BS CP 2008). A range of rainwater goods is available in vitreous-enamelled finish (permanently coloured) and another in pvc-coated steel. Bitumen-coated galvanised steel rainwater pipes with sealed joints can be used internally (see BS 3868). It is one of the cheapest materials.

Lead [19-21]

Lead is expensive and used mainly for forming complex shapes, and valley and parapet gutters. For prestige buildings and restoration of historic buildings, it may well be used for external rainwater heads and downpipes, probably with decorative details which can be produced by casting the lead into moulds, and leadburning the sections together when required. It has an exceptionally long life of over 100 years, if of good quality heavyweight material and provided it is not subjected to corrosive drips.

Stainless steel [22]

Stainless steel is becoming cheaper and is already being used for rainwater goods in the US. Details would be similar to pressed steel (see BS 1091[14]). The recommended grade is 18/10/3 molybdenum stainless steel.

Zinc [23, 24]

Zinc gutters are made to the same sections as copper. Downpipes are made only in welted, locked seam form and are available in the following standard sizes: round section 2, 2½, 3 and 4in (50, 64, 76 and 100 mm) internal diameter; rectangular section 2½in (69 mm) wide × 2in (50 mm) deep and 3½in (89 mm) wide × 3in (76 mm) deep internal sizes. Other sizes can be made to different sections if required. Zinc is rarely painted, but has a medium-length life of about 40 years under average conditions. It is cheaper to replace it at the end of its life than to protect it by painting.

5 Plastics

Glass fibre reinforced polyester (grp)
This material can be moulded to any desired shape before it sets and is suitable for special sections or decorative work. It can be given a variety of finishes and colours, and can be made as strong as required.

Rigid polyvinylchloride (pvc)
Extruded sections with injection-moulded fittings are produced by several manufacturers. A wide range of fittings and accessories is available. Colours are limited to black, white, cream, grey and blue-grey as many colours fade in sunlight. Thermal expansion movement is considerable: 9 mm in a 3·7 m length over a temperature variation of 50 deg C. (Coefficient of thermal expansion is 5×10^6 per deg C). Manufacturers' joints are designed to permit this movement to take place, but site fixing needs attention. Life of pvc is unknown but is more than 10 years. Ease of fixing and replacement, no maintenance, low cost and neat design have put this material in the forefront.

Standard sizes
Gutters: half-round 3, 4, 4½, 5, 6in (76, 101, 114, 127, 152 mm) internal diameter. Thickness varies. Box-section chamfered 4in (101 mm) wide × 2in (50 mm) deep.
Downpipes: round 2, 2½, 3, 4, 6in (50, 63·5, 76, 101, 152 mm)—last two being soil sections; o-ring joints. Rectangular section 2½in (64 mm) wide × 2in (50 mm) deep internally.

6 Advisory organisations

Aluminium Federation, Broadway House, Five Ways, Birmingham, B15 1TN (021-455 0311)
Copper Development Association, Orchard House, Mutton Lane, Potters Bar, Middx (01-77 50815)
British Steel Corporation (head office), 33 Grosvenor Place, London SW1 (01-235 1212)
Lead Development Association, 34 Berkeley Square, London W1 (01-499 8422)
Zinc Development Association, 34 Berkeley Square, London W1 (01-499 6636)
Stainless Steel Development Association, 54 Vincent Square, London SW1 (01-834 6737).

7 References

1 BS 569: 1967 Asbestos-cement rainwater pipes, gutters and fittings [(38)]
2 BS 582: 1965 Asbestos-cement soil, waste and ventilating pipes and fittings [Ih1]
3 BS CP 143: Part 6: 1962 Sheet roof and wall coverings: Corrugated asbestos-cement [(47) N]
4 NURALITE CO LTD Nuralite technical handbook. Higham, near Rochester, Kent, 1971, The Company [Ls]
5 BS CP 143: Part 8: 1970, Semi-rigid asbestos bitumen sheets [(47) Rf6]
6 BS 2908: 1957 Precast concrete eaves gutters [(38)]
7 BS 2997: 1958 Aluminium rainwater goods [(38)] *Amendment PD 6403*, 1968
8 BS CP 143: Part 7: 1965 Sheet roof and wall coverings: Aluminium [(47) N]
9 ALUMINIUM FEDERATION Aluminium rainwater goods. London 1958, The Federation [(38)]
10 BS 416: 1967 Cast iron spigot and socket soil, waste and ventilating pipes (sand-cast and spun), fittings and accessories [Id1]
11 BS 460: 1964 Cast iron rainwater goods [(38)]
12 BS 1431: 1960 Wrought copper and wrought zinc rainwater goods [(38)]
13 BS CP 143: Part 4: 1960 Sheet roof and wall coverings: Copper [(47) N]
14 BS 1091: 1963 Pressed steel gutters, rainwater pipes, fittings and accessories [(38)]
15 BS 3868: 1965 Prefabricated drainage stack units: Galvanised steel [(52)]
16 BS CP 143: Part 2: 1961 Sheet roof and wall coverings: Galvanised corrugated steel [(47) N]
17 BS CP 2008: 1966 Protection of iron and steel structures from corrosion [Du1]
18 BRITISH STEEL CORPORATION Leaflet SC6 Steel sheet rainwater goods. London, 1965, The Corporation [(38)]
19 BS 1178: 1969 Milled lead sheet and strip for building purposes [Md8]
20 BS CP 143: Part 3: 1960 Sheet roof and wall coverings: Lead [(47) N]
21 LEAD DEVELOPMENT ASSOCIATION Lead information sheets. *Architects' Journal*, at intervals from 1947, October 16 to 1961, June 15 [Rh8]
22 STAINLESS STEEL DEVELOPMENT ASSOCIATION Building with stainless steel. London, 1967, The Association [Md3]
23 BS 1431: 1960 Wrought copper and wrought zinc rainwater goods [(38)]
24 BS CP 143: Part 5: 1964 Sheet roof and wall coverings: Zinc [(47) N]
25 BS 4576: Part 1: 1970 Unplasticised pvc rainwater goods

Information sheet
Roofs 6

Roof drainage

This information sheet provides guidance on general principles involved in designing roof drainage and rainwater disposal; it supersedes Information sheet 1555 (AJ 22.11.67). The method of sizing gutters and downpipes see also AJ Handbook of Building services and circulation (AJ 17 & 24.12.69)

1 General considerations

It is desirable for rainwater to reach the ground by as direct a route as possible, and to avoid potential sources of blockage or leaks, such as valley and parapet gutters and internal downpipes, as far as possible.

Snow however, is probably best retained on the roof where it serves as additional insulation. Snow guards should be placed around the perimeter of a roof steep enough to cause snow-slides. Snow can easily block valley and parapet gutters and cause melting snow to overflow at higher levels, while freezing can split open box gutters with disastrous results to internal finishes.

If the preference is for concealed eaves gutters, they can be boxed in behind fascias, usually at extra cost. Attempts to omit gutters and downpipes, except with thatched roofs in rural areas, tend to be frowned on by local authorities. Omission of gutters and downpipes or the use of gargoyles, apart from causing nuisances may result in the subsoil becoming so soggy as to endanger foundations in non-porous soils.

2 Meteorological data

For sizing gutters and downpipes, certain meteorological data is required and can usually be obtained from the loca meteorological office. This comprises:
● Annual rainfall
● Maximum rainfall recorded in storms
● Local problems such as blown rain in exposed areas
● Possibility of snowfall and maximum depth recorded (relate to exposure to wind).

For general purposes it is usual to allow for a rainfall of 75 mm/h in the design of rainwater systems. However, 25 mm/5 min occurs occasionally in short storms of high intensity in this country. It is important to allow for this in designing gutters where overflow cannot be tolerated, ie valley and parapet gutters. In eaves gutters 6 mm/5 min is the maximum which need be provided for as overflowing there is less critical (see BRS Digest 127[1]).

3 Sizing gutters and downpipes

The methods given in AJ Handbook of Building services and circulation and BRS Digest 107[2] are essential when calculating the size of gutters and downpipes for larger buildings, and especially when considering the size necessary for valley gutters and parapet gutters.

Detail design
Positioning of a gutter in relation to the roof finish must be so arranged that run-off is collected under all conditions and snow can slide off without blocking it. Falls along gutters should be kept to a minimum otherwise the visual

effect is unsatisfactory where the gutter is exposed. With sheet metal box, valley and parapet gutters, the tendency is to forget that drips are necessary every 2·5 m or so to cater for standard sheet lengths and thermal movement of the material. Plastic rainwater goods have an even larger coefficient of expansion, but this is usually taken care of by sliding joints designed by the manufacturer.

Downpipes should be not more than about 9 m apart and not less than 65 mm diameter, preferably with copper wire cages at the gutter outlet to lessen the chances of blockage. Discharge from downpipes should go into:
● Rainwater shoe if the branch drain is discharging to a storm water drain or soakaway, and the downpipe is external; or
● Back-entry trapped gulley if the branch drain connects directly with foul water drain and downpipe is external; or
● Back-entry sealed trapped gulley if the downpipe is inside the building away from the external walls.

N.B. Where a building has a series of internal rwps it may be better to use only a slow bend at the base, picking these up into a single internal drain which can be trapped at its connection to the chamber outside.

Water storage
In areas where water is short, and preferably wherever there is space to provide a tank, at least one of the downpipes should conduct the rainwater into storage, preferably in a cool place underground. An overflow pipe connected to a drain is essential.

Internal downpipes
Where downpipes are inside the building, great care must be taken in designing the connection between roof and downpipe. The pipes should be of greater thickness and weight than external, joints sealed and tested. (Soil grade pipes are normally used.)

4 General

Other points in the design of gutters and downpipes are dealt with in BRS Digest 107[2] and BS CP 303: 1952[4].

5 References

BUILDING RESEARCH STATION
1 Digest 127 An index of exposure to driving rain. 1971, HMSO [(13)]
2 Digest 107 Roof drainage. 1969, HMSO [(52·5)]
3 Digest 80 Soil and waste pipe systems for housing. 1967, HMSO [(Ab8)]

4 BS CP 303: 1952 Surface water and subsoil drainage [(52·5)]
5 AJ Handbook of Building services and circulation. *Architects' Journal*, 1969, December 10 to December 17 & 24 [(5-)]

Information sheet
Roofs 7

Comparative prices of decking and waterproofing

This study by BRIAN PUGH *provides a guide to the comparative prices of types of roof decking and waterproofing listed in technical study* ROOFS 4 *The prices given here are those current in January* 1972. *For reasons explained at the beginning of the book, no attempt has been made to update them, the principal reason being that prices are a constantly fluctuating detail which are only relevant if tied to a date. Such information is really only suitable for publication in journals but is included here because the original intention was to show the comparative cost of different roof systems and the ratios between these remain generally valid although some prices may have increased proportionably more than others.*

1 General

In many instances particular components or materials cannot be compared in isolation, and account must be taken of their effect on the supporting structure, method of achieving falls, rainwater disposal and additional insulation which may be required[1].

The range of rates given includes supply and fixing (exclusive of any preliminaries and so on) and must be applied to the total area of materials involved; eg the area on slope must be taken into account and not just the area on plan.

Exclusions

The rates do not include for cost of additional details at eaves, verges, ridges or other perimeter conditions. In the case of reasonably large roofs these perimeter details can involve an addition of as much as 10 to 20 per cent to the cost of the basic areas, and considerably more than this for small roofs, balconies and similar situations

Cost in use factors

Whenever possible, consideration should be given to cost in use factors when choosing roofing or any building element. For instance, one factor is the effect of varying degrees of insulation on running costs of heating installations. For a building with a life of 30 years and an interest rate of 9 per cent, every £1 borrowed represents an annual repayment (including interest charges) of about 10p, so on this basis it might be worth increasing insulation if for every extra £1 of capital cost that this involved, a saving over 10p per annum could be made on running costs.

This kind of comparison is influenced considerably by the predicted life of the building and changes in interest rates, and taxation allowances must be taken into account, particularly in the type of building where allowances on running costs are much greater than allowances or grants on initial or capital costs[2].

2 Comparative prices

2.01 Roof decking

	Cost £/m²
a Asbestos cement hollow decking	
BS 3717: 145 mm thick; 1800 to 3000 mm long.	4·10–4·70
b Compressed straw slabs	
50 mm standard grade fixed to joists at	
600 mm centres (bitumen-lined soffits).	1·50–1·65
50 mm class I grade fixed to joists at	
600 mm centres (asbestos-lined soffits).	1·75–2·00
c Lightweight concrete panels	
76 mm thick, 1800 mm span.	4·00–4·20
102 mm thick, 2700 mm span.	4·50–4·70
d Profiled metal decking	
Aluminium decking.	3·75–4·50
Galvanised steel decking, including insulation board and felt roofing.	3·50–4·00
e Timber	
25 mm tongued and grooved softwood boarding.	1·40–1·60
18 mm external quality plywood.	2·10–2·25
25 mm chipboard.	1·95–2·10
f Wood wool slabs	
Unreinforced wood wool 2in (51 mm) thick.	1·25–1·45
Edge-reinforced wood wool 2in (51 mm) thick.	1·75–2·00
Pre-screeded wood wool 2in (51 mm) thick.	1·35–1·55
Pre-felted wood wool 2in (51 mm) thick.	1·45–1·60
Edge-reinforced wood wool structural units (combined beam/slab).	5·25–5·50

2.02 Waterproof coverings

	Cost £/m²
g Mastic asphalt	
BS 988 on felt with stone chippings finish.	1·85–2·00
BS 1162 on felt with stone chippings finish.	2·45–2·70
h Built-up felt	
Built-up three layers felt roofing (BS 747 according to specification)	0·90–1·50
Aluminium- or copper-faced bituminous felt, including underlay.	3·00–3·50
j Liquid finishes	
Epoxy polyurethane resin.	2·60–3·00
Butadiene including underlay and shingle finish.	2·30–2·50
k Profiled metal, plastic or asbestos sheeting	
Corrugated asbestos: plain.	1·40–1·50
Corrugated asbestos: lined and insulated.	2·90–2·90
Composite profiled: steel asbestos.	3·50–4·25

	Cost £/m²
Galvanised corrugated steel sheets: 26G.	1·30–1·40
24G.	1·50–1·70
Corrugated aluminium: 0·7 mm.	1·40–1·60
0·9 mm.	1·75–1·95
Troughed aluminium: 1·00 mm.	2·15–2·35
1·20 mm.	2·50–2·70
Profiled clear or translucent plastic sheeting:	
standard,	3·60–3·80
fire-resisting.	4·20–4·40

l Sheet metal roofing

Aluminium sheet (BS 1470):	0·91 mm.	4·60–4·90
Copper (BS 2870):	24G.	7·25–7·75
	23G.	8·00–8·50
Zinc (BS 849):	14G.	4·30–4·45
Lead: BS Code 4.		6·50–7·25
BS Code 5.		7·50–8·75

m Single-layer flexible sheet

Asbestos bitumen.	2·10–2·20
Glass fibre reinforced bitumen.	1·70–1·80
Bitumen polymer, including glass reinforced bitumen underlay.	1·70–1·80
Neoprene and Hypalon.	2·50–3·00

n Slates, tiles, etc

Natural roofing slates 20in × 10in (508 mm × 254 mm), including felt and battens.	3·80–4·00
Plain machine-made clay tiles 10½in × 6½in, (267 mm × 165 mm), including felt and battens.	3·15–3·40
Interlocking concrete tiles (16¼in × 13in), (412 mm × 330 mm), including felt and battens.	1·45–1·70
Asbestos-cement slates (20in × 10in), (508 mm × 254 mm), including felt and battens.	2·60–2·80
Cedar wood shingles (subject to large variations on quotation).	6·50–8·50
Reed thatching (subject to large variations on quotation).	4·00–5·00

3 References

1 See Technical Study ENCLOSURE 1, p35
2 STONE, P. A. Building design evaluation: costs in use. London, 1968, E. & F. Spon [(A4)] *£2.10*

Section 6
Internal division: General

Section 6 Internal division: General

Relationship to rest of handbook

The table at the head of the column shows the contents of the handbook as a whole, with the present section highlighted. The diagram at the foot of the page shows how section 6 acts as a general introduction to the three subsequent sections.

References and keywords

The keyword by which this section is identified is INTERNAL DIVISION; those for other sections are shown in the table above. The notes at the beginning of the handbook (p6) explain how keywords are used to identify the documents contained in this handbook.

Introduction

This is the third of the three general, introductory sections of the handbook. Section 1 provided an introduction to the design of the building fabric as a whole, section 2 provided an introduction to the design of the *external envelope*, and this section introduces the subject of a building's *internal subdivision*.

It will be followed by a series of specific sections giving design guidance on each of the element-groups involved: suspended floors, internal walls and partitions, and ceilings (see diagram).

Section 6 consists at present of a technical study and an information sheet giving useful data on the acoustic performance of internal subdividing elements, ie suspended floors, internal walls and partitions, and ceilings.

Like information sheet EXTERNAL ENVELOPE 1, which gave similar data for a building's external skin, this sheet will describe practical methods of evaluating building performance which have been lacking until now. A design guide, is also included at the end of the book covering both the external enclosure and internal subdivision.

Authors and consultants

The authors of each section will be credited at the start of that section of the handbook in which their material appears. In addition, RAYMOND K. HARINGTON is acting as consultant editor for this and subsequent sections of the handbook. He is an architect in private practice, and senior lecturer in building technology at the Polytechnic of Central London.

Raymond K. Harington

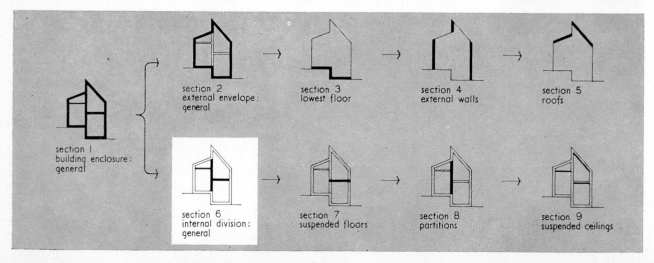

section 1 building enclosure: general

section 2 external envelope: general

section 3 lowest floor

section 4 external walls

section 5 roofs

section 6 internal division: general

section 7 suspended floors

section 8 partitions

section 9 suspended ceilings

Technical study
Internal division 1

Functions of internal subdivision

In this technical study RAY HARINGTON *discusses the functions of the building's internal subdividing elements, thus providing an introduction to the design of internal suspended floors, partitions and walls, and suspended ceilings. He draws attention to the following issues: control of the endoclimate* to cater for user needs; security considerations; structural performance; and design life.*

This analysis should be read in conjunction with technical study EXTERNAL ENVELOPE *in which the basic objectives and means of environmental control are discussed in some detail, as these are also fundamental in ·onsidering the functional design of the internal fabric*
* Endo-prefix meaning within

1 Introduction

1.01 Scope of technical study

This study introduces the third group of sections contained in this handbook, dealing with the design of those elements which subdivide the internal space enclosed by the external fabric. The preceding sections, (Building enclosure: General and Building enclosure: External envelope) have principally been concerned with the modification of external environmental phenomena by the use of suitable intervening fabric to produce an amenable endoclimate for users of the building (see technical study EXTERNAL ENVELOPE 1, 3.01). It is clear, however, that this internal environment, in any reasonably complex building, is comprised of many local and varying environments or micro-environments which individuals or groups require for their specific activities within the external envelope.

1.02 'Insides' and 'outsides' of buildings

Designing the external fabric often involves the resolution of large differences between external climate and endoclimate, and usually produces distinctive building fabric whose form and quality contribute to architectural character. Examples are given in technical study EXTERNAL ENVELOPE 1 (AJ 1.9.71).

Architectural philosophy has frequently taken an attitude requiring close correlation between the 'insides' and 'outsides' of buildings. Yet the appearance and character of internal spaces are not inevitably a direct result of the nature of the enclosing fabric, and there is possibly more than a nostalgic interest in design concepts which intention-

ally differentiate the form of the internal space from that of its protective enclosure.

In certain buildings, particularly those for entertainment, such as cinemas, the internal character has been designed in response to a popular desire for highly emotive qualities, frequently of an escapist nature **1, 2**, and designers may seek to create new forms and experiences by devices such as variable geometry linings combined with changing lighting effects.

Users of internal environment experience and appreciate building quality and performance on a different basis to that of the external observer, and may be oblivious to the external evidence of their occupancy. Within the building, occupants tend to be concerned only about each other when they are conscious of differences in user needs.

The solutions to the physical requirements of internal dividing fabric are capable of quantitive definition and evaluation in much the same way as has been described in the sections dealing with the external envelope. The qualitative requirements, however, may not correlate so closely, as there is frequently more choice of both methods and media which will satisfy both physical and psychological needs—often by superficial means such as temporary surfaces, screens, decorations and placing of furniture **3**.

The design of dividing fabric is therefore primarily concerned with the creation of spaces whose size and character are compatible with the psycho-physical needs and intentions of the users. These are described in AJ Handbook of Building environment CI/sfB (E6)[5].

However, the presence of many users with varying requirements creates the essential design dilemma—the resolution of incompatibilities. These exist between the environmental requirements of individuals and groups, between processes, between varying degrees of danger or nuisance, and between the numerous other variables which any reasonably com-

1a

1b

1c

1d

1a-d *The cinema is a modern building type in which internal appearance has often been intentionally differentiated from external form. The New Victoria* (*London, 1930*) *is a good example; orthodox, repetitive external facades* **a**, *designed to harmonise with streetscape, give no clue to interior, which uses form,*

plex building is required to accommodate and for which it is needed throughout its useful life.

In addition the internal dividing fabric may have to perform permanent structural functions in supporting and stabilising the total building fabric or conversely may be required to be temporary and/or variable in position and dimension.

The foregoing issues are dealt with in this study under the general headings of environmental control, security, structure, and design life.

2 Design strategy

2.01 Interaction with physical planning

In the narrowest sense the designer of dividing fabric needs only to identify the localised problem and solve it within the known constraints. But, as many design problems result from the sheer proximity of incompatible activities and micro-environments, the physical planning strategy for the building as a whole is clearly a basic matter of concern to the designer.

Careful zoning of activities into areas of greater compatibility enables the local problems to be reduced. This results in advantages and savings in material content, complexity and cost **4**.

2

light and colour to create atmosphere of 'an underwater palace'. Design of this kind has usually been thought of as decadent by Bauhaus-influenced architects, but may now be *coming back into favour* **2** *Prince of Wales pub in North London. Behind an unremarkable, restrained exterior is hidden a wild, exuberant and quite unrelated interior*

2.02 The need for rational choice

If the conflicting issues inherent in any design problem and the means of its solution are to be resolved rationally, we must obviously state the problems in terms of the constraints, criteria and priorities deriving from a specific physical context.

The need to separate the feasible from the possible is an inherent part of the designer's problem and a methodology for identifying and comparing feasible solutions is desirable. By defining constraints of various kinds, a 'problem space' can be identified. Proposed solutions falling within the problem space can be regarded as feasible but still require to be evaluated and sorted methodically.

The evaluation must take into account the constituent criteria and their relative importance or priorities. This information can be arranged so as to enable direct proposals to be made either by inspection **5** or by a computer programme, which ranks design proposals by additive scores. Using a formal method of design proposal like this ensures that problems are identified and defined and that solutions are methodically considered and compared on the common basis of user requirements.

3 Environmental control

3.01 Analysis of environmental requirements

In single-purpose buildings the endoclimate resulting from the interpositioning of the external envelope can be considered as adequate for the whole building, whether subdivided or not. However, few modern buildings are simple in use, and differentials will occur between different activities going on within internal spaces or rooms. The most critical 'tolerance differentials' are likely to be those of noise levels, but those of heat, light, smell, other pollution and air movement must also be resolved.

3.02 Noise control

As with the external climate/endoclimate modification the main aim is to reduce transference of noise from the space containing the scource to spaces with low tolerance levels. The problem is often complex, owing to the number of constructional elements which combine to enclose a room or internal space and which are contiguous with those enclosing adjacent spaces.

It is particularly important that sound barriers should be extended through any linings to the basic enclosing surfaces (eg above suspended ceilings) and that they are imperforate, as far as possible. Where apertures, such as doors, are necessary, they should be effectively sealed when closed and direct sound paths avoided when open. Particular attention should be paid to the insulation of any service pipe or duct which runs through adjacent spaces, and to any external skin common to several spaces.

3

Where screens are employed, the diffraction of sound waves should be borne in mind if reasonable privacy is to be maintained. This is important in the design of open spaces such as landscaped offices, within which zones of aural privacy may be desired.

Where privacy cannot easily be achieved by the intervening fabric it may be desirable to deliberately raise the general noise level by use of white noise (a multi-frequency sound) or other continuous masking sound. This may be particularly appropriate where the general sound level is low and aural privacy is required without altering an existing fabric, or designing heavy walling in situations requiring light partitioning.

The finishings of enclosing elements can contribute much to the reduction of sound so consideration should be given to soft floor coverings and absorbent ceiling and wall linings, to attenuate sounds at source and avoid reflections. These issues are dealt with in the AJ Handbook of Building environment Section 5 SOUND[5].

3.03 Heat

Thermal differentials are not often large in buildings of similar use, but significant differences can occur as a result of different occupation patterns (permanent or temporary) and because of variations in use.

Extreme temperature differences can occur when specialised storage or machinery rooms are planned close to habitable areas; an extreme example is the incorporation of refrigerated accommodation within a multiple-use building. In a case like this vapour barriers must be incorporated on the *warm* side of the insulation to avoid interstitial condensation within the insulation zone, which would freeze and cause deterioration to the insulating medium and its finishes.

Openings between refrigerated rooms and normal temperature rooms are usually protected by blown cool air curtains. Hot air curtains can also be used to subdivide contiguous space where appropriate.

Where internal dividing fabric meets the external enclosure, care must be taken to avoid thermal bridging in buildings. This is particularly important in buildings where the internal fabric is of high thermal capacity, such as in

3 *Physical and psychological needs of occupants can often be satisfied by temporary divisions and fittings, and superficial decorations, rather than building fabric*

concrete cross wall flats. The design of fabric in relation to thermal requirements is dealt with in the AJ Handbook of Building environment Section 4 THERMAL PROPERTIES[5].

3.04 Light

The general requirement for surfaces of internal fabric is provision of reflectance characteristics appropriate to the environmental aims. Once attained, the reflecting qualities must be easily maintained without inconvenience to the user. The levels of lighting and surface reflectances appropriate to given building uses are described in the AJ Handbook of Building environment Section 2 SUNLIGHT and Section 9 ELECTRIC LIGHTING[5].

Internal divisions may be required to pass natural light originating from apertures in the external envelope. The degree of received illumination will depend on the relative positions of the light source and the internal opening, and will also be affected by the reflecting qualities of all adjacent surfaces.

In the interests of visual privacy, the clarity of glasses used in internal dividing walls may be deliberately reduced by surface moulding and in many cases this will result in reduced light transmittance values and variations of diffusion. Special light-refracting glass or prismatic glass is available which will reflect light at angles differing in relation to the angles of the prismatic profiles. Such glass may enhance the lighting of internal spaces if suitably positioned (eg lighting a basement from an open 'area').

3.05 Air movement

Care should be taken to ensure that the ventilation rates of naturally ventilated buildings are not unbalanced by an arrangement of internal spaces which induces excessive draughts, or stagnation. The arrangement of continuous, vertical, flue-like spaces connected to zones of high and low external pressure should be avoided, and the stack effect

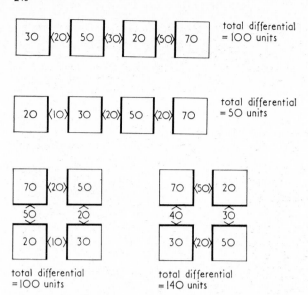

4 *Careful zoning of activities into areas of greater compatibility can reduce local problems. Diagrams show alternative ways of arranging four*

spaces; second arrangement is most efficient, and lower right is least efficient. Figures could be taken to represent various aspects of environment, eg noise level

design solutions	criteria of performance			
	A	B	C	D
X	3	1	4	2
Y	1	2	3	4
Z	1	3	4	2

design solutions	priorities of criteria				total notional values	rank order
	A = 4	B = 2	C = 3	D = 1		
X	$3^4 = 81$	$1^2 = 1$	$4^3 = 64$	$2^1 = 2$	10368	1
Y	$1^4 = 1$	$2^2 = 4$	$3^3 = 27$	$4^1 = 4$	432	3
Z	$1^4 = 1$	$3^2 = 9$	$4^3 = 64$	$2^1 = 2$	1152	2

5 *Formal methods of recording and evaluating alternative design proposals ensure that problems are identified and defined. In above example, three design solutions are recorded (upper table), and ranked in terms of four criteria of performance. Proposal x, for instance, is good in terms of criterion c, not quite as*

good on criterion A, and so on down to B, on which it scores worst. In the next table, the criteria themselves are ranked (A top priority, c next, and so on down to D), and a total notional value for each design solution is found. Proposed solutions can then be ranked as a basis for decision-making

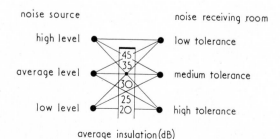

6 *Simple nomogram for estimating average sound insulation required of*

partitions interposed between noise sources and noise receiving rooms.

associated with tall buildings minimised by the use of airlocks and lobbies.

Grilles and registers may be necessary in internal divisions so that air is drawn through spaces by pressure differentials induced by mechanical ventilation. Special care is necessary in the design of dividing fabric to ensure adequate air movement for protection from and removal of smells and the products of combustion (particularly cigarette smoke) even within spaces from which air is being extracted mechanically. AJ Handbook of Building environment—Section 3 AIR MOVEMENT[5] discusses these matters in greater depth.

Similarly, precautions against transfer of bacteria may be necessary in hospital buildings. Such precautions include high air-change rates, disinfectant sprays and treatment by ultra-violet light. The AJ Handbook of Building environment Section 6 HYGIENE[5] should be consulted for further information.

4 Environmental services

In most buildings the environmental services are wholly or partially accommodated within internal fabric or within spaces between internal linings to the main dividing and enclosing fabric. Such arrangements create a need for safe, sufficient means of access to the enclosed installations, and this is dealt with in AJ Handbook of Building environment Section 8 HEATING AND VENTILATING SERVICES[5] and Section 9 ELECTRIC LIGHTING[5] and in the AJ Handbook of Building services and circulation[6].

Service installations for buildings in which dividing partitions are to be movable must be planned so that there are enough potential outlets and attachment points properly positioned in relation to any future arrangement of divisions. This may involve a comprehensive grid of services (particularly electrical power and telephones) installed in a ducting system which allows access at any point, as well as normal access for reorganisation and repair.

In some cases internal services enclosures form major structural elements in combination with staircase and lift enclosures and provision for variable services installations may dominate aspects of the structural concept of a building.

5 Security

5.01 Personal safety, theft

The main aspects of security are personal safety and protection of goods against accidental or deliberate damage or removal. The internal security of a building rests mainly in the provision of structure strong enough to resist various degrees of physical attack. Light prefabricated constructions can in some cases be easily dismantled by removing the beads and cover mouldings, which by their nature allow such fabrications to be easily demountable.

Where extreme security is required, as in bank vaults, the enclosing fabric may have to be heavily protected against possible high stresses resulting from explosive charges and powerful boring equipment.

In all instances the means of access to high security spaces must offer as great a deterrent to disruption as the main enclosing fabric. Such protected means of access must be controlled by highly developed locking devices and systems of keys, together with comprehensive alarm systems. When naturally ventilated, specially designed grilles and registers will be necessary.

5.02 Fire protection

Internal dividing fabric which supports the main loads of a building and any openings in it must be secure against fire. This is dealt with in detail in later issues of the handbook. As a general principle the fire protection function of dividing fabric is to compartmentalise buildings so that fires can be contained and to provide linings of low flame spread to all spaces where there is a risk of fire, or spaces such as escape corridors, where fire would constitute a particular danger. Openings are usually required to provide the same fire resistance standards as the walls or floors in which they are situated. (This issue is governed by Part E of the Building Regulations 1972). In high fire risk situations, openings need to be protected by automatically operated fire resisting shutters controlled by fusible links which respond to high temperatures.

A particular hazard is the spread of fire through enclosed air spaces behind wall linings and suspended ceilings, as well as within hollow structures, and this hazard must be dealt with by breaking down the continuity of these spaces with fire stops. Where service pipes or ducts penetrate enclosing fire protecting fabric they must be carefully sealed (see AJ Handbook of Building services and circulation Section 13 SECURITY[7]).

6 Structure

6.01 Structural function of the dividing fabric

Internal subdividing elements, both horizontal and vertical, may be required to perform major structural functions in the support, bracing and stabilising of a whole structure.

The arrangement of supporting elements will relate to the type of occupancy and the user activities contained within the building. This may result in static cellular spaces permanently positioned, as in blocks of flats, or in a more open space type with subdivisions whose position will vary in time, as in the case of lettable office blocks. The spacing of internal loadbearing vertical dividing structure interacts with the design of horizontal loadbearing spanning structure, and it is important for reasons of economy to attempt an optimisation of these variables **7**.

Particular problems occur in relation to large prefabricated structures where eccentric loading may produce dramatic failures which are the result of non-homogeneous structures formed of jointed panels, loaded near their extremities. The dividing structure must be considered together with that of the external envelope as failure of one element may affect the others, as happened at Ronan Point.

6.02 Provision for fixing building accessories and equipment

Both horizontal and vertical dividing fabric is frequently required to form a basis for the fixing and support of a wide range of accessories and equipment, and these considerations must influence the choice of material. See the AJ Handbook of Fixings and fastenings[8].

7 Design life

7.01 Pattern and mode of building use

The horizontal dividing fabric is likely, to remain permanently fixed during the life of a building unless major

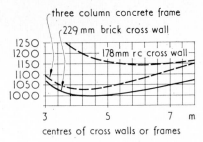

7 *Diagram illustrating the kind of interaction that can occur between vertical dividing structure, horizontal spanning structure, and cost*

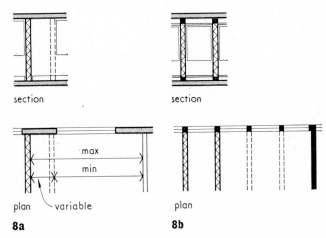

8 *In traditional loadbearing-walled buildings, dimensional tolerances in positioning partitions are usually wide (plan and section a); in framed buildings, there is often much less scope for varying position of partition (plan and section b)*

alterations occur. Vertical divisions other than permanent structural loadbearing fabric may be classified as non-loadbearing—demountable, semi-permanent (ie not specifically made to be demountable but capable of being removed) and permanent (ie non-structural but necessary for other purposes such as fire separation).

Loadbearing divisions may be modified during the life of a building by forming apertures or by infilling existing apertures, provided the structural integrity of the element is maintained. When new openings are formed in loadbearing walls the load carried by the removed portion is transferred to the remaining sections which then need checking. An important aspect, not always considered, is the effect of this redistribution on the foundation loadings.

Designers often refer to their buildings as 'adaptable', 'flexible' or 'responsive to change', so implying the ease with which the dividing fabric can be freely deployed within the external enclosure. The problems of repositioning partitions (other than light demountable partitions or screens used for visual privacy) varies in difficulty depending on the type of construction. In traditional loadbearing walled buildings with solid floors and plastered walls, the problem is mainly one of making good the adjacent surfaces disturbed and evolving suitable cover moulding details to mask junctions. The dimensional tolerances in positioning the partitions are usually wide, due to the mass of brickwork between windows **8a**

In the case of buildings with frames or loadbearing mullion walls the problem is more acute, as there will often be a requirement for closer dimensional relationships between structure and partition positioning **8b**. In effect the width of rooms must become an exact multiple of the structural module used for the mullions (less the width of the partition).

This relationship will be even greater when jointed materials are used for walls and ceilings—particularly if the latter are suspended and sound insulation is required to be of a reasonably high order, needing sound separation above the ceiling level. The use of modular linings with evident joints places a particular responsibility on the designer who wishes to achieve a close correlation between the panels lining walls and ceilings and the positions of lighting fittings, ventilation registers and other visible features.

Clearly any variation in the position of the dividing fabric carries with it the necessity of providing the facility to extend or of having access to related service installations. The extra expense of this may be totally unjustified if the variable planning facility is not used productively during the life of the building (which is by no means uncommon). Additional problems associated with repositioning of the dividing fabric include the poor noise control characteristics of the majority of demountable partition systems due to their inherently light weight and the multiplicity of edge joints which are difficult to seal effectively. Clearly some buildings such as office blocks may require highly manoeuvrable partitions, although the development of landscaped office accommodation **3** is reducing the tendency to subdivide in a cellular manner—separation is achieved by screening and environmental devices such as sound masking, with some degree of personal control of ventilation and heating.

This is, however, an aspect of environmental control very much open to development. The decision to construct large spaces and the necessity for long span structure, comprehensive service installations and variable division systems must be examined in the light of the probable occupancy patterns over the economical life of the building.

Furthermore the ratio of interest on capital expenditure to the equivalent annual value of periodic costs in moving partitions, making good the adjacent fabric disturbed, adapting services and maintaining the components and accessories concerned over the design life of the building is an important issue to be considered in any cost benefit study. This is an aspect of a building owner's financial policy which a designer should fully appreciate from the outset (see information sheet ENCLOSURE 2)[9].

The maintenance of both external enclosures and internal dividing fabric requires similar care in providing safe access, selection of appropriate materials with a particular concern for human behaviour characteristics, cleaning methods and general ability to resist wear by abrasion, impact, water and chemical attack. Maintenance costs are frequently met from revenue and although in many cases they may be set off against tax, the expenditure involved is regarded by management as a burden on company funds—particularly when expressed in terms of the amount of non-profit-making production necessary to provide the money involved. Frequently, however, the opposite situation occurs, causing management to opt for low initial capital outlay at the expense of higher maintenance. This is because there are no capital allowances on buildings but repairs and maintenance costs are allowed in full when assessing tax liability. This is the general rule but the situation is complicated by special grants or allowances in development areas such as Scotland and the North East.

As with external fabric, the appearance of internal surfaces will depend on the selection and disposition of suitable materials and their proper maintenance, although it must be appreciated that many materials perform most of their originally intended functions perfectly well even when superficially in a state of deterioration, and this often leads to less frequent maintenance than may be visually desirable.

Unfortunately there is no simple relationship be. initial cost of materials and their maintenance costs. expensive materials require regular and frequent ma. tenance to preserve their original qualities and many less expensive materials survive neglect remarkably well.

While satisfying all practical criteria, materials are often finally chosen for their intangible qualities, which appeal to those exercising preferences and who are responsible for visual appearance. This factor must be interpreted as a priority which is incorporated in any rational method of selection.

8 References

1 BUILDING RESEARCH STATION (DSIR) Principles of modern building, vols 1 and 2. 1959, HMSO [(9–) (E1)] *Vol* 1 £1, vol 2 87½p

2 FOSTER, J. S. Mitchell's advanced building construction: the structure. London, 1963, Batsford [(9–) (E1)] £1·50

3 STARR, K. Product design and decision theory. Hemel Hempstead, 1963, Prentice-Hall [(A3)] *o/p*

4 AJ Handbook of Building environment. *Architects' Journal*, 1968, October 16, to 1969, July 23 [(E6)]

5 AJ Handbook of Building environment. Section 2 Sunlight: direct and diffused; section 3 Air movement; section 4 Thermal properties; section 5 Sound; section 6 Hygiene; section 7 User requirements; section 8 Heating and ventilating services; section 9 Electrical lighting [(E6)]

6 AJ Handbook of Building services and circulation. *Architects' Journal*, 1969, October 1, to 1970, August 5 [(5–)]

7 AJ Handbook of Building services and circulation. Section 13 Security and fire. *Architects' Journal*, 1970, June 17, July 1, 8, 22 and 29 and August 5 [(5–)]

8 LAUNCHBURY, BILL Handbook of fixings and fastenings. London 1971, Architectural Press £1·00 [Xt5]

9 PUGH, B. Cost considerations. *Architects' Journal*, 1971, August 18, p375-383 [(9–)]

Environmental performance data

This information sheet gives guidance on the environmental performance of various alternative forms of internal subdividing fabric. It therefore forms a counterpart to information sheet EXTERNAL ENVELOPE 1 (p57) *which gave similar guidance for the building's external skin. In the present case only acoustic properties are dealt with, because acoustic insulation is by far the most important environmental control function of internal partitions and suspended floors. The data was provided by* RICHARD LINNELL, *of the Functional Design Laboratory, Department of Architecture, Bristol University, in collaboration with* BRIAN DAY *and* PETER BURBERRY. *All average sound reductions are given in dB.*

WALL & PARTITION CONSTRUCTION *wire 'butterfly' cavity ties used			AVERAGE SOUND REDUCTION (dB)			REMARKS
			no door in partition	lightweight door, with normal gaps, in partition	well sealed heavy weight timber door in partition	
13mm plaster 75mm clinker block 75mm cavity* 75mm clinker block 13mm plaster	13mm plaster 178mm dense concrete 13mm plaster	13mm plaster 228mm brick 13mm plaster	50 — 51	27	37	no advantage in using these constructions if any door is included in the wall structure
13mm plaster 50mm clinker block 50mm cavity* 50mm clinker block 13mm plaster	13mm plaster 75mm clinker block 50mm cavity* 75mm clinker block 13mm plaster	13mm plaster 150mm dense concrete 13mm plaster	47 — 49	27	37	ditto
13mm plaster 114mm brick 13mm plaster	13mm plaster 200mm hollow dense concete block 13mm plaster	100 x 50mm timber studs faced both sides felt on studs 10mm plasterboard 13mm plaster	44 — 46	27	37	if a sealed heavy weight timber door is included in the partition, then no improvement in the wall structure will increase the sound insulation of the partition beyond 37dB
13mm plaster 100mm clinker block 13mm plaster	63mm 'Paramount' 50mm cavity with 25mm glass wool 63mm 'Paramount'	13mm plaster 50mm wood wool 50mm cavity 50mm wood wool 13mm plaster	42 — 43	27	36	if a lightweight door with normal gaps is included in the partition, then no improvement in the wall structure will increase the sound insulation of the partition beyond 27dB

WALL & PARTITION CONSTRUCTION			AVERAGE SOUND REDUCTION (dB)			REMARKS
			no door in partition	lightweight door with normal gaps in partition	well sealed heavy weight timber door in partition	
13mm plaster 75 mm clinker block 13 mm plaster	100 x 50 mm timber studs faced both sides: 13 mm fibreboard 13 mm plaster	13 mm plaster 50 mm wood wool building paper 50 mm woodwool 13 mm plaster	38 — 41	27	34 — 35	if a lightweight door with normal gaps is included in the partition, then no improvement in the wall structure will increase the sound insulation of the partition beyond 27dB
13 mm plaster 50 mm clinker block 13 mm plaster	100 x 50 mm timber studs faced both sides: 10 mm plasterboard 13 mm plaster	13 mm plaster 100 mm hollow clay block 13 mm plaster	35 — 37	27	33 — 34	ditto
plaster skim 75 mm 'Lignacite' plaster skim	100 x 50 mm timber studs faced both sides: expanded metal lath 3 coats plaster	13 mm plaster 75 mm hollow clay block 13 mm plaster	35 — 37	27	33 — 34	ditto
75 mm 'Paramount'	100 x 50 mm timber studs faced both sides: 10 mm plasterboard plaster skim	20 mm plasterboard supported in metal channels faced both sides: 16 mm plaster	31 — 34	25 — 26	30 — 32	
63 mm 'Paramount'	63 x 38 mm timber studs fcd both sides 6 mm plywood two glass wool quilts in cavity	13 mm plaster 50 mm wood wool 13 mm plaster	27 — 30	24 — 25	27 — 29	any sealed heavy weight door included in the partition, has little or no effect on the overall sound insulation; but inclusion of lightweight doors worsens insulation value by several dB
57 mm 'Paramount'	50 x 50 mm timber studs faced both sides: 6 mm plywood	38 mm chipboard, drilled with 20 mm holes, faced both sides: 1 mm Obeche	23 — 26	23	23 — 26	either type of door included in the partition, has little or no effect on the overall sound insulation

FLOOR CONSTRUCTION	AVERAGE SOUND INSULATION (dB)			
	AIR-BORNE NOISE	IMPACT NOISE		
		hard floor finishes	normal floor finishes	soft floor finishes
22 mm floor boarding / timber joists / 10 mm plasterboard	THIN WALLS 29	—	probably 20 dB worse than Grade II	probably 15 dB worse than Grade II
	THICK WALLS 31	—	15 dB worse than Grade II	probably 6 dB worse than Grade II
22 mm floor boarding / timber joists / 10 mm plasterboard / I coat plaster	THIN WALLS 34	—	8 dB worse than Grade II	2 dB worse than Grade II
	THICK WALLS 36	—	5 dB worse than Grade II	probably Grade II
22 mm floor boarding / mineral wool pugging of minimum weight 15 kg/m² / 10 mm plasterboard	THIN WALLS 36	—	10 dB worse than Grade II	4 dB worse than Grade II
	THICK WALLS 40	—	6 dB worse than Grade II	possibly Grade II
22 mm floor boarding / mineral wool pugging of minimum weight 15 kg/m² / 10 mm plasterboard / I coat plaster	THIN WALLS 39	—	5 dB worse than Grade II	probably Grade II
	THICK WALLS 44	—	possibly Grade II	Grade II
22 mm floor boarding on battens / 25 mm mineral wool quilt / timber joists / 10 mm plasterboard	THIN WALLS 39	—	3 dB worse than Grade II	probably Grade II
	THICK WALLS 44	—	possibly Grade II	Grade II
22 mm floor boarding / timber joists / 20 mm lath & plaster	THIN WALLS 40	—	6 dB worse than Grade II	probably Grade II
	THICK WALLS 45	—	Grade II	probably Grade I
22 mm floor boarding / timber joists / gravel pugging weight 83 kg/m² / 20 mm lath & plaster	THIN WALLS 45	—	Grade II	probably Grade I
	THICK WALLS 48	—	Grade II	Grade I
floor finish / concrete slab 220 kg/m² / 10 mm plaster	45	4 dB worse than Grade II	Grade II	probably Grade I
floor finish / concrete slab 370 kg/m² / 10 mm plaster	48	4 dB worse than Grade II	Grade II	Grade I
22 mm floor boarding on battens / 25 mm mineral wool quilt / concrete slab / 10 mm plaster	50	—	Grade I	Grade I

Section 7
Internal division:
Suspended floors

Section 7 Internal division: suspended floors

Scope

This is the first of three sections of the handbook dealing with the specific element-groups comprising a building's internal subdivision (suspended floors; internal walls and partitions; and ceilings). It covers not only the construction of suspended floors, but also the choice and application of sub-floors and screeds, and floor finishes.

Problems of structural strength are not given detailed consideration in this handbook, as they are covered very thoroughly in the AJ Handbook of Building Structure.

Relationship to rest of handbook

The table and diagram show the entire handbook's contents, with the present section highlighted.

This section should be used in conjunction with section 6 INTERNAL DIVISION, which analyses the functions of the internal subdividing elements as a whole.

The information on subfloors and screeds, and floor finishes given in this section, will also be relevant to section 3, which restricted itself to those aspects uniquely connected with the lowest floor of the building, and gave no information on the many finishes which could be applied both to lowest floors and internally subdividing floors. All information on such screeds and finishes is concentrated in the present section to avoid unnecessary duplication.

References and keywords

The keyword by which this section is identified is SUSPENDED FLOORS: the use of keywords is explained on p6.

Author

A. J. ELDER *is a partner in Elder Lester & Partners of Yarm, Yorkshire. In 1966-7 he was president of the Northern Architectural Association.*

A. J. Elder

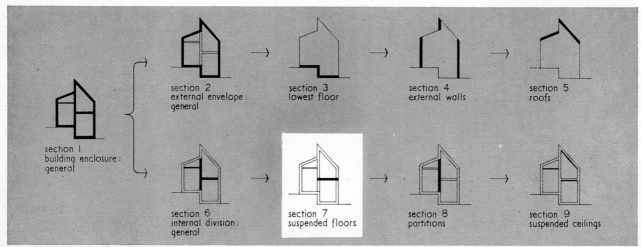

section I
building enclosure:
general

section 2
external envelope:
general

section 3
lowest floor

section 4
external walls

section 5
roofs

section 6
internal division:
general

section 7
suspended floors

section 8
partitions

section 9
suspended ceilings

Technical study
Suspended floors 1

Section 7 **Internal division: Suspended floors**

Upper floors of buildings

In this technical study, A. J. ELDER discusses suspended floors as a support, for dead and live loads from above, or underfixed loads such as services, and the part they play in the enclosure as a whole. Following in this issue is a study (information sheet SUSPENDED FLOORS 1) for use at the drawing board. Information sheets SUSPENDED FLOORS 2 and 3 will be published in sequence

1 Introduction

The gravitational pull of the earth is directed towards its centre, for all practical purposes acting at right angles to the earth's surface and is equally strong no matter which particular point on the earth's surface is being considered. Any differences in the considerable roughness, although large in terms of human scale, are too small when compared with the radius of the planet to have any effect on structural calculations **1**.

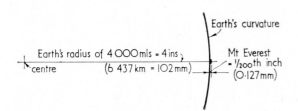

1 *Diagram illustrates minute relationship of even earth's highest topographical feature, Mount Everest, to its total volume. Earth may be regarded as smooth sphere of approximately 8000 miles diameter and, though well-known slight flattening of poles may have some small effect, it is of scientific rather than practical interest in relation to structural calculations*

Over an area such as that in **2**, topographical features would almost certainly make the earth's curvature insignificant. We can therefore safely define the terms 'flat' and 'level' in the context of building as meaning 'without curvature and parallel to the earth's mean surface' (or at right angles to the direction of gravity). There are one or two exceptions to the general rule of 'flatness' for upper floors. These are tiered auditoria such as theatres, where sight lines are involved **3a**, and multi-storey car parks where the whole floor is ramped in two halves so that communicating ramps are unnecessary. This is perhaps the only true example of the deliberate provision of a non-level floor for storage purposes **3b**.

Floors on the ground have already been covered in 3, and quite frequently site conditions and other factors are such that requirements can adequately be met by use of the ground level only. Man had advanced considerably along the road of architectural development before the first truly multi-storey building appeared. Even highly complex structures such as Santa Sophia in Constantinople were basically single storey, although they enclosed a vast space. The modern human 'filing cabinet' is a very recent invention in terms of architectural history and reflects man's efforts

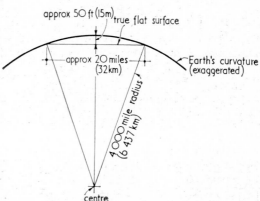

2 *Although a surface parallel to earth's mean surface would be curved in both directions, this is so infinitesimal that all surfaces may be constructed truly flat. To illustrate this, if a building were about 32 km (20 miles) square, rise in floor at centre to keep it parallel to earth curvature would be about 15 m (50ft)*

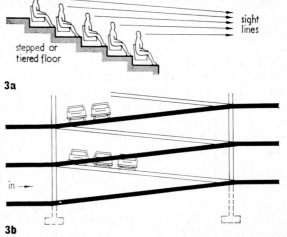

3 *Exceptions to general rule of 'flatness' for upper floors:*
a *tiered auditoria where sight lines are critical;*
b *multi-storey carparks where communication ramps and storage level are same floor slab*

to solve the self-created problems raised by recent developments in science, technology and the accompanying population explosion.

The suspended floor is used to provide a usable floor area in excess of the site area itself (as in multi-storey buildings, the whole sequence of high density and the problem of large scale urban development); also for the basic purpose of keeping people off the ground (ie the early damp-proof course).

As they are the flat level surface necessary for human and other activities, floors are really the basic ingredient to which all else is secondary. They determine, by their extent or area, the extent of activities which can be accommodated. The size of a building is almost invariably defined in terms of floor area; as also is the cost. All other parts of the building are there to serve the requirements of enclosure with respect to supporting structure, enclosure to exclude climatic variations, services to control internal climate and so on.

While it is the primary function of suspended floors to support people, goods and so on, they also act together with internal walls to subdivide space within the entire enclosure. Resulting spaces may have differing environmental requirements and the extent of these differentials will lead to the definition of the standards of performance in terms of insulation required by the intervening structure, ie the floors.

The term 'suspended' floors is used here in its generally accepted sense, as a loadbearing and enclosing surface strategically supported on bearing surface(s), or as in suspended structure, hung from tension members **4**.

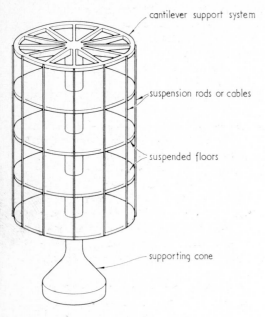

4 *Schematic of suspended structure, floors hung from vertical tension members from rigid framework supported by central stem*

In fact the majority of so-called 'suspended' floors are supported from below by compression members such as walls or props usually known as 'columns', and generally acting in conjunction with beams to form a structural frame transferring the weight of the floor to the ground.

Apart from their principal function of support, upper floors have other functions relating to the subdivision of buildings. These are briefly summarised in 2, and dealt with in more detail later under the headings of: Structural functions, Environmental control, Security and Services and finishes, each of these main divisions has been dealt with in three subdivisions headed:

1 Issues (nature of subject or problem)
2 Factors (factors, conditions, needs and so on, effecting choice of solution)
3 Solutions (alternative possibilities).

Finally mention is also made at the end of each section of constraints imposed by external factors such as, for example, Building Regulations.

2 The functions of suspended floors

2.01 Fundamental

Support

The principal function of upper floors is to provide (sometimes with the ground floor) support for people, goods, machinery and so on, and to provide a surface on which all activities may be safely carried out.

They are also needed to enable greater use to be made of a limited ground area by creating additional space above the ground in multi-storey buildings.

Stability

Sometimes, although not invariably, the function of suspended floors is to contribute to the general stability of the building by acting as horizontal bracing against wind loads.

2.02 Incidental

Insulation

Sound: suspended floors prevent the transmission of sound between zones of the building where these are represented by separate storeys.

Heat: similarly to prevent transmission of heat between zones where a temperature differential is required.

Light: to provide a barrier to light and vision between zones when desirable.

Air Movement

To prevent the movements of air (and smells) between zones.

Security

To provide security between zones of the building against various forms of attack, eg physical attack, burglary, fire, chemical and radioactivity.

Services

To provide support and accommodation for environmental and other services (often in conjunction with suspended ceilings).

Circulation

Openings to permit movement between floors or storeys where and as necessary.

In the subsections which follow, these functions are in certain cases grouped together into the main headings mentioned in 1.

3 Structural functions

3.01 Issues

The provision of support for live and dead loads (including any services) in the form of a flat level surface. Often these must be as free from obstructions as possible, to provide maximum freedom of manoeuvre or flexibility. This need has to be considered against economic facts of life, longer spans cost more.

Floors are often used as bracing membranes to assist in resisting wind loads. Calculations for all types of loading are controlled by the Building Regulations in force according to location. Further reference to this is made in information sheet SUSPENDED FLOORS 1.

3.02 Factors

These include first the type of structure selected for the building, which will have been decided by consideration of many factors in addition to the suspended floor design. These can include availability of material and labour, speed of erection, fire grading of the building and so on. A fundamental choice is between structural steel and concrete for the frame; a decision on which the choice of the floor structure is interdependent.

An important factor here is whether or not the floor slab shall contribute to the strength of the frame beams, thus having a dual function which is usually economical. Freedom from intrusion by structural walls or columns may be a requirement. For example, the normal office slab block with a central corridor and two rows of offices may have a centre spine of columns or be constructed with a full width span, leaving complete freedom of choice in the positioning of partitions or use as open space. In such cases the floor might span across width lengthwise between beams **5**. It is accepted as a general rule (fully borne out by experience) that, given similar conditions of loading and so on, long spans cost more per unit area than short spans, whether considering beams or slab.

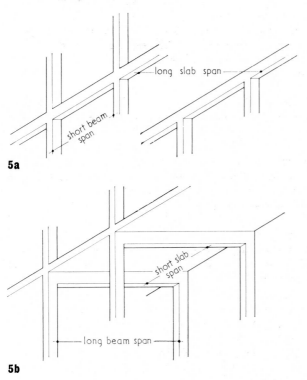

5a

5b

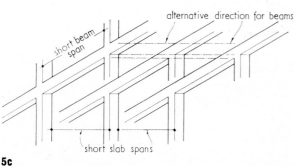

5c

5 *Various support systems which can be used to achieve desired partition or services layout requirements; a short*   *beam span, long slab span;* **b** *long beam span, short slab span;* **c** *short span both ways using central columns*

It is also a general natural law that, other things being equal, long spans involve greater depth to achieve the same strength and given limit of deflection. The most economic compromise, as between column centre, beam and slab spans for any given area of structure, is a design decision which could well be solved scientifically by computer. The alternatives shown in **5** for the typical office floor slab mentioned earlier could clearly be so compared:
a would have a thicker slab but smaller beams
b would have larger beams and a thinner slab
c would have both smaller beams and thinner slab but more columns.

The computer program could be designed to arrive at the optimum spacing for columns in each case and to cost out each scheme. Such calculations are however usually done empirically (or even mentally) as an exact comparison is unnecessary, and there are many other factors affecting the issue. For example, service runs would be easy to accommodate in **a** (uninterrupted by beams). The columns in case **c** might be inconvenient, and in any of the solutions aesthetic considerations could have their effect so that in the end the choice might well be technically intuitive—supported of course by reasonable cost checks.

Fire resistance of floors is determined with respect to building type and will affect the choice of floor construction. Speed of erection may also be important but must be considered within the general building programme. It is not necessarily desirable to build one floor per week if the cladding takes twice as long or if other elements are similarly out of phase.

The need to provide support for services above or below the floor will sometimes control the type of construction chosen. Certain floors (eg precast beam and infill block) are easy to pierce over most of their area for service access and may permit the running of services, at least in one direction, within the depth. Some floors can be pierced with large openings without affecting their structural stability, whereas others will collapse if similar openings are made without special preparation. The provision of apertures for vertical circulation or other reasons must be considered at the design stage.

The subject of system building, and its fellow subject, 'dimensional co-ordination' are not really within the scope of this study, but clearly if some system or module is being used then the choice of floor structure must take account of the appropriate dimensional need and the discipline imposed thereby.

3.03 Solutions

Historical review

Apart from such constructions as the Galleries of the Roman amphitheatres, earlier upper floors were probably of wood. Refinements such as tongued and grooved boarding are recent, but based on the historic principle of beams (or joists) with subfloor spanning between.

In earlier examples the beams were often unsquared, or just roughly squared tree trunks, and the principle that the greatest strength/span ratio was obtained by the use of deep narrow sections did not seem to be understood. Boards, when used, were plain edged and wide; they would clearly have suffered calamitous warping and shrinking in conditions normally applying in modern building interiors.

Another system often used in 17th to 18th century cottage construction was reed and clay, or reed and lime concrete spanning cross joists. It was in a way a rudimentary form of reinforced concrete, capable only of very short spans because of the low inherent tensile strength of the materials.

In such shallow floor-to-floor structures ceilings were usually non-existent but, where used, consisted generally of lathe and plaster and of course in gentlemen's houses and public buildings developed into highly sophisticated media for decorative work. In England the best was the type so frequently attributed to the work of the brothers Adam.

In industrial building, which developed rapidly during the industrial revolution, a three-tier floor construction of heavy timber beams superimposed by large timber joists and finally by flooring 50 to 75 mm thick, was the normal system used for supporting heavy loads **6**.

Beams were supported by brick piers at the ends and usually by cast-iron columns inside, although timber posts were in use. The beginning of composite construction could also be seen in the use of flitch beams and the use of metal for various connections **7**.

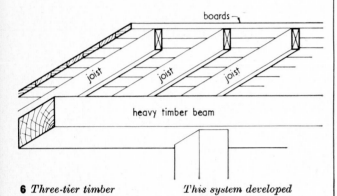

6 *Three-tier timber construction used for supporting heavy loads.*

This system developed rapidly during industrial revolution

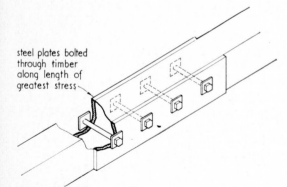

7 *Flitch beam, one sign of beginnings of composite construction*

The true principles of structural engineering in relation to floors were now beginning to be understood. Later came various types of cast-iron beams and finally steel girders, first built up of flats or of triangulated form (the 'Warren' girder) and later the ubiquitous I-section, designed scientifically to obtain the maximum resistance to bending from the minimum of material. Ultimately the full structural frame developed but was often still based on the I-section. Timber was at first still used in conjunction with steel beams as the final infilling material, but had certain obvious disadvantages in relation to fire resistance. From the days of cast-iron beams onwards various systems were tried, from the filler arch through concrete arched filling to today's prestressed concrete **8**.

The principal floor construction types in use today are:

Timber

Generally, because of fire regulations, timber is restricted to domestic construction but may be found as non-compartment floors in other buildings (eg factories, where a partial platform is required and the first floor of maisonettes in multi-storey developments). It is normally used in two-storey constructions in the form of joists supported directly by loadbearing walls or steel beams, and has the advantage of economy.

Other types include composite plywood and softwood structural members, with plywood skins forming a final surface which may be stressed. Long spans can be achieved but usually only with light loadings and, because of fire regulations, this is more often found in roof than floor construction **9**.

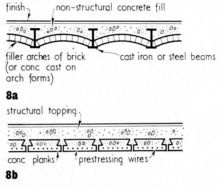

8a

8b

8 *Early and recent structural forms:* **a** *filler arch construction;* **b** *prestressed plank*

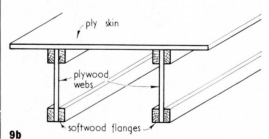

9a

9b

9 *Composite plywood and softwood structural members in conjunction with tongue and grooved boarding or plywood skins forming*

final surface which may be stressed; **a** *normal joint boarding;* **b** *plywood joist or beam construction*

Metal

Sheet steel galvanised or otherwise rust-proofed metal, used alone or compositely with concrete, is the most common material. Aluminium may also be found and both materials, but especially aluminium, are again more commonly found in roof construction as they are more suited to light loadings. The formation of the units is normally profiled or corrugated in some form for strength against bending and is frequently double-skinned to increase strength and provide space for services.

Metal floors which have a full loadbearing capacity without assistance from structural topping are rare in Britain but much more common in the US where a greater premium may be placed on speed of erection and where attitudes to fire risks are often different. Since metal on its own has virtually no fire resistance, provision of an adequate period for such floors would in any case usually require a thick screed to provide the necessary minimum and it is therefore logical to use this by means of shear connectors welded to the steel to provide the compression element in a composite construction **10**.

The other type of composite construction is combined timber and pressed metal beam or joist, again more commonly found in roofs, where long-span light-load situations occur and fire resistance is not a problem. This may however be useful in certain situations such as floors where minimum fire resistance requirements occur **11**.

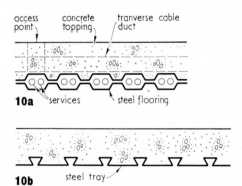

10a

10b

10 *Examples of metal and concrete composite construction:* **a** *composite*   *floor with service provision;* **b** *simple composite floor*

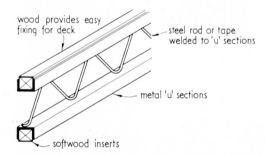

11 *Composite lattice joist: example of timber and metal composite construction for*   *use where minimum fire resistance requirements are enforced*

Concrete

Because of its incombustibility, high resistance to fire and sound insulation, concrete has become the most widely used material for all floors except those in small domestic buildings. The simple in situ reinforced slab can in many cases still be the best choice where speed is not of great importance and where the brief may call for high loadings, a long period of fire resistance or good sound insulation. The choice between a single or two-way slab, and a combination of beam and slab, has usually to be decided on grounds of cost.

Precast concrete floors have gradually expanded in extent of use and number of types, and now contribute a very large proportion of the total floor area constructed. They can be classified into two main types:

1 simple self-supporting beam or slab
2 slab acting in conjunction with structural topping which

may or may not require propping until cast and cured **12**. Obviously the simple unsupported beam has advantages during construction when props can be a nuisance and cause delay. The second type can be cheaper, however, and in certain cases the added concrete can be the screeded finish.

Precast beam floors may sometimes make use of filler blocks, thereby permitting a wider spacing to be used. When this is done the screed may be merely a screed or may again be made to act in conjunction with the beams as a structural topping, in which case the filler blocks require only sufficient strength to act as formwork **13**.

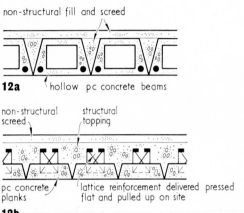

12a   hollow pc concrete beams

12b

12 *Examples of the two main types of precast concrete floors:* **a** *self-supporting precast*   *beams;* **b** *requires propping at least at centre span until topping develops strength*

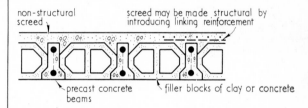

13 *Beam and filler block floor (propping not required unless screed is structural)*

Where long spans are needed (say, 6 m or more) and loadings are not heavy, for example in office floors, it may often be wise to use some device to obtain adequate depth to resist deflection without the weight and unnecessary strength of a solid floor. The beam and light filler block mentioned above is one method, as is the use of lightweight aggregate concrete. Others are the use of deep precast beams with arched soffits or beams of similar profile formed in situ, using patent forms usually of steel or glass fibre **14a**. Where a two-way span can be used in similar circumstances, a coffered soffit formed by using patent shapes of glass fibre, polypropolene, steel or even compressed paper, permits reinforcement to pass in both directions, normally referred to as the 'waffle' floor **14b**.

Where a combination of beam and slab is used, it is normal to use the concrete in the slab as the compression part of the beam, making dual, and therefore economical, use of the same materials. This can be achieved even when using steel beams, by the use of shear connectors and also where precast beams form the structural floor, by cutting back at the ends and infilling with in situ concrete above the beam **15**.

The multiplicity of types of precast or patent in situ floor

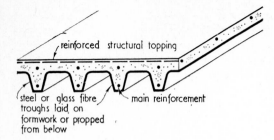

reinforced structural topping

steel or glass fibre troughs laid on formwork or propped from below

main reinforcement

14a

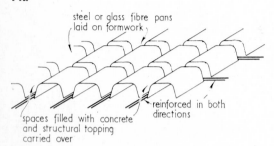

steel or glass fibre pans laid on formwork

reinforced in both directions

spaces filled with concrete and structural topping carried over

14b

14 *Systems for use in long spans, light loadings:*
a *trough type floor;*
b *waffle type floor*

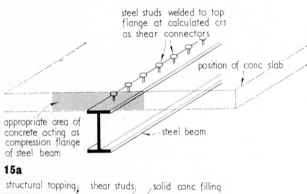

steel studs welded to top flange at calculated crs as. shear connectors

position of conc slab

appropriate area of concrete acting as compression flange of steel beam

steel beam

15a

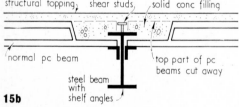

structural topping   shear studs   solid conc filling

normal pc beam

top part of pc beams cut away

steel beam with shelf angles

15b

15 *Examples of composite beam/slab construction:*
a *in situ;* **b** *precast*

makes it impossible to cover the subject in detail. Many ingenious systems are used under factory conditions to produce the components of these various systems, some of which are described in more detail in information sheet SUSPENDED FLOORS 1. In addition there are certain more highly specialised systems which should be briefly mentioned. More important is the principle of prestressing whereby the tensile reinforcement is placed under stress before the concrete is cast around. This has the effect of placing the surrounding concrete in compression through the steel-concrete bond, and when the beam bends or deflects under the applied load the first effect is to relieve this compressive stress so that a greater load can be applied before the concrete actually comes under any tension at all. This considerably increases the feasible span/depth ratio, allowing long spans to be achieved

without undue deflections. Of course it does have an opposite effect of producing reverse deflection, or 'hogging' if the anticipated applied load does not occur. This effect must be allowed for in the building design when using prestressing techniques.

Finally there are specialist erection techniques to be considered. One of the principal disadvantages of in situ construction is the cost and time consumed by erecting formwork. In a patent system known as 'lift slab' the columns are first erected and then all the upper floors are cast on top of each other at ground level, separated by suitable membranes. After a curing period, the roof and floors are hoisted by patent mechanism one by one up to their correct level and fixed in position, thus saving the cost of formwork. Such a system is only suitable for comparatively simple structural forms (multi-storey offices or car-parks).

The ultimate in this category is the system whereby a whole storey is constructed on the ground and then jacked up so that the next storey can be built below it, jacked up again and so on. It has the advantage that all work can go on inside a temporary shelter at ground level, completely unaffected by weather. It is in fact a vertical version of the Swedish shipbuilding system in which the bow is constructed within a shed and then pushed out as sections of the ship are added, again allowing all work to proceed under cover.

An experiment in this type of building was undertaken in Coventry (a city which has pioneered much) some years ago, and it was said then that by the time a storey reached fifth-floor level it was complete with all services and finishes, and went on up from that point completely unchanged. Strangely enough little seems to have been heard from this project—a case where feedback would clearly have been of the greatest interest. The system in fact is still used in Belgium and Holland, but seems to have been proved uneconomic in this country.

Support considerations

The type of supporting structure being used must influence the choice of floor construction and vice versa. An in situ concrete floor will usually, but not inevitably, mean an in situ concrete frame so that the dual use of one mass of concrete, as mentioned earlier, can be made. A steel frame will usually result in the use of either a precast concrete system or steel composite system such as Q-floor.

Columns may be of steel or concrete and composite structures enabling the structural steel sections to act in conjunction with concrete floors are increasingly being used **15**.

The spacing of columns may be dictated by all kinds of factors in addition to structural spans; the principal ones being the controlling effect of room sizes and the use of space. Modular grids are also increasingly imposing their own discipline. A square grid of columns will usually indicate a two-way span slab, whereas a rectangular grid of say two to one proportion will suggest beams and a simple one-way structural slab system.

If structural considerations take precedence, the use of cantilevers to minimise bending moments and create optimum spans, is a good solution. An arrangement similar to that shown in **16** will produce the lowest stresses for any given grid.

Mushroom construction does away with the need for beams in either direction and leads to the use of a square grid. It is suitable only for pure in situ construction and is perhaps one of the more structurally logical ways of using the plastic nature of reinforced concrete **17**.

Floors supported from hangers were referred to in 1, but

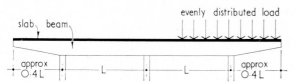

16 *Use of cantilevers to keep stresses to minimum:
optimum span/cantilever proportions*

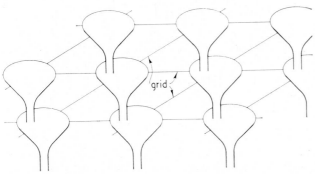

17 *Mushroom construction: seen from below two-way grid*

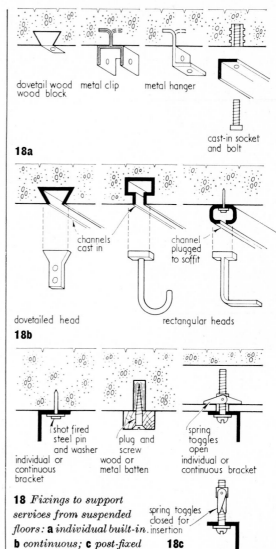

18 *Fixings to support
services from suspended
floors:* **a** *individual built-in*
b *continuous;* **c** *post-fixed*

are rare as although the tensional support is a simple
natural method, the provision of the umbrella from which
the hangers will be suspended is complex and expensive.

Fixings

The support by floors of services 6 and suspended ceilings
(AJ Handbook of Building enclosure, section 9, CEILINGS)
requires the use of fixings usually into the soffit. It is
of course most convenient if these are such that they can be
placed anywhere on the soffit, thus providing no limitation
to the positioning of the supported items.

The loads and frequency of support required vary considerably but generally do not loom large when compared with
the load forming the principal reason for the provision of
the floor in the first place. The fixing can be of two principal
types: built in during manufacture, and fixed *ad hoc* after
the floor is positioned.

The first demands an accurate knowledge of the position
and extent of the loads to be supported and is often used
where suspended ceilings are involved as the grid of the
ceiling and its relationship to the floor grid are design
decisions which can both be taken early. The position of
major services, such as ventilation ducts, are also usually
decided early and may very well be key factors in the choice
of structural system. This provision for fixings can also be
made during manufacture or construction.

Minor services, small pipes, cables and the like, may be a
matter for positioning on site and must therefore depend on
fixings which can be fairly freely placed in any position
within certain acceptable limits. In such cases it may be
desirable to allocate zones for services and ensure that the
structure in these areas is suitable to receive post-positioned
fixings.

Examples of fixings built in during manufacture are metal
supports such as 'bull-dog clips', female section of rawl bolt
and wooden plugs. Fixings attached later could again be
rawl bolts (drilled), rawl plugs, shot-fired fixings which
require sound concrete free of reinforcement, and toggle
type fixings suitable for use with any hollow section such as
clay or concrete infill blocks **18**.

3.04 Constraints

The principal constraints on the structural design of floors
are the Building Regulations, part D (Scottish Standards

and London Regulations as appropriate) and the universal
one of cost. Generally all design decisions are taken with
cost in mind, even if the result is not a saving on the
particular element being considered but merely helps to
keep down the cost of another. An example of this might
be the slight extra cost of a slab, to avoid the use of beams,
and thus making services cheaper.

Part D of the Building Regulations controls the calculation
of loadings, live or dead, for various building occupations
and also wind loads which, since the last amendment, are
now controlled by the newly revised CP 3, Chapter V, part II,
1971, which includes considerably more severe criteria than
those of the 1952 edition. It also contains empirical 'deemed
to satisfy' provisions concerning the design of timber joist
floors and reference to codes of practice covering design in
aluminium, prestressed concrete, precast concrete and
composite steel and concrete.

Since the fifth amendment (which followed the Ronan
Point disaster and now appears as D19 and 20 in the 1972
Regulations), it also contains provisions to limit structural
collapse due to explosion in buildings above five storeys
high. In the case of floors this limit is 70 m² or 15 per cent
of the storey area, whichever is the greater, and such
damage must not occur over more than three storeys.

4 Environmental control

The provision of environmental control is of course mainly
the function of the external envelope dealt with in the

earlier sections. But within any buildings there are often differences in conditions required in separate spaces which must be maintained by the divisions, one of which is suspended floors. The degree of difference required will determine the standard of performance to be provided by the floor. An extreme example might be a turkish bath above a refrigerated store, or, alternatively, a reading room below a sports hall. There are four main aspects of environment which are here dealt with separately.

4.01 Issues

Sound

Sound insulation is a subject frequently confused with sound absorption, but the two are quite separate matters. The first is concerned with preventing the transmission of sound from one space to another, whereas the second is mainly concerned with controlling the period of reverberation and thus the noise level within a particular space. Sound insulation with which we are concerned here has two aspects, airborne sound and impact sound. The latter is usually the greater problem especially as regards transmission downwards through floors.

Heat and humidity*

Humidity is not treated as a separate subject because, although it is an important aspect of environment, it is closely related to and usually controlled by heat (eg in winter internal humidities are usually low because of the low moisture-carrying capacity of cold outside air which is heated and introduced into the building without adding any further moisture). Complete air-conditioning of course overcomes this. The thermal capacity of the floor *and its finish* are here most important.

The heat resistance of an internal floor is frequently unimportant. This is obviously so when the same conditions apply on storeys above and below. Consideration must be given to floors which project through walls, and are therefore more vulnerable. Sometimes careful consideration may be required, and it may also be necessary to consider the prevention of condensation, a problem more usually associated with the roof **19**.

Light

The passage of light through internal upper floors is not often a factor in design but there may be occasions when light from above is needed in a storey below, in which case there can be two design conditions:
1 the floor is still required for support
2 no support is required, permitting an opening or glass laylight.
There may also be occasions when observation is required from one floor to another for supervision or other reasons. Reflection, especially from ceilings, may also on occasions be desirable.

Air

Air movement between storeys is usually undesirable for fire prevention reasons. Natural ventilation normally operates in individual storeys only and mechanical ventilation is controlled. Penetration of floors by air is not normally a problem and would only occur where floor construction was deliberately of the open grid type, such as metal platforms for factories. Air movement is necessarily prevented in ducts and similar vertical shafts which are sealed off at floor levels.

*See AJ Handbook of Building environment section 12 SERVICES DISTRIBUTION

4.02 Factors

Sound

The principal factor influencing the need for sound insulation is the use of adjacent spaces, separated by the floor in question. Sound does, however, differ from other

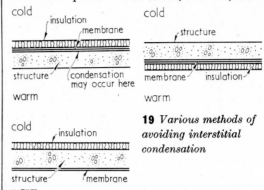

19 *Various methods of avoiding interstitial condensation*

environmental aspects as it is by its nature intermittent, and its transmission between spaces is almost universally undesirable. It differs for example radically from 'heat' which is a continuous condition, so that if two spaces require the same temperature there will automatically be no transfer between them, and the insulation value of the floor will be of no importance.

With sound, even if the two spaces have the same use, for example in offices or classrooms, it is still important to avoid sound transmission, either for reasons of privacy or to avoid diversion of attention from the sounds being produced in the relevant space. If particularly noisy conditions occur in one space, the problem is naturally more acute and can reach such proportions as to make the relevant space unusable (eg a noisy lift motor adjacent to a bedroom).

Factors affecting the prevention of sound transmission through floors depend to some extent on its nature. If impact sound is being considered, three alternatives are possible: use of resilient finish, alternative floor construction, floating floor (see 4.03).

If the sound is airborne, the main preventative measure is just sheer mass. The heavier the floor construction the more effective it will be against sound transmission, and this may often be a factor affecting design decisions on the structure to be adopted, especially in sensitive situations such as multi-storey flats **20**.

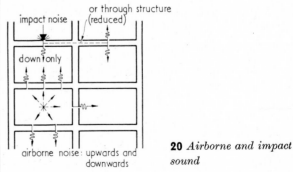

20 *Airborne and impact sound*

The other principal point is to avoid gaps which provide clear routes for the passage of sound.

Heat*

Transfer of heat between spaces is usually far less important, except in unusual circumstances, and the problem is mainly restricted to the external envelope. Floor structure selected on other grounds (structural capacity, sound insulation and so on) will normally be quite adequate in preventing excessive heat transfer. In many cases there will be no differentials and thus no transfer.

If there is a large differential, such as would be created by a refrigerated space or exposed underside, special precautions are necessary against insulation, especially as regards condensation (both surface and interstitial).

The type of heating system may also influence floor construction. In summer, buildings are subject to overheating, as floors have a capacity to absorb solar heat; in this respect too, floor finish plays an important part. Carpet, for instance, will take into the room the heat which would be absorbed by the floor if exposed. This capacity to store heat is deliberately exploited in underfloor heating systems, usually electric, where the floor is used as an accumulator to store heat provided at cheap rates and to emit it during the daytime occupancy period.

Modern lightweight construction with excessive use of glass and rapid heat-up systems, such as warm ducted air, has highlighted these problems. In such structure, the floors tend to form the main heat storage batteries, being the only element with any real thermal capacity. Thermal bridges, for example a floor structure exposed at the edge to the external air and thus becoming cold for some distance into the interior, can cause condensation problems and precautions should be taken **21**.

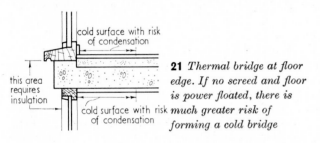

21 *Thermal bridge at floor edge. If no screed and floor is power floated, there is much greater risk of forming a cold bridge*

Light

The extent of the light transmission required between floors, and whether or not support at the upper floor level is still needed, will determine the construction to be used. If actual vision between floors is needed, a simple opening or clear glass will be required, making the use of the floor surface impractical. Examples of this type may be found in departmental stores and public buildings, especially halls, which provide for vertical circulation.

Reflection, usually from ceilings, may be a factor to be considered in deep buildings when natural light is still considered advantageous **22**.

Air

Normal building construction is such that no question of the passage of air between floors arises, except at openings specifically provided for access purposes. Thus the floors do divide the buildings into separate zones so far as air movement is concerned. As odours are airborne, the same applies to them.

Natural ventilation via windows is normally effective within single floor zones only. Artificial or mechanical ventilation is used to ensure air changes in situations where natural ventilation is considered unsatisfactory (eg deep buildings, polluted external atmosphere).

Spread of fire and particularly smoke, considered the greatest danger to life in outbreaks of fire, depends largely on air movement and this is the main reason for preventing the circulation of air between zones; especially between floors. The Building Regulations part E (and appropriate standards in Scotland and London) state that compartment floors shall be imperforate with certain specific exceptions to allow for passage of services and so on.

*See AJ Handbook of Building environment SERVICES DISTRIBUTION

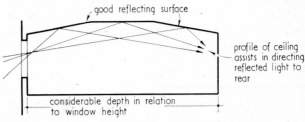

22 *Reflection from ceiling in deep buildings (see* **25** *for specific types)*

4.03 Solutions

Sound

The best solution to unwanted sound transmission is to avoid it completely by appropriate planning, ie do not put noisy spaces adjacent to quiet ones. However, sound transmission between adjacent spaces, if at least one of the spaces is occupied, is always undesirable and floor construction must always take account of this.

Fortunately, except in small domestic buildings, floors are usually of heavy construction (reinforced concrete is much the commonest material). The solid in situ floor will always provide a better barrier to airborne sound than lighter precast or composite floors, and metal floors are less effective still. The effectiveness of a floor as a barrier to airborne

Table i *Table of sound reductions*

No	Construction	Average sound reduction (100 to 3200 Hz), dB
1	Concrete floor (rc or hollow pot slab weighing not less than 220 kg/m²) with floor finish	45
2	Concrete floor with floor finish of wood boards or 6 mm thick linoleum or cork tiles	45
3	Concrete floor with floor finish of thick cork tiles or of rubber on sponge-rubber underlay	45
4	Concrete floor with floating concrete screed and any surface finish	50
5	Concrete floor with floating wood raft	50
6	Concrete floor with suspended ceiling and hard floor finish	48
7	Concrete floor with suspended ceiling and wood board floor finish	48
8	Concrete floor with suspended ceiling and floor finish of thick cork tiles or rubber on sponge-rubber underlay	48
9	Concrete floor with 50 mm lightweight concrete screed and hard floor finish	48
10	Concrete floor with 50 mm lightweight concrete screed and floor finish of thick cork tiles or of rubber on sponge-rubber underlay	48
11	Concrete floor weighing not less than 365 kg/m² (rc slab 150 to 180 mm thick) with hard floor finish	48
12	Concrete floor weighing not less than 365 kg/m² with floor finish of thick cork tiles or of rubber on sponge-rubber underlay	48

NB all these constructions have an average 'slope', ie an increase of insulation per octave of 4 to 6 dB over the range used

sound is in direct proportion to its weight. As an example, Table i shows the sound reduction in decibels for a range of floor constructions of varying weights.

With impact sound, weight again is of paramount importance. Prevention of impact sound penetration is usually dealt with by the use of resilient finishes (carpet or foambacked plastics) on conventional floors, or the use of pugging and hardboard below the finished floor (only in timber joist construction)*. Alternative floor construction may be necessary if the finish alone is inadequate, or the final (and most expensive) resort would be to employ a floating floor, consisting either of a concrete screed or a wooden floor on battens separated from the structural floor by a flexible carpet of glass fibre **23**.

Transmission of sound horizontally via the structure must not be forgotten and the solution to this problem is structural discontinuity; not always easy to achieve **24**. Finally the principal route for sound transmission is via any actual openings between spaces. This is more of a problem in horizontal than in vertical transmission but care must be taken to ensure that all routes by which sound might penetrate (such as gaps around ventilation ducts or pipes) are properly sealed.

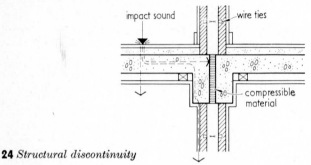

23 *Schematic principles of floating floors*

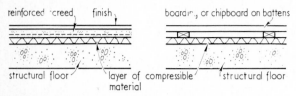

24 *Structural discontinuity*

Constraints

These are contained in the Building Regulations part G which relates only to the sound transmission between dwellings, and also from other purpose groups to dwellings (but not vice versa). G3 is the Regulation concerned with floors and specifies that certain floors shall have 'adequate resistance'. These are floors separating individual dwellings or separating a dwelling and any part of the building not used exclusively with the dwelling, unless used only for repair and maintenance. 'Adequate resistance' is not defined but 'deemed to satisfy' examples are given; these are described in Parts 2 and 3 of Schedule 12 to the 1972 Regulations (Part 1 deals with walls) and the approved constructions are shown here in **25**. But the associated structures (walls, windows etc) must also meet the standard shown in **26**. These requirements are in Regulations G4 (for rooms below the floor) and G5 (for rooms above the floor where only airborne sound is considered). These regulations also refer to a table giving appropriate sound reductions (for airborne) and sound levels (for impact sound) over the frequency range from 100 to 3150 Hz (5 octaves) under certain test conditions laid down in BS 2750:1956.

Heat

As with sound, the best solution is to avoid the problem by designing space relationships so as not to have thermally incompatible spaces adjacent. If impossible, the first approach to a solution is to use a form of structure with heat-resisting qualities. This might conflict with some requirements (eg sound transmission) but might also be compatible with others. Thus hollow reinforced concrete beams have better heat resistance than solid reinforced concrete, and a lightweight screed which lessens structural problems is better than normal cement and sand. Suspended ceilings provide a considerable increase in heat insulation. If the normal structure still proves inadequate to meet

See Sound insulation of traditional dwellings BRS Digest 103, p8

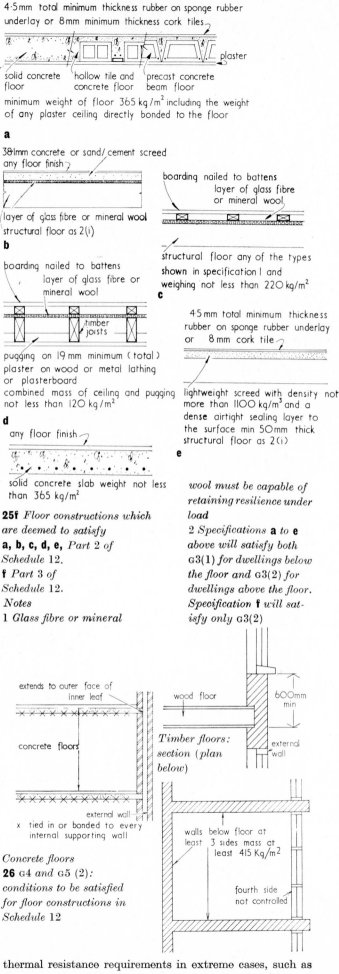

25f *Floor constructions which are deemed to satisfy*
a, b, c, d, e, *Part 2 of Schedule 12.*
f *Part 3 of Schedule 12.*
Notes
1 Glass fibre or mineral wool must be capable of retaining resilience under load
2 Specifications **a** *to* **e** *above will satisfy both G3(1) for dwellings below the floor and G3(2) for dwellings above the floor. Specification* **f** *will satisfy only G3(2)*

Concrete floors
26 G4 *and* G5 (2): *conditions to be satisfied for floor constructions in Schedule 12*

thermal resistance requirements in extreme cases, such as those mentioned earlier, consideration must be given to applying additional insulation. In the case of refrigerated

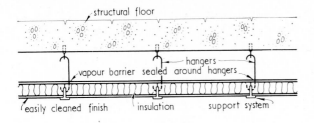

27 *Construction over cold store area. Insulation may* *also be fixed direct to underside of structural floor*

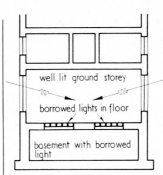

28 *Natural light to basement through floor*

29 *Typical section of glass and reinforced concrete floor light (precast)*

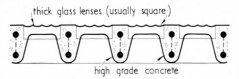

spaces, this is usually carried out by the specialist firms. In the past, cork has been the most usual medium, but recently the considerable range of expanded or foamed plastics has been used. Considerable thickness may be involved (200 to 230 mm is quite usual), and some form of support system is needed for the roof.

This can take the form of hangers from the structural floor above or application of a non-absorbant, easily cleaned finish. In high budget jobs, enamelled steel sheet may be used but a patent spray gloss finish is usually adequate. The question of surface and interstitial condensation also arises, although with modern expanded plastics the struc-ture is usually sealed cell which does not permit vapour penetration; none the less, the use and position of a vapour barrier should be considered **27**.

For less extreme cases, such as an unheated space adjacent to a normal heated space, some applied insulation may be desirable. Rigid types are cork, lightweight screeds (foamed concrete or lightweight aggregate), expanded plastics (such as polystyrene and polyurethane) and fibre boards.

The expanded plastics are much the lightest and therefore the most efficient, but, as might be expected, they have the lowest crushing strength. They may be positioned above or below the structure where crushing strength is not im-portant, but rigidity, permitting widely spaced supports and lightness, is significant. In such situations the ex-panded plastics perform well.

When insulation is placed above the structural floor, crushing strength is important and a suitable finish is necessary. Lightweight screeds are generally suitable for all finishes but expanded plastics would indent under impact if used directly below a flexible finish and either a screed or some rigid material, such as hardboard, would be needed as a sub-base.

One problem of lightweight screeds is the quantity of water they require in laying, and therefore the length of time they take to dry out before finishes can be applied. The flexible types of insulation are glass fibre and mineral fibre, manu-factured in flexible mats and generally used above ceilings, though occasionally used to achieve sound insulation below floor screeds (see preceding section on constraints).

In all circumstances where insulation is necessary, the importance of using a correctly placed vapour barrier to avoid surface and interstitial condensation cannot be overemphasised. The general principles are illustrated in **19**, but in some constructions careful calculations are needed to ensure the avoidance of interstitial condensation*. However, such instances are more frequently found in elements of the external envelope.

Constraints

The Building Regulations part F are concerned only with dwellings and lay down standards for thermal resistance of external elements but do not cover internal subdivision. The same applies to the Thermal Insulation (Industrial Buildings) Act 1957 which affects only factory roofs. Thus

*Condensation in buildings: part 1 MPBW Design guide. HMSO

the only constraint which applies to the thermal resistance of the internal subdivision of buildings are the usual ones of cost and design standards. In most cases other standards tend to exercise greater influence and automatically provide adequate thermal performance. When special insulation has to be introduced the cost is usually low except for the special case of refrigeration.

Light

The only case it is possible to envisage when passage of light between floors is desirable is the transfer of light downwards (eg into the basement area). The old pavement lights are a typical case except that they are really an external element and thus outside the scope of this study, but a similar situation could arise within a building which had a well-lit ground floor and an unlit basement area or, of course, between upper floors **28**. In cases where the floor still needed to be used, the almost universal solution would be the glass lens and reinforced concrete construction usually supplied in precast sections and capable of sustain-ing all normal floor loadings **29**.

Where support is not needed, though vision is usually desirable, the most natural solution would be a simple opening with gallery railings for safety. Museums, art galleries and department stores are typical of buildings where such openings might be found, creating a unity, between several storeys and giving an entirely different aspect to interior environment **30**.

Laylights of obscured or clear glass may be used in situa-tions where sound transmission should be reduced or where clear vision is to be prevented by the use of obscured glass **30b**.

Where deep buildings need the assistance of reflection this will usually be from the ceiling, and the use of a good

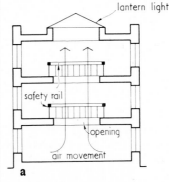

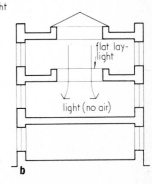

30 *Openings in floors:* **a** *galleried building between storeys permits air movement and through* *vision;* **b** *flat laylight, no air movement and no vision if obscured glass used, but no fire protection*

reflecting surface (light coloured and fine-textured) will assist. A suitable profile may also assist in directing all reflected light to the rear **22**.

Constraints

The Building Regulations part E control the compartmentation of buildings and would make the use of openings in floors impossible in many cases. For example, in industrial buildings and in all buildings more than 28 m high, all floors more than 9 m above ground level must be compartment floors and therefore imperforate.

There are also other restrictions that limit the use of openings between storeys (See The Guide to the Building Regulations 1972, p62, Reg E4). The additional normal constraint of cost also applies and if, for example, a glass and concrete floor were used, the extra cost over normal construction, would need to be weighed against the advantage gained by natural light.

Air

Two aspects have been mentioned, natural and forced movement of air, ie mechanical ventilation. Natural ventilation is frequently adequate and will occur through openings or even through the cracks around them when closed. This will probably be sufficient to supply the needs of the occupants of normal buildings who usually have at least 15 m³ (500 cu ft) of air per person, so that one to two air changes per hour is sufficient. Only in crowded spaces, such as small auditoria, is mechanical ventilation essential.

In multi-storey buildings vertical movement of air currents is not desirable because of the risk of fire spreading. However, openings in floors are necessary for the movement of people and goods. Such openings are difficult to close by normal methods and although one can imagine a horizontal sliding shutter operated by a fusible link or similar system, it would be a clumsy device and other methods are usual. These consist of forming protected shafts around all horizontal openings containing the means of vertical movement (stairs, lifts, services or ventilation air itself). Access to these shafts is through fire resisting doors with some form of automatic closing device. One anomaly of such provisions is that there is nothing whatever to prevent the occupants from propping or fixing the doors open in order to avoid the inconvenience of opening them during normal use. However, it is difficult to see how this can be overcome except by the judicious use of notices appealing to good sense.

When mechanical ventilation is used, ducts are usually supported from the suspended floor (often by using a suspended ceiling), affecting the design of transverse beams.

Some modern high velocity systems can operate through ducts only a *fraction of the size* of normal speed systems (which might operate at say 370 m (1200 ft per minute) to

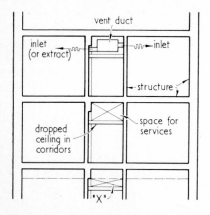

31 *Ventilation ducts above corridors. Note space greatly reduced at* x *if main beams span across building*

avoid undue noise). Such ducts can be surprisingly *large* and in office structures are frequently sited above corridors where ceiling levels can be suitably dropped **31**.

Constraints

The Building Regulations part E control the compartmentation of buildings and the principal intention is to avoid the free movement of air, and hence of smoke and fire, between compartments, which frequently means between floors. Regulation E9 controls openings through compartment floors; E10 protected shafts and E11 fire resisting doors. (See The Guide to the Building Regulations 1972 pp 94 to 98)

5 Security

This aspect is dealt with under the three main headings of fire, actual physical attack (such as theft and burglary) and attack by chemical or radioactivity.

5.01 Issues

Fire

This is the most universal and probably the principal risk to be countered under the heading of security. The main issues connected with fire prevention are first, the need to keep the fire load low by the use of non-combustible materials, second, to restrict the spread of fire by suitable planning and construction and third to use construction which will not collapse for a reasonable time under the effect of fire.

Physical attack

This is only of great importance in certain high risk buildings such as banks, or parts of other buildings which might contain valuables.

Chemical and radioactivity

These are confined mainly to special applications. The existence within buildings such as factories, laboratories and hospitals, of apparatus or processes which produce chemicals (usually in gaseous or liquid forms) corrosive to some normal building materials, or physical rays (x-rays and others produced by nuclear reactions which are harmful to human life or health), call for special protective measures.

5.02 Factors

Fire

The main factor affecting choice of construction in relation to fire is the building type according to occupancy. Some buildings such as residential and institutional buildings (eg flats, hotels, hostels) have a high inherent risk to human life but probably a fairly low fire load. Others such as warehouses might have low risk to life (virtually nil occupancy) but a high fire load due to the type of goods stored, and high risk that outbreaks of fire would not be noticed during the early stages.

The first type do not require a long period of resistance to collapse if good means of escape are provided and these are well protected from the penetration of smoke or fire. In the second type a long period of fire resistance is likely to be required and means of escape will be less important.

Compartmentation to restrict fire spread is probably a factor in all buildings. The most important element in achieving this is suspended floors and frequently all upper floors have, by Regulation, to be treated as compartment floors. Rules affecting these include reference to treatment at the edge of floors to prevent fire spreading from storey to storey via weaknesses in the outer cladding or in the joint between the floor and the vertical wall.

In actual floor construction used, the three points to be watched are:

1 resistance offered to penetration of fire by the whole floor
2 protection of the supporting structure to ensure that it will survive at least as long as the floor
3 prevention or limitation of flame spread along the surface of finishes.

Availability and type of fire fighting appliances does have some effect on building design. For example the fact that there is a Code of Practice covering residential buildings over 24 m high relates to reach of mobile fire escape ladders. Although there are no specific provisions it is customary for planning departments to insist on consultation with the local fire prevention department before approving many types of building.

Physical attack

The principal factors affecting the risk of physical attack are:

1 locations of the relevant space
2 strength of the surrounding structure.

In relation to floors it is necessary in planning to consider ease of access to storeys above and below the space (if any) and the extent of supervision. Apart from this the structure must be of appropriate strength in relation to the likelihood of attack and its likely nature (eg by amateur thieves or professional experts).

A normal reinforced concrete floor will be quite sufficient to deter any attack if what is stored is of little value, but vaults of a safe deposit will call for very special construction. It is important to note that construction with high fire nature will usually be resistant to physical attack.

Chemical and radioactivity

The principal factors involved here are the extent, degree and type of pollution and the possibility of the hazard affecting the building structure and its occupants.

Chemical pollution may be a considerable hazard in certain factories, particularly affecting floor finish and subfloor construction. If gaseous, then the soffit of the floor or ceiling may also need protection. In laboratories protection is normally only needed against occasional spillage, and gases are extracted.

x-rays or sub-atomic radiation are dangerous to human health and, if very severe, to life. Here again the extent of the hazard determines the degree of protection required. The special problems of atomic power stations are really outside the scope of this study, but x-ray rooms in hospitals and laboratories are dealt with. Apart from intensity, the point about all rays is that (like light) they are multi-directional and therefore demand screening of the whole perimeter of the source-containing space.

5.03 Solutions

Fire

Considering first the question of the high-occupancy type building on the basis that the ultimate fire hazard is loss of life, avoidance of fire risk is once more a question of planning, in this case the provision of adequate and properly designed escape routes.

Next in priority is the avoidance of a high fire load, or in other words the use of non-combustible materials. Obviously if a building contains nothing that will burn there is no fire risk. Such an ideal situation never really exists,

because non-combustible structure, services and finishes are always accompanied by combustible furnishings or other goods.

It is however possible to do a great deal towards keeping fire load (quantity of combustible material) to a minimum. In this respect things are not always what they seem; at first sight a multi-storey carpark might appear to be a high risk building but on examination it can be seen that the structure itself is completely non-combustible, as it has no finishes. The combustible contents are limited to the petrol in the cars' tanks, a small quantity compared with industrial installations. Thus the chance of a large-scale fire developing quickly is small and the Government permits relaxation of regulations on compartmentation of this type of structure.

Compartmentation is the next line of defence and is controlled by Regulations (see 5.03 Constraints) which limit compartment size in terms of floor area and volume. Floors must and do play their part in subdividing the building; it is convenient to treat each storey as a compartment. This brings in the question of fire resistance periods; no period is unlimited and no fire can burn for ever. Some reasonable period must be assumed for people to make their escape, for fire services to arrive and act, and so on. Thus the maximum period required of any structure element is four hours, and the minimum half an hour.

In theory these periods have nothing to do with combustibility and a combustible material, say for example a heavy hardwood of substantial thickness, could provide quite a long fire resistance period whereas a non-combustible material such as thin sheet steel has virtually no resistance period at all. Fortunately it is not difficult to achieve long fire resistance periods with ordinary building materials, particularly brick and concrete. For instance, in the case of floors, solid concrete 150 mm (6in) thick, will provide four hours.

Lightweight screeds of foamed slag or vermiculite and sprayed ceilings of vermiculite plaster or asbestos, either direct on the soffit or on to metal lath suspended from the floor, are effective in increasing the resistance period. In this case we have, as might be expected, a similar situation to prevention of thermal transmission, in as much as lightweight mixes are more effective than normal Portland cement concrete for providing long fire resistance periods. (See The Guide to the Building Regulations 1972, pp 78-80). The protection of the supporting structure can be achieved either by making this inherently resistant, as with a reinforced concrete beam with suitable cover to the steel, or by adding protective finishes such as the lightweight mixes and sprays mentioned earlier. The object is to slow the temperature rise of the structural material itself to the point where collapse would occur. When structural steel is used, the protection may either be solid, by casting concrete around the steel member, or hollow by framing out **32a, b**. The same applies to columns. (See The Guide to the Building Regulations 1972, pp 75-77).

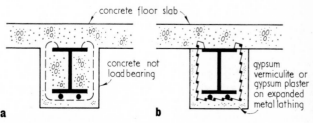

32 *Fire-protecting steel:* **a** *solid protection;* **b** *hollow protection*

Naturally avoidance of unnecessary openings in floors is critical and where these are necessary for vertical access they must be protected. This subject has in fact been covered in 4.03 (Air), but it is important enough to stand repetition.

It is usually necessary to protect vertical circulation by enclosing it in a fireproof ('protected') shaft which, in effect, becomes a vertical compartment penetrating the normal horizontal ones. Access is gained by self-closing fire doors. Where other elements such as ducts and service pipes penetrate compartment floors, the space around them must be fire-stopped, and in trunking a self closing shutter device (damper) must be provided. It is important to realise that the prevention of smoke penetration is as important as flame, if not more so, as this is often the lethal factor in deaths from fire because it causes panic and suffocation.

Where compartment floors join cavity walls it is important to see that the cavity is fire-stopped in line with the floor to ensure that no route for smoke or flame exists around the edge of the floor. The spread of flame from storey to storey at the junction of compartment floors and external walls is not strictly controlled by Regulations, as it would depend on the extent and relative situation of unprotected areas. These are controlled by the distance of the wall from the boundary, obviously intended to control fire spread from one building to another.

At certain distances, the situation is reached where the whole wall can be an unprotected area. This means no fire resistance and would therefore not prevent spread of fire between storeys. The Regulations do, however, state that where compartment floors join external walls, compartment or separating walls, the junction shall be properly bonded and fire stopped (See E9, *The Guide to the Building Regulations* 1972) a measure obviously designed to prevent fire spreading around the edge of compartment floors. There would thus seem to be a gap in the Regulations, and in cases where external walls are permitted to consist entirely of unprotected area, it would still be wise to take some precautions against spread of fire between storeys.

Within compartments, flame spread can (and must by Regulation) be reduced by the use of suitable finishes which are classified 1 to 4 and 0 (totally non-combustible).

Constraints

As might be expected these are extensive, as fire hazard prevention has been one of man's principal problems since the dawn of civilisation and especially since urban communities were built. The subject has therefore attracted much legislation, although unfortunately that concerning building standards and planning is not, as it should be, collected into one publication.

The most extensive legislation affecting building design is contained in the Building Regulations (1972) part E and the similar controls in Scotland and London. But whereas the Scottish and London Standards cover means of escape, the Building Regulations of England and Wales do not, and controls which do exist do not cover all buildings. These include the Factories Act and the Offices, Shops and Railway Premises Act. There are also some non-mandatory advisory publications such as the Code of Practice for blocks of flats over 25 m (80ft) high, mentioned earlier.

As previously stated, any gaps in fire regulations are usually covered by an unofficial arrangement whereby local planning authorities submit proposals received to their local fire department and withhold planning permission unless the architect agrees to follow the fire prevention officer's recommendations. The system seems to work reasonably well but architects may save themselves and their clients trouble by early consultation with the local fire department before making a planning submission. Some gaps now being covered by the 1972 Fire Act.

The Building Regulations (and Scottish and London standards) are mainly concerned with the control of structural standards and finishes so as to inhibit and contain fire outbreaks. Part E of the Building Regulations is typical, classifying buildings into eight groups—three residential, three places of work, one public assembly and one storage. The effect is to limit the size of building or compartment according to class, and to control the resistance period of those elements separating compartments and providing support. Floors are the principal element and the rules include reference to all floor openings and protected shafts used to connect storeys. The Regulations also control the finishes on ceilings and soffits in regard to surface spread of flame, but these particular Regulations do not, perhaps surprisingly, apply to floor finishes.

In conversion jobs (such as a three-storey house into three flats) strict application of the Regulations could make the job prohibitively expensive and thus not viable. In such cases applications for relaxation are usually viewed sympathetically, providing means of escape is good. The recent 1972 Regulations gave local authorities permission to deal directly with this type of case, which had previously to be referred to the minister.

One further important constraint on the effects of fire hazard is the attitude of insurance companies. They exercise control by adjusting premiums to relate to the fire risk, and maintain experts on their staff to advise. So they are frequently responsible for the introduction of expensive preventative measures such as sprinkler systems (capital cost less than extra premiums).

Physical attack

The main defence against theft or burglary must be the use of physically strong materials. The value of contents must control the degree of protection. Strong rooms are the usual solution to the storage of valuables encountered by the average architect and they generally present three points of attack—walls, floor and roof, and access door. In this article we are concerned only with the horizontal elements of floor and roof.

Because of the weight involved only the roof is of concern in the normal single-storey structure. Usually such a roof would not form part of the general floor structure but would be constructed below it preferably with a gap of at least 460 mm between it and the soffit of the floor above to enable observation to be maintained **33**. Lack of storey height might prevent this arrangement. The construction usually consists of 460 mm of heavily reinforced concrete, using both high tensile steel and high grade concrete. The steel is generally far more than is required structurally, and must be closely spaced to make cutting an access opening as difficult as possible. Some of the steel is sometimes supplied in chain link form.

This installation is a matter for specialist firms. Drawings detailing the position of steel are treated as secret documents and never issued to site or the architect who is dependent on the reputation of the firm involved as guarantee of sound workmanship. As ventilation is a problem, condensation may form on the soffit and the use of anti-condensation plasters and paints is normal.

Occasionally a lesser degree of security for, say, confidential documents may be needed and can be dealt with adequately without specialists if the architect simply uses higher grade materials and workmanship for the floors above and below such spaces.

Constraints

There are no statutory requirements and any constraints on the architect will usually arise out of his clients' preference and costs. Most banks have their own specific requirements.

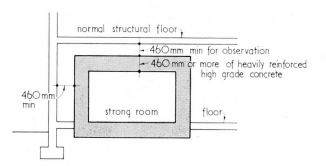

33 *Roofs of strong rooms*

Chemical and radioactivity

Heavy chemical pollution found in factories (usually liquid) is generally dealt with by the use of ceramic tiles. The fully vitrified type is resistant to all normal acids, solvents and alkalis, in fact virtually inert to all chemical activity. The main problem lies in the joints, where any penetration of corrosive liquids through joints or cracks could quickly attack structural concrete with disastrous results. A variety of acid-resisting resins are available, usually as patented mixes for bedding and jointing.

Alternatively, acid-resisting monolithic floors including epoxy resins and some asphaltic compounds are available (see information sheet 3 FINISHES). Thus the maintenance of an impervious finish when chemical spillage is present on upper floors is essential.

To suit less aggressive conditions in laboratories, some plastic sheet floors are suitable. Plastics such as pvc are acid-resistant and, if joints are welded, form an effective barrier against normal spillage. Solvents are another matter and if these are likely to be a problem the use of ceramic tiles is normally advisable.

Gases are not usually a problem, as anything corrosive to buildings would normally be injurious to health and would therefore have to be dealt with by special ventilation. In certain cases, however, their effect has to be considered and the use of special paints (eg chlorinated rubber) is the normal solution. Usually it is the support members rather than the floors themselves which require protection.

Radioactivity, unlike chemicals, does not attack normal building materials but is a hazard to health and life and must therefore be contained within the space where it is generated. Its main attribute (on which its usefulness often depends) is that it will penetrate most normal materials and, like sound, its penetration is best prevented by very heavy materials.

Lead sheet is most effective but expensive. The thicker the lead, the more effective it becomes and expert advice is necessary to determine the weight of lead necessary in any particular situation. As it is not self supporting, lead sheet is most easily laid above floors, but this does raise certain problems as it must be continuous with or lap the lead sheet protection to the walls below **34**.

A cheaper alternative is barium sulphate (Barytes) a heavy mineral which resists x-rays and similar waves. Although a considerably greater thickness is required than the lead equivalent, the cost is still less. It can be used with cement to form barium plaster or concrete and is also manufactured

in blocks similar to normal concrete building blocks. These could be used laid flat on top of structural floors to provide protection, but depending on the degree of protection needed the usual system on floors is to use barium, a plaster ceiling or screed, or both. As with lead, the need for continuity with the wall protection must not be forgotten.

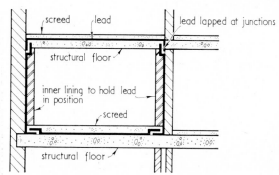

34 x-ray *rooms sheet lead protection*

Constraints

The only situations where these forms of pollution are likely to be encountered are in factories, laboratories and hospitals. The provisions of the Factories Act, Offices, Shops and Railway Premises Act, and Area Hospital Board Regulations will govern the standards of protection to be provided.

6 Services

The three main elements of building are structure, enclosure and services. This handbook deals with the second and this section with intermediate floors, but interaction is inevitable and consideration of the effect of services on such floors is essential. It is also important that services should be considered in the early design stage and decisions on structure and enclosure considered with respect to the service needs for support and accommodation.

6.01 Issues

First, number and type of services supported: these will include the usual environmental services (even the simplest of buildings must have some form of heating as well as water supply and drainage), but in certain buildings such as laboratories they become the controlling factor in the design of the whole building.

Second, location: a choice of above, below or within the depth. The position and number of vertical distribution groups is related to this.

6.02 Factors

These include first and foremost deciding the routes for various service systems. Some form of grouping is usual, controlled by or connected with the structural system. For instance, in a multi-storey office block there may be a choice between a vertical mains system with submains running horizontally at each floor level or a horizontal mains system at ground floor level with submains running vertically at intervals with the columns **35**.

Ventilation differs from other services because of the considerable size of trunking carrying air. Thus it tends to have a disproportionate effect on the structure in comparison with piped services and electric cabling which are usually small. If a full air-conditioning system is used including both input and extract ducts to make the building completely independent of natural ventilation, a considerable space allocation will be needed and inter-floor space must be provided by suspended ceilings. Pipes are normally sufficiently rigid to need only intermittent support, whereas cables require continuous or more frequent support. The contents of pipes are also factors to consider (eg hot water results in thermal movement and can create noise).

The weight to be supported is also a factor although often ignored in structural calculations or taken only as a hypothetical overall unit per sq meter perhaps included with the suspended ceilings. Except in special cases, weight is small compared with the actual dead and live loads which the floor is designed to support.

The need or otherwise for flexibility controls many decisions. A simple example of this is the use of movable partitions which involves at least the reconnection of switch drops. It is possible, however, to have a complex of, say, 15 services, any one or all of which might be required in any modular situation on any floor of the building. Such a degree of flexibility is very expensive.

Accessibility is a separate factor but closely connected with flexibility. A high degree of flexibility needs a high degree of accessibility to enable outlets and connections to be altered. Such accessibility may be from below via removable ceiling panels or from above via removable duct covers, panels and so on (see also section 9 CEILINGS).

A useful feature of certain floor constructions is their ability to contain small services (eg the hollow steel or composite floor and reinforced concrete structures incorporating hollow blocks and screeds) which can at times be usefully exploited. When underfloor heating is used, conduits and water piping can be incompatible with the heating installation and must be carefully detailed.

Finally there is the possibility of using the heat storage capacity of the floor structure as a medium for taking advantage of off-peak electricity tariffs.

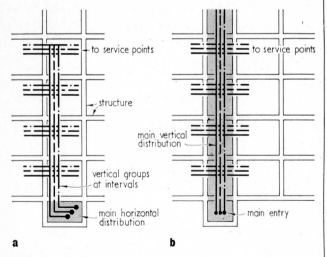

35 *Mains systems:*
a *horizontal;* **b** *vertical*

6.03 Solutions

Probably the most usual solution to the accommodation of services is to run them below the structural floor, exposed or concealed in a suspended ceiling. Services thus accommodated will normally include steel conduit or mineral insulated copper covered cable (MICC), telephone cable and internal drainage.

Ventilation in the shape of sheet steel (or possibly plastic) trunking will also be found in some buildings.

Because ventilation ducts are by far the greatest problem owing to their size, considerable depth might be needed between the soffit of the floor and the suspended ceiling. In plan, these are best located in corridor ceilings where a ceiling height less than that in major spaces is acceptable. This is especially so if the floors span across the building leaving the space free of beams, or alternatively if a double spine of columns is used to keep down beam sizes over corridors. Alternatively ventilation requirements may be subdivided between several ducts and thus accommodated in a smaller depth; this is particularly appropriate when air is to be introduced near external cladding.

The number of alternatives is almost limitless but in **36** an attempt is made to show a few of the principal ones in a normal office or corridor-access type structure.

Such services supported below a floor serve the storey above via small holes in the floor itself except for the central ventilation duct which might serve the same storey **36**.

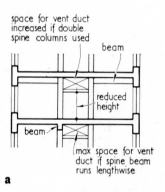

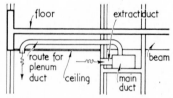

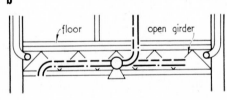

36 *Examples of principal methods of incorporating services into floor construction in normal office or corridor access type*   *structure (see also* **30**)*:* **a, b** *using space over corridor;* **c** *using full span deep lattice girder (or castellated beams)*

In buildings requiring a complex set of services as well as the normal environmental ones, the problem is considerably greater. However, laboratories requiring many different piped services to benches and apparatus, may still be planned on the central corridor system and the space over the corridor can be used to accommodate the main pipe run with groups of branch laterals. Need for a degree of flexibility or the ideal of a modular building with every service available in every module will result in more complicated solutions. These could be removable panel floors above a structural floor, removable panel ceilings to allow services to be fed downwards, or a full intermediate service floor requiring in effect two structural floors per storey **37**.

When only environmental services (including communications) are involved, accommodation within the floor slab is a feasible, neat and economic solution, as it dispenses with the need for suspended ceilings, saving the cost of the supporting grid and reducing storey heights. Certain steel cellular floors are particularly suitable and patent systems are available to overcome the problem of cross-connection between the linear spaces made available by the structural system **10**.

In concrete hollow block floors, the problem of cross-connection can be overcome by using ducts in screed depths or at a point in the structure where continuity is not needed **38**. In all cases, the available space is too small to accommodate more than electrical and communications services. It is, however, sometimes possible to find space for the heating distribution system above floor level around the perimeter and thus still to avoid the use and cost of suspended ceilings.

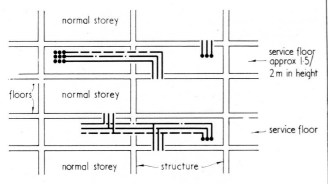

37 *Intermediate service floors; services can run in* *both directions and feed up or down*

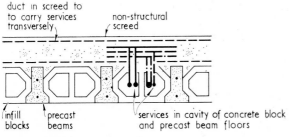

38 *Concrete block and precast beam floors as service distributors*

If the structural floor is unsuitable for services in the normal situation, the possibility of accommodating them above the structure may be considered. Some form of screed is nearly always needed and although thin screeds (see information sheet 2 SCREEDS AND SUBFLOORS) are unsuitable, normal cement/sand or lightweight screeds of around 50 mm are thick enough to take metal, fibre, plastic ducts or electrical conduit.

Various patent types exist and as the structure is not penetrated, the problem of distribution in the two horizontal dimensions can be overcome **39**. Such ducts are particularly useful for the distribution of electrical power and communications as they can be sited to give direct access from floor outlets to office desks or machines. They may either be buried in the screed, covered only by the floor finish, or exposed with removable cover giving immediate access along the full length.

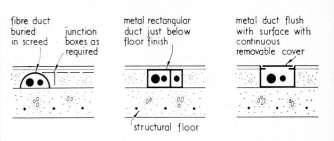

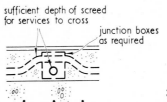

39 *Various methods of installing ducts above floors*

In buildings such as cinemas, large halls and so on, there are normally large spaces, such as that under galleries or raked seating, where services can easily be accommodated, and the large volumes enclosed in the usable spaces create a completely different problem in which suspended floors occupy a place, but a much less dominant one.

In small domestic buildings, services are generally housed on a largely *ad hoc* basis, buried in the plaster and notched into floor joists where the pipes or cables run at right angles to them. The principles to be observed here are to see that buried services (especially electric) are properly protected by metal covers against the casual screw or nail, and that joists are notched only where the effect on structural strength is not important.

Attempts have been made, with some success, to provide prefabricated service cores for houses, and standard kits, at least partly pre-made, for installing heating and electrical distribution systems. No doubt development work will continue on these lines.

The support of services above floors creates no problems, and below floors it may be achieved either by combining with the support system of suspended ceilings or by using a separate system, usually of lightweight metal construction attached to the soffit by fixings such as those illustrated in **17**. The range of patent supports available is adequate to deal with any service support problem and unless there is a particular space/route or weight problem, the choice is unimportant and may be safely left to the contractor, subject to inspection on site.

The combination of various services (eg heating, lighting, ventilation) into one unified system usually occurs within the context of suspended ceilings.

Constraints

There are no legal constraints affecting the relationship of services to suspended floors other than the need already mentioned to fire-stop openings in compartment floors provided for their passage (see AJ Metric Guide to the Building Regulations, p78).

There remains the inevitable constraint of cost and it will be clear from this analysis that the choice of service supports and accommodation systems can have a considerable effect on overall cost. This is why it is important to make decisions on service systems in conjunction with structural design.

7 Finishes

As the subject of finishes is dealt with later in information sheet 3 FLOOR FINISHES, it is only outlined here by summarising the main principles involved.

7.01 Issues

Floor finishes may be defined as the provision of a final upper surface to the structural floor which is aesthetically acceptable and physically suitable in the context of the use envisaged and which where necessary makes a contribution to noise reduction or insulation.

7.02 Factors

This category includes colour, texture, softness and sound absorption which are all important in obtaining the desired ambience within the room.

Other more purely physical or practical characteristics affected by the type of use are anti-slip qualities, resistance to wear, desired life-span, maintenance requirements, prevention of impact noise transmission and possibly resistance to chemical attack and liquids.

7.03 Solutions

The final finish must be controlled to some degree by the structural and subfloor beneath.

Hard monolithic

These include granolithic, terrazzo, asphalt or pitchmastic, magnesite and epoxy resin. The last two are really top-pings laid along with a cement base. There are a number of other patent systems that can be trowelled into the actual structural concrete if required.

Hard tile

These are floors composed of pieces, either manufactured or natural, usually laid and jointed in cement and sand, but sometimes in other materials where special conditions apply (eg chemical attack).

This type of floor includes mosaic (ceramic not glass) ceramic tile, clay tile, concrete tile, terrazzo tile, slate, quartzite, stone and marble. They are available in a wide range of colours and patterns and are usually comparatively costly except for the ordinary (misnamed) quarry tile and concrete tile.

Wood

Types include softwood boarding, really suitable only as a subfloor for carpet or sheet material, hardwood boarding, hardwood block, pine block, parquet (blocks forming patterns), plywood, hardboard and chipboard. The last three are again really suitable only as subfloors but are sometimes stained or lacquered and used as a finished surface in light traffic areas.

Thin tile or sheet

Types include thermo-plastics, vinyl-asbestos, pure pvc, rubber, cork and linoleum. The first two are only available in tile form, whereas the last four are available in tile or sheet. Rubber and pvc are also available with integral foam backings to give extra resilience and quietness. Costs vary considerably from the very cheap thermo-plastics to the rather costly foambacked rubber or pvc. All require a completely flat smooth subfloor, and for most this must be dry and vapour-proof. As might be expected the thermo-plastics are rather noisy whereas the foambacked types are quiet.

Carpet

Principal types available are traditional woven, looped pile, tufted carpets and felts. Those other than the woven types are frequently set in latex rubber and may include an integral underlay. Carpet tiles are a comparatively recent innovation and are often made of animal fibre. They have the advantage of easy renewal of worn sections.

All carpets may be made from a variety of materials including natural wool, other animal or vegetable fibres and a whole range of manmade fibres of which nylon and Tery-lene are but two.

Constraints

There are no mandatory constraints. As stated earlier the Building Regulations which control the flame-spread characteristics of wall and ceiling finishes do not control floor finishes. The principal constraint is likely to be cost, which can vary considerably, and no complicated calcula-tions are required to assess the effect on the total cost per unit of floor area of the building, as there is a simple direct ratio of 1:1.

8 Checklist

8.01 Functions of floors
● Fundamental functions (support; stability)
● Incidental functions (environmental controls; security; accommodation of services; facilitation of circulation)

8.02 Structural functions
Consider the following factors:
● Structural relationship with rest of building
● Loads and spans; materials
● Dimensional discipline (particularly with system or dimensionally co-ordinated building)
● Statutory controls

8.03 Environmental control functions
Consider the following factors:
● Sound insulation (airborne & impact)
● Heat and humidity control; control of passage of light and air
● Statutory controls

8.04 Security functions
Consider the following factors:
● Fire risk
● Other forms of risk (physical attack; chemical and radioactivity)
● Statutory controls

8.05 Incorporation of services
Consider the following factors:
● Grouping and routing of service runs
● Flexibility and accessibility of services
● Support of services

8.06 Floor finishes
Consider functional requirements of finishes:
● Physical (anti-slip; resistance to wear; resistance to chemical attack; lifespan; maintenance; quietness)
● Aesthetic/psychological (colour, texture, softness, appear-ance)
Consider types:
● Hard monolithic; hard tile; wood; thin tile or sheet; carpet

8.07 References
These will be found at the end of information sheet SUSPENDED FLOORS 1, part 2.

Information sheet
Suspended floors 1

Structure

This information sheet covers in greater detail the structural function of the suspended floor already outlined in the preceding technical study.

1 Function of structure

1.01 Support

The implications of this function have been dealt with at reasonable length in the technical study p855; here are covered the types of load which occur.

Normal densities in buildings where people live and work are quite low and never produce anything like the notional loadings used but allowance must be made for their accessories (eg furniture, books, tv sets) and for the occasion, such as a passing procession or special event, when for a short while people might crowd together on one small piece of floor. In such buildings as stadia or auditoria, high densities are normal and are allowed for.

The storage of goods, or warehousing, is a special case. Here again notional figures are available but care is always needed to make sure that the actual load does not exceed these. Surprisingly high figures can be produced by the storage of everyday materials such as paper or canned foods, depending of course largely on the height of stacking and the amount of free space left for access **1**.

A combination of goods and people has already been mentioned and occurs in virtually all human occupancy buildings. Certain areas may need floors of additional strength when it is known that they will be used largely for storage (eg archives) where racking and other equipment designed to reduce storage areas can produce high loads **2**. Finally loads can include moving (eg vehicles) or vibrating (eg machinery) loads. Notional loadings are available for moving vehicles based on certain assumptions (one is that vehicles in buildings move comparatively slowly thereby avoiding impact and braking loads). Machinery can vary from light machines such as lift motors to heavy cranes or large compressors, exerting tremendous actual loads greatly exacerbated by vibration created by moving parts.

Loads of this type are almost invariably transferred directly to the ground by special structure and foundations. Only comparatively small machines such as lathes, drills and so on are treated as part of a notional factory floor load. Even then by far the majority of cases would be sited on ground floors, but 'flatted factories' are becoming more common and the need to concentrate industrial processes at high densities is only a parallel example of the smaller argument in favour of high human density.

Vibrating machinery is usually mounted on anti-vibration mountings **3** to reduce its effect on the structural support system and also (often of greater importance) to reduce structure-borne sound transmission.

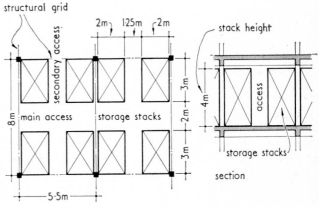

1 *Effect of stacking heights and access on overall loading in warehouses. Assume actual weight of material to be stored is 408 kg per m³. Load over area of actual storage stacks:*
$4 \cdot 0 \times 408 = 1632 \; kg/m^2$
$= 16 \cdot 0 \; kN/m^2$. *Total area of structural bay*
$= 8 \cdot 0 \times 5 \cdot 5 = 44 \; m^2$.
Area of storage stacks

$= 4 \times 2 \cdot 0 \times 3 \cdot 0 = 24 \; m^2$.
Then actual average load on floor is:
$$\frac{16 \cdot 0 \times 24}{44} = 8 \cdot 73 \; kN/m^2$$
Note: some extra allowance would be needed for weight of mechanical stackers (eg fork lift trucks) and floor is designed to ensure distribution of load over whole area

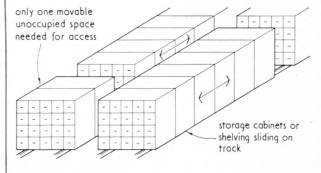

2 *Highly concentrated archive storage*

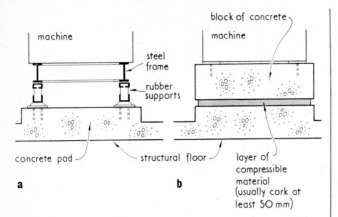

3 *Anti-vibration mountings and pads. Note in method* **b**, *the thicker and heavier*

the block of concrete, the more effective is whole system

1.02 Structural bracing

As well as providing normal resistance to gravitational loads acting directly downwards, floor structure may, and often does, serve a second structural function as bracing for the whole building (or part of it) against horizontal stresses created by wind loads, transferring these through the building by acting as a very thin horizontal plate girder and enabling the whole building to act homogeneously to resist wind force. Such a reaction is dependant on the strength of connections **4**.

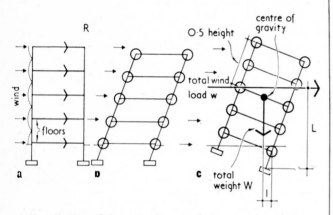

4 *Contribution of floors (and beams) to resistance to wind:* **a** *floors transmit loads through to rear wall* R; **b** *effect on building if joints*

marked o *are pin-points with no rigidity;* **c** *effect of wind if joints* o *are rigid connections. For stability:* Wl > wL

1.03 Insulation

The structural part of floors usually plays the major part in all insulation systems. To play its designed role of load support, structure is essentially the thickest and heaviest part of the total element, making it a good insulator. The possible exception is heat which is better resisted by light cellular-type materials but even here the structural floor will often be the main contributor, especially when of the hollow block and beam type.

Air and light penetration are clearly simple matters which any normal floor will prevent, although perhaps the example of very slight air penetration through floors, as illustrated by pattern staining on wood joist, or even hollow block floors after a period of years, ought not to be ignored if only because of its aesthetic nuisance value **5**. Heat and sound are both complicated matters usually requiring to be dealt with empirically by reference to tables showing

u-values and sound reductions respectively for a variety of normally used composite constructions which have been laboratory or site tested (**22**, p863 gives some examples of sound reductions). The capacity of the floor to retain heat must be considered and either used to supplement the heat supply, or eliminated completely. Finish can prevent absorption by the floor. Neglect of this property can lead to overheating in the summer. Possible impact noise can also be dealt with to a large extent by use of the appropriate finish (see **7**). As the only useful figures are those for a complete composite element, there is no point in quoting any for the structural floor alone, which is the subject of this information sheet.

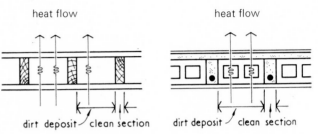

5 *Pattern staining due to heat flow causing convection currents*

2 Physical shape

2.01 Flatness

The essential quality of floors is the flatness of their top surface; the underside may assume a variety of shapes (arched, ribbed, waffle and so on) according to the structural solution adopted in order to permit easy movement of people; permit easy movement of objects or goods; support internal subdivisions; permit flexibility of internal subdivisions. As economical building demands that any element be as thin as possible (this may at times conflict with aesthetic choice), the development of floor structures has proceeded along the lines of achieving maximum spans with flat slabs of minimum thickness.

2.02 Exceptions

There are a few exceptions to the 'flat and level' rule for suspended floors. As discussed previously, they include ramps (if these are regarded as floors at all rather than means of vertical access), stadia and auditoria, where stepped floors are needed to achieve satisfactory sight lines, and sloping storage floors in some multi-storey carparks to serve the double purpose of storage and vertical access, and to avoid the need for additional ramps (**3b**, p855).

The stepped floors of auditoria may well often assist the structural engineer, as they provide an inbuilt vertical depth in the risers between tiers, which can be most valuable in stiffening the structure, enabling actual slab thickness to be reduced **6**. A further possibility is the need for self-draining floors (eg in wet areas of factories), more usually found at ground level. In such cases a decision must be taken on whether to rake the structural slab, and in turn whether also to rake the beams, or whether to form falls only in the screeds, involving thicknesses and therefore loads **7**.

3 Loadings

Loadings or total load to be supported is, with its span (in either one or two directions) the main factor controlling

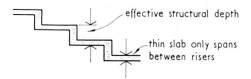

6 *Structural advantage of stepped floors*

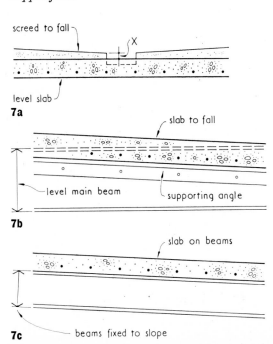

7a

7b

7c

7d

7 *Methods of forming falls.*
7a *Superimposed screed, level slab. Note: depth needed at x to form fall in gutter unless this can be*
recessed into structural slab (depending on direction of span); **b** *level beam, slab to fall. No screed;* **c** *beam fixed to fall;* **d** *finishing screed*

the design of the structural floor. Total load is a combination of the dead load, the imposed load, the effect of any live (moving) load and the wind load. Dead and imposed loads are infinitely the more important as regards floor design in most cases.

Determination of all loads sustained by a building is completely controlled by mandatory regulations: the Building Regulations 1972 in England and Wales and the appropriate standards in Scotland and London. In the original Building Regulations, dead and imposed loads were dealt with in full, and only wind loads were controlled by reference to a BS Code of Practice (CP 3: Chapter V), although in fact CP 3 also covered the other aspects of loading. There were slight differences between the two documents.

With the issue of the 1972 Regulations all loadings are now controlled by reference to CP 3: Chapter V: part I; 1967

(Dead and imposed loads) and part II, 1970 (Wind loads). CP 3: Chapter V is basically a metric document (imperial conversions also given) which ties in with the new metric Building Regulations 1972.

3.01 Dead loads

This is defined in the Building Regulations as 'the force due to the static mass of all walls, partitions, floors, roofs and finishes including all other permanent construction'. CP 3: Chapter V: part I: 1967, lays down that the unit weights of materials shall be those given in BS 648 or the actual known weight of material used. If partition positions are fixed, their actual weight or an overall equivalent solid load not less than that of the patritions must be allowed for. If open floor space is left for movable partitions, the allowance for these is to be one third of the weight per metre run of the partition per square metre of floor with a minimum of 1 kN/m² in office buildings. Actual weight of tanks and their contents are considered as dead load but account must be taken of the effect when empty on the structure.

3.02 Imposed loads

This is defined in the Regulations as 'the load assumed to be produced by the intended occupancy or use, including distributed, concentrated, impact, inertia and snow loads but excluding wind loads', and are to be calculated in accordance with CP 3: Chapter V: part I: 1967. This document has been considerably revised and the original subdivision of all buildings into eight classes abandoned. Table I now contains the basic information on unit-imposed loads to be used for each type of building and is much more comprehensive than the original table, covering in all over 60 types of building arranged alphabetically from 'flat galleries' to 'workshops'. Some building types have a number of subdivisions, each with different loadings (eg colleges, subdivided into assembly areas with fixed seating, assembly areas without seating, bedrooms, classrooms, corridors, dining rooms, dormitories, gymnasia, kitchens). There are also classes which are not strictly buildings but merely associated, such as 'balconies, catwalks, driveways and ramps' and so on. Figures are given in kN/m² but also in kgf/m² and lbf/m².

The highest loading shown is 12·5 kN/m² (type storage areas), higher than the old class 8 which converted to 9·58 kN/m². The lowest is 1·5 kN/m² (houses, dormitories maisonettes, flats). This compares with the old class 1 (houses for single families) which converted to 1·44 kN/m² but is less than the old class 2 (other residential buildings) where the figure was 1·92 kN/m² so that the new rules represent a degree of relaxation in certain cases. This, however, is not universal. For example hospital wards which were included in the old class 2 are now fixed at 2·0 kN/m². Generally the figures compare quite closely with similar types in the old code and are in effect a metric 'rounding off' of the old imperial units, with a more extensive degree of subdivision into types.

Another change is that the old system of specifying a minimum load to be carried by any 12in (304·8 mm) wide strip of slab spanning between supports and a further minimum load to be carried by any length of beam supporting a slab (obviously designed to prevent overloading occurring at certain points due to the possible occasional heavy concentrated load), has been replaced by a simpler system of specifying a single concentrated load to be

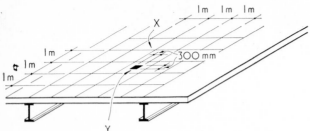

8 CP 3; Chapter V; part I; 1967. Application of distributed and concentrated loads. Distributed load considered as applied evenly over each square meter: X. Concentrated load considered as applied over area 300 mm × 300 mm at position where it will cause greatest stress in slab: Y

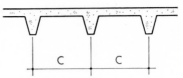

9 Definition of ribs or beams, Building Regulations, if dimension C is over 1 m / considered as beams; if less: considered as ribs forming part of slab.

applied over any square of 300 mm side. This load has to be considered to be applied in such positions as would cause maximum stress or deflection (whichever is the design criterion) and is considered separately from the distributed load, ie the slab is not designed to carry both together **8**. The relationship between the intensity of the concentrated load and the distributed load per unit area varies from about 10:1 up to about 25:1, according to the type of building. Those buildings where heavy point loads are likely (eg x-ray rooms) come at the top of the range. Beams must be designed to carry the distributed load of the appropriate slab and the term 'beam' includes joists, ribs and trusses over a certain spacing. As some slabs are of ribbed nature, it is necessary to define which are part of the slab and which are beams. In the seventh amendment the minimum distance remains as before at 914·4 mm, but in CP 3: Chapter V: part I, it has been rationalised to 1 m **9**. Relaxation on the design load of beams where large floor areas are supported is retained and remains unchanged except for the metric rounding off of the figure of 46·45 m² (500 sq ft) to 46 m² at 5 per cent reduction and multiples thereof every extra 5 per cent up to 25 per cent maximum, Table I.

Table I* Reductions in imposed loads which can be made when an area of slab is supported by one single span of beam and exceeds 46 m²

Area exceeding (m²)	Reduction (per cent)
46	5
92	10
138	15
184	20
230	25

*Adapted from The Guide to the Building Regulations 1973 p22

The reductions allowed in column design according to number of storeys have been increased but are not recorded here as this section is concerned only with floors. The point is made both in the seventh amendment itself and in the Code of Practice that if any actual imposed load is known or is likely to exceed the specified notional load, then the actual load must be allowed for.

The amendment also includes a specific reference to houses of not more than three storeys and to be occupied by one family, offering the alternative of either using the Code of Practice or provisions given in the code itself which are in fact the same as those which applied in the old class 1, giving figures for a 1 m width of slab and single span of beam in addition to a unit floor loading **10**.

3.03 Dynamic loading

The Code is necessarily vague on the subject of moving loads. It states merely that where the possibility of using

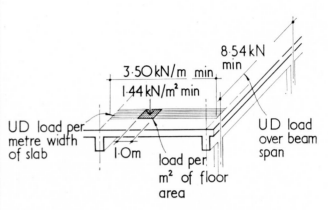

10 Regulation D2 (3) Alternative to CP3: Chapter V: part I, for floors of houses of not more than three storeys for occupation / by one family. (Note: cantilevers are to be treated as beams or slabs counting projection as span)

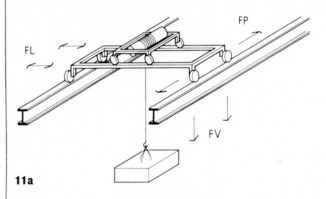

11a

11b

11a Dynamic loads or gantry cranes. Force lateral (FL) to rails to be taken as 10 per cent of crane plus load lifted if electric; 5 per cent if hand operated. Force parallel (FP) to rails taken / as 5 per cent of static load on wheels. Vertical loads (FV) to be taken as actual static load plus 25 per cent.
11b Lifting floor slab into place with crane

mechanical stacking exists (eg fork lift trucks) 'special provision shall be made in the design of the floors'. However it is specific on allowances to be made in the design of gantry crane rails, **11**, because although not strictly related to floors, may give some guide as to how far the effect of rolling loads increases stress as compared with normal static loads.

3.04 Wind loading

The Regulations define wind load as 'all loads due to the effect of wind pressure or suction' and make the basis of calculation CP 3: Chapter V: part II: 1970, but with two provisos mentioned later.

There is something of a history behind this which goes back, along with a number of other fairly vital matters, to the Ronan Point collapse. This episode led to an examination of large panel construction in tall buildings which led eventually to the production of the fifth amendment. The Building Regulations 1965 had always used CP 3: Chapter V: 1952 as the basis for wind load calculations and this was not officially changed until the seventh amendment, presumably because the revised Code has not been issued. In the meantime the BRS published a series of three digests (99, 101 and 105) followed by a revised digest 119 which replaced all three. This in effect was an advanced publication of CP 3: Chapter V: part II: 1970 which is almost identical, and BRS Digest 119 had for some time been the accepted basis for wind calculations although the actual Buildings Regulations were not brought into line until November 1971.

Wind loads are usually of much more significance in the design of walls and roofs, and stability of whole buildings, and usually have little effect on the design of intermediate floors. However, these do play their part as bracing and in the transference of loads across buildings **4**. This is an important function especially in high slender buildings, although in most structures the beams will be designed to take the major part of this duty. This however cannot apply in plate floor types of building where the duty of providing lateral stability, must be assumed by floors and columns alone **12**. Consideration should also be given to the effect of internal pressures on floors where differential pressures may exist on different storeys. Usually the air pressure inside a building would be approximately the same on each storey. CP 3: Chapter V: part II does give methods of approximately assessing the coefficient of the internal pressure (Cpi) as a proportion of the calculated external wind pressure. In tall buildings one would expect a greater pressure inside the upper storey due to high wind velocity, but the differences from storey to storey are too small to require special consideration in the design of the floor slab. However, this might not be so with a building in which what is known as a dominant opening occurs on one side of the building at one storey level and the other side in the adjacent storey, in which case a positive internal pressure on one side of the floor and a negative pressure on the other side would exist. This would create either an upward or downward force on the floor in question according to the direction of the wind, and although such conditions are generally unlikely, they are quite feasible during the construction period **13**.

The Code stresses the necessity of checking the design in respect of temporary conditions which might exist during construction. One such quite common condition which will occur on many sites is when a building is completed to the stage of having frame and floors but no enclosing envelope. In this case the wind pressure against the edge of the floor beams and columns and the frictional drag on the floors

themselves can create a critical load **14**. Because wind direction is usually horizontal, frictional drag on the floor slab itself occurs both above and below and does not therefore produce a bending moment in the slab but only a lateral force. The figures given in 14 are from BRS Digest 119 as the CP gives no actual guidance.

3.05 Collapse loads

Regulation D19, contained in the fifth amendment is designed to avoid the type of collapse which occurred at

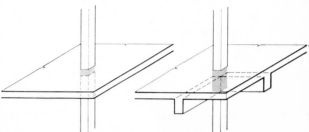

12 *Plate floors, rigid connections. On plate floors area available for forming rigid junction between vertical and horizontal structure is only fraction of*

that available in beam and slab floors. This may sometimes necessitate thickening slab locally around columns

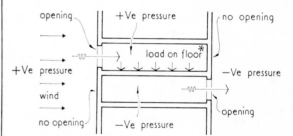

13 *Differential internal pressures (Cpi) between adjacent storeys. Unit load*

on floor* = positive pressure + negative pressure

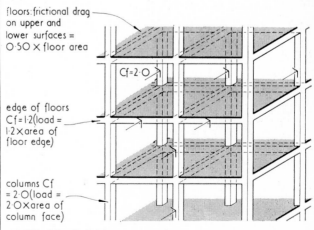

14 *Wind loads during construction*

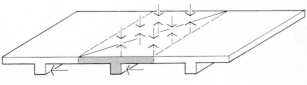

15 *Collapse loads on floors where no alternative support*   *exists*

Ronan Point and is mainly based on the provision of alternative routes for loadings in the event of the removal or collapse of a single structural member. If however no alternative route can be provided then the member must be able to support a load of 34 kN/m² considered to act over the whole area supported by the beam. The effect as regards floor slabs and supporting beam is illustrated in **15**. (For a full description of the effect of Regulations D19 and 20 see AJ Guide to the Building Regulations 1972 pp50/54. Regulation D19 also lays down that any structural failure shall be localised within each storey, and Regulation D 20 defines this as not exceeding 15 per cent of the area of the storey with an absolute maximum of 75 m². Regulation D 21 provides that buildings using rc storey height panels are deemed to satisfy D 19 if they comply with CP 116 Part 2 1969 and are classified as Gp 1 Structures in Addendum No 1: 1970 to that code.

4 Supporting structure

4.01 General

Floors may be integrated with (see 5.04) or act entirely independantly of the supporting structure. This may depend to some extent on the materials used. For example, if both beams and floor are of in situ concrete it is natural to make use of the floor as part of the beam in assessing its size. On the other hand a precast concrete floor supported by a steel beam would usually not contribute to its strength, although they can be made to act together and in certain cases this would be economically advantageous. With a wood joist floor, however, it would be virtually impossible to make the floor and beam act together.

Thus the choice of support system depends very much on the type of floor being used, and here again in almost all design decisions the two are interrelated in such a way as to affect each other.

4.02 Types of supporting structure

The principal alternatives are comparatively few and can be summarised as follows:
● Walls, single span direction or two-way
● Beam and column, single span direction
● Beam and column, two-way span
● Column only, plate floor
● Column only, mushroom type.

It is of course quite common to find more than one system of support in a single building, for example walls and beam column. These arrangements are illustrated in **16**.

4.03 Stages of structure and spans

Floors may in theory be classified in accordance with the number of separate stages making up the total structure, usually limited to a maximum of three. Thus a floor comprising main beams, joists and boarding is a three-stage structure. Similarly a concrete floor using tee-beams and infill blocks with a structural screed spanning between main beams could be called three-stage. A simple reinforced concrete slab spanning between beams would be two-stage as would joist and boards spanning directly between walls. A plate-type floor spanning either one way between walls

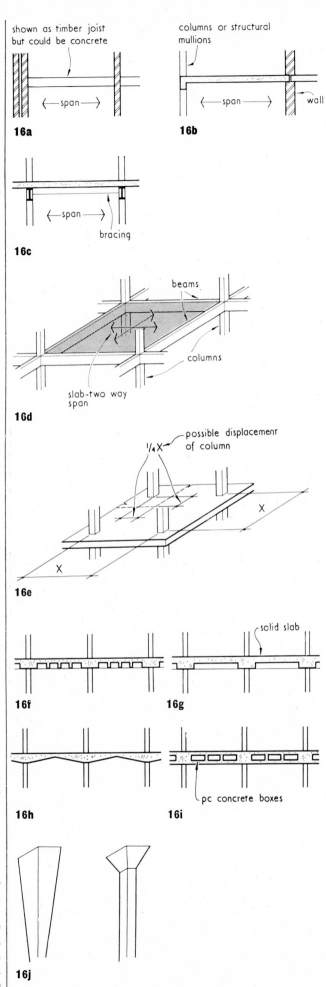

16a — shown as timber joist but could be concrete

16b — columns or structural mullions — wall

16c — bracing

16d — beams — columns — slab-two way span

16e — possible displacement of column — ¼X — X — X

16f

16g — solid slab

16h

16i — pc concrete boxes

16j

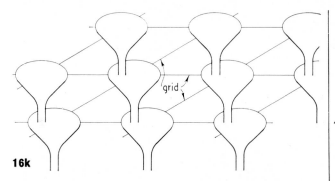

16k

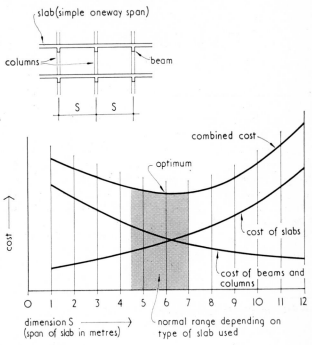

16 *Possible support systems:*
a *full wall support;*
b *spinewall to beam and column system;* **c** *full frame: one way span;* **d** *full frame: two way span (suitable for square or near square grids);* **e** *simple plate floor. Square grid two-way span;*
x = *maximum controlled by punching shear at columns in turn controlled by size of column and floor thickness, usually about 5 m. In some circumstances individual column may be displaced*
from its normal grid position by up to $\frac{1}{4}$x:
f-i *devices for increasing depth of floor at column positions without adding greatly to weight:*
f *coffered floor;* **g** *bonded plate;* **h** *tapered plate (one- or two-way);* **i** *hollow-celled floor;* **j** *tapered or capital-headed columns may be used to spread punching shear;* **k** *mushroom-headed columns and no beams, normally used for heavy loads*

17 *Graph illustrating cost: span relationship*

or two-way between a grid of columns would be a one-stage construction.

The question of whether or not to introduce an additional stage is a matter of economical spans. As spans increase so the cost of the floor slab or joists increases, as greater depth and more reinforcement is needed. Against this the introduction of a beam and possibly columns to split the span also means extra cost and at a certain span the 'break-even point' will be reached. The cost/span relationship for simple one-way span systems is illustrated in the graph **17**. Of course the situation is complicated by such considerations as whether or not to use single or two-way spans and the choice between beams and beamless or plate floors.

In addition there are frequently other design factors which affect or even control column spacings and support systems generally. For example the need for maximum flexibility of layout may be extremely important and demand a column free space say 15 m wide. This would almost certainly prohibit the most economical structural solution, but the additional cost would be acceptable.

4.04 Level

A further point concerning the support system is the amount of space occupied by it (depth) which is in turn affected by the relationship of top of supporting structure to top of floor slab. The most natural relationship is for the bottom of the slab to rest upon the top of the support systems, but there are variations **18**.

One of the advantages of plate floors is that no depth is occupied by beams, hence overall height and cladding costs are saved. On the other hand it may be desired that the beams are visible so that no height is lost, or alternatively space may be needed for services between the soffit of the slab and a suspended ceiling which can also accommodate the beams without adding to the overall storey height, providing that the beams are of a type which can contain openings for the passage of services. In some cases it may

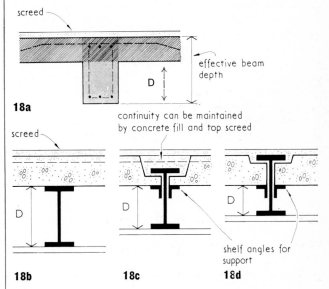

18 *Relationship of top of beam system to slab;* **a** *in situ concrete construction. Note: in this form of construction concrete hatched is all acting as beam, and that toned as slab hence that hatched and toned is in dual use* **b**
d *Cast in situ rc or pc beams cut away. Note: in* **a**, **b** *and* **c** *continuity of slab*
giving increased load or span and less deflection is possible whether precast or in situ concrete is being used, but this is not so on **d**, *where beam completely separates two spans in order to achieve minimum depth below slab soffit.* D *equals minimum depth to suspend ceiling support system in each case and depth for services*

be critical to maintain minimum overall storey height. An example of this could be a multi-storey car park where minimum headroom below beams must be maintained and where it is desired to obtain the maximum number of parking floors in a given height, perhaps controlled by the planning authority. In such cases the choice of materials is important, as if concrete is used for both slab and beams, the full depth of the slab becomes in effect part of the beam which can then be kept to minimum depth below the slab. Against this, the use of steel beams may result in a smaller effective depth and there would then be a case for positioning the upper flange within the depth of, or even level with the top of the slab. All these points are illustrated in **18**.

5 Accommodation of services within the structure

Large services such as ventilation ducts can only be accommodated in specially provided spaces such as are created by suspended ceilings. However, some services can be accommodated within the depth of the structural floor. Usually these are only the cable type services carrying electricity for lighting, power and communications.

The only other feasible possibility is small pipes, but problems of access for lagging or repairs and the general clumsiness of bends and junctions usually prevents this. One possibility which has been tried is to use the actual cells of composite steel and concrete floors as conductors of air for ventilation systems.

Fire protection and heating

In America steel structures have been given adequate fire resistance by filling hollow structural members with water, thus avoiding the need for casing, and it would seem feasible to carry this principle into cellular steel floors which could then have inherent fire resistance without adding concrete. In the event of a fire the whole building would become a natural thermo-syphon carrying the heat away from the source and distributing it rather in the manner of a normal boiler and radiator system. It is not beyond the bounds of possibility that such a system could be deliberately employed to heat the building. However, these possibilities are in the realms of conjecture and to be practical it is better to consider only the cable-borne services as suitable for placing within the structure.

In considering these, the type of floor most suitable is the hollow steel cellular type, but other types which have possibilities are those containing hollow clay tiles or concrete blocks which provide continuous hollow spaces in the direction of the span. Such a use is somewhat unusual and it is more common to place services either below the structure (if a suspended ceiling is provided) or above in shallow ducts in the screed, or both.

The use of spaces in the slab may nevertheless occasionally be worthwhile, especially if this can save the need for a suspended ceiling, and the additional storey height involved. The principal problem is that these spaces run in one direction only and if they are to be used some method must be devised to give one or more links at right angles.

This can usually be done by providing a metal duct in the screed above the slab, but if the screed is structural it would break the structural continuity and would have to be arranged at a point where this did not matter (such as above a beam or at a joint where a break in structural continuity is designed).

Breaking through at isolated points either upwards or downwards gives no problems as the hollow tiles or blocks have no structural significance other than as permanent formwork.

Timber floors are also generally useful for the accommodation of services and in this case even ordinary small pipes usually provide no problem. The space between joists or plywood web beams is adequate and services running at right angles to the direction of span can be accommodated

by drilling through the joist or web on the neutral axis or notching the top or bottom close to the point of support.

*Frank Lloyd Wright's
Johnson Wax building, US,
shown under construction
when each floor is evident*

6 Types of floor structure

6.01 General

Reasons for the universal use of concrete lie in its versatility, comprehensive strength and its non-combustibility and high degree of fire resistance which make compliance with the Building Regulations (and relevant Standards in London and Scotland) a matter of checking that the construction chosen on structural grounds has adequate fire resistance. The almost universal use of the simple joisted floor for two-storey housing has survived all attempts to find something cheaper and equally satisfactory. Furthermore it is not generally realised that timber joist floors can provide up to one-hour fire resistance. There are quite a lot of buildings outside the residential classes where compartment floors are not essential. This means that combustible material may be used and therefore timber floors are possible within certain size limits in all classes of building.

The 1972 Regulations also make possible the use of combustible material in compartment floors in group 3 (other residential) buildings up to four storeys in height and in floors in buildings of purpose groups 4 to 8 if altered, and after alteration not exceeding 15 m in height. These amendments are clearly designed to enable the use of existing timber floors to be maintained in alteration and conversion jobs.

Metal floors are non-combustible but have extremely little inherent fire resistance and are therefore more often found used in combination with concrete. The occasional special situation such as galleries in factory buildings, where steel grids or chequer plate are a natural part of the general structure are about the only examples of pure metal floors. Perhaps because their total area probably forms much the largest quantity of any single building element, floors seem to have attracted the attention of a host of specialist manufacturers and constructors. This is particularly so in the precast concrete field. Thus it is impossible to include in this Information sheet, descriptions and illustrations of all available proprietary types. Instead as a general guide one example of each main type is illustrated and the general characteristics described in Table II.

7 References

BRITISH STANDARDS INSTITUTION
CP 3: Chapter V: part 1: 1967 Dead and imposed loads [(K4)]
2 CP 3: Chapter V: Loading: Part 2 1970. Wind loads [(K4f)]
3 BS 648: 1964 Schedule of weights of building materials [Yy(F4)] *revised October* 1969
4 BRITISH RESEARCH STATION The assessment of wind loads Digest 119 1970, HMSO [(K4f)]
5 Building Regulations 1972 [(A3j)]
6 ELDER, A. J. The Guide to the Building Regulations 1972. London, Revised 1973, The Architectural Press [(A3j)(F7)]

Table II Types of suspended floor construction

Timber

Joist floor

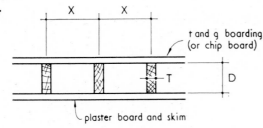

Normal timber joist floor: Building Regulations give span load tables for domestic buildings using joists at various centres up to 600 mm and differing dead loads. The range of spans runs from 1 m up to just over 5 m for joists 225 mm × 75 mm at 400 mm centres but it is probable that over 4 m spans, some of the other timber forms would become more economical or a beam should be introduced

Laminated

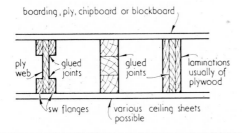

Laminated beams: using modern glueing techniques take possible economic single span range up to about 10 m

Formers

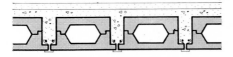

Formers: in situ tee-rib floors spanning in one direction can be produced by using permanent solid or hollow formwork spanning across beams and requiring only propping (usually at mid span) instead of standard soffit formwork. They have this advantage over hollow tile floors but are otherwise similar as they provide soffit for plastering. Material is usually cement-bound wood wool. This type usually prevents the underside of the rib being seen after concreting and poor construction can go undetected

Concrete precast (self centring)

Precast beam

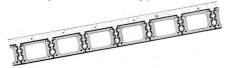

Precast beam: most common type is rectangular hollow beam containing its own reinforcement and designed to carry full loadings without assistance from in situ toppings or screeds. Usually sides are slightly tapered to allow for concrete grouting between beams and placing of top steel above main supports to give structural continuity between bays. Most economical spans in the 3 to 5 m range with depths from about 100 to 200 mm. Widths usually 300 to 400 mm

Wide slab

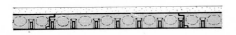

Wide slab: virtually the same as precast beam but in much wider sections, reducing number of pieces to be handled. Suitable for system building where appropriate handling equipment is available.

Precast beam and filler block

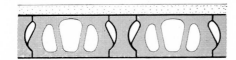

Precast beam and filler block: narrow solid precast beams usually of I-section and spaced at about 600 mm centres with hollow blocks of clay or lightweight concrete spanning between to provide floor which is structurally independent and has continuous top and bottom surfaces as in previous two cases

Trough

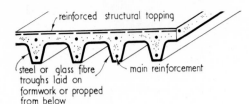

Trough: similar to the normal precast beam but having an open soffit and not suitable therefore for direct plastering. When suspended ceilings are required, however, this is no disadvantage and might even be helpful in providing a route for services within the troughs above main beams

Multi tee-beam

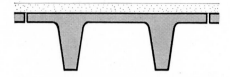

Multi tee-beam: bears the same relation to the last type as wideslab bears to normal precast beam. Simply a wide section of the trough with ribs at intervals; a minimum of two but can be manufactured with more if suited to the module and the depth/span/load requirements. This type is sometimes used in considerable depths up to about 75 mm for long spans

Precast I-beam

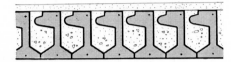

Precast I-beam: series of concrete I-beams rebated to fit together. This is one of earliest types of precast floor and still popular for many situations in non-modular building because the narrowness of the individual unit (about 140 mm) gives greater flexibility and they can be handled without heavy or complicated lifting gear

All the preceding six types are fully self-centring and require no propping during construction, a considerable advantage when speed of erection is important

Concrete precast and in situ

Precast plank

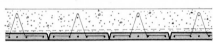

Precast plank: shallow precast flat member usually about 50 mm thick, reinforced with further reinforcement projecting from top. Serves dual purpose of forming part of structure and acting as formwork for in situ part of slab. Requires propping at intervals from below until in situ work has developed strength. A special development of the plank is a 50 mm soffit with protruding steel lattice allowing units of the order of 9 m² or more to be transported and erected

Precast beam and block

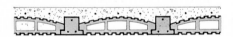

Precast beam, block and structural topping: very similar to precast beam and filler block except that precast beam and block are not structurally complete without assistance of screed, described in such cases more accurately as structural topping. Some reinforcement is normally left projecting from top of precast beam as shear connection and screed itself is reinforced with mesh. In such construction blocks may be regarded as formwork only for once screed has hardened it will span between precast beams as well as forming part of these in achieving necessary strength in direction of the span. Thus screed is doing two structural duties in addition to its normal one of providing suitable subfloor to receive finish. Therefore theoretically such floors should be economical, and generally are over appropriate range of spans (approximately 4 to 6 m). Not suitable if services are to be buried in screed which would break structural continuity

Wideslab panels

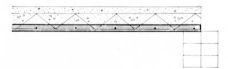

Wideslab panels: similar to precast plank but in much wider units with reinforcement projecting at intervals to integrate panel with in situ concrete to be poured to required thickness (probably about 100 mm) according to load and span. Panels can be made to any size, to suit room sizes if reasonable and given a high finish, only requiring decoration. Propping is necessary until in situ pour has hardened

Precast plank and filler block

Precast plank and filler block: very similar to precast beam block and structural topping but using only narrow plank at intervals instead of deep beam. The plank incorporates reinforcement for in situ concrete tee-beam resulting from filler block formers. Being shallow, planks will clearly need more propping during construction than precast beam type

Precast beam and slab

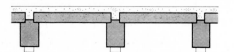

Precast beam and slab: simple form of construction consisting of precast beams with shear reinforcement projecting from top to connect with structural screed and give tee-beam effect. Space between beams is spanned by 2in woodwool or lightweight concrete slabs, leaving ribbed soffit

These have the disadvantages of requiring propping (sometimes only at midspan) until the structural topping has hardened which can hinder other operations and also it is not possible to bury ducts in the screed unless running with span, and not always then. The obvious advantage is that of giving the full value of the integrity of the in situ floor.
On the question of economic span/load factors they are very similar to the types described under precast concrete and are generally best used in the 3 to 5 m range with depths of 100 to 200 mm but have been used successfully at 8 m

Prestressed concrete

Prestressed concrete: technique of tensioning the reinforcement in order to place surrounding concrete in compression and thus limit deflection enables considerably longer spans to be achieved using any given depth of structure. It is however fairly complex and precise, and so far as floor slab construction is concerned, is only suitable for factory made units, not for use on site. This means that it is limited to types of floor containing some element of precast concrete work. Methods used for manufacture of precast concrete beams and planks are particularly suited to pre-tensioning techniques. Long casting beds are usually used along which wires can be stressed and sections can be formed or cut to length as required after casting. Post-tensioning is technique more suited to large beams

Plank

Concrete plank based floors are particularly suitable for pre-tensioning and in fact really need this technique to make them reasonably handleable on site. Pre-tensioning is also suitable for use in normal hollow precast beams or through sections enabling simple one-way spans of up to 15 m to be achieved without excessive depth

Beam and filler

Precast beam and filler block are also suitable and example shown is economical up to spans of 10 m with depth of only 225 m. No propping is needed. A point to be remembered is that precast beam floors are designed to carry super-imposed load which in such buildings as dwellings and offices will hardly ever occur. Result may be tendency for upward deflection to occur particularly over long spans and this can cause difficulties especially at junctions with vertical elements. Such deflections also tend to vary a little between individual beams, and use of good thick screed containing some reinforcement should be considered with view to avoiding trouble from differential movement after placing. It is well to remember that added floor screed or added plaster to cover discrepancies are costly and add weight. They should be considered in the overall economics when making a decision to use pre-stressed precast floor units

Metal

Open-grid

General: Metal is very seldom used on its own because of its low inherent fire resistance (metal used with concrete is dealt with in next section). There are, however, a few situations where some form of pure metal floor, usually steel, has advantages. These situations are galleries in factories or storage buildings where flexibility may be required, and metal grids with suitable associated bolt-together type support structure are easiest system to erect and dismantle. They are not light in relation to strength and although without fire resistance are totally non-combustible. Main types are:
Open-grid: gratings manufactured from strip steel bent and welded to form open grids with sufficiently close pattern to support normal foot traffic (but lethal to stiletto heels). Span depends on depth of steel strip but usually panels are small with supports at joints spaced at 1 to 2 m intervals (see illustration)
Embossed plates: solid steel normally up to 9·5 mm thick according to span required and embossed with pattern to provide anti-slip qualities. Normal diamond pattern is known as 'chequer plate'. Used in similar way to open grid but tends to be heavier. Nothing can drop through

Pressed steel planks

Pressed steel planks: known in the trade as PSP and used in vast quantities for temporary runway construction during the wars. Similar effect to open grid but manufactured in long lengths about 300 mm wide from galvanised sheet obtaining necessary rigidity by being formed into trough section and anti-slip qualities by having flat surface cut and bent to form separations. Placed side by side to form continuous open grid floor

Composite

General: normal reinforced concrete floors are in fact composite construction since they make use of the two materials, concrete and steel, to take advantage of properties of both. This process in which steel, always in form of bars or wires, is embedded in concrete is now so widely used that reinforced concrete has become accepted as single material in element analysis. In this section we are concerned with floors which use two materials (mainly same two) in different way. Because all types illustrated employ some concrete they do have degree of fire resistance which is usually adequate. Where steel is left exposed it is usually zinc treated. Principal types are:

Ribbed expanded metal

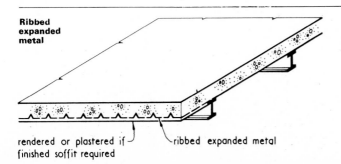

rendered or plastered if finished soffit required — ribbed expanded metal

Ribbed expanded metal: patent type of expanded metal including pressed steel solid ribs at close intervals. Expanded metal has close enough mesh to enable it to serve as formwork for concrete and rigid enough to only require propping at intervals. Its cellular form enables it to bond with concrete and act as reinforcement as well as formwork. A coat of rendering or plastering from below produces complete finished soffit if suspended ceilings are not being used. Fire resistance problems may arise with the exposed bottom of the filler beams which need protection

Filler beam

**Ribbed steel
and concrete**

Filler beam : modern version of old brick arch and filler beam construction using steel beams at suitable centres bridged by curved ribbed expanded metal and filled with concrete. Very suitable where heavy loads or machinery have to be carried as centres of beams can be varied at will to meet any particular circumstances. Fire resistance problems may arise with exposed bottom of filler beams which will need protection

Ribbed steel and concrete : profile is such that it provides sufficient bond to concrete to enable sheet to act as tension element or reinforcement in concrete structure. It is also such that if service requirements permit it can form attractive exposed soffit or alternatively suitable system of grooves for use of patent hangers. Requires propping until concrete develops strength but principal advantage is speed as several floors can be erected and poured at once. Frequently sheet steel is welded or shot fired to the main beams which provides necessary shear connection to enable part of concrete slab to act as compression flange of main beam, thus making it smaller

**Hollow steel
and concrete**

Hollow steel and concrete : similar in principle to last type, but steel portion of floor is formed in two profiled sections which when joined form series of hollow cells to contain services (usually only electrical and communication). Floor may frequently be strong enough to support poured concrete without propping. Shear connectors are provided to enable finished floor to act as composite structure. Very complete system of cross ducts and accessories is supplied to link cells of structural floor and provide virtually 100 per cent coverage of whole floor area as regards positioning of electrical or communication services. This can be very useful in offices especially of the open plan type where maximum flexibility is required

Special systems

Lift slab

Lift slab : study of types would not be complete without reference to special system of erection known as lift slab. This is development of ordinary plate floor in which all floor slabs and usually roof are cast in stack at ground level, after having erected foundations and columns, and subsequently jacked into position starting with roof or top floor and following on in sequence **1**. This means in effect that cost and time spent in erecting formwork in sequence floor by floor is replaced by cost and time of jacking whole floors up columns and then fixing. The system obviously involves patent apparatus and problems of accuracy and stability in erecting columns. It is always executed by specialist contractors. Floor plate itself may be either normal solid slab or any of number of types of beamless floor

8 Checklist

8.01 Function of structure
- Support
- Structural bracing
- Insulation

8.02 Physical shape
- Flatness
- Exceptions

8.03 Loadings
- Dead loads
- Inposed loads
- Dynamic loading
- Wind loading
- Collapse loads

8.04 Supporting structure
- General
- Types of supporting structure
- Stages of structure and spans
- Level

8.05 Accommodation of services

8.06 Types of floor structure
- General
- Selection and comparison of types and characteristics

1 *William Batchelor House, Coventry. Architect: M. W. Weedon and Partners. Example of high rise block of flats under construction using the lift slab system.*

Information sheet
Suspended floors 2

Screeds and subfloors

This information sheet continues detailed discussion of a further element of suspended floors—that between the wearing surface and the structural floor.

1 General

Usually some form of finish or wearing surface is needed on floors. Between this and the actual structural floor it is often necessary to provide an intermediate element as a suitable surface to receive the finish and possibly for other reasons. This material used in conjunction with concrete floors is usually a cement-based mixture and it has become customary to use the word 'screed' to describe such layers and then to extend the term to include all such layers below a floor finish. Included in this heading is the more general term 'subfloors' as there are many situations where other materials not accurately described as screeds are used.

2 Function of subfloors

When considering concrete floors the principal function of screeds can be classified as follows:

2.01 Surface

Generally surface finish which can be provided on the structural concrete floors is insufficiently smooth for thin tile or sheet floor finishes. Screeds, trowelled or floated to a smooth level surface, overcome this difficulty. However, when the floor finish is in itself a cementicious or similar mixture, the roughness of the structural floor surface is a positive advantage providing a mechanical key for surfacing material. Probably the smoothest surface of all is that provided by an asphalt subfloor. With certain very thin and flexible sheet materials such as pure pvc, this is the only subfloor really suitable.

2.02 Structural strength

If screeds are necessary it sometimes makes economic sense to make them contribute to the floor's structural strength by introducing shear reinforcement to ensure that they act in conjunction with the structural floor below. This however leaves no "making good" element in the process (see 2.07). This principle is fully described and illustrated in information sheet SUSPENDED FLOORS 1.

2.03 Services

Where screeds are not structural they can be used to accommodate shallow service ducts for electric power or communications. These are either buried, covered by the floor finish or left exposed for access at any point **1**. If the buried duct is close to the surface of the screed it may be necessary to cover the duct with small size mesh to avoid cracking.

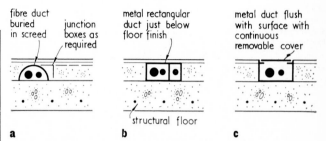

1 *Arrangements of service ducts in screeds:* **a** *buried;* **b** *covered by finish;* **c** *fully exposed*

2.04 Insulation

Screeds assist as part of the composite element in preventing transmission between storeys of sound, heat, light and air. The main role here is usually played by the structural floor itself. Screeds do, however, have a significant part to play especially in lowering sound transmission. Special systems to improve resistance to sound are discussed later. Heat transmission is normally only important in elements of the outer envelope (eg roof and lowest floor) and reference will be found in the relevant parts of the handbook to the use of screeds as heat insulation. Prevention of light and air movement are not normally considered in connection with screeds.

2.05 Security

The three hazards under the general heading of security discussed in the technical study SUSPENDED FLOORS 1 (AJ 19.4.72) were fire, physical attack and chemical or radioactive attack. Physical attack is not really a matter for screeds, nor is chemical attack which is usually a matter of choice of finish. Radioactivity can be resisted by the use of barium sulphate screeds and plasters in which case it is essential to ensure continuity **2**.

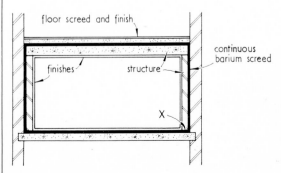

2 *Continuity of barium screeds. Note: lead sheet may be used at* x *to maintain continuity if load is excessive for barium sulphate screed*

Fire resistance can be ultimately determined by the screed, especially in hollow tile or hollow beam floors where the total concrete thickness due to the hollow construction may not be sufficient to provide the notional fire resistance period required. In such cases screed thickness may be considered part of the floor thickness.

2.06 Falls

Roof screeds are frequently used to provide falls necessary for self-drainage. Upper floors are normally flat but there are occasions, especially in factories, certain warehouses and laboratories, where falls to drainage gulleys are required either because the process contained in the building is wet or more usually to assist in washing down, especially where noxious or perishable substances are involved. Such falls may be provided by tilting the structural slab (see information sheet SUSPENDED FLOORS 1, figure **7** AJ 19.4.72) but it is usually more convenient to use a tapering screed and virtually essential if two-way falls are involved. This condition occurs usually only on the lowest floor of buildings.

Degree of fall depends on the nature of the floor surface and the importance of freedom from 'ponding'. If the surface can be relied upon to be true and smooth the traditional formula of 1:120 (25 mm in 3 m) should meet most requirements [now often 1½in (38 mm) to 2in (50 mm) in 10ft (3 m)]. In metric terms this might be rounded off to 1/100, a slightly better gradient, but screed thickness and hence dead loads rapidly build up if falls have to be provided over long distances (for example a continuous fall over say 6 m about 1/100 would be 60 mm which, allowing screed thickness of 40 mm, gives a maximum of 100 mm and an average of 70 mm thickness).

The arrangement of falls is always a matter of compromise between screed thickness and the frequency and extent of the drainage system. Certain floor finishes (eg quarry tiles) having the possibility of slightly lipped joints, might need greater falls to ensure reasonable run off. As an example only it is common to lay ordinary concrete slab footpaths to a cross fall of 1/40. Lightweight screeds are often used to keep down deadweight when falls are required **3**, but these tend to have longer drying times.

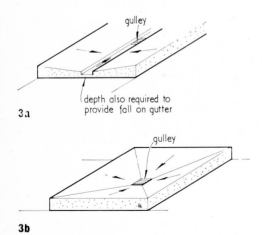

3a

3b

3 *Falls:* **a** *one-way falls;* **b** *two-way falls*

2.07 Construction damage

One case for using screeds is that, providing certain safeguards are taken, they can be applied late in the programme, even after the plastering of walls if necessary (but see 5.04—time for drying). This means that any damage to the

structural floor due to the building process (eg the use of internal scaffold, formwork props and so on) is automatically made good when the screeds are applied, leaving a surface unlikely to be damaged again before floor finishes are fixed. Of course the importance of this function will depend to a great extent on the method employed for construction of the main structure and the general discipline exercised by the builder during construction. If these are adequate, it may often be possible to finish actual structural floors ready to receive finishes direct, making good any minor defects with latex cement (see Power floating and trowelling, AJ 22.3.72, p637). Much will also depend on the type of floor finish being used, as with types such as clay tiles bedded in sand or cement, a very smooth surface is not needed.

3 Types of screeds

There are a number of different types of screed under the general heading of mixtures which are placed or poured and then set into a rigid layer. Those in general use follow:

3.01 Dense cement-aggregate mixture

These might be regarded as normal construction and are doubtless most widely used. They consist of a mixture of Portland cement and coarse sand; 1:3 being the traditional proportions. This, however, is often stronger than necessary and weaker mixes down to 1:4½ will reduce shrinkage. In thick screeds (over 40 mm), it is advantageous to use a graded aggregate so as to form a fine concrete which will have less voids and hence a lower cement ratio.

3.02 Cement and lightweight aggregate

Screeds of lighter weight down to about 50 per cent of dense screeds (or less in the case of vermiculite) can be produced using Portland cement and lightweight aggregate in place of sand. The lightest of all are exfoliated vermiculite and perlite but these materials are so water absorptive that drying out problems are invariably encountered. Others a little heavier and less physically fragile are expanded clay shale and slate, foamed slag and sintered pulverised fuel ash. Of these foamed slag is probably the most widely used; any problems arising out of residual sulphur in the raw material completely overcome by manufacturers.

Screeds of this type are generally used to avoid excessive weight where considerable thicknesses are needed to provide falls or bury services. They also provide good heat insulation, but are less effective in preventing sound transmission. For this reason they are more likely to be found on roofs than on suspended floors. They should not be laid in thicknesses less than 40 mm and will usually, unless the finish has good load spreading qualities, require a topping of at least 10 mm (preferably 15) of normal dense screed laid monolithically. On vermiculite/perlite screed this is always necessary regardless of finish.

3.03 Aerated concrete

Another method of lowering screed density without using lightweight aggregate is to introduce a foaming agent into a fine sand/cement/water mixture. These are usually liquids which must be used strictly in accordance with manufacturers' instructions. *Great care is necessary to ensure the correct proportions of each ingredient*, especially water which is affected by the water content of the sand being used. It is normally advisable to employ a specialist firm to carry out the laying.

The foaming agent creates a screed containing a multitude of tiny air pockets which reduce the density and therefore the weight of any given thickness with the same advantage of increased heat insulation and disadvantage of reduced sound insulation. As with lightweight aggregates they have less physical strength than dense screeds and unless a structurally strong finish is being used they should be finished with a 15 mm dense topping laid integrally (ie within three hours) to avoid indentation. At densities over 1280 kg/m³ this may be dispensed with unless heavy traffic is expected on the screed before the finish is laid. They can be laid in densities from 480 to 1200 kg/m³ with quite reasonable strength at 1200; a specially hardened top can be provided. They should not be laid in thicknesses less than 40 mm excluding the topping.

3.04 Anhydrite

Perhaps the most difficult problem to be overcome in laying all other screeds is that of drying shrinkage which, if adequate precautions are not taken, leads to the breaking of the bond between the screed and the floor below, warping or curling at edges and hollowness, all of which can lead to failure. Avoidance measures are dealt with later but the principal one is *adequate thickness in relation to area covered*. In recent years increasing use has been made of synthetic anhydrite (anhydrous calcium sulphate), virtually the same material as most hardwall plasters. Used with a specially graded aggregate at about 1:2½, it has the unique advantage of having virtually no drying shrinkage, allowing large areas to be laid without risk of curling at a thickness of about 25 mm. Furthermore as almost all the water is used up in chemical action there is little left to dry out and the normal drying time is only about 10 days. Volume for volume it is considerably more expensive than cement-based screeds but as it can be laid so thinly it can compare reasonably providing depth is not required for other reasons. It also compares reasonably in cost with other materials having similar characteristics, such as asphalt, but does not of course have their advantage of water resistance. Anhydrite screeds must be laid by specialist firms who are usually the same firm dealing with floor finishes, a satisfactory arrangement which avoids responsibility disputes.

3.05 Modified cement and sand

Many attempts have been made to increase the versatility of ordinary cement/sand screeds by the preparation of admixtures which affect the quantity of water necessary for workability, and therefore the drying time and theoretically the shrinkage. Similar admixtures are often used in concrete for similar reasons. Some screed admixtures are designed to improve adhesion to the base concrete. The architect would be well advised to exercise great caution in specifying such admixtures to be used by the general contractor. Results are always dependent on site conditions and failures can be the cause of unpleasant responsibility disputes with great risk of consequential loss (eg floor finishes) also arising.

Quick-drying thinner screeds

There are proprietary screeds laid by specialist firms where the success rate is an important technical advance. They are usually based on the inclusion of materials in emulsion form aimed at improving adhesion to the base and allowing thinner screeds to be used. They also tend to reduce cracking in spite of the fact that the drying shrinkage tends to be higher than with normal water mixes. *These screeds dry out faster than normal mixes; the fact that they may be used in reduced thicknesses will assist in this aspect.* The materials used include butimen, pva, acrylic resins and synthetic rubber.

3.06 Asphalt

Several types of asphalt normally used as flooring are highly suitable as subfloors for other materials, particularly thin sheet and tiles. Types used are either mastic asphalt to BS 1410 or 1076 and pitchmastic to BS 1450. All are the normal black colour and although coloured grades are available in both types, there would be no point in using these at extra cost in the role of subfloor. All grades are used as finished floors in their own right and will be dealt with later in information sheet SUSPENDED FLOORS 3

As a subfloor, asphalt may be laid in a single coat not less than 13 mm thick. Normally it can be laid on any reasonably finished concrete surface but requires an underlay of ordinary black sheathing felt. It has advantages over cementicious screeds:

- Small depth required keeps down weight and storey height
- Surface can be finished really true and smooth
- Serves as a waterproof membrane on ground floors
- Has virtually no drying time and is ready for finishes immediately it has cooled
- No shrinkage problems; expansion/contraction joints are not necessary
- Can easily be made resistant to acids, oils and other chemicals.
- May suffer indentation under heavy point load.

Its comparative cost is high (depending on whether a thick screed is needed). As a subfloor the surface could be matt finished with a dusting of sand or suitable fine powder rubbed in and any surplus removed.

4 Preparation and thickness

When applying normal dense screeds, there are three main conditions which might be encountered on new concrete (monolithic), cured concrete or on old concrete surfaces. In the latter two cases there is the possibility of a separating membrane being required.

4.01 Monolithic construction

This refers to a screed laid while the base concrete is 'green' (within three hours so that complete bonding is obtained). Thus screed and base can shrink together and any potential differential shrinkage will be due only to differences in mix and therefore slight. A thickness of 12 mm is sufficient.

The base should be prepared by brushing away any residual water or laitance. Undoubtedly this method offers the least risk of problems of cracking or curling but has the same disadvantage as a power floated concrete surface in requiring protection from an early stage of the contract and possibly a good deal of patching before finishes can be laid.

4.02 On cured concrete

It is frequently convenient or necessary to place the screed late in the contract when the structural concrete has completely hardened. This will always be the case where services are to be buried. The necessity then is to ensure a good mechanical key which may exist if the concrete surface has been left suitably roughened when laid, otherwise it is advisable to have the surface well hacked.

The base must then be cleaned and dampened to reduce suction. It should be brush grouted with either a neat cement grout or bonding agent. If a good standard of preparation can be achieved the screed can be laid to a minimum thickness of 40 mm. Thicknesses are also related to bay sizes, but in this case the minimum is based mainly on the assumption that the bond obtained will be strong enough to resist differential shrinkage stresses even if relieved by vertical cracking.

4.03 On old surfaces

If good quality concrete, reasonably free from grease, oil or similar anti-bonding substances it may be quite practical to merely wash down well and treat the floor as a normal newly-matured concrete slab. Otherwise the safest procedure will be to introduce a membrane and treat the screed as unbonded. This will certainly be essential if the concrete is judged to be of weaker strength than the screed.

4.04 Unbonded

If conditions such as those described in 4.03 exist or if for other reasons such as the need for a damp-proof membrane or the laying of a screed on concrete containing a water repellent admixture, it may be necessary to assume that no bond can be achieved. Such conditions usually arise on ground floors and sometimes in upper floors where some movement in the structural floor can be expected.

In all such cases preparation will consist of filling any large cracks and ensuring a reasonably smooth surface before laying the membrane suitably lapped to ensure complete separation of screed from base. Screed thickness must be sufficient to resist curling and warping in itself. The recommended minimum[1] is 50 mm but it is suggested here that 60 mm is a more reliable figure, **4**.

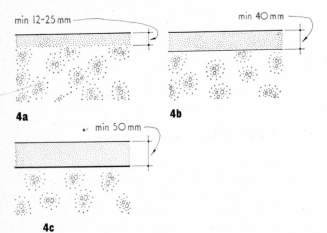

min 12-25 mm

min 40 mm

4a

4b

min 50 mm

4c

4 *Types of screed:* **a** *monolithic—screed placed within three hours of base;* **b** *separate—more than three hours' interval;* **c** *unbonded—membrane separates screed from slab.*

5 Mixing and application

Shrinkage and the various problems associated therewith can be reduced by:
- good mix design
- restraint (ie bond strength to the floor below)
- correct relationships between screed mixes and those of the layer below
- careful curing.

5.01 Mixes

For screeds up to 40 mm a normal Portland cement/sand mix is recommended at 1:3 to 4½ by weight. Less rich mixes will have lower drying shrinkages but also lower strength. Selection will depend generally on the degree of smoothness required to receive the selected finish. Above 40 mm it is better to use a fine concrete which gives equal strength with a lower cement ratio and tends to keep down shrinkage; 1:1½:3 with 10 mm coarse aggregate is suitable and should be capable of taking a good trowelled finish.

Any difficulty arising can be overcome by either finishing the top 5 to 10 mm in cement/sand laid monolithically or by slightly increasing the amount of sand in the mixture.
- Good grading of aggregates is essential to improve workability with low water ratios and the most suitable gradings are those specified in BS 882.
- It is important to use only sufficient water to ensure workability.

A test is to squeeze a handful of mix which should ball together without any water being squeezed out. Workability admixtures can help to keep down water content, thus reducing shrinkage and also drying time. A lower water content is possible if machine instead of hand compaction is used.

Conversely, failures have occurred due to the use of too dry a mix preventing adequate compaction, resulting in a weak layer next to the base leading to poor bond and differential stresses between the top and bottom of the screed.

5.02 Laying and bay sizes

Screed should be spread and levelled with a screed board ensuring even compaction, preferably using a beam vibrator. The slightly rough surface left by the screed board is acceptable for some floor finishes but thin flexible floors usually demand a steel floated finish. This process is carried out after the screed has stiffened slightly to avoid bringing the cement to the top where it will craze and dust and result in a weaker mixture below.

For some time now it has been recommended *that screeds be laid in alternate bays with two or three days allowed to elapse before filling in between.*

It is now suggested in BRS Digest 104 that even if laid in the comparatively small bays recommended, it is still difficult to avoid slight curling at corners which will show undulations under thin floors. The random cracks which will occur when screeds are laid in continuous sections are, it is stated, usually easily repaired and therefore the use of bay construction is no longer recommended except where heating cables are bedded or when in situ floorings are used.

Where bays are used, the size should be related to the thickness but should not exceed 15 m². The proportion of the sides should be as near as possible 1½:1 and *when screed is bonded* bays should preferably be staggered so as to avoid cruciform junctions (when screed is laid on polythene, cracks can still occur).

Joints should be vertical and close butted, no expansion joint material being required except where the bay joint coincides with a movement joint in the structure below (and they should always be arranged this way). This is unlikely to occur at intervals of less than 30 m **5**.

When a screed is laid monolithically, joints will only occur above those in the structure.

5.03 Construction and expansion joints

As stated these are only necessary in screeds where they correspond with such joints in the structure itself. Preferably they should be arranged at positions where they can be concealed by vertical elements of structure in which case they need have no effect on the screeds and floor finishes. If it is essential to create a movement joint in an area of open floor, some device similar to that shown in the sketch may be used **6**.

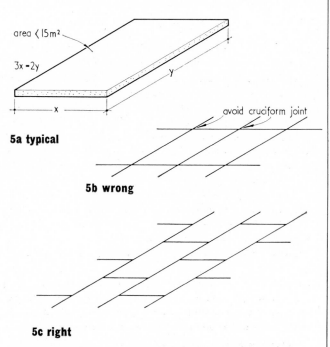

5a typical

5b wrong

5c right

5 *Bay sizes and arrangement:* **a** *typical bay of screed—recommended arrangement;* **b** *wrong arrangement of bays;* **c** *right arrangement of bays*

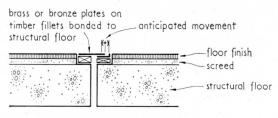

6 *Typical construction of movement joint*

5.04 Curing and drying

The newly laid screed should always be 'cured' under cover of polythene sheets or similar impervious material for at least seven days. As the amount of water used for mixing is always necessarily greater than that needed to hydrate the cement, the screed must dry out before floor finishes are laid. The drying period will be determined by a number of factors, principally temperature and relative humidity of air in the building. These will usually be controllable to some degree even if there is no completed heating system, for example by opening or closing windows or covering similar gaps with polythene.

Generally the longer the drying period the less the shrinkage, with correspondingly less risk of trouble. Building programmes are, however, usually 'tight' and the temptation is to accelerate the drying process to permit flooring subcontractors to start. This should always be resisted at least for the first four weeks. No hard and fast rule can be given but a common rule of thumb is one month for every inch (25 mm) of thickness. The effect of this on a programme if 3in screeds (75 mm) are used can easily be imagined. There is clearly a strong case for laying screeds early, not using thick screeds and finding some other means of housing

services. There are cases where thick screeds are essential and the time penalty has to be accepted.

No finish should be laid (unless of a water mixed type) before a reliable test has shown the screed to be dry enough. Testing methods are discussed in BRS Digest 18[2] and CP 203[3]. The accepted test involves enclosing a small volume of air in contact with the screed and establishing by a hygrometer that the relative humidity of this air does not exceed 75 per cent after a period of four hours during which time the air should reach moisture equilibrium with the concrete base. (If in spite of all precautions 'hollowness' indicating loss of bond does develop in places, these should only be treated as serious defects and justify renewal if the screed actually lifts and is likely to fracture under load.)

5.05 Level

Information on tolerances in floor surface is given in CP 204: 1965[4]. These can be assumed to relate also to screeds, as floor finishes of the thin sheet or tile type have constant thickness and there is no room for correction. The acceptable limits are shown in **7**.

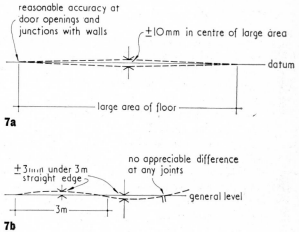

7a

7b

7 *Recommended maximum variations:* **a** *in floor level overall;* **b** *in floor level for localised areas*

6 Membranes

These may be defined as thin layers effectively separating one element of floor construction from another.

6.01 Functions of membranes

Membranes have one or more separate functions. On floors in contact with the ground or subject to wet conditions from above, these can include the function of preventing water and vapour transmission. In such cases this is normally the principal function, making any other effects subsidiary or merely consequential.

On upper floors, however, the question of water or vapour movement is not usually present and one or more other functions are the reason for introducing the membrane. These include separating the screed from the slab deliberately so that separate shrinkage rates and thermal movement can take place independently allowing freedom in the positioning of expansion joints, and preventing the screed coming into contact with undesirable contamination on the surface of the slab, particularly old slabs, such as oil or grease patches, dirt and dust.

There is also the function of preventing too rapid initial drying due to the suction of the slab below, usually achieved by wetting when no membrane is used. In special cases described later, the membrane may assist in preventing impact noise transmission or damage by chemical spillage.

6.02 Main types

There are two main types of normal membrane; first, the liquid poured and spread (either hot or cold) and second, the thin sheet variety laid with lapped joints to ensure continuity.

The first type includes bitumen poured hot and spread usually to a thickness of ⅛in (3 mm) in one coat and a number of emulsions poured cold based on bitumen or synthetic rubber which are spread in at least two coats. Membranes are usually restricted to ground floors, their main function being to prevent rising damp and indeed if finished with a dusting of sand they do in fact offer a degree of bond to the screed above.

The second type includes building paper (quite adequate where meant only to prevent bond and allow free differential movement), polythene sheet of varying thickness up to grade 1000 which is vapour-proof (thinner grades are not), bituminous felts based on hessian, glass fibre or asbestos and aluminium foil, although this is seldom used for this purpose being rather delicate. Polythene sheet is nowadays the most common membrane for upper floor work and if water movement is a factor the joints should be not only lapped but sealed using patent adhesive supplied by the manufacturers (usually a combination of polythene and bitumen).

7 Special situations

There are a number of special situations which can affect screeds or subfloors. As most of this information sheet has been concerned with screeds or concrete floors, the subject of timber subfloors is included in this section as a matter of convenience.

7.01 Floating floors

To reduce impact noise transmission, the normal system is either to provide a compressible floor finish (eg carpet or foam backed pvc or rubber) or to provide a compressible layer of material between structural floor and subfloor. This principle applies regardless of whether the floor is of concrete or timber. The resilient layer can be glass fibre or mineral wool, usually a nominal 25 mm, and the top surface must be covered with an impervious material (polythene or building paper will do) to prevent cement-sand mixes soaking through the layer and forming solid bridges. Blanket materials with a suitable covering material already incorporated or expanded polystyrene are possible types. The screed itself is normal but must not be less than 65 mm thick or 75 mm if incorporating heating cables. It is advisable to reinforce with 25 to 50 mm wire netting laid directly on top of the impervious sheeting. Room-sized panels are best but if these greatly exceed 15 m², laying in bays may be advisable.

7.02 Heated floors

Particular care is required in laying of heated screeds as the temperature gradient across the thickness increases curling tendency. Cables may be incorporated in the structural slab and use a monolithic screed, but this may involve problems with reinforcement **8a**. Also, they are only good at ground floor level and can result in heating ceiling

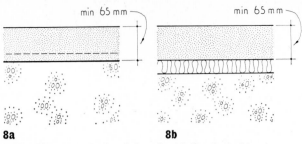

8a   **8b**

8 *Screed types:* **a** *unbonded and with heating cables;* **b** *floating—on compressible material*

below when used in upper storeys (unless adequately insulated). Otherwise the screed must be at least 65 mm thick if bonded and 75 mm if separated or floating.

Frequently the separating layer may take the form of insulation which must be protected against penetration as with floating floors, unless it is in itself non-absorbent (eg expanded polystyrene or polyurethane). Where insulation is involved a thickness of at least 75 mm would be needed to provide an adequate heat storage medium for off-peak supply.

The cables are placed on a thin bed of cement and sand, 10 to 15 mm thick, after which the remaining screed must be immediately placed and tightly packed around the cables. Avoidance of hollow spots is very important as they cause overheating which in turn results in cable failure. During screeding the cables should be continually monitored so that any faults can be corrected before the screed has set. Heated screeds should be laid in bays not exceeding 15 m², and where cables pass from bay to bay they should be looped and wrapped to avoid fracture by shrinkage. *Any movement joints must be taken right through the insulation.* Slow natural drying is essential. Cables must not be used for at least 28 days and then only for a very short time each day gradually building up to full use.

The need for an insulating layer below the screed or floor **8b** depends on the situation. On ground floors it is generally used only around the perimeter. On upper floors if the building is designed for a single corporate occupant (eg offices for one company) it might be omitted, as heat emitted downwards will contribute to the floor below which is in the same ownership.

Conversely, in buildings such as blocks of flats where each floor is in separate occupation, insulation is necessary to prevent loss of heat to another occupant. Cases have been known of flat dwellers, surrounded except on one side by other flats whose owners liked warm conditions, never needed to use their own systems as enough heat leaked through the surrounding divisions to provide livable temperatures.

7.03 Refrigerated floors

These constitute a very special case, restricted generally to cold stores and ice-rinks. In both cases the likelihood is that the structure will be supported on the ground where the principal hazard to be combated is 'ground heave' or lifting of the subsoil due to sub-zero temperatures being allowed to develop in the soil, with consequent disastrous results to the structural floor and finishes.

Even in cold stores it is not the floor itself which is cooled, only the air within the space above, so that perhaps ice-rinks are the only class of building which actually contain refrigerated floors. It is possible that such a floor would be needed at an upper level and at least one ice-rink exists in England situated above a 10-pin bowling centre. The problem is not ground heave but condensation forming on the underside of the floor or even artificial fog forming in the room below due to the lowering of the air temperature next to the ceiling. Because insulation can only slow down the rate of heat transfer and not completely prevent it, these severe conditions of a floor necessarily at a sub-zero temperature may require in addition to insulation some form of heating on the underside to prevent undesirable conditions in the space below **9**.

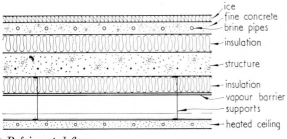

9 *Refrigerated floor*

7.04 Timber subfloors

As stated earlier, apart from small domestic building the majority of upper floors consist of some form of concrete construction on which sand/cement screeds or similar mixtures are the obvious choice as subfloors. The same cannot be said for timber floors where the upper surface usually consists of tongued and grooved boarding. This in itself is quite suitable for most commonly used domestic coverings, mainly carpets, but is unsuitable for most other floor finishes.

After a period linoleum and cork, perhaps next most suitable, tend to show joints in the boards, a generally unattractive effect. If then floor finishes on boarded floors are contemplated, a subfloor of some rigid sheet material such as hardboard, plywood or chipboard would be used, thus reducing the number of joints which can show through. The effect of the joints is further reduced if both are rebated or tongued together to prevent lipping. If the material used is chipboard or blockboard it is more likely to be used directly on the joists as a floor surface in its own right rather than a subfloor.

There are, however, certain floor finishes of the monolithic type which are not really suitable for laying on wood-based materials, for example epoxy resin or magnesium oxychloride. In these cases it may be desirable to lay a screed on top of the timber floor. CP 204 gives guidance on this to the effect that the timber floor itself should be checked to ensure that it is rigid, sound, dry and adequately ventilated on the underside and that there are no loose boards.

A mechanical key should be provided consisting of wire netting or light expanded metal fixed at 75 mm centres and the wiring not to be more than 6 mm above the floor surface. Screed thickness should be not less than 50 mm.

A timber subfloor might sometimes be more suitable even though the structural floor is concrete. For example, if a flat final floor finish is to be carpet perhaps provided by tenants in blocks of flats, space might be required above the structural floor for services. A case for a similar construction might even be made purely on grounds for saving time as timber subfloors completely eliminate the drying time required by thick screeds.

The simplest method of providing this type of subfloors is the use of battens and a suitable surfacing material such as chipboard or plywood. Alternatively if sound transmission is also a problem the use of hardboard on a layer of dry sand has provided a successful subfloor for sheet materials. These various alternatives are illustrated in **10**.

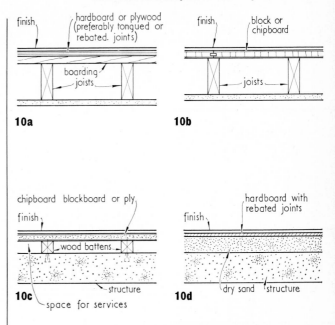

10a   **10b**

10c   **10d**

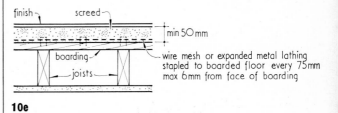

10e

10 *Timber subfloors:* **a** *timber joists and boarding;* **b** *timber joists and block or chipboard;* **c** *concrete slab with services cavity;* **d** *concrete slab with sand fill;* **e** *timber joists with dry and wet floor finish construction*

8 References

BUILDING RESEARCH STATION
1 Digest 104 Floor screeds. 1969, HMSO [(43) Ey]
2 Digest 18 Design of timber floors to prevent decay. 1962, HMSO [(23) Hi (S4)]

BRITISH CODES OF PRACTICE
3 BS CP 203: 1969 Sheet and tile flooring (cork, linoleum, plastics and rubber) [(43) Ty]
4 BS CP 204: 1965 In-situ floor finishes [(43)T]

9 Checklist

9.01 Main categories
- General
- Function of subfloors
- Types of screeds
- Preparation and thickness
- Mixing and application
- Membranes
- Special situations

Information sheet
Suspended floors 3

Section 7 **Internal division: General**

Floor finishes

In this third and last information sheet on the subject of floors, finishes are discussed in detail with regard to the function, methods of preparation, protection and available types, grouped in relation to their principal functional characteristics

1 General

The performance of any particular flooring will be affected by its situation within any particular space and as floor finish cannot always change in accordance with anticipated traffic patterns, the value of accurate wear-resistance tests is clearly somewhat doubtful (reference to this subject will be found later).

2 Functions

Not all functions listed will be necessary in every situation and it hardly needs stating that with certain of these some of the functions listed will be highly important whereas others may be of little or no importance. Later reference will be made to the functions for which particular types of flooring are best suited.

2.01 Appearance

All internal surfaces of spaces within buildings contribute to the total aesthetic effect achieved **1**. The part played by floor finishes within the total aesthetic effect depends on how exposed or conversely how completely covered it is by other items such as furniture. For example a theatre or auditorium is affected more by the colour and texture cf seat upholstery than by carpets or other floor covering, little of which will be visible; whereas large galleries, foyers and similar spaces usually sparsely furnished may well gain a considerable proportion of their total aesthetic from the floor.

2.02 Wear resistance

This is usually the more important physical aspect in selecting floor finishes and the finish may be subjected to various degrees of wear, usually foot traffic but occasionally in factories and warehouses, to what is known as trucking.

2.03 Comfort

The principal factors contributing to the general concept of comfort are probably softness, resiliance, and warmth. The last is not a matter of temperature alone as certain materials feel warm at lower temperatures than others. For example, a clay tile floor with underfloor heating at about 75° might feel as warm to bare feet as an unheated carpet floor at about 65°, but if both at the same temperature the tile would feel colder.

Scientifically this is just a question of rate of heat transfer from the bottom of the foot to the surface in question, in other words a matter of insulation value. Quite unscientifically there is no doubt that soft material such as carpets give a general atmosphere of comfort never achieved by other materials. This of course again presumes a climate where we are not deliberately seeking a cold surface as a relief of excessive atmospheric heat.

2.04 Acoustics

A degree of sound absorption in a floor finish assists in lowering the period of reverberation in a particular space. This can be a good thing, reducing the sound level in the room. Noise is generally regarded as a form of pollution. Hard surfaces on the other hand are reflective to sound and so tend to increase the period of reverberation and, therefore, the general noise level.

2.05 Sound transmission

Floor surfaces can be a considerable factor in reduction of impact sound transmission to the floor below and suitable materials laid on a solid floor can be as effective as the more sophisticated system of using a floating floor. These are also the materials which perform well acoustically in the space itself (see 2.04).

2.06 Heat insulation

One function of total floor construction is prevention of heat transfer from storey to storey where temperature differentials exist. Good insulators frequently perform well acoustically and prevent impact sound transmission.

2.07 Safety

This is usually a question of slipperiness. Certain floor finishes, usually of the hard, non-yielding type, can prove to be slippery especially when wet. This can frequently be overcome by specialist treatment to impart a reasonable anti-slip quality to the floor. Soft resilient floor finishes are normally anti-slip and hence inherently safe.

2.08 Non-combustibility

Although not controlled by the Building Regulations in the same manner as walls and ceiling finishes, it is clearly desirable that floor finishes should be non-combustible. Virtually all hard monolithic or tiled types are non-combustible and most soft or resilient finishes are either non-combustible or do not encourage flamespread (one or two exceptions are mentioned later).

2.09 Crack resistance

It is clearly desirable that floor finishes should have a high enough degree of flexibility not to crack as a result of slight shrinkage, settlement or thermal movement in the structural floor and subfloor.

2.10 Water resistance

This may be important in certain circumstances, for example on ground floors where the finish can function as a water- and vapour-resistant membrane, an obvious convenience. Alternatively there are cases on both ground and upper floors where water may escape or be used for washing down and the floor surface must necessarily be impervious to prevent penetration into the structure or the space below. In such cases care must be taken to ensure continuity with skirting and upstands at projection through the floors to ensure that water, even if it ponds, does not penetrate through weak spots.

2.11 Chemical resistance

In certain cases risk of spillage of diluted or concentrated chemicals or solids which will subsequently require washing down may call for a surface which is both impervious (see 2.10) and resistant to chemical attack. This is usually classified under three headings, ie acids, alkalis, and solvents or oils, and it is necessary to know the likelihood of each of these occurring. The possibility of all three occurring can be quite a problem.

The screed or subfloor with membrane can provide a second line of defence against chemical attack so that this does not reach the structural floor. This may be important as chemical-resisting floors are often formed of tiles with joints which can develop weaknesses and the main danger involved is to the structure itself, especially steel reinforcement.

3 Types of floor finish

The actual number of proprietary floors is so great that it is only possible to describe the principal types and even then to give only brief information on each type. This however should be sufficient to enable the architect to make his early design decisions on the finish to be used in each situation. This is important as decision on finish is invariably interrelated to the choice of subfloor and structural floor, again integrally tied up with the structural design.

Principal classifications used have been made in terms of the nature of the material comprising the floor finish. The details given are related to the functions, described previously with additional information on materials and methods of application. They are categorised as follows:

- Components and mixing
- Type of subfloor and need for membrane
- Application and thickness
- Hardness, softness and resilience
- Wear resistance and cracking
- Colour and pattern
- Insulation and warmth (or coldness)
- Water and chemical resistance
- Flammability
- Safety (non-slip properties)
- Noise and acoustics
- Ease of repair or replacement
- Cost
- British standards, codes of practice, digests and so on.

1 *The total aesthetic effect achieved is a matter with complicated derivatives:* **a** *and* **b** *are comfortable or uncomfortable, pleasant or unpleasant; it is a matter of opinion*

3.01 Hard monolithic

These are floors laid in situ on the site in a plastic condition and subsequently hardened off as a result of chemical action, drying out or cooling. They are described as monolithic and sometimes referred to as jointless but in certain cases have to be subdivided by expansion joints in order to restrict the risk of cracking or warping.

Concrete
Normal concrete with a fine aggregate (say 9 mm down) may be used as a finished surface **2**. The mix is usually comparatively strong ($3\frac{1}{2}$:1) so as to give a hard, smooth surface. The use of surface hardener can improve its performance. It is usually laid direct on to structural concrete roughed or left rough to provide a good bond. Thickness (preferably about 75 mm) can be laid thinner, down to 60 mm, but as it is a cement-based material it is preferable to err on the safe side and use a thickness sufficient to avoid any risk of lifting and warping. Concrete is hard, noisy, easily stained, unattractive grey colour unless pigments are used (not particularly attractive); suitable for factory and warehouse use. CP 204 applies.

Granolithic
Essentially similar to concrete but using granite chippings as aggregate. BS 1201: 1965, should be specified and typical cement/aggregate mix (10 to 5 mm free of dust). As with sand/cement screeds, the safest method of laying is direct on to green concrete, ie within three hours, in which case

it can be said to be monolithic and the thickness should be approximately 20 mm. When laying by this method the bay size will automatically be the same as the area of concrete floor laid below it. Expansion joints are unnecessary except where they occur in the structural slab.

It can also be laid on matured concrete, which must be prepared as described earlier, in which case the thickness should be at least 40 mm, preferably more. Its appearance is really no more attractive than concrete and here again pigmented cement may be used. The surface is noisy, cold and reasonably non-slip unless polished. Abrasive aggregates may be dusted in to improve non-slip quality; surface hardener may also be used to reduce dusting; attacked by weak acids and some oils but resistant to alkalis and mineral oils; essentially unattractive but suitable for factory, warehouses, storerooms and so on. CP 204 and BRS Digest 47 (second series) apply.

Terrazzo

This type of flooring is traditionally in situ but is nowadays frequently laid as precast tiles in which form it is described later. It consists of an aggregate, usually crushed marble, free from dust and impervious and graded in sizes from 1 mm up to 20 mm. It is laid on a screeded bed not less than 19 mm thick into which dividing strips are anchored. These strips may be of brass, copper, zinc, ebonite or plastics and the size of the panels formed by the strips should not exceed 1·2 m².

If bonded, a good mechanical key is necessary but if any movement is anticipated, the use of a separate layer of bitumen felt or building paper is recommended. The water cement ratio should be kept as low as possible to keep down shrinkage. Thickness with aggregates up to 9 mm should be at least 12 mm and with larger aggregates at least 15 mm. The mix should be laid while the screeded bed is still green, ie within three hours; both the mix and the screeded bed are compacted together and trowelled smooth. Borders or decorative design should be laid before the main body of the flooring.

Curing is essential, as for normal cement screeds, and the final finish is a grinding process carried out by machine, using abrasives. The first grinding is started about three days after laying and the second with a finer abrasive approximately five days later. Skirtings are also applied in situ using a 9 mm screed finished with 6 mm of terrazzo. When the screeded bed is laid on a separating membrane, it must not be less than 14 mm thick and lightly reinforced with mesh.

The finished product is hard and has no resilience. Its resistance to wear is high but so is the tendency to crack: thus the subdivision into small panels. The range of colour is wide and can be varied by the use of different aggregates and pigments in the cement. Similarly it can be used to produce virtually any desired pattern (incurring extra expense).

The surface is cold and it will contribute nothing to sound deadening or insulation. It is reasonably resistant to solvents but not to acids and is of course totally non-combustible. Because it is usually highly polished, it tends to be slippery and treatment with carborundum or a similar agent to reduce this tends to destroy the attractive appearance. It is not easy to make invisible repairs to cracks and even the replacement of complete panels would give difficulties in colour matching. The cost is higher than most tiled floors, but less than the luxury materials such as marble. CP 204 applies.

Mastic asphalt and pitch mastic

These are similar finishes. The first is based on rock aggre-

2

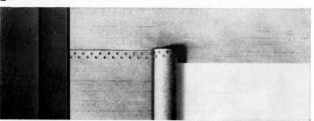

3

2 In situ concrete surface with cast in non-slip profile
3 Underlay for asphalt to prepare subfloor and prevent staining to ceiling below

gates and asphaltic bitumen, the second on silica aggregate bound with coal or pitch. Both are spread hot and laid in thicknesses as from 16 to 25 mm depending on the anticipated traffic intensity. 16 mm is suitable for domestic floors and offices with light traffic.

No damp-proof membrane is necessary in the ground floor as the material is in itself water- and vapour-proof but an underlay is sometimes necessary, depending upon the quality of the base or subfloor. Ordinary concrete is suitable without an underlay but if of porous or open texture, such as pumice or slag concrete, if cracked or dusty or contaminated by foreign matters such as oil or grease, then an underlay should be used.

On wood-boarded floors an underlay fixed with clout-headed nails should be used in addition to ensuring that the boards are securely fixed. The eventual hardness and wearing quality of the surface will depend on the mix used and the material can give quite long service even under heavy conditions (eg factory).

Normal grades are attacked by oil and acids, but special grades can be used to resist attack. Special grades can in fact be produced to suit almost any condition met in industry. The final surface tends to be slippery when laid but can be treated with an anti-slip agent such as carborundum grit. Normal surfaces are reasonably quiet and warm with a small degree of resilience. They are not easy to chip and are completely dustless. They will suffer indentation under heavy point loads. They are also comparatively cheap. The appearance is somewhat unattractive, especially if used in the natural black, but pigment can be used for dark colours such as red and green.

CP 204 gives further information and the appropriate British Standards are 1162, 1418, and 1410 for mastic asphalt and 1450 and 3672 for pitch mastic **3**.

Fleximer

Note. 'Fleximer' is actually a trade name of Dunlop-Semtex but has become accepted as generally describing all floors of this type.

These are jointless floorings, comparatively flexible and based on rubbery or resinous binders, pigment and an aggregate or filler. Binders used include rubber latex, bitumen emulsions and pva emulsion. Aggregates used include granite, cork, wood spar or marble chippings and the setting agent is normally hydraulic cement. When wood is used, these floors are sometimes known as wood/cement floors. Pigments are used for colouring but the finished colour is limited to the darker ranges, although somewhat brighter colours can be produced in resin-bound floors.

After mixing the material is spread with a straight edge, steel floated and usually given a second trowelling to produce a smooth, fine finish. Curing is not necessary. The thickness is usually about 6 mm and the material adheres well to most surfaces. Furthermore on ground concrete no damp-proof membrane is required as the material is not adversely affected by rising damp (pva would be).

It is however not impervious and a membrane may therefore be needed to satisfy Regulation c(3) of the Building Regulations. Crack resistance is good and large areas may be laid without joints. Depending on the aggregate used, the floor is reasonably quiet and slightly resilient; it is also moderately warm to the touch and with good anti-slip qualities. Resistance to water and chemicals depends entirely on the mix and if conditions are known suitable mixes can be used, for example rubber based types have good water-resistance quality and pva types have high oil and grease resistance. There is no tendency to chip or dust and because they are jointless these floors are highly recommended for schools, offices and so on and of course in domestic areas. The material does not support combustion; it has some degree of thermal insulation and acoustic absorption. The cost is comparatively low depending on the binder used. Further information may be found in cp 204.

Polyvinyl acetate (pva) and acrylic emulsions
These materials are not really finishes in themselves but are added to sand/cement mixes, in quantities between 10 and 20 per cent of the cement weight, to improve their properties. They provide increased adhesion and resilience to avoid lifting and cracking, enabling such mixes to be laid down to about 6 mm thickness on top of ordinary concrete or sand/cement surfaces **4**. Wear resistance is good and the surface will be non-dusting and resistant to oil, fat and grease. The mix is not, however, really resistant to water, and at ground level a damp-proof membrane is necessary; situations involving a lot of washing down are unsuitable.

As with epoxy resin the surface is hard and noisy and generally similar to concrete, especially as it only has limited colour possibilities using cement pigments. It is comparatively cheap because of the low resin content. It can be made reasonably non-slip.

Magnesium oxychloride

Generally this material seems to have few advantages over asphalt floorings and quite a number of disadvantages, including cost. In earlier days it no doubt served a useful purpose, but nowadays seems to be a rather outmoded floor finish for which it would be difficult to make a good case, especially as examples of flaking of the top surface are fairly common, no doubt due to inferior workmanship. Further details in cp 204.

Epoxy resin

This is perhaps the most common of a series of thin jointless floorings, based on polymer compositions, which can be spread thinly on to a concrete or screeded subfloor and are sufficiently hard and tough not to wear or crack.

Developed after the war initially as a solution to the timber shortage, they were then frequently used in domestic situations. Their high cost and lack of resilience, coupled

4 *Example of plastic mixed with cement to form durable and grease-resistant industrial flooring*

with the rapid development of other materials, has left them in use virtually only in industrial situations where they may have definite advantages.

Epoxy resin floors are compounded of a resin and hardener mixed 1:1 together with appropriate fillers which can be aluminium oxide, different types and sizes of aggregate and mineral fillers, and which give a wide choice of finish as regards both colour and texture. They are preferably applied by a specialist, but if the work is done by the general contractor, supervision by the materials supplier is essential. Their special quality is a tremendous adhesion and toughness which means that the subfloor must be thoroughly clean and free of all dust and laitance which could prevent adhesion to the solid material.

These same qualities, plus the high cost of the resin, lead to very thin floors (down to about 1·5 mm) which in turn demand a high degree of accuracy in the subfloor level. There are no movement or cracking problems, so that expansion joints are not needed, except for any in the subfloor. Wear resistance is excellent. Damp-proof membranes are not necessary.

The material is resistant to all chemical liquids and to water, which makes it ideal for certain situations such as laboratories and chemical process spaces. Its anti-slip qualities can be varied by suitable choice of aggregates and fillers, but when high chemical resistance is needed a greater proportion of resin in the mix will result in a smooth surface. One type, known as self-levelling, is simply flowed on to the floor and has a tendency to a gloss finish.

Repairs create no difficulty other than colour-matching. The finish tends to be rather hard and cold and therefore noisy and non-absorptive: much the same as concrete. An unusual advantage is that no curing is needed and traffic can use the floors in a matter of hours. The principal disadvantage is cost which is in the medium to high range, and only justified in special situations.

Polyester resins and polyurethane
Polyester resins have very similar qualities to epoxy resins, especially in terms of hardness and excellent adhesion. They are also considerably cheaper. The main disadvantage is their high shrinkage rate during curing which necessitates the use of a heavy inert filler or the use of fillers in fibrous form. One method is to lay the material on to a glass fibre mat, a system similar to the production of reinforced polyester laminates **5**.

Another system is to use coloured aggregate chips as well as normal fine fillers to form a kind of resin-bound terrazzo, subsequently ground down as for normal terrazzo, leaving the coloured aggregate exposed and reducing the area of binder and resin where fine shrinkage cracks can appear. In other respects the material is similar to epoxy resin surfaces but considerably cheaper.

The use of clear polyurethane is a recent development introduced from America. The resin is applied in several coats and then sprinkled with small flakes of coloured resin, finally finishing off with several more coats so that the coloured chips are sealed in transparent polyurethane. The final finish is high gloss but stippled due to the flakes.

The material is resilient and therefore not slippery but tends to show wear on the high spots first, which lose their gloss. There is no risk of hair cracks, as with polyester, and the surface is resistant to virtually all normal chemicals, oils and so on. It is also fairly quiet and, because of coloured flakes, available in a wide colour range.

Repair requires very careful surface preparation to get adhesion. This however may well be justified in certain situations, such as laboratories where chemical resistance and good appearance are both important.

In all resin-based floors, skirtings can be formed in the same material by simply applying it to the vertical surface and cove, formed in the same way as the subfloor.

3.02 Hard tiles

In this section are included all materials (not only tiles) laid in separate pieces, small or large (such as mosaic and stone), as the general process of placing such units to produce a complete floor is similar despite the large disparity in size of unit. They may however be divided into the principal subdivisions of manufactured tiles, asphalt and composition blocks and naturally occurring materials such as slate and stone.

Although there are a multiplicity of different tiles, methods of laying are virtually the same and are therefore described together, followed by details of the main types of tile. BRS Digest 79, second series, is the current reference for this process and three alternative methods are suggested. The principle adopted, contrary to previous practice, is to ensure separation of the tiles and bedding from the subfloor so that shrinkage or movement in the one does not affect the other.

Method 1: Separating layer

A separating layer such as bitumen felt or building paper is used on top of the subfloor and the tiles are then bedded in a normal 1:3 mortar mix, usually 13 mm but up to 19 mm thick. It should always be thinner than the tile itself. Joints are grouted with a similar mix possibly stronger up to 1:2.

Method 2: 'Thick-bed'

'Thick bed' employs a 'semi-dry' mortar of cement/sand not richer than 1:4 and at least 20 mm thick. With this method falls can be formed if needed in the bed, which can be up to 75 mm at its thickest point. Just enough water is used to hold the mix together. No separating membrane is needed because so dry a mix will not bond in any case.

Dry cement or a cement grout is used to finish the top surface before tapping in the tiles. Joints are filled with dry mix topped off with 1:1 grout. Large areas must be laid alternately or chequerboard fashion to allow initial shrinkage to occur before infilling.

Method 3: 'Thin-bed'

Resilient mortars based on latex or similar materials are

5

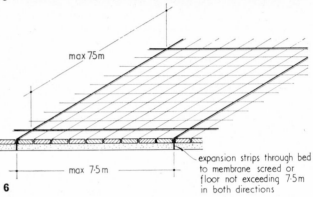

6

5 *Polyester resin used in conjunction with glass fibre reinforcement to increase impact resistance*
6 *Recommended layout for expansion joints in hard tile floors to accommodate drying, shrinkage or temperature movement*

used, which permanently retain sufficient flexibility to allow small differential movements without losing bond. Such bedding will not normally exceed 5 mm, requiring an accurate subfloor, as there is little or no room for adjustment in the bedding. Such mortars can provide better resistance to chemicals and more tolerance to vibration than ordinary sand/cement mixes.

With all methods some degree of movement is to be expected and some clay tiles have a tendency to slight expansion when wet. To accommodate this and the possibility of drying and shrinkage or temperature movement in the subfloor expansion, joints at not more than 7·5 m centres in both directions should be provided passing through the full depth of tile and bed **6**.

The various types of tile for which these preparations and fixing methods are appropriate are briefly described below. All have hard surfaces with no acoustic absorption. They are cold to the touch and generally unaffected by water, requiring no membranes at ground level except as necessary to comply with Regulation c3 in occupied buildings. All are non-combustible and, being made up of small units, comparatively easy to repair or renovate if damaged.

Metric rationalisation

Sizes of the various floor tiles and blocks which follow are given in metric units but they are of course conversions of imperial sizes (eg 305 mm is 12in). When manufacturers convert to metric (some have already done so), the difference will be very slight. Clearly 305 mm will become 300; 102 mm which is in fact 4in will become 100; 914 mm which is 36in will become 900 and so on. The officially recommended key size for all floor units is 300 mm × 300 mm.

All such units should then be manufactured so as to form subdivisions of multiples of this size. They will then co-ordinate with other building components.

Concrete and terrazzo tiles

Concrete tiles are made in moulds with a mixture of coloured cement and hard aggregate on a normal concrete background **7**. Sizes range from 101 mm (4in) to 457 mm (18in) square thicknesses varying from 16 mm to 36 mm. Probably the most common size in general use is 305 mm square (12in). When vibrated, no surface finishing is necessary which means extremely hard aggregates may be used giving hard-wearing and good anti-slip characteristics. They are usually cast with keyed backs. Being concrete, they are attacked by oils and weak acids, but are resistant to surface water. Various surfacings including carborundum, steel filings and even epoxy resin may be incorporated in hydraulically pressed tiles to give a surface which can resist heavy trucking. Floor warming systems may produce hair cracks and so they are not recommended in such situations. BS 1197 and CP 202 are relevant.

Terrazzo tiles are similar in all respects, except that a marble aggregate is used which gives the tile the same character as in situ terrazzo (see 3.01). The manufacturing system is similar but must involve surface grinding and polishing to expose the aggregate. Various sizes are available from 152 mm (6in) up to 610 mm (24in) square, in thicknesses from 19 mm to 38 mm. Probably the most frequently used size is 457 mm square (18in).

Anti-slip characteristics are generally poor, as even if special grits are sprinkled into the surface, the final polishing to expose the aggregate must inevitably leave a smooth surface and it is said in the flooring trade that there is no such thing as a non-slip terrazzo floor—tile or in situ.

The general recommendations as to laying apply to both concrete and terrazzo tile, except that in the case of terrazzo its particular susceptibility to cracking in response to even very small movements make it advisable to use expansion joints at much closer intervals; in fact at the same spacing as recommended for in situ terrazzo to produce panels not exceeding about 1·2 m². 2 m × 0·5 m panels have been used successfully.

Water and chemical resistance are similar to concrete tiles but terrazzo is not suitable for situations where trucking (except very light trolleys) takes place or where there is vibration. Its main advantage over other tiles lies in its attractive appearance and the pleasant effects which may be achieved, especially when using very large aggregate. (This may involve a different method of manufacture, by casting two tiles in a block and sawing in half to expose the aggregate for final polishing.) CP 202 is again relevant. Both types can be supplied with precast skirtings but with terrazzo it is usual to form these in situ.

Terrazzo tile floors tend towards the higher end of the cost scale, but are not in the luxury section. Concrete tile floors fit in the cheap to medium range.

Quarry and clay tiles

The term 'quarry tile' has always been misleading, suggesting some form of stone or slate, whereas in fact 'quarries' are produced like some bricks, from ordinary unrefined clays pressed into dies and burnt hard in kilns. The word is a corruption of the French 'carré' meaning 'square'.

Sizes vary from 101 mm square (4in) to 305 mm square (12in) and thicknesses from 16 mm to 50·8 mm. Sometimes the same size tile is made in more than one thickness, depending on the manufacturer and the clay used. They have a pleasant rustic appearance, usually with a slightly

7

8

7 Concrete paving slabs with non-slip inserts for durable indoor/outdoor surface

8 Ceramic tiles matching beauty with durability. Increasingly more popular in this country to bring back into hard finishes the colour and patterning too often limited to soft

rough surface and a tendency to slight inaccuracies in shape. Colours available are reds, blues, browns, heather mixtures and buff.

The essential character of a 'quarry' is that unlike other clay tiles it is not consistent in texture, having a hard impervious exterior skin and comparatively soft interior. Wearing qualities are good providing the outer skin is not cracked or worn away. For this reason the tiles are not classed as frost-proof and are not suitable for heavy trucking. They are mostly used in domestic areas.

Undamaged, they have good resistance to oils, acids and water and are also suitable for use over heated subfloors. BS 1286 and CP 202 apply.

Clay tiles are made from refined natural clay to much greater accuracy and fired at higher temperatures (1000° to 1200°C) which results in a fully burnt body of even consistency throughout. However, they are not what is known as vitreous tiles, which contain other materials and are fired at higher temperatures. Normal sizes are 76 mm, 101 mm, 108 mm and 152·4 mm square (3in by 3in up to 6in by 6in) all 12·7 mm thick. They are produced with smooth, grooved or studded surfaces and are sometimes grooved or profiled on the underside for key. They are unaffected by water and resistant to most oils, fats and chemicals—the joints are the weaker element in such situations.

Wearing qualities are first class and a good range of colours is available, although as with quarries the natural colour is red or blue. Unlike 'quarries' they are of even colour. Suitable situations are similar to those for quarries. As they are a better quality article, the cost is higher than quarries but still in the medium range, BS 1286 applies where they are classified type B and CP 202 is relevant.

Ceramic (or vitreous) tiles and mosaic

These are the ultimate class of burnt clay tiles and in fact incorporate other materials such as calcium, flint and feldspar. They are also burnt at temperatures well above 1200°C, resulting in a fully vitrified, virtually indestructible product, resistant to all oils and chemicals and completely impervious to water and frost. A very wide range of colours is available including pleasant mottled marbled and 'flamed' effects **8**.

Surfaces are normally slightly grainy, giving good non-slip qualities and ribbed or studded surfaces are also available. With suitable jointing (see section 3 LOWEST FLOOR) they will withstand any type of chemical attack or physical wear, with the added advantage of good appearance. The cost is naturally on the high side but not in the luxury class. Most tiles of this type are imported but sizes are generally similar to those for type B clay tiles, 100 to 150 mm square by about 12 to 16 mm thick being normal.

There is no appropriate BS except 1286, but these tiles far exceed the standards of type B clay tiles. CP 202 is applicable.

Ceramic mosaic

This is simply a form of vitrified tile made in smaller units. Squares of about 20 to 25 mm are normal, being usually delivered attached to sheets of thick paper in squares about 300 mm square. Fixing and grouting is similar to tiles, except that the paper has to be soaked off after laying. Both normal sand/cement and thin bed methods are used.

When laid, the characteristics are virtually the same as for tiles, except that the increased number of joints is a disadvantage if aggressive chemicals are present. Normally, however, mosaic would not be chosen for such situations but rather for positions where a decorative floor of excellent wearing quality is needed. The small unit, and virtually limitless colour range, offer the designer plenty of opportunity to experiment with colour variation and pattern.

Glass mosaic

This is differently manufactured and less suitable for floors being less regular in shape. It has its own particular character more suited to cladding.

On the Continent, especially in Italy, a tradition of glazed floor tiles has developed and these now have a successful market in Britain. They are frequently made in a variety of interlocking shapes. The colour range is limitless and both exotic and traditional patterns are commonly found. An ordinary glazed tile, without relief, is available in sizes of 300 mm × 150 mm and 150 mm × 75 mm. Transparent over-glazes on ordinary quarries are being used to provide the best of two types. Hand-applied finishes give a pleasing ripple in the glazed face, if desired.

The high gloss does tend to be slippery but one type overcomes this problem very well by having a profiled surface with projecting ridges and confining the coloured glaze to the lower surfaces. The final product is an excellent anti-slip yet glossy, fully vitrified patterned tile in an excellent range of colours and patterns (naturally expensive).

Industrial asphalt tiles

There are two types of asphalt tile, one based on natural rock asphalt and the other made by mixing asphaltic bitumen and fillers. Various other additions may be made to the mix in both cases. The general process is to heat the mixture and place this under pressure in suitable moulds.

Natural rock asphalt tile

Normal sizes for this type are 254 mm, 203 mm and 140 mm square and 203 mm by 102 mm rectangular, in thicknesses from 19 to 50 mm. Laying procedure is as for other tiles, but if vibration is likely the tiles may be bedded in mastic asphalt at least 10 mm thick.

The floor is reasonably hard-wearing, non-dusting and water repellent. Special mixes can give a degree of chemical resistance. Normal asphalt colour is usual but red and brown can also be achieved. The finished floor must obviously have similar characteristics to in situ asphalt floors but the convenience of the tile form makes repairs easier. Thick tiles are suitable for industrial use where a degree of wear is to be expected. BS 1324 applies to these tiles.

Asphaltic bitumen/filler mixed tile

These are made in one size 228 mm × 114 mm and from 25 to 64 mm thick. Obviously the considerable thickness is intended for use in heavy industrial situations, where a gradual wearing down of the surface can be expected. They may have square or tapered edges. They are fixed as for other tiles but normally with staggered joints, and always on sand/cement, as bituminous adhesives are not recommended. Tiles are laid close together without jointing material.

Composition block

This type of floor appeared in the 1920s as a substitute for wood block but has a character of its own, with both advantages and disadvantages.

The composition includes cement, wood dust, gypsum, pigment and pressed and cured linseed oil. Normal size is 152 mm × 50 mm (6in × 2in) × 16 mm thick. They are laid like tiles on a normal sand/cement bed. On ground floors a membrane is necessary against damp. Expansion joint requirements are also as for tiles, but joints are grouted with a material of similar composition to the blocks.

Colours available are oak, mahogany, green and black. The blocks can be laid in herring-bone or basket-weave patterns. They are maintained like wood floors but have rather better wear and non-slip qualities. Their resistance to cracking is not, however, so good and anything more than slight movement can cause cracks across blocks as well as on joints. Cost is reasonable (less than normal wood block).

CP 202 includes reference to this type of floor. The latest method of manufacture uses a vinyl bonding agent which will no doubt give improved crack resistance.

Naturally occurring materials

Grouped under this heading are all the quarried materials including quarzite, slate, marble, limestone, sandstone and granite. They are the most expensive types, and can be placed in the luxury class.

Quarzite and slate can in some ways be compared to manufactured types, in that the size and the thickness of the units require a somewhat similar fixing method. The other materials, really all stones, are however quite different in character as they are usually supplied in much larger units, also much thicker and heavier. They will thus remain in position purely because of their own mass, and the question of adhesion or bond does not arise.

Quarzite tiles

These are obtained from a natural crystalline rock or schistous formation which is about 97 per cent silica. Sizes vary according to the quarry but are normally within the range 152 mm to 228 mm in squares and rectangles. Random widths up to 900 mm can be obtained. The mica schist determines the thickness which is usually around 16 mm.

The natural surface is matt and of pleasing colours varying from silver grey to olive green and yellow. As with other tile floors, the surface is hard, noisy and cold, though it gives a warm appearance, and its non-slip quality is extremely good even when wet; it is also very hardwearing and will not chip or crack and is fully resistant to oil, grease, acids, and frost. Because the material is so dense, dirt does not penetrate and the flooring is easily cleaned and completely non-combustible. It is suitable for all positions where a prestige-type floor, nevertheless hard wearing, is required; similar to vitreous tiling.

The method of laying has to be very similar to that used for clay and vitreous tile, but some form of additive to give increased bond will normally be necessary. Because the tiles have certain irregularities of shape, the laying is a skilled job and has to be carried out by trained craftsmen.

Slates for paving can be supplied in slabs up to 1·5 m × 1 m although 1·2 m × 0·6 m is more usual. For normal use a thickness of 32 to 38 mm is considered adequate. This type of paving is perhaps more common outside than internally, and certainly comparatively rare in upper floors. For interior use polished slate in thicknesses from 6 mm to 13 mm is used, in particular where underfloor heating is specified.

The slates should not exceed about 457 mm × 228 mm and are laid like tiles direct on to the cement screed, finished with a fine slurry to which a suitable vinyl adhesive has been added to improve bond, slate being a material which does not bond easily. The material is well known in this country, available in blue, blue-green or green from Wales and the Lake District and some blue-black material imported from Norway. Its general characteristics are similar to tiles: cold, hard and therefore noisy and without acoustic value. It is however quite hard wearing and reasonably non-slip. In normal circumstances it is easy to clean but oil and grease will leave stains and it is not resistant to chemicals. It has the appeal of the 'natural', perhaps indigenous material but otherwise has no advantage over tiles and is more costly.

Marble

This is in itself a vast subject and so only brief reference can be made here. Basically it is a limestone rock within which other materials have caused the beautiful colours and patterns which form its main attraction **9**. As a paving it is used in a vast variety of sizes and thicknesses but because of its high cost it is normally cut as thin as possible and slabs of about ¾in thickness are used for general work.

For special applications cut slabs up to 2 m × 1 m are available, in which case the thickness would probably be in the region of 50 mm. The thick slabs referred to earlier

9 *Patterned marble floor exhibiting quality of material and variety of pattern possible because of innumerable colours and self-patterns available*

would generally be in sizes around 500 mm × 700 mm. Paving should be bedded solid in cement/lime/sand mortar 1:2:6 and 13 mm thick. Joints would not normally exceed 1·5 mm; expansion joints are essential, as with normal tiling, and it is recommended that they be filled with a polysulphide mastic.

Physical characteristics are virtually the same as for slate but the material is even more expensive, depending of course on the type. The range of colours and markings is enormous and marbles are imported from virtually every country in Europe. There are very few true marbles in England and they tend to be the less interesting varieties.

Stone

Stone for paving is obtained from sandstone and the coarser varieties of limestone and granite. The most used are Yorkshire sandstones which are self-laminated and have traditionally been used for paving for many years. Concrete slabs have superseded the old Yorkshire stone.

Sizes depend on the quarry source but average maximum sizes for granite are 2 m × 1 m, sandstones 3 m × 1·3 m and limestones 2 m × 1·3 m. The average size used is however considerably smaller than this and thickness varies from about 50 mm up to 150 mm, depending on the overall size of each stone.

Appearance of stone when properly laid, although not bright and limited in colour range, has once again the attraction of a natural material. Granites vary from light grey to pinks and reds, sandstones from grey to yellow, brown and red and limestones from grey-white to cream, yellow and brown. The material has much the same physical characteristics as slate or marble but is not usually finished to a high polish. All stones are relatively non-slip but granite can become slippery after considerable wear. Wear resistance is generally good when compared with many floor materials but is not unlimited by comparison with, say, ceramic tile. One has only to look at a medieval flight of steps to realise the truth of this. Limestone and sandstone are generally resistant to water, alkalis and oils, but attacked by acids. Granite is also unaffected by weak acids, oils and grease which will however stain limestone and sandstone.

Externally stone is normally bedded on sand but this is not practical for upper floors where smaller units may be expected and these are usually bedded in either a straight cement/sand 1:3 with a plasticiser or cement/lime/sand 1:2:6 and the joints grouted with a similar mortar using crushed stone instead of sand. CP 202 includes reference to stone flooring.

Nowadays very little stone paving is used internally as it is generally restricted to situations where a special effect is required or in the replacement of existing paving in buildings of historic interest. It is expensive and virtually in the luxury class but not normally as costly as marble.

3.03 Wood

In spite of the proliferation of flooring materials since the war, wood in various forms still makes a satisfactory floor surface and, like the stone described in the last section, has the appeal of a natural organic material even when it has been broken down and reconstituted, as for example in plywood. Timber flooring can generally be classified into two main types: boarding, which spans between timber joists and is therefore a structural material as well as a finish, and various types of block which require a complete subfloor to receive them. The principal varieties are described below.

Hardwood block

Blocks, being comparatively small in size, can be produced from timber (off-cuts) useless for other purposes. The range of hardwood now available is extensive and it has its own particular characteristics. The method of laying is however normally the same. Blocks are usually made in widths up to 89 mm and in lengths from 150 mm to 380 mm. Thicknesses can vary from 19 mm to 30 mm, but an allowance has to be made of roughly 9 mm for sanding down and finishing; 25 mm nominal overall is most generally used.

The blocks may be laid on any solid level subfloor, screeded concrete being the normal provision. This is coated with black varnish and each block dipped in a hot mastic, usually bitumen, then placed in position. The blocks are tongued, grooved and may be laid in a variety of patterns eg single herring-bone, double herring-bone, basket weave, square herring-bone, all of which assist in providing an interlocking arrangement which gives additional strength. Today it is becoming increasingly common to use a cold latex/bitumen emulsion instead of hot pitch or bitumen, as it has greater adhesion and obviates the need for priming. The principal risk involved in the use of wood block floors is shrinkage, usually across the grain. This varies considerably with the variety of hardwood, but it is always important to ensure that the blocks themselves are dried down to the correct moisture content before delivering supplies in properly sealed packages, and that the relative humidity inside the building is maintained at a reasonable level once the blocks are unpacked and fixed. *If these precautions are not observed a disastrous degree of shrinkage can occur.*

The material has good physical characteristics, as it has a high insulation value. It is warm to the touch and although not soft, it has a degree of resilience and is not unduly noisy. Wear resistance depends on thickness or rather on the depth down to the tongue, but most hardwood blocks have a satisfactory useful life and repair and replacement is not difficult. Colour is a matter of the natural colour of the timber which can vary from almost white to very dark

brown and red, and there are attractive grain effects in certain timbers. Timber is of course inflammable but the likelihood of setting fire to a hardwood block floor is extremely low. Hardwood blocks are not particularly susceptible to chemical action but are easily stained by oils and grease and of course extremely susceptible to damage by water.

End-grain block

These are laid with the grain vertically, in which position they are considerably more resistant to wear, and are specifically used for heavy-duty situations where severe abrasion or impact loads are anticipated but where a degree of flexibility is desirable. The blocks are normally 76 mm × 228 mm. They range in thickness from 63 mm to 114 mm according to the extent of wear anticipated. Shorter block sizes are also used. Usually they are thoroughly impregnated under pressure with creosote and laid either on a screed or power floated concrete. They may be laid dry with close joints. Alternatively, they may be laid in the manner of normal wood blocks by dipping in hot pitch and grouting with a bituminous grout. They are intended strictly for utilitarian purposes and, although expensive, will survive conditions which would destroy other floors while at the same time providing the floor with flexibility and sound, deadening qualities and strong character.

Parquet and plywood parquet

Parquet is a patterned floor made from specially selected decorative hardwood cut to various sizes and shapes to form either overall patterns or special designs. The sections might be laid direct on to a suitable subfloor (this would be true parquet) or pressed on to a backing to form panels which can then be laid complete in sections. The parquet blocks usually vary in thickness from 6·4 mm to 9·4 mm and the total panel which might be up to 610 mm square will usually be between 25 mm and 32 mm thick. When the blocks are laid direct, the subfloor must have a good level surface. Most wood boarding may need a plywood or hardboard covering fixed with clout nails as preparation. The prepared panels are normally secret-nailed to the subfloor and also grooved together.

The floor will have the same structural characteristics as all wooden floors. This special technique has been used historically to create floors of special beauty.

Plywood parquet

This is a special type formed of plywood tiles with a thick top laminate of at least 3 mm hardwood to ensure a reasonable degree of wear. Usual sizes are 228, 305, 457 and up to 914 mm square. Fixing is normally to wood subfloors with or without glue, pinned at 150 mm to 225 mm centres. Tiles of adequate thickness (9·5 mm to 19 mm) may sometimes be laid directly on to joists without a subfloor. Usually, however, a boarded subfloor is provided which must be level. If at all uneven, an intermediate plywood subfloor (5 mm to 10 mm) may be needed. Such a subfloor, if of adequate strength, may be laid direct to joists sometimes with a layer of bituminous felt or fibreboard below to improve insulation. It may also be laid above concrete floors on suitable subfloors.

The finish has similar characteristics to other wood block floors particularly as regards hardness, resilience, colour, warmth, combustibility, safety, noise and ease of replacement. It is suitable only for light traffic and not resistant to water. When laid on concrete ground floors a damp-proof membrane is essential. Cost is lower than other hardwood floors. CP 201 Part 1 gives further guidance.

Wood mosaic

Similar to glass or ceramic mosaic, here small rectangular hardwood strips are used, about 114 mm × 26 mm × 13 mm thick arranged in groups of four giving squares of 114 mm side. 16 squares are arranged basket-weave pattern to form a large square about 457 mm side, all mounted on a sheet of flexible backing material or papered together on the top surface. They are usually laid in a bituminous adhesive with the backing material down. If papered together, they are laid paper upwards, this being stripped off after laying **10**. Colour range is as for other wood floors. The floor has some degree of resilience and is comparatively warm, being a good insulator. Wear resistance is good owing to reasonable depth of material but depends to a large degree on the hardwood used. It is reasonably quiet, easy to repair, but needs protection from damp. BS 4050 applies.

Chipboard

Sometimes known as particle board, this is a reconstituted timber formed of chips from timber not suitable for conversion into board or strip, with a plastic resin binder. It is produced in comparatively large sheets 2440 mm × 1220 mm and in a number of grades; one of which is known as flooring grade available in thicknesses of 19 mm and 25·4 mm. It is more suitable as a subfloor for thin sheet materials but in domestic use it may be laid as a finished surface in its own right especially if finished with polyurethane and regularly maintained. The advantage over normal softwood boarding is lack of joints and appearance, which when appropriately treated can be attractive having similarities with cork; normally laid direct to joists or battens and nailed with heads punched home. The use of ring-shanked nails may prevent subsequent loosening and consequent creaking; slightly less resilient than normal wood floors; no tendency to crack unless badly maltreated, but will distort if subjected to water. Colour is usually natural light wood but can be stained. Wear resistance is much the same as softwood, but can be preserved indefinitely by suitable surface treatment; warm and good insulator; not incombustible but less likely to burn than timber; not unduly hard and has a reasonable degree of acoustic effect; easily replaced; cost approximately the same as softwood boarding.

Board and strip

All natural timbers have similar characteristics so that much of what has been written regarding wood blocks applies to board and strip **11**. However, these are more difficult to produce requiring the best quality large standing timber for conversion. Strip is used to describe long timber of less than 102 mm nominal width and board everything above this width. Both may be quarter or flat sawn; the quarter sawn giving less variation in the angle between the annual rings and the face and hence less tendency to curl across the width owing to moisture changes **12**.

Timber today is usually kiln dried down to a specified moisture content according to its ultimate destination. This may be as high as 15 per cent for building without central heating and down to as low as 6 to 8 per cent where under-floor heating is used. It is always important to ensure that once dried to the correct moisture content, the timber is not subjected to conditions on site which will cause this to change significantly.

The timber trade still quotes sizes as nominal, 'when delivered to site is usually about 5 mm less in each direction'. This can make a considerable difference on comparatively thin boarding when for example a nominal 22 mm comes

10

11

10 *Wood mosaic and grain flooring exhibits variety of wood's texture and colour*
11 *Timber board flooring here suspended and laid in large basket pattern*

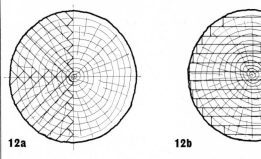

12a   **12b**

12 *Two methods of sawing timber:* **a** *quarter sawn;* **b** *flat sawn*

down to 17 mm actual. In dealing with widths of tongued and grooved boarding, there is the overlap of the joint to allow for in addition to finish so that the actual covering width is usually about 13 mm less than the nominal. Standard sizes vary and nominal widths are from about 50 mm to 150 mm (thickness from 22 mm to 38 mm); only softwood in over 100 mm.

Softwood tongued and grooved boarding

This is normally fixed direct to joists at not more than 450 mm centres, or alternatively to wooden bearers or splines set into or clipped to concrete. The Building Regulations (c3) lay down certain rules as to damage to materials used as finishes on ground floors and Regulations c4 and c5 give 'deemed to satisfy' conditions for timber floors. These are illustrated in the AJ Guide to the Building Regulations. On upper floors this problem does not exist but fixing is important.

Hardwood strip

These floors are sometimes fixed direct to joists or battens or alternatively may be used in thinner sections above softwood boarded subfloors which provide continuous support. Such a subsurface may be needed where the direction of the hardwood strip is changed to suit a particular activity (eg a dance floor) **14**. Hardwood strip is secret-nailed **13** and softwood board face-nailed with two nails per joist. Strip floor may be fixed direct to a screed 50 mm thick of clinker concrete by bedding in bitumen and nailing into the clinker concrete. There is, however, a risk of nails loosening and battens are preferable.

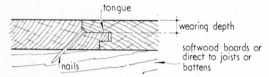

13 *Hardwood boards secret fixing*

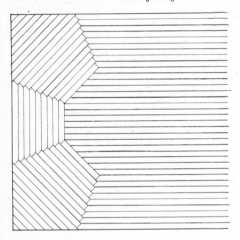

14 *Special arrangement of hardwood strip for dance floors*

Physical characteristics are similar to other wood floors and need not be repeated but if spanning joists or battens there is rather more resilience. Wear resistance depends on the depth down to the tongue **14** but can be counted as good. Well laid and maintained appearance is probably superior to any other type of timber floor depending on the natural beauty of the timber grain. The floor is of course combustible; more so than solidly bedded types. Safety depends on the finish used. Sometimes low-slip resistance is deliberately cultivated for specialist reasons, as on dance floors. Floors are moderately noisy as regards impact but have some acoustic absorption due partly to the diaphragm effect. Repair or replacement is easy. Cost is in the middle to high bracket if good quality timbers such as afzelia or teak are used. These are also the woods with the lowest movement range owing to moisture content changes, an important point in maintaining good appearance. Being good insulators, wood floors are warm but not particularly well suited to heated floors. Resistance to greases and chemicals varies with the wood selected. Water penetration must be avoided.

Softwood boarding is generally only used as a structural subfloor to other finishes, but if stained and polished or treated with a clear plastic varnish such as polyurethane, it can be attractive and can, by proper attention, be maintained indefinitely. It would usually be used in light traffic areas such as room parameters around carpets. BS 1297 covers grading and sizing of softwood boarding and CP 201 covers wood board and strip.

3.04 Thin tile or sheet

This type of floor finish is almost certainly the class which has developed in use and variety more than any other since the war, again partly as a result of the timber shortage. It includes all the sheet materials most of which are also available in tile form, this being a simple matter of cutting by guillotine. The main classifications are naturally occurring materials such as cork and rubber. The more traditional manufactured materials are those using natural mineral or vegetable fillers bound with linseed oil and compressed on to a backing such as hessian (ie the various linoleums); the so-called thermo-plastic tiles which in fact are mainly based on mineral asphalt or pitch but contain plastic resin additives; and the true plastic sheet materials which are virtually all based on polyvinyl chloride resin. The greater the quantity of resin in the mix, the more flexible and hard-wearing the material becomes at normal temperatures. It also becomes more expensive and therefore pure pvc is seldom used unless as a thin facing to a backing containing fillers of some kind. The latest development in this type is sheet material with integral foamed backing giving resilient quiet flooring with high resistance to impact sound.

Preparation for all these thin sheet materials is discussed in 3.01, the principal point being that a flat level surface is essential. This applies to all these materials, but it is most important with the very thin and flexible pvcs and least important with heavy linos and foam-backed sheets **15**.

Properties which the materials hold in common are described together here before dealing with individual types. Application is virtually always by adhesive. Most types remain reasonably resilient and quiet, but the thermoplastics are hard at normal temperatures and can be noisy. For the same reason they are the only type with any tendency to crack. Wear resistance is generally good and throughout the range providing proper maintenance is carried out. All have an unlimited colour range and are available in a wide variety of mottled, marbled and flamed effects. Thermoplastics become more costly when lighter colours are used. All are easy to repair or replace but particularly so in tile form. The cost varies from cheap thermoplastics in dark colours to rubber, pure pvc and heavy linoleums which are in the medium to high range.

Thermoplastics

These are available only as tiles and quite brittle at normal temperatures; contain asphalt and resin and proportions affect cost; fixed with bituminous adhesive. Thickness varies but normal domestic grades are about 0·75 mm; not affected by water; insulation value low therefore cold to the touch, affected by solvents and should be treated only with water-based polishes; non-inflammable; poor resistance to impact loads; cheapness is principal advantage; not suitable above heated subfloors. BS 2592 applies.

Vinyl asbestos

This is a development on the thermoplastic tile using only pvc resin as the binder and asbestos fibre with mineral fillers and pigments as the base. The quality of the tile will depend on the percentage of pvc resin which can vary from 20 per cent up to 50 per cent. This will affect the colour range, flexibility, wear resistance and cost. Fixing is by suitable adhesive and, as with thermo-plastics, it is necessary to warm the tiles. These tiles, however, are not subject to cracking even when cold. They can also be used over heated subfloors. The floor feels a little warmer and a little more resilient than thermoplastic but less so than linoleum; water resistant; reasonable resistance to grease and suitable for domestic kitchens but not for industrial situations; not inflammable; thickness varies according to quality, 2 to 3 mm being normal. BS 3260 applies.

Flexible pvc sheet and tile

These contain a much higher percentage of pvc resin which gives the material great flexibility making it suitable for use in sheet form, also highly resistant to wear and chemical corrosion. Tiles normally are 305 mm square and sheets up to 2·4 m wide. Joints may be welded. It can be imprinted with photographic reproductions of expensive natural materials, then protected with a further coating of clear pvc. The material is extremely tough and therefore usually laid in thin sheets; it thus has a tendency to show all irregularities in the subfloor or adhesive. It is also extremely impervious to dirt and only needs washing to maintain good appearance. It has good non-slip properties. Because it is so hard wearing, it is often combined with other materials such as cork, cellular rubber or foamed pvc which improve resilience, reduce impact sound and avoid the high cost of thicker pvc. BS 3261 applies and BRS Digest 33 is relevant.

Linoleum

Here cork and wood powders are used as fillers and the whole pressed on to a jute canvas backing. Various thicknesses are available according to the amount of wear expected, these being 2, 2·5, 3·2, 4·5 and 6·7 mm. It is produced in plain, printed or inlaid types, the printed variety being only for domestic use in thicknesses of 1·4 mm and 1·8 mm. Inlaid linoleum covers all types in which the colours go right through and are therefore not susceptible to change by wear. A wide variety of patterned and natural effects are available. Standard sheet width is 1·8 m but 2 m is also made. Lino tiles are cut from sheets in various sizes; 305 mm sq being usual. Fixing is by adhesive although not always essential with sheet. It is quiet, resilient, hard-wearing and should have a long life in the greater thicknesses. Easy to maintain; it is resistant to oils, fats and most weak chemicals. Also being comparatively stiff, it does not tend to show minor subfloor imperfections although it is not rigid enough to crack.

A cheaper form is felt-backed linoleum mainly supplied in tile form 2·5 mm or 3·2 mm thick (bonded into impregnated paper felt).

Cork

Granulated cork

This is compressed and baked into blocks, the natural resins forming the bonding agent. Tiles cut from the blocks are usually 4·8 mm upwards according to wear conditions and available in three shades of the natural colour. Density also varies. Tiles are usually 305 mm or 457 mm sq, but non-standard sizes can be supplied. Fixed by various adhesives, but standard practice is also to use nine hard steel pins per tile. A suitable sealer is essential to prevent dirt absorption but the floor is then very hard-wearing, quiet, warm and of pleasant appearance **16**. It does not stand up well to sharp point loads and went out of popularity with the advent of stiletto heels. That period being over, it may again be safely used for all normal foot traffic and is reasonably cheap. It is non-slip if properly surfaced. BS CP 203 applies.

15

16

15 *Vinyl flooring. Flexible sheet*
16 *Cork tile flooring with ease of laying advantages of synthetic types and appearance of natural material*

Cork carpet

This is another version which consists of cork granules, bonded with linseed oil on to a jute canvas backing. Produced in 3·2 mm and 4·5 mm thickness and 1·8 m width, it is similar to linoleum and is fixed in the same way. Principal differences are that it is a little less impervious, but less hard-wearing and available only in natural colour. Surface sealing is most important to avoid dirt absorption. Impact sound resistance, warmth and insulation are very good as with cork tile.

Sometimes rubber latex and cork granules are mixed to form a composite tile vulcanised under pressure. It is produced in slabs 4·8 mm and 6·4 mm thick and about 610 mm × 762 mm which can be cut down; fixed by adhesive. They combine some of the characteristics of each material and provide a quiet, resilient, warm floor. Plain and mottled colours are available.

Rubber

Rubber is another of the traditional sheet materials and although a certain amount of synthetic rubber is used the natural material still makes the best flooring. The sheet material is produced in thicknesses of 3·2, 4·8 and 6·4 mm and widths from 0·9 m to 1·8 m. With natural rubber, a full range of clear colours and marbled or mottled effects are available. They are fixed by a rubber-based adhesive to any suitable subfloor and have excellent wear and anti-slip properties. The thicker grades are particularly suitable for areas where heavy wear takes

17

18

17 *Rubber tile floors with raised texture surface for quiet, anti-slip surfaces*
18 *Typical good quality carpet in contemporary pattern*

place but quietness is also important (eg hospital corridors). Resistant to surface water and weak acids but susceptible to oils and greases; maintenance is a matter of washing down; comparatively warm to the touch but less so than cork—similar to pure pvc in this respect.

It is resilient and quiet, qualities which are enhanced by the use of a foamed rubber backing. This type of floor has become available recently and is particularly resistant to impact sound. Tiles are simply cut from the sheet in sizes from 152 mm to 1219 mm sq. Heavy-duty tiles are available with ribbed surfaces **17**.

BS 1711 and CP 203 are applicable; BS 3398 covers anti-static flooring; and BS 3187: electrically conductive flooring. Cost tends to be high particularly in the heavier and foamed back grades.

3.05 Carpet

The idea of using animal hair as a basis for woven materials was followed by the development of mineral fibres such as cotton jute, kemp and ultimately, the so-called man-made fibres developed recently by the plastics industry. The principal plastic materials used in carpets are nylon, acrylic yarn and rayons. The principal natural fibre is wool used either on its own or in combination with one or more plastics. Table I (from D. Phillips[16]) rates the four materials: A (best); D (worst).

Table I Carpet use characteristics

	Wool	**Nylon**	**Acrylic**	**Rayon**
Dirt resistance	A	D	C	B
Strength	C	A	B	D
Resilience	A	C	B	D
Cheapness	B	D	C	A

A successful mixture often used is 80 per cent wool, 20 per cent nylon. This takes advantage of the good dirt resistance and resilience of wool adding the strength of nylon without increasing the cost appreciably owing to the comparatively low content **18**.

While carpets and rugs are a vast subject in themselves and Persian, Indian or Chinese rugs are a lifetime study, the use of carpets in this way is a comparatively recent development and still largely confined to domestic premises, if we include hotels within that category. Certain types of carpet are, however, now penetrating the commercial field

(eg in office buildings). Table III shows carpet as the most expensive of all flooring materials, but this does not take into account all related costs, eg maintenance, which is a simple matter of vacuuming. The carpet industry has evidence to prove that when all such subsidiary costs are included, carpet can be cheaper in overall annual cost than a number of other finishes commonly used. Carpets represent the ultimate in comfort and attractive aesthetics.

Most carpets would be damaged by damp conditions and although not impervious, they require a flat, dry, even subfloor which means a membrane is required at ground level. They should always be laid on an underlay, giving greater resilience and longer life, fully justifying the extra cost. The material may be wool or synthetic, often bonded with latex or it may consist entirely of foamed rubber latex. Both carpet and underlay should be moth-proofed (unless inherently so). Some carpets have an integral foam latex backing making an underlay unnecessary. Fixing is either by nailing or hooking on to a special grip-fast strip around the perimeter (smooth edge) or by adhesive. In most cases stretching is necessary and the job is one for experts. Thickness varies according to type and quality but generally, including the underlay, will be in the range of 12 to 25 mm but naturally compressible under weight. Softness and resilience qualities are generally excellent as are quietness and acoustic absorption. Colours and pattern are infinite. Heat insulation is excellent and therefore the surface feels warm to the touch, although this quality makes carpet less suitable for underfloor heating situations. Anti-grip qualities are also excellent.

However, they are costly, although in capital cost even a top quality carpet comes well below such materials as stone or marble, their comparatively short life makes annual cost high. Of course if one tries to quantify a subjective quality, such as psychological effect on staff, a different answer might emerge from the computer. Another disadvantage is that carpet laid in large areas may wear unevenly and a lot of good material is wasted. (Carpet tiles described later are one answer to this.) It is generally inflammable but not dangerously so. Size varies, so-called body carpet being supplied in rolls 27in and 36in (686 mm and 915 mm) wide and broad loom generally up to 12ft (3·6 m) but sometimes up to 18ft (5·5 m). BS 3655 gives a code for informative labelling of carpets, carpeting and rugs.

Traditional woven
Axminster and Wilton

These are the two main types. In Axminster the pile is separate and each tuft is woven into a backing material. The pile is always cut, there are a greater variety of colours and designs than are possible with Wilton, and the pile is less dense than Wilton. In Wilton all the colours used in the pile are woven into the carpet in continuous strands **19**. Plain woven carpets are usually Wiltons. Special designs can be obtained for lengths over 100 m.

Cords

Cords are also woven carpets made in a similar manner to Wilton, the uncut pile looped tightly over the backing. Fibres other than wool, such as goat hair, are sometimes used giving rise to the term 'hair-cords', a particularly hard-wearing comparatively cheap carpet.

Top quality Axminster and Wilton carpets are generally regarded as the ultimate in floor finish comfort other than very special items, such as hand woven Donegal, the cost of which is prohibitive for all normal purposes. More than 9000 samples at the British Carpet Centre are evidence of varieties possible.

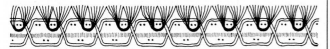

19a

19b

19 *Two types of carpet weave:* **a** *Axminster;* **b** *Wilton (from D. Phillips[16])*
20 *Needleloom carpeting where synthetic fibres are needled to a jute/hessian backing*
21 *Felt flooring made from durable synthetic fibres for high-wear areas*
22 *Carpet tiles: if any area is damaged or worn it can be quickly and easily replaced*

Tufted

The principal difference between tufted and woven carpets is that the pile is stitched into a pre-prepared jute backing and not woven with it. It is then secured by a latex backing. At first colours were restricted to plain or mottled, but more sophisticated processes now permit several colour combinations. Materials used were first rayon for cheapness, but as the reputation of these carpets grew, wool and nylon mixtures were used, some 100 per cent acrylic. Quality, ie meaning wear-resistance, depends on the density of tufts which varies from about 8 to 16 per sq cm. The lower densities being more common. Pile can be cut or looped.

Needleloom

This is a comparatively new type in which nylon or other fibres are needled into a jute/hessian backing; polypropylene is also used; hard wearing and cheaper than traditional carpet; designed to be fixed by adhesive **20**.

Felts

These are not woven but are blankets of compressed fibres stuck to a hessian backing or sometimes implanted through the hessian, so as to be double-sided. Sometimes a further backing of jute is fixed with a bitumen composition. Goat hair, hog hair, and man-made fibres are used. Hard-wearing if made in thickness of 12 mm or more **21**.

Carpet tiles

These were introduced recently from Scandinavia, manufactured in squares about 610 mm wide. They may be laid to produce draughtboard patterns of texture or colour or simply 'straight', when the joints tend to disappear. Being

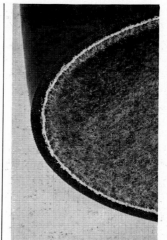

20   **21**

22

about 25 mm thick, they need no adhesive and simply remain in position by virtue of some slight interlocking of fibres. Thus heavily used areas which may become worn are simply replaced. The same firm now makes five different types, some based on nylon and polypropylene fibres needled to a base and bonded with acrylic material. Many similar materials are being introduced in both tile and sheet form, and this type of flooring is now competing with the thick sheet and tile materials as a general floor finish with some, if not all, carpet-like qualities **22**.

3.06 Metal

There are a few types of metal paving which are strictly for industrial use in very heavy-duty floors. They are seldom required and therefore dealt with only briefly here.

Anchor plates

Steel plates formed from 10 gauge material with projecting twisted anchors. Sizes are 305 mm sq and 305 mm × 152 mm, with a depth over the anchor of about 22 mm. They are laid on 48 mm of fine concrete 1:2:1½ while still plastic, buttered underneath with fine grout and tapped into position until solidly bedded and concrete projects through holes in the surface. Suitable for heavy traffic and impact loads.

Metal clad flags

Virtually the same as the last item but manufactured already combined with highly compressed concrete. Sizes are the same and 48 mm thick. They are laid on a 13 mm bed of 1:2½ cement sand, buttered underneath with grout, close butted, and levelled with a mallet. Suitable for same conditions as above.

Metal paving tiles

Iron castings triangular of 305 mm side with shallow projecting feet at each apex. According to surface pattern, which may be plain, studded or ribbed, they are 22 to 25 mm deep, laid on a well dried-out concrete subfloor, and should be damped, spread with a cement mix. The tiles are worked down through the mix until the feet sit on the cured concrete floor. This causes the mix to work up through the joints which show about 6 mm. These floors can stand virtually any rough treatment including oil, grease and weak acids, high-temperature vibration and heavy impact loads. Suitable for situation where spillage of liquids at high temperatures (even molten metal) might occur, and for breweries, dairies, *abattoirs* and the like.

4 Preparation and protection

4.01 Preparation

Correct preparation for type of finish being used is most important. Finishes laid on thick cementious beds need a good key which can be obtained either by leaving a rough surface on the subfloor or by subsequently hacking the surface before applying the bed to receive the finishing tiles or other material. Generally it is also necessary to wash down, not only to remove dust but to reduce the suction of the subfloor which would otherwise cause too rapid drying out and probably result in hollowness.

Another method of producing an adequate key is 'spatter-dashing' with sand and cement, usually combined with a suitable admixture designed to ensure adhesion. This type of preparation is normally required when clay or ceramic tile finishes are being used. These may however also be laid on a cement/sand bed of medium thickness (about 12 mm) above a separation membrane so that any movement in the subfloor or structure is not transferred to the bed and tiles. In this case a comparatively smooth surface is required such as would normally be obtained by the use of a wood float. Absolute accuracy is however unnecessary as the 12 mm does permit a degree of adjustment in the final finish. This is not so when the 'thin bed' method of fixing is used. In this case the tiles are in effect fixed by means of an adhesive and spread on the subfloor (which might be only 2 or 3 mm thick). Not being based on cement, this retains a degree of flexibility and does not therefore suffer from the same risks as a cement base. In this case a wood float surface is satisfactory but a high degree of accuracy as regards level is necessary as there is no room for adjustment in the actual laying.

Thin sheet or tile

Preparation for thin sheet or tile floors generally involves a steel float finish, again laid to reasonably accurate tolerances as there is no possibility of adjustment in the application of the finish itself (see AJ information sheet SUSPENDED FLOORS 2).

The actual degree of smoothness required varies according to the flexibility of the floor finish, and maximum care is required with pure pvc sheeting which moulds itself to even very small projections or hollows in the surface of the sub-floor. The use of mastic asphalt as a subfloor is often recommended for this type of material because of the very smooth surface which can be obtained.

Thin monolithic

Thin monolithic types such as epoxy resin and polyurethane require a similar preparation although in this case some degree of adjustment can be made to the level when the finish is being applied.

In practice it is most unusual for a flooring contractor to find a perfect subfloor and defects usually have to be 'made good' either by cutting out small areas and refilling or by the use of materials such as rubber latex cement, applied in very thin layers and trowelled down to a feather edge.

Wooden floors

Wooden floors such as wood block and parquet normally bedded either in bitumen or adhesive, need similar preparation to that for thin sheet or tile floors. Boarded floors laid on concrete are normally fixed to battens which may be fully embedded, partly embedded or fixed to the surface of the concrete by suitable clips.

Carpet

Carpet is a tolerant material as regards the surface to be covered but this should preferably not be too rough. The underlay normally used will take up most ordinary discrepancies in the subfloor surface.

Economy

A point to be noted in relation to economy is that the tendency to use carpet as an overall flooring material rather than just in the centre of a room has reduced the tendency to regard a boarded wooden floor as essential for the laying of carpets in domestic situations. All that is really necessary is a waterproof membrane in the site concrete and possibly a nailing strip in the perimeter of the room. The use of a good underlay will give the carpet adequate resilience so that the additional cost of a wooden subfloor can be avoided.

It is also normally necessary for the subfloor to be reasonably dry in the case of most finishes although some, such as clay tiles, are unaffected by moisture. Others, mainly impervious thin sheet materials, are highly susceptible **23**. (See information sheet SUSPENDED FLOORS 2, p283 for method of testing.)

4.02 Protection

This takes two forms, namely protection *of* the finish and protection *by* the finish.

Protection of the finish

Against water or vapour

This normally applies to the ground level only. Certain floor finishes are damaged by water, and adhesives are susceptible to damage. Flooring contractors will not lay these floors until the screed or subfloor has attained a satisfactory level of dryness. Other finishes are completely unaffected, but under Regulation c(3) of the Building Regulations it is still necessary to prevent ground moisture. Certain materials such as thermoplastics can be laid on concrete surfaces without protective membranes because they are slightly permeable and any rising water vapour can disperse. Nevertheless a water- and vapour-proof membrane is certainly advisable.

Against rising moisture

This takes two principal forms: the waterproof membrane or alternatively a screed which is itself waterproof. Another possible form of attack from below is heat where heated floors are used. This is generally not a problem as the actual surface temperature is comparatively low (usually below 25°C) and most finishes are perfectly tolerant to temperatures of this order. It is however always essential to inform the flooring subcontractor of the conditions anticipated when the heating is in use (see 4.07).

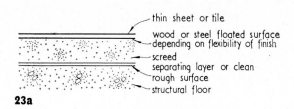

thin sheet or tile
wood or steel floated surface
depending on flexibility of finish
screed
separating layer or clean
rough surface
structural floor

23a

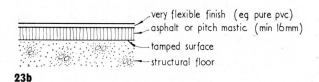

very flexible finish (eg pure pvc)
asphalt or pitch mastic (min 16mm)
tamped surface
structural floor

23b

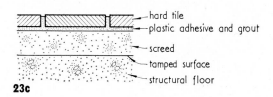

hard tile
plastic adhesive and grout
screed
tamped surface
structural floor

23c

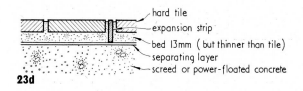

hard tile
expansion strip
bed 13mm (but thinner than tile)
separating layer
screed or power-floated concrete

23d

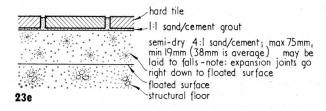

hard tile
1:1 sand/cement grout
semi-dry 4:1 sand/cement; max 75mm,
min 19mm (38mm is average) may be
laid to falls – note: expansion joints go
right down to floated surface
floated surface
structural floor

23e

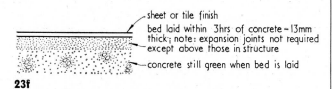

sheet or tile finish
bed laid within 3hrs of concrete – 13mm
thick; note: expansion joints not required
except above those in structure
concrete still green when bed is laid

23f

23 *Preparation for various types of floors*

Protection by the finish

This is normally a question of preventing the penetration of water or liquid chemicals into the structure where the concrete, steel or both might be attacked. Types of floor finishes suitable for providing such protection (depending on the type of chemical involved) include epoxy resin and other applied plastics, pvc sheeting with welded joints, ceramic tiles with suitable jointing materials and acid-resisting asphaltic mixes.

When tiles are used the jointing material must have sufficient flexibility to permit minor structural movements due to shrinkage, settlement or temperature changes without cracking the joint, as such cracks would form a point vulnerable to penetration. Furane resin cement

probably has the best all round performance, giving good protection against acids, alkalis and solvents, but as might be expected it is the most costly and therefore used only in joints between tiles bedded on less expensive mixes. This of course is satisfactory providing no cracks appear in the joints.

Because of the high cost of the jointing material there is tendency to keep joint width to the minimum, best done by selecting tiles with the minimum of size variation. Some tiles are sufficiently accurately sized as not to require selection. Narrow joints do however reduce the amount of movement which an area of tiling can tolerate in the subfloor. Although the narrow joint might at first sight appear to offer less risk as there is less of it, it is not advisable to reduce joints to the absolute minimum. No actual dimension can be given and it is usually best to accept the recommendations of a specialist.

Two further important points

1 It is normal to assume that finishes may fail at some time and to include a second line of defence in the form of a membrane, resistant to the chemical encountered

2 Such floors are best laid to falls to ensure that spillages are drained away as rapidly as possible.

From the protection point of view, falls should be as great as possible but there are of course disadvantages in the use of floors with excessive falls and 1:40 is usually the maximum that can be provided; normally it is less. When laying tile floors a broken joint arrangement should be used in such a way as to avoid continuous joints in the direction of falls **24** (see BRS Digest 120, second series).

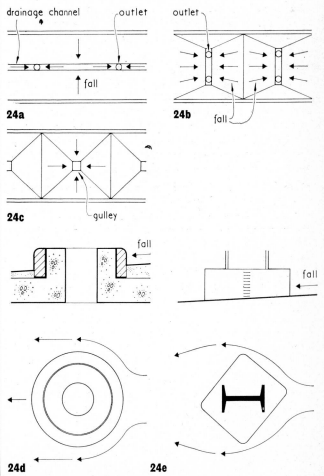

24 *Laying finishes to falls:* **a** *transverse slope;*
b *longitudinal slope;* **c** *saucer slope;* **d** *opening with kerb
(section and plan);* **e** *shape and place projections to give least
resistance to flow (section and plan)*

It is important always to consider the possibility of corrosive spillages, because some quite common materials which might superficially be regarded as safe can attack structural materials. Two examples are petrol in a motor showroom and milk in dairy premises.

Finally, cases do arise of protection being required to small areas of buildings only. Typical of these are lead trays usually used below urinals on upper floors and similar protection below shower trays or even whole bathrooms as a second line of defence against overflowing sanitary fittings 25.

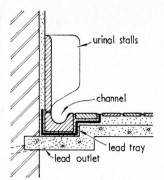

25 *Additional protection at risk points (eg lead tray below floor channel on upper floors)*

5 Schedule

Table II attempts to classify the various main types of floor finish according to their performance under 10 different headings. A to D are the author's own and are not based on any official testing procedure. In such case A is best and D is worst.

Table II *Comparative performance information of floor finishes* (A, *best;* D, *worst*)

Main group	Subdivision	Wear resistance	Appearance	Comfort (warmth softness)	Quietness (impact)	Acoustic absorbtion	Water resistance	Chemical resistance	Crack resistance	Useful life	Safety (anti-slip)	Remarks
Hard monolithic	Concrete	B	D	D	D	D	C	C	D	B	C	
	Granolithic	B	D	D	D	D	C	C	C	B	B*	*if surface treated
	Terrazzo	B	A/B	D	D	D	C	D	D	A	B	
	Mastic asphalt	B	C	C	C	C	A	B	B	C	C*	*can be surface treated
	Pitch mastic	B	C	C	C	C	A	B	B	C	C*	*can be surface treated
	Fleximer (plastics or rubber latex)	C	C	C	D	D	C	C	B	C	C*	*can be surface treated
	Magnesium oxychloride	C	C	C	D	D	C	C	C	C	C	
	Epoxy resin	A	C	D	D	D	A	A	A*	B	C	*depends on subfloor
	Pva and acrylic resin	B	B	C	B	C	A	B	B	C	C	
	Polyurethane	A	B	C	C	C	A	A	A*	B	B	*depends on subfloor
	Polyester	B	C	D	D	D	A	B	B	B	B	
Hard tile	Concrete tile	A/B	C	D	D	D	B	C	B	B	B	Includes artificial stone
	Tarrazzo tile	B	A	D	D	D	B	D	C	B	D	
	Quarry tile	B	C	D	D	D	B	B	B	B	B	
	Clay tile	B	C	D	D	D	B	B	B	B	B	
	Ceramic tile and mosaic	A	A/B	D	D	D	A	A	A	A	A	
	Industrial asphalt tiles	B	D	C	C	C	A	B	B	B*	B	*depends on thickness
	Composition block	B	C	C	C	C	C	C	C	C	B	
	Quarzite	A	A/B	D	D	D	A	B	B	A	A	
	Slate	B	B	D	D	D	A	C	C	B	B	
	Marble or limestone	B	A	D	D	D	B	C	C	B	C	
	Sandstone	B	B	D	D	D	B	B	C	B	B	
	Granite	A	B	D	D	D	A	B	A	A	B	
Wood	Hardwood block	B*	B	C	C	C	D	B	A	B*	C	*depends on thickness
	Parquet	C	A/B	C	C	C	D	C	A	C	C*	*depends on finish
	Plywood parquet	D	B	C	C	C	D	D	A	D	C*	*depends on finish
	Wood mosaic	B	B	C	C	C	D	C	A	C	C*	*depends on finish
	Chipboard	D*	C	C	C	C	D	C	B	D	C	*improved by finish
	Softwood board or strip	D	C	C	C	C	D	C	A	C	A	
	Hardwood strip	B	B	C	C	C	D	B	A	B	D*	*if polished
	End-grain block	B	C	C	B	B	C	B	A	A*	A	*depends on thickness
Thin tile or sheet	Rubber (solid)	B	B	B	A	B	A	D	A	B	A	
	Rubber (foam backed)	B	B	A/B	A	A/B	A	D	A	B	A	
	Cork and cork tile	C	C	A/B	A	A	D	C	C	C	A	
	Cork carpet	C	C	A/B	A	A	D	C	C	C	A	
	Rubber and cork	B	C	B	A	A/B	B	C	C	C	A	
	Linoleum	C/B*	B	B	C	C	C	C	B	C/B*	B	*depends on thickness
	Felt-backed linoleum	C	B	B	C	C	C	C	C	C	B	
	Thermoplastic tile	D	C	C	C	D	C	D	C	D	C	
	Vinyl asbestos tile	C	B	C	C	C	B	B	B	C	B	
	Pvc tile or sheet	B	B	B	B	C	A	A	A	B	A	
	Cork or circular backed pvc	B	B	A/B	A/B	B	A	A	A	B	A	
Carpets	Traditional woven	C/B*	A	A	A	A	D	D	A	C/B	A	*depends on quality
	Tufted	C	B/A	A	A	A	D	D	A	C	A	
	Cords	C	B	B	A	A/B	D	D	A	C	A	
	Needleloom	C	B	A	A	A	D	D	A	C	A	
	Carpet tiles	C/B	B/C	A/B	A	A	C	D	A	C/B	A	
Metal	Anchor plates*	A	D	D	D	D	A	C	A	A	C	*steel
	Metal* clad flags	A	D	D	D	D	A	C	A	A	C	*steel
	Metal* paving tiles	A	D	D	D	D	A	C	A	A	B	*iron profiled

Table III *Vital statistics of common floor finishes with cost references*

Floor finish	Relative cost bar/m² (excluding screed) increasing	Life in years (max)	Add cost of screed (new pence)	Total cost per square meter	Cost per annum/m² (new pence)
Thermoplastic tiles		10	12	1·44	● ~13
Granolithic paving		20	—	1·08	● ~6
Mastic asphalt		15	—	1·49	● ~8
Flexible vinyl tiles 2 mm		15	12	2·51	● ~15
Linoleum sheet 3·2 mm		15	12	2·72	● ~20
Magnesium oxychloride		20	—	2·15	● ~9
Thin epoxy, self levelling		20	12	3·07	● ~13
Quarry tiles 150 mm by 150 mm (6in by 6in)		50	10	3·11	● ~5
Hardwood block 25 mm (1in) nom		25-50	10	3·25	●→● ~5 to 13
Hardwood strip 25 mm (1in) nom		25-50	6	3·43	●→● ~5 to 13
Nylon felt squares		20	12	3·95	● ~23
Polyurethane and granite chips		25	10	3·91	● ~17
Thick rubber tiles		25	12	4·31	● ~20
Thick screed epoxy binder		25	10	4·33	● ~20
Carpet light domestic grade		20	10	4·54	● ~27
Terrazzo in situ		50	10	4·90	● ~6
End grain hardwood block		50	10	5·08	● ~7
Thick screed polyurethane and metallic chips		25	6	5·38	● ~23
Thick screed epoxy and special aggregates		25	6	5·74	● ~25
Fully vitrified tiles		50	6	6·10	● ~10
Carpet, light contract grade		20	12	7·53	● ~39
Carpet, heavy contract grade		25	12	8·61	● ~36
Slate, 1in thick, random		50	6	8·97	● ~22
York stone 50 mm (2in) thick		75	6	10·41	● ~18
Reconstituted marble		75	6	10·76	● ~18
Marble		100	6	11·84	● ~24

Cost per annum/m² (new pence) scale: 5 10 15 20 25 30 35 40

6 Cost

As costs of all building elements including floor finishes are constantly escalating, no attempt has been made to state actual costs of various finishes.

However, Table III gives an indication of the comparative capital cost of each type of finish, an addition for the normal subfloor needed, an anticipated useful life and hence a cost per annum, which may be the really important item. The table has been taken from an article by Dex Harrison and Penelope Whiting[14]. If upgraded for cost increases of say 20 per cent, the horizontal scale would run from about 60p to £10 per sq yd in stages of about 31p (75p to £12/m² in stages of $37\frac{1}{2}$p). In calculating the annual cost, no account is taken of maintenance costs or the constantly changing and complicated effects of company taxation. Consideration of environmental effects on efficiency are also relevant.

7 References

BRITISH CODES OF PRACTICE
1 BS CP 201: 1951 Timber flooring [(43)Yi]
2 BS CP 202: 1959 Tile flooring and slab flooring [(43)Sy]
3 BS CP 203: 1969 Sheet and tile flooring (cork, linoleum, plastics and rubber [(43)Ty]
4 BS CP 204: In situ floor finishes Part 1: 1965 Imperial units Part 2: 1970 metric units [(43)Py]

BUILDING RESEARCH STATION
5 Digest 18 Design of timber floors to prevent decay. 1962, HMSO [(23)Hi(S4)]
6 Digest 33 Sheet and tile flooring made from thermoplastic binders. 1963, HMSO [(43)Tn6]
7 Digest 47 Granolithic concrete, concrete tiles and terrazzo flooring. 1964, HMSO [(43)Yq5]
8 Digest 59 Protection against corrosion or reinforcing steel in concrete. 1965, HMSO [Hh2(S2)]
9 Digest 79 Clay tile flooring. 1967, HMSO [(43)Sg]
10 Digest 98 Durability of metals in natural waters. 1968, HMSO [(53·3)Yh(S)]
11 Digest 120 Corrosion-resistant floors in industrial buildings. 1970, HMSO [(43)Yy(S2)]
12 BULLIVANT D. and ACKHURST, P. Product selection for architects: carpets. RIBA *Journal*, 1970, January [(43)Ty]
13 ELDRIDGE, H. J. Flooring materials 1: hard surfaces. *Building*, 1970, June [(43)Yy]
14 HARRISON, D. and WHITING, P. Floor coverings. RIBA *Journal*, 1969, March [(43)Yy]
15 HUMPHREYS, H. R. Noise reduction in buildings. *Architects' Journal*, 1965, March 24, p719 [(23)(M2)]
16 PHILLIPS, D. Flooring. London, 1969, Macdonald & Co with COID [(43)]
17 HARRISON, D. (ed). *Specification* 1972, Vol 2, Architectural Press, p2-313 to 2-332 [Yy(A3)]
18 WITHERS, M. Floor finishes. *Architect and Building News*, 1967, March 22, April 5 and 12 [(43)]

8 Checklist

8.01 General

8.02 Functions
● Appearance
● Wear resistance
● Comfort
● Acoustics
● Sound transmission
● Safety
● Non-combustibility
● Crack resistance
● Water resistance
● Chemical resistance

8.03 Types of floor finish
● Hard monolithic
● Hard tiles
● Wood
● Thin tile or sheet
● Carpet
● Metal

8.04 Preparation and protection
● Preparation
● Protection

8.05 Schedule

8.06 Cost

8.07 References

Section 8
Internal division: Partitions and walls

Section 8 Internal division: Partitions and walls

Relationship to rest of handbook

The table and diagram show the contents of the handbook as a whole, with the present section highlighted.

This section should be used in conjunction with section 6 INTERNAL DIVISION: GENERAL, which analyses the functions of the whole internal subdivision of the building, and so provides a background against which the functions of partitions can be better understood.

Scope

This section of the handbook deals with the design and selection of internal partitions. Detailed problems of load-bearing partitions, and the effect they have on the structure as a whole, are considered in the AJ Handbook of Building structure.

References and keywords

The keyword by which this section is identified is PARTITIONS; those for other sections are shown in the table. See the notes at the beginning of this handbook (p6) for an explanation of how keywords are used.

Author

Bill Launchbury RIBA, is an associate of Watkins, Gray, Woodgate International and frequent contributor to the AJ Information Library. He is author of the AJ Handbook of Fixings and Fastenings.

Frontis photograph by permission of Bethnal Green Museum | *Bill Launchbury*

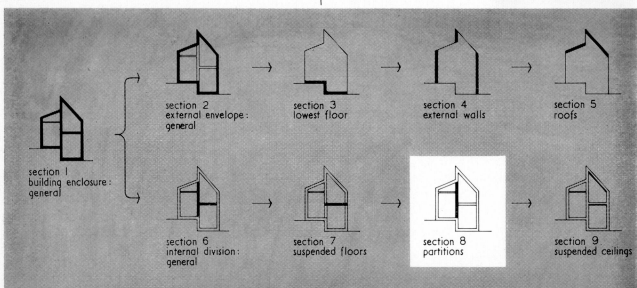

section 1
building enclosure:
general

section 2
external envelope:
general

section 3
lowest floor

section 4
external walls

section 5
roofs

section 6
internal division:
general

section 7
suspended floors

section 8
partitions

section 9
suspended ceilings

Technical study
Partitions 1

Partitions: design and selection

This technical study by BILL LAUNCHBURY *deals with factors involved in the design and selection of internal partitions, and considers how the most significant of these factors inter-relate*

1 Introduction

This type of basic building component has several definable characteristics. To simplify evaluation, information is presented in four stages:
● Primary selection factors (see 2)
● Secondary selection factors (see 3)
● Compatibility and design detail (see 4)
● Special factors (see 5)
The breakdown of these 'consideration stages' is based on the relative significance of individual factors in most design or selection decisions. But there will be many situations where factors other than those in the primary and secondary stages can dictate or influence choice.

1.01 Performance specifications

In 1966 the first performance specification for partitions and internal linings[1] was prepared by DES. This was produced to rationalise requirements for partitions to be used in CLASP, CMB, SCOLA and SEAC systems, and gave detailed descriptions of tests to prove performance.
Since then various departments, notably MPBW[2] and DOE[3], have published similar standards.
Technical descriptions and test data in manufacturers' trade literature are still far from standardised, and great care is necessary in comparing claimed performance of proprietary products.
It is also important to note that performance requirements usually vary for partitions in different parts of the same building.

1.02 Scope

Internal partitions include both opaque and glazed screens, and loadbearing and non-loadbearing components. Interior linings of external walls are not considered, but in evaluating certain factors of partitions, particularly those relating to the surface finish, it is important to achieve compatibility with the inner face of the external wall.
Doors and openings are considered as integral parts of partitions; ironmongery is however outside the scope of this study.
Junctions with ceilings and floor finishes (skirtings) are evaluated in the compatibility and design detail stage (see 4).

Classification
The most effective general classification of partition types is by ease of demountability; this is dealt with under Primary factors (see 2).

Statutory requirements
Reference is made to relevant local authority and other regulations under the various headings of factors to which they apply.

Appearance
Although appearance is inevitably a major influence in the design and selection of partitions, references in this study are confined largely to the preservation of surface characteristics, ie their resistance to damage by impact or abrasion. Damage can also be caused by scorching or chemical action, and surfaces can become unsightly by stains, graffiti and other marking.
Consideration of any finish should allow a study of the relative ease or difficulty in cleaning, redecorating, repairing or replacing finishes. In proprietary systems where the frame or joint is visually expressed, the appearance of 'make up' pieces and junction details should be carefully considered.

Integrated partition/ceiling design
There is a growing tendency for more overall responsibility by one subcontractor for the provision and fixing of all work in definable zones of the building. Examples of fully coordinated partition and ceiling systems are illustrated in 4.

2 Design considerations: primary selection factors

The primary factors are illustrated in **1**, in general they will most influence choice and design of partitions.

2.01 Demountability

The ease with which internal divisions can be removed varies from the fingertip control of a door or 'curtain' construction to the virtual permanence of a loadbearing wall.
A classification of partitions by demountability is shown on page 330. Minor inconsistencies in defining these ranges are accepted by the manufacturing industry. For example:
● Most proprietary partitions can be obtained with glazing in the units, but there is also a clearly identifiable market for glazed screens, closely related to the shopfitting industry.

● Full height concrete slab partitions are shown as physically similar to other 'masonry' types, although their breaking down may be achieved in less time and result in less debris.

Though the term 'demountable' is used widely in the field of proprietary partitions, it should be noted that *any* non-loadbearing wall is demountable but not necessarily re-erectable. Systems finished with plaster, plasterboard or tiling are not generally re-usable, and many proprietary frame and panel types are not designed for re-use. The characteristics of re-usability and a brief description of the types defined in Information Sheet Partition 1, Diagram **1** are tabulated in 6.

Demountability is often difficult to evaluate accurately at design stage. For example, the breaking down and rebuilding of non-loadbearing brick and block walls may cause considerable disruption during the work, and the removal of debris may provide difficulties. But it has been proved in many cases that repartitioning presents so many other design problems in the reprovision of lighting, ceilings and ceiling trim, services and other components, that the disruption in removing and resiting masonry walls is outweighed by the advantages, especially those of superior sound insulation, fire resistance and fitment-carrying characteristics at relatively low cost **1**.

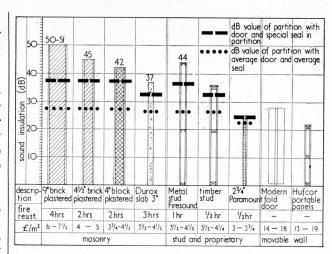

	9" brick plastered	4½" brick plastered	4" block plastered	Durox slab 3"	Metal stud Firesound	timber stud	2¾" Paramount	Modern fold door	Hufcor portable panels
descrip-tion									
dB value	50-51	45	42	37	44				
fire resist.	4hrs	2hrs	2hrs	3hrs	1hr	½hr	½hr	–	–
£/m²	6 – 7½	4 – 5	3¾–4½	3½–4½	3½–4½	3½–4¼	3 – 3¾	14 – 18	13 – 19
	masonry				stud and proprietary			movable wall	

■■■ dB value of partition with door and special seal in partition
●●●● dB value of partition with average door and average seal

2 *Several points are illustrated: the relationship between sound insulation and demountability—partitions with low demountability usually have high sound insulation (and high fire resistance) and vice versa. The height of the partition on the chart is related to the sound reduction (in dB) which it can produce. The effect of including a door with a special seal is also shown, this seal in a solid wall produces far better results (compared with ordinary seal) than a special seal in a stud wall. Costs shown are as at early 1972. See general note on costs in preface.*

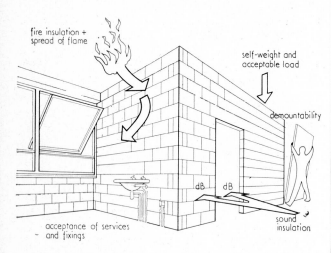

fire insulation + spread of flame

self-weight and acceptable load

demountability

acceptance of services and fixings

dB   dB

sound insulation

1 *Properties illustrated here are those on which architect's first decisions will probably be based when choosing partition type. (Next decisions—secondary factors—are shown in part* II)

In buildings where proprietary partitions are likely to be moved around often, it is absolutely vital to maintain level and accurate ceiling and floor planes with constant height dimensions between them. Inaccuracies of over 3 mm can cause problems in resiting partitions, though sometimes interchangeability has dictated, and succeeded in obtaining, such accuracy. In one instance, where a manufacturer adapted their design to suit a high re-use requirement, a survey of the building made 10 years later revealed that the number of partitions which had been moved was nearly 100 per cent of the total. Conversely there are examples where no changes have been made at all in a similar time.

2.02 Strength and weight

Ability to support load

Internal walls designed to support superimposed structural loading are mainly confined to monolithic concrete or brick and block materials, and their selection will usually involve a major contribution by the structural engineer.

Choice of this type of partition may influence the whole structure: for instance if a multi-storey building with small cell planning (eg residential) can have permanent walls, a masonry structure may be cheaper than concrete for up to 15 to 18 storeys.

More detailed structural implications of choice are given in the following publications: BS 187[4], BS 3921[5], and CP 121 101[6] for bricks for loadbearing internal walls; and BS 2028[7] CP 111[7] and CP 122[9] for blocks and slabs for loadbearing internal walls. BS 2028: 1364:1968[7] specifies seven grades of strength for type A blocks and two grades for type B. The strongest grade in type A requires average comprehensive strengths up to 35 N/mm² and the availability of a unit of this load capacity should give rise to greater use of block-work in multi-storey buildings[10].

With brick and block loadbearing partitions, the control of quality of work will normally require monitoring of the loadbearing quality of the mortar by the use of test cubes.

Transverse strength
Recommended widths for brick and block walls of various heights are shown in table I.

Table I Non-loadbearing walls or partitions should be such that one dimension, either the length or height, should not exceed the following:

Thickness	64 2½	76 3	102 4	152 6	219 8⅝	mm in
Maximum length or height	3·050	3·660	4·570	6·100	7·620	m

The above figures are maximum values and should only be used when there is little possibility of the wall being subjected to avoidable lateral forces (from BS CP 122[9])

For sandwich panel or 'frame and panel' non-loadbearing partitions the effects of side-applied pressure or impact can be critical: this has been recognised in the performance specifications published by several government departments[1-3]. These documents describe tests in detail. For example MPBW *Performance specification*[3] requires units to sustain the following loads:

● sideways uniformly distributed load of 200 N/m²—maximum deflection must be 1/125 of the height or 20 mm (whichever is less)

● temporary point load of 500 N/m²—maximum deflection as above

● soft body impact (three impacts with body weight of 30 kg, 120 Joules energy)—maximum deflection as above. Residual deflection of 1 mm is permitted, and there must be no permanent deterioration of subsequent performance of any sort described in the specification. Similar tests are included for door slamming impacts.

Self weight
Where heavier types of partitions are selected, their weight may affect the general structural capacity of the building. In particular, attention should be paid to any local restrictions which may be placed on the siting of internal walls by structural engineers. For example **3** shows the use of brick or blockwork partitions on a concrete/clay pot slab construction. In certain conditions, depending on floor section and wall height it may prove unsafe to site partitions on a line between ribs without plate reinforcement. This restriction can cause serious problems to anyone changing the partition arrangement several years after the original building, and if such a change is a possibility the floor should be designed to accept partition loads anywhere.

2.03 Sound insulation

Each space in a building should be considered as both a source and a receiver of noise, and special problems should be identified early enough in the planning stage to allow

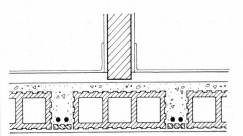

3 *Relationship of partition to ribs in pot floors may be critical*

them to be eliminated or reduced by room arrangement. It is often very expensive, and sometimes impossible, to reduce severe noise in an adjoining space to an acceptable level by later treatment of an existing partition.

The sound-resisting requirements of a partition are affected by the level of noise in the adjoining room and by the acceptable standard in the 'receiving' room. The latter is affected by the general level of ambient noise, and if there is little external noise, or if that noise has been minimised by the use of an insulated external wall, the sound reduction characteristics of internal divisions will be more stringent.

In high-rise city buildings with little control over the entry of street noise, insulation requirements for partitions will vary between the noisier lower levels to the quieter upper floors (street noise does not decrease significantly till about the tenth floor). A nomogram for estimating average sound insulation required of partitions interposed between noise sources and noise receiving rooms is shown in Technical Study ENCLOSURE Internal Division **1**.

Mass law
The loudness of a sound is dependent on its intensity in a complex way. The intensity can be measured in decibels (dB) related to a standard reference pressure, and a measurement in dBA is a good guide to loudness for a very large number of common sounds, such as traffic noise **13, 15**. In ideal circumstances a partition with an average insulation over the frequency range 100 to 3150 Hz† of say 35 dB will reduce an airborne sound of 75 dBA on one side to a level of about 40 dBA on the other.

The stiffness of a partition may control the insulation at *any* frequency and certainly does so in the range 100 to 3150 Hz for many kinds of partition. However, it is agreed that the major controlling influence is the mass (*not* the density; a very thick partition of low density material will give as good insulation as a thin one of high density material provided it is of equivalent mass). The graph **4** shows the average sound insulation (100 to 3150 Hz) related to partition mass (in kg/m²).

This performance applies only to airborne sound, and to non-porous wall materials. The sharp difference in insulation standards between a porous wall before and after sealing with plaster is shown in **5**.

Above all, the ability of a partition to sustain in practice the performance which its weight (or manufacturer's claims) suggests is possible, will depend upon the absence of weaknesses in or around the partition. These can give rise to 'flanking paths' or areas of local weakness **6**. Proprietary partitions may 'leak' sound at the head, sill or joint, and all partitions have weak spots at junctions with structure ceiling voids, through-services and door openings. These spots can cause dramatic loss of insulation performance, even in high rated walls. For example a 10 m² partition of any mass with a 700 mm² hole in it, cannot provide insula-

†Frequency is measured in Hertz. One Hz=1 cycle per second (cps)

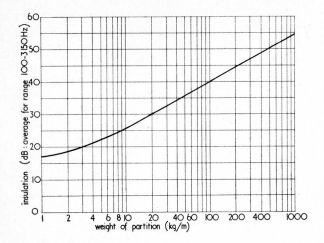

4 *Average sound insulation related to mass*

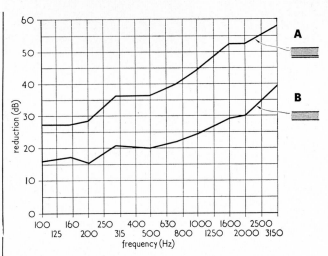

5 *Effect on sound reduction of sealing one side of porous construction* **A** *75 mm clinker block with one face 12 mm plaster (117 kg/m²) gives mean average 40dB; plaster both faces shows mean of 42dB.* **B** *75 mm clinker block unplastered (82 kg/m²) shows mean average 23dB*

tion greater than 42 dB. Where the door area is 7 per cent of the total partition area, with average edge leaks (150 to 200 mm²) then there is no advantage of selecting a wall with a rating greater than 35 dB, and the overall value will be about 27 dB. Comparative performance figures in **2** show the effect of including a door in the construction.

Statutory regulations

There are very few references to sound insulation criteria for partitions in by-laws and other regulations. Requirements for walls separating dwellings or spaces used for other purposes from dwellings, and for walls separating habitable rooms from refuse chutes are expressed in the Building Regulations 1972[17] (part G, Sound insulation), in 'deemed to satisfy' clauses describing acceptable weights of wall materials.

The Building Standards (Scotland) Regulations[18] 1963 require reductions in sound by party walls of houses and flats according to two grade curves which define the insulation at 16 different frequencies over the range 100 to 3150 Hz. The regulations also give 'deemed to satisfy' constructions which include details of flanking wall construction designed to avoid excessive insulation loss from flanking sound transmission[11,14,15].

Methods of testing and presentation of data

Unless more exactly defined, the sound insulation rating of partitions usually refers to the average insulation over the range 100 to 3150 Hz. As insulation is invariably greater at high frequencies than at low ones, it is important to know over what frequency range the average is taken. For example, suppliers of some products originating in the US quote a STC (sound transmission class) value based on measurements over the frequency range 125 to 4000 Hz. This fact, together with other features of the American method of specification results in STC numbers being consistently higher than the averages over 100 to 3150 Hz, sometimes by as much as 10 dB.

Similarly some manufacturers choose to quote an average value over a restricted frequency range (at the higher end of the spectrum), often without acknowledging the restriction.

In the UK the approved methods of testing and defining sound insulation of partitions, both in the laboratory and in the field, are given in BS 2750: 1956[16]. This provides for measurement at 16 different ⅓-octave interval frequencies, and quotation of these 16 values reveals any weakness, such as low insulation in a resonant region, perhaps as a result of the 'coincidence effect'.

In assessing partition performance based on a test measure-

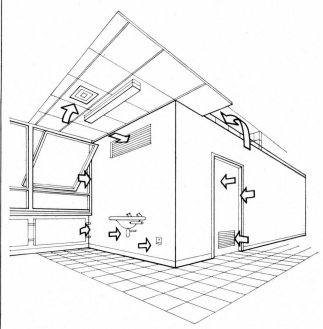

6 *Arrows indicate weak points through which sound can travel, reducing the sound insulation of the wall as a whole*

ment result, the fact that in a laboratory test there will have been very little or no flanking sound transmission must be borne in mind. When a partition is erected in a normal building there will always be some flanking sound transmission and this will inevitably reduce the practical insulation to some extent below the value obtained in a laboratory test. Reductions of up to 10 dB are not uncommon[14,15].

Attempts have been made by various government departments to codify partition performance, in spite of the inherent difficulties outlined above. In *Common performance standards for building components*[2], DES gives five grades of sound insulation standard. These grades are based on insulation values at ⅓-octave intervals as specified in BS 2750[16], with permitted tolerance rules. These rules are now incorporated in the Building Regulations which define how the tests are to be done by reference to BS 2750 (Reg. G6). Another concept of sound insulation performance which has been proposed is one based on speech privacy. Apart from the fact that the loudness and character of background noise in the receiving room have a major effect on the suggested insulation requirement[13], the criterion can never be a very exact one, because some people speak much more clearly and loudly than others.

Sound absorption

Absorbing materials can be used in the room which contains the source of noise, to give some additional control. But direct sound to the partition is not affected, and absorption must be doubled to achieve a noise level reduction in the source room of 3 dB. Similarly, additional absorption in the sound receiving room will also lower the level of incoming sound by a small amount.

Most statements of sound insulation refer to the value to be expected between two 'domestic' size, averagely reverberant rooms (ie with a reverberation time of 0·5 to 1·0 seconds). If the reverberation time (which depends on the amount of sound absorbent present) in the source and/or the receiving room varies widely from this value, the effective sound insulation may be either increased (low reverberation times) or decreased (high reverberation times). Practical limits of this effect are about ±5 dB.

Sound insulation in excess of mass law value

Certain types of partition construction are capable of giving sound insulation in excess of the value which would be expected when considering only their weight. Broadly, these are constructions which consist of two or more 'leaves', or partitions separated by air spaces in such a way that a certain degree of discontinuity is preserved between the leaves. A simple sheeted stud partition can, to some extent, qualify for this increased insulation but to achieve the greatest discontinuity the partition should be double studded and staggered so that there is no connection between the sheeted faces **7**. Further improvement can be obtained by hanging absorbent material in the cavity. Some materials specially weighted by incorporating barytes powder in mineral or glass wool are available.

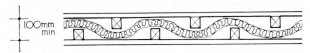

7 *Discontinuity between opposite leaves of partition. Studs are staggered and separated by an absorbent blanket.*

Another technique which can provide unusually high degrees of insulation is the incorporation of mass by means of a pliable material, such as lead or lead-loaded plastic into a partition.

All claims for insulation exceeding the 'mass value' should be carefully scrutinised, and should only be accepted if substantiated by valid test measurements, preferably in field conditions.

2.05 Fire resistance

By-laws and regulations

Mandatory requirements can have considerable influence on design and selection of partitions. Regulations are based upon the principle of preserving life in the case of fire; this is done by providing means of escape and by dividing the building into a series of compartments to stop the fire spreading.

Section E of the Building Regulations (England and Wales) 1972[17] classifies buildings by use, and lays down the maximum size of compartments for each purpose group in accordance with stated height limits.

The regulations are specific as regards detailing of walls forming fire compartments, and **8** shows the main areas where special attention is necessary[19].

Requirements in Scotland are covered by Building Stan-

If in 'unprotected shaft' where duct-work perforates compartment wall, opening requires firestopping in space between duct and opening, and duct requires automatic fire shutter

Firestopping required at wall junction with slab and other structural junctions especially in cavities

Perforations for pipes are permitted with limitations on diameter depending on material used and requirement for firestopping

Automatic fire shutters required if conveyor belts or escalators penetrate compartment

Impact damage can weaken fire resistance of wall

Doors must be self-closing and when giving access to protected shafts must be held shut when not in use

8 *Detailing of fire compartments* [19]

dards (Scotland) Regulations, 1963[18]. In the GLC area the controlling document is the London Building Acts (Amendment) Act 1939[20]. The GLC publishes guidance information dealing with means of escape and a schedule of fire resistance of various materials (obtainable from the Information Centre, South Block, County Hall SE1).

The regulations define the required fire resistance of compartment walls and other conditions. In the Building Regulations (England and Wales) 1972[17] these are scheduled in table A to Regulation E5, Parts 1 and 2. In general, requirements range from a half-hour resistance (which applies for instance to all one- and two-storey private dwelling houses above ground) to a four-hour resistance (which applies to certain above and below ground conditions in group VIII buildings of 27·4 m high and over; and some below ground cases in groups V and VI).

Although BS 476[21] defines fire resistance up to six hours, the regulations consider four hours' resistance as the maximum requirement. The minimum requirement for all separating walls is one hour, and except for certain easements regarding property, fire-stopped pipes must not be perforated.

Insurance

In addition to precautions taken to safeguard life, by compartmenting and using fire resisting materials, additional provisions may be asked for by insurance companies. They may demand extra compartments, and prohibit certain materials which in burning or smouldering give off damaging gases without spreading flame.

Testing

Tests are described fully in BS 476: Part 1: 1953.

Proprietary partitions

Proprietary partitions with one-hour resistance are specially treated to achieve continuity of the protection at junctions and joints between units. But resistance of one hour and over is more likely to be provided by masonry or concrete materials, and as an example of average require-

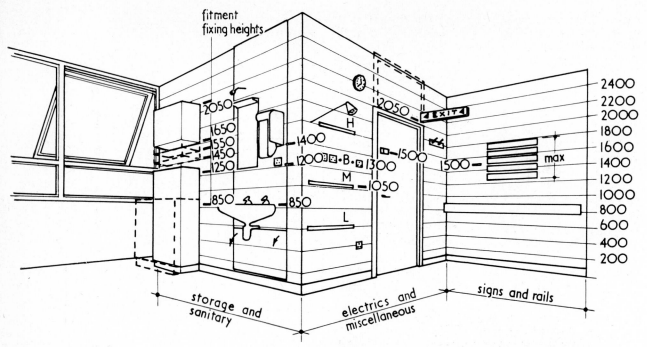

9

9 *Range of dimensions suitable for co-ordinating fixings to internal partitions based on* MPBW *performance specifications for fittings in hospitals*

ments, the MPBW *Partitions: Performance Specification*, 1970, calls for only half-hour and nil resistance.

2.06 Spread of flame

BS 476: Part 1: 1953[21] classified wall surfaces in ascending order of resistance the surfaces were defined as: class 4: rapid flame spread; class 3: medium flame spread; class 2: low flame spread; class 1: very low flame spread.

The Building Regulations[17] acknowledging certain inadequacies in the classification, added a further more stringent category class 0: a surface of a material which:

● is non-combustible throughout, or

● The surface or (if bonded to a substrate) the surface and substrate have an index (I) not exceeding 12 and subindex (I_1) not exceeding 6 in accordance with BS 476: part 6: 1968.

● If however the face is plastic with a softening point below 120 deg c when tested by method 102c of BS 2782:1970 it must either

be bonded to a substrate which is not plastic and the combined material must comply with the preceeding rule, or it must satisfy the test in the above rule and be so used that if the lining were not present, the surface below would not be plastic with a softening point not exceeding 120 deg c and would itself satisfy the test criteria.

For each purpose group the Building Regulations defined locations in a building where the various classes are applicable (table to Reg. E15 in the Regulations). Class 4 is considered too low a standard for inclusion anywhere. Class 0 is required in all purpose groups except group I (small residential buildings) for circulation spaces and protected shafts. Manufacturers providing partitions within the *Partitions: Performance Specification*, 1970 of the MPBW must supply class 0 and class 1; class 0 coinciding with the 'hard wearing' requirement, ie internal walls enclosing areas with low spread of flame risk (class 0) need high wear resistance.

2.07 Ability to accept fixings

Dimensional criteria for a wide range of fixings to internal partitions are given in **9**. Although specific to health buildings, this range of fittings is fairly typical.

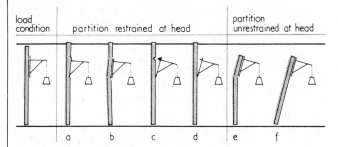

10 *Ways in which partitions under load may fail*

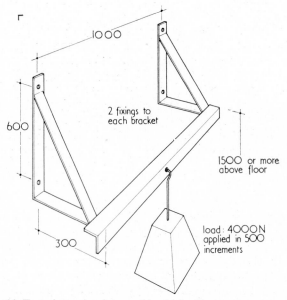

11 *Test rig to simulate washbasin loading*

Official performance specifications[1-3] separate light and heavy fittings, and partitions are usually required to accept the former, eg pinboards and nameboards.

DOE s *Performance requirements for partitions*[3] lays down a testing standard for 'lightweight fixtures', eg small fire extinguishers and coathooks, which require a good anchorage. The fixing specified must support, without loosening or

12a   **12b**

13

14a

14b

damaging the partition, a load represented by
- a force of 100N applied both parallel and at 45° to the face (in any direction) and
- a force of 250N applied at right angles to the face.

For heavier fittings, it is possible that some partitions cannot provide adequate support over the whole face, or even at all. Several of the main factors which can cause or influence this failure are indicated in **10**, in the later stages of planning the condition of internal walls required to carry such loads should be checked, particularly where partitions are of light construction or are unrestrained at the head.

Tests for heavier fittings are included in specifications[1-11]. Another important factor is the time at which the fixing is to be carried out, and this may be critical where areas of permissible fixings are known to the partition specifier, but not necessarily to the building user. Resiting of cupboards and washbasins can also create serious problems if, for instance, the recognised fixing method requires the provision of a backplate on the other side of the partition.

Available fixings are illustrated in the AJ Handbook of Fixings and fastenings[22]. But devices for fixing objects to internal walls will use one of the following principles:
- Back-clamping to the inside of the panel skin (toggles and cavity fixings)
- Threading into fibres of face or core materials (wood screws, or special screws for chipboard, woodwool, etc)
- Threading or displacing metal (self-threading and self-tapping screws)
- Expansion into the face or core material (nails or screws into plugs, bolts in self-drilling anchors, expansion bolts)
- Pressure of the face or core material (nails)
- Mechanical clamping through the wall (bolts with washers or backplates on other side)
- Adhesion (glues).

Manufacturers of partitions using certain materials for face or core have developed special devices in collaboration with the fixings industry—particularly in the case of plasterboard. Manufacturer's recommendations should be followed, and after taking over the building the user should be made aware of these recommendations, and of any limitations to which the partitions may be subject **12**.

Failure of fixings is a common complaint about buildings in use, and fixing devices should be carefully specified, and their application accurately described, in contract documents, or adequate performance requirements given in quantifiable terms. Particular care should be taken with regard to fixings into concrete blockwork, the relative density of which will influence the specification.

2.08 Ability to accept services

If pipework and electrical wiring or conduit must run in the partition 'zone', it can run either along the main wall face,

12 *Some proprietary partitions:* **a** *have special channels to which light shelf brackets can be clipped. Heavier fittings* **b** *are supported on timber grounds behind the lining. Note small hole to allow for services.* (**a** *Magnacon,* **b** *Gyproc metal stud*)
13 *Electric services chased into a brick or block partition could reduce sound insulation considerably*
14a, b *If a 'service run philosophy' is not developed at early planning stages,* **a** *and* **b** *are likely to occur, especially at skirtings.* **a** *shows the importance of taking into account the bend in the conduit, which prohibits satisfactory fitting at both skirting and floor level.* **b** *illustrates the importance of remembering the lighting conduits on the floor below, when designing the partition on the floor above*

15 *Electric cables can travel through vertical posts in
proprietary partitions (Unilock Compactum)*

16 *Inside of double skin steel partition, showing services
and access panel (Gyproc)*

on the reverse face (ie on the wall in a less important room,
or in a duct), or in the thickness of the partition itself. It is
vital to establish a 'service run philosophy', and apply this
when developing details at early planning stage; serious
misunderstandings between architect and consultant can
occur unless these principles are agreed and understood.
It is possible to coordinate terminals in fairface work with
competence, even with concrete block partitions **13**. It is also
possible to attempt on site a miracle detail at the skirting
where conduit changes from its agreed run in the screed to
its agreed run up the wall face **14a**.

Electrical services

If wiring in plastered brick, block or storey-height concrete
slab partitions cannot be incorporated within the depth of
the plaster then chases should be cut. Depth of chase cuts
should be kept to the minimum. Note that back-to-back
outlet boxes weaken the sound insulation value of an
otherwise high performance wall **13**. Note also that Clause
D15 Schedule 7 of the Building Regulations strictly limits
the depths of horizontal and vertical chases in relation to the
total thickness of the wall, inner leaf or partition.
Nearly all proprietary partitions offer facilities for running
electrical wiring. Horizontal runs are usually available at
the base, often with clipped-on removable skirtings.
Vertical runs are taken either through voids in the panels,
or through posts in frame constructions, in which case
switch terminals are usually designed to fit within the face
dimension of the post **15**.
Heights for electrical fittings in hospitals are shown in **9**.
In the MPBW performance specifications requirements vary
slightly (low level outlets at 350 mm, switches at 1350 mm
and clock spurs at 2250 mm). Minimum horizontal spacings
are given as optional installation points.

Mechanical services

The design of partition systems capable of accepting internal
pipework has been strongly influenced by the requirements
of Hospital Board building programmes, and has resulted
in the use of one or two skins of plasterboard fixed to
pressed steel studs, **16** shows a detail of this.
Partitions which have an overall width of 100 mm are
severely limited in the size of pipes which can be incorporated (25 and 38 mm overall sizes are possible). Check
carefully that pipe crossings can be accommodated. The
MPBW specifications refer to larger pipe sizes of 51, 60, 70,
73, 82 and 150 mm, but recognises the need for vertical runs
only and acknowledges that the larger sizes may be incorporated in ducts formed within the system from two walls.
The system described in the DHSS 'CUBITH' manufacturers'
basic data allows for pressed metal vertical studs with
several knockout holes to accept small diameter horizontal
runs.
Any system allowing internal pipe runs must include
access panels for inspecting pipework, operating valves and
cleaning eyes. Local water authorities should be contacted
before this sort of pipe run principle is adopted, to ensure
that it is permitted by the particular regulations affecting
the building **16**.

2.09 Conclusion: primary factors

In comparing these primary factors (ie those which have
the greatest influence on partition selection and design)
note that the traditionally constructed 'masonry' wall of
brick or blockwork shows a high score as regards strength,
fire and sound resistance, acceptance of fixings and incor-

poration of services, and with cost evaluation. The possible problems of 'demounting' this type of partition should be reconsidered in this light and in the light of other changes to services in floors or ceiling which may need altering regardless of type of partition used, so that demountability might not always give the flexibility which it superficially appears to do.

Note also that many factors have a bearing on each other: incorporation of internal services affects sound insulation and demountability; weight and general mass affects sound insulation and ability to receive and support heavy fitments, and so on.

3 Design considerations: secondary selection factors

3.01 General

Secondary factors (ie the second check) are shown in **17.** They are concerned mainly with qualities of finish, rather

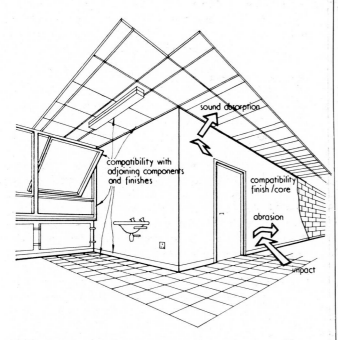

17 *Primary decisions were illustrated in* **1** *(part 1). The next decisions—secondary factors—are illustrated here*

than the core material of the partition. Some factors are strongly interrelated, and high performance in one way may imply low performance in another. For example, finishes with good sound absorbent characteristics usually have low resistance to abrasion and impact.

Consideration is given (3.06) to compatibility of partitions with adjoining elements, such as the external wall. The dimensional aspects of this are dealt with in 4.

3.02 Sound absorption

Sound insulation *reduces* sound transmission *through* the wall, and relates to the construction of the whole partition; absorption—the prevention of reflection—is controlled by quality of finish or construction of the surface. These two factors are not directly related, though absorbent surfaces in a noisy room can reduce the reverberation level of that room and improve levels in adjoining spaces. But even doubling the area of absorbent finish in a room will only reduce noise level 3dB, and 8dB reduction is the maximum possible.

Absorptive materials lining air ducts which pass through partitions, will reduce sound reverberation and lessen the effect of this weak point in the wall. Some proprietary partitions use air spaces and absorbent materials inside cavities to improve the overall insulating quality.

Besides controlling reverberation times in rooms where quality of speech or music is important, absorbent materials can also be used in machine rooms to change the character of noise. These should be as near as possible to noise source, and are usually suspended from the ceiling (though partitions are sometimes used to form screens).

Sound absorption efficiency is measured by the sound absorption coefficient, giving performance figures for the octave frequencies of 125, 250, 500, 1000, 2000 and 4000 Hz[12].

Types of absorbent materials
Absorbent materials fall into three main categories:
● porous materials which have highest performance at high frequencies. Increasing the thickness of the absorptive material to 25 mm assists performance at the middle and the lower frequencies. Porous materials include mineral and glass wool, wood wool, felts, foamed connecting-cell plastics, fibreboard and sprayed asbestos and soft furnishing materials
● resonant panels, more efficient at low frequencies (50 to 200 Hz), and used where selective performance is required
● cavity resonators (Helmholtz resonators) are even more selective, and can control noise over a narrow band of frequency.

From the partition design aspect, sound absorption is mainly dealt with by porous materials, which may be mounted to act as resonant panels. For example, battens placed behind any kind of acoustic tile (to leave a space) will improve low-frequency absorption.

Some proprietary acoustic products consist of perforated panels over an air space with porous absorbent, thus combining the effects of all three categories.

Ceilings are usually treated as absorbent surfaces in preference to walls, as they are less susceptible to staining, and to damage by impact and abrasion.

Where absorbents must be used on the wall and are also likely to get worn, materials with rigid faces should be used. Where hygiene is important, eg in hospitals, it is difficult to obtain good sound absorbent qualities as well, as there are few materials with good sound absorbing qualities which do not harbour bacteria.

3.03 Abrasion and staining

Marking, scratching or serious permanent damage can be inflicted on surfaces by building users including cleaners **18**. In hospital spaces where trolleys pass continually, protection rails should be used, and the designer should liaise with the client to co-ordinate rail design with trolley type and size. Resistance to mechanical wear is a difficult factor to quantify, and there is no overall British Standard which is applicable.

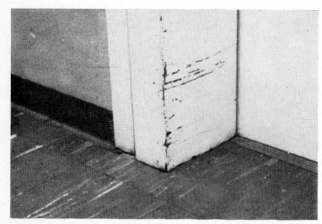

18 *Impact and abrasion damage on architrave of lift shaft; stoved enamel was used instead of stainless steel, and the false economy of this decision shows only too clearly*

Performance specification

The DOE performance requirements for partitions (1970)[3] refers, as do other performance specifications, to tests developed by the Furniture Industries Research Association Laboratories at Maxwell Road, Stevenage, Herts.
The following tests are described:
● Resistance to water. This test, which requires no marking after a saturated pad has been left on the surface is detailed in BS 3962: part 4[23]
● Brittleness of finish. In this test, steel blocks are dropped on to the finish, which is then examined and given ratings from 0 (severe cracking) to 4 (no surface damage)
● Adhesion of finish. In this test a grid is scratched on the surface with just sufficient pressure to penetrate the material below. The finish is rated by amount of loose material from 0 (65 per cent or more removed) to 4 (clean scratches)
● Resistance to scratching. A standard scraper is drawn across the finish under a gradually increasing load, and the load recorded when the material below is first visible
● Resistance to wear. The DOE specification notes that a test is being developed. However in the MPBW performance standards a test is described which involves rubbing the surface with a silicon carbide disc for 40 revolutions with a load of 2·72 kg. Assessed ratings are shown in five grades from 'slight surface marking' to 'finish removed'.
Some finishes are resistant to marking agents such as pencils, paints, inks and wax crayons. It is important to check whether the finish is resistant to acid and/or alkali.

3.04 Impact resistance

There are two types of impact resistance test:
● Effect on a partition of a hard blow from a relatively large soft body, ie three impacts on each side with a bag filled with 30 kg of dry sand (impact energy 120 J), after which no damage which is not easily repaired shall be sustained, and no residual deformation noted in the partition's perform-

ances (MPBW specifications allow maximum 1 mm deflection and no lowering of any other factors). One further impact on each side is required with the energy increased to 240 J, without any shattering or breakage causing danger.
● The effect on the finish of a lighter blow from a steel ball. A solid steel ball of 50 mm diameter is allowed to drop on each side of the partition. All partitions are required to withstand such blows at an impact energy of 2·5 J without visually unacceptable indentation (in most finishes 0·5 mm maximum) and at 10 J without damage which is not easily repaired and without causing dangerous fragments. For 'hard-wearing' situations such as teaching spaces the impact energy level for the first part of the test is increased from 2·5 to 6·25 J.

3.05 Compatibility of finish with core

Proprietary partitions

Selection of finish to match core characteristics would obviously be tested before production runs start. The adhesion of decorative coating can be tested by the scratch method described in 3.03.

'Masonry' partitions

The basic principle in choosing a finish to match the core is: always choose a finish which is *weaker* than the core behind. There is always danger in putting a stronger skin on top of a weak background, eg it may be inadvisable to fix ceramic tiles on a cement/sand base applied to a concrete block core with high shrinkage potential without taking special precautions and seeking expert advice. Clay bricks or blocks are a better base for hard skin materials (ie tiles) as they have no shrinkage problems although in such cases shrinkage of the tile bed may be a problem. Full details of finish/core compatibility are given in BS CP 211[24].
Where there is little mechanical key on the face of the material, the horizontal joints should be raked out—always provided that this is acceptable to the structural performance of the wall.
Where grounds are fixed to walls to support panelling and similar finishes, enough tolerance should be left to take up dimensional discrepancies in the vertical planes, particularly where concrete columns are incorporated. All joints between dissimilar materials should be considered, especially in the case of plastered or rendered finishes.

3.06 Junction with other finishes

The point where the partition meets the external wall requires particular study. The additional thermal insulation requirements may result in different core and/or finish materials, even if brickwork or blockwork is used both for internal partitions and external wall lining. Also this zone may have to accommodate penetrating service pipes and conduits. Dimensional and setting out implications are considered in 4.
Where loadbearing and non-loadbearing brick- and block-work join, the finishes at that point must take up differential movement **19**.
If demountable partitions are attached to fixed parts of the building, this junction must allow the partitions to be removed with the minimum of repair work to areas exposed by removal. (This applies equally to floor and ceiling finishes, especially the latter, where the junction detail depends on whether or not the partition penetrates the ceiling void). The practical problems of top retention of partitions are referred to in 4.
When the partition penetrates the ceiling plane the ceiling

finish must accommodate the junction by allowing a standard treatment of the wall zone (to take all occurring partition thicknesses). Alternatively a satisfactory trimming philosophy should be followed **20**.

Where plaster finishes are used for adjoining wall and ceiling planes (or adjoining walls of differing loadbearing characteristics where the walls are tied but not bonded), anticipated movement cracks can be limited by using shellac-treated junctions if it is too costly to incorporate more sophisticated movement joints.

There are three types of skirtings:
● continuation of the partition finish
● continuation of the floor finish
● a third material to separate the partition and floor finish.

Choice may depend on trade responsibility and sequence for large areas of the finishing work in the building. When selecting skirtings it is also important to consider intended treatment at all internal and external corners, at door frames and architraves, and—most important of all—the meeting with other types of skirting, both at corners and in the same plane.

Skirtings protect the base of partitions from floor-cleaning operations; they protect less resistant surfaces from wet processes, and take the marks which cleaning machines usually make and which are often conspicuous on light painted architraves penetrating the skirting line.

19

20

19 *A 'birds eye view' (taken before casting slab) looking directly down on head of loadbearing wall with flexible ties to receive non-loadbearing wall. Movement joints are then incorporated in plaster finish.*

20 *Recessed trim (detailed enamelled pressed metal) allows use of uncut ceiling tiles*

4 Setting out and design detail

4.01 General

This section deals with dimensional co-ordination in manufacture and setting out of partitions, and with joints, junctions and edge conditions. These are indicated in **21**.

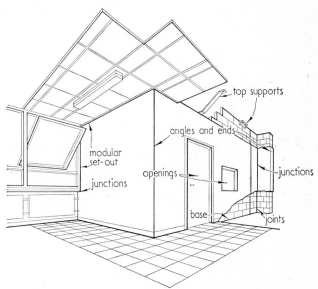

21 *Important areas where partitions must relate to other building elements*

4.02 Dimensional co-ordination and setting out

British Standards

Two British Standards are concerned with rationalised component dimensions: BS 4011[25] gives preferred size increments; components which comply are known as 'modular building components'. First preference is 300 mm, the second 100 mm. Third and fourth preference are 50 mm and 25 mm, but only for multiples up to 300 mm. So the 1000 mm (1 m) dimension is only a second preference.

BS 4330[26] shows preferred heights for spaces in various building groups, and gives controlling dimensions for partitions whether made of panels, blocks, or bricks. These controlling dimensions are in increments of 100 mm, and the standard shows how to deal with skirtings and other applied trim which may encroach on controlling zones.

PD 6444[27] limits the permutations available from the BS 4011 recommendations by indicating the most applicable sizes for components fitting the controls in BS 4330.

Setting out

Earliest consideration should be given to:
● column/partition relationships (ie whether partition runs will avoid columns, or how they will meet)
● window wall/partition relationships. Allowance must be made for all thickness variations (including applied finishes). Detailing of blockwork and brickwork must not demand impossible performance standards in laying. Accurate setting out of such partitions at floor level will not necessarily result in the accuracy at ceiling level which ceiling components may demand. If precise junctions with uncut ceiling tiles are required, it is recommended that checks are made on length and room-diagonal dimensions directly after

completing the blockwork in the first few spaces.

Also, if architects get involved in the minutiae of 100 mm, or 300 modular terms they can lose sight of the 'coarser' modular condition—the window mullion grid, or ceiling tile grid—both of which will have an eventual visual impact far greater than the smaller unit.

4.03 Partition base detail

Demountable proprietary partitions are usually built on a finished screed, with or without final finish **24**. Brick and block walls are constructed on the structural slab **24a** or on the screed **24c**.

'Masonry' partitions

If on the slab, removal of partitions will inevitably reveal differing floor finish levels on each side of the removed wall. The screed must be protected from damage if a brick or block wall is built on top of it, and this may prove quite expensive. Screed strips can be used below partition runs **24b**. The base course may need to be cut, or special height blocks used, to obtain neat coursing at soffit level of lintels to openings. (Or, if built from slab level, to give the appearance of a full base course in fairfaced blockwork).

Proprietary partitions

Some partition systems use fixed floor plates, or jacking principles to secure the base. Often the base area of the core, or the applied skirtings, are used to run services, and if electrical or piped runs penetrate the slab, considerable accuracy is required in co-ordinating the setting out of partitions and holes. The MPBW performance specification: Partitions 1970[3] refers to tolerance allowance of 5 mm for variations in the horizontal plane of the floor finish. In all systems, the sealing method, or lack of seal, at the junction of partition and floor will influence sound and fire insulation ratings, especially those optimistic figures sometimes referred to in trade literature, **22**, **23**, **24**.

22 *Erection of uprights in pressed metal stud partition. The pressed metal members can be cut to fit on site (Gyproc)*

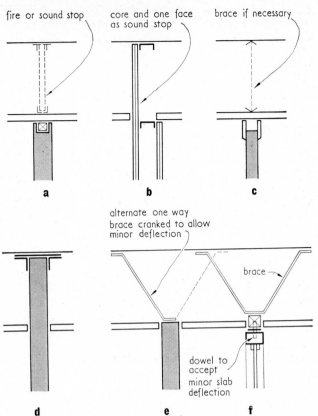

23 *Heads of some types of partitions can be restrained by fixing to ceiling membrane, directly **a** or by compression devices in the head member **c**, to structural slab above **b** and **d** or at ceiling level but braced to slab **e** and **f***

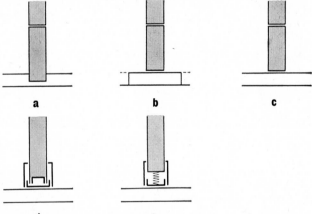

24 *Alternative base details **d** and **e** show principles used in two types of proprietary partitions*

4.04 Partition head detail

Partitions may have to cut through a suspended ceiling to the underside of the structural slab for three main reasons—firestopping, sound insulation, or general stability (**25**). Partitions are made structurally stable by being pinned to the underside of structural beams or slabs. This can be difficult and expensive if any anticipated deflection makes direct fixing impossible (or 'pinning' with mortar in the case of masonry work).

Areas where this problem is likely to arise should be checked with the structural engineer at an early stage of the design programme. Triangulated brackets in the ceiling space may be used to restrain certain types—especially high-weight partitions fixed at the fitting-out stage of the contract, which tend to overturn unless held back by the structure, rather than at the ceiling plane.

25

26a

26b

25 *Full height concrete panels using method of stop restraint shown in 23e (Durox)*
26 *It is very difficult to achieve a neat appearance at **a** the junction of a loadbearing internal wall and in situ concrete slab. The same problem **b** occurs between brickwork and rc lintel*

When choosing between partition systems, it is important to examine how the head is sealed and the effectiveness and appearance of any trim used. Movable partitions of the 'lift-away' type have a variety of head-clamping details using magnetic, pneumatic, pantograph, spring and other mechanical devices.

When using any fixing which exerts pressure on the ceiling plane, the architect must ensure that the ceiling design and its method of suspension allows for this. In the MPBW performance specification[3] the maximum expected tolerance allowing for variations in horizontality of the ceiling plane is 5 mm, plus 20 mm for possible deflection of the ceiling. Junctions between loadbearing brickwork and the concrete slab may also cause problems **26**.

4.05 Joints and junctions

This deals with two/three and four way junctions, and free ends, plus relationships with columns and the external window wall **27**.
Free ends and outside surfaces of right-angle junctions are particularly prone to damage and may need protection. Joints between panels, or panels and posts of proprietary systems should satisfy all requirements, particularly in strength, fire and sound insulation, colour and durability. Many systems use the exposed post to carry electrical

27 *Detail of proprietary partition (Paramount) showing how a T-junction is made. A vertical batten is nailed to timber plugs driven into the panel*

switch terminals, or to accommodate hooks and brackets for wall furniture or equipment. In certain areas, especially in hospitals, holes and slots in the visible surface of the post are regarded as a health hazard because they may support bacteria.
Brick partitions may require vertical joints extending through the finish, particularly where loadbearing walls meet non-loadbearing partitions **19** movement joints are essential in concrete block construction, to control shrinkage and other movement[9] [10].

4.06 Openings

Openings represent the weakest point in the partition with regard to
● ability to resist the through passage of sound, fire and smoke, and
● concentration of traffic, which increases the likelihood of abrasion, impact and mechanical damage 18.
Where damage is likely, additional protection should be considered to doors and surround trim.
Note that without protection, the base of doors, their frames and architraves may be damaged and stained by floor-cleaning equipment, even though the partition itself is protected by a suitable skirting.
Doorsets are increasingly used in all types of partition. Preferred dimensions are now given in BS 4330[26] first preferences being 2100 mm high and 900 mm wide, with variations in 100 mm increments.

5 Special factors

As well as the factors described in 2, 3 and 4 certain building types may require the partition to have other properties, such as:
● Thermal insulation greater than normal eg special walling to coldrooms, when specialist advice should be sought
● Humidity and moisture resistance. In a moisture-laden environment a requirement like this may lead to a careful appraisal of all core and metal materials likely to deteriorate. Plasterboard and flaxboard materials are particularly vulnerable
● Toxicity (may occur in some process buildings)
● Odour (ditto)
● Security (See also Section 3 lowest floor)
● x-rays (See also Section 9 para 4.03)
● Particular health risks (isolation of bacteria etc confined

mainly to pharmaceutical labs and hospitals.

Note. There are also many other aspects of partition design which could be classified as special factors and so qualify for inclusion in this section. They have however been generally covered in Section 2 (primary factors) are illustrated in **6**, **8** and **9** and hence not repeated here.

6 Checklist

6.01 First selection factors

Those on which the architect will choose the *basic* partition type, include:
- demountability
- strength and weight
- sound insulation
- fire resistance
- spread of flame
- ability to accept fixings
- ability to accept services

6.02 Secondary selection factors

Those on which the architect will consider the partition finish, include:
- sound absorption
- abrasion and staining
- impact resistance
- compatibility of finish with core
- junction with other finishes

6.03 Setting out and design detail

Setting out
Check dimensional relationships between the partition and columns, window openings, ceiling tiles, light fittings, and internal openings. Consult BS 4011, 4330 and PD 6444.

Design detail
Check what happens at:
- partition base
- partition head
- joints and junctions
- openings

6.04 Special factors

Certain building types may require the partition to have other properties such as:
- high thermal insulation
- humidity resistance
- resistance to toxicity, odour
- security
- resistance to x-rays

These factors will depend on building type.

7 References

1 DEPARTMENT OF EDUCATION AND SCIENCE
Performance specification for partitions. 1966, HMSO [(22) (A3)]

2 Common performance standards for building components. 1970, HMSO [(9–) Xy (E) (Ajp)]

3 MINISTRY OF PUBLIC BUILDING AND WORKS (now DOE)
Performance specification: Partitions. 1970, HMSO [(22) (A3)]

BRITISH STANDARDS INSTITUTION
4 BS 187: Part 2: 1970 Calcium silicate (sandlime and flintlime) bricks. Metric units [Ff1]
5 BS 3921: Part 2: 1969 Specification of bricks and blocks of fired brickearth, clay or shale. Metric units [Fg]
6 BS CP 121: 101: 1951 Brickwork [(21) Fg]
7 BS 2028: 1364: 1968 Precast concrete blocks. Metric units [Ff]
8 BS CP 111: Part 2: 1970 Structural recommendations for loadbearing walls. Metric units [(21·1) (K)]
9 BS CP 112: 1952 Walls and partitions of blocks and of slabs [(2–) Yi (K)]
10 GAGE, M. Concrete blockwork. 1971, Architectural Press [Ff]
11 BS CP 3: Chapter III: 1960 Sound insulation and noise reduction [(M)]
12 NATIONAL PHYSICAL LABORATORY The airborne sound insulation of partitions by E. N. Bazley. 1966, HMSO [(22) (M)]
13 AJ Handbook of Building environment, Section 5 Sound. *Architects' Journal*, 1969, 2 January to 12 February [(E6)]
14 DEPARTMENT OF THE ENVIRONMENT Sound insulation in buildings, by H. R. Humphreys and D. J. Melluish. 1971, HMSO [(M)]
15 PARKIN, P. H. and HUMPHREYS, H. R. Acoustics, noise and buildings, 1969, Faber revised edition [(M)]
16 BS 2750: 1956 Recommendations for field and laboratory measurement of airborne and impact sound transmission in buildings [(M4h)]
17 Building Regulations 1972, HMSO [(A3j)]
18 Building Standards (Scotland) 1963 [(A3j)]
19 Fire prevention design guide. 1969, Fire Protection Society [(R1)]
20 London Building Acts (Amendment) Act 1939 [(Ajn)]
21 BS 476: Part 1: 1953 Fire tests on building materials and structures [Yy (R4) (Aq)]
22 LAUNCHBURY, W. AJ Handbook of Fixings and fastenings. 1971, Architectural Press [Xt5] £1
23 BS 3962: Part 4: 1970 Method of test for clear finishes for wooden furniture: resistance to marking by liquids [(82) Yu 3 (Aq)]
24 BS CP 211: 1966 Internal plastering [Aa8]
25 BS 4011: 1966 Basic sizes for building components and assemblies [(F4)]
26 BS 4330: 1968 Recommendations for the coordination of dimension in building: controlling dimensions [(F4j)] *Metric units*
27 PD 6444 Recommendations for the coordination of dimensions in building: basic spaces for structure, external envelope, and internal subdivision. Part 1: 1969 functional groups 1, 2 and 3 [F4j)] £2

Information sheet
Partitions 1

1 Types of internal partitions

In this information sheet BILL LAUNCHBURY *describes 'masonry', demountable, and movable wall types of partition. A list of proprietary types follows, with information on properties, illustration of joint details, and the name and address of manufacturers.*

1 Generic types

A breakdown of generic types under the headings below, is shown diagrammatically in **1**.

1.01 Masonry partitions (bricks, blocks and slabs)

Bricks

Advantages over concrete blocks include a relatively smaller movement potential—offering very slight expansion compared with a possibly significant shrinkage in the case of blocks—but they are generally more expensive. Reverse sides of fairface 4½in (114·3 mm) and 9in (228·6 mm) walls can give visual problems, and in the latter case it may be necessary to select lengths of through bricks. For half brick walls needing good appearance both sides, calcium silicate or similar bricks of consistent dimensional accuracy are very suitable.

Blocks

Care should be taken to choose blocks with the right performance. Some ranges include blocks with high thermal insulation qualities which may have relatively high shrinkage potential. High thermal insulation is rarely needed for internal partitions, and blocks with more relevant properties (eg high sound insulation) should be considered. Costs of similar products from different manufacturers vary, and significant savings are often possible by 'shopping around' at specification stage.

Concrete slabs

Full height slabs (600 mm wide) are available from at least three suppliers (one offering fixing). They are fairly light and easy to handle, but sound insulation is slightly less efficient than the equivalent width of average brickwork—(eg 100 mm thick panels at around 60 to 65 kg per m² are claimed to give about 36 dB unplastered). Panels can be sawn; supports for heavy fixings may require special plates on other side of the wall, and accurate location of these may be necessary when ordering units although they can be drilled on site.

1.02 Demountable partitions (stud, panel and frame systems)

Panel/panel

Systems using plasterboard for skin, or for skin and core, with the joints of face panels flushed, are usually not re-erectable. Panel/panel systems with visible joints make use of battens or tongues of timber or asbestos. Thicknesses are usually between 50 and 65 mm, and sound insulation is likely to be around 25 to 30 dB. These can be re-erected.

Stud and skin

Following an impetus given by hospital and other building programmes, several firms now provide pressed steel stud systems, usually clad with plasterboard, using two skins per face when higher dB ratings are required. (Partitions 100 mm thick using double skins of 12·5 mm plasterboard over 50 mm framing, claim 44 dB and 1 h fire resistance). Incorporation of heavy fixings into partitions by user after occupation of the building can cause difficulties (although this problem arises with many types). Service pipe and conduit runs can be incorporated, but pipe sizes and incidence of pipe crossings should be carefully checked at planning stage, as the cavity is only 50 mm.

Post and panel

A very wide range is available in hardwood, pressed steel, and extruded aluminium. Extrusion allows the hollow post to contain wiring and receive fixing accessories as well as retaining the panels. At least one pressed steel unit is now available which offers similar facilities. Panel thicknesses vary considerably, but most are around 50 to 65 mm, with sound insulation characteristics similar to the panel/panel systems.

Glazed screens

This set of components is usually associated with the shopfitting industry. Aluminium systems are based on hollow rectangular box framing around 100 mm × 45 mm with thin-frame doors. The latter are mechanically jointed by some firms, welded by others. Top springs housed in the transom box section are used widely. Optional details are available for profile, fixing of beads, colour and anodic methods. Sound reduction is low or virtually nil where screens stop short of ceiling.

Wc cubicles

These can be off the ground on posts, or down to the ground, or suspended from above. The top frame creates a marked improvement in rigidity. A recognisable component 'family'. The 'off the ground' system is generally assumed to have hygienic advantages.

Low-level screens

These are available in glass, aluminium and melamine laminates, and used mostly to subdivide space in 'Burolandschaft' offices **2**. Walls cantilevering from the floor without top retention present obvious difficulties, and cross wall arrangements or right angled junctions are usually required for bracing.

1.03 Movable walls—doors and panels

Tracked doors
Some systems allow unlinked panels to stack in cupboards at the end of the rail run, as well as those using the more familiar sliding and slide-fold techniques **3**. Weight provides suspension problems, and sound ratings claimed to be in excess of 30 dB should be checked.

Portable panels
Now used more frequently in hotels, restaurants and other places where quick subdivision is necessary, these panels, which have rebated or grooved edges, are designed to be lifted away and stored out of sight after the top or bottom edge fixing is retracted. Various firms offer a vast array of mechanical, pneumatic and magnetic devices to provide retention pressure, and stabilising of the ceiling plane may be necessary. Such systems are claimed to improve the dB reduction by sealing all gaps around edges.

2 Proprietary types

Masonry partitions
As properties and methods of construction will not vary greatly between bricks, blocks and slabs of different manufacture, proprietary types are not listed in this sheet.

Demountable partitions
The following list gives properties of demountable partitions based on primary selection factors. A plan showing a joint detail through the partition is given where available. (2.01).

Movable walls—doors and panels
A short list of tracked doors and movable walls is also included. (2.02).
The details which follow of patented systems for both demountable and sliding door/partitions are as supplied by manufacturers. They are brief in order to cover the widest possible field but even so there will be other manufacturers not represented. It should also be understood that the information given may not necessarily be on a uniform basis. The item likely to be most widely interpreted is the sound reduction which will vary over a wide range of frequencies. This range is normally taken as from 100 to 3150 Hz, and where two figures are given they usually imply the results at the top and bottom of this range (unless stated otherwise). Where one figure is given it is usually accepted as the average or median figure for the same range. Considerable differences may be observed in the upper and lower ranges so that it is always important to check the type of sound likely to emanate from the source room and the performance of the selected partition at this frequency. The Building Regulations 1972 Part G (which are only concerned with dwellings but nevertheless can be taken as a good guide) lay down very specific conditions as to the testing of walls and partitions for sound transmission which must be based on methods described in Section 2A and 3A of BS 2750: 1956 and even specify the method of normalising tests (clause 3C (ii)). There are also further conditions. None of this applies to other types of building (eg offices) where demountable partitions are most likely

but it is well to check with the makers how the quoted sound reductions are arrived at.

MASONRY	DEMOUNTABLE	MOVABLE
bricks, blocks, slabs	stud, panel and frame systems	door and curtain systems

increased ease of demountability ⟶

1

2

3

1 *Partitions divided into 'families' or generic types*
2 *Low level partitions dividing space in open plan offices (Unilock)*
3 *'Concertina' type doors, which slide fully back when not in use. (Brockhouse Modernfold)*

2.01 Demountable partitions

'Firesound'
Sound reduction
33 to 39·3 dB
Fire resistance
Up to 1 hour obtainable
Surface spread of flame
Class 0
Demountable
Fully
Finishes
Various

Unilock-Compactom Ltd,
176-184 Vauxhall Bridge
Road, London sw1
(01-834 1155)

'Harvey'
Sound reduction
33 dB
Fire resistance
Up to 1 hour
Surface spread of flame
Class 0
Demountable
Completely

G. A. Harvey Office
Furniture Ltd (Harveypac
Division), Woodwich Road,
London se7 (01-858 3232)

'Easerect'
Sound reduction
23 dB
Fire resistance
Up to 1 hour
Surface spread of flame
Class 1
Demountable
Completely

Down & Francis Ltd,
Ardath Road, Kings
Norton, Birmingham,
b38 9pn (021-458 6571)

'Dixaplan'
Sound reduction
28 dB
Fire resistance
½ hour
Surface spread of flame
Class 0 (asbestos)
Demountable
Completely

Dixaplan Partitioning Ltd,
Environment House,
875 Sidcup Road, London
se9 (01-850 7716)

'Intercon'
Sound reduction
30 dB average
Fire resistance
½ hour (steel and asbestos)
Surface spread of flame
Class 0
Demountable
Fully
Finishes
Pvc, veneer, or to order

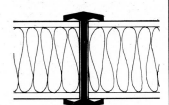

Sherwood Fibreglass Co Ltd,
44-46 New Road, Chatham
(Medway 0634)

'Soundlok'
Sound reduction
40 dB (depends on core)
Fire resistance
Up to 1 hour
Surface spread of flame
Up to and including Class 0
Demountable
Fully
Finishes
Painted, pvc, laminates,
wood veneers

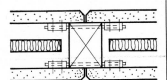

Wm Mallinson & Sons
130 Hackney Road,
London e2 (01-739 7654)

'Templan'
Sound reduction
35-45 dB (expanded
polystyrene with
plasterboard skin)
Fire resistance
Non-combustible
Surface spread of flame
Class 1
Demountable
Fully
Finishes
Range includes pvc and
hessian

Office Planning Ltd,
6 Mercer Street, London,
wc2h 9qg (01-836 9597)

'Tranwall'
Sound reduction
32 dB
Fire resistance
½ hour (hardwood frames)
Surface spread of flame
Class 0
Demountable
Yes
Finishes
Variety

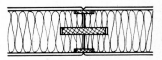

James Scott Environmental
Services, Minerva House,
26/27 Hatton Garden,
London ec1
(01-242 7682)

'Clifford' aluminium
Sound reduction
28-30 dB (single skin)
35 dB (double skin)
Fire resistance
½ or 1 hour
Surface spread of flame
Class 0, single skin
Class 0 or 1, double skin
Demountable
Fully
Finishes
Natural wood, veneers,
vinyl, corkboard etc or
glazed

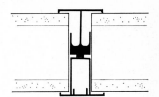

Clifford Contracts Ltd,
Champion House,
Burlington Road, New
Malden, Surrey, kt3 4nb
(01-949 1621)

'Flush V' timber
Sound reduction
35 dB approx
Fire resistance
½ hour
Surface spread of flame
Class 1 or 0 obtainable
Demountable
Fully
Finishes
Various timber finishes,
vinyl, veneered doors or
glazed

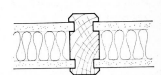

Clifford Contracts (see
above)

'Eiderline'
Sound reduction
Up to 33 dB (solid wall)
Fire resistance
½ hour
Surface spread of flame
Class 0 or 1
Demountable
Fully
Finishes
Textured vinyl, or
others

EI Environments Ltd,
Knightcott Works, Old
Hutton Road, Banwell,
Weston-super-Mare,
Somerset (Banwell 2241)

'Vencoustic'
Sound reduction
42 dB
Fire resistance
½ hour
Surface spread of flame
Class 0
Demountable
Fully
Finishes
Anodised aluminium frame; panels in grained pvc, melamine or timber veneer

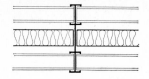

Venesta International, Construction Materials Ltd, West Street, Erith, Kent (Erith 36900)

'Component'
Sound reduction
27 dB
Fire resistance
Nil
Surface spread of flame
Class 1 (hardboard)
Class 0 (asbestos)
Demountable
Fully
Finishes
Aluminium frame; panels of grained pvc, melamine, timber veneer

Venesta International, Construction Materials Ltd, (see above)

'Howick A'
Sound reduction
27-30 dB
(Type A achieves 35 to 38 dB)
Fire resistance
Nil (Type AS achieves ½ hr)
Surface spread of flame
Class 0
Demountable
Fully
Finishes
Wood veneer vinyl laminates, hessian

R. Howick & Co, Holmethorpe Avenue, Redhill, Surrey, RH1 2NF (Redhill 62794)

'Versi-Wall'
Sound reduction
28-35 dB
Fire resistance
½ hour
Surface spread of flame
Class 0
Demountable
Fully
Finishes
Wood veneer, vinyl laminates, hessian

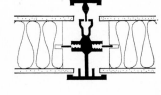

Versatile Fittings Ltd, Bicester Road, Aylesbury, Bucks (Aylesbury 83481)

Shearwater
Sound reduction
26-29 dB single skin
46 dB double skin
Fire resistance
½ hour
(1 or 2 hours possible with double skin)
Surface spread of flame
Class 0
Demountable
Not without difficulty, as

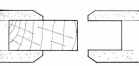

Shearwater Ltd., Dennis

---

jointing is a wet process
Finishes
Primed for decoration

OAST 'composite'
Sound reduction
28 dB
Fire resistance
Not available
Surface spread of flame
Class 0
Demountable
Fully
Finishes
Anodised aluminium frame vinyl panels

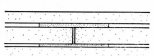

Road, Tanhouse Industrial Estate, Widnes, Lancs (051-424 5435)

Office & Storage Techniques Ltd, 27 Burnt Mill, Harlow, Essex (Harlow 32041)

Gyproc 'laminated'
Sound reduction
32 dB (50 mm thick)
Fire resistance
1½ hour (50 mm thick)
Surface spread of flame
Class 0
Demountable
Not fully
Finishes
May be decorated as required

British Gypsum Ltd, Ferguson House, 15-17 Marylebone Road, London, NW1 5JE (01-486 1282)

'Planline'
Sound reduction
41 dB
Fire resistance
½ hour
Surface spread of flame
Class 0
Demountable
Fully
Finishes
May be decorated as required

British Gypsum (see above)

'Silverline'
Sound reduction
30 to 38 dB
Fire resistance
½ hour (demountable)
Surface spread of flame
Class 1
Demountable
Fully
Finishes
Paper backed vinyl, trims in grey pvc

Grafton Magna Ltd, Magna Works, Biscot Road, Luton, Beds (Luton 20005)

'Magnacon'
Sound reduction
28-35 dB
Fire resistance
½ hour (demountable)
Surface spread of flame
Class 1 or 0
Demountable
Fully
Finishes
Paper backed vinyl panels

Grafton Magna (see above)

333

Bridge Walker Mk II
Sound reduction
32 dB (single skin)
44 dB (double skin)
Fire resistance
½ hour
Surface spread of flame
Class 1
Demountable
Fully
Finishes
Vinyl, painted, veneer

Bridge Walker Ltd,
91 & 93 Effra Road, London,
sw2 1DD (01-733 3351)

'Tenonflex'
Sound reduction
26-28 dB
Fire resistance
Incombustible
Surface spread of flame
Class 0
Demountable
Fully, and re-erectable
Finishes
Painted, pvc, wood veneer

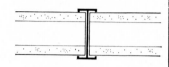

Tenon Contracts Ltd,
42 Upper Berkeley Street,
London w1
(01-262 1644)

'Context'
Sound reduction
24-26 dB
Fire resistance
Incombustible
Surface spread of flame
Class 0 obtainable
Demountable
Fully
Finishes
Painted, pvc, wood veneer

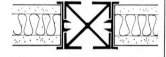

Tenon Contracts Ltd
(see above)

'Opus 4'
Sound reduction
30-45 dB
Fire resistance
½-1 hour available
Surface spread of flame
Class 0
Demountable
Fully
Finishes
Aluminium frame: panels
finished pvc; veneer; painted;
melamine; hessian

Opus 4 Ltd, Draper Street,
Southborough, Tunbridge
Wells, Kent
(Tunbridge Wells 32225)

'Panacoust'
Sound reduction
30-32 dB (according to
panel thickness)
Fire resistance
½ hour
Surface spread of flame
Class 0 (asbestos faced)
Demountable
Fully
Finishes
Ready for decoration or
laminated plastic, veneer

Richard Graefe Ltd, Mahtal
Works, Gomm Road, High
Wycombe, Bucks
(High Wycombe 20791)

'Moduline'
Sound reduction
27 dB, standard range
Fire resistance
Nil
Surface spread of flame
Class 3 or 4
Demountable
Fully
Finishes
Paper backed pvc

Sankey Sheldon-Unistrut,
Division of GKN Sankey Ltd,
PO Box 214, Hadley Castle
Works, Telford, Salop
TF1 4RE (0952 4321)

'AC11' composite
Sound reduction
27 dB, standard range
Fire resistance
Nil
Surface spread of flame
Class 3 or 4
Demountable
Yes
Finishes
Pvc, melamine, veneer

Sankey Sheldon-Unistrut
Ltd (see above)

'Econowall'
Sound reduction
36·3 dB
Fire resistance
½ hour
Surface spread of flame
Class 0
Demountable
Fully
Finishes
Paint, pvc, wood
veneer

Tenon Contracts Ltd
(see above)

'Flushform'
Sound reduction
32 dB (400-3200 Hz range)
Fire resistance
½ hour
Surface spread of flame
Class 0 or 3
Demountable
Fully
Finishes
Various laminates

Firmin and Collins Ltd,
Dover Road, Northfleet,
Kent (Gravesend 64844)

'Executive'
Sound reduction
33 dB (150-4000 Hz range)
Fire resistance
½ hour (untested)
Surface spread of flame
Class 0
Demountable
Fully
Finishes
Pvc painted
Stove enamel

Norwood Steel Equipment
Ltd, Howard Way, Harlow,
Essex (Harlow 26741)

BIE 'O type'
Sound reduction
32-40 dB, double skin
Fire resistance
½ hour, standard partition
Surface spread of flame
Class 0
Demountable
Fully
Finishes
Various

British Industrial
Engineering Co (Staffs) Ltd,
Hainge Road, Fivedale,
Warley, Worcs
(021-557 1222)

'Plaslin'
Sound reduction
27·7 dB
Fire resistance
1 hour
Surface spread of flame
Class 0
Demountable
Not easily, as receives
plaster finish
Finishes
Skim coat of plaster
ready for decoration

Stramit Ltd, Eye, Suffolk
(Diss 2821)

'Movaflush'
Sound reduction
27 dB
Fire resistance
½ hour, hardboard faced
½ hour, asbestos faced
Surface spread of flame
Class 3: hardboard faced,
Class 1: hardboard or
asbestos partition board faced,
Class 0: asbestos wood
Demountable
Fully
Finishes
Variety

Stramit Ltd, Eye, Suffolk
(Diss 2821)

'Paramount' 2¼in
Sound reduction
29 dB (43 dB with quilt)
Fire resistance
½ to 2 hours, depending on
types of plaster finish
Surface spread of flame
Class 0
Demountable
Not easily, as board is
nailed to studs
Finishes
Prepared for painting,
or pvc covered or plastered

British Gypsum Ltd,
15-17 Marylebone Road,
London NW1
(01-000 0000)

'Superflex T'
(timber frame)
Sound reduction
27 dB, single skin
Fire resistance
½ hour
Surface spread of flame
Class 0
Demountable
Yes
Finishes
Pvc covering

Swiftplan Ltd, 345 Ruislip
Road, Southall, Middx.
(01-845 1266)

'Grangewood Flush'

Sound reduction
28-31 dB
Fire resistance
½ hour (asbestos board finish)
Surface spread of flame
Class 0
Demountable
Yes
Finishes
Painted; vinyl; veneered
ply; melamine

Grangewood Partitions Ltd,
Grangewood House, Wilton
Mews, Wilton Way,
London, E8 1BQ
(01-254 1131)

'Corelok'
Sound reduction
37 dB, standard wall
Fire resistance
2 hours, standard wall
4 hours, double skin (untested)
Surface spread of flame
Class 0
Demountable
Fully
Finishes
Painted vinyl wood veneer
cork; glazed tiles

Moveable Drywall Construc-
tion Ltd, Alvechurch Road,
West Heath, Birmingham,
B31 3PQ (021-475 5258)

'Permalok'
Sound reduction
36·5 dB, standard range
(40 dB with quilt)
Fire resistance
½ hour for standard range
(1 hour or 2 hour obtainable)
Surface spread of flame
Class 1
Demountable
Fully
Finishes
Prepared for decoration
painted vinyl etc

Expamet Contracts Ltd,
PO Box 130, Ashburton
Grove, London N7 7AD
(01-607 6332)

Cinplan
Sound reduction
26 dB approximately
Fire resistance
1 hour available
Surface spread of flame
Class 0
Demountable
Fully
Finishes
Pvc; veneers; melamine;
felt; etc

Cinplan (Installations) Ltd,
Cinplan House, 30-38 High
Road, Byfleet, Surrey
(Byfleet 48011)

Baywall
Sound reduction
33-45 dB
Fire resistance
½ to 1 hour
Surface spread of flame
Class 0
Demountable
Partially
Finishes
Plasterboard ready for
decoration

Baileys Roofing Ltd,
Brookland House, Pennywell
Road, Bristol, BS5 0TG
(Bristol 551436)

Alpac
Sound reduction
28 dB
Fire resistance
½ to 1 hour
Surface spread of flame
Class 0
Demountable
Fully, and re-erectable
Finishes
Pvc, painted, hessian,
felt, cork

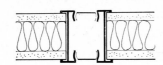

Alpac Contracts Ltd,
Bernard Avenue, Wallasey,
Cheshire (051-638 8814)

'Executive'
Sound reduction
34 dB (unless glazed)
Fire resistance
½ hour
Surface spread of flame
Class 0
Demountable
Fully
Finishes
Double panelled metal,
stove enamel finish

Ayrshire Metal Products
Ltd, Church Street, Irvine,
Ayrshire (Irvine 2671)

Clip-grip
Sound reduction
00 dB
Fire resistance
½ hour and 1 hour
Spread of flame
Class 1
Demountable
Completely

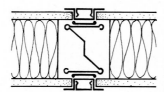

Cubitts/Neslo, New
Chester Road,
Bromborough, Cheshire
(051-334 4020)

Profilit
Sound reduction
23 dB (single glazed)
31 dB (double glazed)
Fire resistance
None
Spread of flame
AA
Demountable
Fully

Profilit Glass Ltd,
44 Wellesley Road,
Croydon, CR9 3PD
(01-686 8241)

Roneo Vickers DLA
Sound reduction
26·4 dB
Fire resistance
½ hour
Spread of flame
Class 0
Demountable
Fully

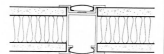

Roneo Vickers Ltd,
Acornfield Road, Kirby
Industrial Estate, Kirby,
Liverpool, L33 7UX
(051-546 2050)

2.02 Movable walls—doors and panels

'Monoslide'
Sound reduction
28-31 dB (45-76 mm door
thickness, single skin);
37-42 dB (63-76 mm door
thickness, double skin)
Fire resistance
½ hour
Finishes
Veneered panels pvc sheet

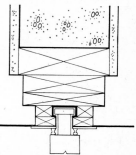

British Fairwall Ltd,
Equity House, Central
Square, Wembley,
Middlesex (01-903 0332)

'Sonafold'
Sound reduction
32 dB
Fire resistance
None
Finishes
Coloured leathercloth

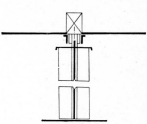

Bolton Gate Co, Turton
Street, Bolton, Lancs,
BL1 2SP (Bolton 32111)

'Acousti-Seal'
Sound reduction
41·7 dB
Fire resistance
Not available
Surface spread of flame
Depends on finish
Finishes
Laminated vinyl

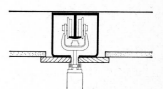

Brockhouse Modernfold
Ltd (see next page)

'Esavian 100S'
Sound reduction
28 dB (48 dB for double
partition)
Fire resistance
½ hour
Surface spread of flame
Class 1
Finishes
Primed for painting, vinyl,
polished veneer, hessian

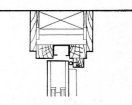

Esavian Ltd, Esavian
Works, Stevenage, Herts,
SG1 2NX (Stevenage 3355)

'Track Lockwall'
Sound reduction
20-30 dB
Fire resistance
½ hour
Surface spread of flame
Class 1 or class 0 available
Demountability
Flexible within ceiling-mounted guide track

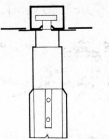

SMP (Lockwall) Ltd, Ferry Lane, Hythe End, Staines, Middx (Wraysbury 2225)

'Soundmaster'
Sound reduction
37 stc*
Fire resistance
Not available
Surface spread of flame
Not available
Finishes
Laminated vinyl

Brockhouse Modernfold Ltd, 25 Hanover Square, London, W1R 0DQ (01-629 8783)

'Pella' 558 series
Sound reduction
18-20 dB average
Fire resistance
Not applicable
Demountable
Completely
Finishes
Wood veneer, mahogany, limba, pine, oak, teak, mansonia, walnut (supplied polished or unfinished)

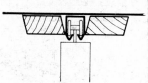

Alfred G. Roberts (Exports) Ltd, 235 Southwark Bridge Road, London SE1 (01-407 7591)

'Hufcor' portable walls
Sound reduction
26 stc*
Fire resistance
Not available
Surface spread of flame
Depends on finish
Demountable
Fully
Finishes
Vinyl laminates; wood grains; enamelled hardboard; natural hardboard for painting

Henderson Doors Ltd, Romford, Essex, RM3 8UL (Ingrebourne 45555)

'Panelfold'
Sound reduction
38 stc* ('Sonicwall')
Fire resistance
Not available
Demountable
Completely
Finishes
Hardwood veneers, melamine, and others

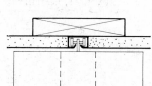

Lenscrete Ltd, 153 Battersea Park Road, London SW8 (01-622 1063)

'Thamesply-Partifold'
Sound reduction
Not available
Fire resistance
Not available

Demountable
Completely (track remains)
Finishes
Hardboard for painting, or veneered

Thames Plywood Manufacturers Ltd, Harts Lane, Barking, Essex (01-594 5511)

'Hufcor' folding partitions
Sound reduction
30 to 36 dB
Fire resistance
Not available
Surface spread of flame
Depends on finish
Finishes
Vinyl, hardboard

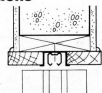

Henderson Doors Ltd, Romford, Essex, RM3 8UL (Ingrebourne 41122)

* stc = sound transmission class measured over 125-1250 Hz range

Section 9
Internal division: Ceilings

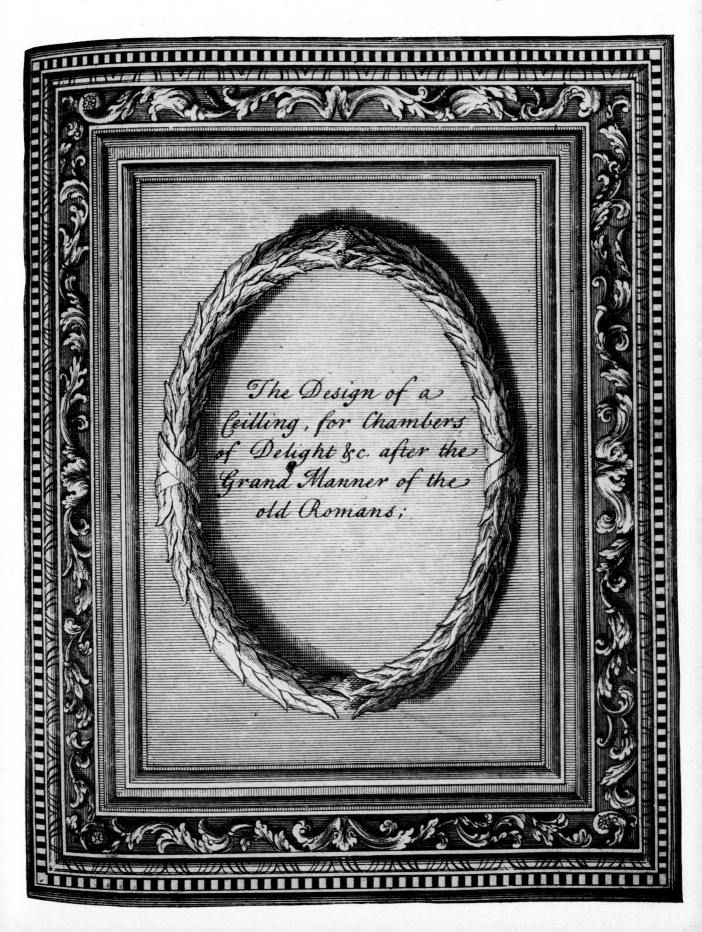

The Design of a Ceilling, for Chambers of Delight &c. after the Grand Manner of the old Romans;

Section 9 Internal division: Ceilings

Building enclosure		Reference keywords
Section 1	**Building enclosure: General**	ENCLOSURE
Section 2	**External envelope: General**	EXTERNAL ENVELOPE
Section 3	**External envelope: Lowest floor and basement**	LOWEST FLOOR
Section 4	**External envelope: External walls**	EXTERNAL WALLS
Section 5	**External envelope: Roofs**	ROOFS
Section 6	**Internal division: General**	INTERNAL DIVISION
Section 7	**Internal division: Suspended floors**	SUSPENDED FLOORS
Section 8	**Internal division: Partitions and walls**	PARTITIONS
Section 9	**Internal division: Ceilings**	CEILINGS
	Design guide	DESIGN GUIDE
	Appendix A: Legislation	
	Appendix B: Specialist advice	
Appendix 1	**Summary of references**	ENCLOSURE: REFERENCES
Appendix 2	**Index**	ENCLOSURE: INDEX

Relationship to rest of handbook

The table and diagram show the contents of the entire handbook, with the present section highlighted. This section should be used in conjunction with section 6 INTERNAL DIVISION which analyses the functions of internal subdividing elements as a whole. The information on service enclosure and acoustic insulation will also be relevant to section 8 PARTITIONS as partitions are often closely related to ceiling design and construction.

Scope

This is the last of the three sections in the handbook dealing with the specific element-groups comprising a building's internal subdivision (suspended floors; internal walls and partitions; ceilings). It covers the construction and function of in situ and suspended ceilings, the choice and application of the various finishes, and decoration.

References and keywords

The keyword by which this section is identified is CEILINGS: the use of keywords is explained on p6.

Author

A. J. ELDER is a partner in Elder Lester & Partners, Yarm, Yorkshire. In 1966-7 he was president of the Northern Architectural Association. He is a frequent contributor to the AJ and author of the *Guide to the Building Regulations* 1972.

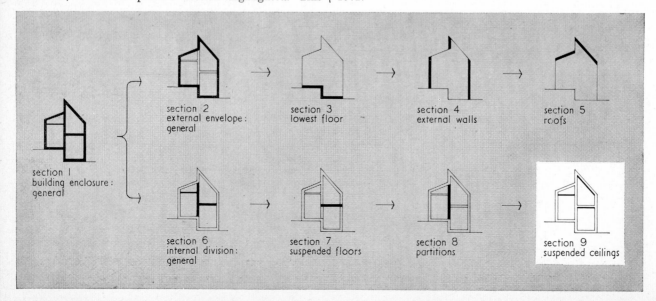

section 1
building enclosure:
general

section 2
external envelope:
general

section 3
lowest floor

section 4
external walls

section 5
roofs

section 6
internal division:
general

section 7
suspended floors

section 8
partitions

section 9
suspended ceilings

Technical study
Ceilings 1

Functions of ceilings

In this study A. J. ELDER *describes generally the initial demand for, and subsequent development of ceilings. He describes both in situ and suspended types. Two information sheets will follow, the first concerning suspension and grid systems for suspended ceilings, the second, in situ or monolithic ceilings*

1 Introduction

1.01 Recent developments

Complex services networks, plus structural developments, have led to the use of suspended ceilings. At first ignored **1**, eventually the concept of services as part of the overall building design has grown and been accepted.

The architect sought means of concealment by lowering the ceiling level. In a single operation he could also conceal structural beams and provide a ceiling surface as flat and level as the floor below—a great advantage when the idea of flexibility in the shape of movable partitions became a consideration. Service runs can be left exposed as an expression of function in the same way as structure, or even picked out in different colours according to function **2**.

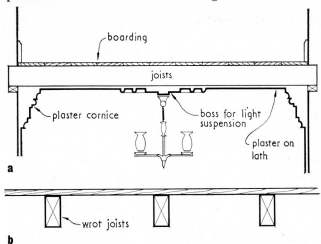

1 *Traditional construction:* **a** *traditional enriched ceiling with cornice;* **b** *cottage type construction—no ceiling effective height increased relative to air content of room*

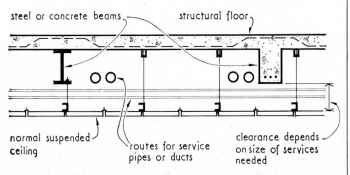

2 *Normal role of suspended ceiling* (NB *if ceiling does not provide fire protection, steel beam needs casing*)

1.02 Variations

A shaped or profiled interior may be desired. This can be a repeated profile within a grid, of limited depth (possibly no more than 300 mm), which could still be used in a typical multi-storey building. Alternatively they can create a totally different internal form, only loosely related to that of the building.

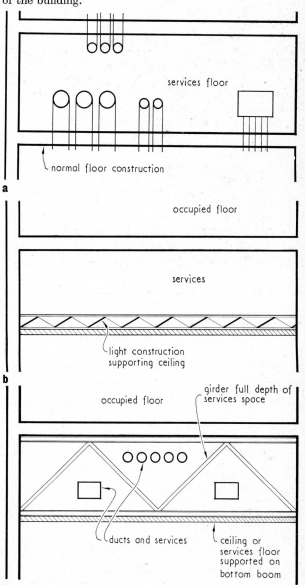

3 *Various means of providing space to run services:* **a** *full service floor;* **b** *independent ceiling (not suspended);* **c** *full depth girder*

2 Functions

2.01 Physical

● To provide a finish to the underside of a structural floor, concealment for the main structure and space for services run below and supported from the structural floor or frame.
● To provide support and space. There are a variety of possibilities here, including lighting fittings, services (if not directly supported from the structure), cat walks for access, and a top fixing for partitions (which may or may not be movable) **3**.
● To provide acoustic absorption. Most suspended ceilings are inherently acoustically absorptive.
● To contribute to the prevention of transmission of sound and heat between storeys and sometimes to help control air movement.
● To provide security. In the case of ceilings this is really restricted to their role in fire protection.

2.02 Aesthetic and psychological effects

Ceilings can create interior shapes bearing little relation to the external envelope. Cinema auditoria of the 1930s are perhaps the best example of this use.* It is sometimes desirable to lower the room height. See technical study SUSPENDED FLOORS 1, 4.02, fig **22** (AJ 19.4.72).

2.03 Access

Where services are concealed above suspended ceilings strategic access is often necessary.
Virtually all grid and panel systems are claimed to be demountable. It is usually possible and preferable to arrange special fixings for certain panels. In monolithic ceilings, special hatches must be provided at access points **4**.

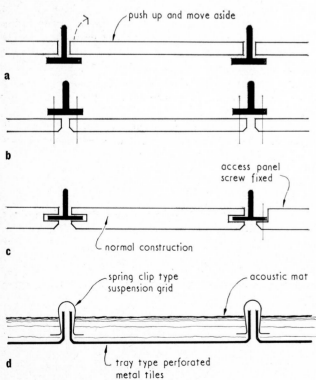

4 *Access systems:* **a** *exposed tee-section grid, full access;* **b** *screw fixing, full access;* **c** *concealed grid, special arrangements for access;* **d** *full access*

*This aspect of interiors is covered by Raymond Harington in his technical study INTERNAL DIVISION 1 (AJ 5.4.72) where he quotes and illustrates the cinema as an example of such techniques

3 Environmental control

Suspended ceilings can play a significant part in separation between storeys: first as part of the total barrier acting with the floor and second as a barrier in their own right between occupied space and the space between ceiling and floor soffit. Relative importance of these two functions varies according to aspects of environmental control.

3.01 Noise

This is probably the most important aspect because its transmission between spaces is always undesirable.

Issues
These are prevention of sound upwards or downwards, including the space left between the top of partitions and the structural soffit when the partitions stop at that level leaving open a route for sound reflection from the soffit **5**.
There is also the question of acoustic absorption designed to reduce the reverberation period and noise level and prevent echo in large spaces. Ceiling surfaces can also be used as reflectors to direct or reinforce sound towards particular situations (eg the sounding board above a stage or pulpit) **6**.

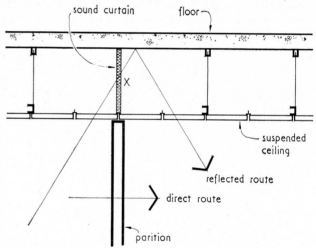

5 *Sound transmission above partitions: sound resisting curtain needed at* x *or ceiling must be sound resisting*

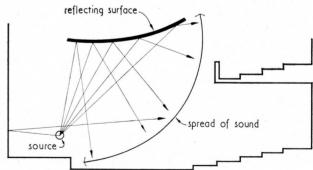

6 *Deliberate reflection of sound to specific areas*

Factors
These include:
● sound reduction value of the structural floor and finishes, frequently adequate without assistance from the ceiling.
● general sound level and sound spectrum anticipated and considered acceptable within each space.
● need for flexibility in partitioning (consider the problem of the sound route via space above the ceiling and partition).
● importance of sound privacy (eg is some degree of sound transmission acceptable provided that actual words cannot be distinguished?).

Solutions

Where prevention of sound transmission upwards is important, the ceiling might be used as a partial barrier in addition to the floor. In such cases a ceiling of some weight might be used (eg thick plaster on expanded metal or thick plaster board) and the ceiling might be 'pugged' (a layer of some heavy material such as sand placed on top). Such a ceiling would reflect part of the sound created in the space below and its effectiveness could be further improved by the use of special hangers to provide a degree of discontinuity on a similar system to anti-vibration mountings **7**. Such a system would also assist in prevention of impact sound transmitted from above.

Acoustic correction, rather than prevention of sound transmission, is the usual role of suspended ceilings. They are eminently suitable for this as they constitute a large area of light sound-absorbing materials. Most of these rely on the principal of a perforated surface allowing sound to penetrate and be absorbed in the backing or body. Acoustic correction is not always necessary but most rooms benefit from some degree of absorption to lower the reverberation period.

In open plan situations, a high degree of acoustic absorption is essential for sound privacy between working areas. Such open plan spaces have a natural background noise level. One solution to this problem is to deliberately introduce a certain level of background noise ('white' sound) which reduces the area over which any particular sound source can be distinguished. A ventilation system often serves this purpose.

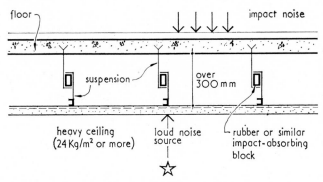

7 *Use of heavy ceilings and broken suspension system to reduce transmission of impact noise from above or excessive noise from below*

Constraints

Part G of the Building Regulations lays down minimum standards for certain floors but applies only to dwellings. These are described on pages 117 to 119 of the *Guide to the Building Regulations* 1972.

3.02 Heat

Although not all spaces within a single building necessarily have the same temperature requirements, differences are small and heat insulation is unlikely to present problems.

Issues

These are:

● prevention of heat transmission from storey to storey and

● the top storey to the outside atmosphere.

In both cases the ceiling will play its part in the total composite resistance (U-value) of the floor or roof. It may also perform a secondary role in maintaining temperature differential between the occupied space and any unoccupied space above, which does not need to be heated, thus saving

running costs. This is probably a minor role, since the spaces involved are usually neither large, well ventilated nor exposed, but considerable savings can be made in heating costs of old houses with high rooms by introducing suspended ceilings.

Factors

These include temperature differentials between storeys, insulation (or U-value) of floor construction and the need to provide other controls such as fire protection, sound absorption or resistance and accommodation for services. The last item may well determine whether or not the ceiling should be suspended. If sound absorption is required no conflict should arise, as materials which are resistant to heat transmission are generally also sound absorptive. They are not, however, resistant to sound transmission. Use of the ceiling as a fire barrier may well lead at times to provision of greater thermal resistance than required.

Solutions

Whether or not the ceiling is directly applied to the structure, materials available in sheet or panel form contain a high percentage of thermally resistant elements. Original wood-based fibre boards are still available, followed in historical order by mineral fibre boards and tiles and the whole range of cellular plastics such as polystyrene and polyurethane. The plastics offer no fire protection; even though they have high thermal resistance as they melt at comparatively low temperatures. Also available are rigid sheets or strips of metal, plaster and asbestos, which can be backed with glass or mineral fibre blankets; these fibres themselves can now be produced in rigid form and faced so as to require no additional support over normal grid spans of say 610 mm.

Monolithic

For monolithic ceiling construction there is a range of plaster mixes based on gypsum, asbestos and vermiculite, which give good thermal resistance. Heated ceilings using either hot water pipe grids or electric cables always require thermal insulation above the heating elements to direct the heat downwards **23**. Further information is given in information sheet SUSPENDED CEILINGS 1. Normal internal floor/ceiling structures should not present the architect with the danger of interstitial condensation. The principles are shown in **8**.

Examples are all based on assumptions concerning the most adverse likely conditions; more detailed information is contained in BRS Digest 110[2].

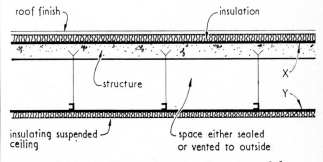

8 *Principles for avoiding condensation above suspended ceilings below roofs.* NB *risk of condensation is greatly reduced if space above ceiling is vented to outside air but this reduces effectiveness of roof insulation. Vapour barrier is not needed at* X *if space below is vented or if insulation is itself impermeable to water vapour (eg closed cell plastics). Vapour barrier always essential at* Y *unless ceiling itself is impervious (eg foil-baked plasterboard with sealed joints)*

Constraints

Part F of the Building Regulations lays down certain minima for heat loss in dwellings. These include losses through ceilings and roof spaces where the U-value must not exceed 1·42 w/m² deg. C when the sum of the surface resistances is taken as 0·15. The Thermal Insulation (Industrial Buildings) Act (1957) also lays down a minimum thermal resistance value for factory roofs.

3.03 Light

Suspended ceilings play their part in the transmission, diffusion and reflection of natural and artificial light.

Issues

These are:
- type of light to be transmitted—natural, artificial or both
- need to conceal or blank off direct view of light source
- intensity of illumination required and avoidance of glare.

Factors

These include the overall storey height, shape and depth of space from windows to interior wall. Determine whether the ceiling is an overall source of artificial light or only a means of accommodating or supporting lighting fittings. In the first case it cannot also serve as a good natural light reflector. Consider PSALI (permanent supplementary artificial lighting) for solving the deep space problem. Also consider any purely decorative lighting.

Solutions

Ordinary depth offices or rooms do not require special provisions for improving natural lighting but where (for design reasons) spaces are deep from the window wall, the ceiling becomes important as a reflector, indirectly increasing the quantity of natural light reaching the rear. Apart from adoption of special ceiling profiles, the surface itself should be highly reflecting white, but reasonably matt to avoid unpleasant highlights. If natural light is from above, a laylight below a rooflight may be used **9**.

Design of a good lighting-layout involves a degree of technical sophistication, but it should be noted that light intensity at desk level (where it is normally considered) depends on its distance from the light source, as well as its intensity; also the effective light spread from any particular source and therefore the distance apart of fittings, depends on their height above the working surface. In a factory or similar building of considerable interior clear height, power and spacing of fittings must be considered when deciding on actual suspension height.

In multi-storey office buildings with suspended ceilings, it is convenient to fix fittings directly to the ceiling, or incorporate them into it. Here spacing will be influenced by ceiling grid. This and the fittings output will be controlled by the desired standard of illumination at working level and ceiling height.

For a fully illuminated ceiling, suitable moulded plastic translucent panels and continuous corrugated strip laid between tees are available. Obscured glass is another, rarer, alternative. In such cases, available height above the suspended ceiling is most important. This is not normally great and keeping the lighting fittings as far away as possible from the ceiling ensures even light distribution. Suitable reflectors behind fittings improve efficiency.

Where natural light is desired electric lighting is placed above the lay lights so that both natural and artificial light come from the same source. A suitable switching system can make the changeover at dusk almost indiscernible **10g**. Where fittings are ceiling fixed, a trunking which also carries supply cabling as part of the suspension grid system is used. Fittings are attached by removing a section of the cover. Such trunking can also serve as a top fixing for movable partitions, giving an all-round adaptable system. Modular lighting fittings are also designed to form part of an integrated ceiling design. Common sizes are 305 m × 1220 m, 610 m × 610 m, 610 mm × 1220 mm and 610 mm × 1830 mm (or multiples of 300 mm in metric grids).

A type of suspended ceiling, sometimes known as a 'Rotterdam ceiling' is simply an open grid of fins, about 300 mm deep, hung some distance below the soffit. This, according to fin spacing and depth, provides a suitable cut-off angle, enabling services (probably painted black with the soffit) and lighting fittings to be fixed above, unseen and yet directly accessible. The system is particularly suitable in shops, showrooms and display spaces.

The main principles involved in these various systems are illustrated in **10a**.

Constraints

None, other than those imposed by cost and other design considerations.

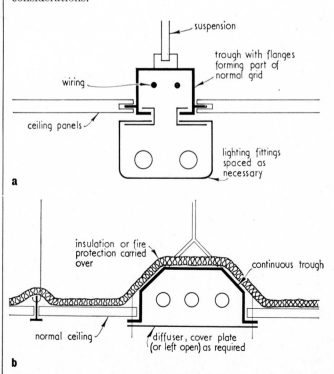

10 *Typical types of ceiling mounted light fixtures:* **a** *wiring and fixing trough;* **b** *recessed trough*

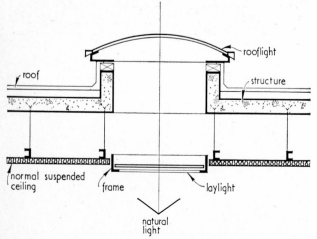

9 *Lay lights, traditionally obscured glass set in tee-section members within frame*

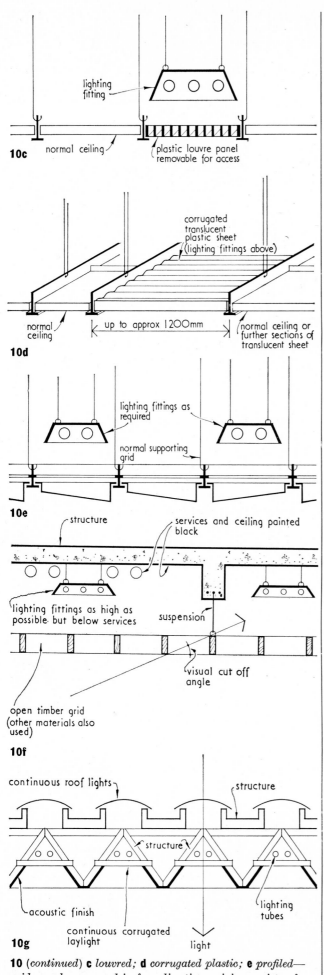

10c

lighting fitting

normal ceiling

plastic louvre panel removable for access

corrugated translucent plastic sheet (lighting fittings above)

normal ceiling

up to approx 1200mm

normal ceiling or further sections of translucent sheet

10d

lighting fittings as required

normal supporting grid

10e

structure

services and ceiling painted black

lighting fittings as high as possible but below services

suspension

visual cut off angle

open timber grid (other materials also used)

10f

continuous roof lights

structure

structure

acoustic finish

continuous corrugated laylight

light

lighting tubes

10g

10 (continued) **c** louvred; **d** corrugated plastic; **e** profiled—grid may be arranged in four directions, giving variety of patterns; **f** Rotterdam ceiling; **g** natural and artificial light from same direction

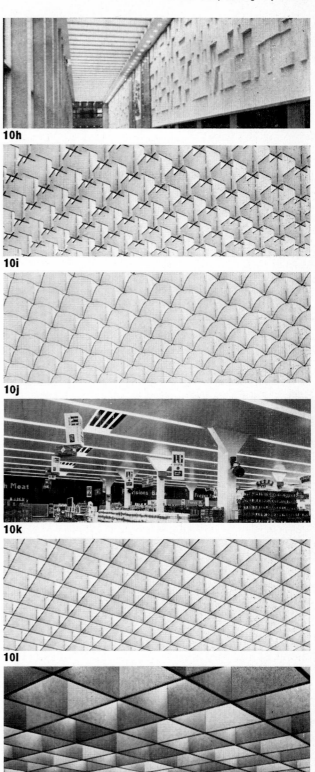

10h

10i

10j

10k

10l

10m

10g *example of integrated ceiling system where ceiling panels and lights are installed as one;* **h** *circle grid ceiling at Manchester law courts. Reflecting nature of floor pattern;* **i** *aluminium louvre panels with rectangular cutouts on undersill to form homogeneous decorative ceiling;* **j** *ripple-textured aluminium louvre panels with scalloped louvre edge;* **k** *aluminium louvre panels in pattern emphasising every other grid intersection;* **l** *aluminium louvre panels in range of eggcrate cell sizes;* **m** *cruciform ceiling formed in fibrous acoustic boards suspended on wire or rod*

3.04 Air

Air movement is normally restricted to that within individual storeys. Use of suspended ceilings keeps down air volume to be handled and provides a route for controlled air movement above (either ducted or not).

Issues

Certain minima are laid down in various acts as to the volume of air per person occupying buildings.

Determine number of air changes needed and whether by natural or artificial means. Check fire and smoke prevention roles involved (see section 4).

Factors

Anticipated occupancy density. Building shape and siting establishing choice between natural and artificial ventilation (affected also by decisions on natural lighting). Type of heating system (eg warmed air automatically means controlled air movement). External environment—degree of pollution determining need for air filtration.

Solutions

Factors described are principally related to the need or otherwise for providing controlled air circulation. It may often be possible to accommodate all services other than ventilation in small floor ducts in the screed; in a small space provided by say 50 mm battens below the soffit and in perimeter casings below windows. In this way storey heights can be kept to a minimum and cost of suspension systems avoided.

Should conditions make controlled ventilation necessary there are three basic alternatives:

● A normal low-speed system demanding ducts of some considerable size: 1200 mm × 900 mm would not be unusual. Depth can be reduced by increasing width but a proportion of over 2:1 is not considered good practice. Such systems require considerable space above suspended ceilings.

● A high velocity system with small circular ducts and sound attenuating systems. They also move less air and work by entraining air movement in the room itself over water-heated elements. These require much less void.

● Ducts can be dispensed with altogether and the ceiling void used as a plenum. This naturally demands a reasonably impervious ceiling. Methods of inlet or outlet from rooms vary, but one system is a continuous slot on a grid line with means of controlling the opening provided (a type of linear hit-and-miss ventilator).

Recent experiments, particularly by some electricity boards, have been made in designing heat-balanced buildings. By minimising external glazing and using high insulation standards, it is possible to almost balance heat losses with gains from lighting fittings, and occupants. Heat from lighting fittings is recovered by inducing air flow around them and transferring this back to a central exchange, where it is either heated further or cooled as necessary before being returned to the occupied space. In this operation the suspended ceiling plays an important part in controlling air movement.

Constraints

There are no constraints on air movement except in its capacity as a carrier of smoke and flame in the event of fire. The Building Regulations lay down conditions under which suspended ceilings can only be counted as contribution to the fire resistance of floors if in some circumstances they are monolithic and hence impervious (see 4.03).

4 Security

When considering suspended floors, three aspects of security were studied—protection against fire, physical attack, and chemical or micro-wave attack. Of these, only fire is generally relevant to ceiling construction although certain plasters or other means may be used as ceilings in rooms containing radioactive apparatus, such as x-ray machines.

4.01 Issues

These are:
● need for protection against fire and radioactivity.
● use of a directly applied ceiling (or suspended) can have considerable influence in increasing the effective resistance period of various floor constructions.
● use of a fire resisting suspended ceiling system to protect exposed steel structural members

4.02 Factors

These include fire resistance of the floor and whether or not this is adequate without the ceiling. In addition there is the question of the choice of structural system, in turn dependent on the nature of the building and client requirements*. When considering radioactivity the principal factor is the power of the source, which will control the type and thickness of material used. Expert advice will be needed.

4.03 Solutions

The Building Regulations 1965 lay down criteria for suspended ceilings which can be counted as contributing to the total fire resistance of the floor (ceilings applied direct to the soffit can be included). The actual regulation, E5 table B, is fully explained in the *Guide to the Building Regulations* 1972.

Its principal effects are that the usual type of suspended ceiling, consisting of a grid containing panels, cannot be treated as contributing to the fire resistance of the floor in buildings more than 15 m high when the period required is one hour or less, nor in any building when the period is over one hour. In these cases only jointless ceilings may be counted as contributing, and there are also rules about non-combustibility of the ceiling and its supports and/or surface spread of flame rating of the upper surface.

If the floor itself is adequate without the ceiling, it may be assumed that a modular type ceiling can be used to provide protection for the steel **11**. This means that a much wider choice of suspended ceiling structure is available when the floor itself (plus screed and finish if suitable) is self sufficient. When ceilings of the panel type are used, they must give continuous protection and any breaks (perhaps caused by introduction of lighting troughs, fittings or cable ducts) must be closed against fire penetration.

This is done by backing with a fire-resisting material such as mineral wool across the top, ie above the top surface of the ceiling **11**. In such cases the type of ceiling which relies for its fire resistance (and probably its acoustic value) on a suitable blanket-type backing material laid on the exposed rigid strip or panel surface (which may often be of perforated metal) is suitable.

Where a monolithic ceiling is necessary, the usual solution is to use expanded metal, reinforced by ribs and plastered

*These factors are examined in technical study SUSPENDED FLOORS 1 (AJ 19.4.72 5.02, p866)

on the underside. Normal gypsum plasters are usually adequate but if long periods are necessary, asbestos or vermiculite mixes may be used.

A ceiling can help to provide resistance with comparatively thin or hollow concrete floors Table 1.

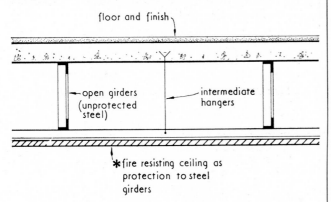

11 *Fire protection of structure. Fire resisting ceiling (at ✻) as protection to steel girders permitted even if of grid type, but not permitted to count as contributing to total resistance of floor itself where period is one hour in buildings up to 15 m high or in any buildings where period is more than one hour (unless monolithic and non-combustible). Other conditions apply to shorter periods (see Regulation E5, table B of Building Regulations)*

Table 1 Fire resistance of concrete floors showing thickness of solid material for various types of floor construction and giving different periods of fire resistance. NB *the thicknesses of screeds can be included, but voids do not count*

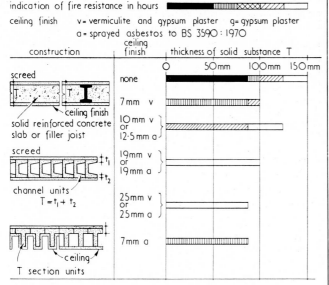

The above is a diagrammatic representation of certain deemed to satisfy descriptions in schedules of the Building Regulations. Further examples may be found in *Guide to the Building Regulations* 1972 p.80

In rooms containing radioactive rays ceiling treatment can be continuous with wall treatment without the rays passing through the structural floor above **12**.

Constraints

The Building Regulations control combustibility, surface spread of flame on upper surface, and jointless construction when ceilings have to contribute to the total fire resistance of the floor construction

*When the ceiling is applied direct to the underside of the floor it may always be counted as contributing to the total resistance of the floor and the effect of certain ceiling finishes on various types of floor in increasing the resistance period are illustrated diagrammatically on pages 78, 79 and 80 of the *Guide to the Building Regulations* 1972

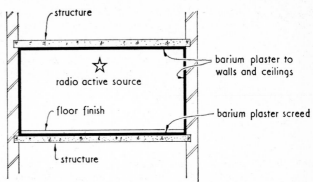

12 *Protection against radioactivity.* NB *barium sulphate concrete blocks may also be used in walls. Lead is a further alternative, but barium sulphate plaster is the only suitable material when protection is placed on ceiling*

5 Services and structure

5.01 Issues

The issues involved are the positioning of services and their size, number, weight and position. In particular, whether or not they include ventilation ducts. A further point at issue is whether or not it is important to conceal the services.

5.02 Factors

There are a considerable number of factors affecting design decisions to be taken when considering ceilings in relation to services. These concern first the necessity of using a suspended ceiling at all. Other possibilities might almost certainly be cheaper, such as placing services in floor ducts either in the screed or the floor itself and creating a small space of say 50 mm by using battens on the soffit.

If services are complex and the decision is taken to use a suspended ceiling, other factors are whether the ceilings are required for other reasons such as the various aspects of environmental control and security already discussed.

Degree of accessibility to the services needed will also influence the design. A high degree of accessibility would clearly conflict with the use of a monolithic ceiling which might be needed for sound insulation or fire protection. The nature of the services (eg rigid pipes, pliable cables, circular or rectangular ducts) are all factors to be considered when deciding how they should be supported. Rigidity is particularly important as it controls the frequency of support points required.

Suspended ceiling grid systems are usually of very light pressed metal frames as the panels used are also normally light. However plaster is sometimes used but generally not in great thickness, so the overall weight of a ceiling would seldom exceed 25 kg/m². Such systems are not therefore able to support heavy services such as large pipes. It is nevertheless convenient if the ceiling grid can be used as support instead of making separate provision.

5.03 Solutions

Principal services other than lighting are hot and cold water, drainage, heating, ventilation, electric power and communications.

When the wet services are put above ceilings, it is normal to support them from the floor above. Any leakage is critical and it is necessary to ensure a high standard of workmanship and testing and/or put in a second line of defence, such as a lead channel.

Heating consists of moderate size pipework (diameters above 50 mm are rare except in main ducts). These are usually supported on the main structure as they are generally fixed before the ceiling and because branch supplies etc usually feed upwards through the floor and are shorter if the main is fixed directly to the soffit. In addition fixing is firmer.

Frequency of support varies according to pipe diameter, material and wall thickness and is normally decided by the heating engineer. Metal pipes are still considerably more rigid than plastic ones, even those suited for use with hot water **13**.

Ventilation ducts are hardly ever supported on ceilings. Constructed of thin galvanised sheet (nowadays sometimes of plastics) and having considerable depth, they are capable of reasonable spans. Typical support is by a metal angle below the duct, fixed by screwed rods and bolts at each side from the floor above. Occasionally the bay size of the main structure and duct size may be such as to enable the duct to span the full bay and be supported at the beam positions only **13**.

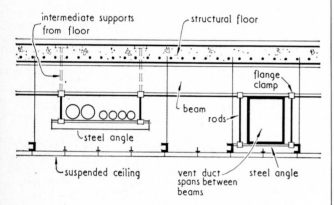

13 *Support of service pipes and ducts*

Electric and communications services require continuous support. MICC cable, though comparatively rigid still needs frequent support. Continuous support for ordinary insulated cables will take the form of small ducts, circular conduits or open trays. Floor trays can also be used and may be supported from the ceiling grid or floor above.

Other systems are open side multi-cell ducts and normal conduit, both of which will usually be independently supported **14**. It is more common to find power and communications wiring located in ducts above the floor where it is immediately available for provision of extra outlets or alterations to existing ones.

Careful detailing is required at the ceiling/wall junction where pipes may have to turn sharply.

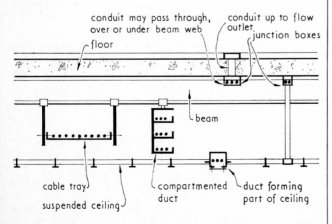

14 *Support of electric cables*

Systems of light lattice construction or similar are worth examining where a great many or large services are involved. The ultimate development is the construction of a second service floor below the main floor as mentioned in 2.03. Alternatives are illustrated in **3**. Where access to the space above ceilings can be limited to certain specific situations (eg rows of lighting fittings, lighting galleries in theatres), the best solution may be a catwalk forming part of the ceiling structure or hung from above **15**.

Constraints
Local authorities fire and public health departments in buildings for public entertainment.

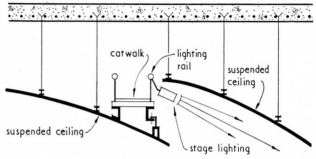

15 *Catwalk access above ceilings*

6 Fixing requirements

Ceilings are often used to secure other elements of enclosure or fittings.

6.01 Issues

● The nature of the building, mainly whether or not it is cellular (divided permanently into small spaces), mainly one or more large spaces or adjustable by means of movable partitions
● Whether other aspects of the design call for suspended ceilings
● Need for ventilation and lighting.

6.02 Factors

The client's brief will determine the degree of flexibility of layout*. The structural floor will determine the hanger type and the ceiling structure type will determine number and spacing.

The lighting installation design will control the system of fixing and supplying light fittings, integral, suspended from the ceiling (consider weight) or from the floor above **10**.

Top fixing of movable partitions is something of a problem as the typical ceiling grid is not strong enough to withstand any upward pressure such as might be created by wedging or jacking partition systems. Ordinary grid members are not wide enough to receive the partition thickness, leading to untidy detailing. Furthermore the ordinary ceiling will not withstand much lateral force. There is also the question of sound transmission routes above partitions **5**.

Type of ventilation is also a factor; although ducts are normally separately suspended (see 5.03) provision generally has to be made in ceilings for fixing inlet or extract grilles or diffusers.

*Flexibility of partition layout is discussed on page 315

6.03 Solutions

Dealing first with partitions, the degree of flexibility needed must be established. In a modular discipline the best solution is to construct the ceiling with a member wide enough to accept the partition and designed to receive the top fixing system on every module*.

If full flexibility is required, without even a modular discipline, the best answer is a monolithic ceiling, presenting a completely flat surface. Fixing would then be on an *ad hoc* basis, involving either plugging and screwing or accepting wedging as adequate. Corresponding adjustment of lighting fitting positions would be equally awkward, but possible.

Support of lighting fittings is well achieved by the system described earlier for partitions. Other methods have also been dealt with in 3.03. Where non-modular fittings are used in conjunction with a modular grid, it will be necessary to provide an arrangement to span across two grid members, to take the fitting attachments. There are plenty of suitable devices, such as 'Lindapters'; which provide for fixing to virtually any type of structural section.

Ventilation outlets are usually supported from the ductwork. They may be designed to fit into a modular ceiling grid but if not, a special panel is provided to receive them. In such cases and in monolithic ceilings the grille or diffuser is normally fitted with a cover flange to conceal any crudities in the hole cutting **16**.

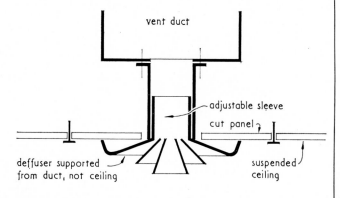

16 *Fixing ventilation outlets*

7 Types available

Ceilings may be divided into three main types:
1 Flat directly fixed to soffit
2 Flat suspended
3 Profiled suspended
The third type is confined to special types of building, such as auditoria. The first two types each form the subject of an information sheet to follow, but in order to make this study a useful reference in itself the principal subdivisions are classified here.

7.01 Flat directly fixed to soffit

Ceilings in this class can include the following main types:
● Plaster, two or three coats direct on concrete
● Plasterboard and skim coat of plaster to bottom of floor joists or battens fixed to concrete soffit
● Thick sprays such as asbestos fibre mixes and vermiculite mixes normally from about 10 mm to 25 mm according to design requirements

*See Technical Study Partitions 1. p. 315 ff.

● Thin sprays usually based on cement or resins and available in mottled effects. Normally not thick enough to conceal the profile of the soffit
● Fibreboard or foamed plastic boards fixed to joists or battens. Joints usually taped
● Acoustic tiles fixed to joists or battens at suitable centres
● Acoustic tiles fixed by adhesives to concrete soffit **17**.

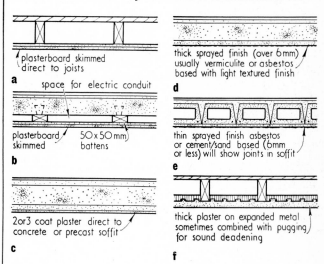

17 *Types of direct (non-suspended) ceilings:* **a** *skim coat on plasterboard;* **b** *skim coat on plasterboard with battens;* **c** *plaster to soffit;* **d** *spray to soffit (monolithic structure);* **e** *spray to soffit (individual structural units);* **f** *plaster on expanded metal*

7.02 Flat suspended

These consist of main structural sections spanning between hangers and cross noggings at panel junctions. Most are of galvanised pressed steel, a few of aluminium. There is an even wider variety of panels, boards and strips to be used in conjunction with the grids. There are also types not based on the grid system.

Grid systems

● Rectangular or square grids of main members and cross noggings to receive ceiling panels. Lower part of metal grid is exposed and panels are removable for access
● Similar grid but with panels grooved for secret fixing. Not removable
● Rectangular or square grid of members designed to receive 'push-in' fixings (noggings or metal tray type tiles) to provide accessibility.

Tiles and panels

The panel frequently has acoustic and/or thermal insulation properties. Materials used are ordinary fibre board, mineral-based boards, asbestos board expanded plastics (polystyrene and polyurethane) and plaster or metal tiles, perforated and backed with a blanket of flexible mineral or glass wool. These backing materials can also be made in a form sufficiently rigid to span the normal grid system without support **18a,b,c,d**. In this case they are usually faced with a sheet material which takes decoration.

Strip

Various types of profiled strip which require support in one direction only (no cross noggings) are available. They can be holed or plain and are manufactured from aluminium or galvanised sheet steel, finished on the underside with a variety of materials including melamine, pvc, epoxy resins and normal enamel in various colours **19a,b,c**.

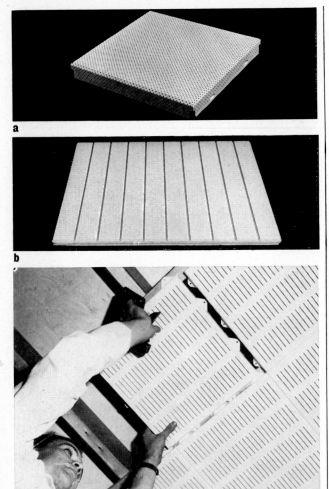

a

b

c

d

18a *Thermo-acoustic ceiling panel with accent grooves;*
b *metal tile with holes for sound absorption. Fibrous mat can
be laid on top for extra sound-deadening quality. Note
grooves on left-hand edge to receive tool used in pulling tile
down;* **c** *pvc-moulded tray tile shown during installation;*
d *acoustic ceiling panels with modular light fittings
incorporated*

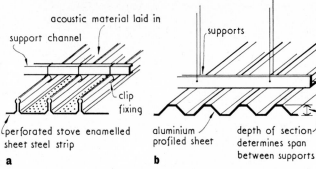

19 *Strip ceilings:* **a** *perforated stove-enamelled sheet steel
strip;* **b** *aluminium profiled sheet—may be solid or
perforated and backed acoustically*

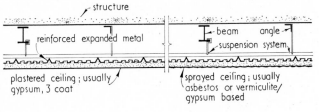

19c *Profiled strip metal tile, stove-enamelled finish*

Monolithic

The normal system is to use a stiffened expanded metal,
suspended by a suitable system of hangers and horizontal
sections, and to apply a finish from below. This may be
normal gypsum plaster, vermiculite, or, if fire resistance is
important, asbestos plaster mixes or some form of spray
based on asbestos and vermiculite aggregates. (Sprayed
types usually have good acoustic qualities though these are
reduced by redecoration) **20**.

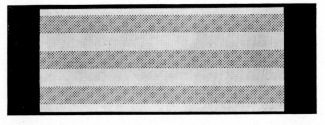

20 *Monolithic ceilings. Choice of finish and thickness
depend on characteristics required, eg fire resistance,
acoustic correction*

Stretched plastic

A new development in ceiling systems is the use of a sheet
of plastic material such as pvc stretched tight and fixed
round all four sides. Backing quilts may be used to give
acoustic and thermal qualities, and holes for lighting
fittings and so on may be cut at any point. This type of
ceiling is quick to erect, cheap, but does not provide fire
protection **21**.

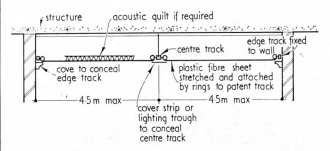

21 *Stretched skin ceilings*

Integrated ceilings

These include functions such as lighting, acoustics, ventilation and thermal insulation, sometimes (but not necessarily) all together.

When ceilings also incorporate lighting, as opposed to merely providing support for lighting fittings, three main systems may be used:

1 Lighting troughs between sections of normal ceiling
2 Translucent panels or corrugated sheet in suspended grid (permits tubes above ceiling)
3 Open grilles of various dimensions and materials (permits tubes above ceiling and may also be used to introduce ventilation, if normal diffusers are placed above).

Types 2 and 3 may be used together, with the open grilles limited to the areas where air is being introduced or extracted. In such cases ducts can be dispensed with and ventilation allowed to permeate the space above the ceiling and enter the room via the open grille panels. Various lighting systems are illustrated in **10** and **22** illustrates the principles of integrated ceilings.

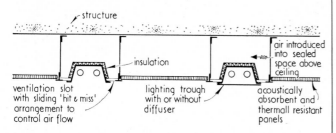

22 *Integrated ceiling. This type of installation combines lighting, acoustic correction, thermal insulation and ventilation. Other systems may be used for same purpose eg introduction of ventilation louvred panels into translucent ceiling lit from above (see 10) although in this case acoustic correction would be minimal. If fire protection is also required, best solution is metal tray type ceiling with acoustic/fire resistant blanket backing taken over top of lighting fittings; ventilation must then be ducted*

Decorative ceilings

All except the plainest of suspended ceiling can be described as decorative to some degree, but some types are designed (usually in combination with lighting) in which a variety of aesthetic effects is achieved by different means. These include silk screening on translucent panels, profiled panels arranged in various ways, deep louvres with varying bottom profiles and colours which permit a heavily textured effect enhanced by lighting from above, and a variety of patterned or gridded panels in translucent plastic or plaster **23**.

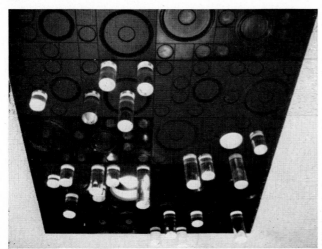

a

b

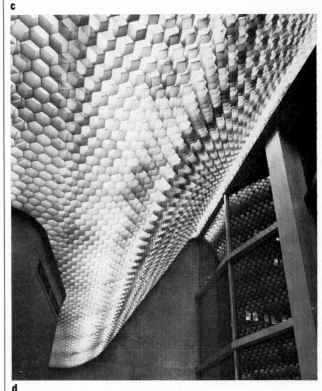

c

d

23a *Decorative light/ceiling panel set into modular filled ceiling;* **b** *glass fibre illuminated ceiling panel with relief pattern;* **c** *profiled panels forming illuminated ceiling with random pattern;* **d** *decorative suspended eggcrate-hexagon ceiling in New York office building shows versatility of this type of installation*

Open grid ceilings

This description could be applied to a number of the types described in 7.02 but this final section really refers to the large-scale open grid (originally christened the 'Rotterdam ceiling') referred to in 3.03. The early examples of such ceilings were usually simply a grid of timber or plywood vertical intersecting ribs comparatively large intervals apart.

The depth of the ribs, the spacing and the height above eye level, determined the visual cut-off angle **10f**. The grid was suspended by wires from the floor above and generally provided a tidy finish to conceal services, lighting and so on, while leaving complete accessibility. Patent forms using other materials are now available.

Metrication

Most manufacturers of modular ceiling grids and patterns are in the stage of change-over to metric, and are at the moment making both metric and imperial sizes. The most common imperial sizes were 12in, 24in and 48in; 24in × 24in being used more than any other. This converts to 610 mm and is being rationalised as expected to 600 mm, which ties in with the agreed key dimension for flooring units of 300 mm × 300 mm.

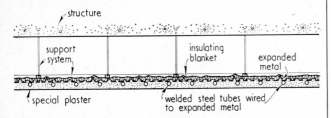

23 *Water panel heated ceiling, yet a further use for a suspended ceiling*

24 *Ceilings have always been a visual expression of structural form, but they were also frequently plastered to improve the quality of the finished surface* **1**. *In later domestic architecture the ceiling was used to reproduce classical cornice details at the junction with the wall or at intermediate beams. Low relief patterns on the flat surface, perhaps centred on some feature such as a chandelier, were often picked out in colour.*

25 *Detail of ceiling in Horace Walpole's Strawberry Hill, Twickenham*

8 Checklist

8.01 Introduction

● Recent developments
● Variations

8.02 Functions

● Physical
● Aesthetic and psychological effects
● Access

8.03 Environmental control

● Noise
● Heat
● Light

8.04 Security

● Issues
● Factors
● Solutions

8.05 Services and structures

● Issues
● Factors
● Solutions

8.06 Fixing requirements

● Issues
● Factors
● Solutions

8.07 Types available

● Flat directly fixed to soffit
● Flat suspended

Information sheet
Ceilings 1

Section 9 **Internal division: Ceilings**

Suspension systems

Following general discussion of ceilings in Technical study
CEILINGS 1, *this sheet deals with types of suspension*
systems, statutory constraints and the question of
integration of the functions of the ceiling with environmental
services, a subject of considerable research and
development in recent years

1 Types of suspended ceiling

1.01 Grids

Light structural grids supporting panels of various sizes
and materials are perhaps the most common form of
suspended ceiling. Since various types of grid may be used
with a variety of infill panels, the two items are treated
separately. As panel materials are usually lightweight, grids
also tend to be of light construction: galvanised pressed
steel and occasionally aluminium. They can be subdivided
into those systems with exposed grid members (usually
stove-enamelled or plastic coated) and those with concealed
grid. Virtually all grid systems are proprietary.

Special circumstances or a special module might require an
independent design to be used, sometimes adopted as
standard by the manufacturer. Grid systems, required to be
particularly robust and rigid to accept top fixings of movable
partition systems, are the most likely to require individual
design. Proprietary grid systems are generally either two-
or three-stage, consisting in the first case of main runners
and cross noggings and in the second of main bearers usually
channel section, supporting by clips a system of main
runners and cross noggings **1** and **2**.

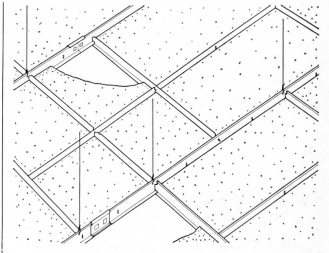

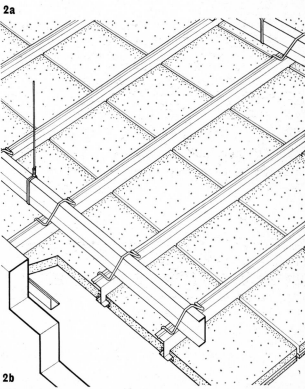

2a

2b

1 *Light suspended ceiling based an a grid system*

2a *suspension wires are fixed directly to grid;* **b** *wire fixed*
to channel above grid

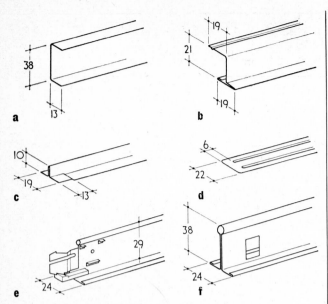

3a *Channel main bearer;* **b** z-*tile section;* **c** *nogging tee;*
d *spline;* **e** *heavy section nogging tee;* **f** *main runner*

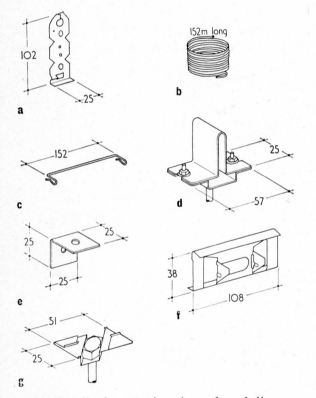

4a *Nailing clip;* **b** *suspension wire;* **c** *channel clip;*
d *support clamp;* **e** *angle fixing bracket;* **f** *main runner
splice;* **g** *twist clip*

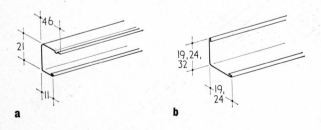

5a *stop section;* **b** *angle edge trim*

Sections used vary according to function. Main runners are
usually what is known as z- or T-sections, and cross noggings
either T or flat (splines). The z-section is often not a true z

but an inverted T with a half top flange **3b**. There is a variety
of jointing sections, fixing clips and suspension wire or rods **4**.
At room edges or openings, different sections are used **5**.
Sizes used are generally multiples of 12in (305 mm). Most
popular is probably 24in × 24in (610 mm × 610 mm),
which gives a reasonable degree of modular flexibility with
fewer grid members. A 4ft × 2ft (1200 mm × 610 mm) panel
size is probably the most economical, particularly if it is an
exposed two-stage system with main tee at 4ft centres and
cross noggings at 2ft. Possible grid arrangements are shown
diagrammatically in **7**. Metric round dimensions have been
used here although most manufacturers publish their
catalogues in imperial notes on metric conversions.

Metrication

Imperial sizes convert to multiples of just over the accepted
metric module of 100 mm. Thus 12in is 305 mm, 24in is
610 mm and 48in 1220 mm. (rounded off to 300, 600 and
1200 now from most manufacturers). Metric equivalents
will be used from this point on and imperial sizes ignored.
Need for accessibility to the space above is related to the
type of system used. If the grid is exposed and panels
merely laid, the latter can be easily lifted and moved aside.
Holding down clips are used from above with certain panels
to limit risk of distortion due to changes in temperature and
humidity. This applies especially with larger panels such
as 1200 × 600 mm. In such cases the panel may still be
lifted, as the clips will spring off under pressure but they
cannot be replaced, and it is clearly advisable to use panels
which will not distort when merely laid into the grid. If
access can be localised, special sections can be used to
frame these panels and avoid distortion.
Concealed grid systems, used in conjunction with 'kerfed'
panels (see next section) need similar arrangements to
provide access at specific points. Alternatively, overall
access can still be achieved by using split noggings, ie 2 × L,
instead of a single inverted T and cutting back the kerfed
edge along one other side. With tiles which do not need
cross noggings, eg plaster tiles, the system is simpler **8**.
Metal pan type acoustic tiles are used with spring T-bar
main runners into which the edges of the metal pan can be
pushed from below and retained. These can also be used
for ordinary solid tiles or panels, using a suitable cross-
nogging with upturned ends pushed into spring section **9**.
Many panels described in the next section have inherent
fire resistance of up to two hours. Four hours is possible,
but the grid is the limiting factor. In concealed systems
panels protect the grid but exposed or lay-in systems may
also be fire rated, which is achieved by use of slightly
heavier sections and provision for expansion to prevent
distortion. The web is cut away at specific points in long
main sections to allow flanges to buckle without twisting **6**.
There is no problem with short cross noggings. There are
however limitations on the type of ceiling considered as
contributing to a floor's overall fire resistance (see 3).

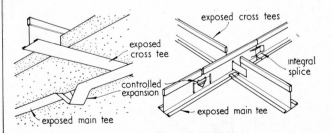

6 *Fire-rated grids. Each main tee has controlled buckling
point and each end of cross tee overrides main face tee to
accommodate expansion*

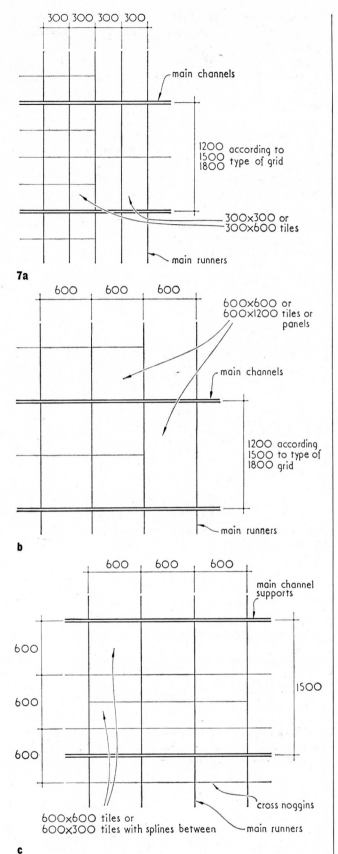

7a

b

c

600x600 tiles or
600x300 tiles with splines between — main runners

cross noggins

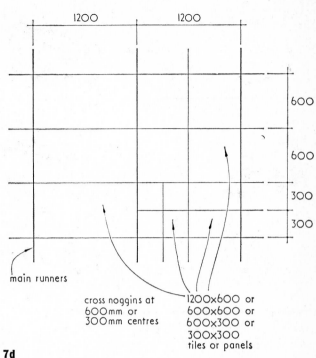

7d

7a,b,c,d *Schematic plan of typical suspension systems: more
possible combinations involving two- and three-stage layouts;
spacing of vertical support rods or wires (whether
attached to main channels in three-stage systems, or to main
runner in two-stage systems), depends on strength of
members and weight of panel, but in both cases normal
spacings are in the order of 1200 to 1500 mm and seldom
exceed 2000 mm*

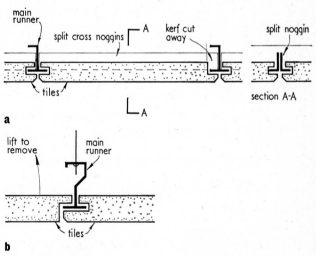

8a,b *Two methods of maintaining complete accessibility with
concealed grids*

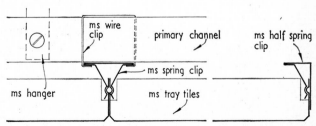

9 *Clip-in metal tray tiles, manufactured from zinc-coated
perforated mild steel sheets, formed into trays. Edges are
chamfered on all sides to produce bevelled joints. Finished
stove-enamelled, pvc coated or epoxy resin painted for
above average humidity areas*

1.02 Tiles and panels

There is a wide choice of materials available for tiles and panels, most of which are comparatively light-weight. Choice of material will depend on the nature of the performance characteristics required. These will include some of the following, (the choice will always be a compromise): appearance, acoustic absorption, prevention of sound and/or heat transmission, ease of cleaning and redecoration, ease of removal for access, light transmission, fire resistance, weight, air transfer and cost.

Fire resistance, lightness, acoustic absorption and thermal resistance are all characteristics of mineral fibre panels. On the other hand, sound resistance is not compatible with lightness, nor is fire resistance with light or air transmission. Sizes are available to fit the nominal grid dimensions (less normal tolerances) and larger. This is normally due to their lightness and natural rigidity or resistance to warping which makes them suitable for use in large grids, reducing number of grid members and therefore cost. A list of the usual materials, which is not claimed to be comprehensive, is given in table I with brief comments on the principal characteristics.

Table II Typical ceiling tile and panel materials

Material	Weight	Fire resist-ance[2]	Acoustic absorp-tion[2]	Thermal resist-ance[2]	Cost
Asbestos based	high	good	low*	good	medium
Mineral fibre	light	good	good	good	medium
Wood fibre (fibreboard)	very light	nil	good	good	low
Glass fibre (rigid vinyl faced)	very light	nil	good	very good	low
Cane fibre	light	nil	good	good	low
Steel (galvanised enamel finish)	medium	nil	nil	poor	medium
Steel pans perforated filled mineral wool	light	good	very good	good	high
Wood fibre—asbestos surface	light	nil	low	good	low
Plaster	heavy	low	low	low	medium
Plaster holed and backed with quilt	heavy	medium	very good	good	high
Plasterboard	heavy	low*	low	low†	low
Plasterboard holed with quilt backing	heavy	medium	good	good	low

*Can be made good if board is perforated and backed by a quilt of glass mineral fibre

†Can be improved as to fire resistance by plastering to various thicknesses, but this then changes the type of ceiling to monolithic. Thermal resistance can be improved by using foil-backed plasterboard

Materials which have a NIL fire resistance may still usually be supplied to either Class 0 or Class 1 surface spread of flame standards

Virtually all materials listed may be obtained either plain or with varied finishes. Surfaces may be lightly or heavily textured, holed in various sizes to regular patterns or random spacings, fissured, grooved or ribbed, marked in imitation of other materials (eg travertine), striated, slotted, ribbed and holed, profiled to various patterns, regular and irregular and surfaced with other materials. Manufacturers naturally vie with each other to produce materials with interesting and attractive finishes.

1.03 Strip and sheet

Certain materials, particularly asbestos and profiled metal, may be conveniently used in strip form, thus needing support in one direction only. Asbestos strips are manufactured in only two metric sizes both 200 mm wide × 9·5 mm thick, in lengths of 2400 and 3000 mm. Fixing is normally by self-tapping screws to suitable metal sections at 600 mm centres.

Aluminium is used in both strip and sheet form. In both cases the material may be plain, unpierced, in which case it has no acoustic value. Alternatively it may be pierced or holed in various ways and backed with a suitable mineral wool quilt for both sound absorption and fire resistance values. Both are comparatively recent materials and no figures are yet published for fire resistance periods—presumably tests are still awaited. Sound absorption values for the profiled sheet with backing indicate figures similar to normal metal pan tiles with a maximum of 0·78 at 500 Hz **10** and **11**.

Finish on the strip is stove enamel, 18 colours, and on the sheet pvc organosol, nine colours, with additional colours for large quantities. Support centres vary according to whether or not an acoustic pad is used, continuity, and in profiled sheet, metal gauge. Generally however the maximum for the strip is 1800 mm while the sheet having several profile depths varies a good deal—assuming a permitted deflection of 1/400 from 2·2 to 7·9 m if continuous (reduced 20 per cent if perforated).

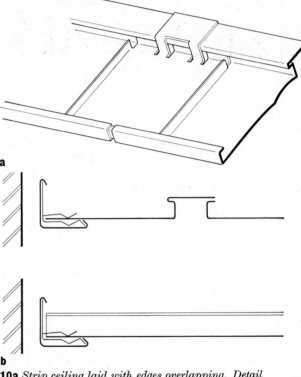

10a *Strip ceiling laid with edges overlapping. Detail where strip meets wall is shown in* **b**

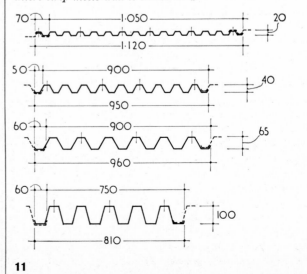

11

11 *Profiles of some typical sheet ceilings*

12 *Mineral fibre ceiling panels on concealed metal suspension, used at Infants School in Burnley*

1.04 Monolithic

These ceilings present a continuous surface and are not modular in any way. They are far more resistant to air and smoke penetration than jointed ceilings and are therefore required by the Building Regulations in certain circumstances.

There are two principal methods of construction, use of reinforced expanded metal suspended from the floor and finished on the underside with either normal plaster or a sprayed finish and use of plasterboard laid in a normal grid built up of main runners and cross-noggins plastered on the underside to a thickness appropriate to the required degree of protection **13**—(see **20** in technical study CEILINGS 1).

Special hatches must be provided for access. But these ceilings provide a better degree of sound insulation due to their inherent weight, which can be increased by pugging. Sprayed asbestos or vermiculite mixes should be used if sound absorption is required.

1.05 Plastic sheet

A comparatively recent development in the field of suspended ceilings is use of pvc sheet, which can be stretched sufficiently tight to keep deflection within acceptable limits over moderate areas. Until recently such ceilings were limited to small rooms such as hotel bathrooms where perimeter fixing (usually timber battens) was all that was necessary. The system provides a quick, easy, dry method of concealing services and drains, and is fixable without mess after all other trades have finished and plumbing etc been tested. A beading is necessary around the perimeter to conceal fixings.

More recently still this system has been developed to cover a much wider range of applications. The principal difference is in the use of a tough woven plastic material, instead of the normal monolithic plastic sheet. This enables considerably greater spans to be achieved within acceptable deflection limits, using a stretching tool and ring fixing system. Rings are attached to the material and hooked on to the special

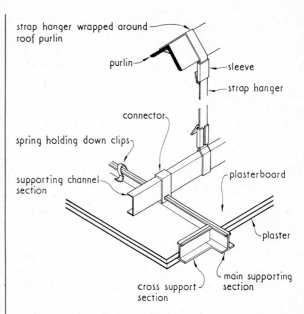

13 *Monolithic ceilings (plasterboard grid)*

perimeter or separating track. Maximum width in one span is 4·5 m, no limit on the length. Colour is matt white.

If greater width is needed, a jointing system, used at 4·5 m maximum intervals is available complete with cover strip, and the joint may be exposed as a modular element to accommodate items such as partition tops or lighting track. Holes can however be cut at any point in the sheet to accommodate lighting fittings, ventilation diffusers and so on. A clip-on cover covers edge fixings. **14** (see also **21**, technical study CEILINGS 1.) The system can be backed with glass fibre to give both sound absorption and thermal resistance. It does not however, even when quilt-backed, provide any fire protection although it is graded **class 1** spread of flame.

This is comparatively cheap and clearly provides a quick, clean system for concealing services or lowering the height of rooms. Being non-modular there are no dimensional restrictions, but it is of no use if fire resistance is required.

1.06 Decorative ceilings

This term is used here to describe ceilings where deliberate attempts are made to produce decorative effects regardless of functional need. There are three main types:

1 Moulded or sculptured solid tile (usually plaster) used in a normal grid.
2 The translucent panel using prismatic or grid effects, or patterns on solid glass or plastic, usually combined with illumination from above.
3 Louvred ceilings mostly using metal fins where effects can be achieved by cutting the base of the fins to a profile and varying spacing and height.

The last two types overlap with the integrated ceilings described later, as they combine illumination with decoration. The last type also overlaps with the open grid ceiling described in 1.07; in this next case, the main purpose of the open grid ceiling is functional rather than decorative. (For illustrations see Technical study Ceilings 1, **23**.)

1.07 Open grid ceilings

Construction of the open grid ceiling (see technical study CEILINGS 1) was originally simple, consisting of timber fins running both ways, of sufficient depth to form a rigid grid suspended from the floor above. The module was large

a   b

c   d

14 *Sequence of erection of stretched-skin ceiling:* **a** *first two sides clipped into place by hand;* **b** *second two sides stretched with clamps;* **c** *clip-in covering fitted at edge* **d** *ceiling completed*

(say 1200 mm × 900 mm) and depth of fins, say 300 or 400 mm. They were particularly useful in large shops and stores, where there were frequently a large number of services which presented an untidy appearance, but to which access was often needed. The grid provided a visual cut-off (especially if everything above painted black) without impeding access. It also assisted in preventing glare from lighting placed above, did not interfere with ventilation, and was not expensive.

Proprietary types have now been developed using a metal grid suspension system supporting vertical fins of mineral fibre board, so that the ceiling also performs an acoustic function **15**.

Metal fins are also used, in their simplest form identical in purpose, but usually made on a much smaller module. They are classed as decorative because of the many variations. The last type of open grid ceiling is the plastic or metal open grid panel for use with normal suspension grids, which overlaps into integrated ceilings since they are designed both for illumination and ventilation from above (for illustration see Technical study Ceilings 1, **10k**).

2 Integrated ceilings

Here the function of the integrated ceiling, rather than their method of construction or nature of materials is discussed. 'Integrated' is used to indicate that ceilings of this type are multi-purpose and furthermore in themselves form part of the building security and/or services systems in addition to typical ceiling requirements (see 7.02 of technical study CEILINGS 1).

All principal services can be concealed if used as a plenum it is again performing as an integrated element. If the panels are also illuminated it virtually forms part of the whole environmental control system.

Ceilings almost always serve more than their single primary function of providing the upper limit to the enclosed space. Probably one of the earliest additional functions is that of sound absorption; another is that of fire resistance providing protection particularly where structural steel is used. 'Integrated ceilings' most common example is the illuminated translucent ceiling lit from above (Technical study **10**). Unfortunately this type of use is not compatible with fire resistance, there being no known translucent, fire-resisting material. Similarly these materials are not

15

16

15 *Mineral fibre open grid ceiling*
16 *Integrated ceiling with continuous strip lighting*

sound absorbing, although by using double panels a reasonably high thermal resistance can be achieved.

The most sophisticated type of integration is no doubt the use of the ceiling as a means of distributing ventilation air by eliminating ductwork and introducing air into the space above the ceiling. Volumes of 0·15 to 2·5 m³ of air per minute can be introduced, giving air change rates of three to 30 per hour. The air is introduced by porous tiles or panels, or specially slotted panels or hollow T-section, which can then accommodate any type of panel. Both latter systems are controllable by using the hit-and-miss ventilator system using sliding control splines inside the slots. Air being introduced through narrow slots entrains the adjacent air as it enters and stimulates a gentle air movement in the room. Such systems are compatible with the use of illuminated ceilings and with fire protection but not with both.

If the maximum integration is required, the only solution is to use a grid system with suitably slotted mineral fibre tiles or panels and inset lighting units into the grid as needed, fire protected by mineral felt backing. Metal tray type ceilings with such backings could also be suitable, providing the felt is protected against disintegration due to air movement.

Perhaps the ultimate in integration is in recent experimental buildings with high external insulation values and low window/wall ratios, in which attempts have been made to balance as nearly as possible the normal heat losses with the heat produced by sources within the building—including machinery and occupants but mainly lighting. In these cases the air is extracted so as to pass over the lighting tubes collecting heat on the way, ducted to a central plant where it is cleaned, heated or cooled as required, and returned to the room via the ceiling space as described earlier **17**.

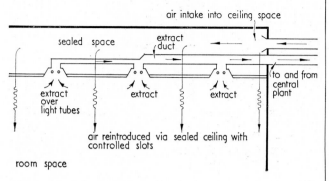

17 *Integrated ceiling with controlled air conditioning*

3 Constraints

There are two forms of constraint imposed on suspended ceilings by the Building Regulations (1972 metric version). These concern, respectively, fire resistance and surface spread of flame. All ceilings directly attached to the floor soffit (ie without a gap) are allowed to contribute to the total fire resistance period of the floor as a structural element.

Suspended ceilings are only permitted to do so in certain circumstances, depending upon the surface spread of flame rating of the upper surface and the type of construction. To be acceptable under all circumstances, suspended ceilings must be monolithic (jointless) and completely non-combustible. Table II indicates the requirements under various circumstances.

The implications of this Regulation are that the normal type of suspended ceiling consisting of separate tiles cannot be counted as contributing to the fire resistance of the *floor* in buildings over 15 m high where the period required is one hour or in buildings of any height where the period required is more than one hour. In these circumstances only jointless ceilings can be considered as contributing.

This Regulation relates only to the contribution made by *suspended* ceilings to the fire resistance of floors. It is not concerned with the protection afforded by suspended ceilings to structural steelwork, which is a separate and distinct consideration.

Surface spread of flame characteristics are controlled by Regulation E15 and are fairly complex. They relate to the underside of the ceiling and the principal controls are summarised in Table III.

Certain relaxations are defined in E15 and E16 to permit use of plastic and resin-bonded fibre glass materials as 'star lighting' in buildings without separate ceilings and as panels in suspended ceilings. These specify maximum size and minimum spacing criteria.

One classic example of the effect of these Regulations is that the stretched plastic sheet type of ceiling described in 1.05 which has a surface spread of flame rating of class 1 could not be used in circulation spaces other than in two-storey houses.

(Reg E5) Table II *suspended ceilings contributing to total fire resistance of floor*

Height of building	Type of floor	Required fire resistance of floor	Description of suspended ceiling
Less than 15 m	Non-compartment	1 hour or less	Surface of ceiling exposed within the cavity not lower than class 1 (as to surface spread of flame)
	Compartment	Less than 1 hour	
	Compartment	1 hour	Surface of ceiling exposed within the cavity not lower than class 0 (as to surface spread of flame) ; supports and fixing for ceiling non-combustible
15 m or more	Any	1 hour or less	Surface of ceiling exposed within the cavity not lower than class 0 (as to surface spread of flame) and *jointless;* supports and fixings for ceiling non-combustible
Any	Any	More than 1 hour	Ceiling of non-combustible construction and *jointless;* supports and fixings for ceiling non-combustible

References are to classes as specified in regulation E15

Table III *Restriction of surface spread of flame (walls and ceilings)*

Residential purpose group	Small rooms (max 4 m²)	Other rooms	Circulation and protected shafts
1 (small residential)	3	1*	1*
2 (institutional)	1	0*	0
3 (other residential and houses of more than two storeys)	3	1	0
All other groups	**(max 30 m²)**		
4 to 8	3	1	0

*Ceilings in group 1 may be class 3 throughout and in group 2 may be class 1 in other rooms (bigger than 4 m²). Classes 1, 2 and 3 are defined in BS 476, Part 1, 1953 and Class 0 is defined in the Regulations themselves as completely non-combustible

Information sheet
Ceilings 2

Directly fixed ceilings

The primary object of this information sheet by A. J. ELDER
*is to provide more detailed information on various types of
directly-fixed ceilings, which were referred to only briefly in
technical study* CEILINGS 1

1 Introduction

1.01 Functions of directly fixed ceilings

Directly fixed ceilings are not as versatile as suspended
ceilings. For instance they:
1 Do not conceal the main structure
2 Do not conceal services (other than small items)
3 Do not normally provide support for services
4 Do not provide fire protection for main structural members which project below them and if necessary must be
separately treated
5 Cannot affect room proportions
6 Are not required to give access for any purpose except
as part of a general access position through the whole floor
structure from storey to storey.
These omissions reduce the extent of real functions to
providing an acceptable visual finish to the upper surface of
the enclosed space, assisting in environmental control in the
space, prevention of transmission of sound, light, heat or
air between storeys, and security against fire by contributing to the total fire resistance of the floor structure or by
resisting radio-active penetration.
Sound transmission between storeys is difficult to prevent;
but transmission of heat is seldom a problem except below
the roof or in the event of large temperature differences in
adjacent storeys.

2 Types

Type of finish selected will depend on the function and type
of soffit to which it is attached. This soffit will be either
continuous (eg concrete or concrete and clay tile or other
materials providing an unbroken surface) or *intermittent*
(eg bottom of wooden joists or channel section concrete
floors which only provide support at intervals, though the
intervals are normally small of the order of 300 to 600 mm
on centres). It is also possible to convert a continuous soffit
into an intermittent one by using battens, usually about
50 mm × 50 mm plugged from below. Principal types of
finish are as follows:

2.01 Plaster direct

If the soffit is continuous, the simplest and most common

finish is a direct application of plaster in only two or three
coats.
Success or failure of plastering depends on the skill of the
individual craftsman and his ability to understand and
comply with instructions issued by the manufacturers or
from official publications, most important of which is
CP 211 :1966[1]. The importance of what appears to be minor
details may not always be apparent and a high degree of
competent supervision at foreman and clerk of works level
is essential following the issue of specifications by the
architect. Because of the nature of the work, this applies
perhaps more than to any other trade.

Materials
The matrix or binding agent for plaster may be used alone
or in combination with a fine aggregate. The latter method
is known as 'coarse stuff' and restricted to undercoats.
Materials used as plaster base are: lime, Portland cement
and gypsum (calcium sulphate).

Lime
This surface is comparatively soft and not generally regarded today as a satisfactory finishing coat. The raw
material varies from place to place and if clay is present a
hydraulic lime is formed which (when mixed with water)
does undergo a chemical reaction similar to cement but
to a lesser degree. Lime is now available in three forms:
1 Quicklime to be slaked sieved and run to putty on site
2 Hydrated lime, dried and bagged as a powder requiring
only water to convert it to putty
3 Already prepared as a putty in polythene sacks ready for
use.
Method 1 is seldom used these days and hydrated lime is
the most common form. The appropriate standard for all
limes is BS 890: 1966[2].

Portland cement
This is now perhaps the most ubiquitous of all building
materials. Normal cement complying with BS 12[3] may be
used for all internal plastering unless there are special
conditions.
It would never be used alone on ceilings but might be an
undercoat mixed only with sand where a high strength coat
is required. Much more common is its use mixed with lime
and sand to add strength to the otherwise weak mixture.
It should never be used in the same mix as gypsum plasters.

Gypsum plasters

These are covered by BS 1191: 1967[4], where they are classified under four main headings:

Class A Plaster of Paris
Class B Retarded hemihydrate gypsum plaster
Class C Anhydrous gypsum plaster
Class D Keene's plaster.

All are based on gypsum. There are two main groups, the first being the hemihydrate type in which the natural gypsum is treated to drive off one of water molecules.

Unadulterated, this is plaster of paris (class A) which sets in a matter of minutes and is therefore only useful for casting. Addition of retarders turns it into a class B plaster, which today is the most commonly used.

The second group (classes C and D) are anhydrous calcium sulphates in which all water has been driven off by using higher temperatures. The plasterer has virtually unlimited time to produce the true, highly polished face associated with these plasters.

The plasters also require less water for a workable mix, leading to greater final strength and impact resistance; this lies behind the traditional use of Keene's for arrises.

In accordance with CP 211, class C and D plasters are only suitable for finishing coats—class D used alone, and class C with not more than 25 per cent lime. Class B plasters are suitable for undercoats and finishing and may be used with lime in various mixes.

Sand

This produces a dense plaster mix. As with concrete it is important that the sand used should be clean, sharp and well graded to give good workability. This applies regardless of the matrix being used. The better the quality of the sand, the higher the plaster strength and the less likelihood of shrinkage.

All sand should conform to BS 1198[5] or 1199[5] (see CP 211[1] for details). Sea sand should never be used as the salts present affect the set, cause efflorescence and recurring dampness. Similarly additives containing chlorides should never be used in plaster.

Lightweight aggregates

These are minerals which have been greatly expanded and so reduced in density by heat treatment. There are other types used in concrete mixes, but the only two normally used in plasterwork are exfoliated vermiculite and expanded perlite. They may be mixed on site but it is more usual to buy the material ready mixed with class B gypsum plasters. Part 2 of BS 1191: 1967[6] covers lightweight premixed plasters and classifies them as follows:

Type A *Undercoat plasters*
- Browning plaster
- Metal lathing plaster
- Bonding plaster
- Multi-purpose plaster

Type B *Final coat plasters*

These plasters have many advantages. Their lightness makes them more acoustically absorbent (although only marginally) and the aggregates used have a very high fire resistance. Their disadvantage is a low resistance to impact, hardly important on ceilings.

2.02 Mixes

A variety of mixes are in common use according to materials selected. It is worth noting that the volume of a suitable mixture of lime and sand is no greater than the sand itself as the lime merely fills the spaces between the sand particles and does not increase the bulk. So if (for example) a 1:2:9 cement lime/sand mix is to be used, the one volume of cement should be mixed with nine (not 11) volumes of the 1:4½ lime/sand mixture.

A wide variety of mixes is possible using three basic materials and sand or lightweight aggregate. Principles to be adopted in selection are chiefly as follows.

Strength

The strength of plaster when set should not exceed that of the background to which it is attached, or shrinkage or thermal movement of either may cause structural failure in the background. Similarly, *strong finish coats must not be applied to weak backing coats.*

Movement

Cement and lime mixes shrink on drying (cement more than lime). Shrinkage of cement mixes can be reduced by adding lime. Gypsum plasters expand on setting and so adding them to lime/sand mixes reduces or eliminates drying shrinkage. Conversely, adding lime to gypsum mixes reduces expansion but tends to accelerate set.

Resistance to impact

Lime mixes and lightweight gypsum mixes tend to be soft and easily indented. Cement mixes are the hardest and Keene's (class D) is the hardest of all gypsum plasters and is normally used on cement/sand or strong gypsum undercoats. For ceilings, this quality is not important and softer mixes are therefore to be preferred, as they present fewer problems.

Use of sand

The quantity of sand in a mix will depend on the strength required, but generally low-strength mixes (ie those with more sand) are less liable to shrinkage or expansion troubles. The best sands are clean and well graded, leaving the minimum unfilled volume for the matrix.

Prepared plasters

Use of premixed lightweight gypsum or cement/perlite plasters eliminates the possibility of errors in site mixing and has many advantages for use on ceilings, especially if difficult bonding conditions exist.

Finishing coats

CP 211[1] defines four main types in general use:

Category 1
Class B or C gypsum gauged with lime from 1/4 up to 1:1. Plasters with less than 1/4 lime content are not included, as they are stronger and require stronger undercoats such as cement/sand or similar mix gypsum.

Category 2
Weak lime. Lime putty gauged with up to half its volume of gypsum, and up to one volume fine sand. Stronger mixes may be used with up to 1:1 lime/gypsum, but require stronger undercoats.

Category 3
Lightweight, premixed, proprietary use on similar undercoats.

Category 4
Cement. Either with sand alone or sand plus varying proportions of lime. Alternatively a plasticiser may be used instead of lime. Use on undercoats of similar composition.

In addition, a recent development from Scandinavia known as 'thin-wall plaster' is available. This is based on minerals with an organic binder and delivered in drums as a paste. It hardens by drying, not chemical set and is often applied by spraying in very thin coats. *Useful (if not essential) for use over difficult materials such as lightweight concrete.*

Undercoats

CP 211[1] defines five main types, some of which are broken down into subtypes, according to strength.

A summary of these follows:

Type G lime/sand (1:2 to 3) gauged with gypsum eg 1:3:9 class B gypsum:lime:sand.

Type B, Class B gypsum plus sand Proportions vary from 1:2 to 3 up to 1:2 to 3 gypsum:sand according to strength required and type of sand. There are four classes and two sands, making eight mixes in all.

Type L Proprietary lightweight gypsum plasters Four types are defined, browning, bonding, metal lathing and multi-purpose.

Type C Based on cement Three classes of strength are defined with three variations, depending on whether the mixes are based on adding lime, plasticisers or using masonry cement (all to give workability and lessen shrinkage). Lime mixes run from 1:0 to $\frac{1}{4}$:3 to 1:2:8 to 9 cement:lime:sand and only two plasticised mixes 1:5 to 6 and 1:7 to 8 are given corresponding in strength to the last two lime mixes.

Type D Premixed lightweight cement.

Compatability

Lime and cement, or lime and gypsum may be used together but as stated earlier cement and gypsum should never be mixed. Apart from this the range is wide and the main principle is never to use an undercoat stronger than the background to which it is applied.

Backgrounds

Choice of plaster mix depends on strength, hardness, smoothness and porosity or suction. Drying shrinkage will also affect length of time which must elapse before application. Strong hard backgrounds can take strong plasters but can equally accept weak mixes or lightweight mixes.

The principal problem is providing adequate bond especially if smoothness is also a characteristic. Porous surfaces with high suction are often also weak. Apart from this they provide good bond but excessive suction can cause failure by too rapid drying out. On the other hand good suction may result in increased strength in some cement based plasters by lowering the water content during the setting period to something like the optimum for strength for development as opposed to workability. CP 211 defines three types of solid background in addition to no fines concrete which is unlikely to be found in soffits. These are:

Dense, strong, smooth materials

This description would generally only apply to in situ concrete cast on a smooth shutter. Obviously it would be better to use a rough shutter if at all possible to provide some mechanical key. If mould oil is used it should be removed before plastering. It is advisable on such soffits to use either a cement/sand spatterdash coat, wire mesh stapled on or a bonding agent such as pva emulsion. Traditionally the soffit is backed to provide a mechanical key but this must be thorough. In situ patent floors using high density clay pots may also be in this category but they are always keyed for plaster and slips are usually provided for the base of the concrete ribs to avoid a change in material **1**.

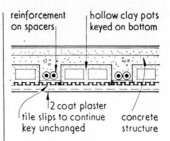

1 *Continuation of key*

Moderately strong and porous materials

These include medium density concrete and most clay or precast concrete blocks found in many types of concrete floor. Such backgrounds should afford some suction and blocks usually also provide a mechanical key either in the form of a keyed profile or deliberately coarse surface. No difficulties should be experienced providing very strong plaster mixes are not used; and time is allowed for the initial shrinkage to develop.

Moderately weak and porous materials

These are mainly of lightweight concrete using aeration or lightweight aggregates. Such concrete can have a high drying shrinkage but is usually used in precast form as part of a patent floor system and delivered properly cured to site. It may also have a fairly high thermal movement, so it is particularly important that mixes are selected which are not stronger than the background. However any typical undercoat may be used providing weaker mixes are selected. Such backgrounds are likely to have a relatively high suction and may benefit from treatment with a bonding agent to reduce this. Lightweight plaster mixes are probably the most suitable on such backgrounds **2**.

No fines concrete

A good surface for key but unlikely to be met on ceilings.

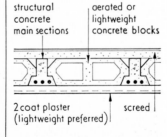

2 *Varying soffits; base of both solid and lightweight concrete may be roughened, but if not spatterdash coat or bonding agent essential*

Slab backgrounds

Sometimes construction might involve use of woodwool or strawboard as permanent shuttering. Shrinkage is low but if they are plastered before the concrete above has completed shrinking movement may occur. Woodwool has good key and low suction and can take strong gypsum mixes or lightweight plasters. Strawboard has poor key but this can be improved by use of a bonding agent or wire mesh. Lightweight plaster is advisable.

Application

Where plastering has to be continued across backgrounds of more than one type expanded metal fixed across the junction will reduce the risk of cracking due to differential movement. Alternatively it may be assumed that the crack will occur and make a straight v cut in the plaster or use metal casing beads to show a straight joint.

When the soffit is likely to be subject to structural deflection (such as might happen in long span prestressed precast concrete floors) it may be wise to avoid use of plaster direct and use some other system, which either provides a degree of independence between ceiling and floor or uses more flexible materials. The principle governing number of coats required is mainly trueness, or otherwise, of the backgrounds. Traditional backgrounds were rough lath reeds etc and so three coats including a haired coat were needed to build up sufficient thickness to eliminate divergencies in surface level and produce a true flat face.

Modern materials are generally much more precise and two-coat work is the most common. It can be used on most slightly rough concrete surfaces including patent systems, keyed clay blocks etc. Normally excluding the keys two-coat work should not exceed 13 mm. If three-coat work is required because of unusually uneven surfaces the total thickness excluding keys should not exceed 19 mm. On smooth concrete two-coat work should not exceed 10 mm and the use of lightweight mixes would be preferable. If the surface of smooth concrete is also true single coat work (ie finish coat only approximately 5 mm) may be preferable. New thin wall plasters based on organic binders may be used since they have excellent adhesion and are suitable for both dense and lightweight concrete.

Accessories

Various plastering accessories are only briefly mentioned since they are little used in ceilings on solid backgrounds. They include scrim of corrosion resistant metal, hessian or other fabrics used to reinforce joints especially at ceiling/wall junctions metal beads to form various angles and stop edges and galvanised wire netting to provide mechanical key. Traditional use of a cornice either run on site or precast in fibrous plaster, to elaborate junction between wall and ceiling has largely died out, although various types of cove usually manufactured in the same way as gypsum plasterboard or from polystyrene are available as a rather pale substitute. As with the cornice they do serve to conceal the crack which often develops on this line. A modern alternative is to use a recess **3**.

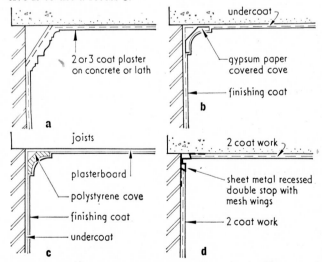

3 *Cornices and junctions:* **a** *traditional cornice in fibrous plaster or on site on lath;* **b** *modern gypsum cove;* **c** *polystyrene cove;* **d** *recessed junction*

2.03 Plasterboards and laths

When the soffit is not continuous some material is necessary to span across the intermittent supports. These may be the bottom of wooden joists, battens attached to a continuous soffit to give space for electrical conduit or merely to lower the risk of cracking, timber inserts or other fixings in the

ribs of T or channel type concrete floors precast or in situ **4**. Much the commonest is plasterboard which consists of a core of set gypsum between two strong paper liners. It is available in ⅜in (10 mm) and ½in (13 mm) thicknesses and for ceilings three types are defined, baseboard, lath and plank. The relevant British Standard is BS 1230[7]. The main difference between these is simply a question of shape. The baseboard comes in a variety of rectangular sizes up to 6ft × 3ft (1830 mm × 915 mm) and the others in a variety of lengths × 1ft 4in (407 mm) or 1ft 6in (458 mm) wide. These narrow types also have two rounded paper covered edges whereas the baseboard has open edges all round. Fixing centres can vary between 14in and 18in (356 mm and 548 mm). At the longer centres it is advisable to use the thicker (13 mm) lath. Both lath and boards are fixed with 32 mm or 38 mm galvanised clout head nails at about 150 mm centres. Joints are staggered and with the lath or plank the rounded joints are filled with plaster before the finish coat is placed. Baseboard joints are reinforced with scrim not less than 90 mm wide and all angles between wall and ceiling are similarly treated.

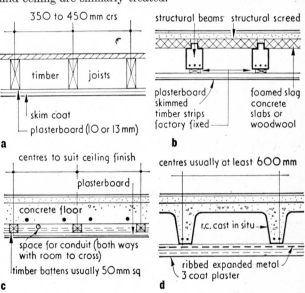

4 *Various intermittent support types:* **a** *normal joists. Expanded metal and three coats can be used instead of plasterboard and skim coat;* **b** *concrete beams and infill panels;* **c** *battens and plasterboard (10 or 13 mm, according to batten spacing) and finish coat (or two coats if necessary);* **d** *expanded metal on concrete channel structure. Ribbed expanded metal is shot fired or plugged to concrete*

Finish on plasterboard is normally a single coat (5 mm) of neat class B plaster, board finish, but if the surface is particularly uneven, two coats. In this case the total thickness should not exceed 10 mm, but as the undercoat will be sanded, manufacturers should be consulted as to the choice of plaster type for undercoat. Lightweight bonding plasters are equally suitable for either one or two coat work.

Although one or two finishing coats are normally applied gypsum plasterboard may be used unplastered especially if decorated with one of the new plastic paints with sufficient body to conceal the joints. For this purpose tapered edge lath is available to receive scrim and plaster to the joint only, so as to leave a level surface **5**.

Insulated fibreboard based on wood and vegetable fibre may be used. When plastered it is fixed in a similar manner to plasterboard with clout nails at 200 mm centres generally and 100 mm around edges. Boards are now available in metric sizes 1 m wide in two thicknesses 13 mm and 19 mm. Fixing should be at centres (maximum 450 mm and 600 mm).

As the material has a high moisture movement it should be exposed on edge in the situation where it is to be fixed for at least 48 hours before fixing. It may also be necessary to dampen or wet the board before plastering. This should be done immediately after fixing. Joints should be reinforced with galvanised wire mesh pressed into a thin coat of plaster before applying one or two coats of plaster. Two coats will normally give a better chance of avoiding cracks and strong mixes should be avoided. Lightweight bonding plaster is to be preferred. BS 1142: 1961 applies.

Expanded plastics. These comparatively new boards usually of polystyrene or polyurethane are useful for situations where good thermal resistance is needed. They are available in a wide range of sizes and thicknesses, are fixed in a similar way to ordinary fibreboard but are *not* subject to a high degree of movement. Plastering is similar to that used on plasterboard.

Other materials. There are of course many other possibilities for direct ceilings not normally associated with this function, eg boarding both hardwood and softwood, wood strip which can be combined with acoustic felts, asbestos plank and others **10**.

Metal lathing

This is nearly always expanded metal, although a welded mesh with clay crosses is available. It should weigh at least 1·6 kg/m² for sanded plasters and 1·2 kg/m² for lightweight plasters. Mesh should be 10 mm or 6 mm fixed with the longway across the supports which should not normally exceed 360 mm centres. It should be packed off slightly to maintain key at supports. If longer spans are required a ribbed variety is available with spans varying according to the depth and spacing of ribs **6**.

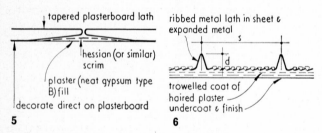

5 *Tapered plasterboard lath—unskimmed*
6 *Ribbed expanded metal. Note: strength and thus span depends on depth d, spacing s and gauge of metal. Spans up to 1500 mm are normal*

Metal lathing should not be treated as a solid background as it will give under shrinkage stresses caused by strong cement mixes which should not be used. Gypsum plasters are preferable and there is a metal lathing grade in both class B and lightweight plasters. This usually contains hair and is used for the first coat of what is normally a three-coat system. BS 1369: 1947[9] applies.

2.04 Thick spray finishes

These are all proprietary mixtures usually applied by spraying apparatus from below. They can however usually be applied to expanded metal by first trowelling on a suitable undercoat. They are based on either vermiculite or asbestos fibre with suitable binders and have considerable advantages over normal cement/lime or gypsum mixes. These include good bond to virtually any backing, a degree of flexibility which virtually eliminates cracking, high sound absorption and very good fire resistance. They are completely non-combustible.

Thicknesses vary from about 10 mm up to 50 mm and this of course influences the degree of sound absorption and fire protection afforded. It is however unusual and normally unnecessary to exceed 25 mm. The natural finish is an attractive coarse texture, but if required a special smooth finish can be applied although this reduces sound absorption **7**.

2.05 Thin spray finishes

These are those finishes usually 6 mm or below in thickness and which at the lower end of the scale really overlap with paints, when they could be described as a built-up paint or a thin finish. They are almost always applied by spray and could be said to include the so-called thin wall plasters referred to in 2.01. As with thick sprays they are all proprietary and usually specialist applied either by the manufacturers own team or by specially trained painting or plastering contractors.

They are based on mineral fillers with a variety of binders including cement, pva or other polymers, epoxy and other resins and chemically treated rubber. Those based on cement usually have polymer emulsions added to give bond and flexibility. Most can be applied to virtually any background and will adhere however smooth (eg dense concrete). However, being thin, they cannot achieve one of the objectives of plastering which is to conceal irregularities in the structure and are therefore only suitable for use on flat true surfaces. But they can be thick enough to conceal the sharp edges of cracks or lipping and if the surface imperfections form a regular pattern the effect is not necessarily unattractive **7**.

Such finishes may require further decoration but some types are self-coloured and even available in mottled effects involving two or more colours. Final finish is normally the result of a build up of several very thin coats, and possibly a final clear glaze.

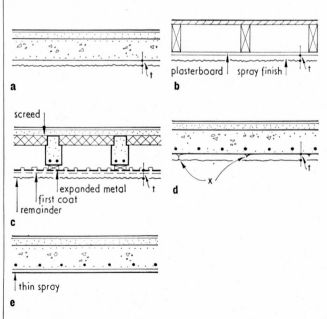

Note thickness 't' may vary from 10 to 50mm (25mm usual)

7 *Sprayed finishes: **a** solid background. Thick spray in one coat or built up in several tough layers; **b** open background using plasterboard and spray; **c** open background using expanded metal. First coat trowelled on, remainder sprayed; **d** surface imperfections; **e** thin sprays (6 mm or less) require perfect surface (eg good concrete)*

2.06 Boards and sheets

With non continuous soffits the ceiling may be provided by a variety of boards and sheets having strength characteristics appropriate to the spacing of the structural supports. Use of plasterboard unplastered as mentioned in 2.02 is one example. The use of insulating fibreboard and rigid expanded plastics as a base for plaster has also been described in the same section. These sheet materials can also be used on their own with suitable fixing and jointing arrangements.

Thicknesses are normally 13 mm or 19 mm and using the latter these boards are quite rigid enough to be fixed at 600 mm centres. When used with plaster clout head nails are used but these would be unsightly if exposed and the use of adhesive in conjunction with panel pins until set is a suitable method. Joints may be expressed by using cover strips or a suitable recessed or other profiled metal or plastic section or merely taped with adhesive tape which becomes almost invisible after decoration **8**. Principal types available are as follows:

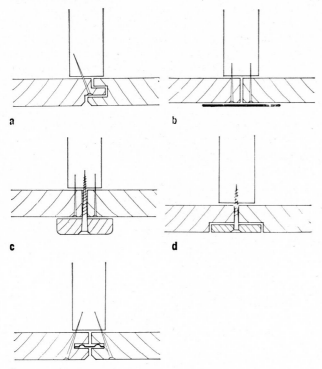

8 *Joints in unplastered board ceilings:* **a** *secret nailed;* **b** *butt joint, taped and decorated;* **c** *butt joint and cover lath;* **d** *recessed joint and lath;* **e** *grooved and chamfered with spline*

Wood fibre insulation board

A material of which there are many well-known manufacturers. Available in large sheets. Combustible but can be treated to give class 1 spread of flame. Wood fibre boards have quite good sound absorption especially if drilled.

Expanded polystyrene

Is now the commonest form of board insulation and quite suitable for ceilings. Extremely light but of low crushing strength (not important with ceilings). Very good insulation value. No value for fire resistance, as it melts at quite low temperatures. (Should not be used over 80 °C.)

Expanded polyurethane

Similar to polystyrene but has improved characteristics. Slightly more dense it has a higher strength/weight ratio and even better κ value. It can also be used at rather higher temperatures, its strength being unaffected up to the boiling point of water. Will not spread combustion but still has no fire resistance value.

Expanded rigid pvc

Cannot compete in cost with the two predecessors but is available in rather higher densities and hence is stronger. It could therefore be useful where supports can only be conveniently provided at greater intervals. Other characteristics very similar to expanded polystyrene.

General

These wood fibre and plastic materials are low in weight and rigid in relation to thickness. Traditional fibreboard is naturally heavier at about $2\frac{1}{2}$ kg/m² for 13 mm thickness against 0·2 kg/m² for some polystyrenes with polyurethane at about 0·5 kg/m². All these weights are however negligible in structural terms and result in very good weight/strength ratios especially for the plastics, meaning no tendency to sag between supports. The exception may be fibreboard which will sag if affected by excessive humidity.

None of the materials are of any value as fire resistance since fibreboard is combustible and the plastics simply melt at quite low temperatures although they are available in self extinguishing grades. All have good κ values polyurethane being exceptionally good at 0·02 and fibreboard the worst (although still good at 0·05 (metric) W/m/°C). Being of closed cellular structure the plastic boards have a low water absorption rate, good vapour resistance and only moderate sound absorption.

Mineral fibre board

Although normally only associated with suspended ceilings this material is available in boards, 600 mm × 1500 mm and could be fixed direct to battens in the same way as the cellular plastic boards providing these are at suitable centres (say 300 mm). Apart from providing good acoustic correction these boards have the great advantage of giving good fire protection if needed. Rigid glass fibre is also available in sizes up to 1200 mm × 4800 mm.

2.07 Acoustic tiles fixed to joists

Most types of acoustic tile suitable for suspended ceilings (see information sheet CEILINGS 1 p1464 may be fixed to joisted floors or other intermittent structures providing the structural members are at suitable centres. The fixing system could be either adhesive or concealed nailing and although the smallest normal size of 300 mm × 300 mm would not generally be big enough there is a fairly wide variety including 400 mm × 400 mm, 450 mm × 450 mm, 600 mm × 600 mm, 300 mm × 600 mm and larger sizes including some strip materials in asbestos or metal suitable for direct fixing **9**.

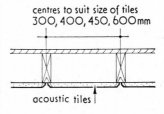

9 *Acoustic tiles on joists. Centres to suit size of tiles:* 300, 400, 450, 600 mm. Note: Detail **8e** *using splines to avoid lipping may be advisable with tiles as well as boards, especially on cross-joists. Many types are supplied suitably grooved. Alternatively, secret nailing system in* **8a** *may be used*

2.08 Acoustic tiles fixed to solid soffits

If acoustic correction is needed without using a cavity for wiring a useful method is to use normal wood or mineral fibre acoustic tiles fixed direct to the soffit with a suitable adhesive, recommended by manufacturers. Dabs of adhesive are used and lipping is prevented either by using a tongued and grooved tile or separate splines **10**. The smaller type of tile is the most suitable for this application 300 mm × 300 mm or perhaps 300 mm × 600 mm.

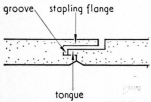

10 *Tongued and grooved edge detail, ensuring level ceiling with concealed fixing*

Naturally the structural soffit needs to be reasonably flat and true but small projections such as might be caused by leakage between shutter joints can be covered in the depth of the adhesive dabs. If asbestos based or mineral fibre based tiles are used, they will also contribute to the total fire resistance of the floor.

3 Special plasters

There are three principal classes of special plaster which might be used on ceilings:

Protective plaster
x-ray rooms require special protection against penetration to spaces outside. Barium sulphate plaster is the most convenient method and is simply a normal plaster based on cement or gypsum but using barium sulphate (barytes) as an aggregate. A normal mix is one part cement (or class B gypsum) to one part barytes fines and three parts barytes sand. Thickness will depend on output of equipment to be housed and is laid down in terms of a 'lead equivalent'. Manufacturers sometimes give National Physical Laboratories figures for the lead equivalent of their plaster. Further advice can be obtained from the NPL.

Acoustic plasters
Normal plaster has little acoustic value and on a solid background the absorption coefficient may be as low as 0·02 at 500 Hz. Special acoustic plaster would give a figure of around 0·20 at the same frequency and 0·25 at 100 Hz. This admittedly is 10 times better but is still very low compared with other materials such as mineral based tiles for which figures of 0·75 at 500 Hz are common. As the technique is difficult and the effect easily reduced by redecoration acoustic plaster (as opposed to sprayed materials) may be regarded as outmoded.

Thermal insulating plasters
As with acoustic absorption plaster is not of much value in thermal insulation and many other materials (including air in the form of a cavity) are much more efficient. However light weight plasters incorporating perlite or vermiculite do give some increased thermal resistance to floor and ceiling constructions probably amounting to something like 10 per cent of the total u value of an average roof construction. They also have some advantage over normal plasters where intermittent condensation is likely.

4 Ceilings below roofs

As with suspended ceilings, the ceiling immediately below a roof is a special case because of the high temperature differential between outside and inside and the need to avoid both surface and interstitial condensation. The principles which apply in the case of suspended ceilings were described in 3.02.03 of the technical study and illustrated in **8**. Exactly the same principles apply to non-suspended ceiling especially when a joisted construction is used leaving an air space which should be ventilated to the external air (care being taken to cross batten or drill joists to all air to flow both ways) in the same circumstances as apply in suspended ceilings. Further examples are given in information sheet EXTERNAL ENVELOPE 1 (section 2) where examples of solid construction may be seen.

5 Constraints

Building Regulations 1972 were described in information sheet SUSPENDED CEILINGS 1. (Table II of Regulation E5 will not apply to ceilings applied directly to the soffit.) Schedule 8 gives examples of the effect of different types and thicknesses of plaster on the fire resistance of the whole floor. These are considerable—for example a concrete floor having an aggregate thickness of 90 mm of solid material can be increased from ½ to 2 h resistance by the addition of 10 mm of vermiculite/gypsum plaster.

Presumably acoustic tiles of mineral fibre fixed directly by adhesive would be allowed to contribute providing the adhesive were not affected by heat penetration through the tile. On the other hand ceilings, fixed to battens even if only 50 mm below the structural soffit would presumably count as suspended for the purpose of table 3 of Regulation E5 and their contribution would be limited accordingly.

Surface spread of flame as controlled by Regulation E15 would not vary from suspended ceilings.

6 References

BRITISH STANDARDS INSTITUTION
1 BS CP 211: 1966 Internal plastering [(42) Pr2] £1·25
2 BS 890: 1966 Building lines [Yq1] £1·25
3 BS 12: Part 2: 1971 Portland cement (ordinary and rapid-hardening), Metric units [Yq2] £1·25
4 BS 1191: Part 1: Gypsum building plasters. Excluding premixed lightweight plasters [Pr2] 85p
5 BS 1198-1200: 1955 Building sands from natural sources [Yp1] 70p
6 BS 1191: Part 2: 1967 Premixed lightweight plasters [Pr2] 70p
7 BS 1230: Part 2: 1970 Gypsum plasterboard, Metric units [Rf7] 55p
8 BS 1142: 1961 Fibre building boards [Rj1] 85p
9 BS 1369: 1947 Metal lathing (steel) for plastering [Jh2] 40p
10 BUILDING RESEARCH STATION Technical information leaflet TIL 34, Timber flat roofs. June 1972 [(27·1) Yi] free on application
11 FIRE RESEARCH ORGANISATION Expanded polystyrene linings for domestic buildings. Fire Note 12. 1971, HMSO [8 Yn6 (R4)]
12 The Building Regulations 1972 [A3j]

Design guide

Building enclosure

Form

This design guide consists of four parts:
- Collect data
- Design of external envelope
- Design of internal division
- Appendices A and B

Scope

The design of the building enclosure and division which is the specific subject covered by this handbook, will normally be tackled *after* the basic position and orientation of the building on the site have been tentatively decided, and *after* preliminary decisions have been taken on general building form and structural type (eg loadbearing walls and pitched roof, or non-loadbearing walls and northlight roof supported on stanchions, and so on).

The user will, therefore, generally come to this handbook after he has consulted the relevant AJ Building type guide and also the AJ Handbook of Building Structure and after the general building form, disposition of spaces, and structural type have been tentatively decided. However, as detailed analysis and design of the enclosing elements proceeds, it may well prove necessary to go back and revise some of the earlier decisions.

How to use

This design guide suggests a broad sequence of decision-taking, and reminds the architect of the points to be considered at each stage. It does not attempt to convey design information; this will be found in the technical studies and information sheets of the relevant Handbook section.

Unfortunately it is necessary for practical reasons to present the guide in the form of a linear sequence of detailed instructions, even though design, in practice, is never a strictly-controlled linear process. We hope that architects will be able to follow the *broad* decision-sequence, while adapting the more detailed sequences suggested in the guide to suit their own needs. Some may adhere to the suggested

procedures quite closely, while others may follow their own well-tried methods, using the guide largely as a checklist to ensure that everything has been thought about.

To aid users, there is a diagram on the next page summarising the sequence of decisions. It is recommended that this be constantly referred to when the guide is being studied or used, so that the reader can orient himself within the whole sequence and keep track of what he is doing.

References

References are given a short title for identification only. Full titles, with details of publication and a brief description of contents where appropriate, are given in the appendix. References in SMALL CAPITALS are to other documents in this Handbook.

Superseded material

This design guide brings together in a single document the whole range of subject matter covered by the six separate element design guides published in the AJ in 1967. The earlier individual guides are more detailed than the present revised, composite version, and readers who have them on file may wish to keep them for background information, even though they are unwieldy and in some respects out of date. Most readers will however probably prefer to consult only the new unified guide in this book; in which case the following material should now be discarded:

Element design guide 1: General (AJ 30.8.67) CI/sfB (9–)

Element design guide 2: Floors on the ground (AJ 30.8.67) CI/sfB (13)

Element design guide 3: Suspended floors (AJ 27.9.67) CI/sfB (23)

Element design guide 4: External walls (AJ 18/25.10.67) CI/sfB (21)

Element design guide 5: Internal walls (AJ 20.12.67) CI/sfB (22)

Element design guide 6: Roofs (AJ 25.10.67 and 15.11.67) CI/sfB (27)

The sfB (1961) classification for all the above guides, which was in use at the time of their publication, was Ba4 (2).

COLLECTION OF DATA

DATA REQUIRED
design requirements
- building type, purpose, occupancy
- flexibility of internal spaces
- security, protection
- users' preferences
- environmental requirements

design constraints
- client's economic policies
- client's building economic policies
- cleaning, maintenance policy
- design life, durability
- availability of resources
- construction programme
- dimensional basis
- insurance, fire brigade, legislation

design context
- site, climate
- programme
- structural context

performance requirements for building fabric
- structural, fire resistance, security
- design life, durability
- cost limits
- environmental performance

DESIGN OF EXTERNAL ENVELOPE

TAKE BASIC DECISIONS
POSITIONS, SHAPES AND SIZES OF OPENINGS
walls and roofs
- consider access and egress
- consider view
- consider daylight and sunlight
- consider ventilation
- consider noise
- consider heat
- review decisions

CHARACTERISTICS OF OPENINGS
walls and roofs
- consider heat, air and sound control
- consider light, view and privacy

CHARACTERISTICS OF SOLID FABRIC
- review earlier structural decisions
- decide solid wall fabric
- decide solid roof fabric
- decide solid lowest floor fabric
- review decisions

TAKE DETAILED DECISIONS
solid. fabric
- decide details of wall fabric
- decide details of roof fabric
- decide details of lowest floor fabric

openings
- decide details of wall openings
- decide details of roof openings

junctions
- decide joint sizes
- decide joint shapes
- decide joint materials

TAKE FINAL DECISIONS
whole envelope
- finalise drainage
- finalise cleaning and maintenance
- finalise appearance
- finalise cost plan
- review decisions

DESIGN OF INTERNAL DIVISION

RELATE DESIGN DECISIONS TO PERFORMANCE REQTS.
partitions/floors/ceilings
- adjacent elements
- structural requirements
- support/fixing facilities
- radio-active screening
- dirt resistance
- thermal performance
- sound control
- light and view
- ventilation
- fire resistance/security
- accommodation of services
- durability, maintenance, appearance
- dimensional considerations
- cost plan check

Collect data

The design process involves the reconciliation of two complementary classes of information: clients' and users' *requirements* (ie what they want or need); and the *constraints* acting upon the solution (ie factors which control, or tend to prevent, the fulfilment of these requirements). The first step in designing the building enclosure is therefore to identify and record both requirements and constraints, as far as they are known, together with the general background information which forms the *context* of the design problem.

Section 1, below, deals with design requirements; section 2 with design constraints; and section 3 with design context. They apply to both the external envelope and the internal division of the building. Section 4 deals with the *performance requirements* of the building fabric; these are derived from sections 1 to 3.

1 Design requirements

1.01 Building type and purpose

See AJ building type design guides listed on page 22 for *planning requirements*, and implications on building form, fabric and finishes. Check *purpose group* of building in terms of regulation E2 of the Building Regulations 1972

1.02 Occupancy

Prepare schedule of periods during which various parts of building will be occupied, and of activities to be performed. Distinguish between activities requiring *continuous* occupancy, and those for which space usage is *intermittent*

1.03 Flexibility of internal spaces

Record degree of adaptability of internal spaces, on suitable scale ranging from *nil* (no rearrangement of building fabric required at all), to *high* (rearrangement necessary at least yearly)

1.04 Security and protection

Establish general *standards*; identify specific *risk areas*

1.05 Users' preferences

Record specific users' preferences, so that possible conflicts with other design considerations can be identified and resolved at later stages in design

1.06 Light

Establish, for each internal space type, users' *daylight requirements**

1.07 Sun

Establish, for each internal space type, users' *sunlight requirements**

1.08 View

Establish, for various users and/or space types, *importance of view out*. Where important, decide what is to be seen: nearby ground, facing buildings and trees, distant views, sky

1.09 Privacy

Establish, for various users and/or space types, importance of *privacy*—both visual and aural

1.10 Air

Establish, for each internal space type, users' *ventilation requirements**

1.11 Noise

Establish, for each internal space type, *noise criterion* (NC) curve; see above table. For lecture rooms, auditoria, etc, establish desired *reverberation time*; see AJ 12.2.69 p465

1.12 Heat

Establish permissible *heat loss rates*, and desirable *thermal storage capacity* (high, medium, or low) for building as a whole

2 Design constraints

2.01 Client's economic policies

● Establish how project is to be financed (government, private, commercial, mortgage)

* See Technical study EXTERNAL WALLS 4 table I

● Establish cost limitations, availability of money, programme of expenditure, capital cost allowance, or official cost limit
● Establish rate of economic return where applicable
● Establish whether expenditure is to be phased in relation to fund-raising efforts or future revenue, etc
● Establish sources of income

2.02 Client's building economic policies

Establish *cost plan* (proportion of total cost allocated to each element); relationship of *capital costs* to *recurring costs*; cost-benefit appraisals

2.03 Cleaning and maintenance policy

Discuss *methods* and *frequency* of cleaning; give special attention to least accessible parts (eg roof glazing); consider relationship between maintenance *access* and security/privacy requirements

2.04 Design life

Anticipate possible future *changes of use*; vertical or horizontal *extension*; adaptation to improved environmental standards; changes in fashion, etc

2.05 Durability

Establish special aspects of building usage which might affect durability requirements; eg traffic intensity, abnormal wear and tear, vandalism, presence of corrosive chemicals

2.06 Availability of resources

Check inbuilt cost penalties of materials, public utilities, labour services not easily available in locality. Check availability of contractors' plant

2.07 Construction procedure

Consider constraints imposed by structural form, construction programme, site equipment, on freedom of design and choice of materials and components

2.08 Dimensional basis

Consider constraints imposed by modular grid, official dimensional co-ordination recommendations, standardised component sizes. See Information sheet ENCLOSURE 1

2.09 Insurance and fire brigade requirements

Consider special constructional requirements; limitations on usage of materials; means of escape; access for fire-fighting appliances

2.10 Legislation

Planning (height and position of building; roof profile; choice of materials; restrictions on eaves profiles and elements such as tanks and lift-motor rooms on roof)
Building (fire resistance and combustibility; positions and sizes of openings, subdivision of building into compartments, and protection of apertures in relation to fire legislation, lighting, ventilation, access and egress, heat transfer, moisture control, quality of materials)
Building uses (eg Factories Acts; Shops, Offices and Railway Premises Act 1963)
(Note: the new Building Bill when produced and approved will combine much, if not all, of this legislation in one Act)

3 Design context

3.01 Site

Soil: bearing capacity; subsidence; water table and underground watercourses; presence of harmful chemicals. See AJ *Guide to site investigation* (AJ 27.10.65)
Note condition of *adjacent property* (eg weathering and effect of pollution); roof and eaves lines; nature and uses of adjacent properties; access facilities
Note *views* (direction and character)

3.02 Climate

Sun (intensity and duration of sunshine, determined from latitude; modifying effect of cloud cover conditions locally prevalent, trees, other buildings, etc)
Air (winter and summer air temperatures; direction and force of prevailing winds, and effect of local topography on air currents)
Water (intensity and duration of rainfall and snowfall; relative humidity in winter and summer)
Noise (local sources of noise; location, intensity and duration)
Pollution (local sources of pollution, eg industry, motorways, dust sources)

3.03 Programme

Investigate speed and phasing requirements; protection of building is strong argument for getting building watertight as soon as possible

3.04 Structural context

Check on decisions already taken, relating to structural type and form, supports, spans, fixing conditions. Note structural requirements to be catered for by enclosing fabric, both internal and external

4 Performance requirements

4.01 Structural requirements

See 3.04. Tabulate dead and imposed loads which will operate upon each element

4.02 Fire resistance requirements

See 2.09. Knowing shape and size of building, and its position relative to boundary, evaluate minimum fire resistance of solid parts of walls, and maximum amount of 'unprotected' area in external walls, and degree of protection required for apertures in internal subdivisions

4.03 Security requirements

See 1.04. *Fabric* should be of physical strength appropriate to degree of risk, and to value of building contents. *Openings* should be so located as to minimise risk of entry (eg in situations where frequent observation is likely) and fitted with locking devices appropriate to degree of security required

4.04 Required design life

From 2.04, establish *design life* required of each group of building elements or components (structure, external envelope, internal division, finishes, decorations, etc)

4.05 Required durability

From 2.05, establish *durability* required of various parts of building fabric and finishes

4.06 Cost limits

From 2.01 and 2.02, establish *cost limits* of elements and components: capital cost, maintenance and cleaning costs, repair and replacement costs

4.07 Sun and light entry

For each space in building, establish sun and natural light entry requirements in detail. From 1.06 and 1.07 *daylight factor* and *insulation* requirements are known; consider also required *visual character* (restful, dramatic, neutral), and desired degree of control

4.08 Air infiltration

For each space in building, establish desired rate of air change, and pattern of air movement

General *rates of air change* requirements, from 1.10, may be modified by special conditions in room (high population density, presence of heat-producing equipment, or presence of internally-produced air pollutants will indicate increased rate of air change required also the direction which should be away from non-polluted areas)

Pattern of air movement influenced by function of room, and seasonal requirements (in summer, air entry and movement at working height may be desirable; in winter, high level would be preferred)

4.09 Sound modification

For each space in building, establish from 1.11 and 3.02 noise-reduction performance of walls and partitions

4.10 Thermal performance

From 1.12, establish the following:
- Mean u-value of external envelope as a whole and, where relevant, specific u-values of particular portions of both external envelope and internal partitions
- Desirable ratio of window area to solid fabric area, for external envelope
- Thermal capacity for building as a whole (high, medium or low)

External envelope: take basic decisions

5 Positions, shapes and sizes of openings

Paras 5.01 to 5.07 list the functional requirements which form the basis for deciding opening positions, sizes and shapes. The decision will often be a compromise between conflicting requirements: to remind the architect of the *opposing* factors to be borne in mind when considering each requirement, these are listed in each case as 'constraints'

Decisions on individual openings must be taken subject to two overall disciplines, which must be kept constantly in mind:
- *Appearance* of building as a whole

● *Environmental performance requirements* of external envelope as a whole
Ratio between area of openings, and area of solid fabric, is of crucial importance to thermal and (to a lesser extent) noise-insulation performance of the envelope. Every glazed opening in the envelope reduces its thermal and acoustic insulation value, and the larger the opening, the greater the reduction in performance. A decision should therefore be taken at the outset on approximate *percentage of glazing* (see Information sheet EXTERNAL ENVELOPE 1, page 57), and decisions on window and door openings checked against this controlling discipline
Technical study EXTERNAL ENVELOPE 1 page 43 and Technical study EXTERNAL WALLS 4 page 143, especially table II, should be constantly referred to when using this design guide

5.01 Access and egress

● Consider *entry/exit* requirements of people, goods and vehicles
● Consider *fire escape* requirements
● Consider access requirements for *cleaning*

Constraints

Main constraints on sizing and positioning of access and egress openings will be *security* requirements (Technical study EXTERNAL ENVELOPE 1, para 4.02)

5.02 Daylight and sunlight

● Consider *available light:* influenced by latitude, orientation, slope of site, obstacles, seasonal variations (see 3.02)
● Consider *daylight requirements* inside each space in building, both statutory (daylight factors for dwellings, schools) and desired non-statutory (illumination intensities, limitations on glare, visual character) (see 4.07)
● Consider *sunlight requirements* inside each space in building (see 4.07)
● Decide most appropriate *permutation* of natural and artificial lighting (total reliance on artificial lighting; or mainly artificial lighting with small amount of natural light to improve modelling and give link with outside; or natural light permanently supplemented by artificial light for deep interiors (PSALI); or major reliance on daylighting). Room depth will be major factor in choice. Conversely a decision to use what is usually known as integrated design (incorporating PSALI) will, in the absence of other constraints, dictate the physical plan
● On basis of above, establish preferred window and rooflight arrangement

Constraints

Main constraints on exploitation of natural lighting, which may require large openings, are the following factors, which generally favour small apertures: *privacy* requirements; need to limit *solar glare*; need to avoid excessive *heat gain* and *heat loss;* need to avoid large *cold surfaces* in winter; *noise* insulation; strength limitations

5.03 View

● Consider *aspects* of external environment to be seen; decide relative importance of each (see 1.08)
● Consider critical *eye-levels* inside building: standing, sitting, reclining positions

Constraints

Main constraints on satisfying view requirements, which may demand large openings, are the following factors, all of which favour smaller apertures: *Privacy* requirements; need to limit *solar glare*; need to avoid excessive *heat gain* and *heat loss*; need to avoid large *cold surfaces* in winter; *noise* insulation

5.04 Ventilation

● Consider *external conditions:* prevailing wind direction and velocities; influence of local topography on patterns of air movement; sources of airborne dirt and pollution (see 3.02)
● Consider *internal ventilation requirements* (see 4.08)

Constraints

Main constraint on reliance upon natural ventilation will in many cases be *noise insulation* requirements, which may rule out use of opening windows. Ducted forced ventilation may then be indicated. Size and position of opening lights may also be limited by *safety* requirements

5.05 Noise

● Consider *external noise sources* (intensity and times of occurrence); and orientation of building in relation to sources (see 3.02)
● Consider desirable *internal noise levels* (see 4.09)
● Establish desirability of openings in fabric: sealed windows can provide some noise insulation, but opening windows, employed for ventilation, cannot

Constraints

Main source of conflict is likely to be incompatibility between *noise insulation* requirements, and *ventilation* requirements

5.06 Heat

● Consider *external* conditions: radiant conditions, and winter and summer air temperatures (see 3.02)
● Consider desired *internal* conditions and degree of control required

● Establish appropriate *ratio* of aperture area to solid fabric area. Large areas of glazing cause problems of thermal control which may prove expensive or impossible to solve satisfactorily by later choice of glazing material, choice of low u-value solid panels, or choice of heating/cooling installation (see introductory notes preceding 5.01)

● Evaluate proposed individual windows and rooflights for *heat-gain* and *heat-loss*, and effect on mean radiant conditions, relative to rooms they serve

Constraints

Main sources of conflict likely to be opposition between thermal requirements, which favour small apertures; and *daylighting* and *view* requirements, which may require large openings. *Aesthetic preference* may also favour large areas of glazing

5.07 Review basic decisions

Having decided tentatively on positions, sizes and shapes of openings, *review* these decisions in terms of the following criteria, before going on to consider most appropriate types of infilling

● Appearance
● Structural stability: assess in terms of 4.01
● Fire resistance: assess in terms of 4.02
● Junctions with internal elements: check arrangement of openings for compatibility with internal structural element, partitions, service elements, and furniture
● Cost considerations: openings are generally more expensive than solid wall or roof, both in first cost, and cleaning, maintenance and replacement costs. Check against 2.02

6 Characteristics of openings

The preliminary layout of openings decided upon in 5 must now be analysed more closely, and the functions of each opening determined in detail. Some openings will have just *one* function, for instance a door opening intended to cater solely for access/egress. Others will be intended to provide the minimum of obstruction to *several* environmental aspects, eg light, view and ventilation simultaneously. Yet others will be called on to perform the more complex function of *selective* control, eg a window required to admit light but exclude heat; or one which must allow occupants to look out, but prevent outsiders from seeing in

The following decisions must be taken at this stage, to ensure that each opening will perform its full range of functions satisfactorily:
● Type of opening (eg fixed window/rooflight; or opening unit)
● Type of infill (eg solid or louvred; opaque, translucent or transparent; one-way or two-way vision)
● Location of opening in relation to thickness of solid fabric
● Additional elements (eg sun or glare shading, burglar-proofing)

Re-examine each opening in terms of the following:

6.01 Heat loss

Knowing external conditions (orientation, winter air temperatures, from 3.02); desired degree of control (from 1.12); and basic sizes and positions of window/rooflights; decide on suitable types of infilling for *heat loss control*. The following measures will reduce heat loss:
● Use of fixed, rather than **opening lights**
● Use of multiple, rather than single glazing
● Use of heavy curtains or blinds
If these measures are not adequate, reconsider earlier design decisions, and study possibilities of:
● Reducing size of opening
● Re-orienting opening towards south (but this may lead to problems of heat gain)

6.02 Heat gain

Knowing external conditions (orientation, summer air temperatures, from 3.02); desired degree of control (from 1.12); and basic sizes and positions of window/rooflights; evaluate alternative infilling types in terms of *heat gain control*. The following measures will reduce heat gain:
● Shading window/rooflights by means of external blinds, louvres, or building projections
● Use of heat-absorbing glazing
If these measures are not appropriate, reconsider earlier design decisions, and study possibilities of:

- Reducing size of opening
- Re-orienting opening away from south

6.03 Air infiltration

If natural ventilation is to be used, decide positions, sizes and types of *opening lights*. Consider need for protection against entry of rain, dust and pollution; and against effects of wind and air turbulence

6.04 Sound infiltration

Open windows are a major source of noise infiltrating buildings. Where an external noise source is present, one or more of the following measures may be indicated:
- Use of double-glazing, spaced at least 150 to 200 mm apart
- Use of edge-sealing, with opening windows
- Using fixed windows, with ducted ventilation

If these measures are not adequate (see Information sheet EXTERNAL ENVELOPE 1), re-orient openings away from noise source

6.05 Light, view and privacy

If large areas of roof or wall glazing are required for natural light, or for view, it may be difficult to satisfy glare-control or privacy requirements. If careful design of aperture size, proportion and arrangement cannot solve problem, following measures may be considered:
- Glare control. With roof glazing, incoming light should be screened from normal view within an angle 40 to 45° to the horizontal. If depth of roof construction cannot provide this, louvres or other shading devices may be necessary; or low-transmission glazing should be used. With windows, louvres or blinds may be used to limit direct view of sky; and sharp contrasts between sky and immediate window surrounds reduced by painting windows and surrounds a light colour, and by directing generous light onto window wall either from other windows, or from reflected or permanent artificial light. Upper portions of large windows can be glazed with low-transmission glass
- Privacy. Consider use of screening devices or, in extreme cases, one-way glazing
- Sun: penetration of direct sunlight can cause discomfort and it should be remembered that the depth (though not the intensity) is greater in the winter because of the low angle of the sun.

7 Characteristics of solid fabric

Basic decisions have now been taken on sizes, positions and arrangement of openings (step 5), and on the treatment of each opening (step 6). The next step is to take similar basic decisions on the *solid* portions of the building fabric; once this is done, a tentative design will have been achieved for the whole of the external skin, and the remaining decisions will be detailed ones

7.01 Review earlier structural decisions

If not already decided at earlier stage (ie at design stage preceding this handbook; see Section 2 EXTERNAL ENVELOPE Technical study 1), decision must now be taken whether enclosure is to be essentially of *heavy* construction (either homogeneous, or built-up units of brick, concrete, etc), or *light* construction (ie secondary supporting framework with light infills)
- Consider external *wall construction*. Are walls to be loadbearing or non-loadbearing; wet or dry construction; relatively heavyweight or lightweight? Probable strength and stability, thermal character, cost and appearance of whole wall-element must be reassessed on basis of known extent and arrangement of window-openings, and earlier decisions amended or confirmed
- Consider relationship of external wall to internal walls or partitions. Settle the basic structural principles of the complete building—eg is it cellular (leading possibly to the use of loadbearing masonry with resulting economy) or open and flexible inside, leading to choice of framed structure. These characteristics affect the basic *nature* of the building and indicate a system for the exterior walls.
- Consider *roof construction*. Is roof to be flat or pitched; dry or wet construction; are earlier decisions on spans and support still valid? Reassess probable performance, appearance and cost of whole roof-element on basis of known extent and arrangement of rooflights; and either confirm or amend earlier decisions on roof-form, method of construction, spans and structural support

7.02 Take basic decisions on solid wall fabric

- Consider required *thermal insulation* value. On basis of known mean U-value for wall-element as a whole (see 4.10), and known ratio of window area to wall area, establish U-values for solid portions to give required overall wall performance
- Consider required *thermal capacity*. From 4.10, and known ratio of window area to wall area, decide required relative massiveness of solid fabric. Note however that

wall fabric cannot be considered in isolation: building structure, partitions, floors and roof will all help determine total thermal capacity

● Consider *water exclusion*. Rain exclusion can be achieved by cavity-construction (relatively cheap, effective and trouble-free, providing bridging problems are overcome); or by impervious outer skin (can function without cavity, but requires watertight jointing, and usually vapour-barrier). Former usually preferred. Interstitial condensation avoidance will be considered in 8.01

● Consider *noise exclusion*. If noise insulation requirements are stringent, relatively massive construction is better than lightweight; wet construction is better than dry for avoidance of soundpaths

● Consider *structural strength* and stability; check solid fabric against 4.01

● Consider *relationship* between external walls and structure (if separate). Decide position of wall-plane in relation to supporting structural frame, and adjacent elements. Consider shading effect of projecting floors, walls, columns, or fins; possibility of access along projecting floors; and appearance

● Consider *cost* of proposed construction (both capital and recurring, eg cleaning, maintenance, replacement)

● Consider *appearance*

7.03 Take basic decisions on solid roof fabric

● Consider required *thermal insulation* value. Roofs are major source of heat loss, particularly on low-rise, extended-plan buildings. On basis of known required mean U-value (see 4.10) of roof-element as a whole, and known ratio of rooflights to solid roof fabric, establish required U-values for solid portions to give required overall roof performance

● Consider required *thermal capacity*; see paragraph under 'walls' above. Similar considerations apply

● Consider *water exclusion*. In *flat roofs*, covering must be totally resistant to water entry, both in itself and at joints. May be basically continuous (eg asphalt, plastic or synthetic-rubber based coating; or built-up felt and bitumen); or basically discontinuous with raised joints (eg metal). Consider resistance to damage by traffic, and danger of interstitial condensation (see 8.01). In *pitched roofs*, covering may consist of overlapping units (slates, tiles, corrugated metal, asbestos-cement, plastic), or fully-supported built-up or single layer covering

● Consider *noise exclusion*, and relationship between roof construction and sound insulation (eg from which direction does sound come)

● Consider *structural strength* and stability; check against 4.01

● Consider *security* requirements. Lightweight, easily dismantled forms of construction (eg boarding, lightweight sheets) are not suitable for occupancies where security is important. Rooflights are also easily penetrated

● Consider *cost* of proposed basic construction (both capital and recurring, eg cleaning, maintenance, replacement)

● Consider *appearance* of roof, both as seen from ground level, and from above (the importance of this depending on relationship to adjacent buildings)

7.04 Take basic decisions on lowest floor

● Decide *position* of lowest floor, relative to ground level

● Consider *structural functions* (imposed loads, spans, loadbearing capacity of soil)

● Consider *environmental functions* (water exclusion; condensation avoidance; thermal insulation; acoustic insulation if floor is raised above ground level)

● Consider *surface characteristics* (functional, and aesthetic)

7.05 Review basic decisions

Review the above decisions 7.01 to 7.04, and assess external envelope as a whole before going on to detailed decisions

External envelope : Take detailed decisions

8 Detailed design of solid fabric

The performance of the external envelope and its parts are now known; and method of construction, cost, appearance, and similar basic attributes have been established in principle

Detailed decisions on specific materials, forms and components, and on their assembly, can therefore now be taken. The suggested decision sequence is solid fabric first (step 8); then openings (step 9); then junctions (step 10); finally, the remaining decisions on external envelope as a whole (step 11)

8.01 Take detailed decisions on solid wall fabric

● Decide details of moisture control:

Rainwater exclusion If *cavity* construction has been selected in 7.02, consider details and avoidance of bridging problems at lintels, sills and jambs; if *impervious* outer skin has been selected, consider jointing and water run-off paths—total prevention of water entry must be achieved if there is no cavity

Condensation control Risk of interstitial condensation is reduced by the following: porous outer skin which allows water vapour to escape to outside air; ventilated and drained cavity; insulation incorporated near outer face of wall; correctly-positioned vapour barrier*

Drainage water collecting on or within wall as a result of rainfall or condensation, must be collected at convenient points and disposed of. Decide positions of collecting channels, gutters, downpipes etc

● Decide details of *thermal control*, to achieve performance laid down in 7.02. Methods for achieving low u-values include rigid insulating slab or sheet materials; low-density block construction; multileaf construction; cavity infilling with insulating foam; reflective surfaces. Decide method, and position within wall. Check u-values in AJ *Metric handbook*; condensation risk in Information sheet EXTERNAL ENVELOPE 1 (Section 2)

● Decide details of *fire control:* fire resistance; combustibility and spread of flame; fire stops. Each must comply with fire legislation

● Decide details of *structural strength* and stability

● Decide detailed incorporation of *services*. Consider vertical and horizontal services distribution; access requirements; possible future alterations of services and fabric

● Consider detailed *appearance*

● Decide form, shape and size, finish, support and attachment method of each panel, to satisfy all the above detailed decisions

8.02 Take detailed decisions on solid roof fabric

● Decide details of moisture control:

Rainwater exclusion In flat roofs, decide: methods of achieving required falls; system of gutters and downpipes; jointing and junction details; flashings and trim. In pitched roofs, decide: system of gutters and downpipes; details of waterproof covering, flashings, eaves and verges; snowguards; sizes and details of gutters and downpipes. For all types of roof decide method of keeping all gutters, fall pipes or any water conducting systems free from clogging by such hazards as birds, air pollution, vegetation. This is usually forgotten during design and discovered when the first cloudburst occurs. At least try something, if only the old-fashioned balloon cage.

Condensation control Basically, interstitial condensation in roofs with continuous sealed coverings may be countered either by incorporating thermal insulation layer plus vapour barrier on warm side of insulation; or by incorporating thermal insulation layer with ventilated cavity between insulation and outer covering. See Information sheet EXTERNAL ENVELOPE 1 Section 2 for examples

In roofs with discontinuous overlapping units, interstitial condensation is not likely to be a problem, because vapour can escape through interstices of roof

● Decide details of thermal control:

In *flat roofs*, required thermal insulation may be provided either by layer of insulation between weatherproof covering and roof structure or deck; by the insulation value of the deck itself; or by an insulating lining beneath roof structure

In *pitched roofs*, where there is a separate ceiling, insulation is usually placed immediately above ceiling, as there is no point in insulating uninhabited roof space

See section 5 of Handbook and AJ *Metric handbook*, for u-values

● Decide details of *fire control*

● Decide details of *structural strength* and stability

● Consider detailed *appearance*: both appearance when new, and likely changes due to weathering, wear and tear

● Consider *weight* of roof and if lightly constructed check whether its mass is sufficient to resist negative wind pressures (suction), especially at edges (see *Guide to the Building Regulations* 1972 pages 25 to 33). Consider need to anchor roof down: they have been known to take off.

● Decide form, shape and size; finish; support and attachment methods for all solid parts of roof

● Decide detailed incorporation of *services*; bear in mind possible future alteration of services or fabric

8.03 Take detailed decisions on lowest floor

● Decide details of moisture control

In *basements*, methods of water exclusion include site drainage; integral waterproofing (using proprietary additives, and waterbars at joints); drained cavity;

* See Information sheet EXTERNAL ENVELOPE 1 (Section 2, para 3.03)

external asphalt or bituminous membrane; or internal membrane*
In *solid floors* (floors in contact with the ground), a waterproof membrane is now generally required to satisfy Building Regulations (apart from excepted buildings)
In *suspended* lowest floors, vapour-proof membrane on warm side of thermal insulation will be required to obviate condensation
● Decide details of *thermal control*, if lowest floor is suspended above ground. Insulation may be positioned either above or below structural slab, and must be on cold side of vapour barrier. See Information sheet LOWEST FLOOR 3 (Section 3)
● Decide details of *structural strength* and stability
● Decide detailed incorporation of *services*. Consider distribution of services; access requirements; and possible future alterations both of services and fabric
● Decide details of construction and finish; see section 3 of handbook

9 Detailed design of openings

9.01 Take detailed decisions on wall openings

● Decide details of *opening method:* hinged, pivoted, sliding, removable; inward or outward opening. Check travel of opening leaves
● Decide details of *frame construction:* material, profile, gaskets
● Decide details of *infilling:* on basis of decisions made in step 6 (solid or louvred infill; opaque, translucent or transparent; one-way or two-way vision; heat-transmission characteristics; noise-transmission characteristics, etc), and weather-resisting requirements, specify type and thickness of infilling material
● Decide *equipment:* operational gear; locks, fasteners and other security devices; ventilators, blinds, louvres, etc

9.02 Take detailed decisions on roof openings

● Decide details of *opening method:* hung, pivoted, sliding, sliding/folding, louvres, removable panels
● Decide details of *glazing system:* materials and finish; shape, size and spacing of glazing members; glazing type and thickness; fixing and bedding methods.
If patent system, consult manufacturer's details
● Decide details of *relationship* between rooflights and solid roof fabric: fixings, treatment and waterproofing of junction, drainage of rainwater and condensation run-off
● Decide on *opening equipment:* operational gear (hand or mechanically-operated; cord, pole or remote-control; louvres and blinds, etc)

10 Detailed design of junctions

Joint function is to connect adjacent components or elements in such a way as to maintain overall performance of external envelope. Therefore joints must be designed in such a way that such properties of adjacent components as thermal insulation, noise insulation, weather resistance and structural strength, are maintained across the space of the junction in sufficient degree (ie check no cold bridges)
In addition, joints must allow for inaccuracies; for some dimensional adjustment during erection; for easy maintenance of materials used in joint, if this should be necessary; and in some instances for movement or dimensional change in the completed building. In some instances, joints must also allow for dismantling adjacent components for repair and replacement

10.01 Decide joint sizes

● Consider minimum and maximum joint widths for satisfactory structural and environmental performance (will vary with material used)
● Consider manufacturing and assembly inaccuracies (tolerances + & —)
● Consider movement in structure and some components: this may be thermal, drying shrinkage or differential settlement. On very bad sites it may be cheaper to accept and design for a considerable degree of movement rather than accept the extra cost of piling or other ground stabilising system.
● Consider appearance of joints
● Decide hierarchy of fits and tolerances for structure and fabric as a whole (dependant on basic modules used)

10.02 Decide joint shapes

● Profiles of prefabricated components or products may influence joint shape
● Consider types of stress expected; magnitude and direction of anticipated movement in adjoining components; need to protect seals; need to prevent thermal by-pass; and assembly method of components. (Overlapping joint types may

* See Information sheet LOWEST FLOOR 1(Section 3)

impose left-to-right assembly sequence, or vice-versa, or create difficulties in placing last component into position)

10.03 Decide joint materials

● Consider stresses to which joint will be subject (pressure, deformation, sunlight or corrosive substances); performance requirements (water exclusion, thermal or acoustic insulation, ability to maintain properties under deformation); and cost
Some systems are designed to accept the penetration of water into spaces in the joint, down which it can pass and be finally collected. This is an alternative to trying to stop the water at the external face and could have advantages: less mastic, more movement tolerance.

External envelope : Take final decisions

11 External envelope as a whole

Detailed design decisions have now been taken on all the individual parts of the external envelope; and all that remains to be done is a final assessment of the design as a whole, to ensure that the parts function effectively as a total assembly; that the total assembly satisfies the performance requirements laid down in step 4; and that there are no design faults or lack of compliance with legal provisions. Equally important, the total *appearance* of the building can now be assessed in detail
These remaining decisions are summarised below

11.01 Drainage

● Consider rainwater, condensation disposal, and cavity drainage; and undertake final co-ordination of drainage system for entire building envelope

11.02 Cleaning and maintenance

● Provide methods of access for cleaning, as well as maintenance and repair, of building fabric finishes and concealed services

11.03 Appearance

● Consider appearance of external envelope as a whole. Not only first appearance, but also likely effects of weathering, staining, and wear and tear must be considered. Effects of rainwater discharge from roof elements, sills, and other projecting features require particular attention. See Technical study EXTERNAL ENVELOPE 1 (Section2)

11.04 General assessment

Carry out final check, covering following points:
● Statutory requirements (fire, light, ventilation, thermal transmittance, structural strength and stability, escape). Some of these are only statutory in respect of a certain type or types of building, but are nevertheless desirable for any type of building. Furthermore the statutory figures are minima (or maxima where the phenomena have nuisance value) and improved values better than the statutory figure are often worthwhile.
● Environmental requirements (amount and quality of daylight; heat gain and loss; sound reduction; ventilation; views of outside; privacy)
● Security requirements (with particular attention to burglar-proofing of doors, windows, rooflights)
● Incorporation of services
● Trade sequence
● Cost

Internal division : Relate decisions to performance requirements

12 Relate design decisions to performance requirements

12.01 Adjacent elements

● Assess in respect of the following factors (12.02 to 12.13) the effect of adjacent elements in constraining the design of the element under consideration
● Identify the effects of compatibility, contextual variability, standards of performance in combination

12.02 Structural requirements

● Consider nature of *support* to element—beams, walls, columns, floor slabs etc
● Identify *structural performance* required of the element in combination with adjacent structure
● Establish the *function* of the element in giving local support, general stability,

horizontal and vertical bracing etc (chiefly against wind forces)
● Consider need to allow for *movement* or conversely need to achieve effective structural *continuity*
● Consider the optimal design of spanning structural elements such as slabs, primary and secondary beams

12.03 Support and fixing facilities required of element

● Consider nature of *loads* acting on the element resulting from the suspension of equipment and fittings eg shear, tension and overturning
● Consider positions, degree of permanence and types of *fixing methods* to be accommodated by the element, and selection of suitable material and form of construction

12.04 Radioactive screening

● Consider positioning and nature of protective screening
● Consider suitability of background for the support and application of screening *finishes* such as lead or barium sulphate plaster, and consider methods of achieving full *continuity* between vertical and horizontal planes and the detailed design of protected openings

12.05 Resistance to dirt, micro-organisms and vermin

● Assess *risk of deterioration* of the fabric due to these causes
● Consider *nature of surfaces*, degree of ability to contain dirt and nurture micro-organisms
● Consider *methods of sealing* small cavities and apertures and densifying porous surfaces
● Consider *ease of cleaning*, redecorating and resurfacing
● Select finishing and core materials which are incompatible with appetites of rodents, insects, birds etc, and which do not sustain fungi or other micro-organisms

12.06 Thermal performance

● Assess *temperature differential* on each side of element, and direction and rate of heat flow
● Consider factors affecting *rate of heat transfer* such as surface configuration, core materials, insulation features such as air spaces, incorporation of materials of low emissivity/high reflectivity
● Consider need for provision of *thermal capacity* and selection of materials of adequate mass
● Consider need for *vapour barrier* in conditions of steep temperature gradient through the structure and large humidity differentials
● Consider problems of *thermal bridging* between spaces of large temperature difference and also where internal elements meet external fabric

12.07 Sound performance

● Assess desired *sound levels* on each side of element and degree of sound reduction required
● Consider *nature* of the source of sound—airborne, impact, vibration from equipment; and continuity of element with other sound conducting elements, both internal and external
● Consider need for *mass, discontinuity* and need for *sound deadening* finishes
● Assess desired acoustic characteristics of spaces and select appropriate materials to provide required absorption, reflection and resonance
● Consider need for multiple forms of construction, eg floating floors, suspended ceilings, multiple leaf walls, multiple glazing

12.08 Light and view

● Assess *nature* of natural lighting required—general, localised, diffused, etc
● Assess need for transparent, translucent or special glazing to give general or directional light or privacy
● Assess necessity for *light control*—refractive glass, blinds, curtains etc
● Assess degree of *reflectance* required of surfaces and characteristics of finishes
● Consider means of keeping glazing clean and accessibility of all surfaces
● Consider means of replacement of glazing with minimal damage and disruption of on-going activities

12.09 Ventilation

● Consider *type* of ventilation and *degree of control* required
● Consider need to seal joints and apertures to prevent air movement
● Consider degree of personal control of ventilation media by occupants in relation to heating and ventilating system employed
● Select suitable permanent or controlled registers to ventilating apertures, and consider further the means of control and cleaning of high level registers
● Establish need to *control* and *purify* air in special cases where there is risk of

cross-infection and the use of devices such as electro-static filters, disinfectant sprays, ultra violet light, ozone infection etc
● Consider the *compatibility of materials* in relation to effects of ventilation system—drying out, discoloration, deformation, dirt deposit and so on

12.10 Fire resistance and security

● Establish fire resistance required of whole elements and resistance of surface finishes and linings to spread of flame
● Consider degree of contribution of materials of construction to fire propagation, structural behaviour of element under fire and mode of collapse
● Determine need to control *smoke* and *flame spread* by protected openings. Test compatibility of protective devices with the structure and fire resistance of the wall in which the openings occur—fire resisting doors, shutters, guillotines, horizontal cut-off shutters etc, all of which constrain the design of the heads and jambs of openings in terms of adequate support and strength of fabric to provide fixings
● Determine methods of *sealing* apertures where services pass through the elements
● Examine the need to break down internal cavities by *fire stopping*
● Consider appropriate *materials* for structural support, protective encasures and select appropriate linings, applied materials (including special fire reducing materials such as intumescent paints)
● Consider problems of incorporating *fire-fighting systems* within the structure of elements eg sprinkler systems, detectors etc
● Consider means of escape
● Consider the need for *special construction* and provision of *protected openings* for spaces of high security risk and the need for specialised protection against explosives, powerful cutting equipment etc

12.11 Accommodation of services

● Identify *types* of services to be installed in association with the element eg electrical conduit, telephones, air ducts, heating pipes, plumbing, air tubes etc
● Decide the *relationship* of the services installations to the fabric—internal, surface fixing or both—their support, protection and means of access
● Consider the need to *dismantle* and *reposition* services whether due to replanning service runs or to repositioning demountable elements
● Consider need to provide pre-positioned connection points on a modular basis for the connection of services and means of blanking off such points when not in use

12.12 Durability, maintenance and appearance

● Establish *types of use*, nature and intensity of wear anticipated eg schools, hospitals, libraries
● Identify character of the desired *appearance* and consider appropriate materials and finishes
● Consider type and nature of decorative finishes in relation to, the frequency of their *renewal*, replacement, restoration and general maintenance
● Consider need for special *protective features*—reinforced corners, metal cover plates and angles, plinths etc
● Identify likely *forms of deterioration*—physical (abrasion, indentation, wilful damage); chemical (ultra-violet light, interaction of acids and alkalis in adjacent materials, electrolytic action, chemical deposits from smoke, deodorant sprays etc)
● Identify likely effects of *cleaning methods*—chemical, abrasive etc
● Consider relationship between *capital costs* and *periodic costs* of maintenance and renewal for the various acceptable methods of construction and finish and analyse by elemental cost-in-use study

12.13 Variability, dimensional and tolerances

● Assess *degree of permanence* required of subdividing fabric—movable, demountable, semi-permanent, permanent—and select suitable types of construction, finishes and jointing methods
● Consider *fixing facilities* offered by adjacent structure, the degree of *disruption* involved in making changes (making good of adjacent surfaces disturbed, sealing off and reconnecting the services, providing continuity of matching surfaces)
● Consider *dimensional constraints*, and relationships between element and adjacent structure, within the context of dimensionally co-ordinated designs and assess need for erection tolerances, use of in-fillers, wedges and distance pieces, cover moulds etc necessary to accommodate dimensional variability when positioning elements within appropriate zones

Appendixes: legislation; specialist advice

Appendix A: legislation

The following list summarises the statutory requirements dealing with various aspects of the building enclosure.

England and Wales:

The Building Regulations 1972

Govern the construction of buildings. Obtainable from HMSO.

Materials and Interpretation

Part A deals with general interpretations. Regulation B3 lists materials which are unsuitable without exception and those which are suitable only in certain circumstances.

Moisture

External walls and lower floors shall resist the passage of moisture (Regulation C3 and C8) Regulation C10 deals with the moisture resistance of roofs.

Loading

Part D. Regulation D2 specifies the method of calculating loadings. Further Regulations define the codes of practice which give 'deemed-to-satisfy' constructions.

Fire

Part E deals with fire resistance, combustibility and surface spread of flame. This part of the Regulations should be studied in detail, as it deals with the whole structure in relation to fire.
E4 deals with providing compartment floors and walls.
E5 (2), E8 and E9 deal with separating walls and Table B to E5 deals with suspended ceilings.
E6 deals with fire resistance tests for compartment walls and floors.
E7 deals with external walls.
E11 deals with fire-resisting doors.
E13 deals with stairways.
E14 deals with fire-stopping of cavities.
E15 deals with restricting flame spread over walls and ceilings.
E17 deals with roofs.
Part H deals with stairways.
Parts L 4 and 5 deal with construction of walls and floors adjoining hearths.
Schedule 6 deals with imposed floor loads and joist sizes.
Note particularly the compartmentation principle which is interpreted in Regulation E1, and the designation of purpose groups (Regulation E2).

Thermal insulation

Part F. Regulation F3 to F6, gives U-values and schedule 11 gives 'deemed-to-satisfy' construction for roofs, walls and floors.

Sound insulation

Part G deals with walls and floors, and gives 'deemed-to-satisfy' constructions.

Railings

Railings on balconies, platforms, etc shall not be less than 1·1 m high (Regulation H6). Other regulations under H also control the main dimensions of staircases.

Light and air

Section K1 governs size of windows in habitable rooms in dwelling houses in relation to a 'zone of open space' outside the window which must be open to the sky. Note that any portion of the window within 1·2 m of the floor is discounted from the calculation. Section K4 deals with ventilation of rooms in dwelling houses. In general, if the window is used for ventilation, the ventilation area must not be less than one-twentieth of the floor area and not less than 1·75 m above the floor. External doors can be used for ventilation if they contain separate opening portions.
Other parts of K are also applicable.

Applicability

The Building Regulations of 1972 like their predecessors of 1965 (with amendments) are not always universally applicable. Some apply only to certain types of building. Those which are not totally applicable are as follows:
Part C. (Resistance to moisture)—excepted buildings not designed for human habitation are only partly controlled.
Part F. (Thermal insulation). Applies only to buildings used as one or more dwellings.
Part G (Sound insulation). As for Part F.
Part H (Stairways). As for Part F.
Part J (Refuse disposal). Restricted to buildings comprising more than one dwelling.
Part K (Open space and ventilation). Deals only with 'habitable rooms' which as defined in the Regulations do not include kitchens. K4 however which concerns means of ventilation expressly provides that for this clause only the term includes kitchens and sculleries.

London:

London Building Acts 1930-1939
London Building (Constructional) By-laws 1972

Applicable in the inner London boroughs only (ie within the boundaries of the former LCC). Obtainable from the GLC

Non-loadbearing walls and cladding

Part VI sets out requirements for four classes of non-loadbearing wall. Important requirements are:
Thickness and height Clause 6.02
Combustibility, fire resistance Clauses 6.03 to 6.07, clause 6.11
Position and area of openings Clause 6.08
Materials Clause 6.09 specifies suitable materials for cladding

Loadbearing walls

Part VII sets out requirements for walls constructed of bricks, blocks, concrete or reinforced concrete, including:
Thickness, height and length Clauses 7.05, clauses 7.07 to 7.12, clauses 7.17 to 7.21
Position and area of openings Clause 7.13
Loading Clauses 7.14, 7.26

Loading Part III defines dead and imposed loads and tabulates minimum imposed loads for design purposes.

Structural design Parts VIII, IX and X cover the structural use of steel, reinforced concrete and timber respectively.

Fire resistance Part XI deals with the fire resistance of the structure as a whole.

Means of escape Guidance on the various statutory requirements for escape from buildings is given in a code of practice, *Means of escape in case of fire* (Document 3868), published by the GLC.

Lighting and ventilation Clauses 11.03 of the 1952 By-laws is still in force and stipulates requirements for lighting and ventilating rooms used for habitation or offices. In general, the superficial area of windows shall not be less than one-tenth of the floor area. In addition, either an area of window not less than one-twentieth of the floor area shall be openable or alternative means of ventilation shall be provided.

By-laws for Good Rule and Government access for maintenance

The Regulations set out in Document 4193 include a stipulation that no person may 'stand or kneel on the sill of any window for the purpose of cleaning or painting such window or for any purpose whatever, such sill being more than 6ft in height from the level of the ground immediately below it, without support sufficient to prevent such person from falling.'

Scotland:

The Building Standards (Scotland) (Consolidation) Regulation 1971 : (with three amendments)

Govern the construction of buildings obtainable from HMSO.

Loading

Part C.

Fire

Requirements for fire resistance and combustibility are set out in Part D. Section D18 deals exclusively with roofs.

Means of escape

Part E. Sections E3 to E8, E13 and 14 deal with exit requirements in case of fire.

Access

Sections E17 and E18 stipulate requirements for access to windows and buildings for fire fighting and escape. Section P4 deals with safe access to windows for cleaning purposes.

Moisture

Roofs and external walls shall resist the passage of moisture (Section G8)

Thermal insulation

Part J deals with resistance to the transmission of heat. Sections J3 and J4 specify U-values for roofs and walls

Ventilation

Section K5 requires a ventilation area of not less than one-twentieth of the floor area in windows or rooflights ventilating an apartment or room in a dwelling house. In some cases, a permanent ventilator is also required.

Light

Sections L4, L6 and L10 cover requirements for windows in housing to give a satisfactory standard of daylighting.

General

The Thermal Insulation (Industrial Buildings) Act 1957 and Thermal Insulation (Industrial Buildings) Regulations 1958 (SI 1120)

This Act is particularly relevant to the design of roofs of industrial buildings (ie factories within the meaning of the Factories Acts 1937 and 1948). The Regulations stipulate minimum standards of insulation. Both the Act and the Regulations are available from HMSO.

The Factories Act 1961

Provides for standards of health, safety and welfare in factories. Obtainable from HMSO.

The Offices, Shops and Railway Premises Act 1963

Provides for standards of health, safety and welfare in offices, shops and railway premises. Note in particular the requirements for temperature, ventilation and lighting.

The Construction (Lifting Operations) Regulations 1961
The Construction (Working Places) Regulations 1966

These regulations govern access to the wall by means of ladders, scaffolding, scaffolds or cradles suspended on cables and all lifting machines restrained by a guide or guides, provided these are used for 'building operations'. They would consequently control the use of such equipment for any cleaning or maintenance work carried out as part of a building contract, but not routine window cleaning.

Appendix B: specialist advice

The following organisations offer specialist advice on various aspects of the building enclosure:

Aluminimum Federation, Broadway House, Five Ways, Birmingham, B15 1TN

Brick Development Association, 3-5 Bedford Road, London, WC1R 4BU

British Precast Concrete Federation, 9 Catherine Place, London SW1

BISRA: Corporate Laboratories of the British Steel Corporation, 24 Buckingham Gate, London SW1

Building Research Station, Garston, Watford, Herts

Cement and Concrete Association, 52 Grosvenor Gardens, London SW1

Copper Development Association, 55 South Audley Street, London, W1Y 6BJ

Fire Protection Association, Aldermary House, Queen Street, London EC4

Forest Products Research Laboratory, Princes Risborough, Bucks

Joint Fire Research Organisation, Fire Research Station, Boreham Wood, Herts

Lead Development Association, 34 Berkeley Square, London W1

Meteorological Office, London Road, Bracknell, Berks

Timber Research and Development Association, Hughenden Valley, High Wycombe, Bucks

Vitreous Enamel Development Council, 28 Welbeck Street, London, W1M 7PG

Appendix 1

Appendix 1 **References**

Summary of references

The most important references from technical studies and information sheets are collected together below. Source documents and general reading matter are not included; nor is legislation, which is summarised at the end of the design guide. The emphasis is on practical reference material

British Standards Institution

1 BS 12: Part 2: 1971 Portland cement (ordinary and rapid-hardening). Metric units [Yq2] £1·25

2 BS 102: 1963 Protection of buildings against water from the ground [(I2)]

3 BS 187: 1967 Calcium silicate (sandlime and flintlime) bricks [Ff1]

4 BS 416: 1967 Cast iron spigot and socket soil, waste and ventilating pipes (sand-cast and spun), fittings and accessories [Id1]

5 BS 449: Part 2: 1969 The use of structural steel in building. Metric units [(2–) Gh2 (K)]

6 BS 459: Part 1: 1954 Panelled and glazed wood doors. Part 2: 1962 Flush doors. Part 4: 1965 Matchboarded doors [(32·2) Xi]

7 BS 460: 1964 Cast iron rainwater goods [(52·5) Ih1]

8 BS 476: Part 1: 1953 Fire tests on building materials and structures [Yy (R4) (Aq)]

9 BS 476: Part 3: 1958 External fire exposure roof tests [Yy (R4) (Aq)] *amended* 1959

10 BS 569: 1967 Asbestos-cement rainwater pipes, gutters and fittings [(52·5) If6]

11 BS 582: 1965 Asbestos-cement soil, waste and ventilating pipes and fittings [(52·5) If6]

12 BS 644 Part 1: 1951 Wood casement windows [(31·2) Xi]

13 BS 644 Part 2: 1958 Wood double-hung sash windows [(31·4) Xi]

14 BS 644 Part 3: 1951 Wood double-hung sash and case windows—Scottish type [(31) Xi]

15 BS 648: 1964 Schedule of weights of building materials [Yy (F4)] *revised October* 1969

16 BS 743: 1966 Materials for damp-proof courses [(9–) Yy (I2)]

17 BS 890: 1966 Building lines [Yq1]

18 BS 952: 1964 Classification of glass for glazing and terminology for work on glass [Ro (Ah)]

19 BS 990: 1967 Steel windows generally for domestic and similar buildings [(31) Xh2]

20 BS 1091: 1963 Pressed steel gutters, rainwater pipes, fittings and accessories

[(52·5) Ih2]

21 BS 1097: 1966 Mastic asphalt for tanking and damp-proof courses (limestone aggregate) [Ps4 (I2)]

22 BS 1142: 1961 Fibre building boards [Rj1]

23 BS 1161: 1951 Aluminium and aluminium alloy sections [Hh4]

24 BS 1180: 1944 Concrete bricks and fixing bricks [Ff2]

25 BS 1186: Part 1: 1971 Quality of timber [Yi (A7)]

26 BS 1186: Part 2: 1971 Quality of workmanship [Yi (A7)]

27 BS 1191: Part 1: Gypsum building plasters. Excluding premixed lightweight plasters [Pr2]

28 BS 1191: Part 2: 1967 Premixed lightweight plasters [Pr2]

29 BS 1198-1200: 1955 Building sands from natural sources [Yp1]

30 BS 1217: 1945 Cast stone [Yf3]

31 BS 1230: Part 2: 1970 Gypsum plasterboard. Metric units [Rf7]

32 BS 1236 to 1240: 1956 Sills and lintels [(31) Gy]

33 BS 1239: 1956 Sills and lintels: cast concrete lintels [(31) Gy]

34 BS 1243 Metal ties for cavity wall construction [(21·1) Xt6]

35 BS 1282: 1959 Classification of wood preservatives and their methods of application [Yu3]

36 BS 1285: 1963 Wood surrounds for steel windows [(31) Xi]

37 BS 1369: 1947 Metal lathing (steel) for plastering [Jh2]

38 BS 1418: 1966 Mastic asphalt for tanking and damp-proof courses (natural rock asphalt aggregate) [Ps4 (I2)]

39 BS 1422: 1956 Steel subframes, sills and windowboards for metal windows [(31) Xh2]

40 BS 1431: 1960 Wrought copper and wrought zinc rainwater goods [(52·5) Ih]

41 BS 1787: 1951 Steel windows for industrial buildings [27 (31) Xh]

42 BS 2028: 1364: 1968 Precast concrete blocks. Metric units [Ff]

43 BS 2503: 1954 Steel windows for agricultural use [26 (31) Xh2]

44 BS 2504: 1955 Wood doors and frames for milking parlours [(32) Xi]

45 BS 2750: 1956 Recommendations for field and laboratory measurement of airborne and impact sound transmission in buildings [(M4h)]

46 BS 2908: 1957 Precast concrete eaves gutters [(27) Gf2]

47 BS 2997: 1958 Aluminium rainwater goods, amendment PD 6403, 1968 [(52·5) Ih4]

48 BS 3235: 1964 Test methods for bitumen [Ys1 (Aq)]

49 BS 3621: 1963 Thief-resistant locks for hinged doors [(32·2) Xt7]

50 BS3868: 1965 Prefabricated drainage

stack units: galvanised steel [(52·1) Ih2]

51 BS 3921: Standard special bricks. Part 1: 1965 Imperial units; Part 2: 1969 Metric units. [(Fg)]

52 BS 3962: Part 4: 1970 Method of test for clear finishes for wooden furniture: resistance to marking by liquids [(82) Yu3 (Aq)]

53 BS 4011: 1966 Basic sizes for building components and assemblies [(F4)]

54 BS 4315: Part 1: 1968 Methods of test for resistance to air and water penetration: Windows and gasket glazing systems [(31) (I2)]

55 BS 4330: 1968 Recommendations for the co-ordination of dimension in building: controlling dimensions. Metric units [(F4j)]

56 BS 4374: 1968 Sills of clayware, cast concrete, cast stone, slate and natural stone [(31) Gy]

57 BS 4471: 1969 Dimensions for softwood [Xi2]

58 BS CP 3 Chapter I, Lighting. Part 1: 1964 Daylighting [(N)]. Chapter II: 1970 Thermal insulation in relation to the control of environment [(J2)]. Chapter III: 1960 Sound insulation and noise. Chapter V Loading. Part 1: 1967 Dead and imposed loads. Part 2: 1970 Wind loads [(K4f)]. Chapter VII: 1970 Engineering and utility services [(5–)]

59 BS CP 98: 1964 Preservative treatment for constructional timber [Yu3]

60 BS CP 101: 1963 Foundations and substructures for non-industrial buildings of not more than four storeys [(1–)]

61 BS CP 102: 1963 Protection of buildings against water from the ground [(I2)]

62 BS CP 111: Structural recommendations for loadbearing walls. Part 1: 1964 Imperial units; Part 2: 1970 Metric units. [(21·1) (K)]

64 BS CP 122: 1952 Walls and partitions of blocks and of slabs [(2–) Yi (K)]

65 BS CP 112: 1967 Structural use of timber [(2–) Yi (K)] £2

66 BS CP 114: Part 2: 1969 The structural use of reinforced concrete in building. Metric units [(2–) Eq4 (K)] £1·50 * Now replaced by single consolidated code.

67 BS CP 115: Part 2: 1969 Structural use of prestressed concrete in building. Metric units [(2–) Yq (K)] * Now replaced by single consolidated code.

68 BS CP 116: Part 2: 1969 Structural use of precast concrete. Metric units [(2–) Gf (K)] £2 * Now replaced by consolidated code.

69 BS CP 117: Part 1: 1965 Composite construction in structural steel and concrete: Simply-supported beams in building [(2–) Gv (K)] * Now replaced by single consolidated code.

70 BS CP 118: 1969 The structural use of aluminium [(2–) Yh4 (K)] £3

71 BS CP 121:101: 1951 Brickwork [(21) Fg]

72 BS CP 143: Part 2: 1961 Sheet roof and wall coverings: Galvanised corrugated steel [(47) N]

73 BS CP 143: Part 3: 1960 Sheet roof and wall coverings: Lead [(47) N]

74 BS CP 143: Part 4: 1960 Sheet roof and wall coverings: Copper [(47) N]

75 BS CP 143: Part 5: 1964 Sheet roof and wall coverings: Zinc [(47) N]

76 BS CP 143: Part 6: 1962 Sheet roof and wall coverings: Corrugated asbestos-cement [(47) N]

77 BS CP 143: Part 7: 1965 Sheet roof and wall coverings: Aluminium [(47) N]

78 BS CP 143: Part 8: 1970 Semi-rigid asbestos bitumen sheets [(47) Rf6]

79 BS CP 144 Roof coverings. Part 1: 1968 Built-up bitumen felt. Imperial units [(47) Ln2]. Part 2: 1966 Asphalt. Imperial units [(47) Ps4] amended 1967

80 BS CP 151: Part 1: 1957 Wooden doors [(32) Xi]

81 BS CP 152: 1966 Glazing and fixing of glass [Ro (D6)]

82 BS CP 153: Windows and rooflights. Part 1: 1969 Cleaning and safety. Part 2: 1970 Durability and maintenance [(3–)]

83 BS CP 201: 1951 Timber flooring [(43) Yi]

84 BS CP 202: 1959 Tile flooring and slab flooring [(43) Sy]

85 BS CP 203: 1969 Sheet and tile flooring (cork, linoleum, plastics and rubber) [(43) Ty]

86 BS CP 204: In situ floor finishes. Part 1: 1965 Imperial units. Part 2: 1970 Metric units [(43) Py]

87 BS CP 211: 1966 Internal plastering [(42) Pr2]

88 BS CP 212: Part 1: 1963 Internal ceramic wall tiling in normal conditions [(42) Sg3]

89 BS CP 212: Part 2: 1966 External ceramic wall tiling and mosaics [(41) Sg]

90 BS CP 221: 1960 External rendered finishes [(41) Py]

91 BS CP 303: 1952 Surface water and subsoil drainage [(11)]

92 BS 2001: 1957 Site investigations [(11) (A3s)]

93 BS 2008: 1966 Protection of iron and steel structures from corrosion [Vu]

94 PD 6432 Recommendations for the co-ordination of dimensions in building: arrangement of building components and assemblies within functional groups, part 1: 1969 Functional groups 1, 2, 3 and 4 [(F4)]

95 PD 6440 Draft for development: accuracy in building, part 1: 1969 imperial units; part 2: 1969 metric units [(F6)] £1·80 each

96 PD 6444 Recommendations for the co-ordination of dimensions in building: basic spaces for structure, external envelope, and internal subdivision, part 1: 1969 functional groups 1, 2 and 3 [(F4j)] £2

97 PD 6445 Recommendations for the co-ordination of dimensions in building: tolerances and joints, the derivation of building component manufacturing sizes from co-ordinating sizes. Metric units [(F4j)]

98 DD 4 Draft for development. Window performance. 1971 [(31)]

Building Research Establishment

1 Digest 9 (first series) Building on made-up ground. 1949, HMSO [(11)]

2 Digest 16 Aerated concrete: part 1: Manufacture and properties. 1969, HMSO [Yq6 (E1)]

3 Digest 17 Aerated concrete: part 2: Uses. 1969, HMSO [Yq6 (E1)]

4 Digest 18 The design of timber floors to prevent decay. 1970, HMSO [(23) Hi (S4)]

5 Digest 33 Sheet and tile flooring made from thermoplastic binders. 1963, HMSO [(43) Tn6]

6 Digest 34 Design of gutter and rain-water pipes. 1963, HMSO [(52·5)]

7 Digests 36 and 37 Jointing with mastics and gaskets: parts 1 and 2. 1963, HMSO [Yt4]

8 Digest 47 Granolithic concrete, concrete tiles and terrazzo flooring. 1964, HMSO [(43) Yq5]

9 Digest 54 Damp-proofed solid floors. 1968, HMSO [13 (I2)]

10 Digest 58 Mortars for jointing. 1965, HMSO [Yq4]

11 Digest 59 Protection against corrosion or reinforcing steel in concrete. 1965, HMSO [Hh2 (S2)]

12 Digest 61 Strength of brickwork, block-work and concrete walls. 1965, HMSO [(21·1) (K)]

13 Digests 63 and 64 Soil and foundations: parts 1 and 2. 1965, HMSO [(16) (L4)]

14 Digest 67 Soil and foundations: part 3. 1966, HMSO [(16) (L4)]

15 Digest 70 Painting metals in buildings: 1. 1966, HMSO [Vv]

16 Digest 71 Painting metals in buildings: 2. 1966, HMSO [Vv]

17 Digest 73 Prevention of decay in window joinery. 1966, HMSO [(31) Xi (S4)]

18 Digest 77 Damp-proof courses. 1966, HMSO [(9) Yy (I2)]

19 Digest 79 Clay tile flooring. 1967, HMSO [(43) Sg]

20 Digest 80 Soil and waste pipe systems for housing. 1967, HMSO [81 (52·1)]

21 Digest 85 Joints between concrete wall panels: Open drained joints. 1967, HMSO [(21) Gf2]

22 Digest 89 Sulphate attack on brick-work. 1968, HMSO [Fg2 (S2)]

23 Digest 90 Concrete in sulphate-bearing clays and ground water. 1968, HMSO [Yq (S)]

24 Digest 98 Durability of metals in natural waters. 1968, HMSO [(53·3) Yh (S)]

25 Digest 104 Floor screeds. 1969, HMSO [(43) Ey]

26 Digest 107 Roof drainage. 1969, HMSO [(52·5)]

27 Digest 108 Standardised u-values. 1969, HMSO [(J4)]

28 Digest 110 Condensation. 1969, HMSO [(I6)]

29 Digest 111 Lightweight aggregate concretes, part 3: Structural application. 1969, HMSO [Yq7 (K)]

30 Digest 116 (first series) Roof drainage. 1958, HMSO [(52·5)]

31 Digest 119 The assessment of wind loads. 1970, HMSO [(K4f)]

32 Digest 120 Corrosion-resistant floors in

industrial buildings. 1970, HMSO [(43) Yy (S2)]

33 Digest 123 Lightweight aggregate concretes. 1970, HMSO [Yq7]

34 Digest 126 Changes in appearance of concrete on exposure. 1971, HMSO [Yq (S)]

35 Digest 127 An index of exposure to driving rain. 1971, HMSO [(I3)]

36 Digest 131 (first series) External rendered finishes. 1960, HMSO [(41) Pq4]

37 Technical information leaflet TIL 34, Timber flat roofs. June 1972. HMSO [(27·1) Yi] free on application

38 Current Paper 36/68 Battery case cladding panels. 1968, HMSO [(41) Rf (B2d)]

39 Current Paper 73/68 Lightweight aggregates: their properties and use in concrete in the UK. 1968, HMSO [Yp]

40 Current Paper 30/69 Large panel structures. Notes on draft addendum 1 to BS CP 116: 1965. 1969, HMSO [(2–) Gf (K)]

41 Current Paper 25/70 The use of cranes on low rise high density industrialised housing. 1970, HMSO [81 (E1e) (B3p)]

42 Principles of modern building: volume 1. 1964, HMSO [(9–) (E1)] £1

43 Principles of modern building: volume 2. 1961, HMSO [(9–) (E1)] 87½p

AJ Handbooks

1 AJ Handbook of Building environment (AJ 2.10.68 to 13.8.69) [(E6)]

2 AJ Handbook of Building services (AJ 1.10.69 to 5.8.70 and 16.9.70) [(5–)]

3 AJ Handbook of Building structure (AJ 8.3.72 to late '73) [(2–)]

4 AJ Legal handbook (AJ 31.3.71 to 15.3.72) [(Ajk)]

5 AJ Handbook of Fixings and fastenings (AJ 24.3.71; 7 and 21.4.71; 5 and 12.5.71) [Xt5]

6 AJ Guide to concrete finishes (AJ special issues 14.2.68 and 26.3.69) [(41) Yq]

7 AJ Guide to concrete blockwork (AJ special issue 8.4.70) [(Ff)]

Nos 5, 6 and 7 were republished as books by The Architectural Press

8 AJ Guide to stainless steel (AJ 22.4.70) [Yh3]

9 AJ guides to building types: see list on contents page in handbook (AJ 21.7.71)

Other references

AGREMENT BOARD

1 Methods of assessment and testing 1: Windows. Hemel Hempstead, Herts, 1967, the board [(31) (Aq)]

2 Information Sheet 1 Windows. Hemel Hempstead, Herts, 1967, the board [(31)]

3 BRICK DEVELOPMENT ASSOCIATION Load-bearing brickwork: design for the fifth amendment, 1970, London, the association [(21·1) Ff (A3)]

BRITISH CERAMIC TILE COUNCIL

4 Recommended methods of fixing frost-resistant ceramic wall tiles. Stoke-on-Trent, the council [(41) Sg3 (J2)]

5 Technical specification for ceramic wall tiles. Stoke-on-Trent, the council [Sg3 (A3)]

6 BRITISH STEEL CORPORATION Leaflet SC6 Steel sheet rainwater goods. London,

1965, the corporation [(52·5) Mh2]

7 BULLIVANT, D., and ACKHURST, P. Product selection for architects: carpets. RIBA *Journal*, 1970, January [(43) Ty]

8 BURBERRY, P. Environment and services. London, 1970, Batsford [(E6)] £2·50, *paperback* £1·60

9 BURBERRY, P., DAY, B. F., and LOUDON, A. G., Condensation in buildings. *Architects' Journal*, 1971, May 19, p1149-1159; May 26, p1201-1208; June 2, p1265-1269 [(I6)]

10 CAPE UNIVERSAL BUILDING PRODUCTS LTD Technical manual 1970/71. England, 1970-71, Page Bros [Yy (Abd)]

11 CEMENT AND CONCRETE ASSOCIATION Concrete practice in building construction. London, 1960, the association [Yq]

12 CLAY PRODUCTS TECHNICAL BUREAU Technical Notes, vol 1, no 10 Movement joints in brickwork. London, 1966, the bureau [(9–) Fy (S6)]

DEPARTMENT OF EDUCATION AND SCIENCE
13 Performance specification for partitions. 1966, HMSO [(22) (A3)]

14 Common performance standards for building components. 1970, HMSO [(9–) Xy (E) (Ajp)]

15 DIAMANT, R. M. E. Industrialised building: Fifty international methods. Vol 1 1964, vol 2 1965. Iliffe Books (for *Architect and Building News*) [E1b] *vol* 1 £3·15, *vol* 2 £3·50

16 DIAMANT, R. M. E. Thermal and acoustic insulation of buildings. London, 1965, Iliffe Books (for *Architect and Building News*) [(J) (M)]

DEPARTMENT OF THE ENVIRONMENT
17 Sound insulation in buildings. H. R. Humphreys and D. J. Melluish. 1971, HMSO [(M)]

18 Sunlight and daylight-planning criteria and design. 1972, HMSO [(N7)]

19 DEPARTMENT OF SCIENTIFIC AND INDUSTRIAL RESEARCH Principles of modern building, vols I and II, HMSO [(9–) (E1)]

CEMENT AND CONCRETE ASSOCIATION
20 External rendering. London, 1970, the association, fifth edition [(41) Pq]

21 ELDER, A. J. The guide to the Building Regulations 1972. London, 1972, The Architectural Press [(A3j) (F7)]

22 ELDRIDGE, H. J. Flooring materials 1: hard surfaces. *Building*, 1970. June [(43) Yy]

23 FARRANT, D. and HOWE, J. Product selection for architects: external doors. RIBA *Journal*, 1971, February, p73-78 [(31) Xy (A3u)]

24 FIRE PROTECTION ASSOCIATION Fire protection design guide: a handbook for architects. London, 1969, the association [(R1)]

25 Fire Regulations. Doors. *Architects' Journal*, 1970, March 18, p691-696 [(5–)]

26 FIRE RESEARCH ORGANISATION Fire Note 12 Expanded polystyrene linings for domestic buildings, 1971, HMSO [8 Yn6 (R4)]

28 FOSTER, D. Clay bricks and blocks: specification in practice. RIBA *Journal*, 1970, April, p171-176 [Fg (A3u)]

29 Failures in brickwork. *Architects' Journal*, 1971, October 6, p767-776 [(21) Fg2 (S)]

30 FOSTER, J. S. Mitchell's advanced building construction: the structure. London, 1963, Batsford [(9–) (E1)] £1·50

31 Go-Con battery casting of concrete panels. AJ 1971, May 5, p998-1002 and 1971, June 16, p1341 [Gf (B2d)]

32 GROEGER, R. G. A guide to the use of sealants and mastics, AJ Information sheet 1603, 1968, June 5 [(Yt4)]

33 HARRISON, D. (ed). *Specification* 1972, vol 2 p2-313 to 2-332 Architectural Press [Yy (A3)]

34 HUNT, W. D. The contemporary curtain wall. New York, 1958, Dodge Corporation [(21·4)]

35 INSULATING GLAZING ASSOCIATION Glazing requirements and procedures for double glazing units, 1. London, 1963, the association [Ro5] *revised* 1968

36 KING, H. and EVERETT, A. Components and finishes. London, 1970, Batsford [(9–) (E1)]

37 KIRKBRIDE, T. W. Loadbearing concrete blockwork for housing. RIBA *Journal*, 1968, November, p516-519 [814 (21·1) Ff]

38 LEAD DEVELOPMENT ASSOCIATION Lead information sheets. AJ at intervals from 16.10.47 to 15.6.61 1961 [Rh8]

39 LONGMORE, J. and ADDLESON, L. Product selection: float glass. RIBA *Journal*, 1970, September, p420-430 [Ro1]

40 MARKUS, T. A. Function of windows: a reappraisal. *Building Science*, vol 2, p97-121, 1967 [(31)]

MASTIC ASPHALT ADVISORY COUNCIL
41 Model specification for mastic asphalt in building. 1965, the council [Ys4]

42 Application of mastic asphalt: tanking, roofing, flooring, paving. 1966, the council [Ys4]

43 MEIKLE, T. A. V. A guide to the use of sealants, part 1: Flexible joints. *Architect and Building News*, 1970, October, p55 [(Yt4)]

44 MINISTRY OF HOUSING AND LOCAL GOVERNMENT (now DOE) Circular 31/67 Vertical dimensional standards in housing. 1967, HMSO [(81) (F4j)]

MINISTRY OF PUBLIC BUILDING AND WORKS
45 Performance specification: Partitions. 1970, HMSO [(22) (A3)]

46 DC 4 Recommended vertical dimensions for educational, health, housing, office and single-storey general purpose industrial buildings. 1967, HMSO [(F4j)]

47 DC 5 Recommended horizontal dimensions for educational, health, housing, office and single-storey general purpose industrial buildings. 1967, HMSO [(F4j)]

48 DC 6 Guidance on the application of recommended vertical and horizontal dimensions for educational, health, housing, office and single-storey general purpose industrial buildings. 1967, HMSO [(F4j)]

49 DC 7 Recommended intermediate vertical controlling dimensions for educational, health, housing and office buildings, and guidance on their application. 1967, HMSO [(F4j)]

50 MINISTRY OF TECHNOLOGY AND FIRE OFFICES COMMITTEE Fire Note 5 Fire venting of single-storey buildings [(R)]

50a MINISTRY OF PUBLIC BUILDING AND WORKS (Post-war Building Study 20 Fire

grading of buildings, 1946, reprinted 1963, HMSO [(R)]

51 MURPHY, W. E. Jointing between precast concrete façade panels: Tolerances achieved in vertical joints. *Architects' Journal*, 1967, November 15, p1231-1234 [(21)]

52 BUILDING RESEARCH ESTABLISHMENT Factory Building Study 11 Thermal insulation of factories. G. D. Nash. 1962, HMSO [27 (J2)]

53 NASH, C. D., COMRIE, J., BROUGHTON, H. F. The thermal insulation of buildings: Design data and how to use them. 1955, HMSO [(J2)]

54 NATIONAL PHYSICAL LABORATORY The airborne sound insulation of partitions. E. N. Bazley. 1966, HMSO [(22) (M)]

55 NISBET, J. Cost planning and cost control (AJ 3, 10 and 24.11.65) [(A4)]

55 NURALITE CO LTD Nuralite technical handbook. Higham, near Rochester, Kent, 1971, the company [Ls]

56 PHILLIPS, D. Flooring. London, 1969, Macdonald & Co with COID [(43)]

57 BUILDING RESEARCH ESTABLISHMENT Condensation in sheeted roofs. A. W. Pratt. National Building Studies Research Paper 1958. 1960, HMSO [(27) (I6)]

58 Production selection for architects: Timber windows. RIBA *Journal*, 1970, February [(31) Xh (A3u)]

59 Protection of openings. *Architects' Journal*, 1970, July 29, p271-276 [(5–)]

60 STONE, P. A. Building design evaluation: costs in use. London, 1968, E. & F. Spon [(A4)] £2·10

61 WEST, H. W. H. Clay bricks and blocks: selection criteria. RIBA *Journal*, 1970, April, p169-171 [Fg (A3u)]

62 WHITE, R. B. The changing appearance of buildings. 1967, HMSO [(9–) (S)] £1·05

63 WITHERS, M. Floor finishes. *Architect and Building News*, 1967, March 22, April 5 and 12 [(43)]

64 REYNOLDS, C. E. Reinforced concrete designer's handbook. London, 1971, Concrete Publications Ltd, seventh edition [(2–) Gf (K)]

65 ROSTRON, M. Light cladding of buildings. London, 1964, Architectural Press [(21)]

66 ROYAL INSTITUTE OF BRITISH ARCHITECTS The co-ordination of dimensions for building. London, 1965, the institute [(F4j)]

67 Screens, louvres: General 3: Shading devices and masks. Information sheet 1184. AJ, 1963, January 2 [(22)]

68 SHACKLOCK, B. W. The design of concrete ground floor slabs. London, 1968, Cement and Concrete Association [(13) Yq]

69 ALAN SILCOCK Protecting buildings against fire: background to costs. *Architects' Journal*, 1967, December 13 p1515-1519 [(R1) (Y2)]

70 SLIWA, J. Accuracy, tolerances, joints: confused advice from BSI. *Architects' Journal*, 1970, 4 March, p553 [(F6)]

71 STAINLESS STEEL DEVELOPMENT ASSOCIATION Building with stainless steel. London, 1967, the association [Md3]

72 Steel designer's manual. London, 1966, Crosby Lockwood, 3rd edition [(2–) Yh2 (K)]

Appendix 2

Index to Handbook

This handbook consists of nine sections plus a design guide and two appendices. Each section contains two types of document: technical studies (TS), followed by information sheets (INF). There is a single design guide for the whole handbook, and this is not referred to in the index, as it contains no information additional to that conveyed in the technical studies and information sheets—it is mainly a procedural checklist.

The document referred to in each of the following entries is identified in the following manner: type of document/reference keyword/number of document. For example: TS LOWEST 1 (= technical study LOWEST FLOORS 1); or INF ROOFS 6 (= information sheet ROOFS 6). To find the document referred to, scan the top strips of the pages of the relevant handbook section; the title of each document, with numbers of paragraph appearing on that page, is printed at the top outer corner of each page. For example: Technical study **Lowest floor 1 para 2.02 to 3.01**; Information sheet **ROOFS 6 para 1 to References.** See also list of contents on page 6

Section title	Reference keywords	Abbreviated keyword used in index
Section 1 Building enclosure: General	ENCLOSURE	ENCLOSURE
Section 2 External envelope: General	EXTERNAL ENVELOPE	EXTERNAL
Section 3 External envelope: Lowest floor and basement	LOWEST FLOOR	LOWEST
Section 4 External envelope: External walls	EXTERNAL WALLS	WALLS
Section 5 External envelope: Roofs	ROOFS	ROOFS
Section 6 Internal division: General	INTERNAL DIVISION	INTERNAL
Section 7 Internal division: Suspended floors	SUSPENDED FLOORS	SUSPENDED
Section 8 Internal division: Partitions and walls	PARTITIONS	PARTITIONS
Section 9 Internal division: Ceilings	CEILINGS	CEILINGS
Appendix 1 Summary of references	ENCLOSURE: REFERENCES	
Appendix 2 Index to Handbook	ENCLOSURE: INDEX	